The Management of Organizations: A Systems and Human Resources Approach

McGraw-Hill Series in Management

KEITH DAVIS, Consulting Editor

ALLEN   Management and Organization
ALLEN   The Management Profession
ARGYRIS   Management and Organizational Development: The Path from XA to YB
BECKETT   Management Dynamics: The New Synthesis
BENNIS   Changing Organizations
BENTON   Supervision and Management
BERGEN AND HANEY   Organizational Relations and Management Action
BLOUGH   International Business: Environment and Adaptation
BOWMAN   Management: Organization and Planning
BROWN   Judgment in Administration
CAMPBELL, DUNNETTE, LAWLER, AND WEICK   Managerial Behavior, Performance, and Effectiveness
CLELAND AND KING   Management: A Systems Approach
CLELAND AND KING   Systems Analysis and Project Management
CLELAND AND KING   Systems, Organizations, Analysis, Management: A Book of Readings
DALE   Management: Theory and Practice
DALE   Readings in Management: Landmarks and New Frontiers
DAVIS   Human Behavior at Work: Human Relations and Organizational Behavior
DAVIS AND BLOMSTROM   Business, Society, and Environment: Social Power and Social Response
DAVIS AND SCOTT   Human Relations and Organizational Behavior: Readings and Comments
DE GREENE   Systems Psychology
DUNN AND RACHEL   Wage and Salary Administration: Total Compensation Systems
FIEDLER   A Theory of Leadership Effectiveness
FLIPPO   Principles of Personnel Management
GOLEMBIEWSKI   Men, Management, and Morality
GLUECK   Business Policy: Strategy Formation and Executive Action
HARBISON AND MYERS   Management in the Industrial World
HICKS   The Management of Organizations: A Systems and Human Resources Approach
JOHNSON, KAST, AND ROSENZWEIG   The Theory and Management of Systems
KAST AND ROSENZWEIG   Organization and Management: A Systems Approach
KOONTZ   Toward a Unified Theory of Management
KOONTZ AND O'DONNELL   Principles of Management: An Analysis of Managerial Functions
KOONTZ AND O'DONNELL   Management: A Book of Readings
LEVIN, McLAUGHLIN, LAMONE, AND KOTTAS,   Production/Operation Management: Contemporary
    Policy for Managing Operating Systems
LUTHANS   Contemporary Readings in Organizational Behavior
McDONOUGH   Information Economics and Management Systems
McNICHOLS   Policy Making and Executive Action
MAIER   Problem-solving Discussions and Conferences: Leadership Methods and Skills
MAYER   Production Management
MUNDEL   A Conceptual Framework for the Management Sciences
PETIT   The Moral Crisis in Management
PETROF, CARUSONE, AND McDAVID   Small Business Management: Concepts and Techniques for
    Improving Decisions
PIGORS AND PIGORS   Case Method in Human Relations
PRASOW AND PETERS   Abritration and Collective Bargaining: Conflict Resolution in Labor Relations.
READY   The Administrator's Job
REDDIN   Managerial Effectiveness
SALTONSTALL   Human Relations in Administration
SARTAIN AND BAKER   The Supervisor and His Job
SCHRIEBER, JOHNSON, MEIER, FISCHER, AND NEWELL   Cases in Manufacturing Management
SHULL, D'ELBECQ, AND CUMMINGS   Organizational Decision Making
STEINER   Managerial Long-range Planning
SUTERMEISTER   People and Productivity
TANNENBAUM   Control in Organizations
TANNENBAUM, WESCHLER, AND MASSARIK   Leadership and Organization
VANCE   Industrial Administration
VANCE   Management Decision Simulation

The Management of Organizations: A Systems and Human Resources Approach

SECOND EDITION

Herbert G. Hicks

Professor of Management
Louisiana State University

McGraw-Hill Book Company

New York   St. Louis   San Francisco   Düsseldorf   Johannesburg
Kuala Lumpur   London   Mexico   Montreal   New Delhi
Panama   Rio de Janeiro   Singapore   Sydney   Toronto

This book was set in Optima by University Graphics, Inc., printed by Halliday Lithograph Corporation, and bound by The Maple Press Company. The designer was Rita Naughton; the drawings were done by John Cordes, J. & R. Technical Services, Inc. The editors were Richard F. Dojny, Hiag Akmakjian, and Sally Mobley. Peter D. Guilmette supervised production.

Cover photograph by J. Paul Kirouac.

To A. G. H.

Contents

Preface

Organizations have enabled man to span oceans in hours, to enjoy an unprecedented abundance of material goods and leisure, and to double his span of life. Organizations also have enabled man to go to the moon. Clearly, organizations are among man's most important creations and servants. Organizations exist because they help man to achieve his objectives.

The purpose of his book is to help the reader understand what organizations are, why they exist, how they work, and how they can be made to work more effectively. Any kind of organization can be better understood by using the tools this book provides.

Because an understanding of organizations and management in our complex world is so important, a large body of literature has grown up on the subject in recent years. This book endeavors to incorporate the significant contributions of differing points of view in a general, interdisciplinary approach to the study of organizations and management.

Organizations are dynamic processes that include in their make-up a number of subprocesses. The basic component of organizations, however, is the *individual person,* and this person is the fundamental unit of study in this book.

This book presents an uncomplicated, broad, introductory systems view of the field of organizations and management. Therefore, many exceptions to and ramifications of the basic ideas have been omitted. Also, it is thought that a beginning course will best serve the student if it presents an integrated study of the field in its present state of development, which is precisely what this book attempts. The merits and disadvantages of comparative management theories, as well as a detailed historical study of the field, can well be studied in subsequent courses.

This book takes an interdisciplinary approach to the study of management and organizations. It is designed to integrate the findings of the behavioral sciences and other fields of study with classical and other theories of management. It also explains how managers can profitably use quantitative techniques of analysis in organizational problems. Each area—classical management theory, behavioral and other sciences, and quantitative analysis—has much to offer in assisting a manager in his crucial role of making decisions. A workable integration of these areas will enhance the worth of all.

The book is divided into four parts. Those readers who are primarily interested in "what" and "why" questions about organizations will find Part I of particular interest. In addition to analyzing why organizations are created, what they are, and the processes by which they assist man, Part I also examines the highly significant relationship of individual and organizational objectives. The vital role that management plays in organizations is explained. Part I places organizations and management in perspective with their larger environments. A study of why organizations stagnate, decline, and die, together with an explanation of organizational life, prosperity, and self-renewal, is included. Part I can be studied as an independent unit, without reference to the remainder of the book, if desired.

Part II explores human behavior because organizations are made up of humans whose interactions lie at the very heart of organizational processes. Behavioral scientists have provided rich insights into the process of human behavior in organizations, and these insights are summarized in Part II. Part II begins with an overview of human behavior and proceeds to a study of behavior patterns of individuals, behavior among individuals, and behavior within groups. It concludes with a study of behavior among groups.

Part II is helpful for those who wish to emphasize the findings of the behavioral sciences in their study of organizations and management. It does not assume that the reader has done any work in the behavioral sciences, although previous study in these areas would enrich and complement this material. Teachers who wish to omit Part II may do so without seriously damaging the continuity of the remainder of the volume.

Part III includes a detailed study of creating, planning, organizing, motivating, communicating, and controlling, six of the most important processes that occur in organizations. These processes are particularly important in an organization with specified objectives—for example, a business firm. For each of these processes, basic concepts are first explained in detail. Desirable managerial attitudes toward creating, planning, organizing, motivating, communicating, and controlling are explained. An explanation of *how* a manager can use each function to improve performance in organizations is also included. The manager's role is seen as central if the six managerial functions are to be performed efficiently and if the organization is to accomplish its objectives effectively.

Part IV integrates traditional concepts and principles of organizations and management with more recent developments. A historical sketch of management thought is included, and the problems of wasteful practices in organizations are emphasized. The book concludes with a summary of a unified, dynamic philosophy of management.

The widespread acceptance of the first edition of this book has been most gratifying. This second edition has been updated and enlarged, but it retains the basic format of the first edition. Chapters have been added or greatly enlarged on the environment of organizations, planning, controlling, systems analysis, and management in the future. More cases and discussion questions are included, and annotated suggested readings for each chapter have been provided. The chapters in Part II have been rewritten and strengthened with the addition of much new material.

This book is intended primarily to serve the needs of a collegiate introductory course in management or organizations; and with this use in mind, most examples have been drawn from organizations with which students have probably had personal experience. Such examples should increase the student's involvement in the course.

Many concepts of organizations are universal; that is, they apply to all organizations. Thus, concepts derived from study of clubs, universities, governments, and businesses all are relevant to better understanding management and organizations, wherever found.

This book has several significant features:

1 Its approach is highly dynamic, rather than static. Time is recognized as a significant variable in the study of organizations.

2 The individual member of the organization is the basic unit of study.

3 Its scope is broad enough to incorporate all organizations and several schools of thought.

4 Interaction of persons is presented as the most important feature of organizations.

5 What organizations are, why they exist, and how they can be made to perform more effectively are explained in detail.

6 More effective management is emphasized as the key to more effective organizations.

7 The organization of the book into clearly defined parts enables one to use all or part of it, according to his need. Any part can be used as an independent unit, although in sequence the four parts give a unified view of organizations and management.

8 Terminology is clearly explained. Jargon and technical language have been almost entirely eliminated.

9 Examples are drawn from the situations that are likely to be familiar to most students.

Teachers who prefer to use another approach for their introductory course may find the book of value for their second course. The book also has been used in advanced courses in organizations and management. It can be supplemented by additional readings or individual research by students. For this purpose, *Management, Organizations, and Human Resources: Selected Readings* and a study guide are available to accompany this text.

Instructors of courses in administration in the fields of engineering, political science or government, sociology, and education have found this book to be a suitable text. Some instructors have successfully used large blocks of material from this volume as collateral reading for a case-oriented course in organizations and management. The book also offers suitable collateral reading in a large number of related courses in business administration, as well as in other fields. Significant use of the book has been made in introduction to business courses. Many junior and community colleges have courses for which this book is suited and in which it offers an alternative to the often unsatisfactory traditional approaches.

The book also has proved useful for practicing managers. Experienced managers can study the material individually, and numerous university- or company-sponsored management-development programs have used the book as a text.

Because the orientation of the book is broad enough to include all kinds of organizations, in any setting, users in countries other than the author's have found the volume of value. The first edition was translated into Japanese.

In preparing the first edition of this book, I was fortunate to have the assistance of Professors John H. Abernathy, James L. Davis, and Morris E. Massey. I continue to appreciate the wise counsel of Professor Keith Davis. I particularly thank Mrs. Thomas M. Smylie for her assistance; she was also my teacher. The present edition benefits from the contributions of Professor W. Jack Duncan who provided the initial drafts of the present Chapters 16, 23, 30, and 32. Of course, a complete list of former teachers and students who influenced this book would be endless. I sincerely thank all who contributed, but I am solely responsible for whatever deficiencies this book may have.

Herbert G. Hicks

The Management of Organizations: A Systems and Human Resources Approach

1
Organizations— An Overview

1
You and Organizations

*The stage is the entire planet. The plot and the settings
are as diverse as life itself.*
BERTRAM M. GROSS

". . . three . . . two . . . one . . . lift-off! This is the voice of Rocket Control. The manned space flight is headed toward the moon as scheduled."

"In closing, may I tell you gentlemen that working with you has been a real pleasure. I'm sure that the merger of our two companies will provide a major new force in our highly competitive industry."

"And so it's up to you to get out there and make *sure* that we reach that total! All our United Fund agencies are counting on it!"

These are the voices of persons—persons engaged in different activities—but their words have a common thread.

"But, darling, we can't get married until I can get mother to realize that it'll be best for her to live with Aunt Joan."

"All right, class, that's all for today's lecture. Next time we'll finish up Chapter 12 and begin 13. Be sure to be prepared."

3

"Yes, officer, I might have been going a little fast, but I'm late for a date and she just wouldn't understand."

"'Tenshun! Presennt arms! Abooout face! Hut! Two! Three! Four! Hut! Two! Three! Four!"

All these persons are involved in *organizations*. They are interacting with other people in purposeful, structured, interdependent behavior. Any time the behavior of individuals is interrelated, some form of organization exists.

"Gentlemen of the jury, show that justice still exists for those who have little materially, but who live a decent life, protecting only what is rightfully theirs. In your heart, you know the verdict is 'not guilty.'"

"Going into the final seconds of the game, State is leading 13 to 8 with Tech threatening on the 4-yard line. Here's the last play! It's a short pass—complete—touchdown! Tech wins the championship!"

". . . and now let us worship with the morning offering. Will the ushers please come forward."

The voices above all reflect organizations at work. Organizations permeate everyone's life in the modern world. You may never have been aware of organizations before, but they have influenced you nonetheless. You, in turn, can influence them, if you understand how they work. Instead of being a helpless pawn, you can help to determine how organizations can operate to make the best contributions to you and society.

THE PERVASIVENESS OF ORGANIZATIONS

As you go about the business of living, you are surrounded by organizations. In a few minutes you can think of many organizations that affect you—large ones, small ones, formal and informal ones, groups that are primarily economic, religious, military, governmental, educational, social, or political. You belong to many groups that you can easily recognize as organizations—the company you work for, your church, a political party, and several social groups. You also belong to others that you may not recognize as organizations. Further, there are organizations affecting you with which you may feel no direct connection: Governmental units such as fire and police departments are constantly protecting you; utility companies provide power for you, even while you sleep; business organizations stand ready to supply you with goods and services when you need them. Thus, organizations are part of the environment in which you work, play, relax— do just about anything. Organizations are a definite, definable, important daily influence on your life and the way you live it. The way you dress, what you eat, where you go, what you do, your values, your hopes and dreams are products, in part, of organizations that influence you.

You have always been a member of some organization. You have been affected by them and dependent upon still others. At birth you became a member of your family, which is basically an organization. We depend on our family organization to care for us until we are ready to care for ourselves. Other organizations probably also began to serve you immediately at birth—the delivery-room staff, the hospital staff, the suppliers of medicine, food, and other needs for babies. The process of growing up brought you into immediate contact with other organizations—the other children in your neighborhood, the educational system, the boy or girl scouts, and many more—as you came to associate with increasingly more persons outside your family circle. And this pattern holds true not only for you but for almost everyone.

The "organization man" in the gray flannel suit was a product of our own civilization, but he had a host of ancestors. Anthropologists have discovered evidence of organizations in the primitive societies of the earliest known humans. For thousands of years the basic organization was the simple family unit, but other forms gradually developed in answer to the demands of tribal living, religious teachings, and barter and commerce.

A study of various peoples around the world today produces living examples of several stages of development. Isolated tribes in Africa, South America, and Australia show how man existed when civilization dawned. Among these primitive peoples, who live only slightly better than some monkeys, man's early organizational efforts may still be studied. As foreign as their techniques may seem, the basic purposes of their organizations and ours may be essentially the same. Both the village open market and a large department store serve some of the same needs in much the same way, by gathering together the things that man wants or needs in a specially appointed place. Tribal witch doctors or a team of skilled surgeons hover over a desperately ill man, both groups trying to save his life. In a primitive society, man may communicate with his fellows by pounding jungle drums; in our own, he uses satellites hovering 24,000 miles above the earth. But the urge to communicate is the same in each case. Efficiency, sophistication, and complexity are the principal changes that have occurred in organizations since their primitive beginnings.

Once we enter the period of recorded history, we can see these early organizations becoming more complex as we study the horde armies of early China, the teams that built the pyramids, the administrative units within the Roman Empire, the crusaders, the merchants of the Middle Ages, the leaders of religious movements, the New World explorers charting new frontiers, and the empires of latter-day industrial Goliaths.

Today diverse organizations are interwoven in a complex tapestry. You and their other members are bonded more and more closely together, day by day. Glistening satellites are linking the world's burgeoning population through live audio and visual communications. Faster and more efficient means of transportation make vast distances shrink into terms of a few hours' supersonic flying time. Mushrooming world trade is spreading the wealth of nations and raising the living standards of millions.

As we become more and more involved with organizations, they sometimes seem to be our masters rather than our servants. We may fear that their growing power and pervasive influence may threaten our individual freedom and dignity.

But when we look at the positive side of organizations, we also see their tremendous benefits: A student pays fees to, and spends precious time in, an organization—a college—and gets a valuable education. In almost every case his benefits far exceed what he gives up. He complains about paying taxes to an organization—his government—but those taxes provide highways, police protection, and medical research. He pays a large sum to still another organization for a new automobile, but the mechanical marvel provided by the car manufacturer offers efficient and comfortable transportation at reasonable cost for many thousands of miles.

It is true that membership in organizations imposes many different costs—money, time, and work. But in a complex society it seems virtually impossible for a person to avoid participating in a number of organizations. The fundamental question for each person is not whether or not he will belong to organizations; rather, the question is how organizations can serve him more effectively. Organizations offer each person the potential for many satisfactions; but if they are to serve him better, he needs to know how they work, in general, and how particular organizations can work for him.

A person joins or forms an organization because he expects that his participation in it will satisfy some of his needs. To gain these satisfactions he is willing to incur certain costs or to make an investment in the organization. These relationships are shown in Figure 1-1. The person expects that his need satisfactions will be larger than his costs, and he evaluates his expected satisfactions and costs in his value system. Thus, before he participates in an organization, a person expects that his

Satisfactions-costs > 0

or, stated alternatively,

$$\frac{\text{Satisfactions}}{\text{Costs}} > 1$$

If events confirm these expectations, the organization is successful. On the other hand, because the individual's participation in the organization is based on expected or perceived values, it may turn out to have been a mistake. In that case his costs exceed his satisfactions, and the organization was ineffective. Thus, an organization creates values,

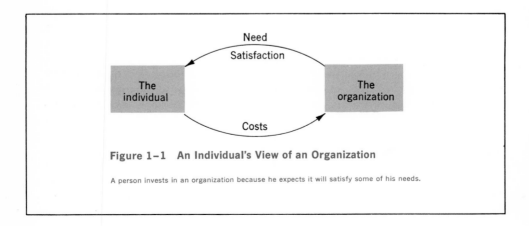

Figure 1–1   An Individual's View of an Organization

A person invests in an organization because he expects it will satisfy some of his needs.

which satisfy personal needs. A successful organization takes resources from persons, but returns more values than were invested.

REASONS FOR ORGANIZATIONS

Organizations meet many different kinds of needs for man—emotional, spiritual, intellectual, economic. Argyris explained their existence by saying simply that they are usually formed to meet objectives "that can best be met collectively."[1]

One of the best discussions of the ability of organizations to do things that individuals cannot do alone is that of Chester I. Barnard.[2] Barnard defined the limitations of an individual as the things that keep him from doing what he wants to do. Limitations fall into one of two groups; they are established by either (1) the biological capacities of the individual or (2) the physical factors of the environment that he faces. Barnard emphasized two things. First, these limitations are directly related to one another—that is, limitations that apply to one of these groupings of factors can only be described in terms of the other set of factors. And second, the individual must clearly define what he wants to do; if he has no specific goal, the term "limitation" has no significant meaning.

To illustrate, Barnard cited a situation in which a man wanted to move a stone that was too large for him. The limitation may be stated in one of two ways: "stone too large for man" or "man too small for stone." The first statement expresses the limitation in terms of the physical environment; and the second, the limitation in terms of the man. For many years—beginning probably with the caveman—man's organizations were designed to overcome limitations of physical environment: to move stones, to kill tigers, to protect himself from cold.

Barnard pointed out, however, that when two men work together to move a stone, they are increasing their individual strengths by pooling them and that when they recognize this, they deliberately form an organization. Thus, we have a clear basis for organizations. Organizations are designed by man to overcome his own limitations. With organizations, man sees that the ultimate limitation for most of his objectives is not individual strength or intellect but his ability to work effectively with his fellows in organizations.

Thus Barnard explained the development of organizations as a device to overcome the limitations that restrict individual action. For, until man conceived the idea that by organized effort a group of men could satisfy some human needs or achieve some objectives more effectively than they could separately, as individuals, all action was limited to individual action. Until the concept of organizations was perceived and acted upon, man was limited by the combined effects of his individual capacities and his physical environment. Once man conceived the idea of joint, goal-directed effort, then *the chief*

---

[1]Chris Argyris, *Integrating the Individual and the Organization,* John Wiley & Sons, Inc., New York, 1964, p. 35.

[2]Chester I. Barnard, *The Functions of the Executive,* Harvard University Press, Cambridge, Mass., 1956, pp. 23–37.

limitation on his accomplishments was determined by the effectiveness of his organiza-tions. Organized action became man's chief means for overcoming restrictions imposed on individuals.

Social Reasons

Man is a gregarious being; he seems always to want relationships with other persons. Even the hippie, who supposes himself to be rebelling against conforming to society, conforms very rigidly to the standards of dress and behavior imposed by his hippie group.

Many organizations exist purely to meet this need for companionship. Others, whose primary objectives may be intellectual or economic, also answer it, whether consciously, deliberately, or in spite of themselves. A large business organization, for example, can provide many satisfying contacts for its employees within the firm itself and with sup-pliers and customers. Sometimes a person's social needs are so completely met by the company he works for that others say of him, "His job is his life." He seems completely happy just to go to work, to associate with his fellow employees, to gear his whole life to his job. Another person may work with a volunteer group—a church, a charitable or-ganization, or even a volunteer fire department—because he agrees with its humani-tarian purpose; but often, however (and perfectly legitimately), he is drawn to a group in which he expects to enjoy his associates. Man, therefore, organizes because he needs and enjoys the social satisfactions organizations provide.

Sports organizations often provide social values. The competition and companion-ship of athletes and teams frequently produce intense personal involvement of spectators as well as players. One star athlete described his involvement with his team: "It's great getting a bunch of guys working together toward a common goal and achieving it."

Material Reasons

Man also organizes for material reasons. Through organizations he can do three things that he could not do alone: (1) he can enlarge his abilities; (2) he can compress the time required to accomplish an objective through an organization; and (3) he can take advan-tage of the accumulated knowledge of previous generations.

Enlarge abilities The first material reason for organizations is that they enlarge man's abilities. That is, through organizations he can do many things more efficiently than he could if he had to work without the association of others. In fact, many things that man wants to do can be done *only* through organized efforts.

When man recognized that as an individual his ability was limited, he probably formed organizations to provide basic needs—food, clothing, and shelter. The results of novel experience were highly successful. These organizations so improved living standards and assisted in man's fight against the elements that the idea of organizations was soon extended beyond achieving basic needs. Man found that many things—for example, mutual defense and production of goods—could be achieved better with organized effort than by individual effort. With organizations, man could develop legal systems and governments; and in today's world, insurance companies, orchestras, and athletic teams. With organizations he could build a rocket to go to the moon, and he could produce a higher and higher standard of living. Organizations produce gains in productivity because they make specialization and exchange possible.

Specialization   Adam Smith in *The Wealth of Nations* (1776) recognized the value of specialization in his famous example of the making of pins. By World War II the same principles, extensively applied, had resulted in harnessing the power of the atom. And every day, specialization enables business organizations to produce more at a lower cost than could possibly be done with individual efforts. Further, each person can do the particular job for which he is best suited and trained.

Often, when persons work together to accomplish a goal, they can divide the work and accomplish the goal with much less total effort than if one person worked alone for the goal. For example, if several individuals want chairs, there is no doubt that given the proper skills and tools each could construct a chair, in time. But if these same skilled individuals with the same tools were to get together and decide on what type of chair they were to make, then each could produce a specific part. Each could specialize. The group would then be able to produce the same number of chairs in a shorter time.

The advantages of specialization can be illustrated with a simple example. Suppose Mr. Taylor worked to produce the chairs mentioned above. He could produce an entire chair by himself. In that case he performs cutting, assembling, sanding, painting, and upholstering operations. When he works in this fashion, Mr. Taylor produces nine units of productivity per day, as shown in Figure 1-2.

On the other hand, it is easily conceivable that Mr. Taylor might be an expert assembler and that he could increase his daily productivity by spending all his time assem-

	MR. TAYLOR'S ACTIVITIES	UNITS OF PRODUCTION PER DAY	
		WITHOUT SPECIALIZATION	WITH SPECIALIZATION
1	Cutting	3	0
2	Assembling	2	12
3	Sanding	1	0
4	Painting	1	0
5	Upholstering	2	0
		9	12
	Gain from specialization = 12 − 9 = 3 units per day		

Figure 1-2   *Comparative Productivity without and with Specialization*

Specialization, which is made possible by organizations, is an extremely powerful way of increasing man's productivity.

bling chairs. Figure 1-2 illustrates that this shift of Mr. Taylor's efforts might result in his producing twelve units of productivity per day, a gain of three units.

The degree of specialization in the modern world is truly astounding. Indeed, a person often identifies himself in terms of a specialization. For example, one may refer to himself as a quarterback, student, engineer, accountant, son, Methodist, Democrat, and in countless other such ways. He thus describes himself in terms of some kind of specialized activity, role, profession, or interest. In the work area alone, thousands of job classifications (specializations) are recognized by the U.S. Department of Labor.

Specialization is advantageous for a number of reasons. First, it is impossible for anyone to become expert in all the skills and areas of knowledge in modern society. Thus, one restricts himself to relatively few activities in which he can become expert. Second, men differ in their interests, nature, capacities, experiences, and skills. The example above of Mr. Taylor specializing in assembling chairs can illustrate these factors. Mr. Taylor may like to assemble chairs. His manual dexterity and other physical and mental factors suit him to this work. Perhaps he has had many years' experience as a chair assembler. In short, he is an expert in that work. Specialization also will permit Mr. Taylor to acquire specialized, expensive tools to assist him.

An organization is necessary for Mr. Taylor to specialize in assembling chairs. If he gives up the functions of cutting, sanding, painting, and upholstering, other persons must perform those functions, working cooperatively with him. Perhaps each of these functions also can be specialized with further productivity gains.

If Mr. Taylor spends all his time assembling chairs, he certainly will have more chairs than he needs. Somebody else must be willing to buy his surplus. Furthermore, other persons—similarly specialized—will have to produce and distribute the food, clothing, and all other goods and services required by Mr. Taylor. Managers (another specialty!) will have to coordinate the production of the chairs and distribute them to customers. The chain of such cooperation is endless; the tremendously complex web of interdependence of modern society could not be fully described with a whole shelf of books.

Some effects of specialization may be undesirable. The monotony of specialized work may be boring. And the large and complex organizations required for high degrees of specialization may be overwhelming to the individual. His work may be so fractionalized that he might spend all day putting one bolt on a car on an assembly line. It may be difficult for him to see himself as worthwhile performing such a task. Also, large organizations may be impersonal; members may have feelings of alienation and nonparticipation. Such problems are serious in the modern world. Despite the problems, it is likely that you participate in or benefit from many instances of specialization.

Exchange As explained above, specialization implies exchange. The exchange process also can be viewed as an organizational process that creates value.[3] Gains from

---

[3]The alternative view attributes such gains to the specialized production process since it is a prerequisite to exchange.

exchange can be illustrated by a simple barter example. Suppose Mr. Fox has five bushels of grapes worth 100 units of value to him. Mr. Sanders has a pair of shoes which he values at 90 units of his values. Mr. Fox would like to have the shoes; they would be worth 110 units of his values. Mr. Sanders would like to have the grapes; they would be worth 120 units of his values. So they exchange, each gaining in the exchange. The transaction is shown in Figure 1-3.

The exchange just described is an extremely simple one. Many exchanges are far more complicated. They involve the enormous complexity of financial institutions, distribution systems, monetary systems, and other means of facilitating exchange. In every case, however, exchange as an organization activity is undertaken by each participant with the expectation that he will benefit from the exchange. Thus, organizations enlarge man's abilities or productivity through the exchange process. Whenever you benefit from any exchange you are benefiting from an organization.

Compress time   The ability of organizations to compress the time required to reach an objective is the second material reason for their existence. In many cases, reducing total elapsed time is more important than ordinary efficiency. Hence an objective that could be accomplished by an individual or a relatively small group might be assigned to a large organization, even though the larger group will expend more effort or money. The elapsed time that an individual or small group would take to do the job might be too long to be acceptable. A "crash" program to get a man to and from the planet Mars might require an extremely large organization, with little emphasis on keeping costs low. For instance the President might in 1976 decide between two alternatives. Alternative A is projected to land a man on Mars in 1984 with each of the eight years' preparation costing $4 billion. Alternative B is estimated to do the job in 1989; each of the thirteen required years will cost $2 billion. These relationships are illustrated in Figure 1-4.

The eight-year plan costs $32 billion, and the thirteen-year plan costs $26 billion. The difference, $6 billion, is the extra price that is paid for getting the job done sooner. Just as an automobile requires more and more gasoline per mile as the speed rises

	MR. FOX'S VALUES	MR. SANDERS' VALUES
Grapes	↓ 100	120 ↑
Shoes	110	90
Gain from exchange	10	30

Figure 1-3   *An Example of Exchange. Arrows Indicate Direction of Exchange*

A successful exchange results in gains to all participants. For this reason, countless individuals and organizations engage in exchange.

ALTERNATIVE	NUMBER OF YEARS	COST PER YEAR (BILLIONS)	TOTAL COST (BILLIONS)
A	8	$4	$32
B	13	$2	$26
		Cost of five years' compressed time =	$ 6

Figure 1-4   *Compressing Time*

Organizations often compress or reduce the time required to meet an objective by putting more resources to work faster. Often this increased speed of accomplishment is more costly.

above about 50 miles per hour, so also do organizations often use more resources to work faster. In choosing between the Mars alternatives, the President would have to decide which is more desirable, $6 billion or getting the man to Mars five years sooner.

The pressure to compress time may demand that a highly specialized scientist be available immediately when needed for the Mars project, although much of his time is not efficiently used. If the organization is not efficient enough to utilize his services all the time, his "free" time might nevertheless be accepted as necessary, because filling the needs for his services quickly after a problem arises may be more important than short-run efficiency. Thus, organizations whose objectives must be accomplished quickly will often be inefficient in other respects.

Another example of compressing time is seen in using a large group of fire fighters rather than a small one, or an individual fireman, to fight a large fire. And military organizations often require troops or planes to remain idle for countless months, just to be available the instant they are needed. Or a company may have an all-out but costly program to get one of its products accepted in the market before a competitor's.

Time is a significant factor in the accomplishment of many, if not most, of man's objectives. By permitting some objectives to be accomplished sooner, organization provides a time value. Both saving total expended time through specialization and compressing total elapsed time can be accomplished through organizations. Saving and compressing time are related but different reasons for organizations.

Accumulate knowledge   The third material reason for organizations is that they allow man to take advantage of accumulated knowledge, to "stand on the shoulders" of those who have gone before him. Without organizations it would be necessary for every man of every era to learn everything by himself, from the beginning. Early man transmitted his accumulated knowledge by word of mouth, sometimes through legends and folk tales handed down within his organization, or tribe. Modern man uses many devices, among which a modern library is an obvious example. Each bit of information that has been produced, accumulated, and stored in the library may provide a foundation for further advances. And a modern educational system provides for quick communication of this knowledge. Clearly, a highly important reason for organizations is that they provide the means for man to take advantage of the experience and insights of those who have gone before him.

The Synergistic Effect of Organizations

The above reasons for the existence of organizations also are explained in part in the concept that organizations can have a synergistic effect. That is, the output of an organization may differ in quantity or quality from the sum of the inputs. In ordinary arithmetic, $2 + 2 = 4$. However, in "organizational arithmetic" 2 units of inputs $+$ 2 more units of input may give 3, 4, 7, 13, A, X, or Z units of output. The units of output may be the same dimensions as the input units and may be equal to or different from their arithmetic sum. In the above statement the outputs 3, 4, 7, and 13 are of this type. The output 3 (meaning an organizational loss of one unit) represents an unsuccessful organization. The output of 4 is a break-even one, and 7 and 13 represent successful organizations. Their output is greater than their costs, or inputs. Outputs A, X, and Z are representations of the fact that the dimension of output may be qualitatively different from input units. The participants have to decide whether or not these organizations were successful.

To illustrate the fact that organizations can have synergy, or a synergistic effect, consider a very simple example—a car stuck in the mud. The car is facing north, and assume it requires 125 pounds of force directed toward the north to free it. Joe and Bob begin to push, with Joe pushing 50 pounds to the south and Bob pushing 100 pounds to the north. This is an unsuccessful organization, for the net effect on the car is 50 pounds to the north—not enough to free it. If the organization is improved by Joe coming around to the other end of the car and pushing his 50 pounds to the north, the total effect is then 150 pounds to the north, which frees the car. The principal synergy produced by this organization may be qualitatively quite different from the expended pounds of force. That is, the two boys are now able to use the car to proceed on their dates with their two beautiful girl friends. The benefits they might gain from this (the outputs of their organization for getting the car unstuck) are, of course, quite different qualitatively from their investment in their organization (pounds of force pushing on the car).

Similarly, one always expects that his benefits from participating in an organization will be greater than his costs. It is possible (although, of course, there are many unsuccessful organizations where one or more participants incur a loss) that all participants will come out ahead, because organizations produce value through this synergistic effect. For this reason organizations—like labor, land, and capital—are considered to be factors of production; that is, they can and do create value.

TYPES OF ORGANIZATIONS

Organizations are infinitely variable. There are as many different organizations as there are persons who are their members. An organization can be either the central focus of a person's life or only an incidental servant. An organization can be rigid, cold, and impersonal; or it can have warm, flexible relationships.

Formal and Informal Organizations

A popular scheme for classifying organizations is to label them as "formal" or "informal," depending upon the degree to which they are structured. Actually, these designations are only extremes, for it would probably be impossible to find a completely formal or a completely informal organization. *Formal* and *informal* define the extremes of a continuum of organizational types. This concept is illustrated in Figure 1-5.

A formal organization has a well-defined structure that may describe its authority, power, accountability, and responsibility relationships. The structure can also define the channels through which communications flow. Formal organizations have clearly specified jobs for every member. The hierarchy of objectives of formal organizations is explicitly stated. Status, prestige, pay, rank, and other perquisites are well ordered and controlled. Formal organizations are durable and planned; because of their emphasis on order, they are relatively inflexible. Membership in formal organizations is gained consciously, at a specific time, and usually openly. Some examples of formal organizations are large business corporations, federal and state governments, and universities.

At the opposite end of the continuum in Figure 1-5 are informal organizations. In contrast to formal organizations, informal organizations are loosely organized, flexible, ill-defined, and spontaneous. Membership in informal organizations may be gained either consciously or unconsciously, and it is often difficult to determine the exact

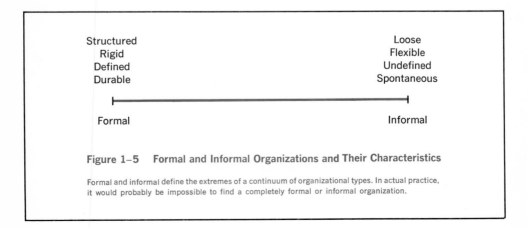

Structured	Loose
Rigid	Flexible
Defined	Undefined
Durable	Spontaneous

Formal   Informal

Figure 1–5   Formal and Informal Organizations and Their Characteristics

Formal and informal define the extremes of a continuum of organizational types. In actual practice, it would probably be impossible to find a completely formal or informal organization.

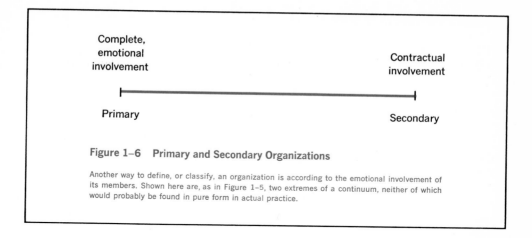

Figure 1–6   Primary and Secondary Organizations

Another way to define, or classify, an organization is according to the emotional involvement of its members. Shown here are, as in Figure 1–5, two extremes of a continuum, neither of which would probably be found in pure form in actual practice.

time when a person became a member. In informal organizations one's membership or involvement may just "grow" through time. The exact nature of the relationships among the members and even the goals of the organization are unspecified. Some examples of informal organizations are a bridge club, a dinner party, passersby who rescue the injured at a car wreck, and a friendship.

Informal organizations can be converted to formal ones when the relationships and activities are defined and structured. Similarly, formal organizations can become informal if the defined and structured relationships are not enforced and are replaced by new, unspecified, and uncontrolled relationships.

Primary and Secondary Organizations

Another way to clarify organizations is as primary or secondary ones, according to the emotional involvement of its members. The terms "primary" and "secondary" also describe the extremes on a continuum, as shown in Figure 1-6.

Primary organizations claim the complete, personal, and emotional involvement of their members. They are characterized by personal, direct, spontaneous, face-to-face relationships. They are based on mutual expectations rather than upon precisely defined obligations. Examples are some families, persons dedicated to their professions, and organizations that espouse causes dear to the hearts of their members. Primary organizations are satisfying ends in themselves.

In secondary organizations, on the other hand, relationships are intellectual, rational, and contractual. Relationships tend to be formal and impersonal with explicitly defined obligations. They are not satisfying ends in themselves, but they have members because they can provide the means (such as pay) to the members' ends. Members involve themselves in only limited ways in these organizations. For many employees, students, and soldiers their respective organizations represent only limited commitment. For example, an employee may, in effect, contract with his employer, agreeing to sell so much of his output or effort for so many dollars per week. Such a contract is limited because neither employee nor employer is expected to perform beyond the boundaries of their agreement.

An organization can have some members for whom the organization is primary; other members of the same organization may regard it as secondary. Obviously, the potential for productivity in primary organizations is vastly superior to that in secondary organizations. In primary organizations the member is willing to commit his total efforts, whereas in secondary organizations he involves himself only partially.

Organizations Classified According to Their Principal Objective

Every organization is formed to achieve some purpose or purposes which can be broadly described as satisfying the wants, needs, desires, or objectives of its members. We can classify an organization according to the particular objectives of its members that it seeks to serve. For example:

1 *Service organizations* that stand ready to assist persons without requiring full pay from each recipient of service (charities, public school boards, park and zoo commissions, highway departments).

2 *Economic organizations* that provide goods and services in return for some form of payment (corporations, proprietorships, partnerships).

3 *Religious organizations* that provide for the spiritual needs of members (churches, sects, orders).

4 *Protective organizations* that protect persons from harm (police departments, the military, fire departments).

5 *Government organizations* that satisfy the need for order and continuity (federal governments, states, cities, courts).

6 *Social organizations* that serve the social needs of persons for contact with others, identification, and mutual support (fraternities, clubs, teams).

SUMMARY

You are surrounded by organizations of all kinds—large, small, formal, informal, primary, secondary, economic, political, social, and others. You are inescapably a part of many of them. Next year you will be affected by additional organizations, and you in turn will have your effect on them. The kinds of organizations to which you are closest, the ways they affect you, and the ways you affect them will change from time to time throughout your life, but organizations of some kind will always be a part of your life.

It has been demonstrated throughout human history that most individuals can achieve more of their goals or achieve them faster, easier, more completely, or more efficiently through organizations. Since the dawn of time, man has learned to use organizations to satisfy an ever-increasing number of his needs. This has meant the creation of more and more organizations, with increasingly complex organizational structures.

Organizations can serve your purposes without governing your life if you understand their purposes and operations. An understanding of organizations can help you determine whether to join a particular organization, stay out, or form a different kind; once within an organization you can help it to help you; you can understand organizations of which you are not a part, and this understanding will enable you to benefit more from them. Finally, through increased knowledge you can improve the effectiveness of your organizations.

Persons often join organizations because of the many social benefits they offer. Fortunately these social benefits frequently are available also in organizations that operate mainly for other purposes. For example, the work relationships in a business may have valuable social dimensions.

Organizations also create value because they permit specialization and exchange. These two factors are foundations of modern society; they account for much of man's time and energy. Time values are provided by organizations when they compress time by accomplishing some objectives faster than would otherwise be possible. And in their ability to store, accumulate, and pass on knowledge, organizations allow persons to build upon the accomplishments of others.

In general, organizations have a synergistic effect. That is, their outputs may differ from the sum of their inputs. Successful organizations create values in that participants' benefits exceed their costs.

Several ways of classifying organizations are available: formal-informal, primary-secondary, and according to the principal objective. These classification schemes can overlap; a given organization can be placed in all three categories.

The more effectively you use organizations, the more valuable they become. This book has been written to give you the tools that you need to understand and improve your organizations.

FOR REVIEW AND DISCUSSION

1 Explain why you are a member of these organizations: your family, a college, and a business firm. Point out the things you give up for membership as well as the benefits you expect to receive in each case.

2 "Sometimes we may feel that organizations are not our servants, but are our masters." Do you agree? Explain your reasons in detail.

3 Suppose a person were not a member of any organizations. What would his life be like?

4 In the modern world, why have organizations become larger and more numerous?

5 List five examples from your own experiences of persons who have been members of organizations to satisfy their social needs. Explain each.

6 Explain the material reasons for organizations. Use examples from your own experiences.

7 How can a business or service organization help to satisfy social needs of its members? Is this a worthwhile and legitimate function of such organizations?

8 Why do we study organizations?

9 Define formal, informal, primary, and secondary organizations.

10 List six organizations, in each of the following four types, of which you are or have been a member: (1) formal, (2) informal, (3) primary, and (4) secondary.

11 Distinguish between an organization's ability to save costs through specialization and its ability to compress time. Use examples not given in the text.

12 Explain in detail how specialization works in organizations. Use examples to illustrate your explanation.

13 How can organizations help to overcome the limitations of individuals acting alone?

14 "Organizations today can fill the gamut of human needs, wants, drives, or strivings. Whether organizations actually succeed in doing these things is a different matter; the fact is they have this potential." Thoroughly explain and evaluate this comment.

15 Discuss a number of disadvantages of belonging to organizations. Use examples from your own experience.

16 Explain the statement: "The chief limitation on man's accomplishments is the effectiveness of his organizations." Do you agree? Explain your answer.

17 Do you agree with the statement: "There are organizations in existence that attempt to satisfy practically every human need"? Explain your answer.

18 Why might the management of a company want to convert the relationships of its employees to the company from a secondary one to a primary one? How might the company go about doing this?

19 The firemen of Fremont City spend their on-duty time roughly as follows: fighting fires, 5 percent; training, 5 percent; playing cards, 90 percent. Using the concept of compressing time as explained in the chapter, justify this apparent gross waste. Suppose, as an economy measure, the city reduced the number of firemen. What effects might this have on the percentage of time the typical fireman spent "working"? What might be the effects on the city's fire losses? Fully explain your answer.

20 Explain in detail and with examples how it might be true that many persons who work free for service organizations may also be doing so to fulfill other needs, that is, needs other than the desire to merely provide the service.

21 Analyze and evaluate this statement: "We may be moving away somewhat from a preference for the enormously complex, impersonal, but highly economically efficient organizations of modern society. We may be moving back toward a preference for the intimate, small group, 'tribal' organizations of the past. The task of the younger generation is to decide which it prefers." Do you agree that such a move is taking place in our society? Explain your answer, using examples for illustration.

22 From library research, write a short but meaningful paper on one of the following aspects of organizations: specialization, exchange, compressing time, relationship of formal to informal organizations, social aspects of business organizations, or other topic as assigned by your instructor.

23 Using a numerical example not in the text, illustrate how an organization can create value through exchange.

24 Explain the advantages and disadvantages of specialization.

25 Explain, with examples, the concept of organizational synergy.

CASES

A   Bob Smith and Elton Jones had been friends for many years. One day, as they were fishing, Bob said, "Say, Elton, why don't we set up an organization to manufacture that special fishing lure you designed? It catches more fish than anything else we've ever used."

"That sounds like a good idea, Bob, but we would have to get some help. I don't know anything about accounting or selling. I just know how to make things."

"Yeh," said Bob, "and all I can do is engineering. But I still think we ought to look into it."

  1 In what ways would an organization enlarge the abilities of Bob and Elton?

  2 Would the organization be a formal or informal one? Explain.

  3 In their conversation how did Bob and Elton recognize the principle of specialization? In addition to accounting and selling what other talents do you think they need to bring into the organization?

B   The S and J Soap Company recently spent several million dollars on a crash promotion program for Magnificent, its new soap. Recently Harold Letts talked with Thomas Shirley, an executive of S and J.

Harold: "Tom, I just don't understand it. Why did you spend so much money so fast on promoting Magnificent? There were all kinds of goof-ups in the program, and I am sure that you would have gotten a much smoother campaign if you'd just taken six months longer."

Tom: "Sure, Harold, you're right. But this way we were certain of getting the market before our competitors."

  1 Explain the organizational principle that was the basis of Mr. Shirley's decision to have the crash program.

  2 How might the right decision in such a case result in apparent waste and inefficiency?

C   Adam Bailey, a freshman at Palms College, was a member of every protest group on the campus. He joined every picket line that sprang up, and on two occasions he had been dragged off to jail by policemen when he lay in the street in front of the car of a leading conservative politician. Each time his friends from the local espresso house bailed him out.

When interviewed by a reporter from the campus newspaper, Bailey made the following statement: "What's wrong with the world is it's overorganized. We must go forward with our plan to do away with all organizations because they enslave us."

    1 What inconsistencies do you see between Bailey's statements and his actions?

    2 Is Bailey's desire to do away with organizations realistic?

    3 Do you agree with Bailey that the world is overorganized? Explain.

    D Mrs. Redlove was president of the Pine Grove Elementary School Parents and Teachers Association. Each month the PTA held a general meeting for the membership, at which some kind of a program—such as a guest speaker—was given. This meeting was usually well attended by several hundreds of persons. The Pine Grove PTA was widely recognized as one of the best and most efficient in the city.

Little, if any, business was conducted in the general meetings. Officers were elected (based on the report of the nominating committee) once each year, resolutions (proposed by the resolutions committee) were sometimes summarily passed, and committee reports were received on occasion.

It was said that the real work of the organization was done by the Board of Directors. This board had about twenty members, consisting of all officers, committee chairmen, and the school principal. The board met regularly the second Tuesday of each month from ten o'clock until noon at the school. Business matters required about half this time, and the other hour was spent chatting, over coffee and cookies. Board meetings were looked forward to by most members as highly enjoyable social occasions. In fact, Mrs. Rutgers, who had recently moved into the city, had requested and gotten a committee chairmanship with the idea that this would be a good way to make new friends. (Many permanent friendships were formed in the Pine Grove PTA in this manner.) She was appointed chairman of the food service for the very popular Halloween Carnival. She, of course, continued to attend board meetings throughout the year, after all work had been completed on the Halloween Carnival.

In November, Mrs. Redlove found that the board had no business to transact. Nevertheless, she called a "meeting" to be held at her home at the usual time. Everyone came and had a good time.

    1 Explain how the Pine Grove PTA Board satisfied human social needs while it conducted its business. Was this social satisfaction available at the general meetings also? Explain the difference between the board and the general meetings on this matter.

    2 Should Mrs. Redlove have canceled the November meeting because of a lack of business to transact? Why?

    3 Should organizations mix business with pleasure as did the Pine Grove PTA? Why?

    4 What could the management of a business learn from the Pine Grove PTA?

FOR FURTHER STUDY

Additional sources can be found in the sources cited in the chapter.

Books

Chester I. Barnard: *The Functions of the Executive,* Harvard University Press, Cambridge, Mass., 1938, chaps. III and IV. Organizations are cooperative systems intended to overcome physical limitations and to satisfy psychological and social needs.

Hadley Cantril: *The Psychology of Social Movements,* John Wiley & Sons, Inc., New York, 1941, pp. 3–21. A person is born into and spends his life in a highly organized society that largely determines his norms, values, standards of judgment, frames of reference, and attitudes.

Luther Gulick: "Notes on the Theory of Organizations," in Luther Gulick and L. Urwick (eds.), *Papers on the Science of Administration,* Institute of Public Administration, New York, 1937, pp. 3–6. Specialization is the economic foundation of organizations. There are a number of reasons for it, and there also are limitations.

James D. Mooney and Alan C. Reiley: *Onward Industry!* Harper & Brothers, New York, 1931, pp. 1–6. Man organizes because it is his natural way of gaining his physical, economic, social, and spiritual objectives.

Adam Smith: *Wealth of Nations,* originally published 1776 (numerous editions currently available), chap. 1. In this classic chapter Smith described the advantages of specialization, or division of labor. The example of a pin factory is used.

Articles

"An Uneasy Sense of Emptiness and Anonymity," *Life,* Apr. 21, 1967, pp. 62–72. The modern mood of uniformity under pressure and of distorted scales of values can lead to a sense of emptiness and anonymity.

Daniel Bell: "Toward a Communal Society," *Life,* May 12, 1967, pp. 112–124. To preserve the importance and freedom of the individual in our increasingly complex society, many changes and adaptations must be made.

Harry Levinson: "Reciprocation: The Relationship between Man and Organization," *Administrative Science Quarterly,* March 1965. Individuals and organizations interact because they mutually contract to provide benefits for each other.

Jon M. Shepard: "Functional Specialization, Alienation, and Job Satisfaction," *Industrial and Labor Relations Review,* January 1970. Increased specialization tends to lower job satisfaction.

"The Search for Purpose," *Life,* Apr. 28, 1967, pp. 66–79. There is an intense search among the young in our complex society for personal commitment to worthwhile goals.

2
What Is
an Organization?

An organization is a system of cooperative human activities. . . .
    CHESTER I. BARNARD

The first tool needed for a serious study of organizations is an explicit definition of just what an organization is. The definition below, expressed in terms that will be used throughout this book, is based on five facts that are common to all organizations:

1 An organization always includes persons.[1]

2 These persons are involved with one another in some way—that is, they are interacting.

3 These interactions can always be ordered or described by some sort of structure.

4 Each person in the organization has personal objectives, some of which are the reasons for his actions. He expects that participation in the organization will help to achieve his objectives.[2]

5 These interactions can also help to achieve compatible joint objectives, perhaps different from, but related to, their personal objectives.

---

[1]Ants, bees, beavers, and baboons have organizations. And an automobile or building may be thought of as being an organization of its many parts. However, this book is concerned only with human organizations.

[2]Even a person who has been forced into an organization against his will may be seen as working to accomplish his objectives—perhaps to keep from being executed. For example, many persons were forced to work for Nazi organizations in World War II. They did so to escape prison, punishment, or death.

Members of organizations work toward these joint, organizational objectives in order to achieve their personal objectives. Therefore,

An organization is a structured process in which persons interact for objectives.

What occurs in an organization are interactions; the organization's structure describes these interactions, setting forth roles, relationships, activities, hierarchies of objectives, and other features of the organization. The nature of the structure and the particular processes of interacting will vary from one organization to another. However, persons are interacting for objectives in every organization, and this interaction can always be described with some type of structure. For formal organizations structure is likely to be recognized as a primary feature; for informal organizations the structure likely is less important.

ELEMENTS OF ORGANIZATIONS

This basic definition gives us minimum but explicit standards that will enable us to identify an organization, sometimes with unexpected results. For example, two strangers walking toward each other on a crowded sidewalk may simply be two individuals going about their respective businesses. However, if they see one another and deliberately change course or pace to avoid a collision, interaction has taken place. Further, each has acted with a purpose peculiar to himself, a purpose compatible with the joint goal: not to collide. Is this brief, accidental interaction therefore a bona fide organization? Yes, it is. Its membership is very small, its duration only a moment, its structure very simple, but it *is* an organization. It may not succeed—the collision may take place in spite of it—but there has been deliberate interaction in response to individual purposes, and the same interaction has also served a joint purpose. The structure of this organization might be described in several different ways: in terms of which person acted first to avoid the collision, or which person was the actor and which the reactor, or which person was the leader and which the follower. Their objectives are also structured in their joint desire to avoid a collision. This is, of course, an extreme example, but it does illustrate an organization in its simplest form.

The local Farris TV Service is an organization. In addition to Mr. Farris, the owner, its membership includes eleven repairmen, a bookkeeper, and a telephone receptionist. All these persons interact for the purposes of providing repair service for television sets and making the Farris TV Service successful.

The definition also identifies extremely complex organizations, such as a university. Here there are countless interactions among thousands of persons—students, professors, cafeteria workers, deans, repairmen, secretaries—each of whom, consciously or not, is pursuing his own purposes while he works for the university. Some of these purposes are lofty and idealistic, some practical, some in conflict with others, some supporting or reinforcing others; but they may be met when the university is carrying on its work; hence these persons have come together and their interactions are centered around the campus. The structure of the university is shown by its organization chart, the identifiable activities in which its deans, professors, and students engage, or its hierarchy of objectives.

Thus an organization can be either casual or exquisitely complex.[3] The term is broad enough and flexible enough to encompass minor collisions on a crowded street, major universities, and corporate behemoths. Large organizations have numerous small organizations within them. A university has classes, social groups, and academic societies. Each is an organization unto itself. Many small organizations come into being, succeed or fail, and often die quietly, perhaps without ever having been recognized as organizations, even by their members.

With all this variety and complexity, however, there are two kinds of elements common to all organizations, the *core element* and the *working elements*.

The core element of any organization is *persons*—the particular persons whose interactions compose the organization. Any organization is constantly changing—hence the use of the term "process" in the definition above, to convey the dynamic nature of organizations. The names on a membership roll may change, but there are always some persons involved and their relationships can be expressed in some sort of structure, or no organization exists. Interacting persons are the necessary—and sufficient—element, and therefore they constitute the core element of organizations. "The necessary condition for organization is interaction between two or more persons who perceive that their individual desires can best be satisfied through the combination of personally possessed capabilities or resources."[4]

The success or failure of any organization is basically determined by the quality of interactions among the core element, its members. But the core element does not exist in a vacuum. As soon as an organization comes into being, the core element begins to be affected by working elements. The working elements determine the quality of interactions. Members interacting make an organization, but the working elements make it effective or ineffective.

The working elements of an organization consist of its human resources—its members' abilities and their personal influence; its nonhuman resources—free and economic goods; and the conceptual resources of a particular group of its members—the managers. The degree to which all members of an organization employ their abilities and influence in the effective utilization of resources depends upon how well the managers of the organization understand and perform their jobs.

This chapter can assist in that understanding, for it explains the relationship of members to their organization and the responsibilities of managers to the individual members as well as to the organization as a whole. There is a clear connection between the personal objectives of individuals in an organization and the objectives of the organization itself, and establishing this connection in practice is a job of the manager.

---

[3] The objectives of some organizations may be known only unconsciously to some of its members. In fact, some members of organizations may not even be aware of their membership. See Eric Berne, *Games People Play,* Grove Press, Inc., New York, 1964.

[4] Ogden H. Hall, An Analysis of Power and Its Role in the Decision-making Process of the Formal Organization, unpublished dissertation, Louisiana State University, Baton Rouge, La., 1964, p. x.

THE CORE ELEMENT: PERSONS

Persons are the essential core element in organizations. Things interact—for example, chemical elements—and animals interact. But interactions of things and animals differ from human interactions, in that only humans can experience a sense of purpose. Animals act instinctively or merely by training or experiences, and apparently are not aware of the ways in which they benefit from their actions, even habitual actions such as finding food.

Humans, on the other hand, can work consciously toward their individual objectives. They may not always be conscious of what these objectives are, but they are *capable* of being conscious of them, and when they join with other persons in an organization, they have done so for their individual purposes. In terms of the definition above, when persons interact in some structured way, an organization exists. But the interaction would not have taken place except for their objectives.[5] Objectives come first, both in the history of any organization and in the study of organizations as a whole.

Persons and Their Personal Objectives

"Why should I join that club?" "Should I stay with this company or look for another job?" "What will happen if I stay outside of the student association or the hospital insurance plan—will I be penalized?" Such questions are always a part of a person's decision to go into, remain in, or stay out of any organization. Without persons, an organization cannot come into being in the first place, so their reasons for forming, joining, or rejecting it are of crucial importance to the organization. An individual supports an organization if he believes that through it his personal objectives are being attained; if not, he loses interest.

Importance of personal objectives in organizations
Not everyone stops to analyze consciously just how a particular organization fits in with his personal objectives; in fact as was said above, not everyone is completely aware of his personal objectives. A specific person may not even be aware that he *has* objectives. Yet, effective organizations exist, in spite of these deficiencies. Why then is it important for managers to recognize that the personal objectives of each member of an organization are related to that member's participation in the organization? *Because the effectiveness of the member's participation is directly related to his idea of how the organization helps him to achieve his own objectives.* If he believes that it does, he can participate in a highly productive cycle: he works wholeheartedly toward his own objective (he understands that it is most likely

---

[5]Modern psychology assures us that persons always have reasons for their actions—actions that do not involve other persons as well as those that do (that is, interactions). Persons need or want something, and they act or interact accordingly. Without arguing the point as a general principle, this text suggests that it is a valid, practical one as far as organizations are concerned. Individual objectives and organizational objectives will be dealt with separately to emphasize that individual objectives are distinct from (although related to) the objectives of the organization as a whole. Activity unrelated to other persons, even though undertaken for individual objectives, does not qualify as an organization because no interaction exists.

to be accomplished when he contributes to the organization), thus helping to move the organization toward the organizational objectives, which moves him closer to his own, which moves the organization closer, and so on.

The member's and the manager's job of relating personal and organizational objectives would be rather simple if each member had one objective at a time, if each knew what this objective was, and if it were directly related to the agreed objective of the organization. But personal objectives—even for one person—are very complex. Everyone is capable of short-range, medium-range, and long-range objectives, and everyone probably has all of them at any given time, some more important to him than others.[6] When he is associated with other persons in an organization, their combined objectives overlap, conflict, and reinforce one another. If managers are aware of this, they can minimize conflicts and make the most of reinforcements. Numerous tools exist to help in this process once the basic sequence is clear:

1 Persons are the core element of all organizations.

2 All persons have personal objectives.

3 Organizations are both the result of these objectives and the means by which persons attain them.

Interactions—the expression of personal objectives An organization comes into being because of personal objectives; it functions through interactions among persons. These interactions are, in fact, the only processes by which organizations can function.

We often speak of accomplishments "by" a club, a church, a government—any organization—and this kind of generalization is certainly helpful; a complete description of the interactions among all the individuals who helped to design, build, and launch a rocket would be endless. This familiar organizational terminology permits grouping personal interactions into several levels and thus to speak of the whole or of components of complex organizations as tangible, identifiable entities. However, it should be kept in mind that this is only a sort of verbal short cut; "the government" that launches the rocket *is* the persons (and their interactions) who are associated in the project and, by extension, also the persons whose only contributions were to pay taxes and watch the television screen when the rocket was launched. With these qualifications, any set of complex interactions will be referred to in this book as an organization, capable of accomplishing objectives in and of itself. But the interactions of persons are always present, on any level of interaction.

---

[6]Generally, if a person can see an important objective close at hand, he will work harder and endure difficulties more willingly than for a distant, equally desirable objective. The dimension of time is therefore as important as the ultimate values persons give to their own objectives. For example, in June a college student may take a back-breaking construction job that will pay well, knowing that in September he will have made enough money to go back to college. The same job would not attract him on a long-range basis; one of his medium-range, major objectives is his college degree, and one of his long-range, major objectives is the professional life he pictures for himself fifteen years hence.

Levels of interaction   The individual interaction that takes place in organizations can be described on four levels.[7] These levels appear to grow progressively less personal.

Individuals interact.
Individuals and the organization interact.
Organizations and other organizations interact.
Organizations and their total environment interact.

Even on this last level, however, as organizations and their environment interact—as when General Motors embarks on a huge expansion program—persons are always present and constitute the interaction.

1 *Individuals interact.* The first of these levels is visible and immediate; we need look no further than ourselves to see an individual doing something that evokes a response from other individuals.

This response is both physical and mental. When a student is in a classroom, the interaction of his thoughts and those of the professor is a mental response; his presence in the classroom is a physical response and may be due to the fact that the professor expects him to be there. Even in the unintellectual task of ditch digging, the obviously physical interaction among the diggers is coordinated by some sort of mental interaction; otherwise ditches would vary erratically in depth, width, and direction.

Recognizing the presence of these countless, continuing, individual interactions is crucial to an understanding of organizations, because a person's relationship in and to a particular organization, and hence his productivity, is expressed through them.

In any group, even if the relationships are not formally imposed at the beginning, they will soon begin to become evident. For example, the leaders and subleaders of the group will emerge, and the activities and contributions of each member can be identified.

2 *Individuals and the organization interact.* Consider a member of a large organization interacting with that organization. If a private literally hates the army and all it stands for, he will very likely evoke a response. However, the private is actually reacting to army policies as carried out by a *person* (or persons) acting in assigned capacities and influenced by all sorts of military traditions. The response of the army to the private's individual repugnance will also be carried out by a person. For a second example, consider an outside person who interacts with a large organization. When a young woman from a small town goes on her first trip to New York she may go to a great deal of trouble to visit Macy's. She may think of herself as visiting something more than a vast department store—an institution, a landmark, a monument to the American woman's thrift as well as to her good taste. Macy's has waged a long and vigorous campaign to create this image in her mind, but the organization understands very well that once she has

---

[7]Cf. the grid inside the covers of Merwin M. Hargrove, Ike H. Harrison, and Eugene L. Swearingen, *Business Policy Cases,* Richard D. Irwin, Inc., Homewood, Ill., 1963.

entered the doors of the store itself, her satisfaction depends upon *persons*—not a mammoth abstraction—and sales personnel are repeatedly reminded of this.

3 *Organizations and other organizations interact.* Rival service stations engage in bitter price wars—and cooperate to establish a community chest and Better Business Bureau—and once again we can see, beneath the banner of each organization, the individuals who are interacting. By the time this level of interaction is reached, there may be a large number of individuals between the persons who decide on a particular policy and those who carry it out, and so interactions are even more numerous and complex than those between two individuals. The interactions may travel down a long chain of command, from an oil company division manager who decides to cut prices, to a high school boy who works after school at a service station; but the boy's action in painting out the old price of gasoline is directly connected with the manager's decision. Conversely, the boy's experiences with the buying public and with employees at the rival station across the street can travel back to the manager through the same channels to play their part in the next decision. Once again, interactions among individuals are the heart of all interactions, including those among organizations.

4 *Organizations and their total environment interact.* No organization exists in a vacuum. It exists in association with many other organizations and with many individuals. This complex in which an organization exists is called its "environment." To some degree every organization is influenced by its environment; and it, in turn, can to some extent influence its environment. What General Motors does affects the entire economy, and vice versa—changes in the economy affect General Motors.

Personal interactions are taking place on all four of the above levels. The term "the organization" is used to refer to a concept of these interactions. This way of looking at interactions relates them to one another in terms of a structure. When large organizations are involved, interactions appear to be impersonal when we focus on structure instead of interactions. Because of the difficulty of dealing with numerous and complex interactions, it is tempting to forget that interactions always take place within every structure.

Persons and Their Organizational Objectives

Effectiveness of a given organization is determined by how well the objectives of that organization are being achieved. One group may be effective if everyone within it is learning to speak Spanish; another, if the stockholders are making money. Probably no organization is fulfilling its objectives as well as it might, but if it continues to exist, it is because some persons view it as at least partially effective.

We speak of an organization as a thing unto itself (the verbal short cut discussed above), an entity with its own objectives, in terms of which its effectiveness can be measured. But within the organization are its members, each of whom has his individual objectives. When we begin to speak of objectives of the organization, are we ignoring the objectives of individuals? Is there, after all, a valid relationship between individual objectives and organizational objectives, and if so, what bearing does this relationship have on the effectiveness—and thus, on the continued existence—of an organization?

First, there is indeed a close relationship. Next, the relationship is important because the manager who understands it can then apply resources to their best uses—uses that satisfy both individual and organizational objectives.

The relationship of individual and organizational objectives comes about in this way:

1 The objectives of individuals lead to action by those individuals.

2 When action by one individual involves another individual in some way, the second individual reacts, in accordance with individual objectives of his own. This interchange of action and reaction constitutes *interaction,* which can be described by a structure. This interaction by persons (the core element) makes up the productive part of an organization.

3 The individual objectives that lie behind the actions and reactions thus are responsible for the existence of the organization.

4 Each member of the organization has two sets of concepts about himself and the organization: a, his concept of his objectives that he expects to achieve by participating in the organization; b, his concept of the objectives of the organization. Of course, he does not think of them as "concept a" and "concept b"; he may not consciously think of objectives at all. If he did formulate concepts a and b ("I need money," and "this company is trying to sell houses"), they would appear to be compatible to him ("I can sell houses; the company will pay me to do it"). Thus, if he joins the organization, he does so either to achieve something positive or to escape something negative, and he expects that by helping this organization he will help himself. As an example of escaping something negative, consider a young man who eagerly enlists in the Air Force to avoid something he would dislike—being drafted by the Army.

5 The most effective organizations are those in which, first, concepts a and b are compatible for all members; not only do the members *think* they might be—they are.[8] Second, all the concepts b, which we may call b_1, b_2, b_3, etc. (that is, all the individual concepts of the objectives of the organization) are substantially in agreement.[9]

This fifth step does not come about automatically. For example, Figure 2-1 shows the concept of a member in conflict—one whose concept a and concept b are pulling in opposing directions. This personal conflict, if not resolved, very likely will adversely affect that member's performance in the organization. The manager cannot assume that concepts a and b are compatible for each member or that the individual concepts b are in

---

[8]Members think their a's are compatible with their b's, or else they would not be members. But the facts may not support their beliefs; the organization may be a failure.

[9]Cf. Chester I. Barnard, *The Functions of the Executive,* Harvard University Press, Cambridge, Mass., 1938, pp. 72, 73, 75, 81, 94, 240; and "Famous First: Composer of Management Classics," *Business Week,* Nov. 27, 1965, pp. 84–86.

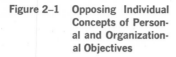

Figure 2–1   Opposing Individual Concepts of Personal and Organizational Objectives

The individual's concept of the organization's objective b is opposed to the individual's personal objective a. If this conflict is not resolved, it will likely affect adversely that member's performance in the organization.

agreement. More likely, neither of these conditions exists except in an incomplete way, and herein lie two clear-cut directives for the manager:

First, a continuing responsibility of the manager is to help members of the organization to integrate their concepts a and b.[10] He shares this problem with the individuals themselves, and whether or not the problem is resolved is ultimately their personal business. The manager can help—and he can certainly hinder—but he cannot do the whole job. If an individual cannot see some compatibility between his own objectives and the organizational objectives, his membership will be unsatisfactory to him, and the effectiveness of the organization as a whole will suffer correspondingly. Figure 2-2 shows the two concepts of a well-integrated individual—one whose concept a and concept b are pulling in essentially the same direction.

The second responsibility is a direct one, however. The manager must integrate all the concepts b—the individual concepts of what the organization's objectives are—in such a way that they can be stated as "concept B," the overall objective for the organization. This concept B, even with its capital letter, is not necessarily a static one. It needs

[10]Cf. Chris Argyris, *Integrating the Individual and the Organization,* John Wiley & Sons, Inc., New York, 1964.

Figure 2–2   Well-integrated Individual Concepts of Personal and Organizational Objectives

If the individual is well integrated, his concept of the organization's objective b moves essentially in the same direction as his own personal objective, and the effectiveness of the organization is strengthened.

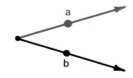

to be restated and reinterpreted continually if the organization is to continue to move toward it. ". . . people work most fruitfully when they know the goals toward which they should be striving."[11] Selection of the best ways of moving toward it and the evaluation of this progress are also the province of the manager, and the working elements of the organization are the tools that he uses. Figure 2-3 shows an example of several members' individual concepts of the organization's objective that are relatively well integrated with the overall organizational objective. If all objectives in the organization were perfectly integrated they would pull in only one direction.

By recognizing the relationship of individual objectives and organizational objectives and by employing resources to achieve organizational objectives, a manager can make his organization increasingly effective.

WORKING ELEMENTS: RESOURCES

The working elements of an organization are those resources within it that can determine whether or not it is effective. Since the manager is the person most responsible for making the organization effective, he must know what these resources are and how they are available to him.

Resources available to an organization fall into two broad categories: nonhuman and human. They include every thing, every person, every concept, and every condition that an organization has to work with.

Nonhuman Resources, Tangible Assets of Organizations

Some nonhuman resources are free and easily accessible to organizations, and others are not. Nature provides free goods in abundance—air, climate, and in some cases even water. For example, a fishing party (a simple organization) in a Gulf Coast town has a

---

[11] Harwood F. Merrill (ed.), *Classics in Management*, American Management Association, New York, 1960, p. 178.

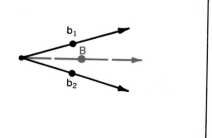

Figure 2–3   Well-integrated Individual and Overall Organizational Objectives

This diagram shows relatively well-integrated individual concepts of the organization's objective and the overall concept of the organizational objective. All the b concepts, b_1, b_2, and so on, are integrated and expressed as concept B—the overall objective for the organization. All concepts of organizational objectives are dynamic; they need to be continually updated.

free ocean in which to fish, as well as free fish. Other kinds of tangible resources are sometimes free in particular cases, as when a church provides a meeting room for a secular organization that discusses famous literature.

However, most tangible resources are not free. The first problem for any organization is to provide itself with the materials and facilities that will be needed to accomplish its objectives.

Human Resources

Human beings—the core element of the organization—now appear again as working elements. Persons within the organization utilize free resources and arrange for the organization to acquire other necessary resources. Without effective management, resources are likely to be wasted; and if the organization's objectives are accomplished at all, they will be accomplished only accidentally. Resources should be channeled or directed or—the most accurate term of all—"managed"; and this is done, of course, by the manager.

The manager needs to recognize that in their role as a working element, humans can bring to the organization three kinds of resources—their own ability to do, their ability to influence others to do, and their ability to comprehend and use concepts.

Ability to do   First, there is the ability to do. A chemical firm needs chemists and chemical engineers, and a baseball team needs expert baseball players. A university needs faculty members who can teach, and the Air Force needs pilots to fly its airplanes. Every organization needs some members who can themselves perform the activities needed to achieve its objectives.

Ability to influence   Second, there is the ability to influence others to do. A person's influence may be derived from his economic power, his social position, his political power, or his individual personality. Ability to influence is essentially the same as power, because power can be defined as the ability to alter the behavior of others. [12]

The power distribution determines whose objectives the organization serves and the weight or consideration given to each member's objectives. Members with extensive power or influence will have a large voice in determining the objectives and operations of the organization; members with little power or influence will be considered but slightly. [13] For example, through the power of their ownership, the proprietors of a business firm will direct the objectives, membership, and activities of their firm. Of course, their power may not be absolute; they must operate within the boundaries of legal,

---

[12] Cf. Ogden H. Hall, *op. cit.,* pp. 2–9.

[13] It is not judged here whether or not any distribution of influence, or power, is best or equitable; that is the task of moral and political philosophers. However, it is emphasized that the manager's values and morals are inextricably involved in *every* decision he makes (even if his decision is to continue the status quo). An excellent source on this subject is Robert T. Golembiewski, *Men, Management, and Morality,* McGraw-Hill Book Company, New York, 1965.

moral, and social restrictions—in effect, these restrictions represent power held in the hands of others. The distribution and application of power ultimately determine the objectives of the organization, its membership, and the way it operates.

Ability to use concepts: The functions of managing The manager needs both influence, or power, and the ability to use concepts to coordinate all the resources of the organization and to direct them effectively toward accomplishing organizational objectives. He ". . . is the dynamic life-giving element in every [organization]."[14] He uses concepts as tools, which may be divided into the areas of creating, planning, organizing, motivating, communicating, and controlling.

Creating   The first task of the manager is to create (or to see that others create) ideas. Creating supplies valuable ideas for products, services, and methods for the organization's use. With creativity the organization can help to assure its prosperous future. It can find better means of achieving its objectives or it can find better objectives to achieve. Without creativity, the organization will eventually die, for man is constantly seeking better things and experiences from his organizations. The organization that fails to take this into account does so at its peril, for if it does not provide these better things, it will be replaced by another organization that does.

Planning   The second task of a manager is to determine what the objectives of the organization are (concept B). Planning includes determining the general way that objectives are to be accomplished.

Organizing   The third conceptual area that managers use is organizing. After the planning has been completed, the manager will determine exactly what activities are required to accomplish the objectives. He will then group these activities into workable units by structuring roles, activities, objectives, authority-responsibility relationships, and the flow of information and communication in the organization.

Motivating   The fourth function of managers is motivating members to accomplish the organization's objectives. Briefly, motivating means discovering the stimulus for particular individuals that will lead to desired behavior. This means making the individual concepts a and b as compatible as possible with concept B. The organization's system of rewards is used to help each individual accomplish his concept a; that is, his objectives for himself in the organization. In other words, members are motivated to work for organizational objectives when their concept of the organization's objective is closely comparable to the actual organizational objective and when their work will lead to the satisfaction of their individual objectives for themselves.

Communicating   Except by accident, nothing is done in organizations without the fifth area, communicating. Communicating may be both verbal and nonverbal, but no interaction can take place without some form of communicating. Communicating is important in discovering what the influential persons desire the organizational goals to be, in translating these goals into terms meaningful to all organizational members, and in

[14]Peter F. Drucker, *The Practice of Management,* Harper & Row, Publishers, Incorporated, New York, 1954, p. 3.

further communicating these goals to all members of the organization. Communicating is also important in discovering what the individual's objectives are for himself and for his organization. When communicating has provided all of this information, the several concepts a and b can be integrated as much as possible and related to the concept B. Because the work of all members must be coordinated, the opportunity for faulty communicating can exist at every point in the organization's performance.

Controlling   Organizations need to know how well they are accomplishing their objectives. Well-administered controlling procedures can tell them. Controlling, the sixth area, compares the events that took place in the organization and the objectives that were attained with those that were desired. If deviations are discovered, appropriate correcting action is taken. On the other hand, if results were satisfactory, members should be told that their behavior was acceptable; they should be appropriately rewarded.

Controlling reduces the amount of uncoordinated behavior; it leads toward more order, discipline, and coordinated performance in the organization. Controlling provides the answer for whether or not the current performance of the organization should be continued, or what corrections might be needed to make the performance satisfactory. Planning sets goals. Controlling tells how well the organization is working toward achieving them.

Each person has his unique concept b (his concept of the organization's objective); concept b is likely different for every member of the organization. Controlling aids in working toward concept B, a generally agreed upon concept of the organization's objective. Without controlling, each member likely would work toward his individual concept b, rather than the organizational concept B. Controlling compares actual performance with concept B; if accomplishment in terms of concept B is not satisfactory, controlling suggests that corrective action be taken. This corrective action will be done with creating, planning, organizing, motivating, and communicating.

Each of the managerial functions of creating, planning, organizing, motivating, communicating, and controlling will be studied in detail in later chapters of this book.

SUMMARY

When persons interact for individual and joint objectives, an organization exists. It can be structured in terms of roles, relationships, activities, and objectives. It can be simple or complex, ranging from two-person interactions to giant, complex groupings involving thousands of persons. And the life span of an organization can range from a few moments to centuries.

Each member of an organization has two concepts: his concept of his own, personal objectives in the organization, and his concept of the organization's objectives. For personal and organizational effectiveness, both concepts must be integrated. Further, organizational effectiveness requires an integration of all the individual concepts of the organization's objectives into a joint, overall concept of the organization's objective.

This overall organizational objective provides direction for the activities of every member of the organization.

The core element of an organization is persons interacting, and such interaction is the necessary and sufficient condition to establish the existence of an organization. However, an organization also can have working elements, the resources that determine effectiveness. Working elements consist of nonhuman resources and the abilities of persons. Human abilities include the ability to do, the ability to influence others, and the ability to use concepts of creating, planning, organizing, motivating, communicating, and controlling. When all resources are well employed or managed, an effective organization exists, if its objectives are being effectively accomplished.

FOR REVIEW AND DISCUSSION

1 What is the necessary and sufficient condition for an organization to exist?

2 What are the things that can be structured in organizations?

3 Explain your view of the objectives of the following organizations: (a) American Legion, (b) Daughters of the American Revolution, (c) General Electric, (d) a family, (e) an orchestra, (f) a college fraternity, (g) a student religious group, (h) Eastern Air Lines, (i) your college or university, and (j) the class in which you are using this book. Can you think of any organizations for which there are no objectives? Why?

4 List five human activities that do not involve organizations.

5 A corporation president was asked, "What is your organization?" He pointed to a chart on the wall and said, "Here is my organization." Do you agree? Why?

6 Explain the role and functions of managers in organizations.

7 Explain the relationship of a person's objectives to his participation in organizations.

8 Differentiate and explain the following: (a) a person's personal objectives, (b) a person's concept of his organization's objectives, and (c) the overall objectives of that organization.

9 Explain the process of integration of individual and organizational objectives.

10 Explain the difference between the core element and working elements of organizations.

11 What three types of abilities do humans bring to organizations? Explain each. Give five examples, from your own experience, of the use of nonhuman resources by organizations.

12 Explain each of the four levels of interactions in organizations.

13 How can a manager help to integrate individual and organizational objectives? Is this one of his responsibilities?

14 Can an organization be totally ineffective and continue to exist? Why?

15 What determines whose objectives the organization will seek to serve?

16 Through library research, find two definitions of organizations. Cite your sources. Compare these definitions of organizations with the one given in this book.

17 Explain and evaluate the statement: "An organization can best be viewed *simultaneously* as a whole and as subunits. Every unit and the interactions among all units must be considered."

18 Explain and evaluate the statement: "An organization is a slice of the world in buzzing confusion."

CASES

A   At a military training base enlisted men between assignments were assigned to a "holding" company while awaiting orders. The company commanding officer insisted that the men stand reveille formation at 5 each morning. The next required formation was at 8:30. Members of C barracks immediately observed that the commanding officer did not bother to count the troops—he quickly took the barrack chief's report and retired to the mess hall for hot coffee.

Never more than half the men in C barracks stood reveille at a time; yet everyone was reported "present or accounted for." Each barracks member had a buddy on the other floor. On Mondays, Wednesdays, and Fridays the members of the first floor stood reveille; on Tuesdays, Thursdays, and Saturdays those from the second floor were present. Each person at roll call would answer for himself and his buddy.

    1 Describe the organization that existed within the barracks. What were its objectives?

    2 Did an organization involving the troops and the commanding officer exist? Explain.

    3 Must the objectives of an organization be good for it to fully qualify as an organization?

B   Stanislaus Brodskey, a recent immigrant, had to walk past a public playground on his way home from work each day. Members of the Vultures, a teen-age gang, often hung around the park. The Vultures continually harassed new immigrants; they had on two occasions roughed-up Stanislaus as he walked past the park.

Stanislaus learned that if he delayed his walk for about five minutes, he could keep pace with Kirby, a policeman, making his regular rounds by the park. Thus, Stanislaus could avoid trouble from the Vultures. Stanislaus and Kirby always had a pleasant chat as they walked together.

    1 Explain the organization that existed between Stanislaus and Kirby.

    2 Was the organization formal or informal? Explain.

C   For several years the eight founding members of POF (Protect Our Freedoms) had met once each week to discuss political, economic, and moral philosophy topics. Through informal means the members had decided upon the questions that came up before the group, including when and where they would meet.

Recently, several members of the group have expressed the opinion, "We ought to get organized." They said that better organization would make it possible to handle the many new persons who wished to join, would make POF into a political force of real power, and in general would cause the group to be more effective and efficient. Two members violently disagreed, and they threatened to quit if any changes were made.

Around the first of September each member received a notice through the mail that an "organization meeting" of POF would be held the seventeenth of the month. The notice went on to say that a president, vice-president, and secretary-treasurer would be elected and that a proposed constitution would be presented for adoption.

    1 Did an organization exist before the organization meeting? Explain.

    2 If the proposed changes are adopted how will they affect the operation of the organization?

    3 Explain some of the reasons why the two members who were vigorously against the organizational meeting might have objected. Could they be justified in their threat to quit?

D   The First Trust Bank published an advertisement containing the following sentence: "Although we're a large bank, you'll deal personally with someone very much like yourself." This advertisement was one of a series instigated by Mr. Carter, the president. His purpose was "to increase the bank's business with both individuals and organizations by reducing the impersonality of the bank. Our bank must become very personal if we are to reach our objectives."

    1 Is Mr. Carter's approach to improving business a good one? Why?

    2 Which of the levels of interaction described in the chapter are involved in this case? Explain your answers.

    3 Does the bank really do business with organizations? Explain.

FOR FURTHER STUDY

Additional sources can be found in the sources cited in the chapter.

Books

Chester I. Barnard: *The Functions of the Executive,* Harvard University Press, Cambridge, Mass., 1938, chap. VI. A formal organization is: "A system of consciously coordinated activities or forces of two or more persons."

Peter M. Blau and W. Richard Scott: "The Concept of Formal Organization," *Formal Organizations,* Chandler Publishing Co., San Francisco, 1962, pp. 2–8. The formal organization is a structure of relationships and ideas. Informal organization in practice modifies this structure.

Joseph A. Litterer: *The Analysis of Organizations,* John Wiley & Sons, Inc., New York, 1965, pp. 5–10, 135–136. Organizations are made up of purposes, behavior, individuals, boundaries, structure, and other elements.

Richard A. Johnson, Fremont E. Kast, and James E. Rosenzweig: *The Theory and Management of Systems,* 2d ed., McGraw-Hill Book Company, New York, 1967, chap. 3.

Several models of organizations are available: traditional, bureaucratic, neoclassical, professional, decision making, and systems.

Herbert A. Simon: *Administrative Behavior,* 2d ed., The Macmillan Company, New York, 1957. A set of concepts and a vocabulary suitable for describing an organization and the way an administrative organization works is needed.

Articles

Chris Argyris: "The Individual and Organization: Some Problems of Mutual Adjustment," *Administrative Science Quarterly,* June 1957, pp. 1–24. Mutual adjustment of the complex relationship between the individual and the organization is often difficult.

Solomon E. Asch: *Social Psychology,* Prentice-Hall, Inc., Englewood Cliffs, N.J., 1952. pp. 240–272. There are two extreme doctrines in organization theory: the individual thesis and the group-mind thesis. One arrives at vastly different conclusions depending upon which doctrine he selects.

Rollin L. Burns: "Organic Organization," *Personnel Journal,* September 1963. Organizations are dynamic systems of people, products, and places.

Lawrence Haworth: "Do Organizations Act?" *Ethics,* October 1959. Both organizations and individuals act, although there is a distinction between the two in this regard.

Herbert A. Simon: "Comments on the Theory of Organizations," *American Political Science Review,* December 1952. Organizations are systems of interdependent activities directed toward compatible objectives. Decision making, power, rationality, environment, stability and change, and specialization are important dimensions.

3

Individual Objectives in Organizations

Human hopes and human creeds
Have their roots in human needs.
EUGENE FITCH WARE

Organizations exist because persons need them—to do things that they need to do or want to do, and that they either could not do as well or could not do at all without people organizations. The things that people need or want—their objectives—thus are responsible for the existence of organizations. Further, how effective any organization is (that is, how well it meets its own objectives as an organization) is ultimately determined by the degree to which it helps its members to achieve these individual objectives. Unless the persons responsible for managing an organization understand this role of the individual objectives of its members, the organization cannot be accurately understood, nor operated at its full potential.[1]

[1]This is not to say that an individual's particular objectives must always be defined in order for an organization to serve him, or vice versa; the manager may not recognize all of his own objectives, let alone those of other persons. However, it is fairly easy to see that everything a person does is an expression of his personal objectives, whether he knows it or not. The manager who functions most effectively is one who pushes this line of reasoning one stage further and recognizes that everything an organization does is also an expression of objectives of individuals.

39

BIOLOGICAL AND SOCIAL NEEDS

Every person is different from all other persons. He has a unique set of needs or wants, which can be extremely varied. For example, Murray included inspiration, water, food, feeling, sex, avoidance of heat, avoidance of cold, avoidance of harm, acquisition, order, achievement, recognition, autonomy, aggression, play, understanding, and twenty-six others in his list of forty-two needs.[2] A person's needs such as these are the forces that impel him to act or react.

Because he is a goal-seeking being, everything a person does is an expression of his personal objectives, whether he knows it or not. The manager who functions most effectively recognizes that everything an organization does is also an expression of objectives of individuals. An individual's particular objectives need not always be defined in order for an organization to serve him, or vice versa; the manager may not recognize all of his own objectives, let alone those of other persons. But the more the manager understands the objectives of individuals, the more effective he can be.

Human needs can be grouped into two broad categories—*biological needs* and *social needs*. Biological needs are common to all mankind; man's survival depends upon whether he can supply them. Every man everywhere, at any time, in any place, needs food, water, oxygen, and some form of protection from extremes of weather.

Once these biological needs are satisfied, social needs develop—needs that vary greatly in kind and in degree from person to person. Satisfying them is not usually necessary for a person's survival, but they are always principal influences upon his actions. They include the desire for power, for companionship, or for love and affection. A person's need for social experiences can be very strong. This desire for human involvement

> . . . may be viewed as a hunger, not unlike that for food, but more generalized. . . . it may be expressed as a desire for contact, for recognition and acceptance, for approval, for esteem, or for mastery. . . . Persons not only universally live in social systems, which is to say they are drawn together, but also universally act in such ways as to obtain the approval of their fellow men.[3]

The relative importance of social needs is determined by the values of a society, and it is even possible for them to dominate the biological needs. For example, personal pride has been so important in many Oriental societies that in some situations when a person "loses face," suicide is obligatory.

Biological and social needs often become interdependent, because social needs exist in persons who are biological entities and because the way biological needs are satisfied is influenced to a high degree by the society in which these biological entities exist. For example, man's biological need for food can be satisfied by a great many

---

[2]H. A. Murray, *Explorations in Personality,* Oxford University Press, New York, 1938. Also see K. B. Madsen, *Theories of Motivation,* 4th ed., The Kent University Press, Kent, Ohio, 1968, pp. 317–318, which compares human needs as listed by several leading psychologists.

[3]D. A. Hamburg, "Emotions in the Perspective of Human Evolution," in P. H. Knapp (ed.), *The Expression of the Emotions in Man,* International Universities Press, Inc., New York, 1963, p. 312.

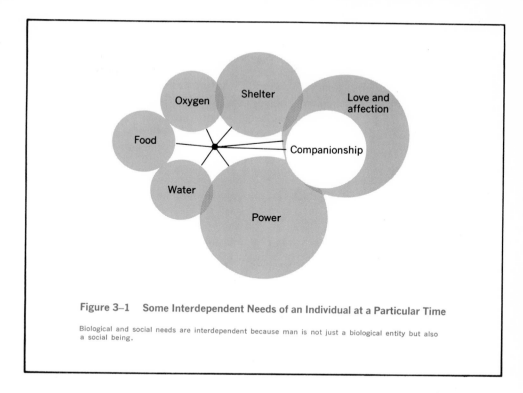

Figure 3–1   Some Interdependent Needs of an Individual at a Particular Time

Biological and social needs are interdependent because man is not just a biological entity but also a social being.

different kinds of food. Which kinds a man "wants" are determined by his society. For example, snake meat is repugnant to most persons reared in the United States, but it is a normal and attractive entree to a native of Thailand.

The interdependence of individual needs is illustrated in Figure 3-1.[4]

At the core of this complex of needs, the physical person exists. The surrounding complex is a variable mixture of needs, some that he recognizes, others that he does not. The person whose needs are diagrammed in Figure 3-1 may be at a particular time aware of his needs for food and companionship, and unaware of his needs for oxygen and power, but all these needs affect his actions both as an individual and as a member of an organization.

If such a diagram could be accurately drawn at a particular time for a human being, it would become inaccurate immediately, because needs are continually changing in intensity—and even in composition. Some may vanish altogether and others appear, gradually or with dramatic rapidity. For example, if the needs that are diagrammed in Figure 3-1 were those of an individual who was suddenly abandoned on a desert, they

[4]The principle that psychological forces can be diagrammed, as in this chapter, was explained by Kurt Lewin, *Principles of Topological Psychology*, McGraw-Hill Book Company, New York, 1936. See especially pp. 47 and 97.

might change to those shown in Figure 3-2. Love, affection, and power may still exist as part of his complex of needs, but their relative importance is overshadowed by his immediate and critical needs for water and shelter from the sun (and also by his persisting need for oxygen).

Most of this continuing change is gradual, as individuals mature and as their circumstances vary. The brash young college graduate needs to get ahead, to make his place in the world; the middle-aged man needs to provide security for old age and retirement. An organization that employs both men can function at maximum effectiveness only if it provides advancement and challenge to one and the prospect of adequate retirement to the other. It is most likely to be able to do this if it recognizes their different, but equally valid, needs.

Simultaneously satisfying all these continually altering needs is virtually impossible, because different activities may be necessary to satisfy each of them. An individual consequently arranges his objectives (as determined by his needs) in an order of preference that reflects the relative importance of his various needs, and that changes as the needs change. The precise arrangement of this hierarchy at a given time is prob-

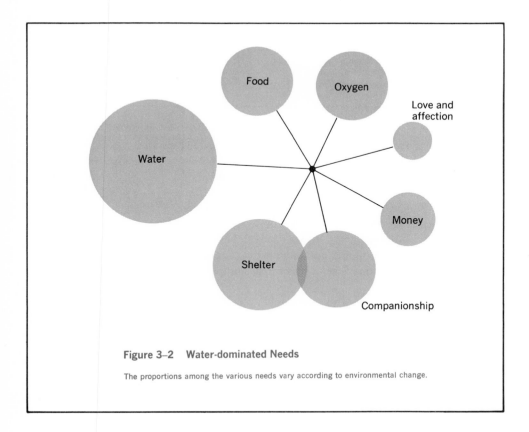

Figure 3–2 Water-dominated Needs

The proportions among the various needs vary according to environmental change.

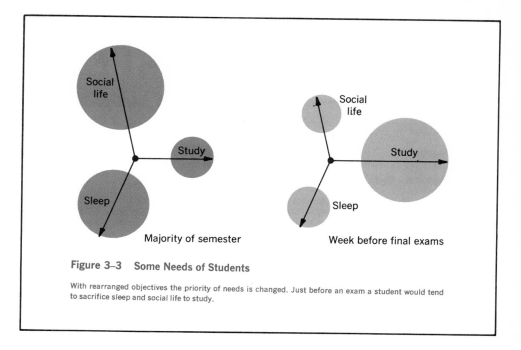

Figure 3–3   Some Needs of Students

With rearranged objectives the priority of needs is changed. Just before an exam a student would tend to sacrifice sleep and social life to study.

ably impossible to determine, even for the most systematic individual, because he may have needs of which he is not aware, but his actions reflect his needs. He can therefore diagram approximately some of his most important needs—and others can observe his actions and presume the needs behind them.

The principle of a changing priority of needs is illustrated by the two diagrams of the man in the desert, but a less dramatic example may be even more instructive: The study habits of many college students change drastically just before final exams, showing that they have rearranged their objectives. Study rooms that have been almost deserted are suddenly packed, as desperate students try to cover a semester's work in a week. As shown in Figure 3-3, formerly important objectives such as sleep—or social activities—are minimized or even completely forgone.

No single need is likely to be satisfied completely once and for all. Above, for example, the need for study will dominate some lives; and individuals will study as much as they can, but as they enter the examination room, they will probably feel that they have not studied enough. Once the examination is over, the needs will probably change again, in still another pattern.

The progress of an individual toward the satisfaction of any need is likely to be erratic. Even as he is working toward a particular objective, his needs may change and he may move in another direction, as shown in Figure 3-4. Here he has set out to accomplish objective A, but before he reaches it, objective B becomes more desirable.

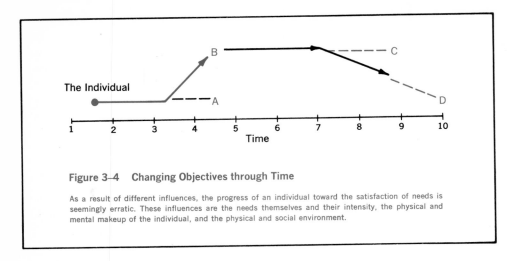

Figure 3-4   Changing Objectives through Time

As a result of different influences, the progress of an individual toward the satisfaction of needs is seemingly erratic. These influences are the needs themselves and their intensity, the physical and mental makeup of the individual, and the physical and social environment.

When he reaches B, objective C takes on increased importance, and so on. These shifts in objectives, which are reflected in changed behavior, are the result of several kinds of influences on the individual.

HOW ACTIONS ARE INFLUENCED

Three major factors influence the particular action a person will take in response to a need. These three factors operate whether the need is biological or social, and whether or not it is consciously felt.

1 The first factor is what the need is, and how intense it is. Intense hunger demands direct action; a person's sensation of slight hunger may be "satisfied" simply by his deciding to wait for half an hour before going to lunch, the decision making being the only form of action that takes place. A student feeling pressures from many sides may go to a movie to help himself relax; but if his tensions are extremely severe, he may take additional measures to relieve his tensions.

2 The second factor that influences the action of an individual is the physical and mental makeup of that individual. His sensory organs, his physical strength, and the sensitivity of his nervous system all affect his behavior, both in making him aware of his needs and in helping him satisfy himself. It would never occur to some students to go to a movie to relax; a fast game of tennis for them might be a different matter —their way of working off tensions.

3 The third factor that affects individual action is the environment of the individual—not only the physical environment but the social environment as well. Obviously, the tense student can play tennis only if a court is available—and if his past experiences have brought him in contact with tennis.

The strength of each of these three interrelated factors fluctuates continually, so they probably never exist in identical degrees in any two persons at the same time. It is even less likely that any two persons in a given organization would be simultaneously affected by *identical* combinations of these factors. However, the mere existence of organizations shows that human beings frequently ally themselves with other human beings in response to *similar* combinations of influences. The compatible human needs that are the reasons for the organization enable the organization to answer those needs by joint effort. The organization man is in the organization because he has some needs that are similar to those of his fellow members, but within the organization he remains a man. A key to an effective organization is the recognition by the manager of this *man* within the *member,* a particular man whose numerous and continually changing needs are directing his behavior

HOW HUMAN NEEDS OPERATE IN ORGANIZATIONS

The pattern of human needs is very important for organizations. Unless an organization is helping an individual satisfy his particular needs, he is probably not giving the organization his full efforts and may eventually leave it. If it is hindering him, he may even fight it. An individual does things for an organization because it has done (or he expects that it will do) things for him—things that are more important to him than the sacrifice or inconvenience involved in his membership. Ordinarily, a person gives up something to the organization, but he expects membership in the organization to more than repay him for his loss.

Each individual is unique in his set of needs, but there is enough similarity among many needs to enable persons to use organizations to achieve satisfaction. Persons of similar backgrounds, for example, have similar wants, needs, and desires; and many successful organizations are based on this fact. However, similarity of background is not so important as another factor; the key requirement is that individuals must have the opportunity to satisfy whatever needs they have via the organization. They either form an organization or join an existing one. Persons form such organizations as a marriage, a joint effort to fix a flat tire, a cooperative business, a committee with a special purpose, a rescue operation, or a children's neighborhood backyard circus. They join existing organizations such as religious orders, established businesses, armies (although membership is not voluntary in many established armies), and governments.

Figure 3-5 shows the basic key to organizations—mutual or compatible satisfaction of objectives. A, B, C, D, and E are individuals with very simple, limited needs, but the set of needs of each differs from that of the others. Individuals A and E have a similar need for money; individual B needs companionship; an organization can help them to meet their own needs. The organization may already exist for the purpose of helping its members acquire money, and providing them with companionship; if it does not exist, A, B, and E will form it. C and D have other needs that are more compelling to them, so they are not interested. Should they be forced to join the organization or should they perhaps join it accidentally, neither can receive any real satisfaction of

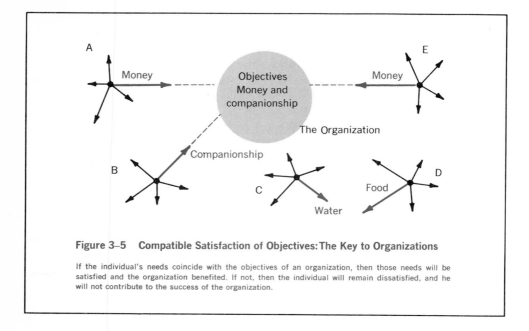

Figure 3–5   Compatible Satisfaction of Objectives: The Key to Organizations

If the individual's needs coincide with the objectives of an organization, then those needs will be satisfied and the organization benefited. If not, then the individual will remain dissatisfied, and he will not contribute to the success of the organization.

a need, as neither possesses in significant degree a need that this organization will help satisfy. If they remain with the organization, they probably will not contribute toward its success, and may actually hinder it, because their objectives may be at cross purposes with those of others.

As the individuals in an organization work to accomplish their own objectives and the broader objectives of the organization itself, the interactions among these persons will influence their future individual objectives. This influence will eventually alter the form, direction, or intensity of the individuals' objectives. The same interactions also exert influence in the opposite direction—that is, the individuals will alter the organizational objectives. The process of change and movement is inherent in every living thing. Organizations and the individuals within them are continually changing processes.

The organization in Figure 3-5 is very simple in comparison with most actual organizations. Most organizations involve more people, more resources, more inter-actions, and more objectives; and they often are a very significant influence on the people within them. And, of course, the sets of needs of real people may be much more complex than those of the hypothetical individuals in Figure 3-5. Yet the basic points illustrated in this simple example hold true for all organizations, regardless of how large or complex they might be: organizations exist because individuals see them as means of accomplishing their personal objectives.

Only one of the needs of each individual is labeled in the diagram above, the need that determined whether or not he would be a member of a particular organization. His other needs are important to him—and equally important to the organization—because they influence his behavior and thus his effectiveness. Some of the most important needs of an individual can be estimated; ways to meet these needs can then be realistically considered. This is the procedure a manager uses when he suggests as a motivating influence how an organization can help a person satisfy his needs. For example, individual A of Figure 3-5 might be represented as in Figure 3-6.

An examination of A's needs shows that they are not necessarily in conflict, even though they are directed toward different objectives. First, A exists in an environment that will influence him, and he in turn will influence his environment. (Generally, the influence of the environment will be the stronger.) Our hypothetical individual, A, has four distinctive needs—love and affection, status, self-esteem, and money—and one set of biological needs, which all individuals possess. (The biological needs are treated here as a single drive to simplify the analysis.) To derive a relationship among the needs, the environment and the area lines can be removed, leaving the basic vectors, representing the needs, as shown in Figure 3-7.

A's needs pull him in different directions, but some of them may be compatible. Figure 3-8 shows how the vectors for each need are "added" together by connecting

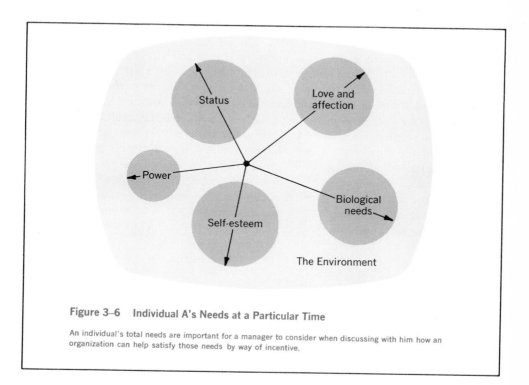

Figure 3–6   Individual A's Needs at a Particular Time

An individual's total needs are important for a manager to consider when discussing with him how an organization can help satisfy those needs by way of incentive.

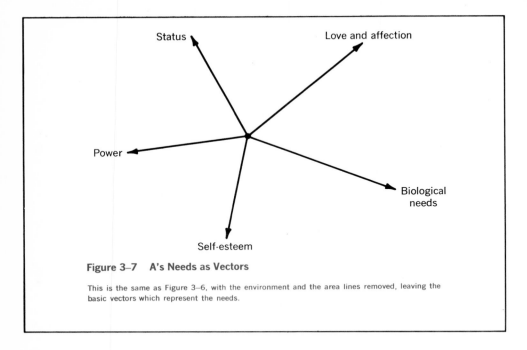

Figure 3–7   A's Needs as Vectors

This is the same as Figure 3–6, with the environment and the area lines removed, leaving the basic vectors which represent the needs.

them end to end in a sequence, while keeping the original lengths and directions.[5] Then the starting point and the open end of the chain are connected, producing a new dimension that is called the "resultant" of all the forces. This resultant is an abstract representation of A's total needs, and the resultant can be substituted for all the other needs. This operation is carried out in part *b* of the diagram, and the resultant it produces is placed in the original model in part *a*. The implications of this derived resultant are very significant for organizations because the resultant shows the net direction that this particular individual can move in to best satisfy his needs.[6] His net effective objective, then, can be thought to be his resultant vector. The resultant represents the net effect of the individual's desires at a particular point in time with his particular set of needs. If an individual can find an organization that is moving in the same general direction that he is (toward organizational objectives that coincide with his resultant vector), then he should be willing to devote his efforts to it.

By adding the vectors, it is possible to conceive of the direction and intensity of an individual's next move. For example, two equally strong and opposite needs might cancel one another, leaving the individual in conflict, as in Figure 3-9.

Such conflicting needs can make a person very uncomfortable. He must change

[5] The procedure is simply to add the tail of each to the head of another, in any sequence.
[6] Vector analysis of objectives is at this point only a conceptual tool. Much research will have to be done to measure an individual's objectives, both in strength and direction.

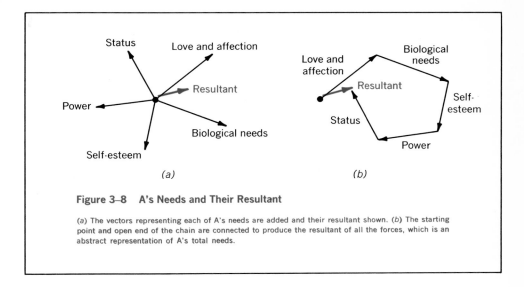

Figure 3–8   A's Needs and Their Resultant

(a) The vectors representing each of A's needs are added and their resultant shown. (b) The starting point and open end of the chain are connected to produce the resultant of all the forces, which is an abstract representation of A's total needs.

his needs or achieve a compromise to prevent complete frustration. Time, which is always at work on an individual's set of needs, may settle such a quandary. Needs that tend to cancel each other out may change over a period of time, and one of them can then be satisfied to some degree. Or, unhappily, the conflict may remain unresolved if the person is unable to achieve a solution. In such a quandary, he may push the problem into his unconscious mind, thereby producing a possible permanent neurosis (unconscious conflict).

As the individual's set of needs changes in composition, strength, and direction, the direction of the resultant will also change. But always, to achieve satisfaction, the individual is directing his behavior at a moving objective whose changing position is a function of time and his own changing needs.

A person's needs and the objectives that they direct him toward are therefore important to the organization of which he is a member. The relationship between his objectives and his performance as a member of an organization is one of simple cause and effect: two individuals work together to do something that each believes will ac-

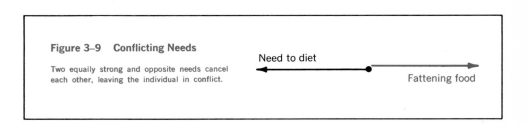

Figure 3–9   Conflicting Needs

Two equally strong and opposite needs cancel each other, leaving the individual in conflict.

complish something he wants. This combined effort spawns or perpetuates an organization.

THE RELATIONSHIP BETWEEN INDIVIDUAL AND ORGANIZATIONAL OBJECTIVES

If individuals are members of organizations primarily to achieve their own individual objectives, and if organizations may be assumed to have distinct objectives of their own, what is the relationship between these two kinds of objectives? In successful organizations they are, or have been, compatible. There is no assurance, however, that they will remain compatible—unless some action is taken by the managers of the organization. The interactions between individuals and the organization, between the organization and individuals, and between individuals and other individuals can separate rather than correlate individual and organizational objectives. Thus, managers must recognize the wide range of possible relationships between individual and organizational objectives. Figure 3-10 demonstrates the range of possible meshing relationships between individual and organizational objectives. The complete range of relationships sometimes can be found within a single organization.

Totally Opposing

In the first category on the scale in Figure 3-10, "totally opposing," the objectives of an individual member are diametrically opposed to the objectives of the organization. For example, the objectives of subversives "boring from within" established organizations (governmental, religious, labor, etc.) or of prisoners trying to escape are totally opposed to the organizations of which they are a part. In the business world, sometimes a single individual within an organization wants effectively to destroy it so that he can buy it at a low price. For the organization to function most effectively, the influence of

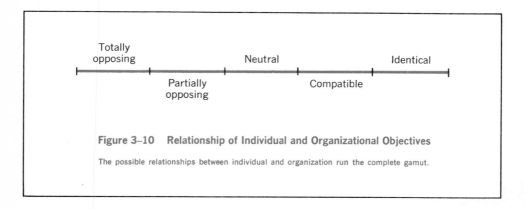

Figure 3–10   Relationship of Individual and Organizational Objectives

The possible relationships between individual and organization run the complete gamut.

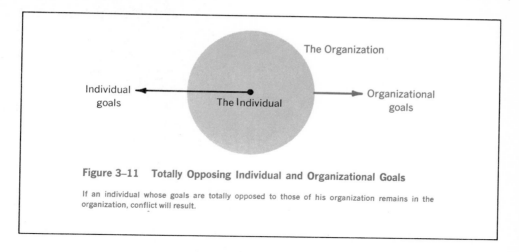

Figure 3–11   Totally Opposing Individual and Organizational Goals

If an individual whose goals are totally opposed to those of his organization remains in the organization, conflict will result.

these individuals must be nullified or their or the organization's objectives must be changed.

The relationship of the directions of "totally opposing" individuals and the organization's activities can be diagrammed, as in Figure 3-11. The black arrow represents the resultant of the individual's objectives and consequent behavior patterns, and the colored arrow represents the organization's resultant objectives. If this individual remains in the organization, conflict obviously will result.

Partially Opposing

In the next situation the objectives of the individual member are partially opposed to those of the organization. The major difference between this category and the preceding one is that some of the goals of the individual are in agreement with organizational goals. A visual concept of partially opposing objectives is shown in Figure 3-12.

Perhaps the clearest example of this type of relationship is that of the armed forces with a conscientious objector, who abhors war but volunteers to serve as a medic. In this situation the individual does not agree with and is even mentally opposed to the "grand design" of the organization—waging and winning a war in minimum time. But the individual does feel that the relief of human suffering is a desirable goal, and to this extent his objectives and those of medical care are in basic agreement. In addition, the individual does not actively hamper the overall organizational objective.

Neutral

In the neutral case, the objectives of an individual member of the organization neither oppose nor are compatible with the objectives of the organization. The individual is

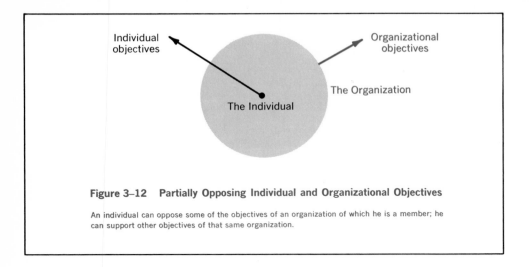

Figure 3–12 Partially Opposing Individual and Organizational Objectives

An individual can oppose some of the objectives of an organization of which he is a member; he can support other objectives of that same organization.

a nominal member, but he does not take an active role in the work of the organization. The organization, in the neutral case, is aiming for its objectives and the individual for his—each going his merry way, and not in conflict with the other. Schematically, this situation may look like Figure 3-13.

The individual and the organization do not really need each other; no involvement exists. The individual does not function in the organization in Figure 3-13, although he may technically be a member.

Compatible

In the compatible case the majority of the individual's objectives are compatible with the objectives of the organization. Both individual and organizational objectives can be reached simultaneously without undue sacrifice to either. The individual retains his identity within the organization, but at the same time he respects the organization's need for coordination.

A research scientist in nuclear physics who joins the staff of an organization engaged in nuclear research is an example of this type of compatibility. The objectives of the scientist and the research laboratory are compatible—not completely identical. The scientist provides his knowledge and experience and inquiring mind in return for research facilities and monetary rewards. The research center does not necessarily provide him with unlimited facilities or allow him to conduct whatever experiments he desires. The scientist recognizes the right of the organization to assign projects that lead to the accomplishment of the organization's goals—even though he himself may wish to see another priority established. He does have the option of voicing objections and having these objections heard, and he also has the option of striving to

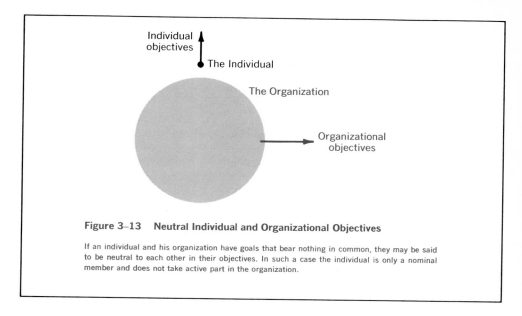

Figure 3–13   Neutral Individual and Organizational Objectives

If an individual and his organization have goals that bear nothing in common, they may be said to be neutral to each other in their objectives. In such a case the individual is only a nominal member and does not take active part in the organization.

become a member of the group that determines priorities and assignments. If his proposals are not approved, he will abide by organizational demands as long as he can continue to achieve his own objectives within the framework of the organization's objectives.

Figure 3-14 shows how individual and organizational objectives can exist compatibly. The individual's objectives move in the same general direction as the objectives

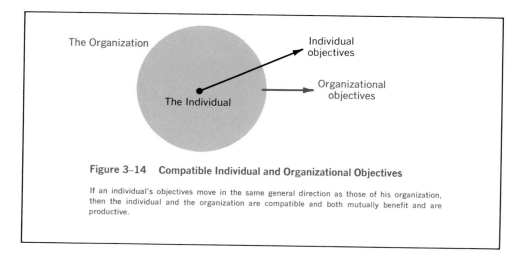

Figure 3–14   Compatible Individual and Organizational Objectives

If an individual's objectives move in the same general direction as those of his organization, then the individual and the organization are compatible and both mutually benefit and are productive.

of the organization. If the individual is a member of the organization, he will benefit from the efforts of the organization, and the organization will benefit from his efforts. Such a situation is mutually productive. The majority of successful organizations are due to the existence of individual and organizational objectives that are compatible.

Identical

It sometimes is impossible to separate the goals of the individual from the organizational goals. Members may completely subordinate themselves to the desires of the organization, allowing themselves to be controlled like puppets. This situation is found quite often. Examples can be found in some owner-manager one-man businesses, in members of superpatriotic organizations, in religious orders, and in military groups. The man in the gray flannel suit was an example of an individual who subordinated himself to an organization.[7]

The individual's complete identification (or subjugation, as the case may be) of personal objectives with the organization's objectives is shown in Figure 3-15.

Unfortunately, this situation is considered desirable by some practicing managers —particularly owner-managers. We find this feeling exhibited in such statements as "They don't have the interests of the organization at heart," or "They are not dedicated enough." This is the view of an individual who expects everyone to have the same identity with the organization that he has. In view of the whole range of possibilities and the smaller stake that these other members have in the organization, this position is untenable and unattainable for most organizations. Organizations may have several

[7]Serious questions immediately arise as to whether such total subjugation is healthy for the individual or, in the long term, for organizations.

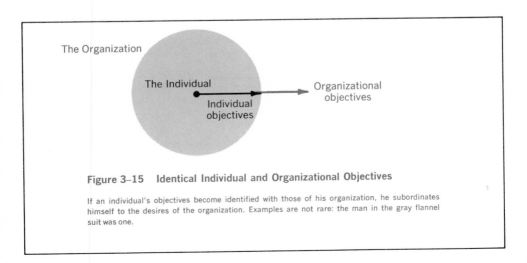

Figure 3–15   Identical Individual and Organizational Objectives

If an individual's objectives become identified with those of his organization, he subordinates himself to the desires of the organization. Examples are not rare: the man in the gray flannel suit was one.

members who have voluntarily made their goals identical with those of the organization, but it is too much to expect this to be true for all members.

The organization should try to bring individual and organizational goals into a working relationship that will contribute to the success of both, but this does not mean that the goals must be identical. Far from it. For most persons and organizations *compatibility*, not *uniformity*, is the most desirable relationship.

SUMMARY

Organizations exist because persons expect that some of their objectives can best be accomplished by joint effort. Persons often seek satisfaction of biological needs necessary for the maintenance of life through organizations. Organizations are also called upon to satisfy social needs.

The personal objectives that individuals call upon organizations to serve will be different for each person and will also depend upon the particular time and circumstances. However, there often is enough similarity in these personal needs to accomplish them best through joint and coordinated effort. The key to successful organizations is joint effort to satisfy personal, compatible objectives.

Personal objectives may be wholly opposed to, partially opposed to, neutral, compatible with, or identical with organizational objectives. For most members of organizations the most desirable relationship is that their personal objectives be compatible with organizational objectives. Thus, when organizational objectives are accomplished, personal objectives are also achieved.

FOR REVIEW AND DISCUSSION

1 What is the basic reason for the existence of organizations?

2 Define biological and social needs. Explain how biological needs can sometimes dominate social needs.

3 Explain how the changing circumstances within which an individual finds himself can change the relative strength of his different needs.

4 Explain the three major factors that influence the particular action a person will take in response to a need.

5 Do the needs of a particular person always remain the same? Explain.

6 Under what conditions are the needs of a number of persons likely to encourage them to join together in an organization?

7 What is the significance of the resultant of a person's complex of needs?

8 What are the possible courses of action for a person who has two needs that are equally strong but directly conflicting?

9 Describe the following relationships between individual and organizational objectives: (a) totally opposing, (b) partially opposing, (c) neutral, (d) compatible, and (e) identical. Give an example to illustrate each relationship.

10 For an effective organization, must all members have identical objectives? Must all have compatible objectives? Explain.

11 List about twenty human needs that can be satisfied wholly or partly in organizations.

CASES

A Glenn Camden, who flew a private airplane as a hobby, invited his friend, Adam Felts, who had never been in an airplane, to go up for a sight-seeing ride. The air contained a lot of smoke and haze which made visibility extremely poor.

Glenn's intention had been to navigate exclusively by visual reference to landmarks. However, shortly after the flight began, Glenn and Adam discovered that they were lost. Visibility was so poor that no familiar landmarks could be seen. Glenn flew around for ten minutes searching for something they recognized, but was completely unsuccessful. By this time both men became very frightened; their sole objective was to find a landing field. Glenn began to work with the radio navigation equipment in the plane, but he had never had any formal training in its use.

    1 How did changing conditions change the objectives of Glenn and Adam?

    2 Before he got in the plane Adam had felt a bit hungry. Do you think he was hungry after they got lost? Why?

    3 What effect is this experience likely to have on Glenn's flying hobby (assuming he gets down safely)? Explain your answer.

B Wilber Laslie had just had a backyard visit with his new neighbor, Fred Taylor. After a long conversation Wilber concluded three things: (a) that the vast majority of his and Fred's interests were completely unrelated, (b) that Fred was an outspoken Republican (Wilber was an equally outspoken Democrat), and (c) that Fred's enthusiasm for golf matched his own. As Wilber left he said, "Fred, let's go for a round of golf Saturday."

"O.K.," Fred answered.

    1 What is the basis for a possible friendship between Wilber and Fred?

    2 What effect is politics likely to have on the friendship?

C Jesse Gill, owner of Gill Enterprises, always stayed at his office working long after all his employees had gone home. In addition, Mr. Gill could often be found at his office during weekends.

Over the past several years Mr. Gill had hired a number of recent college graduates in the hope that he might get someone to supervise his office staff. However, each man he hired soon quit and went to work for a large company.

In describing his problems Mr. Gill said, "They just don't want to work. They expect to be a success by working forty hours per week. If a man's going to get ahead in my business, he's got to work just as hard as I do. He's got to have the interest of the business at heart, just like I do."

    1 Why was Mr. Gill unsuccessful in keeping an office manager?

    2 Was it reasonable for Mr. Gill to expect that his men should be as interested as he in his business?

    3 Is there any particular reason why the men who wanted to work only forty hours per week will not be successful with the large companies?

D   Andy Browne, youngest member of an extremely wealthy family, had received an expensive sports car as a graduation present from prep school. The next fall Andy enrolled as a freshman at State University. In addition to his expenses Andy was given an allowance of $400 per month by his family.

Andy felt greatly inconvenienced by having to park his car in the student parking lot two blocks away from his classes. The university assigned a parking space to each faculty member close to the classroom building, and Andy privately arranged to park in Professor Clark's space for the semester. For this privilege Andy paid Professor Clark $100. Professor Clark was pleased with the arrangement since he walked to his office anyway.

When the university administration heard of this situation it brought disciplinary action against both Andy and Professor Clark.

1 What were the objectives that led to the formation of the organization of Andy and Professor Clark?
2 Explain the problems that this arrangement might cause for the university.
3 Explain the conflict that existed among Andy, Professor Clark, and the university. Is this sort of conflict typical in organizations?

FOR FURTHER STUDY

Additional sources can be found in the references cited in the chapter.

Books

Saul W. Gellerman: *Motivation and Productivity,* American Management Association, New York, 1963, part II. Until recently, research on motivation in industry has focused on management and its role rather than on the individual and his own drives. The focus now is on the individual's needs for competence, affiliation, achievement, prestige, security, and money.

Douglas McGregor: *The Professional Manager,* McGraw-Hill Book Company, New York, 1967, pp. 24–30. Social needs and values profoundly affect the behavior of managers and other members of organizations.

Leonard R. Sayles and George Strauss: *Human Behavior in Organizations,* Prentice-Hall, Inc., Englewood Cliffs, N.J., 1966. Physical, security, social, and egoistic needs are satisfied by working in organizations.

Robert A. Sutermeister: *People and Productivity,* McGraw-Hill Book Company, New York, 1963, chap. 5. It is important to recognize the wide diversity of factors which can influence the needs of a single individual. Furthermore, the needs of an employee change with time.

Articles

Alexander W. Astin and Robert C. Nichols: "Life Goals and Vocational Choice," *Journal of Applied Psychology,* February 1964. A number of life goals of individuals are related to their vocational choices.

William D. Guth and Renato Taguiri: "Personal Values and Corporate Strategy," *Harvard Business Review,* September–October 1965. The theoretical, economic, aesthetic, social, political, and religious values persons have vitally affect their behavior in organizations.

George H. Labovitz: "The Individual versus the Organization (No Easy Answers to Industrial Conflict)," *Advanced Management Journal,* January 1970. Individual and organizational goals are different, but the organization can achieve both satisfactorily by adjusting them.

Brian J. Loasby: "The Decision Maker in the Organization," *Journal of Management Studies,* October 1968. Individuals make decisions to satisfy their personal goals in organizations.

Robert N. McMurry: "Conflicts in Human Values," *Harvard Business Review,* May–June 1963. "To deal realistically with problems in labor relations and public relations, morale and performance, communications and teamwork, management must be realistic about conflicts in human values."

Burt K. Scanlan: "Is Money Still the Motivator?" *The Personnel Administrator,* July–August 1970. Wages and equity are crucial components of motivational packages.

4
Organizational Objectives

Organizational objectives should give the organization meaning to man . . . and man meaning to the organization.
 JAMES L. DAVIS

[Alice said], "Would you tell me, please, which way I ought to go from here?" "That depends a good deal on where you want to get to," said the Cat. "I don't know where . . . ," said Alice. "Then it doesn't matter which way you go," said the Cat.
 LEWIS CARROLL, Alice's Adventures in Wonderland

Organizations are created and maintained by their members as means of satisfying their personal objectives, but organizations themselves also have objectives, distinct from the objectives of individual members, but derived from them. As shown earlier, individual objectives can be extremely diverse—so diverse that probably no organization could ever satisfy them all. But, on the other hand, an organization cannot operate effectively unless it is satisfying *some* of them—and the more it can satisfy, the more effective its operations will be. Therefore, every organization should first recognize the existence of its members' individual objectives and then develop organizational objectives that will help satisfy some of them. This process is directed by the manager, and is the first step in planning.

IMPORTANCE OF ORGANIZATIONAL OBJECTIVES

The importance of clearly defined objectives is generally recognized. Managerial literature is sprinkled with such statements as:

Objectives serve as reference points for the efforts of the organization.

Objectives are necessary for coordinated effort.

For coordination the first step is to state the objectives the organization desires to achieve.

The organization that wishes to compete effectively and grow must continually renew its objectives.

Organizational objectives are the ends toward which all organizational action is directed.

Objectives are prerequisite to determining effective policies, procedures, methods, strategies, and rules.

Organizational objectives define the destination of the organization; they move forward as rapidly as they are approached or attained.

Clearly defined organizational objectives are analogous to a star which can be used for navigation by ships and airplanes.

These varied statements have a common denominator—the importance of providing stated objectives for organizations. All point out that when objectives, missions, or targets are planned for the whole organization and for its component parts, coordinated action can result—and this is, after all, the way the organizational objectives are accomplished. Even in the simplest organization—say, three men cooperating to push a car out of the mud—the objective must be clearly established before they act, and a plan must be derived from the objective. No one has to explain this to the three men; hastily and informally they agree to push the car forward at the count of three. This same simple and obvious principle of cause and effect is overlooked, however, in many formal organizations. Many organizations seem to feel that it will be enough if they solve each problem as it comes up, without the benefit of a unifying objective.

Well-defined and integrated organizational objectives or goals have numerous advantages, including the following:

1 Effective objectives encourage all members to work toward the *same* organizational objectives. Otherwise there likely will be many different ideas among members as to what the objectives of the organization are or should be. Each person under such circumstances works toward his own idea of the organizational objectives. Much such work likely will be in conflicting directions or may be otherwise ineffective. Thus good objectives make behavior in organizations more rational, more coordinated, and thus more effective, because everyone knows the accepted goals to work toward. A person can justify doing anything if any objective is as good as another.

2 Effective goals give objective yardsticks for measuring, comparing, and evaluating performance. They provide objective, rational bases for settling disputes.

3 Effective objectives also can be good motivators because they make it easier for a member to relate the accomplishment of his personal goals to the work of the organization. He knows what is expected of him and is thereby more secure in what he needs to do to be successful in

the organization. In setting effective objectives, managers help members at all levels of the organization to understand how they can "best achieve their own goals by directing their behavior toward the goals of the organization."[1]

The Problems of a State Government without Well-defined and Agreed-upon Objectives

[The state's] ox is in the ditch. We all wish it wasn't. But it is. And the people who are supposed to be getting it out aren't making much progress. Some of them just can't seem to see it, although it is lying there, on its back, all four hooves in the air, big as life, kicking and bellowing. Some apparently think the beast ought to be left in the ditch as a penalty for its clumsiness. Some think that before they get the ox out of the ditch it would be best to plan a long-range ditch-filling project, so it won't fall in again. Some would rather not get involved until they have written invitations to a barbecue to be held after the ox is lifted from its reclining place.

Among those who say they want to help, there is a paralyzing disagreement on methods. Some want to haul it out by the tail, others by the ears. Some want to slide a pole under it and prize it out, others to build a derrick. Some would like to try dynamite.

Maybe that isn't an exact description of what has happened so far at the special session. But it comes pretty close. A tremendous amount of heat has been generated but virtually no light.

Blocs and factions have defended their interests, as they see them. The legislature has made plain its reluctance to increase any kind of taxes, least of all taxes paid directly by the consumers. . . . The governor's tax program has been shot to pieces.

Unfortunately, this kind of negative action simply will not be enough under the present circumstances. There are few situations in this life in which it is enough simply to do nothing and this is not one of them. There are urgent needs in state government that must be met and if they are not met unfortunate and painful things are going to happen that few if any people in [the state] really want to happen.

We believe that the great majority of legislators understand the situation the state now faces and want to do something about it. We are certain that when they come back Monday after their long Thanksgiving weekend they will be eager to put behind them the confusion and bickering of recent days and either deal constructively with the revised tax program which the governor has said he will present or propose effective alternatives of their own. No one needs to tell them that this is as much their responsibility as it is the governor's. The latter can say, at least, that he tried, and we don't think any member of the legislature wants to be obliged to say less.

(Excerpted from a newspaper editorial.)

CHARACTERISTICS OF ORGANIZATIONAL OBJECTIVES

Four characteristics of organizational objectives are useful to the manager:

1 Organizational objectives are structured in a hierarchy.
2 They reinforce individual objectives, and vice versa.
3 They are—or should be—compatible with individual objectives.

---

[1]Douglas McGregor, *The Professional Manager,* McGraw-Hill Book Company, New York, 1967, p. 13.

4 Higher level, superordinate objectives contain subordinate objectives and can be accomplished effectively only through cooperation.

Hierarchies of Objectives

In complex organizations, objectives are structured in a hierarchy in which the objectives of each unit contribute to the objectives of the next higher unit. And a broad objective (the grand design) states the purpose of the entire organization. This is true of all organizations—military, educational, governmental, and business.

A significant article on this subject is introduced thus: "There are objectives within objectives, within objectives. They all require painstaking definition and close analysis if they are to be useful separately and profitable as a whole."[2]

Means-ends chains   A useful technique in portraying the hierarchy of objectives for an organization is to describe its objectives in a means-end chain.[3] Figure 4-1 shows such a hierarchy for a hypothetical company.

[2]Charles H. Granger, "The Hierarchy of Objectives," *Harvard Business Review,* May–June 1964, p. 63.
[3]Cf. Herbert A. Simon, *Administrative Behavior,* 2d ed., The Macmillan Company, New York, 1957, pp. 62–66, and James G. March and Herbert A. Simon, *Organizations,* John Wiley & Sons, Inc., 1958, pp. 31–32, 152, 190–191.

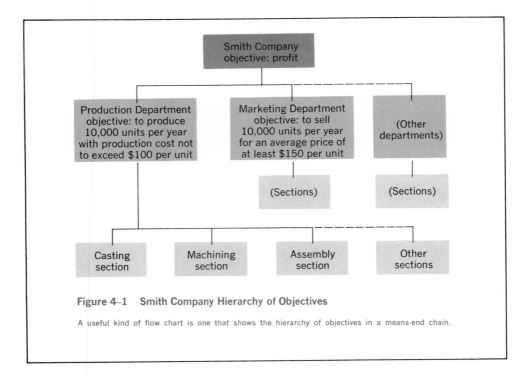

Figure 4–1   Smith Company Hierarchy of Objectives

A useful kind of flow chart is one that shows the hierarchy of objectives in a means-end chain.

In the hierarchy of objectives the objectives (ends) of component units become the means by which the broader objective is achieved. For example, in the Smith Company if the casting, machining, assembling, and other production sections work together effectively, they will accomplish the production department's objective. And if the production, marketing, and other departments accomplish their departmental objectives, they contribute to the overall profit objective of the company. The objectives (ends) achieved on lower levels are the means by which objectives at a higher level are reached. Each level of objectives stands as an end relative to the levels below it and as a means relative to the levels above it. Thus, this means-end chain, or hierarchy of objectives, directs the behavior of every member and every department toward the highest objective of the organization. This procedure can be used to define and relate the objectives of any organization, no matter how complex.

The structure of complex organizations   A complete hierarchy of objectives that is generally recognized and accepted provides an organization with a logical, consistent standard, enabling it to determine what activities are necessary and how these activities can best be grouped. The more complex an organization, the more necessary such a standard.

For example, a typical business organization can be divided in descending order into divisions, departments, sections, and work groups, as shown in Figure 4-2. The overall objectives of an organization may be determined in many ways, including votes, consensus, edict, coalitions, and others. The objectives for the whole organization are restated as objectives for each division. Each division's objectives are in turn converted to objectives for each of its departments. A department's objectives determine the objectives of each of its sections. Finally each section's objectives are converted to objectives for its work groups. Under the influence of the objectives for the whole organization, the objectives for each level are developed in sequence, starting with the highest level.

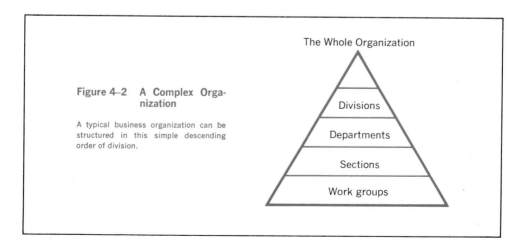

Figure 4–2   A Complex Organization

A typical business organization can be structured in this simple descending order of division.

The Whole Organization

Divisions

Departments

Sections

Work groups

A large public utility firm asked each of its departments to report its plans for the next ten years. When all these departmental plans were assembled it was discovered that based on the plans submitted the firm would be bankrupt within eight years! At this point a consultant was called in who pointed out that the missing ingredient was overall, top-level, unifying objectives for the firm. For this firm, top objectives simply were not present. Too often managers fail to recognize that overall objectives do not automatically exist. In fact these objectives must be created and communicated by the top managers.

Division objectives should be compatible with, and should help to accomplish, the broad objectives of the whole organization. The objectives for each division should also be compatible with the objectives of all the other divisions.

In turn, departmental objectives should be compatible with, and should help to accomplish, divisional objectives. If the same requirements are met for each lower level —sections and work groups—the organization then has a hierarchy of objectives on each level that supports and contributes to the accomplishment of the overall organizational objectives.

Each level in the hierarchy may contribute differently. The lower levels typically are more concerned with operations than are higher levels, which are more likely to deal in concepts.

Failure to develop, maintain, and communicate such a hierarchy of objectives will eventually lead to a failure of subordinate units to contribute to the achievement of higher-level goals. For example, a large data-processing firm that designs companywide information systems often discovers, in the course of studying companies in order to improve their communication, that whole departments of customers' organizations contribute practically nothing to overall objectives. Because they had not kept their hierarchy of objectives in mind, these firms simply did not know which departments were contributing to overall objectives and which were not. Paradoxically, some of these useless departments were hard-working and apparently efficient, but they simply had not been required in the first place. Another example: A B-52 bomber group may operate with high efficiency based on the accepted performance standards for B-52 bomber groups. But the group may possibly make little if any contribution to national defense if its purpose could better be accomplished by other means—perhaps guided missiles, if missiles were available.

Mutual Reinforcement of Objectives

When individual and organizational objectives are accomplished together, the process is spoken of as "mutual reinforcement." This mutual reinforcement explains a point that is central for understanding the life and success of organizations: Organizations benefit when they assist individuals in reaching individual objectives; and, similarly, individuals benefit when they help organizations reach organizational objectives. This concept is illustrated by Figure 4-3.

In Figure 4-3, Bill Smith is a salesman working for Excel Company. He has accepted

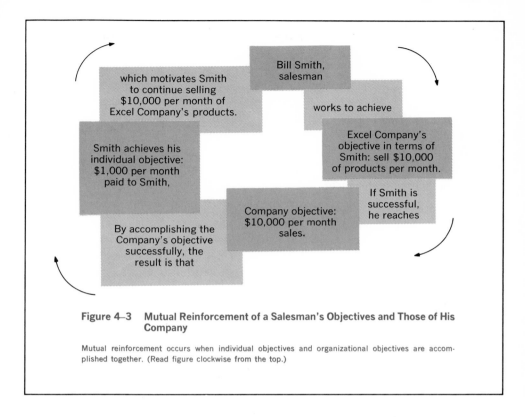

Figure 4–3   Mutual Reinforcement of a Salesman's Objectives and Those of His Company

Mutual reinforcement occurs when individual objectives and organizational objectives are accomplished together. (Read figure clockwise from the top.)

the Excel Company's objective for him, to sell $10,000 of its products each month. At the same time Smith wishes to earn his $1,000 per month pay. When Smith is successful in selling his $10,000 quota, Excel continues to employ him at $1,000 per month. Thus, Smith accomplishes his individual objective of making $1,000 per month at the same time that he achieves Excel's objective of sales worth $10,000 per month. The two objectives are mutually reinforcing: successful achievement of one contributes to success of the other, and vice versa, ad infinitum.

This principle is working in every organization. To see it in operation, one has only to discover what the individual and organizational objectives are for the particular instance at hand. For example, a professor is successful when he effectively teaches his students, which makes the university successful. In turn students support (through their parents, in many cases) the university that pays the professor, giving the professor incentive to teach another group of students. Another example: A good coach by winning games brings money and prestige to the university. In turn the university rewards the coach with prestige, pay, and other benefits.

If there is no mutual reinforcement, the organization and the individuals concerned will suffer. For example, if a coach's team consistently loses, he will find it difficult to recruit excellent new players; ticket sales will decline; and the coach may be fired, completing the chain.

Mutual reinforcement of objectives in organizations can also be viewed in terms of the law of effect—that is, successful behavior is rewarded and tends to be repeated. Unsuccessful behavior, on the other hand, is not rewarded and therefore tends not to be repeated.

In a successful organization, objectives and the individual objectives of all of its members are continually reinforcing one another. Thus, the organization continues to prosper, along with its members.

Compatibility of Objectives

For effective performance, some objective(s) of each individual or part of the organization must be compatible, though not necessarily identical. This fundamental concept is illustrated in Figure 4-4. Here S and W represent two objectives of an individual person or part of an organization (1). An organization (3) exists when (1) interacts with another individual person or organizational unit (2). Two of the objectives of (2) are shown as B and G. The highest level (3) of the organization may have objectives L and R.

If objectives W, R, and B are compatible, and if W and B can help to accomplish R, an effective organization can exist. For example, in the Smith Company, W might represent the objective of the production department to produce 10,000 units per year, B might represent the marketing department's objective to sell those units, and R may represent the profit objective of the company. None of these three objectives is the same, but together they may form the basis for effective performance in the organization.

Superordinate Objectives

The concept of superordinate objectives provides an excellent vehicle for summarizing the study of organizational objectives. It also explains a central feature of organizations: organizations exist because they are capable of accomplishing some things that individuals cannot accomplish alone.

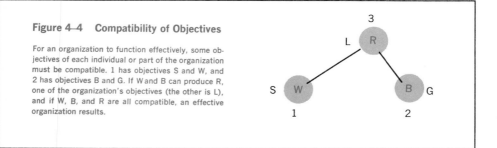

Figure 4-4   Compatibility of Objectives

For an organization to function effectively, some objectives of each individual or part of the organization
must be compatible. 1 has objectives S and W, and
2 has objectives B and G. If W and B can produce R,
one of the organization's objectives (the other is L),
and if W, B, and R are all compatible, an effective
organization results.

Figure 4–5 Simple Superordinate Objective

The superordinate objective is the organizational objective. John's primary objective is to meet Jim for a soft drink. Jim's primary objective is to meet John for companionship. Their superordinate objective is to meet for soft drinks each afternoon.

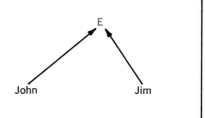

A superordinate objective is an objective that appeals to all subordinate persons or departments and that can best be accomplished through cooperation. Further, a superordinate objective is broad enough to include all subordinate objectives.

Simple organizations The basic operation of superordinate objectives can be seen when only two persons are cooperating to achieve some objective. This concept is illustrated in Figure 4-5, where John and Jim are cooperating to achieve a superordinate objective E. John likes soft drinks (and, secondarily, companionship); Jim likes companionship (and, secondarily, soft drinks). They meet at the corner drugstore for a soft drink each afternoon. John's primary objective is to get a soft drink; Jim's primary objective is companionship; their superordinate objective is to meet for soft drinks each afternoon.

In Figure 4-5, John and Jim cooperate to achieve objective E, which is desired by each. Objective E, their superordinate objective, can also be called their "organizational objective." Objective E can be accomplished best, or only, by the cooperation of John and Jim. Achieving objective E may reward John and Jim in different ways, in terms of their individual objectives.

Complex organizations Perhaps John and Jim are members of a more complex organization. Again, the concept of superordinate objectives gives us insight into organizational relationships. Figure 4-6 shows this more complex organization. At the drugstore John and Jim happen to meet Ted and George, who are present because of F, the super-

Figure 4–6 Complex Superordinate Objective

The complex superordinate objective is the superordinate objective of John, Jim, Ted, and George and of E and F.

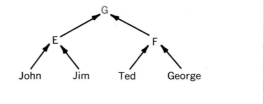

ordinate objective of Ted and George. Suppose all four—John, Jim, Ted, and George— play a fast game of darts. Thus, the four have set up a complex organization whose over- all objective is G, to play darts.

In Figure 4-6, objective G (playing darts) is the superordinate objective of the entire organization. John and Jim work together to achieve objective E (companionship and soft drinks); Ted and George cooperate to achieve objective F (whatever brought Ted and George together); objectives E and F in turn contribute to objective G. Objective G is a superordinate objective for John, Jim, Ted, and George, and for objectives E and F. The means-ends chain, described earlier in this chapter, also can be seen developing in this example. Being present in the drugstore provided the means whereby the end (dart game) for the whole organization could be accomplished. These concepts of superordinate objectives and means-ends chains can be applied to any organization, no matter how complex.

The hierarchy of objectives also can be viewed from the top down. In that case, E and F are subordinate objectives of G; the objectives of John and Jim are subordinate to E; and the objectives of Ted and George are subordinate to F. Finally, the objectives of John, Jim, Ted, and George, as well as E and F, are all subordinate to G.

In a business organization the manager accomplishes the superordinate objective at his level by effectively delegating authority to subordinates and by holding them ac- countable for accomplishing their respective objectives. For example, if the organization in Figure 4-6 were a business firm, objective G might be the responsibility of the presi- dent, and objectives E and F might be the responsibility of two vice-presidents or depart- ment managers.

ORGANIZATIONAL OBJECTIVES AND TIME

Practically nothing can be accomplished instantaneously, so any human activity, which of course includes man's activities within organizations, can be related to some measure- ment of time. For instance, the effectiveness of organizations can most understandably be expressed by measuring their objectives against a structure based on time; that is, by determining to what extent an organization is achieving its *immediate objectives*, its *attainable objectives*, and its *visionary objectives*. Of these three levels, only immediate and attainable objectives can be related to standard units of time; we can say that four- teen hours are required to assemble a complete automobile, sixty days to build a three- bedroom house, four years to finish college, or five hundred years to build a pyramid. Visionary objectives relate to the unmeasured future, and defy an exact time table. Fig- ure 4-7 shows the hierarchy of their relationship in terms of time for accomplishment.

Visionary Objectives

Visionary objectives are at the top of the hierarchy. These objectives are ultimates toward which the organization is moving—the most desirable accomplishments for the organization. Although none of them can be realistically anticipated by any particular

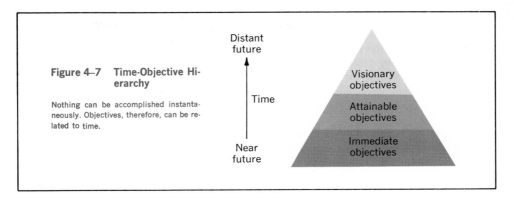

Figure 4–7   Time-Objective Hierarchy

Nothing can be accomplished instantaneously. Objectives, therefore, can be related to time.

Distant future

Time

Near future

Visionary objectives

Attainable objectives

Immediate objectives

time, visionary objectives stimulate advances and improvement, and eventually they are often achieved. The small organization that consisted of Orville Wright and his brother Wilbur had such an objective: they anticipated that one day man would be able to fly in machines, and they began to work toward this "impractical" idea.

As man's level of knowledge advances and as all the conditions that influence an organization change, the visionary objectives will also change. In a sense, working toward a visionary objective is like trying to reach the point at the end of an infinitely long, straight railroad track; as one moves toward that point it recedes into the distance.

Visionary objectives are frequently considered unnecessary—they are often said to be "too theoretical," "blue sky," "presently unattainable," "abstract." But they are very beneficial for any organization that intends to continue to better its accomplishments; they have in fact been the primary stimuli for some of mankind's greatest accomplishments. Practically every modern-day advance in transportation, communications, energy production, synthetics, medicine, and all the other areas that contribute to the highest standard of living man has ever known can be traced to visionary objectives that acted as spurs until the visionary became attainable and then immediate.

The Futurists: Looking toward A.D. 2000[4]

Men in business, government, education and science itself realize that they must look at least two decades ahead just to keep abreast, must learn to survive under totally different conditions.

*   *   *

The exploration of the future has become a sizable business. General Electric has set up Tempo (Technical Management Planning Organization) in Santa Barbara, where 200 physical scientists, sociologists, economists and engineers contemplate the future on a budget that tops $7,000,000 a year. The armed forces have long been in the future business. The Air Force, at Wright-Patterson A.F.B., conducts studies of the whole problem of scientific prediction, also contributes $15 million a year to Santa Monica's Rand Corp. to think—and not necessarily

[4]Excerpts from *Time*, Feb. 25, 1966, pp. 28–29. © Time, Inc., 1966. (By permission.)

about weapons systems. The nonprofit Hudson Institute investigates the possibilities of war and peace along with the future in general. At the University of Illinois, Dr. Charles Osgood is conducting a "computerized exploration of the year 2000," and the Southern Illinois University is providing money and facilities for Buckminister Fuller's World Resources Inventory. The American Academy of Arts and Sciences helped to support the Commission on the Year 2000, headed by Columbia Sociologist Daniel Bell. The Ford Foundation has allocated $1,400,000 this year to a group called Resources for the Future.

*   *   *

That closer inner space, the ocean, will be . . . radically transformed. Rand experts visualize fish herded and raised in offshore pens as cattle are today. Huge fields of kelp and other kinds of seaweed will be tended by undersea "farmers"—frogmen who will live for months at a time in submerged bunkhouses. The protein-rich underseas crop will probably be ground up to produce a dull-tasting cereal that eventually, however, could be regenerated chemically to taste like anything from steak to bourbon. This will provide at least a partial answer to the doomsayers who worry about the prospect of starvation for a burgeoning world population. Actually, the problem could be manageable before any frogman wets a foot; Oxford Agronomist Colin Clark calculates that if all the presently arable land were farmed as the Dutch do it, it could support a population of 28 billion. Even the gloomiest forecasts assume a world population of not more than twice the present size, or 6 billion by the year 2000.

*   *   *

Medicine is in a similar state of exhilarated anticipation. Already widely discussed today, artificial organs—hearts, lungs, stomachs—will be commonly available by the year 2000. An expected development in immunology will make possible the widespread transplanting of organs from either live donors or the recently dead.

*   *   *

In automated industry, not only manual workers, but also secretaries and most middle-level managers will have been replaced by computers. The remaining executives will be responsible for major decisions and long-range policy. Thus, society will seem idle by present standards. According to one estimate, only 10% of the population will be working, and the rest will, in effect, have to be paid to be idle. This is not as radical a notion as it sounds. Even today, only 40% of the population works, not counting the labor performed by housewives or students. Already, says Tempo's John Fisher, "we are rationing work. By 1984, man will spend the first third of his life, or 25 years, getting an education, only the second one-third working, and the final third enjoying the fruits of his labor. There just won't be enough work to go around. Moonlighting will become as socially unacceptable as bigamy."

By 2000, the machines will be producing so much that everyone in the U.S. will, in effect, be independently wealthy. With Government benefits, even nonworking families will have, by one estimate, an annual income of [$50,000 in 1970 dollars]. How to use leisure meaningfully will be a major problem, and Herman Kahn foresees a pleasure-oriented society full of "wholesome degeneracy."

Attainable Objectives

Attainable objectives are those objectives that "could be done"; the time required for accomplishment can be estimated. Although visionary objectives are typically too far in the future for an organization to set up a program designed to accomplish them, attainable objectives are not. Most research programs are in fact specifically designed to work toward attainable objectives.

For example, the Borden Company began to market a low-calorie food-drink for weight control. A pamphlet enclosed in each carton of *ready diet* contained the following statement, [5] explaining the company's attainable objective while developing the food.

Attainable Objectives

Borden's *ready diet,* now being presented to the medical profession and the public, has been developed according to these objectives:

1. To build our product on the concept of scientifically balanced nutrition — including high-quality milk protein providing *proportioned* indispensable amino acids.
2. To provide in a 900 calorie food-drink all the important nutrients for which recommended dietary allowances and minimum daily adult requirements have been established.
3. To make and market *ready diet* in strict adherence to the standard of quality and ethics long associated with the Borden name.

The basic knowledge and processes had existed for producing a dietary food-drink, and Borden's had realized that they could develop the product they wanted by extending existing processes. They thereupon established their objectives and were able to attain the product they wanted.

Immediate Objectives

Once Borden's attainable objectives became feasible, a new set of objectives—immediate objectives—were necessary to manufacture, distribute, and sell the product. All new products, techniques, methods—all innovations—are examples of attainable objectives that have been reached and that then become immediate objectives.

Immediate objectives can be accomplished with existing knowledge and technology; knowledge need not be extended, as would be the case in reaching attainable objectives; nor new knowledge sought, as with visionary objectives. The sales budget for the Rogers Company, shown in the table on page 72, also illustrates immediate objectives.

The Hierarchy of Objectives for Exploration of the Sea

Another real-life example will show the operation of this hierarchy of objectives in terms of time. Although the exploration of outer space is more widely publicized, the exploration of "inner space"—the unexplored areas of the earth—presents equally exciting and promising challenges to man, for two-thirds of our own planet, the sea and the land beneath the sea, has largely been untapped. A leader in the exploration of the sea, Captain Jacques-Yves Cousteau, a French scientist and explorer, has been instrumental in discoveries and innovations that have already brought new benefits from the sea.

[5] By permission of the Borden Company.

Immediate Objectives

ROGERS COMPANY SALES FORECAST AS OF JULY 1, FOR COMING YEAR

July	$ 100,000
August	90,000
September	90,000
October	75,000
November	70,000
December	90,000
January	125,000
February	150,000
March	180,000
April	190,000
May	200,000
June	250,000
Total budgeted sales for year	$1,610,000

For decades men have thought seriously about living in the sea, but Cousteau's project was the first major step in that direction. First the captain had to think out for himself and then explain to others what his objectives were. In Captain Cousteau's own words,

> To begin with, I have long felt that undersea exploration is not an end in itself. It must lead to scientific research, to prospecting for wealth, and to greater utilization of the oceans. Finally, it must lead to human occupation of the sea floor—not only for the brief moments that man has known before, but for days, weeks, even months at a time.[6]

With this visionary objective in mind, a research expedition in September 1962, began working on attainable and immediate objectives, directed toward the visionary objective.

As of August 1962, the *immediate* objectives were:

1 By September 1962, to enable men to live for a week at 33 feet below the surface of the sea and to dive to, and work at, 85 feet. (This location is referred to as "Conshelf One," *Conshelf* being a contraction of Continental Shelf Station.)

2 By June 1963, to enable five men to live for a month at 36 feet below the surface, and to dive to 280 feet (Conshelf Two).

The *attainable* objectives at this same time were:

1 By August 1964, to enable five men to live for two weeks at 165 feet below the surface and to dive regularly to 280 feet (Conshelf Three).

2 By May 1965, to enable five men to live for two weeks at 330 feet and to dive to 525 feet (Conshelf Four).

3 By August 1965, or August 1966, to enable five divers to live for two weeks at 590 feet and to dive to 900 feet (Conshelf Five, the drop-off line of the continental shelf).

[6]Capt. Jacques-Yves Cousteau, "At Home in the Sea," *National Geographic Magazine,* April 1964, p. 472.

The *visionary* objective for the entire project is that ultimately men will be able to occupy the sea floor, even for "months at a time." They will live at 660 feet and dive to 1,300 feet. Most of these objectives were attained as planned. The implications of this visionary objective in economic as well as military terms are fantastic.

Using the familiar pyramid to represent the hierarchy of these objectives, the project may be plotted, as in Figure 4-8. Similar hierarchies can be built for any organization that plans to accomplish more than its immediate objective. The preciseness of the Conshelf hierarchy shows that this organization was directing its activities toward objectives that were spelled out.

Statements of some objectives for the space program and for Inland Steel Company are shown on the next page as additional descriptions of organizational objectives.

INTERACTION OF TIME AND ORGANIZATIONAL LEVEL HIERARCHIES

An organizational objective has two principal dimensions. The first dimension is the level of the organization to which the objective applies. The second dimension is the period of time when the objective is expected to be accomplished. The two dimensions interact to determine the objectives of the organization.

Lower objectives are more detailed, restricted, and limited in their influence on the total organization. The higher one goes up the hierarchies, the more limited the objec-

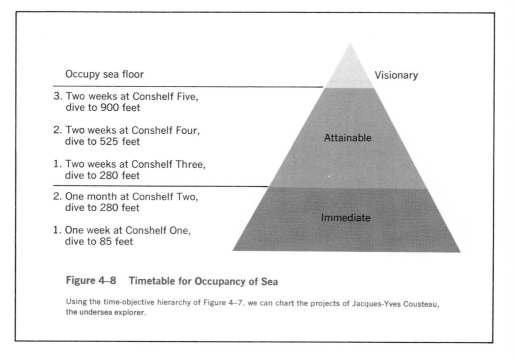

Occupy sea floor   Visionary

3. Two weeks at Conshelf Five,
   dive to 900 feet

2. Two weeks at Conshelf Four,
   dive to 525 feet   Attainable

1. Two weeks at Conshelf Three,
   dive to 280 feet

2. One month at Conshelf Two,
   dive to 280 feet
                                        Immediate
1. One week at Conshelf One,
   dive to 85 feet

Figure 4–8   Timetable for Occupancy of Sea

Using the time-objective hierarchy of Figure 4–7, we can chart the projects of Jacques-Yves Cousteau, the undersea explorer.

Some Attainable and Visionary Objectives for the Space Program

- Vastly improved propulsion, using both nuclear and chemical energy.
- Marriage of major features of both aeronautics and astronautics via development of lifting bodies and winged spacecraft with maneuverable reentry ability, launched by means of recoverable and reusable launch vehicles, with landings and take-offs from spaceports.
- Operational astronaut rescue and spacecraft repair capability.
- Establishment of one or more lunar bases, possibly international in nature.
- Development of manned earth-orbiting permanent space stations.
- Unmanned probes of the solar system; manned exploration of planets.
- Satellite communications of radio and TV directly to home receivers.
- Operational and research satellite advances in meteorology, mapping, navigation, and observation.

Edward C. Welsh, "Why Have a Space Program?" *The General Electric Forum,* Autumn 1967, p. 9.

The Objectives of Inland Steel Company

First: To endeavor constantly to improve the caliber of our personnel at all levels of our operations with the objective of having the best team in the field. This can only be done by employing the most careful methods of selection, training and promotion. Without attaining this goal most of the others can never be reached. With it, they are all possible.

Second: To conduct all phases of our business under the highest standards of ethics and morality. This includes a policy of non-discrimination in employment and promotion. Merit and experience alone should govern, and all should have equal opportunity irrespective of race, color, or creed.

Third: To foster harmony throughout our organization; provide satisfactory working conditions; properly reward our employees by adequate compensation, and offer them the opportunity of acquiring a stock ownership in the company. The objectives of these moves are, of course, to make Inland a place not only where men and women want to work, but where they will be happy in their work, and seek to do their best in the common interest.

Fourth: To continually improve our methods and our facilities so that our costs will be as low or lower and our quality as good or better than our competitors.

Fifth: To serve our customers so well that we will merit a volume of business from them relatively as great or greater than that enjoyed by any of our competitors.

Sixth: To expand our plants and enter new lines of activity whenever the undertaking appears wise and the investment sound in relation to the financial condition of the company.

Seventh: To encourage our people to play their full part in the affairs of their community —civic, philanthropic, religious, educational—and thus take their places as good and useful citizens.

Eighth: To lend our best efforts to improve and assist the communities in which our operations are located.

Ninth: To inform our employees, stockholders, customers and the public fully and regularly regarding our plans, our progress and our problems.

Tenth: To make an annual return on our sales and our invested capital as good or better than any other company in the industry.

(Used by permission of Inland Steel Company.)

tives become in number, but the more important they are in relation to the whole organization. Each level of the hierarchies synthesizes the objectives of the level below. Top-level objectives are, therefore, abstractions of the entire hierarchy of objectives of the organization. All subordinate objectives, and the activities directed toward accomplishing these objectives, are determined by these highest objectives.

Figure 4-9 shows a mix of time objectives with organizational-level objectives. Figure 4-9 might represent a large organization such as an automobile manufacturer, an aerospace corporation, or a university. The particular mix of objectives is read horizontally. The higher the organizational level, the more the concern with visionary and attainable objectives. Lower levels are more concerned with immediate objectives. No matter what the level, there is still some concern with all three types of objectives. Thus, every member of the organization has at least some interest in all of the organization's objectives, at every level and for every point in the organization's future.

SUMMARY

Organizations exist because they can achieve personal objectives of their members when they successfully accomplish their own organizational goals. Organizational objectives are derived from the personal objectives of members. Thus organizational objectives give purpose and meaning to the organization.

The development and communication of organizational objectives are important because organizational objectives provide the framework for coordinated effort. With-

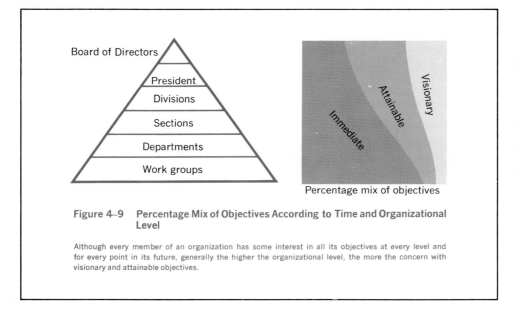

Figure 4–9   Percentage Mix of Objectives According to Time and Organizational Level

Although every member of an organization has some interest in all its objectives at every level and for every point in its future, generally the higher the organizational level, the more the concern with visionary and attainable objectives.

out mutually understood organizational objectives, individual members or units are likely to wander more or less aimlessly, not working together effectively.

The objectives of an organization can be arranged in a hierarchy. Objectives in this hierarchy should be compatible with and reinforce individual objectives. When organizational objectives are accomplished, individual objectives are also achieved, and vice versa. Higher-level, superordinate organizational objectives coordinate subordinate individual and organizational objectives. Thus, higher level objectives are achieved when subordinate objectives are successfully met.

The concepts of superordinate objectives and means-ends chains explain the importance of every individual and his work in an organization. If one persons fails, his failure may adversely affect the accomplishment of every objective of the organization, because accomplishment of objectives at any level depends upon the successful accomplishment of every subordinate objective.

The failure of an individual probably also unfavorably affects the objectives of parallel units, since they would have benefited if he had contributed to objectives superordinate to both him and them; or they may have to spend their efforts on doing the work of the one who failed, delaying their own primary work.

Organizational objectives should be developed, renewed, and communicated in a sequence, starting at the highest level of the organization. The objectives for each successive lower level are then developed in turn.

Finally, organizational objectives can be related to time. Visionary objectives are the ultimate or "dream" objectives for the organization. No specific timetable can be set for their achievement. Attainable objectives will require investment in research to develop or perfect a technology, but good estimates can be made of the time and expenditure required. Immediate objectives can be achieved now without new technological developments. Lower levels of complex organizations are primarily interested in immediate objectives. Higher levels become increasingly more concerned with visionary and attainable objectives. One of the jobs of managers is to see that objectives for every part of the organization are always available.

FOR REVIEW AND DISCUSSION

1 What is likely to occur in an organization without well-defined objectives? Explain the advantages of well-defined and integrated organizational objectives.

2 Explain a manager's responsibility in the formulation of organizational objectives.

3 Explain in detail what is meant by the statement: "Organizational objectives are structured in a hierarchy." Include in your discussion the concept of organizational objectives as means-ends chains.

4 Explain the sources of the top-level objectives of an organization. Describe how the objectives for a complex organization (for example, a large business) could be determined for every unit and person in the organization. Why must this be a "top-down" rather than a "bottom-up" process?

5 Consider the statement: "Too often managers fail to recognize that overall objectives do not automatically exist." If this statement is true, what effect will such a condition have on the operations of a large organization?

6 How is it that a department within a larger organization could work with apparent efficiency and still contribute little or nothing to the overall objectives of the larger organization? Include in your discussion two illustrative examples not given in the text.

7 Explain the concept of mutual reinforcement of individual and organizational objectives. Give three examples not in the text.

8 Define subordinate objectives and give three examples not in the text.

9 Explain the concept of compatibility of individual and organizational objectives and give three examples not in the text.

10 Define visionary, attainable, and immediate objectives. Give two examples not in the text to illustrate each.

11 Is the top management level or the foreman level more concerned with visionary and attainable objectives? Explain.

12 Are lower levels of an organization concerned solely with immediate objectives? Explain.

CASES

A   Bartex Mud Company, which supplied drilling mud for oil drillers, employed 200 persons. No formal management procedures had ever been used by the firm until two years ago. At that time Mr. Barton, the president, requested that each department supply him after every quarter with a statement of that department's objectives.

Mr. Barton took no action on the objectives which were supplied him. He saw a number of inconsistencies, conflicts, and overlaps, but he was reluctant to say anything to his managers because he had noted a decided improvement in the operations of the company.

> **1** What effects do you think Mr. Barton's requirement for each department to submit its objectives had upon the operation of the firm? Could this have been responsible for the improvement in operations?
>
> **2** Suggest a better approach for Mr. Barton to use in dealing with his organization's objectives.

B   Foster Paper Corporation, which had sixteen large mills employing a total of 30,000 employees, recently hired a firm of management consultants to suggest ways of improving its operations. The consulting firm made an extensive study of the company's operations, after which it submitted a report to the president, Mr. Lucas. The following comments are taken from the report of the consultants:

"In our opinion, the most significant opportunity for improving the operations of the company is in the area of organizational objectives. We suggest that you undertake, with our assistance, a comprehensive program for improving your objectives at every level. We propose that every employee and manager agree with his direct supervisor in writing at the beginning of each quarter on exactly what his or his department's work objectives will be. At the end of each quarter an appraisal will be held in each case by the parties concerned to determine how well stated objectives were met. Adequate provision should be made for improving these objectives each quarter."

    1 What problems do you foresee in implementing the consultants' plan?

    2 What effect do you think the plan would have on the company's operations?

    3 Considering all factors, do you recommend that Mr. Lucas accept or reject the consultants' proposal? Explain your answer.

    C In 1867 two brothers, Silas and Jupiter Marion, decided to go into the buggy business. The venture was highly successful, and after the turn of the century the firm had become one of the world's largest automobile producers.

When they decided to go into business with each other, Silas and Jupiter had entered into the following contract:

    I, Silas Marion, agree to make all the buggies my brother Jupiter can sell.

    I, Jupiter Marion, agree to sell all the buggies my brother Silas can make.

(Signed) Silas Marion

Jupiter Marion

July 29, 1867

    1 Construct the hierarchy of objectives as you see it for the Marion brothers.

    2 Do you think the contract of the Marion brothers improved or harmed their operations? Explain. How might the contract be improved?

    D During recent years the Student Council of the College of Social Sciences of State University had become increasingly active. From time to time the council submitted questionnaires to students of the college soliciting student opinions about the operations of the college.

In one instance the council demanded that the dean discharge an unpopular teacher. The council also pressed for a grade review board, for voting representation on all college committees, and for a voting voice in all matters of hiring, firing, promoting, and awarding tenure to faculty members.

Dr. Sholter, Dean of the College, had at first been quite willing to cooperate with the council because he thought it represented desirable student participation in matters which legitimately concerned them. Yet, the dean had become increasingly resistive to the demands of the council. In a speech to the local Lions Club he said, "We must be careful that we do not let militant students destroy the university. They, like almost everyone else in life, have some legitimate complaints. But if we go much further we will destroy the quality of the university, and the students themselves will be the biggest losers."

A week after Dean Sholter's speech, the council presented a statement to him from which the following is excerpted: "We demand the elimination of required courses. We demand that a degree be awarded to a student whenever he completes any 128 semester hours in the university." The statement contained several other similar demands, and ended with the following sentence: "The students of the college have approved these demands by majority vote."

Dean Sholter had no doubt that the demands had indeed been voted for by most of the students of the college.

    1 What response should Dean Sholter make to the demand to eliminate required courses? Why?

    2 Should the students be allowed to set the objectives of the college by majority vote? Why?

FOR FURTHER STUDY

Additional sources can be found in the references cited in the chapter.

Books

Dalton E. McFarland: *Management: Principles and Practices,* 3d ed., The Macmillan Company, New York, 1970, chap. 7. "Objectives assist executives in performing their leadership roles by providing a basis for uniting the efforts of workers in the business. The objectives help to identify the company and to give the company recognition and status. In addition, objectives motivate individuals and provide a basis for evaluating the total performance of the organization."

William H. Newman: *Administrative Action,* 2d ed., Prentice-Hall, Inc., Englewood Cliffs, N.J., 1963, chap. 2. Goals serve a dual purpose in administration. They are vital links in the planning process, and they are also essential elements in the process of control.

Herbert A. Simon: *Administrative Behavior,* 2d ed., The Macmillan Company, New York, 1961, pp. 4–8, 16–18, 62–64, and 112–117. Organizational objectives are determined by facts and values, and form means-ends chains in organizations. They also provide inducements for individuals.

George R. Terry: *Principles of Management,* 5th ed., Richard D. Irwin, Inc., Homewood, Ill., 1968, chap. 2. "The primary need of most enterprises is a single target or several major ones toward which all members, and particularly, the leaders, are directed with the greatest force."

Stanley Young: *Management: A Systems Analysis,* Scott, Foresman and Company, Glenview, Ill., 1966, chap. 4. This chapter is a good, general discussion of the meaning and importance of organizational objectives.

Articles

George J. Berkwitt: "The Rocky Road to Company Goals," *Dun's Review,* September 1968. Many managers do not even know what a corporate goal is, much less how to set one.

Charles H. Granger: "The Hierarchy of Objectives," *Harvard Business Review,* May–June 1964. This important article explains the framework of objectives in complex organizations. It also shows how objectives at all levels can be chosen, established, and profitably used by managers.

Walter Hill: "The Goal Formation Process in Complex Organizations," *The Journal of Management Studies,* May 1969. Organizational goals are formed by coalitions and are affected by the environment, the internal social system, and the motives of members.

J. R. Maker and D. T. Pierson: "Perceived Clarity of Individual Job Objectives and of Group Mission as Correlates of Organizational Morale," *Journal of Communication,* June 1970. Clear individual and organizational job objectives increase job satisfaction.

Charles Perrow: "The Analysis of Goals in Complex Organizations," *American Sociological Review,* December 1961. "An understanding of organizational behavior requires close examination of the goals of the organization reflected in operating policies."

5

The Organization and Its Environment

*The environment is the sum of factors that make it up,
such as war and peace, science, ethics, international
economic and political attitudes and alliances, cultural
and traditional patterns, national and local political and
economic conditions, unionization, community attitudes,
and the interests of consumer groups, stockholders, and
the general public.*
    *THOMAS MORANIAN, DONALD GRUNEWALD,
    and RICHARD C. REIDENBACH*

An organization does not exist in a vacuum. It exists in association with its environment, which provides resources and limitations. If it is to remain prosperous an organization must continually adapt to its environment, which is constantly changing. Failure to adequately adapt to the environment is a major cause of organization failure.

An organization and its environment are interdependent, as shown in Figure 5-1. The organization depends upon its environment for the resources and opportunities necessary for its existence. Too, the environment determines the limits of the organization's activities. As shown in Figure 5-1, the environment will contribute valuable resources to the organization only if the organization provides desired goods or services to the environment. The activities of the organization when doing this must be acceptable to the environment. For example, a manufacturer must produce his product without excessively polluting the air. Through feedback, the environment reacts to the goods and services produced by and the activities of the organization. The envi-

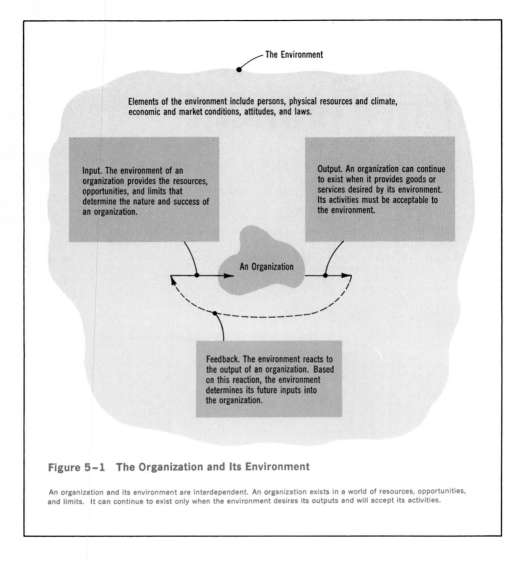

The Environment

Elements of the environment include persons, physical resources and climate, economic and market conditions, attitudes, and laws.

Input. The environment of an organization provides the resources, opportunities, and limits that determine the nature and success of an organization.

Output. An organization can continue to exist when it provides goods or services desired by its environment. Its activities must be acceptable to the environment.

An Organization

Feedback. The environment reacts to the output of an organization. Based on this reaction, the environment determines its future inputs into the organization.

Figure 5-1   The Organization and Its Environment

An organization and its environment are interdependent. An organization exists in a world of resources, opportunities, and limits. It can continue to exist only when the environment desires its outputs and will accept its activities.

ronment evaluates these and determines the future resources that it will contribute and the restrictions that it will place on the organization.

ELEMENTS OF THE ENVIRONMENT

The elements in the environment of an organization are persons, physical resources and climate, economic and market conditions, attitudes, and laws. These are included in Figure 5-1. All these elements that make up an organization's environment affect it in one way or another. Some of these are important because they help the organization to attain its objectives. Other environmental elements get in the way. And every organization's environment is different. A city university, for example, may be housed in towering buildings crowded together in the midst of busy city life apparently unrelated to the univeristy. Yet this university is vitally affected by its city environment, which gives it many opportunities and problems that do not exist for a university in a small town (and vice versa). The character of each university will be largely determined by its environment.

Persons

The first element in an organization's environment is persons. Without persons to interact and to do the work of the organization, there in fact would be no organization. A manufacturing plant can be successful only if its community can provide workers with the necessary skills. And a college will prosper only if students want to go there and instructors want to teach there. Thus, persons are the indispensable resource of an organization.

Persons determine the availability of other resources to the organization and what the organization does and the ways it functions. Thus, persons are involved in the other elements of environment discussed below.

Physical Resources and Climate

Physical resources often determine the location or affect the operation of an organization. Manufacturing businesses must have the raw materials required to make their products. They also must have the necessary plant facilities and machines. Lumber mills are usually located near forests, refineries near oil fields, and canning and freezing plants near vegetable and fruit growing centers.

In the opposite direction, inadequate parking facilities has been a factor contributing to the relative decline of business in center-city stores. In another area, whether special classroom facilities are available might determine the way a course is taught. Library resources, laboratories, and housing will affect a college's operations.

Climate affects the location and operations of an organization. A snow skiing resort requires cold weather, lots of snow, and mountains. Even curricula are affected by climate and other geographical factors. Sugar and rice are studied at one southern university while astronomy is emphasized at another in the West where clear skies prevail. Schools of mining are located in mountain states.

Economic and Market Conditions

Is the market (environment) able to pay a satisfactory price for an organization's goods or services? If so, the organization may prosper; if not, it almost surely will fail. In periods of prosperity labor and other resources may be scarce. In depression periods, many businesses may be hard pressed just to survive. Governmental monetary and fiscal policies are closely watched by millions because of their profound effects.

Shifting tastes of consumers profoundly affect those who supply goods and services. During some recent years a trend toward longer hair for men threw many barbers out of work. At the same time, organizations producing pollution-control devices have prospered due to rising demand.

In a broader sense, some environments may emphasize individual capitalism; others may value socialism, facism, or communism.

Attitudes

Social, cultural, religious, political, and philosophical attitudes are significant factors in an organization's environment. A university may have a tradition of a winning football team. Football weekends, which bring great hordes of people to town, may be an integral part of the tradition. Opinions vary about these weekends; operators of restaurants and motels think they are great; homeowners who live near the university and do not want out-of-towners parking on their lawns disagree. As long as the team is winning, the homeowners may be caught up in the general enthusiasm and stifle their complaints. Let the team begin to lose, however, and along with cries to fire the coach, there will be bitter stories about the ruts in the lawns.

The importance of attitudes as environmental factors sometimes may not be fully appreciated because attitudes are intangible. Various concepts of freedom are hard to define, for example, yet they affect practically everyone and every organization. Religious attitudes about ethics, morals, and life's meaning are vital factors in the environment of organizations. For instance, attitudes toward birth control and welfare measures for the poor have great effects on countless organizations. Similarly, one nation may adopt an educational philosophy designed to educate the masses, while another may view education as a privilege of the elite. Numerous organizations must respond accordingly. Some environments may emphasize individualism; others may emphasize the common good.

In recent years, attitudes of increased interest in protecting the quality of the physical environment have emerged. Many demands are made that those organizations that use resources must not unduly pollute the environment. One steel producer, in trying to meet these demands, in one year invested $50 million on waste water treatment facilities. Increasingly the cry has been heard that organizations, particularly business firms, ought to be "socially responsible." That is, there are many who demand that a business contribute to the larger good of society and not just focus on maximizing profit. In addition to controlling pollution, businesses are told to be socially responsible by hiring and training the hard-core unemployed, by practicing conservation, and contributing to other community improvement programs.

Laws

Laws are the "rules of the game" under which society says an organization must operate. Some organizations, such as corporations and government agencies, are set up by law.

On the other hand, laws sometimes forbid the existence of an organization, such as organizations that would perform illegal acts. In most cases, however, laws are more in the background, but they do influence—directly or indirectly—a very large portion of organizational activities.

THE EFFECTS OF THE ENVIRONMENT ON THE ORGANIZATION

Environmental factors affect an organization in two ways: they set limits, and they provide opportunities and challenge.

The limits, like the factors themselves, are sometimes visible, tangible ones: a river or a cliff decrees that a building may go here but not there. Sometimes they are invisible, but still very real: the social situation in which an organization exists specifies what kind of behavior will be tolerated. A noisy manufacturer may be in for difficulty if he locates himself within a quiet neighborhood. The neighbors may be able to call on or pass laws to force him either to move altogether or to alter his equipment, or influence alone may be all that is necessary; the neighbors may know (or be) the "right" people politically.

In addition to setting limits, environmental factors also provide opportunities and challenge. The environment provides the market for a new product that might be highly successful. And the fact that the moon is there seems to have inspired man to go to it.

THE EFFECTS OF THE ORGANIZATION ON ITS ENVIRONMENT

The effects of the organization on its environment may be equally as important as the effects of the environment on the organization. The influence of one on the other is reciprocal, and constantly changing in kind and in degree. The organization exists within an environment, and all the goods, services, money, or other factors that come out of the organization affect the environment. In recent years, this interrelationship has been appreciated more than ever before as the effects of widespread pollution have been felt.

There are some environmental factors over which the organization has a high degree of control. However, all too often an organization does not even recognize these factors, or may not see their importance. More awareness and effort for improving environmental factors will help both organizations and the environment, at least in the long run.

WHICH ENVIRONMENTAL ELEMENTS ARE IMPORTANT?

A dynamic organization is constantly changing and is surrounded by thousands of environmental elements. An organization can respond to its environment in two ways: (1) it can adjust to the environment, or (2) it can, if it has the ability, change the environment. These elements are acting upon it, and being acted upon by it. They are constantly changing, thus presenting a confusing picture.

Every organization should be aware of environmental elements; that they are numerous; that they are changing; and that some of them are important to its success or failure. Which ones? The important factors are those that, directly or indirectly, help most to achieve the organization's goals or keep it from achieving them.

A healthy organization knows what its objectives are, knows which environmental factors are affecting it in its progress toward these objectives, and realistically deals with them. The goal is to have a healthy interrelationship of the organization and its environment, for their mutual benefit.

SUMMARY

In all its operations, an organization is affected by its environment. In turn the organization affects its environment by the factors that it sends into the environment. The elements of the environment include persons, physical resources and climate, economic and market conditions, and attitudes and laws. The environment thus provides opportunities and limitations for an organization.

The effective organization tries to be as compatible as possible with its environment. It recognizes which environmental factors are important, and asserts itself in changing those factors over which it has some control. It tries to adapt to those that are beyond its control. Thus it can employ its resources to best accomplish organizational objectives, avoiding a needless expenditure of resources on conflicts with its environment. The socially responsible organization also tries to improve its environment.

FOR REVIEW AND DISCUSSION

1 Explain how each of the following environmental factors can affect an organization. Give an example not in the text to illustrate each factor: (a) persons, (b) physical resources and climate, (c) economic and market conditions, (d) attitudes, and (e) laws.

2 Explain how factors in the environment can set limits on an organization's operations. Give two examples not in the text.

3 Explain how factors in the environment can provide opportunities and challenges for an organization. Give two examples not in the text.

4 What are the two kinds of responses an organization can make to its environment? Illustrate each with an example not in the text.

5 Explain the concept of social responsibility for an organization. Do you agree that an organization has social responsibility?

CASES

A For several years, San Cristo, a large western city, had experienced a severe drought. Normal water supplies were so low that the city had been forced to use water from underground wells. This underground water, although safe to drink, had a very unpleasant taste and odor.

During the drought, Bill Ralls had sold Mountain Sparkle water, which he had brought from the mountains 200 miles away. The business had been extremely successful during the drought, but recent heavy rains have allowed the city to return to using good water from its reservoirs.

Since the rains, sales of Mountain Sparkle water have dropped to the point where the business is no longer profitable. Bill wondered what action he should take about his business.

    1 How have changing environmental conditions affected Bill's business?

    2 What alternative courses of action do you think are available to Bill? Which should he take? Why?

B The following item recently appeared in a daily newspaper.

Mine Shutdown Brings "Ghost" to Utah Town

Latuda, a small mining town in central Utah, officially becomes a ghost town July 20.

That's when the power goes off for the town that once had 600 residents and now has only 53. The reason: Shutdown of the Liberty Fuel Coal Mine started in 1917 by Frank Cameron and Frank Latuda, for whom the town was named.

Latuda's son, Frank, Jr., says the mine no longer can continue to operate because of rising labor and delivery costs.

    The last coal was mined Friday.

    1 Explain how changing environmental conditions caused the shutdown of the mine.

    2 Explain how, in turn, environmental conditions caused the town to close. Take the viewpoint of a merchant in the town.

    3 Suppose you were a farmer who sold vegetables to the merchant. How have changes in the environment affected your operations?

C Melbo City has just learned that the government will locate a large missile complex just outside the city limits. Many persons think the success of Melbo City in attracting the installation was largely due to the efforts of Senator Fishburne, one of the most powerful members of Congress. Of course, Melbo City had all the resources required for the missile agency, but so did twenty other cities who vigorously sought the complex.

    1 What was the most important environmental factor that made Melbo City's effort successful?

    2 Assume you are in the following business or organizations in Melbo City. How will the announcement affect your organization: (a) real estate agency, (b) drive-in restaurant, (c) church, (d) Committee to Preserve Historic Melbo City, and (e) Melbo Junior College?

D Recently the state legislature passed a law rigidly controlling stream pollution by new manufacturing plants. The law became effective during the time Mr. Summer, mayor of Woodville, was negotiating with Atlantic Paper Company to build a large papermill near Woodville. Atlantic decided that it wanted to accept Mr. Summer's proposal for the location of its plant, but informed him it would be impossible to meet the state's new stream pollution law. Consequently, Atlantic was thinking about building its plant in Gerdts, which was 50 miles away from Woodville and across the state line. The state in which Gerdts was located did not have a stream pollution law.

Woodville was an old mining town which had suffered more and more unemployment over the past several decades due to reduced mining operations. Currently, its unemployment rate was twice the national average. Mr. Summer thought the paper mill was the last opportunity to improve the economy of the town. He decided to petition the governor to call a special session of the legislature to repeal the stream pollution law.

> **1** Do you agree with Mr. Summer's action to get the stream pollution law repealed? Why?
>
> **2** Is Atlantic justified in moving to the other state? Explain the pollution control problem that exists because of the different laws for the two states. How could this be resolved?

FOR FURTHER STUDY

Additional sources can be found in the sources cited in the chapter.

Books

Keith Davis and Robert L. Blomstrom: *Business and Its Environment,* McGraw-Hill Book Company, New York, 1966. "The discipline of business and its environment covers relationships of a business institution to values and institutions outside its own formal organization."

William T. Greenwood: "Business and Society: Contemporary Issues and National Goals," from *Issues in Business and Society,* Houghton Mifflin Company, Boston, 1964, pp. 512–536. Social and political factors affect business management.

Paul R. Lawrence and Jay W. Lorsch: *Organization and Environment,* Richard D. Irwin, Inc., Homewood, Ill., 1969. The relationships between organizations and their environments are examined.

Joseph W. McGuire: *Business and Society,* McGraw-Hill Book Company, New York, 1963. The relationship between business and its social, political, and economic environment in the United States is studied.

Articles

James R. Bright: "Opportunity and Threat in Technological Change," *Harvard Business Review,* November–December 1963. Dealing with technological innovation is becoming a more serious, more frequent problem for all society as well as for business management.

Jules Cohn: "Is Business Meeting the Challenge of Urban Affairs?" *Harvard Business Review,* March–April 1970. Guidelines for businessmen's involvement in pressing social problems are suggested.

Fortune, February 1970. This issue has several articles on environmental pollution.

Stephen A. Greyser: "Business and Politics," *Harvard Business Review,* September–October 1964. "Businessmen generally believe that improvement in the political climate toward business awaits more activity by business itself."

William K. Reed: "Our Future Business Environment," *Conference Board Record,* January 1970. Future political, economic, and social conditions affecting organizations are estimated.

Dow Votaw and S. Prakash Sethi: "Do We Need a New Corporate Response to a Changing Social Environment?" *California Management Review,* Fall 1969. Corporations must make a new response to social problems.

6
Viability of Organizations

*Only birth can conquer death. . . . there must be—if we
are to experience long survival—a continuous "recurrence
of birth" to nullify the unremitting recurrence of death.*
    JOSEPH CAMPBELL

How does an organization survive? Why does one grow and flourish while a similar one withers and dies? Chances are that sooner or later you will find yourself faced with this question.

At the time that it becomes important to you, you will not be concerned with abstract theories about organizations; you will want to know, in terms that apply to your particular organization, what it is that determines whether *that* organization will live or die. Your personal happiness, your paycheck, or your life itself may be at stake.

An organization is not inherently short- or long-lived. The first factor that determines the length of its life is whether the persons with power in it want it to be long lived. But even if they do, other factors must be in operation before they can get what they want.

Organizations that are clearly temporary have a number of characteristics that differ markedly from the characteristics of organizations that function for a relatively long time (as determined by comparing their life span with that of similar organizations). Because one set of characteristics is found so consistently in short-life organizations and the other so consistently in long-life organizations, these characteristics can be regarded as determining ones—that is, an organization with long-life characteristics will have a long life. Further, an organization with short-life characteristics that wants to survive for a long time can do so by reshaping these characteristics.

The determining characteristics fall into three categories. The length of an organization's life can be predicted by comparing its view of survival, its philosophy of objectives, and its structure with those in Figure 6-1.

An organization may be designed at the outset to be a long-life organization, but in practice its early life will show many of the characteristics of the short-life organization. Its structure, for example, may begin in a very simple way. But the persons who have power in the organization want it to survive, and they consciously and deliberately work to that end.

Short-life organization		Long-life organization
Long-term survival is not seen as important.	VIEW OF SURVIVAL	Long-term survival is a goal; operations are directed toward it.
Organization has only immediate objectives. Development for renewal is not important. Little effort is made to closely relate individual and organizational objectives. Organization has no hierarchy of objectives.	PHILOSOPHY OF MANAGEMENT	Organization has immediate, attainable, and visionary objectives. Development for renewal is important. Elaborate attempts are made to keep individual objectives compatible with organizational objectives, and vice versa. Organization has an elaborate hierarchy of subordinate and superordinate objectives.
Organization has little concern for environmental factors.		Attempts are made to keep organization in harmony with environment, either by controlling it or by adapting to it.
Organization has simple, informal, and unstable structure.	STRUCTURE	Organization has complex, formal, and relatively stable structure.

Figure 6–1   Viability of Organizations

Organizations are not inherently short- or long-lived. Many start out as short-lived and then develop the characteristics of a long-lived organization in an effort to become one.

Such an organization, if it is to become long-lived, will go through three phases: in phase I, most of its characteristics are temporarily those of the short-life organization; an important exception is that it wants to survive. In phase II, its characteristics are moving closer to those of the long-life organization. In phase III, its characteristics are those listed on the right in Figure 6-1: it *is* a long-life organization.

Some organizations, on the other hand, set out to be only short-lived; they accomplish their simple, immediate objectives and die, never aspiring to progress—and so never progressing—beyond phase I. Others, having started their operations with no long-range plans, want to continue.

For example, two students at a university decide to sell snacks in the dormitories during exam week. This is a short-term organization, with no plans for the future. The students expect to pool their money, invest it in snacks, advertise and market the snacks, divide their returns, and dissolve their organization.

Perhaps, however, the organization turns out to be very profitable. Its "managers" decide that they want it to continue. They have therefore taken the first step to change it from a short-term to a long-term organization; the time that had been expected to be its whole life now becomes merely its first phase.

What do they do next? They plan; they consider what changes in the organization will be necessary to keep it going. The two of them may have lost as much sleep as they want to—more personnel may be needed. Who will hire them? How much will they be paid? What university regulations are involved?

Immediately the young organization is involved with objectives; its environment becomes more important, and it must set up some sort of structure to define the responsibilities and activities of employers and employees. This period of transition, phase II, will come to an end when the organization has an orderly system of day-to-day operation. This simple progression can be portrayed as in Figure 6-2.

Once an organization has safely arrived in phase III, what then? Stability is, unfortunately, only an illusion. This brings us back to the question at the head of the chapter: Why does one organization grow and flourish while a similar one withers and dies? The organization that withers and dies has slipped from phase III back into phase II, and from there to phase I, and so into oblivion.

The viability chart given in Figure 6-1 is therefore important in two ways: It enables an organization to measure itself on the way "up"—in the process of becoming a long-term organization—but it also enables an organization to discover that it is in danger, that its very life may be threatened. Obviously, the sooner this is discovered, the better. If an organization can recognize that one of its established long-term characteristics has changed (for example, if one of the partners in Dormitory Snacks, Incorporated, should be drafted—this is a challenge that must be met), and that as an organization it is therefore already back in phase II, it can pinpoint its problem and deal with it, moving itself back to phase III. (Perhaps the other partner can buy him out; perhaps someone else wants to buy in. Whatever the solution, its success or failure will soon show up in the other characteristics.) Organizations that attain phase III must *continually and consciously work* to maintain their position there.

Thus whether an organization is short-lived or long-lived depends upon its view of

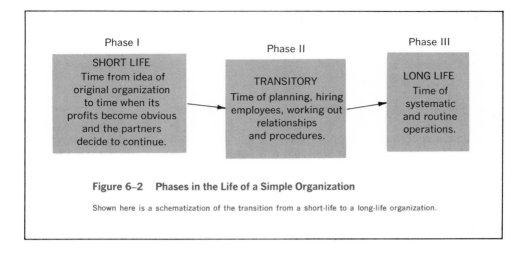

Figure 6–2 Phases in the Life of a Simple Organization

Shown here is a schematization of the transition from a short-life to a long-life organization.

survival, its philosophy of management, and the structure of its relationships. Each of these three factors is discussed below in more detail for both short- and long-life organizations. The transitory phase is not discussed separately because it is merely an intermediate stage between short and long life.

VIEW OF SURVIVAL

The first determinant of the permanency of an organization is the view that it takes of its survival.

Short-life Organizations

The question of survival will ordinarily not be a major concern of a short-life organization. This organization will be concerned only with living in the present—it has no concern with what will become of it in the future. Long-term survival is not an objective.

Long-life Organizations

In striking contrast to a short-term organization, a long-term organization has a vital and continuing concern for its survival. It makes survival one of its objectives. Without this decision it has scant chance of long life; with this decision it takes the first major step towards long life.

PHILOSOPHY OF MANAGEMENT

The second determinant of short- and long-life organizations is the philosophy of management. The organization's way of dealing with its objectives, development, members, environment, and relationships is important.

No overt management philosophy is needed for short-life organizations; the organization plods along its way meeting as best it can situations that present themselves. But long-term organizations need a well-developed philosophy to guide their decisions.

Short-life Organizations

Objectives of short-life organizations are static, limited, and do not change to meet the changing conditions in which the organization must operate. Objectives are stated in terms of accomplishing a specific task—raising a certain amount of money, meeting a deadline, gathering information about some anticipated project, or investigating and evaluating a proposal. Almost all the objectives of the short-life organization are immediate ones.

The objectives of short-life organizations are usually singular; they do not form a complex hierarchy. For example, what subordinate objectives are necessary if the basic objective is to get a car out of the mud, or to quickly earn some extra income? Therefore, short-life organizations generally do not find it necessary to construct complex hierarchies of objectives. Objectives of the short-life organization can usually be stated very simply. Few, if any, have attainable or visionary goals, nor do they need them.

Short-life organizations do not change their objectives. Things continue to be done a certain way for no other reason than "they have always been done that way." The old "mom and pop" corner grocery stores are excellent examples of enterprises that tried to conduct "business as usual" even as the chain grocers and the supermarkets were revolutionizing food marketing. Problems are usually dealt with on a "crisis-to-crisis" basis. Only when the problem becomes unbearable does management try to cope with the problem and its ramifications. In many cases, by this time it is too late to solve the problem, and the organization is doomed.

Long-life Organizations

The objectives of long-life organizations are dynamic. Changes in its environment will cause a long-life organization to change its objectives. A long-life organization may also adopt new objectives even if its environment does not change significantly. It simply may improve its position within a given environment.

Following the life of ice companies provides an example of this reorientation process. Before the widespread use of electric refrigerators, ice was considered a necessity, and ice companies regarded themselves as long-life organizations. Most towns had several producers. But the development of household electric-refrigeration units reduced the demand for commercially produced ice. Thus, to continue to exist, ice producers had to change their objectives. Some ice companies diversified; others moved into the refrigeration field; the stronger companies purchased their weaker, nearly bankrupt, competitors; most of those who did not change their goals ceased to exist. A more recent example of adapting to environmental changes can be seen in the response of automobile companies in the United States to the increasing importation and sale of small foreign cars; instead of trying annually to produce the "biggest" car, they began to emphasize compactness and sophisticated styling. Large steel companies are attempting to offset an anticipated decline in per capita use of steel by developing new uses for steel.

Decision making for a long-life organization is usually directed toward attempting to anticipate problems before they arise. The costs in time, efforts, interruptions, or lost opportunities that are saved are usually far greater than the cost involved in planning, if the planning enables the organization to anticipate problems and eliminate them before they appear. Even if problems are not eliminated, solutions can be worked out in advance so that the problems can be solved faster and their effects minimized. An ounce of prevention is indeed worth a pound of cure, for many organizational problems.

Subordinate objectives of long-life organizations are usually multiple. There is a consciously and deliberately constructed hierarchy of objectives that includes attainable and visionary objectives.

STRUCTURE

Short-life Organizations

Short-life organizations are usually not highly or formally structured. Relationships are defined casually and without much consideration for long-term effects.

Long-life Organizations

There is usually a formal and clearly defined structure for long-life organizations. This formal structure allows information to be communicated to all members so that coordinated effort is possible. Responsibility, accountability, authority, power, and activities are defined.

Thus, whether an organization is short or long lived will depend upon its attitude toward survival, its managerial philosophies, and, if it is large, how well it can make an orderly structure of its complex relationships. If long life is desired, a key factor will be the organization's approach to growth and development—the topics we will study for the remainder of this chapter.

GROWTH, DEVELOPMENT, AND THEIR INTERACTIONS

Consider organizational growth to be any increase in the size of the organization or any movement toward a given objective. And consider organizational development, on the other hand, to be the formation of new combinations of resources or the formulation of new attainable and visionary objectives. Development involves policy decisions that change organizational objectives. Growth, on the other hand, involves technical or administrative improvement (originating either within or outside the organization) by which it is possible to more effectively accomplish old objectives.

Development is the broader of the two concepts; it occurs through innovation and it provides the framework within which growth can occur. Growth, being narrower, occurs within a given stage of development. Reaching or attaining the maximum output with a given stage of development is a process of attaining maximum growth. Growth asks: How does the organization get more out of what it now has? Development asks: How can the organization achieve something different? Short-term organizations are concerned only with growing in size or moving toward a given objective that is usually narrowly defined. In contrast, long-term organizations develop by reaching new attainable and visionary objectives. Because development changes "the system," it often is resisted. It is untidy and difficult to control, and its outcome frequently is uncertain. Growth thus usually is more comfortable.

Growth and development are in many respects separate and distinct phenomena, but they are also interrelated. Development creates the potential for new growth, and as growth reaches the limits or ceiling imposed by the existing stage of development, pressures will often occur for development. New innovations lead to higher stages of development and new growth potentials. This interaction is shown in Figure 6-3. Creativity leads to innovation, which leads to new development, which gives the potential for increased growth. But even though the potential for new growth exists, growth does not necessarily follow.

If growth does occur, it will reach a ceiling. This is an application of the principle of diminishing returns, taught in sophomore economics courses.

The vertical lines in Figure 6-4 (I, II, III, and IV) represent distinct stages of development. The part of the stage of vertical development that is higher than that of the previous stage represents the increase in growth potential that occurs when an organization moves from a lower to a higher stage of development. Thus, moving from stage I to stage II increases the growth potential by AB; moving from stage II to stage III increases the growth potential CD, etc. Compare the first three stages. The movement from stage I to stage II represents a new process, which results in a relatively large improvement in the growth potential. Moving from state II to stage III represents another new process.

For example, over 200 years ago, sulfuric acid, a basic industrial chemical, was produced by an expensive, inefficient process (stage I). Sulfur compound was burned,

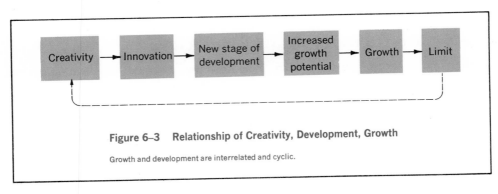

Figure 6–3   Relationship of Creativity, Development, Growth

Growth and development are interrelated and cyclic.

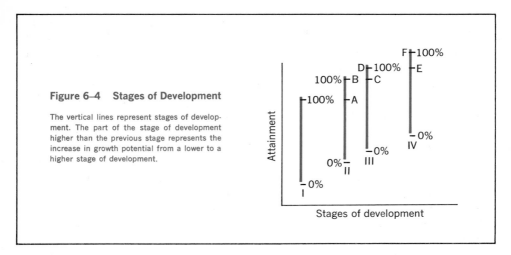

Figure 6–4   Stages of Development

The vertical lines represent stages of development. The part of the stage of development higher than the previous stage represents the increase in growth potential from a lower to a higher stage of development.

and the resulting gases were condensed in lead containers. This was strictly a batch-by-batch process. Around 1880 the first continuous-process producing units were installed (stage II). Weak acid was first made by chemical reaction and then was concentrated by being run through a chain of distillation units. The potential for growth improved greatly. Far greater output was now possible. The external environment was extremely favorable and growth continued. In the 1920s, another improved process was developed (stage III). It eliminated a big step in the old process. Again the capacity for growth increased, and again growth resulted. The process has again been improved (stage IV) by the introduction of electronic operating and control systems. Similar examples exist in the historical changes in the manufacturing processes of many other products.

Each development has a ceiling, or a limit to the growth that can result. And as the ceiling is approached, additional units of growth become more and more difficult to achieve.

As continued growth within one stage of development becomes more difficult, the competition for the discovery of new and successful innovative changes becomes exceedingly keen; for in this race, to the victor belongs the first choice of the spoils. This keen competition can result in several innovations, each by a different firm, occurring within a single industry in a relatively short period of time.

GROWTH, DEVELOPMENT, AND THE HIERARCHY OF OBJECTIVES

The interaction between growth and development can also be viewed in terms of organizational objectives, using the hierarchy of objectives developed in Chapter 4. As a quick review, the basic concept of this hierarchy is that an organization may have three levels, or types, of objectives. The short-life organization typically has only a set of immediate goals, which when reached represent the completion of the organization's purpose, and its approaching death. An organization that anticipates a long life has all three types of objectives—immediate, attainable, and visionary.

When reduced to a visual conception, this idea of a ceiling for growth becomes much more manageable—thus, Figure 6-5.

Immediate objectives provide a ceiling for accomplishments. Reaching this level of attainment, the short-life organization has accomplished all its objectives.

How can an organization that wants to have long life hope to achieve it? The answer is deceptively simple—an organization can achieve long life by developing new objectives, rather than by merely striving for more efficiency in old objectives.

The entire process whereby the time-accomplishment hierarchy allows an organization to achieve development rather than be restricted by some growth ceiling can be seen in Figure 6-6. This diagram embodies the concept of organizational objectives that evolve over time to allow the organization to reach higher and higher levels of development. The shift that occurs in the hierarchy of objectives is important. Visionary and attainable objectives shift downward as the organization becomes more able to accomplish them. Visionary objectives become attainable, and attainable become immediate. The growth of the organization will reach its peak at growth ceiling I unless the objectives change. A change in the objectives will allow the organization to reach a higher level.

Moving to time period II, there has been an increase in the growth potential of the organization (growth ceiling II is in operation), brought about by development. How did the development occur? The development in the organization came when formerly attainable goals$_1$ became immediate goals—now these goals are part of the immediate goals$_2$ in the time-accomplishment hierarchy of time period II. Another significant

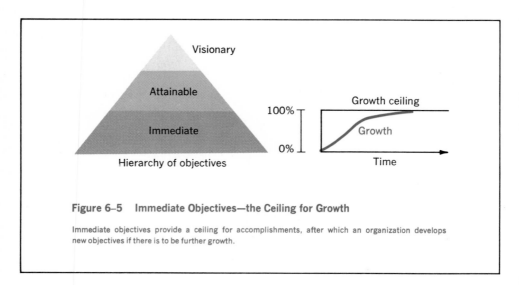

Figure 6–5   Immediate Objectives—the Ceiling for Growth

Immediate objectives provide a ceiling for accomplishments, after which an organization develops new objectives if there is to be further growth.

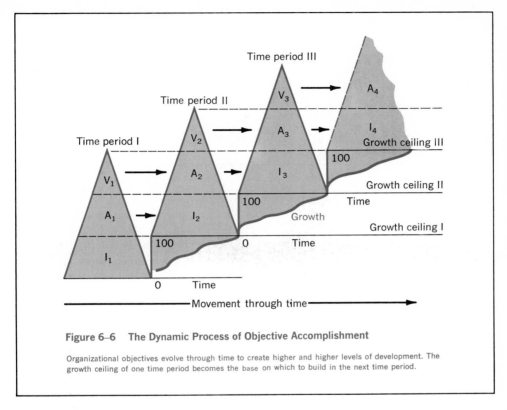

Figure 6–6   The Dynamic Process of Objective Accomplishment

Organizational objectives evolve through time to create higher and higher levels of development. The growth ceiling of one time period becomes the base on which to build in the next time period.

change in the goal hierarchy has also taken place. The visionary goals$_1$ of time period I are now part of the attainable goals$_2$ in time period II.

Time period II shows the original visionary goals$_1$ converted into immediate goals$_3$. The growth ceiling has risen twice, and development has been responsible for the rise each time.

If an organization continually renews and updates its hierarchy of objectives, the goals feed down from the top until they become attainable. Note that the visionary goals$_2$ become attainable goals$_3$ in time period III and will be immediate goals$_4$ in the future time period IV. This then is how developing new objectives renews an organization.

Evolution of Objectives

As an organization moves to accomplish its objectives, the process of redefining objectives is an evolutionary one. The upward shift in development may be smoother than in the separate and distinct stages that can be labeled "time period I," "time period II,"

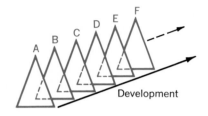

Figure 6–7   Evolutionary Development of Objectives

The process of development in an organization may consist of small, gradual rises through time.

"time period III," and so on. A major innovation may allow the organization to make a sudden leap forward, but the total process is often one of small, gradual rises, as shown in Figure 6-7.

The line connecting the lower right corners of each hierarchy shows that the movement can be relatively smooth—the hierarchy changes slowly unless there are revolutionary breakthroughs that suddenly allow the attainable or visionary goals to become immediate. The possibility of a dramatic breakthrough is present in any organization that actively seeks to innovate and to advance its development, as in Figure 6-8. Rather than continuing in small steps, the potential for the organization in Figure 6-8 makes a giant step forward because of some innovation that allows the organization to revamp its objectives almost completely. The innovation suddenly makes the visionary goals of hierarchy C into immediate goals, which become the base of the hierarchy for hierarchy D. Examples of such dramatic innovations are:

The first drilling rig that bored to pools of subsurface oil. Oil had been dipped up on the earth's surface, but now "Drake's Folly" cut costs, boosted output, and brought a revolutionary potential for light, heat, and power in the United States.
A workable concept of mass production. Henry Ford put a nation on wheels and made possible tremendous increases in volume in production by many other

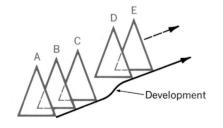

Figure 6–8   Effect of Revolutionary Development

Sometimes a dramatic breakthrough in development occurs, and an innovation allows an organization to revamp its objectives almost completely in one big giant step.

Figure 6–9   Composition of Hierarchy of Objectives

The composition of a new hierarchy is a mixture of the goals that move downward from attainable goals to immediate goals. In this figure immediate goals$_2$ are composed of those attainable goals$_1$ that have become immediate plus old immediate goals still being pursued by the organization.

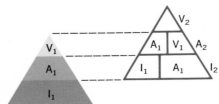

manufacturers.

The "safety hoist" of Elisha Otis. This device led to the modern elevator, which made tall buildings feasible and which has shaped the characteristics of cities around the world.

Composition of the Hierarchy of Objectives

A second qualification needs to be made: As objectives move downward, the composition of a given level in the new hierarchy is a mixture of the goals that have moved downward to become immediate, and some of the former immediate goals that are still relevant. Thus, in Figure 6-9, immediate goals$_2$ are composed of those attainable goals$_1$ that have become immediate plus the carry-over of immediate goals$_1$ that are still being used by the organization. This same concept applies to the composition of the other categories of goals: attainable goals$_2$ are composed of the visionary goals$_1$ which have become attainable plus a carry-over of the attainable goals$_1$ that are still not immediate.

Expansion of the Hierarchy

As time goes on and the organization evolves new hierarchies of objectives, the hierarchy may expand. These expanding hierarchies would look like Figure 6-10. American Tele-

Figure 6–10   Expansion of Hierarchies of Objectives

Organizations exist in time, and therefore they can evolve new, expanding hierarchies.

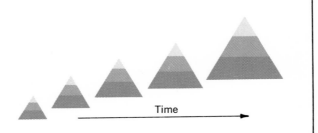

Time

phone and Telegraph Company is a good example: the corporation owes much of its success as the world's leader in communication to the fact that it has had expanded hierarchies of objectives.

A visionary objective for the voice communications operations of A. T. & T., as stated by an A. T. & T. chief engineer, was this:

> In the ultimate, whenever a baby is born anywhere is the world, he is given at birth a number which will be his telephone number for life. As soon as he can talk, he is given a watch-like device with ten little buttons on one side and a screen on the other. Thus equipped, at any time when he wishes to talk with anyone in the world, he will pull out the device and punch on the keys the number of his friend. Then, turning the device over, he will hear the voice of his friend and see his face, in color and three dimensions. If he does not see him and hear him, he will know that the friend is dead.[1]

Contrast this visionary goal with an attainable goal for A. T. & T., the installation of coast-to-coast dialing at a flat monthly charge to each person with a telephone. Technically, this goal is now obtainable, but all telephones in the United States must be on dial or push-button systems. Thus, an immediate goal of the company is to convert all of the telephone systems in the United States to dial or push-button systems. Direct-distance dialing equipment was, in the early years of telephones, only a dream. That vision became technically feasible, and now is being implemented as an immediate goal.

It has been suggested that someday telephones will be so small they can be contained in the rims of a pair of glasses. Perhaps this vision also some day will become reality.

RESPONSIBILITY OF MANAGERS

Overconcern for "how it is done" is one of the diseases from which organizations die, so it is up to managers to ensure that organizations do not become so preoccupied with growth that development is overlooked.

> Little by little, preoccupation with method, technique, and procedure gains control over the whole process of goal seeking. How it is done becomes more important than whether it is done. Means triumph over ends. Form triumphs over spirit. Method is enthroned. Men become prisoners of their procedures, and organizations that are seeking to achieve some permanent goal become obstacles in the path of that goal.[2]

As an ideal, if all organizations continually changed their objectives to ensure continuous growth and development, what could be attained would be self-renewing organizations.

SUMMARY

Organizations have no inherent life span. Whether they are short lived or long lived depends upon their objectives and the activities of their members—particularly mana-

---

[1]"American Telephone and Telegraph," *Forbes,* June 1, 1964, p. 26.

[2]John W. Gardner, *Self-renewal—The Individual and the Innovative Society,* Harper & Row, Publishers, Incorporated, New York, 1963, p. 47.

gers. For long life, an organization must meet three requirements: (1) it must desire long life, (2) the philosophy of its managers must permit long life, and (3) its managers must structure relationships within the organization to permit effective operations. An organization can be classed as short- or long-life by how well it meets these requirements.

Within a given set of immediate objectives there is a limit to the growth potential of an organization. Thus, a key to achieving long life in organizations is to renew them with new objectives. This is done by developing new visionary and attainable objectives and converting these new objectives to immediate objectives. With the necessary managerial decisions and renewed objectives an organization has the potential for long life.

FOR REVIEW AND DISCUSSION

1 What is the first factor that must be present if an organization is to be long lived? Does the presence of this factor necessarily ensure the long life of an organization? Explain your answer.

2 In your own words compare the following characteristics of short- and long-life organizations: (a) view of survival, (b) philosophy of management, and (c) structure.

3 Is an organization that succeeds in reaching phase III, long life, guaranteed that it will remain there? Explain your answer.

4 From your personal experience list three organizations in each of the following classifications: (a) short life, (b) transitory, and (c) long life. For each organization on your list give the important factors you observed that caused you to put that organization in its particular classification.

5 As the text uses the terms, distinguish between growth and development.

6 Explain how creativity can lead to both further growth and development.

7 Explain the statement: "If an organization has only immediate objectives, there will be a limit to its possible accomplishments."

8 Describe how the creation of new visionary and attainable objectives can, through time, lead to higher levels of attainment for the organization.

9 Consider the statement: "Overconcern with how it is done is one of the diseases from which organizations die." What responsibility does this statement place on managers?

10 Do you think an organization necessarily has an inherent life cycle? Fully explain your answer.

11 Describe the essential characteristics of a self-renewing organization.

12 In the text it was pointed out that a self-renewing organization must continually develop new visionary and attainable objectives. Does this necessarily mean that all present immediate objectives must be discarded for the future?

CASES

A   The Benis Harness Company had been founded in 1854. The firm had, until the 1920s, been extremely successful. Its product line included all sorts of harnesses, collars, and other items needed for working horses. Through the years Benis had made many improvements in the design and quality of its products.

By the late 1920s a sharp decline in the number of working horses in the United States had begun as more and more work was done by tractors. Horse population in the country, which at one time had been as high as 40 million, by the middle of the century was only a small fraction of its previous high.

In 1938 the company was managed by the fifth generation of the Benis family. The product line was unchanged, but because of the reduction in the number of working horses, sales and profits continued their long-term downward trend. The company had no plans for changing its product line.

> **1** How have company policies contributed to the decline in sales and profits?
>
> **2** Why do you think the company has made no substantial changes in its product line? Do you think its policy has been wise? Include in your analysis a discussion of the advantages and disadvantages of the policy.
>
> **3** For many years the Benis family has invested the money earned from the Benis Harness Company in widely diversified additional ventures, most of which have been quite successful. How might this additional information change your answers to the first two questions?

B   President Braves of Patrick College, a small, liberal arts college, appointed Susan Green, Jean Smathers, Michael Yates, and Thomas Arant to the committee to plan and coordinate the annual spring convocation and dance. These students represented the freshman, sophomore, junior, and senior classes, respectively. The committee met for dinner each Thursday for several months. All details were handled informally, and the committee did not elect officers. The committee failed to meet again after the highly successful spring convocation and dance.

> **1** Was the committee a transitional, short-, or long-life organization? Explain your answer.
>
> **2** Should the committee have organized by electing officers from among its members?

C   Consider the following company slogans: (a) "Progress is our most important product"—General Electric Company, (b) "Better things for better living through chemistry"—E. I. du Pont de Nemours & Co., Inc., (c) "Changing to meet a changing world"—Ethyl Corporation, and (d) "The energy company"—Humble Oil and Refining Company.

> **1** How can such slogans (and the managerial attitude they might represent) affect the life of a company?
>
> **2** Consider the names of the four companies. Which of them have names that might work against long life? Why?

FOR FURTHER STUDY

Additional sources can be found in the sources cited in the chapter.

Books

Warren G. Bennis et al. (eds.): *The Planning of Change,* 2d ed., Holt, Rinehart and Winston, Inc., New York, 1969. Change is natural, but is occurring more and rapidly. Responsible and effective agents of change are needed.

James R. Bright: *Research, Development, and Technological Innovation,* Richard D. Irwin, Inc., Homewood, Ill. 1964. A textbook on technological innovation in organizations.

Don Fabun: *The Dynamics of Change,* Prentice-Hall, Inc., Englewood Cliffs, N.J., 1967. A remarkable overview of change and innovation.

John W. Gardner: *Self-Renewal,* Harper & Row, Publishers, Incorporated, New York, 1964. We are beginning to understand the conditions under which individuals and organizations can renew themselves.

Gordon L. Lippitt: *Organizational Renewal,* Appleton-Century-Crofts, Inc., New York, 1969. "The organization that will remain viable, creative and relevant must engage in the process of search that the renewal effort involves."

Articles

James R. Bright: "Evaluating Signals of Technological Change," *Harvard Business Review,* January–February 1970. Political, social, and other factors signal markets for new products and services.

Theodore Levitt: "Exploit the Product Life Cycle," *Harvard Business Review,* November–December 1965. Products have a life pattern of development, growth, maturity, and decline. Managerial knowledge of and action based on this pattern can make organizations more successful.

Theodore Levitt: "Marketing Myopia," *Harvard Business Review,* July–August 1960. Failure to set new organizational objectives inevitably leads to stagnation and decline, but effective new objectives can lead to continuing prosperity.

James E. McNulty: "Organizational Change in Growing Enterprises," *Administrative Science Quarterly,* June 1962. Research findings have substantiated the need for a company to provide, through programs and motivational techniques, for flexibility in its organization to permit automatic adjustments to take place when they are needed.

E. E. Scheuing: "The Product Life Cycle as an Aid in Strategy Decisions," *Management International Review,* no. 4-5, 1969. A product's life cycle includes introduction, growth, maturity, saturation, and decline.

Robert B. Young: "Keys to Corporate Growth," *Harvard Business Review,* November–December 1961. "Of all the tasks confronting persons in the highest echelons of corporate management, perhaps the most crucial is that of providing for and protecting the future of the company."

II
Human Behavior — the Basic Resource in Organizations

7

Behavior in Organizations — Interdisciplinary Contributions

This is new, and it is also very old. We have come from the tyranny of the enormous, awesome, discordant machine, back to a realization that the beginning and the end are man—that it is man who is important, not the machine, and that it is man who accounts for growth, not just dollars or factories.
Above all, that it is man who is the object of all our efforts.
   PABLO CASALS

Human behavior is an ever-present element of organizations. Therefore, the student of organizations or management finds valuable assistance in the fields of psychology, social psychology, sociology, and cultural anthropology. This chapter and the four that follow describe some of the contributions these behavioral science fields have made that are valuable in the study of management and organizations.

INDIVIDUAL BEHAVIOR

The study of individual behavior examines the personal factors that influence an individual in his behavior; the individual person is the unit of study or analysis. Psychologists have taken this viewpoint and have focused on motivation, judgment, perception, learning, remembering, imagination, personality traits, and other such factors that constitute the world of the individual person.

ORGANIZATIONAL BEHAVIOR

In a sense, all behavior is individual behavior. So-called "group or organizational behavior" is still individual behavior—a special category of individual behavior. That is, organizational behavior is individual behavior that occurs in association with others.

The term organizational behavior has meaning because research almost always has shown that when persons undertake activities in relation to others, or even simply in the presence of others, certain patterns of behavior—called organizational behavior—can be described. Studying organizational behavior is important because the average person spends a large portion of his life participating in organizations. Organizational behavior includes the topics of cooperation and competition, social organizations, institutions, values, languages, kinship, technology, ascendance and submission, and other social and cultural dimensions. Theories about individual behavior that focus only on factors such as psychological traits or personality types give only limited insight; studying organizational behavior provides additional understanding.

AN INTERDISCIPLINARY APPROACH

It is clear that behavior in organizations cannot be divided totally into neat packages paralleling fields of study, such as psychology, sociology, and so forth. The organizational member or manager studying organizations is interested in the overall effect of behavior within the organization. He is not concerned primarily with the classification of that behavior as psychological, sociological, or in terms of any other field of study.

Nevertheless, because of the complexity of the subject, it often is helpful to take varying viewpoints or to have particular points of emphasis, depending upon the objectives and the situation. For example, both psychology—which focuses on the individual person—and sociology—which focuses on the group—might provide helpful insight into the same organizational behavior. The perspectives are different—as are likely to be the findings—but they will be helpful if they provide additional insight by complementing one another.

Consider the study of a mountain, for comparison. A geographer is interested mainly in the gross anatomical features of the mountain. A geologist or mining engineer focuses on the kinds of rock in the mountain. A botanist has interest in the plant life supported by the mountain. Artists, road builders, hunters, and many others see the mountain differently. Each looks at the same mountain, but depending upon his interests and perspective perceives something different. All can contribute to a better understanding of the mountain.

The same sort of thing is true of organizations. Many different viewpoints yield different, but complementary, ideas about organizations. This concept is illustrated in Figure 7-1. The point also is illustrated by the old story of three bricklayers who were asked what they were doing. One replied, "Laying bricks." Another said he was "Making a wall." The third said he was "Building a great cathedral." The point is illustrated further by the story of the president of a large chain of short-order restaurants who had much

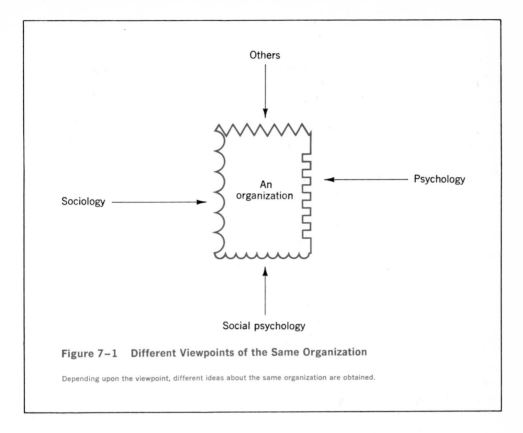

Figure 7–1   Different Viewpoints of the Same Organization

Depending upon the viewpoint, different ideas about the same organization are obtained.

conflict between his male cooks and female waitresses.[1] He called in a psychologist, a sociologist, and a cultural anthropologist as consultants. The psychologist reported the problem was caused by unresolved family conflicts brought over to the work situation. Transferred sibling rivalry caused workers to be unduly competitive with each other, he said. The sociologist emphasized status conflicts as causing the problem. He said conflict is bound to result when cooks (higher status) take orders from waitresses (lower status). Finally, the anthropologist saw the problem and its solution in terms of different cultural values of cooks and waitresses. As the story goes, all three behavioral scientists recommended the identical, practical solution, regardless of their different viewpoints. All recommended that waitresses leave written orders for food on a spindle. These were to be picked up and filled by cooks without talk. The conflict would be settled by eliminating direct contact of the cooks and waitresses. Thus, the views of all three behavioral scientists were valuable; each provided additional insight into the problem, from his particular viewpoint.

[1]See Elias H. Porter, "The Parable of the Spindle," *Harvard Business Review,* May–June 1962.

Each of the several behavioral science fields, in looking at behavior in its particular way, has made large contributions. However, it has become increasingly evident that there are organizational problems that cannot be understood by any one of them alone. The experimental psychologist can go his own way with little concern for the findings of sociologists and anthropologists. However, these fields become important when he tries to apply his findings to organizations. Similarly, the social worker is confronted with concrete problems which must be solved within the framework of individuals and the culture. The cultural anthropologist can help the social worker in understanding this culture. Moreover, social workers have learned from psychologists, and the indications are that this collaboration will increase.

Thus, workers in the fields of personality psychology, social culture, cultural anthropology, organizational behavior, and management practice find themselves drawn together by common interests.

In such fashion the interdisciplinary approach has emerged, characterized by a willingness to follow organizational problems regardless of disciplinary boundaries and to use any data or techniques that seem pertinent to the problem at hand.

THE STUDY OF ORGANIZATIONS

The above sections have described the need and value to the study of organizations and management of an interdisciplinary approach to the behavioral sciences. However, the study of organizations is so broad that even more fields must be included in an even broader interdisciplinary approach for the most useful study of organizations and management. In addition to the behavioral sciences, the fields of administrative management theory, bureaucracy, scientific management, communication theory, economics, ecology, and numerous others are relevant.[2] This pervasive view can be described as organization theory. In advocating this approach Ackoff wrote: "We must stop acting as though nature [and man] were organized into disciplines in the same way universities are."[3] This entire book takes an interdisciplinary viewpoint; the present group of chapters surveys contributions of the behavioral sciences to the study of management and organizations.

Chapter 8 studies characteristics of an individual person not engaged in organizational activity. Then Chapter 9 explores interpersonal behavior, or behavior between two or more individuals. Chapter 10 examines the relationship of individuals to an organization or group. Finally, in this part, Chapter 11 describes relationships between two or more groups or organizations. The orientation of these chapters is depicted in Figure 7-2.

[2]See David L. Huff and Joseph W. McGuire, "The Interdisciplinary Approach to the Study of Business," *Washington Business Review,* June 1960, for a long, representative list of relevant fields.
[3]Russell L. Ackoff, "Systems, Organizations, and Interdisciplinary Research," *General Systems,* vol. 5, 1960, p. 6.

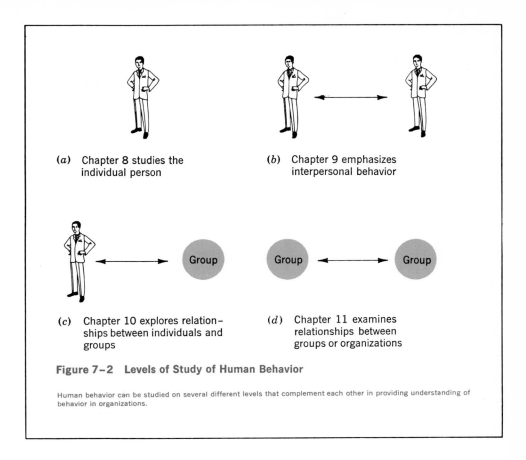

(a) Chapter 8 studies the individual person

(b) Chapter 9 emphasizes interpersonal behavior

(c) Chapter 10 explores relation-ships between individuals and groups

(d) Chapter 11 examines relationships between groups or organizations

Figure 7-2   Levels of Study of Human Behavior

Human behavior can be studied on several different levels that complement each other in providing understanding of behavior in organizations.

PROBLEMS OF AN INTERDISCIPLINARY APPROACH

Every discipline has its own methodology, terminology, and objectives, so when several fields try to work together this diversity causes problems. There are two important problems in successful collaboration among psychologists, sociologists, anthropologists, and organization and management theorists. First, one usually is comparatively ignorant of other fields, which is natural because as a specialist he usually has intensive training only in one. This difficulty can be overcome by cross-field study and cooperation.

The second problem is the lack of consistent terminology. Because each field has developed its own jargon, or specialized language, it often is difficult to understand what one in another field is saying. This problem can be seen firsthand by simply looking through a journal of another field.

Much progress has been made in developing an interdisciplinary approach, and the further gains in this direction can be expected.

SUMMARY

Psychologists, social psychologists, sociologists, anthropologists, and researchers from many other areas have studied various aspects of man and his significant contributions. The emerging field of organization theory synthesizes these findings into an interdisciplinary approach seeking to give better explanation of human behavior in all types of organizations. This part of this book emphasizes contributions of the several behavioral science fields to this endeavor.

The student of organization theory or the practicing manager must consider *total man* to understand, explain, or improve organizational performance. This total man's behavior, personality, and environment are inextricably interwoven. For the manager it does not matter if a behavioral problem is classified as psychological, sociological, or whatever. Traditional boundaries of academic disciplines must be ignored in favor of a broader, integrated approach.

The following four chapters analyze the individual person and the interactions that result when he inevitably becomes associated with others. The emphasis is first on the individual outside organizations; then on his interactions with other individuals; then on his behavior within a group; and finally, on the interactions of his groups with other groups.

FOR REVIEW AND DISCUSSION

1 List the academic disciplines that help us understand human behavior in organizations. Explain the contribution of each.

2 Define an interdisciplinary approach to the study of organizations. What fields are included? Why is an interdisciplinary approach necessary? What are some of the problems in this approach?

3 Describe the field of organizational theory.

4 Explain how different points of view can yield different ideas about the same thing. Illustrate your answer with an example not in the text.

5 What is the difference between individual and organizational behavior?

6 What is meant when it is said that *total man* must be considered in the study of organizations.

CASE

Transcon Computer Company had become famous for the innovations it had made in managerial practices. The company had received many requests from academic specialists who wished to study its operations. Last summer the company invited Dr. Berry, a psychologist; Dr. Tims, a sociologist; Dr. Hann, a cultural anthropologist; Dr. Romano, a psychiatrist; and Dr. Gunn, a management and organization theorist, to spend two months studying the organization.

During the two months the five professors were friendly on a social level, but they seldom discussed their observations of Transcon. On professional matters each found that the other four "spoke a different language."

In due time each professor wrote an article, in a journal in his field, reporting his study of Transcon. None of the articles was ever read by any of the other four researchers who had been at Transcon at the same time.

1 Why didn't the five professors communicate with each other about their observations of Transcon? Were the professors really observing "five different worlds"? Explain your answer.

2 What was lost by the failure of the professors to talk about and read each other's articles about their experiences?

3 What do you think the attitude of the company management was toward the failure of the five professors to communicate on professional matters?

4 What recommendations would you make to: (a) the professors, (b) the company, and (c) the president of the university of which all five professors were faculty members?

FOR FURTHER STUDY

Additional sources can be found in the sources cited in the chapter.

Books

Chris Argyris et al.: *Social Science Approaches to Business Behavior,* The Dorsey Press and Richard D. Irwin, Inc., Homewood, Ill., 1962. The research findings of the behavioral sciences are relevant to managerial decision problems.

W. W. Cooper et al. (eds.): *New Perspectives in Organization Research,* John Wiley & Sons, Inc., New York, 1964. This volume is a collection of papers on interdisciplinary behavioral and management science topics.

Articles

George F. Farris: "The Drunkard's Search in Behavioral Science," *Personnel Administration,* January–February, 1969. Better methods, interdisciplinary collaborations, and open systems theory can make behavioral science more meaningful.

Mason Haire: "The Social Sciences and Management Practices," *California Management Review,* Summer 1964. Developmental research needs to be done to turn behavior science theories into practical applications.

David L. Huff and Joseph W. McGuire: "The Interdisciplinary Approach to the Study of Business," *University of Washington Business Review,* June 1960, pp. 48–60. This article describes how a number of academic fields of study can be useful for studying business administration.

J. L. Meij: "Management, A Common Province of Different Sciences," *Management International,* no. 50, 1962, pp. 37–46. Managerial problems can be studied from several viewpoints including human relations, economics, formal organization, management science, and a synthetic approach.

Hollis W. Peter: "Using Behavioral Science in Management," *Advanced Management Journal,* October 1964. In the area of managing people, the professional manager cannot rely exclusively on behavioral scientists, as he must himself develop skill in working with people in order to do his job.

Harold M. F. Rush: "A Case for Behavioral Science," *Conference Board Record,* September 1968. Behavioral science knowledge applied in a company resulted in new growth and profits.

M. F. Rush and Walter S. Wikstrom: "The Reception of Behavioral Science in Industry," *Conference Board Record,* September 1969. Behavioral science findings are favored by managers.

Maneck S. Wadia: "Management and the Behavioral Sciences: A Conceptual Scheme," *California Management Review,* Fall 1965. Businessmen can gain from the findings of the three major behavioral sciences.

8
The Individual

*All the world's a stage, And all the men and women
merely players. They have their exits and their
entrances. And one man in his time plays many parts, His
acts being seven ages.*
   WILLIAM SHAKESPEARE

*Know then thyself, presume not God to scan; The proper
study of mankind is man.*
   ALEXANDER POPE

The drama of life unfolds in fantastically broad and intricate patterns—from the nursing infant to the lonely, senile adult; from the rebellious teens to the stable fifties; from the idealistic to the realistic; from tragedy to comedy; from birth to death. The journey of an individual through life can take an almost infinite number of paths. The particular path a person takes is determined in large measure by his characteristics. Behavior of a person in an organization can be understood better with a knowledge of his individual characteristics and their origin.

DEVELOPMENT OF INDIVIDUALS

Man is extremely complex. His interests and abilities are diverse. On the other hand, he has many common characteristics. Generally, a person's characteristics are products of his genetic inheritance and physical being and learning experiences.

117

Genetic Inheritance and Physical Being

Each person starts life with a certain set of characteristics. Each newborn baby is unique; no one else has the same brain and other body components. No one else has the potential to grow up into the same person. Even "identical" twins upon closer observation will be found to be different.

Physical traits such as height; color of eyes and hair; skin complexion; and shape of nose, mouth, and ears are largely hereditary. A person also is endowed with his basic sensitivity in the sensory areas of sight, sound, taste, touch, and smell. His basic intelligence, muscle coordination and dexterity, aptitudes, and instinctive drives are inherited. Whether an individual is short or tall, weak or strong, thin or fat, well-developed or defective, well-coordinated or awkward, gifted with stamina or not, and smart or not is affected by his genetic inheritance.

In large measure, except for disease, an individual's physical makeup is determined biologically. However, the person himself and his environment determine how he will develop with his natural resources and restrictions. Someone might be born with fine physique and coordination, but he can become and remain an expert athlete only if he continually trains and practices. Similarly, even the most gifted pianist must devote hundreds of hours perfecting his skill. Some persons not so generously endowed by nature achieve success—whether in sports, on the concert stage, in a work skill, or wherever—because they devoted unusual effort to perfecting their skills. For example, blind persons often develop highly acute senses of hearing and touch to compensate in part for their lack of sight.

The most significant of man's physical endowments, so vital to his coping with the world around him, is his brain. With a higher degree of intelligence, man is able to deal with his environment on a far more sophisticated level than other living beings.

Man's mental capacities combined with the versatility of his body give him an almost endless variety of responses to the world around him. His capacity to understand abstract thought, to reason, and to analyze is a more powerful asset than his physical abilities. Had the builders of the pyramids not used levers, inclined planes, and other devices developed through thinking, the pyramids might still be under construction.

Given fairly standardized physical attributes, why do individuals act so differently? The answer is that they think differently. Man's mental processes provide him with a wide range of possible actions based on his thoughts, feelings, interpretations, and responses to his environment. His ability to learn and his other mental functions are inherited to some extent—geniuses are born, not made. However, contrary to the old assumptions that intelligence is unalterable and that its development is predetermined by heredity, there is fairly general agreement that even a person's basic intelligence (IQ) may rise with favorable and decline with unfavorable learning experiences. (Intelligence as used here refers to a person's capacity for learning; it does not refer to the amount he has learned.) This correlation is particularly true in preschool years, which accounts for recent increased emphasis on kindergarten, Head Start, and similar programs. It has been estimated that favorable early school experiences can raise a person's IQ by 10 points.

However, even more dramatic is the evidence of some research that a stimulating and challenging home environment can add as many as 25 points to one's IQ. Like his muscles, a person's mind must be exercised to achieve and maintain its best condition.

Learning

Even before birth a person is affected by his environment. Disease of the mother during pregnancy may cause temporary or permanent injury to the baby. After birth, one's physical condition depends upon the characteristics with which he began life modified by growth, diet, medical and parental care, and numerous other factors.

A person starts life with certain biological mental features. These inherited mental characteristics are modifed by learning experiences to produce a complete personality, the individual that participates in organizations. This relationship is shown in Figure 8-1.

Learning is a change in behavior based on experience. It does not include maturation, or change in behavior due to organic factors such as fatigue, drugs, or illness. Learning greatly affects the ways man thinks, feels, and acts, and his beliefs, values, and objectives. Thus learning is an extremely powerful determinant of man's behavior.

Whether a person is loud or quiet, submissive or dominant, and passive or assertive is largely determined by learning experiences. How an individual attempts to fulfill his needs, make adjustments to his frustrations, and resolve his conflicts are affected by learning. Through learning he forms in large measure his concept of himself and the world in which he lives. Biological drives or instincts remain important, but in modern life more and more of man's needs or wants are determined by learning. And the ways physical and instinctive needs are satisfied often are learned. Interests, attitudes, and motivations are also greatly affected by learning.

The question often is asked: Which is more important in a person's development,

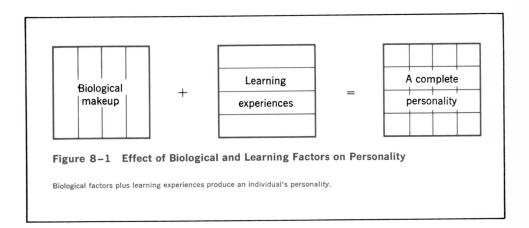

Figure 8–1   Effect of Biological and Learning Factors on Personality

Biological factors plus learning experiences produce an individual's personality.

genetic inheritance or learning experiences? There is no simple answer, for both are inextricably interwoven in each person. By analogy, a similar question is: Which is more important in a cake, the ingredients, the recipe, or the preparation procedures? All are important.

The personality   Thus, heredity and learning experiences combine to produce a personality—the sum total of what a person was, is, and aspires to be. Personality is

> the way a man looks and talks and thinks and feels, the things he likes and the things he hates, his abilities and interests, his hopes and desires, the way he wears his hat or whistles a tune or throws a ball. . . . The fact that a man is fat is as much a part of his personality as the fact that he has a deep voice. If his greatest desire is to play big-league baseball, that's as much a part of his personality as his politics. If he's always suffering from head-aches, if he loves sweet, rich desserts, if he hates his mother-in-law—these things are also his personality. Personality simply means the total person. . . .[1]

It is this total person with which a manager works. Everyone is different because he has different heredity and experiences. Because he *is* different he will behave differently from everyone else; the manager is well advised to remember this.

Ways a person learns   There are several ways a person learns. First, one learns by imitation, or copying others. Imitation can be seen clearly in children, who often pick up the characteristics of parents or·others who are respected or admired. Similarly, a manager might imitate the managerial approaches of another manager he admires. Imitation often is unconscious and subtle, but it is extremely powerful. Also, it truly is the "sincerest form of flattery." Vicarious learning, the second way, is closely related to imitation. Vicarious learning occurs if one learns because he sees another get a reward, and he consciously or unconsciously changes to get a similar reward. Imitation occurred because one wanted to be like another; vicarious learning seeks the rewards another has. Third, learning occurs by habit, or doing something over and over until it becomes automatic. Fourth, learning can occur by "putting through." For example, a physical therapist may "put through," or move a patient's legs for him. Eventually it is hoped that the patient will be able to learn to do the movements by himself. Some complex movements in a manufacturing or assembly process might be learned by having the instructor "put through," or guide the movements of the learner.

Effects of learning   The learning process profoundly affects one's personality, including habits, knowledge, and personal and cultural values. A person enters the world totally dependent; years are required before he can survive alone. His experiences during his developmental—and usually to a lesser extent his adult—years deeply affect his personality. An infant, for example, has no independent concept of himself;

[1]William C. Menninger and Harry Levinson, *Human Understanding in Industry,* Science Research Associates, Chicago, 1956, p. 18.

he develops his self-concept mainly through his interactions with others, particularly family members.

Secondly, learning produces habits. Although they sometimes can be criticized for keeping one in a "rut," habits are extremely valuable. Without habits acquired through learning, every situation would require a new analysis—which would severely limit one's capabilities. Through habits, one can more easily drive a car, tie a shoelace, and interact successfully in groups. Thus, habits acquired from learning enable man to more easily and quickly cope with many situations.

Thirdly, learning is responsible for a person's store of knowledge about the universe in which he lives. The human mind has the capacity to remember countless facts, experiences, and ideas with which a person comes into contact.

Fourthly, learning has a great effect upon one's values. Generally, a person adopts as his own the values of his society. Consider, for example, the various standards of beauty found around the world. Some tribes in Africa regard the fattest women as the most beautiful, whereas others ask only that women have fat lips. Some measure a woman's attractiveness by the number of brass rings adorning her ears, neck, and nose. And there are great differences of concepts of feminine beauty among European countries and in the United States. Similarly, no society uses all available edibles. Many foodstuffs consumed with relish in one society are considered totally repugnant in others. Is a drink of fermented ox blood and milk any more or less palatable when compared with a milk shake in the United States? A person probably prefers the one with which he has had experiences. His answer depends largely on his learning experiences.

Stimulus and response   Persons learn through a sequence called "stimulus and response." A *stimulus* is any event that an individual can sense. A *response* is what the individual does because of the stimulus he has received. To illustrate, reflexes are stimulus-response patterns. Saliva flows when food is put in the mouth; a leg moves when hit just below the knee; the eye blinks against a puff of air; one's body assumes a typical contracted position when he is startled. Such automatic, or "wired-in" responses are the only ones available before a person begins to learn. After learning, a person can have a wide variety of new responses.

There are overt and covert responses. Overt responses are observable as such and hence readily understandable. In contrast, covert responses are more internal or disguised and not so understandable. However, with training, the meaning of many covert responses can be understood. For example, an ulcer is likely to be a warning sign that the person is under stress, in addition to being a purely physical condition.

A stimulus might produce a number of responses, either from one person or several. For example, a certain person given a milk shake had these responses: his saliva flowed more freely; his stomach prepared to receive food; he thought pleasant thoughts; and his expression changed. Further responses occurred when he drank the milk shake. Another person might have an entirely different set of responses if given the same

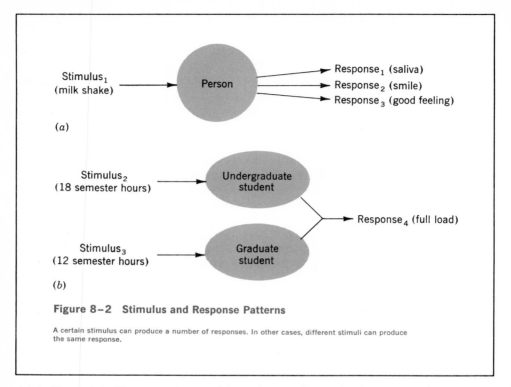

Figure 8–2   Stimulus and Response Patterns

A certain stimulus can produce a number of responses. In other cases, different stimuli can produce the same response.

drink. Figure 8-2a illustrates the condition where a given stimulus can produce a number of responses.

It also is possible that different stimuli can produce the same response. For instance, the stimulus "eighteen semester hours" might produce the response "full load" in an undergraduate student. The different stimulus "twelve semester hours" might yield the same "full load" response from a graduate student. This possibility is shown in Figure 8-2b. Many other stimulus-response patterns exist.

Learning has been defined as "a change in the stable relationship between (a) a stimulus that the individual organism perceives and (b) a response that the organism makes, either covertly or overtly."[2] This change can take place in two ways. First, a person may transfer a response from one stimulus to another. Major learning occurs when a baby's responses are switched from liquids to solids and then to widening varieties of food.

Second, a person may make a new response to an old stimulus. Experiments have shown that children are not inherently afraid of snakes. However, a child may become afraid of snakes after being warned about them. Similarly, upon joining a new work

[2]David K. Berlo, *The Process of Communication,* Holt, Rinehart and Winston, Inc., New York, 1960, p. 76.

group, a person may be aloof, but after becoming acquainted with his fellow workers, he may be warm and friendly.

Deliberate thought often is an important ingredient in the learning process. Figure 8-3 shows how deliberate thought is used to change an old habit into a new one.

In Figure 8-3a a person has a stable, habitual response to a stimulus. With the introduction of deliberate thought the same stimulus may begin to produce new responses during the learning process as shown in Figure 8-3b. Finally, the new response can become a stable habit, as illustrated in Figure 8-3c. Once a habit is formed, it is not necessary to give concentrated, deliberate thought to produce the habitual response.

Factors that affect learning   The newborn human has a few innate responses that function for his survival; he is somewhat like a partially programmed computer. Soon the infant begins to learn from the results of his own responses, from other persons, and from his social and cultural setting. He also restructures through thinking the world he perceives. Beginning with initial simple thoughts, he develops increasingly complex thought patterns. Everyone receives a constant stream of stimuli, interprets them, makes new responses, reinterprets, and so on. Several factors influence the learning process.

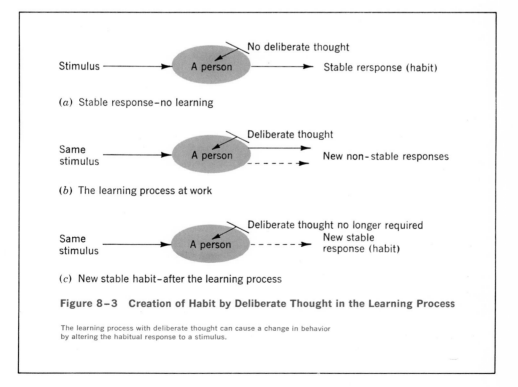

(a) Stable response–no learning

(b) The learning process at work

(c) New stable habit–after the learning process

Figure 8–3   Creation of Habit by Deliberate Thought in the Learning Process

The learning process with deliberate thought can cause a change in behavior by altering the habitual response to a stimulus.

First, a person tends to continue a response if he views the response as rewarding. Similarly, he tends to discontinue unrewarding behavior. This phenomenon of tending to repeat rewarding behavior and eliminate unrewarding behavior is called the "law of effect."

A second factor is the frequency of stimuli. Frequent, repeated stimuli tend to develop stable patterns of reaction, whereas infrequent stimuli tend to be responded to with more variation.

Third, the strength of the reward affects learning. If the reward is great, learning is rapid; insignificant rewards do not command the same attention.

The fourth factor is the time lag between performance and reward. An immediate reward is likely to produce learning faster than a delayed reward. To illustrate, native Indians working at a mine in South America performed adequately only if they were paid every hour or so. More sophisticated persons can tolerate a longer time lapse between performance and reward.

The fifth factor is the difficulty of "unlearning" old, conflicting patterns. Pavlov provided insight here with his famous experiments on dogs. He found that three conditions were necessary to restore to mental health dogs that had been intentionally abused. These conditions were new handlers, time, and a new environment. If taken back into the old, abusive conditions, the dogs became sick again. Similarly, adequate rewards and conditions are required for persons if they are to unlearn old things to acquire new ones.

Sixth, learning is affected by the effort required to make the response. Some responses are much more difficult than others. For example, a person might not be willing to go through the difficult learning required to be a scientist. Many more persons are willing to learn the relatively easy pastime of fishing. If a person can achieve what he wants through several paths, he will tend to choose the easiest one.

Levels of learning   Persons learn both consciously and unconsciously. In conscious learning one is aware that he is learning. He understands that the learning process is taking place, and he is aware of what he has learned. In contrast, unconscious learning takes place without one's being aware that he is learning or has learned. Ethical, religious, clothing styles, and other values often are acquired unconsciously.

Learning can occur at several levels, which describe the degree the person has integrated the learning into his personality. Beginning with the most shallow and proceeding generally to deeper learning, a number of levels can be described:

1 *Awareness.* The most shallow learning exists if one simply becomes aware of something. For example, one might know that electronic computers exist, but know practically nothing else about them.

2 *Recognition.* If one has the ability to recognize something for what it is, he moves to a deeper level. To continue the electronic computer example, he now would be able to recognize a computer if he saw one.

3 *Description.* Still deeper learning occurs if one can recite or describe something. The one interested in computers now must be able to describe a computer to others. On this level he does not have to have detailed knowledge; he simply must have the ability to describe the computer's general features.

4 *Comprehension.* Another level of learning occurs if one understands something. The computer man now must understand what a computer is and why it exists. (This level and level three above can be interchanged. Often one can understand something without being able to describe it, and vice versa. For example, one could understand a theory without having the ability to describe it.)

5 *Use.* The fifth level of learning occurs if one can use it. Now the computer man is able to use the machine to solve problems.

6 *Generalization.* Still deeper learning gives one the ability to make generalizations at this level Our computer man can generalize his knowledge to apply the computer to new problems.

7 *Internalization.* The deepest learning occurs when one internalized it, or makes it a part of himself. Now he is able to perform comfortably and without much thought. The computer is now "second nature."

Managerial applications of learning concepts   Much that occurs in organizations can be viewed as teaching-learning situations. In a broad view the manager wants members to learn to contribute to organizational objectives. Thus, learning concepts have direct relevance for the manager. McGehee had the following advice based on learning theory for managers:[3]

1 Give rewards for proper responses as quickly as possible. The shorter the time lapse, the greater the reinforcement. (A managerial implication: Pay bonuses for work above standard as quickly as possible.)

2 Give the learner knowledge of the results of his responses as quickly as possible. Is he right or wrong? The more a wrong pattern is repeated, the harder it is to change. (A managerial implication: Talk to an employee about an improper work procedure he is using as quickly as possible after it comes to the manager's attention.)

3 Make the learning experiences as close to the real thing as possible. (A managerial implication: Use supervised on-the-job training techniques. Also use devices that closely simulate the real procedures.)

4 Space learning so that learner has some "absorption" time. Give time to "work through" problems and solutions. (A managerial implication: Carefully space training

[3]William McGehee, "Are We Using What We Know about Training?—Learning Theory and Training," *Personnel Psychology*, vol. 2, 1958.

activities to let learner absorb knowledge consistent with the need to expeditiously complete training. Too many hours per day of intensive training may be less effective than a more leisurely pace with some time devoted to routine activities.)

The Self

At any time, a person is the product of his biological inheritance and learning experiences. Because he has a will of his own, he can to some extent determine his future self. He does this by choosing among alternative future learning experiences.[4] He understands situations and decides on the basis of his own motives, knowledge, assumptions, and feelings. For example, if a student decides to quit college and enlist in the army, by his decision he determines in part his future personality. He will be a different person, with the military experiences, from what he would have been had he remained in college. The degree of freedom or ability or alternatives one has varies widely. When one has been drafted in the army, one has virtually no choice (except to defy the law) but to go. In contrast, in the United States one often has a virtually unlimited (barring interference of family) choice of occupation and marital partner.

It often is difficult to express oneself in deciding difficult matters. William James expressed his frustration about this in these words:

> I am often confronted by the necessity of standing by one of my empirical selfs and relinquishing the rest. Not that I would not, if I could be both handsome and fat and well-dressed, and a great athlete, and make a million a year, be a wit, a bon-vivant, a lady-killer as well as a philosopher, a philanthropist, statesman, warrior, and African explorer, as well as a "tone-poet" and saint. But the thing is simply impossible. The millionaire's work would run counter to the saint's; the bon-vivant and the philanthropist would trip each other up; the philosopher and the lady-killer could not well keep house in the same tenement of clay. Such different characters may conceivably at the outset of life be alike possible *to a man.* But to make any one of them actual, the rest must more or less be suppressed. So the seeker of his truest, strongest, deepest self must review the list carefully, and pick out the one on which to stake his salvation. All other selves thereupon become unreal, but the fortunes of this self are real. Its failures are real failures, its triumphs real triumphs, carrying shame and gladness with them. This is as strong an example as there is of that selective industry of the mind. . . . Our thought, incessantly deciding, among many things of a kind, which ones for it shall be realities, here chooses one of many possible selves or characters, and forthwith reckons it no shame to fail in any of those not adopted expressly as its own.[5]

Because of the frequent difficulty of making decisions on important matters, it can be comforting if the decision is made for one by another. For example, parents, faculty, the government, and "the system" often make decisions for a person. Although he frequently may protest vigorously such a decision, on a deeper level it may be satisfying because it provides a sort of security. Too much decision-making freedom or

---

[4]Some authorities thus view the self as a third determinant of personality. See, for example, James C. Coleman, *Psychology and Effective Behavior,* Scott, Foresman and Company, Glenview, Ill., 1969, pp. 60–69.

[5]William James, *The Principles of Psychology,* Dover Publications, Inc., New York, 1950.

responsibility can produce extreme anxiety. (Balanced against this factor is the individual's legitimate desire for freedom.)

Self-development is a long, laborious, and difficult process. Initially, an infant does not distinguish between himself and others. Through time, interaction with others causes a child to begin to think of himself as a separate and distinct being. His concept of self is formulated in terms of how people react to him; it is in great measure a mirror of how others perceive him. For example, if a child repeatedly is told he is bad, he will likely act bad; if he is told he is good, then his behavior is likely to be good.

The values of the groups with which one associates are important in self-development. The individual tends to accept group norms as his own. Witness the rigid acceptance of and adherence to fads by teen-agers. The family exerts strong influence over its members and is the most important reference group for children. Of course, individuals do change, and as they change, so do the broader norms and standards of a group as a whole.

Several factors affect an individual in his decisions. First, his capabilities are important. Someone who thinks of himself as being exceptionally capable will establish higher goals than one who considers himself average or inferior. Second, an individual's knowledge of the possible goals will influence him—a person who has never been more than 25 miles from the farm where he grew up will probably have a very limited horizon of career opportunities. Third, a person's experiences of success or failure will affect the level of attainment he sets for himself. A manager who fails in settling a dispute may not be as confident in the next crisis, and if failure occurs again, he may lose even more confidence. Repeated failures can lower one's confidence until he is incompetent whenever a difficulty arises. Fourth, an individual's idea of his status in a group will influence him. If he is "in," he tends to conform to group norms; if he is "out," he tends to go in other directions.

Similarities of Individuals

Every person is unique; no one else has the same body; no one else has had the same learning experiences. This chapter has emphasized differences among persons. However, looking at differences shows only one side of the picture, for persons have many characteristics shared with others. These similarities provide the basis of predictive knowledge about how persons behave, both alone and in association with others in organizations. Many of man's similarities are well understood; the present purpose is to describe briefly several characteristics every man has that differentiate him from other human beings. Knowledge of those characteristics shared with other beings is assumed.

Intelligence   Man's intellectual ability is far above that of other beings. Man can determine cause and effect relationships, infer, deduce, have fantasies, and make generalizations from his insights. He can create totally new things and ideas, and he has a conscious will. Man uses his intelligence to adapt to an extremely wide range of climates, soil conditions, and other environmental factors.

Self-reflexiveness   An apparently unique characteristic of man is his self-reflexiveness. Man not only knows so much; he also knows that he knows. This self-reflexive ability has profound implications for civilization and other organizational participations. Self-reflexiveness gives man the power of choice. He can deliberately set an objective and determine how to get there.

Toolmaking   Man vastly increases his power by making the tools that are essential for higher orders of productivity and for the complex specialization and exchange systems of modern society.

Language   Language is a building block of complex organizations because effective cooperation demands good communication. Man has by far the most effective audio languages and the only written ones.

Externally registered gains   Man has the great ability to record and carry forward, besides his genetics, his accumulated gains. Thus he can pass on to later generations the whole fabric of civilization. Otherwise, each generation would have to start without a culture, language, civilization, and so forth. Libraries are eloquent evidence of this ability.

Other special characteristics   Man can bind time; he can think not only of the present but also of the past and future. He has the most complex family and social systems. He seeks through religion to understand his existence. And, finally, he consciously and deliberately controls change. He does not have to wait until random events produce what he wants.

Understanding these and the more obvious characteristics he shares with others not described here aids in understanding man's involvement in and use of organizations.

PERSONALITY AND EMOTIONS

Persons have emotions or "feel," often very strongly, about most subjects. Studying basic features of complexes and personality structure gives understanding of how emotions affect individual behavior alone and in organizations.

Complexes

A complex is a system of interrelated feelings, memories, impulses, and emotionally charged ideas. It readily prompts associations. It is demonstrated when an individual is faced with a situation that triggers the expression of the complex. Generally, if a complex causes an individual to accomplish something useful or beneficial, it is considered constructive. Similarly, if the expression (or repression) of a complex is detrimental, the complex is considered destructive. The merits of complexes, then, are measured in terms of effects, not in terms of the complexes themselves.

Characteristics of complexes   A person's complexes have a direct bearing on his actions and reactions in an organization. He may have a whole range of emotionally colored feelings on almost any subject—from women's styles, to governmental intervention, to moral standards, to tropical fish. Complexes encompass such a variety of topics—many that are common—that if they were undesirable, anyone really enthusiastic about any subject would have to be condemned—all the golfers, Republicans, stamp collectors, tennis players, art lovers, football fans, and so on. Persons start acquiring complexes early in life and continue developing them as they experience new situations.

Some subjects generally do not create strong feelings one way or another. For example, there is usually a rational reaction to such subjects as mathematics, chemistry, biology, logic, and physics. These subjects lend themselves to authoritative, objective verification, and feelings will not change the results. Complexes are not involved in such rational, objective thinking.

On the other hand, nonrational or emotional behavior—expressing complexes—is colored by emotional experiences and personal perceptions of the individual. Consider the following topics: the relative merits of the popular makes of automobiles, taxation, religious beliefs, the value of labor unions, what constitutes honesty, and the moral standards of the younger generation. In these topics, the cool, logical approach of rational thinking found in objective topics gives way to expression of complexes. When logical reasoning and pure facts will not substantiate one's opinion, he may use vehement emphasis and a steadfast manner in attempting to convince the other party.

Despite the obvious difference between complex-directed and logical thinking, individuals often make emotionally toned pronouncements as if they had been arrived at through clear, logical thought processes. Few will readily admit their thoughts are being influenced by their feelings; most will insist that they are using logical thinking. Yet thoughts based on emotions probably outnumber logical ones.

An individual's complexes are strictly personal. Some emotionally tinted ideas may be held in common by several persons—for example, those in a religious group, political party, or fraternal order—but although they are generally accepted, the ideas are nevertheless unique in their absolute meanings to each member of the group. Even within a close-knit group there always is some variation.

Another distinguishing characteristic of a complex is the ease with which associations to it are made. Seemingly unrelated subjects can be readily tied together by the complex. Thus, a proud grandparent can relate any subject to his new grandson; a dedicated public servant sees everything according to its effect on the public welfare; or an engineer may relate everything to his personal concept of the importance of engineering. The personal feelings of each are constantly influencing his thinking; and based on these feelings, associations are often made that would not be made by anyone else.

Expression of complexes   Complexes insist on being expressed; they simply refuse to lie dormant. They continually influence a person's perceptions, thinking, and actions. The typical reaction of any individual to situations and to other persons is not initially neutral and then rationally analytical; rather it begins with a set of feelings. Conscious actions and thoughts often are expressions of complexes. For example, many persons immediately react in a definite way—often hostile—toward a person of another nationality. They never give the other person a chance to be considered rationally on his own merit; instead they express their emotional complexes, derived from past experiences, in determining how they will treat the person.

A person might readily justify his complex-determined behavior to himself, but others might find it intolerable. Similarly, some social groups might find a particular expression of emotional thinking appropriate, and others would severely condemn the action. It is often incorrectly thought that complexes are expressed only through socially unapproved behavior. To be sure, theft, murder, rape, and suicide probably are acts in which complexes are at work. But complexes and the often accompanying conflicts also are active in the normal, everyday life of everyone. If one decides against direct expression of a complex, he still can express it in a more acceptable form. Thus, complexes are expressed even if they are disguised into approved behavior.

Most of an individual's complexes are hidden from himself and from others, just as most of an iceberg is hidden beneath the water level. Rarely are these underlying feelings recognized for what they are. Thus, a person acts and reacts in many instances because of the deep-rooted feelings which even he does not recognize or understand.

Self, sex, and herd—some major complexes   Many of man's emotions can be grouped into three major complexes: self, sex, and herd. All three involve person-to-person (interpersonal) feelings, and many personal and organizational conflicts can be traced to opposing demands of these three complexes.

The self complex includes emotions about oneself. Feelings of elation, anger, fear, pride, amusement, disgust, and self-assertion are in the self complex. A person's concept of himself is a significant determinant of his behavior with others. If he feels inferior, he is likely to act quite differently than if he considers himself equal or superior to the other person. Feeling inferior, he may make sarcastic remarks, try to undermine the other person, or grasp any means available to gain control over the other person. Or, a highly ambitious individual may take many chances in order to get ahead, while someone who is satisfied may resist change. If a person is satisfied, then the prospect of change may bring a hostile reaction from him.

The sex complex includes feelings of love, affection, and tenderness; the mating and reproduction instincts; and parental impulses. Sex complexes are at work in an organization in something so commonplace and obvious as office romance. But the expression of this complex can be much more subtle and intricate. Such is the case of the classic frustrated "old maid." Lacking the normal expressions of marriage, she might express these feelings in another fashion on the job. Because she badly wants to be needed, she becomes more and more dominating in the office. Eventually, she may gain an iron grip on her co-workers. She may dictate the operating procedures of the office and try to exert as much control as possible over everyone she encounters—even her supervisors. By so expressing herself, the frustrated woman has gained some satisfaction of her feelings, even though in an indirect way. Certainly, many women have chosen their jobs for other reasons, and not because of a failure to find a rewarding expression of their sexual feelings. Yet the lack of such expression apparently does influence others in their actions. Of course, men are just as likely as women to behave in organizations in ways that express feeling in sex complexes.

The herd complex contains feelings of loneliness, nostalgia, sympathy, trust, attachment, gregariousness, imitation, and appeal—in short, the feelings which tie an individual to his friends, associates, and society. A person often considers others before acting, and frequently he modifies his behavior to gain the most favorable response. In some cases, the need of a manager to be liked by his employees is so strong that it hinders the operations of his organization. His desire to be liked or the fear of making people angry at him or hate him causes him to try to please everyone. He may retain employees who are incompetent, hire someone for whom he feels sorry, or overlook poor performance. Thus, the manager may compromise organizational needs in seeking the friendship of his subordinates. To be effective, often a manager must forgo the friendship and association of his subordinates.

Often complexes are in conflict. For example, the desire of the manager described above to be liked by all his employees (herd complex) may stand in the way of his being a successful manager (self complex). Conflict of complexes also is seen in a romantic affair (sex complex) that is in violation of the couple's cultural or religious norms (herd complex). Because complexes can exist on so many topics, it indeed is difficult, if not impossible, to live in complex society without numerous conflicts.

Selected Classical Structures

Closely related to concepts of complexes are theories of personality structure. These structures are not physically identifiable parts of the human anatomy; rather they are models that describe the mental makeup of persons. Two classic structures developed by Sigmund Freud and Eric Berne are presented here as somewhat oversimplified samples of personality structure theories available in the literature.

Sigmund Freud's structure   Sigmund Freud, often thought of as the founder of modern psychology, suggested there are three forces directing all human behavior—the id, the superego, and the ego. Like complexes, these forces exist only in the mind. Also, like complexes, they are apt to be unrecognized. As a basic foundation they have allowed researchers to develop explanations for many facets of human behavior.

The id   Freud suggested that the id encompasses the most ancient and primitive aspects of man's mental makeup. The id is instinctive, is often unconscious and unrecognized, and is unaffected by socially or culturally determined restrictions. The id represents man's natural urges and feelings as developed through hundreds of thousands of years.

The superego   The superego according to Freud stands in contrast to the id. The superego represents the noblest thoughts of man—ideas and feelings gained from parents, teachers, friends, religions, and organizations. The superego tends to be expressed unconsciously, and it is always there to act as a censor on the individual. His thoughts, feelings, and actions are weighed and judged by it in the light of the standards which have been instilled in him. As a censor, a too strong superego is likely to be in constant and pronounced battle with the id. The urges of the id, the natural primitive feelings of man, are often contrary to the standards of behavior and thought established through social restraint. The conflict between the id and the superego can be thought of sometimes in highly oversimplified terms as unacceptable behavior (id) versus acceptable behavior (superego). The id tells a person what he would like to do if he had no self-imposed or social restraints. The superego, on the other hand, tells the person what he "ought" to do. Thus, there is need for a third part of the personality—the ego.

The ego   Freud suggested that the ego is man's conscious mediator. The ego brings the demands of the id in line with the restrictions imposed by the superego. As such, the ego is practical and works in an executive capacity. The ego is the reality-oriented part of man's thinking; it works constantly to keep a healthy psychological balance between the id's impulsive demands and the superego's restrictive guidance. The ego governs how people act, what they say, and what they think about consciously. It tries to find acceptable answers to the many needs and demands of an individual. If it succeeds, the individual is content; if it falls short of success, he has ambivalence and mental stress.

Eric Berne's structure   Closely related and parallel to Freud's structure is one recently developed by Eric Berne.[6] Berne's structure includes child, parent, and adult. Berne suggested that parts of everyone's personality can be described in these terms. According to Berne they all are desirable elements of one's personality; trouble occurs only when they get out of healthy balance.

The child   Everyone, in Berne's view, is part child. Irresponsibility, selfishness, seeking pleasure, and other childlike attributes are found to some extent in everyone. These traits are archaic and instinctive and are undesirable only when one becomes fixated ("stuck") on them. More positively, a person's child component contributes charm, pleasure, and creativity to life.

The parent   Berne wrote that everyone also has a parent within. This parental component is derived from parents and other authoritative influences such as religion and culture. One's internal parent can be oppressive, but it also has positive functions. It contributes stability to life and society. Further, by providing traditions, it frees man from countless decisions. In its purest form, the parental component says, "It's done that way because that's the way I say it's done."

The adult   According to Berne, man is part adult. Again, this attribute is found in everyone, and is necessary for survival. The adult in one gives an objective appraisal of reality, and enables him to deal effectively in the world. The adult mediates objectively

---

[6] Eric Berne, *Games People Play*, Grove Press, Inc., New York, 1964, pp. 23–28.

between the parent and child components. For example, one might say: I (parent) am angry because I (child) dropped soup on my tie. However, I (adult) will remove the spot when I get home. One is effective and feels comfortable when he has a happy integration of his child, parent, and adult components.

SUMMARY

Man indeed is complex, and he lives many roles in life as Shakespeare so eloquently stated. A person is born with certain genetic biological features and impulses. Learning through experiences combines with this basic endowment to produce a complete personality—the sum total of a person. A person's future personality is influenced by himself, by deciding among alternative life experiences.

Persons learn by imitation, vicarious experience, forming habits, and "putting through." A person's habits, knowledge, values, and other personality characteristics are acquired through the learning process, which involves stimulus-response patterns. A number of factors affect the learning process, and learning can occur on several levels ranging from vague awareness to internalization. Managers can improve organizational performance by applying learning theory concepts to everyday problems.

Although everyone is unique, humans share a number of characteristics including high intelligence, self-reflexiveness, toolmaking, language, and externally registered gains. These are in addition to the more obvious characteristics of persons.

Complexes and other emotional factors affect behavior, even if the individual thinks he is acting totally rationally. Though they often are repressed, complexes insist on expression, even if they must be disguised by being expressed in acceptable terms. Major complexes include self, sex, and herd.

Sigmund Freud provided a classic structure of personality when he described the id, superego, and ego. These were later paralleled respectively by Eric Berne in his concept of the mind as consisting of child, parent, and adult attributes. A healthy person has achieved a favorable balance of these factors.

Because it does sometimes require painful examination of one's own actions and thoughts, and because such examination can be conveniently avoided, a great many people go through life failing to understand themselves or other people. Perhaps the familiar advice of "know thyself" is really the best key to understanding individuals. Each person must understand himself before he can understand others. By studying inherited human characteristics and human traits of perception, learning, emotions, and complexes, one can gain a better understanding of himself and an appreciation of other persons' actions in organizations. An understanding of these parts of human behavior can significantly improve a supervisor's effectiveness.

FOR REVIEW AND DISCUSSION

1 Suppose a child had been left in the jungle without human contact since birth. Would you expect this child, if he grew up, to be more like a human or more like an animal of the jungle? Explain your answer.

2 Define personality. Describe the two major determinants of a person's personality. Is one necessarily more important than the other? Why is every individual unique? How does the self affect one's future personality?

3 Explain the statement: "A person's mind must be exercised to achieve and maintain its best condition."

4 Explain the statement: "Learning enables man to cope with his current situation through use of past experiences."

5 Explain how different persons might have different responses to the same stimulus or similar responses to different stimuli. Include illustrative examples from your own experience.

6 Define learning. What is the place of thought in the learning process? When a habit has been formed, is thought still necessary? Explain.

7 What is the law of effect? Illustrate your answer with three examples from your own experience.

8 What is a complex? Who has complexes? How can a complex be evaluated as to whether it is good or bad? Explain the self, sex, and herd complexes. Give three examples of complexes in action that you have observed recently.

9 What are some subjects that usually do not stimulate the expression of complexes? What are some subjects that do? Do you agree with the statement: "Thoughts based on emotions probably outnumber logical ones"? Explain.

10 Explain the statement: "Complexes are expressed even if they assume the disguise of approved behavior."

11 Explain the functions of the id, superego, and ego and the child, parent, and adult components.

12 Parents of more than one child frequently remark about the differences in the personalities of their children. Often, they claim, these differences have been evident since birth. Explain the factors that could account for these differences.

13 Habitual responses permit a person to conserve "thinking time." Below is a list of things most of us perform regularly and habitually. For each item write a description of how you normally (habitually) perform each task. Then deliberately perform the task a different way. Record your feelings and problems in having to "think your way through" the new way of: (a) tying a shoelace, (b) putting on a coat, (c) striking a match, and (d) writing.

14 Describe the factors that affect learning. Illustrate each factor with an example from your own experience.

15 Describe the levels of learning and illustrate each level with an example from your own experience.

16 Describe four managerial applications of learning concepts not given in the text.

17 Describe in your own words the similarities persons have. Include several not described in the text.

18 Describe several ways persons learn. Illustrate each with an example from your own experience.

19 Describe several effects of the learning process. Illustrate each with an example from your experience.

CASES

A   Years ago a grade school child might have been disciplined by being required to write many times a statement that he would not repeat an offense.

One day Miss Strum, a second grade teacher, noticed that Henry was dipping Mary's pigtail in his ink bottle. (Mary sat in the seat just in front of Henry.) Seeing Henry doing this, Miss Strum went over to him and said, "Henry, write this sentence 100 times." She handed Henry a slip of paper on which was written, "I will never put Mary's hair in my ink bottle again."

    1 How was Miss Strum applying the law of effect?

    2 What effect did the requirement that Henry had to write the sentence many times have on learning? Would this lead to deeper learning?

    3 Would similar punishment be appropriate for workers in a plant who were constantly causing problems because of practical jokes and horseplay?

B   The Larsen Oil Company, which had had several serious fires recently, put into effect the following "no-match" regulation: "No matches, lighters, or other fire-producing devices are permitted inside the plant. Violation of this rule will mean automatic and permanent dismissal for any employee." Each employee was required to sign a statement that he had read, understood, and agreed to the terms of this regulation.

Previously, many employees had brought matches and cigarette lighters into the plant. The old "no-smoking" rule in the plant had been widely respected, although there was considerable evidence that two of the recent fires may have been caused by illicit smoking. This evidence had led to the publication of the new no-match rule.

Jake Stapler had for twenty-five years been one of the best mechanics in the plant. Two weeks after the no-match rule had been put into effect, Jake was working on one of the processing towers in the plant. As he was climbing up the tower, a book of matches fell from his pocket and landed right at the feet of Mr. Bellows, Jake's supervisor.

Mr. Bellows: "Come on down, Jake. I'm going to have to report these matches. It'll mean your job."

Jake: "Please don't, Mr. Bellows. In all my twenty-five years here I've never smoked in the plant. I just forgot about the new rule."

    1 If you were Mr. Bellows what would you do? Why?

    2 Did the company take adequate steps to teach the new rule to Jake? Explain.

    3 How might the company have handled this situation better?

C   Professor East was a famous chemist. His neighbor, Professor March, was an equally highly regarded biologist. For years the two men had been fast friends, and had discussed at length many topics of mutual professional interest.

During the last political campaign, relations between the men became strained.

Professor East, a dedicated Republican, claimed that March was blind to the creeping socialism that was sweeping the country. March, on the other hand, loudly proclaimed that East was against all social progress. He said he had thought that East was a smart man but now he was beginning to wonder.

Just before election day the two men had a violent argument. Each questioned the intelligence and honesty of the other. They parted in a rage, and six months passed before they even spoke to each other again.

      1 How is it that politics could break up the long friendship?

      2 What advice would you give the two men that might help them renew and keep their friendship?

      3 Is there any reason to think that either man was dishonest or had lost his intelligence? Explain.

FOR FURTHER STUDY

Additional sources can be found in the sources cited in the chapter.

Books

James C. Coleman: *Psychology and Effective Behavior,* Scott, Foresman and Company, Glenview, Ill., 1969, chap. 2. Heredity, environment, and the self are determinants of personality.

O. Spurgeon English and G. H. J. Pearson: *Emotional Problems of Living,* W. W. Norton & Company, Inc., New York, 1955. A scholarly but readable presentation of the psychoanalytic view of personality development.

Abraham H. Maslow: *Toward a Psychology of Being,* 2d ed., D. Van Nostrand Company, Inc., Princeton, N.J., 1968. A developmental philosophy for individual self-actualization is described.

William C. Menninger and Harry Levinson: *Human Understanding in Industry,* Science Research Associates, Chicago, 1956. To be most effective a supervisor must understand personality development, structure, and expression of his workers.

Edward A. Strecher and Kenneth E. Appel: *Discovering Ourselves,* 3d ed., The Macmillan Company, New York, 1962. "It is of great importance to every human being to know something about behavior and moving forces in human nature and society in order to understand some of the underlying feelings, motivations, and directions in civilization today."

Robert S. Woodworth: *Dynamics of Behavior,* Henry Holt and Company, Inc., New York, 1958, chap. 9. Elementary learning concepts are explained.

Articles

Hadley Cantril: "The Human Design," *Journal of Individual Psychology,* November 1964.

There are many different demands that human beings impose on any society or political culture because of their genetically built-in design.

Edward T. Hall, Jr.: "The Anthropology of Manners," *Scientific American,* April 1955. A highly readable explanation of the effect of cultural experiences on learned behavior and expectation patterns of individuals.

Harry Levinson: "What Killed Bob Lyons?" *Harvard Business Review,* January–February 1963, pp. 127–143. A remarkable paper describing the psychological forces at work in man and how they shape his relationships to others—indeed his whole life.

Robert C. Ziller: "Individual and Socialization: A Theory of Assimilation in Large Organizations," *Human Relations,* November 1964. "The theory of individuation evolves from a consideration of the socialization process whereby the individual becomes assimilated by various groups and yet strives to maintain a degree of individuality, to preserve a stable self-concept which serves as a point of reference."

9
Interpersonal Behavior

People need people. Laurie was about three when one night she requested my aid in getting undressed. I was downstairs and she was upstairs, and . . . well. "You know how to undress yourself," I reminded. "Yes," she explained, "but sometimes people need people anyway, even if they do know how to do things by theirselves." As I slowly lowered the newspaper a strong feeling came over me, a mixture of delight, embarrassment, and pride; delight in the realization that what I had just heard crystallized many stray thoughts on interpersonal behavior; anger because Laurie stated so effortlessly what I had been struggling with for months; and pride because, after all, she is my daughter.
WILLIAM C. SCHUTZ[1]

Most human experiences involve interaction or relationship with other persons. In the previous chapter, attributes of an individual person and his developmental processes were described. The present chapter analyzes typical patterns through which individual persons interact, or relate to each other.

No one has ever fully described or explained human interaction because of its great richness and variety. Indeed, in many ways the more that is known, the deeper the mystery seems to become. Nevertheless, certain typical patterns of cooperation, conflict, adjustment, and response can be described.

COOPERATION

Before taking up the problem-oriented material of the majority of this chapter, it is emphasized that persons cooperate in countless satisfying interactions in organizations. There is a tendency to cooperate in an organization whenever two or more persons think

[1]William C. Schutz, *FIRO: A Three-dimensional Theory of Interpersonal Behavior,* Holt, Rinehart, and Winston, Inc., New York, 1958, p. 1.

their best interests will be served by it. Describing the elements of cooperation is a major objective of this book, because understanding cooperation contributes to improving the productivity of organizations. Several entire chapters and portions of others analyze cooperation-related topics in detail. Because this material is presented elsewhere, it is not included in the present chapter. However, when studying the somewhat negatively or problem-oriented material on conflict, defense mechanisms, and other such topics in the remainder of the present chapter, it should be remembered that cooperation is a pervasive feature of human interaction. It is easy to forget this if only problems are considered.

A MODEL OF INTERPERSONAL BEHAVIOR

Figure 9-1 is a model of persons interacting. The model $person_1$ has a core personality that typically is surrounded and obscured by conflicts and psychological mechanisms. His perception of his environment is colored by conflicts and psychological mechanisms because he sees the world through them. These give him a singular and probably distorted view of things, just as if he were wearing colored glasses. He seeks to satisfy his goals, and the particular behavior he selects is distorted by his conflicts and mechanisms. That is, his actual behavior is different from what it would have been if he had no conflicts or mechanisms. His behavior has certain consequences or feedback, which is also distorted by his conflicts and psychological mechanisms.

Person$_2$ has a similar situation except that, as the model shows, his perception of satisfying goal-seeking behavior is not significantly distorted by conflicts. Likewise, he does not distort the feedback, or results, with mechanisms.

If the behavior of the two persons is related—if there is interaction—then interpersonal behavior exists, as shown in the model. Many elements of this interaction are analyzed elsewhere in this text; the remainder of this chapter studies the effect of conflict, psychological mechanisms, and response traits on interpersonal behavior.

CONFLICT

Conflict underlies or accompanies much human interaction; some degree of it is typical. Conflict may be minor, manifested only by a slight feeling of uneasiness of one or more participants. Or conflict may be serious; in some cases it is the major component of interaction. In severe cases it destroys successful interaction.

Conflict can be between persons if they have different objectives or ways of achieving them. Where there are no vested interests, conflict of this type often can be fairly easily resolved, particularly if it is discussed openly with mutual good will. More subtle conflict often springs from within a person; frequently, it spills over into his relationships with others, causing conflict between him and them. Surprisingly, internal conflict is to blame for many problems of interaction. Several types of such conflict, including approach-approach, avoidance-avoidance, and approach-avoidance, can be described. Any of these can profoundly influence interpersonal behavior.

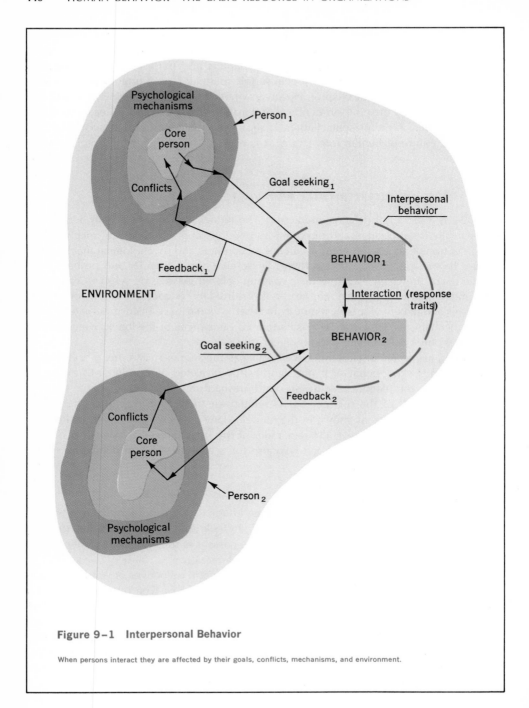

Figure 9–1   Interpersonal Behavior

When persons interact they are affected by their goals, conflicts, mechanisms, and environment.

Approach-Approach Conflict

In approach-approach conflict a person is attracted to two or more goals that seem roughly equally attractive. For example, a person might be torn between two attractive jobs, as shown in Figure 9-2a. Or, he might be in great conflict over whether to spend some available money to purchase a new car or a new boat.

Avoidance-Avoidance Conflict

Avoidance-avoidance conflict exists when a person is torn between two or more things he wishes to avoid. For instance, a young man may wish to avoid serving in the army, but to do so he might have to leave the country, as depicted in Figure 9-2b. In another case a businessman may wish to avoid suing a customer for nonpayment of a bill, but he also may want the money.

Approach-Avoidance Conflict

The third type of conflict, approach-avoidance, exists when there are both good and bad elements in a certain action. For example, a college graduate may be offered an excellent job in a bad location, as diagrammed in Figure 9-2c. Or a student may be in conflict over whether to take a desired course because he thinks it will require too much work.

All these types of conflict can be serious. In extreme cases a person may become incapacitated if he is unable to successfully resolve them. More often conflicts within or among persons simply make life more difficult, and often more interesting.

PSYCHOLOGICAL MECHANISMS

Persons have certain typical ways, called psychological mechanisms, by which they relate to their environment. As shown in Figure 9-1, psychological mechanisms act somewhat as filters or colored glasses through which a person sees and understands events. In the other direction, these mechanisms also determine in part the ways he behaves. Thus, psychological mechanisms tend to affect both a person's understanding of his environment and the ways he interacts with it. Because they are integral parts of his personality, a person usually is not aware that he is using a psychological mechanism; he can much more easily see another person using one. Typically, these mechanisms are used by persons as a means of coping with mental problems or conflicts. Because such problems are so prevalent, the presence of mechanisms in behavior is the rule rather than the exception. In fact, it probably would be difficult to find any behavior that does not involve one or more of the mechanisms.

It is tempting to consider psychological mechanisms as being totally negative factors because they stand between a person's direct relationship with his environment. However, like complexes, psychological mechanisms are best judged in terms of their effects. If a mechanism has a constructive effect, it is considered good; and if it is

(*a*) Approach–approach conflict
In approach–approach conflict a person wants two positive situations but can have only one.

(*b*)   Avoidance–avoidance conflict
In avoidance–avoidance conflict one wishes to avoid two unpleasant things but must take one of them.

(*c*)   Approach–avoidance conflict
In approach–avoidance conflict one desires certain elements of a given action but finds other aspects of that same action undesirable.

Figure 9–2 . Types of Conflict

There are several types of conflict including approach–approach, avoidance–avoidance, and approach–avoidance.

destructive, it is thought to be bad. Almost always the use of a mechanism involves a sort of self-deception in that the person uses it to see reality in his preferred, usually somewhat distorted way. Similarly, he often uses a mechanism (frequently involving self-trickery) in selecting or explaining his behavior. Nevertheless, a person always —in his view—has a reason for using a mechanism; that is, he perceives it as serving some useful function for himself. The overall effect may be generally constructive or destructive.

The psychological mechanisms described in the following paragraphs are arranged in rough order from constructive to destructive. This order is not precise, but it does suggest that the effects of mechanisms can vary over a wide range. Figure 9-3 shows this approximate ordering of the mechanisms.

Sublimation

Sublimation redefines instinctive drives, and directs this energy into acceptable expressions. For example, an athlete sublimates aggressive feelings into vigorous and successful action on the playing field. His play may be greatly admired by his team's supporters. He benefits by releasing pent-up aggression and from the rewards of his good play. The employee who was angry at his boss and named one of his golf balls after his boss is another example of sublimation. It is wiser to hit the ball rather than the boss, and the amazing thing is that such vigorous physical activity does reduce interpersonal aggression. Success in business or other endeavors can spring from sublimation. Energy coming from hostility, anger, and other such sources—that would be

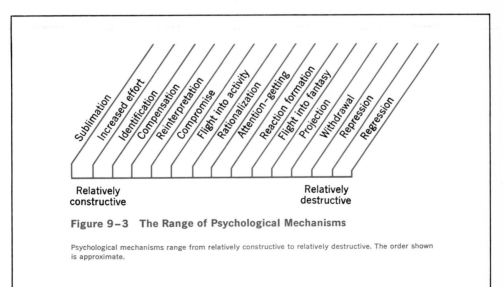

Relatively
constructive

Relatively
destructive

Figure 9–3   The Range of Psychological Mechanisms

Psychological mechanisms range from relatively constructive to relatively destructive. The order shown is approximate.

destructive if expressed directly—is converted by sublimation into other expressions, with positive results. This is almost always desirable, so sublimation is rated here as the most constructive mechanism.

Increased Effort

When one is not satisfied with the results of his behavior, he can use a mechanism called increased effort. He may expend more energy, work longer, use more approaches, or use more courage in his increased effort. For example, to increase his income, a salesman may decide to spend more time, use new techniques, and call on prospects that he has neglected because he feared them.

Identification

Identification is the practice of imitating the behavior of someone who is admired. Often a person's identification with another is quite obvious—he may dress similarly or identically, speak with the same mannerisms, try to look like the other person (for example, hair style), read the same books, or go to the same places. Through identification one can vicariously have the achievements or fame of another. Identification is at work when teen-agers imitate idols, when women try to look like Paris models, and when an employee dresses like his boss. Through identification one may absorb another's belief, values, and attitudes. For example, children often grow up holding similar attitudes as their parents. In fact, positive identification with respected authority figures generally is necessary in a person's healthy development. Identification is necessary if one is to be an integral part of most any group. Identification is seen as good if there is approval of the group and its leader. On the other hand, most persons would think that identification with a bad group or leader (for example, Hitler) is undesirable.

Sometimes a leader has ardent followers who feel he can do no wrong. Or a person may feel such a strong attraction for another that he idolizes. Many persons felt this way about President Kennedy. This extreme form of identification is called idealization. Another form of idealization is seen in some men who think that a beautiful woman is bound to be a splendid cook, mother, and conversationalist—which of course is not necessarily true.

Compensation

The next mechanism shown in Figure 9-3 is compensation, which often is highly constructive. A person who is deficient in one attribute or talent may substitute a high degree of proficiency in another. A student who lacks the ability to get along well socially with others or to compete effectively on the athletic field may devote his energies to studying. He may gain compensating satisfaction from a straight A record. Similarly, an athlete may excel on the field to compensate for his lack of prowess with academics. Also, a blind person may compensate by developing acute hearing and touch senses. A more destructive form of compensation is seen when parents try to compensate for their lack of satisfaction with their own lives by living through their children. Often such parents drive a child to succeed in sports, music, school, or other areas because they think they will be more important because of the child's outstanding performance. Frequently the child deep-down hates the thing he excels in, and—to top it off—he also often hates his parents for pushing him.

Reinterpretation

In reinterpretation one takes a goal that he has not attained and reinterprets or revises it. He might see his goal in a new light or seek to attain it by different means. He also may substitute another goal or decide to accept a lower goal. Or he may decide to "stretch out" or take longer to achieve the goal. For example, a man (now a vice-president) had a lifelong ambition to be president of his company. It became obvious that he never would achieve this goal after another man was elected president. By reinterpreting his goals the disappointed man might accept his vice-presidency as a satisfactory terminal position. Or a student rejected for a doctoral program might come to enjoy the job that he took as a substitute. Similarly, a rejected suitor, through reinterpretation of his goals might learn to completely love another.

Flight into Activity

Sometimes a person handles a problem by distracting himself with other activities. This flight into activity often is frenetic, and may seem to be an end in itself. When using this mechanism a person's principal objective may just be to keep busy, and thus avoid thinking about his more basic problems. An anxious person may try to relieve his tension by going shopping, taking a trip, or just keeping busy at anything. This is flight into activity if the basic reason is to avoid something else, such as uncomfortable feelings. Another example is seen in the man who works harder than ever as an escape from his feelings of grief for his deceased wife. Flight into activity frequently produces good things from the activity—for example, extraordinary work. And perhaps something, at least some temporary relief, is obtained while one has distracted himself. Thus flight into activity can have some constructive effects, but it is destructive to the extent it masks the basic internal problems rather than solving them.

Rationalization

Rationalization is a psychological mechanism that is at work when one uses a "good" rather than the real reason for justifying his action to himself or others. Perhaps a person does not want to do the work he brought home from the office. He may be unable to admit even to himself that he does not want to work. He then may convince himself that by going to a movie he will be more relaxed, enabling him to work better. He may further rationalize a trip for a snack or a visit with a friend after the movie, now claiming that he does not have enough time to work anyway. The work remains undone. Thus he has developed a rationale through rationalization that allowed him to do what he really wanted with a clear conscience. Rationalization also is frequently used to justify the purchase of a new car. A person may say that it will cost too much to do the repairs on the old car. More likely, he wants the new car for other reasons but does not understand or is unwilling to state them. Rationalization often is present in alibis or excuses; the person may be unable to directly face his failure, so he comes up with "good" reasons to justify it. The "sour grapes" pattern also typically involves rationalization. When one cannot have what he wants, he often claims he did not want it anyway. Some degree of rationalization seems to be present in most behavior, since persons rarely, if ever, are fully aware of the reasons for their actions.

Attention Getting

If a person wants to be noticed more, he may employ the mechanism of attention getting. His behavior may be shown in loud or excessive talking, ostentatious purchases, or the seeking of a highly visible job merely to call attention to oneself. Or a teen-ager may get in trouble simply to force his parents to notice him. A woman who wears seductive clothing merely to be noticed also is indulging in attention getting. Unusual hair styles—both for men and women—and flashy cars also can be used for this purpose. Attention getting is partly destructive because it diverts attention away from real problems or issues to the rather false attention-attracting devices or behavior.

Reaction Formation

A person may dislike certain behavior, values, or things. He may then go exactly opposite, utilizing the reaction formation mechanism. For example, a boy may very much want to be liked by a girl, but fearing the possible involvements, he may act in such a way that the girl cannot possibly like him. A once-popular song, "You Always Hurt the One You Love," seems to illustrate this mechanism. In recent years long hair for men has often represented a reaction formation to the short-hair styles of the "establishment." Similarly, in some earlier times short hair was a symbol of protest against prevailing long-hair styles. Reaction formation is not very constructive since by his reaction to something one still is—perhaps unwittingly—attached to the very thing he despises. In the purest sense, he is not doing his "own thing" after all, because even when reacting to something he remains involved with it.

Flight into Fantasy

Instead of thinking about what is going on in the here and now one can think about something else. When used as an escape mechanism this is known as flight into fantasy. For example, a woman might be bored with keeping house and changing diapers and may secretly long (perhaps unconsciously) for a chivalrous knight in shining armor on a white horse to take her away to wonderland. (Many commercials for household products are based on this theme.) A man might use this mechanism in imagining that he is too good for his job and he ought to be president. Everyone sometimes thinks the grass is greener on the other side of the fence. Milder versions of flight into fantasy are ordinary daydreaming, watching TV, and going to movies. These often are constructive in providing fun, relaxation, and a change from routine.

Projection

Projection is an obnoxious mechanism whereby a person attempts to hide his own feelings or position by focusing on another person. For instance, if one felt hostile to another person and wanted to hide that fact, he could allege that the other person hates him. Then he may say, "Since he is out to get me, I will get him first." An employee with projection may justify his failure to do his job. He may claim that everyone with whom he had to work was hostile and uncooperative. They may have been behaving quite normally. (Although if they are subjected to the unfair projection, they may react to it in anger.) Or a student may use projection to cover up his inability to answer an exam question. He may claim the question was unclear, which may not be the case if the other students had no difficulty in understanding it. Projection is employed whenever one attempts to hide his attitudes or deficiencies by unreasonably blaming others or by focusing on alleged characteristics of others. Projection is destructive in interpersonal behavior although—like all other mechanisms—it is designed to perform some function for its user. Perhaps this dimension of projection was illustrated in the lower than usual suicide rate in London during the blitz of World War II. By focusing on the bombing perils, many persons seem to have been relieved of internal distress.

Withdrawal

Sometimes a situation is so frightening that a person removes himself physically by using the mechanism of withdrawal. For instance, a student took one look at an examination, had an overpowering fear reaction, told his instructor he could not take it, and walked out. Sometimes withdrawal is used if a person appears to be enjoying or exploiting an illness that limits his activities. Withdrawal is constructive if through it a person removes himself from a situation that is truly dangerous.

Repression

Repression is the mechanism of putting distasteful, guilt-producing, painful, and shameful experiences, memories, and information out of the conscious mind. They are, of course, retained in the unconscious mind. The attempt is to try to eliminate these objectionable things, as if they simply did not exist. In repression one consciously forgets or blocks the offending material. A student who "forgot" an assignment that would have interfered with activities he desired more may have repressed it. Repression also often is used in an attempt to escape painful feelings associated with traumatic experiences. A woman once saw a rat at a vacation cabin and became so upset that the whole vacation had to be cancelled. Until she saw the rat she was not even aware of her unusual fear of rats, which had its source in early childhood experiences. For more than twenty-five years she had repressed this feeling.

Regression

The final mechanism, regression, is used when a person reverts to earlier, often childish, behavior. Something in present or recent experience has been so frightening that the person regresses to an earlier adaptation. In effect, he says, "I cannot cope with my present life so I will go back to some time when I was more comfortable." Regression can dominate a person's personality, but often is more subtle and applies to particular situations. For example, organizational members frequently transfer parental feelings to their supervisors. A person doing this wants or expects his supervisor to treat him as his parent did, or as he wanted his parent to treat him. Such transference blankets the relationship with inappropriate out-of-date feelings. Numerous conflicts result. When they feel threatened or weak (like they may have felt as children), some persons revert to a high-pitched voice more appropriate for children. Regression also was shown by the club member who stormed out of a meeting in a temper tantrum because the club refused to let her dominate its activities. Because regression is based in the past, rather than the present, it seldom is constructive.

The use of psychological mechanisms often is called misdirected adjustment. These mechanisms often are seen as defenses against impaired self-esteem, feelings of guilt or anxiety, and other threatening or uncomfortable situations. The fact that they are unconscious adaptation devices gives additional weight to this negative view. However, it must be remembered that a person always expects a mechanism to serve some useful function for him; often it does. Further, a mechanism often produces valuable interpersonal or social effects which must be considered in any evaluation. Also, one never is aware he is using a mechanism as such. He simply is behaving according to his understanding. Finally, it should be recalled that persons use one or more mechanisms in almost all behavior, so if they all are condemned almost everyone will be included. Clearly, psychological mechanisms profoundly affect interpersonal behavior.

NEUROSES AND PSYCHOSES

If psychological mechanisms as a first line of defense prove inadequate to protect a person when he feels inadequate or insecure, he may employ a second line of defense, a neurosis. A neurosis is a severe, unresolved unconscious conflict. It is "reflected in our ways of thinking, feeling, and behaving, produced by severe emotional tensions."[2] A neurosis produces behavior that is more maladjustive than that of defense mechanisms. Neurotic behavior is unconscious conflict. The neurotic is in touch with his

[2]George F. J. Lehner and Ella Kube, *The Dynamics of Personal Adjustment*, 2d ed., Prentice-Hall, Inc., Englewood, N.J., 1964, pp. 145–146.

environment, but his behavior in certain situations may be inappropriate, rigid, or compulsive. Anxiety, fears, obsessions, and depression often are felt by the neurotic. Everyone, of course, has all these from time to time. For example, practically everybody feels anxious before and during an interview for a new job. The normal person can get satisfactory release from such tension by exercise or by diversion, such as going to a movie. If the anxiety is neurotic, adequate relief cannot be obtained by such ordinary measures. As another example, almost everyone might shrug off not being invited to a party, but a neurotic may be greatly offended if he were not invited.

Most persons have neurotic (unreasonable) fear of some things such as high places, rats, snakes, windowless buildings, the dark, and so forth. Further, almost everyone feels compelled by some often seemingly mysterious force to do some things to excess —such as visit relatives, wash hands, and criticize others. The examples of neurotic behavior are endless, and are so prevalent that practically everyone can be said to exhibit at least mild neurotic behavior in some situations. Neurotic behavior often is very much like normal behavior. The neurotic simply overdoes it. A neurosis is serious only when the person suffers significantly from it or the maladjustive behavior it produces.

Sometimes even neurotic behavior is not sufficient protection for a person, and he uses psychotic behavior as a sort of third line of defense. The neurotic seems unreasonable about certain things. In contrast, the psychotic has lost touch with reality, and his totally unrealistic personality is involved in everything he does. Unlike the neurotic, who may be aware that his actions are unreasonable, the psychotic has no appreciation that anything is wrong with him. The neurotic has "one foot on the ground"; the psychotic has both off. The psychotic may have hallucinations and delusions. His behavior is almost totally maladjustive. He usually must be hospitalized because he may be dangerous to himself or others.

A more complete analysis of neuroses and psychoses is beyond the scope of this book. The principal objective here is to have a basic understanding of them and their effect on interpersonal relationships.

RESPONSE TRAITS

Persons often use certain typical patterns of behavior—known as response traits—when interacting. Twelve response traits, described below, are typical of interpersonal behavior.[3] Each trait has an opposite which is given in parentheses.

1 *Ascendance (social timidity).* The person defends his rights, does not mind being conspicuous, is self-assured, and forcefully puts himself forward.

2 *Dominance (submissiveness).* The person is confident and assertive, desires power, is tough, tends to give orders, and is strong-willed.

[3]Adapted by permission from David Krech, Richard S. Crutchfield, and Egerton L. Ballachay, *The Individual in Society,* McGraw-Hill Book Company, New York, 1962, p. 106.

3 *Social initiative (social passivity).* The person is an organizer and wants to lead.

4 *Independence (dependence).* The person works things out his own way, does not seek advice, and is emotionally self-sufficient.

5 *Acceptance of others (rejection of others).* The person believes in, trusts, and sees the best in others.

6 *Sociability (unsociability).* The person is active in social affairs, likes to be with others, and is outgoing.

7 *Friendliness (unfriendliness).* The person forms relationships easily, is warm and genial, and is easy to approach and meet.

8 *Sympathy (antipathy).* The person is concerned with the feelings and wants of others, defends underdogs, and exhibits kind and generous behavior.

9 *Competitiveness (noncompetitiveness).* The person sees every relationship as a contest—others are rivals to be defeated, and he is noncooperative.

10 *Aggressiveness (nonaggressiveness).* The person attacks others directly or indirectly, resents authority, quarrels readily, and is negatively oriented.

11 *Self-consciousness (social poise).* The person exhibits stage fright, is embarrassed in front of others, does not volunteer in group discussions, does not like to be watched at work, and feels uncomfortable if he is different from others.

12 *Exhibitionism (self-effacement).* The person goes to extremes in dress and behavior, seeks attention, recognition, and applause and shows off for attention.

Everyone has all these traits to some degree. However, the frequency of use, intensity, and the situations where the traits are used vary from person to person. Also, a trait can be expressed in a number of ways. For example, an aggressive person may show his aggression in several ways—he may be a bully, be sarcastic, or use profanity.

Response traits have several important characteristics: (1) stability, (2) pervasiveness, and (3) consistency. Response traits tend to be stable over long periods of time. Married couples, school children, and adults who were studied and reexamined as much as twenty years later showed remarkable stability in their interpersonal response traits. Perhaps this characteristic explains the difficulty that often occurs when a small business attempts a large expansion. The president, in becoming a manager rather than a supervisor who operates from his head or back pocket, has to change his relationships with almost all members of the organization. This is very difficult to do; many businesses fail attempting it.

Pervasiveness is the extent to which a trait is found in a person. He may express certain traits in only a limited number of situations, whereas others may be aired frequently. For instance, social poise can be exhibited only when one faces a group of strangers, but competitiveness can be expressed in most interactions. A person also can place limits on the use of a trait—he may be sociable with members of his own ethnic group but unsociable with others.

Consistency, the third characteristic, describes the probability that one will express a trait. If a person has high trait consistency, it is easier to predict what he will do in a certain situation.

HEALTHY ADJUSTMENT

Healthy persons interact in ways that are generally mutually satisfying. According to one writer, a healthy person has the ability to deal constructively with reality, to adapt to change, to be relatively free from symptoms that are produced by anxieties and tensions, to find more satisfaction in giving than receiving, to relate to others in a consistent manner with mutual satisfaction and helpfulness, to direct his hostile energy into creative and constructive outlets, and to love.[4] These certainly are ideal characteristics and give almost everyone a great deal to work toward.

To improve his adjustment a person can alter his environment or adapt better to it. Today—in contrast to earlier decades—one does not have to merely live with his problems of adjustment and interactions. With effort and help, he can get an improved awareness of self, others, and the problems of life. Fortunately, a wide range of opportunities for such improvement exists. For example, a manager can attend seminars on business problems, join a sensitivity group, get professional counseling on problems he has in dealing with others, or use thousands of other means for improving his interactions with others.

SUMMARY

A multitude of factors are involved when persons interact. Each person is unique, and his behavior is influenced by his personality and environment. Despite the many potential difficulties, persons do very often successfully interact in organized, cooperative behavior. Quite often, however, such interpersonal interaction is affected by conflicts. Conflicts can be approach-approach, where one must chose between two desirable alternatives. Or the conflict can be avoidance-avoidance, where the person must select between two undesirable alternatives. In the third type of conflict, approach-avoidance, a person sees both good and bad in an alternative and has difficulty in deciding upon it. A person can use one or more of some fifteen psychological mechanisms in adapting to his environment. Some of these are relatively constructive, while others produce severe maladjustive behavior. Even more serious maladjustments are exhibited in neuroses and psychoses.

Because interpersonal behavior is so complex, pat formulas about supervisor-employee relationships, communications flow, or roles in organizations are not very useful. However, a manager who understands the dynamics of interpersonal behavior has a real

[4]Anonymous.

advantage in motivating and coordinating the activities of the members of his organization.

Improvement of interpersonal relationships in organizations can come from increased awareness of self, others, and the problems of organizations. For improvement, a person can evaluate his attitudes, try to resolve conflicts, and become more aware of how others react to him. He can gain understanding of others' feelings and attitudes and develop more respect for and acceptance of them as individual persons. Of course, it is much more difficult to take these steps than it is simply to list them. Fortunately, many sources can assist in these endeavors. Usually the gains made through such efforts far outweigh their costs, because successful interaction with others is among man's most rewarding experiences.

FOR REVIEW AND DISCUSSION

1 Define a psychological mechanism. What is the purpose of a psychological mechanism?

2 Describe each of the following psychological mechanisms, and give an example from your own experience to illustrate each in action: (a) sublimation, (b) increased effort, (c) identification, (d) compensation, (e) reinterpretation, (f) compromise, and (g) flight into activity.

3 Same as question number 2 above, but take these mechanisms: (a) rationalization, (b) attention-getting, (c) reaction formation, (d) flight into fantasy, (e) projection, (f) withdrawal, (g) repression, and (h) regression.

4 In your own words describe these response traits and their opposites: (a) ascendance, (b) dominance, and (c) social initiative. Give an example from your own experience to illustrate each trait, and another to illustrate each opposite.

5 Same as question 4 above, but take these traits: (a) independence, (b) acceptance of others, and (c) sociability.

6 Same as question 4 above, but take these traits: (a) friendliness, (b) sympathy, and (c) competitiveness.

7 Same as question 4 above, but take these traits: (a) aggressiveness, (b) self-consciousness, and (c) exhibitionism.

8 Describe the following kinds of conflict and illustrate each with an example not given in the text: (a) approach-approach (b) avoidance-avoidance (c) approach-avoidance.

9 Define neuroses and psychoses. Give an example of each.

10 Describe criteria that indicate healthy adjustment.

CASES

A   Cross Continent Gas Pipe Line, Inc., has just completed its new line to the Midwest. The company decided that the new Midwest Division would be operated just like the other two older divisions, the Eastern and Western.

To staff the maintenance department of the Midwest Division the company asked for nominations from the appropriate managers in the two older divisions. Quite naturally, employees who had been in trouble, who had poor reputations in their work, or who did not get along well with their present managers or co-workers were nominated. The first foreman of the maintenance department of the Midwest Division, Ben Todd, was also such a reject.

At his first meeting with his employees Ben made the following statement: "All right, men, let's not kid ourselves. We had just as well face it. We are all a bunch of culls. But if we all pull together, we can be the best maintenance crew the company has."

Company records since the formation of the Midwest Division have shown that, based on every measure, Ben Todd's crew has consistently been the best maintenance crew in the company.

    1 How did Ben turn an apparent liability into an asset?

    2 What psychological mechanisms were at work in Ben's new crew?

B   Louis Clark, an engineer with Astro Airplane Company, had always secretly wanted to work at the firm's headquarters office. That office was located in Crescent City, a small town on the West Coast. Crescent City also was near Blayville, the town in which Louis had spent his childhood years.

Each year the company offered the opportunity to move to Crescent City to a very small number of its top flight engineers. Year after year Louis had hoped to be on the list, but it finally became apparent to him that he would never have the opportunity to move to Crescent City.

Over coffee one day Louis was heard to say: "Even if they offered me the chance to move to Crescent City I wouldn't take it. It's too close to my old home. I like things just like they are. I hope they never make the offer; I wouldn't want to say no to the company."

    1 Explain the psychological mechanisms Louis may be using to hide his true feelings.

    2 What types of conflict might Louis have about his old job and the possibility of the new job?

C   When Marty was three years old, he had fallen from a tree and been severely injured. Although he had been confined to bed for many months, Marty's recovery was apparently complete, and Marty dismissed the fall from his mind.

After Marty graduated from engineering school, he accepted a job with Blade Oil Corporation. Company policy required that all new engineers must spend two years as a "rough-neck" on drilling rigs before being assigned to engineering work.

During Marty's first day at the rig the tool pusher (foreman) told him: "Go up on top of the rig and straighten out that cable, Marty."

"Sure," Marty replied.

Halfway up the 150-foot-tall tower Marty "froze." He couldn't move up or down; finally the tool pusher went up and carried him back to ground. Marty had no idea what caused his paralyzing fear of high places.

    1 Describe the psychological mechanism Marty had used that would explain why he did not know the reasons for his fear.

D   Jay Pesson had accepted employment with Consolidated Corporation when he received his engineering degree from a midwestern university. Consolidated's beginning salary offer to Jay was significantly higher than the other offers Jay had.

Jay had always wanted his permanent home to be close to where he grew up in a small Midwestern town. However, he decided to go with Consolidated because of the higher salary even though he had to move to the Consolidated plant, which was located on the West Coast. Because Consolidated had only this one plant, there was no possibility of ever working with them closer to home.

Jay's intention was to work for Consolidated for a few years, save his money, and return to his section of the country for his career employment. After ten years with Consolidated, Jay had received several promotions and numerous raises reflecting his very successful work with the company.

Because of Consolidated's unique products Jay's technical knowledge was worth much less to another firm. This meant that Jay could return to his home state to work only by taking a severe pay cut. Jay liked his work with Consolidated, but after ten years with that company his desire to return to his home area was as strong as ever. Jay could not decide which to do—keep working with Consolidated or give up his job to return home. Jay became more despondent after several months of trying unsuccessfully to make a decision. Recently he began to consult a psychiatrist about his very painful feelings about the matter.

   1 What kinds of conflict does Jay have?
   2 What do you recommend that Jay do? Why?

FOR FURTHER STUDY

Additional sources can be found in the sources cited in the chapter.

Books

Chris Argyris: *Personality and Organization,* Harper & Row, Publishers, Incorporated, New York, 1957, pp. 36–47. Defense mechanisms are used by an individual to protect himself against threat.

James C. Coleman: *Psychology and Effective Behavior,* Scott, Foresman and Company, Glenview, Ill., 1969, chap. 7. A person uses numerous adjustive reactions and mechanisms to meet his requirements.

Keith Davis: *Human Relations at Work,* 4th ed., McGraw-Hill Book Company, New York, 1972. "Human relations, an art rather than a science, requires a basic philosophy and framework if it is to be effectively taught and practiced in business."

George F. J. Lehner and Ella Kube: *The Dynamics of Personal Adjustment,* 2d ed., Prentice-Hall, Inc., Englewood Cliffs, N.J., 1964. A highly readable explanation of the sources and dynamics of human behavior.

Abraham Zaleznik and David Moment: *The Dynamics of Interpersonal Behavior,* John Wiley & Sons, Inc., New York, 1964. "The energy for interpersonal relations, as with all action, belongs to the individual. The meaning of the technical, social, and organizational environments in which interpersonal relations unfold and the process of behavior itself can be viewed as an extension of the individual's tendency to define symbolically the world in which he lives."

Articles

Grady D. Bruce and Richard F. Dutton: "The Neurotic Executive," *Personnel Administration,* September–October 1967. Executive neuroses cause severe problems for organizations. Procedures should be established to prevent neurotics from becoming executives.

George C. Homans: "Social Behavior as Exchange," *American Journal of Sociology,* May 1958, pp. 597–606. A view of interpersonal behavior as social exchange. For example, A gives social values to B in the expectation that in return B will give some social values to A.

Melvin J. Lerner and Sylwyn Becker: "Interpersonal Choice as a Function of Ascribed Similarity and Definition of the Situation," *Human Relations,* February 1962. An individual will be more motivated to maintain or gain agreement in social judgment with a "similar" person rather than a "dissimilar" one.

Carl R. Rogers: "Interpersonal Relations: U.S.A. 2000," *Journal of Applied Behavioral Science,* July–August–September 1968. Rogers, a noted psychologist, offers his views of future interpersonal relationships in the U.S.A.

Abraham Zaleznik: "Managerial Behavior and Interpersonal Competence," *Behavioral Science,* April 1964. The objective of most training efforts, by both universities and corporations, is to modify behavior, usually interpersonal, according to some set of norms that related to organizational effectiveness or improved individual and group performance. This approach is quite often not the proper one to adopt.

10
Intraorganizational Behavior

Many of our satisfactions and frustrations grow out of our participation in groups and our strivings, with others, toward group goals.
    JAMES C. COLEMAN

Almost everyone is deeply affected by groups.[1] Involvement in some sort of group or organization occupies the major portion of the lives of many, if not most, persons. Numerous benefits can come from improved relationships between individuals and groups. For example, the success of a business typically depends upon productive behavior of individuals in work groups. Also, someone must deal successfully with customers, suppliers, governmental units, and the general public. The same is true of a college classroom which depends upon the successful interaction of the professor and students in their group. And students often join cliques outside class to exchange old tests, "obtain" new ones, try to outguess the professor, or sometimes even to study together! Further, parents, wives, husbands, sweethearts, friends, and administrators continually interact with the larger college or university.

[1]For purposes of this text, group and organization are the same.

This chapter analyzes several dimensions of intraorganizational behavior, with emphasis on the relationship of a person to a group and, in the other direction, of a group to a person. This relationship often is extremely complicated; seldom is it completely understood. Yet, behavioral scientists have provided rich insights into the meaning, structure, dynamics, and many other aspects of human groups.

MEANING OF GROUPS

Do groups exist? Or, are groups merely figments of the imagination? These questions may be surprising because almost everyone has some idea of the nature and importance of groups. However, the questions do have validity because groups, unlike individuals, do not exist as physical entities. Individuals certainly exist regardless of the viewpoint, but it can be argued that groups are merely the individuals comprising them.

This negative view of group existence sees groups as nothing more than mental abstractions. According to this view, ascribing reality to groups can indeed be destructive, because to do so results in "group-think," which emphasizes group importance. Then there may be demand for blind group loyalty, social prejudice, and subordination of the individual to the group. These problems can be avoided, according to this negative view of group existence, if it is maintained that only individuals, and not groups, exist.

The opposite, positive view about groups holds that groups exist. Coleman expressed this view in perhaps an extreme form when he wrote:

> Groups, like individuals, have structural and integrative characteristics and operate in physical and social settings. Like individuals, they strive to maintain themselves and resist disintegration and to grow and develop their potentials. Like individuals, too, they may solve their problems in either task-oriented or defense-oriented ways, and if their problems are beyond their resources—or believed to be—they may show evidence of strain, decompensation, and pathology.

> Groups have power structures, leadership structures, role structures, communication structures, and sociometric structures. They develop norms and ideologies and characteristic atmospheres and degrees of cohesiveness and morale. . . . Many groups show a "life cycle" not unlike that of individuals.[2]

Perhaps the two above extreme views of groups can be at least partially reconciled with the concept of synergy. Synergy recognizes that an aggregate may be different from the sum of its component parts. In the physical sciences synergy has been recognized widely. For example, the combined action (synergistic effect) of two drugs taken together may be significantly different from their action if taken separately. Also, chlorine—a highly poisonous substance—combines with sodium—an unstable and explosive substance—to produce common salt. The salt has characteristics (stability nonpoisonousness, etc.) that are almost unrelated to its component elements of chlorine and sodium.

[2]James C. Coleman, *Psychology and Effective Behavior*, Scott, Foresman and Company, Glenview, Ill., 1969, p. 298.

So it is with individuals and groups. A group may have characteristics that are significantly different from the individuals that compose it, just as salt is different from chlorine and sodium. Thus, a group has what can be called "social synergy." But a group does not have a mind that makes decisions.

Two sets of entities, therefore, can be considered in the study of a group—individual persons and groups. Both points of view have merit, and it often is valuable to shift analysis from one to the other—from the individual to the group and vice versa—depending upon one's purposes. Ironically, because of synergy, different answers to the same question often will be obtained, depending upon whether the point of view of the individual or the group is taken. For example, an individual employee may serve his interests if he is able—perhaps by threatening to quit—to force a pay raise for himself. But the interests of his company (group) may be harmed if the raise for this one employee destroyed the integrity of the firm's salary schedule. Optimizing the interests of an entity (individual, group, subgroups, supragroup, and so forth) does not necessarily optimize (indeed, it may harm) the interests of component or supra-entities. However, one of the purposes of this text is to raise the degree to which individuals and groups at all levels mutually benefit each other.

It seems best, then, to avoid either extreme view of the existence of groups. The viewpoint recommended here is to think of groups as aggregates of persons with certain typical features of interaction, structure, leadership, subunits, supra-units, and so forth. However, groups do not per se think, have life or soul, make decisions, or have or accomplish goals. Groups do exist as inevitable, ubiquitous, and powerful human structures. They, like almost all human experiences, can be used for either good or evil. Groups do exist, if not as physical entities, certainly as social entities. They are important, but it always should be recalled that they are made up of individuals who also are important.

GROUP MEMBERSHIP

Practically all individual effort takes place in association with others in groups. Group associations range from spontaneous, informal social gatherings, to work on an automobile assembly line, to a large army. Most of man's knowledge, attitudes, and values come from group experience. Man's objectives and his ways of achieving them are largely devised from groups. There indeed is little that can be understood about behavior in organizations without reference to group phenomena. Man has developed in groups for untold years; it is unlikely he could do without them now. Only through groups or organizations has man been able to achieve his goal of a better life.

Gaining Membership

Membership in a group can be gained in several ways including birth, application, invitation, and mutual consent. One gains membership in his family, ethnic, and national group by *birth*. When he gets older, he chooses and makes *application* to organizations to which he wishes to belong, such as a university, professional society, or a neighborhood. Sometimes he joins groups by *invitation*—for example, an alumni association, the army (perhaps enforced invitation!), or a great books study group. Finally, one joins many organizations by *mutual consent,* if it is not clear who—himself or the organization— took the initiative on soliciting membership. Examples of mutual consent include side-walk gangs that just grow without plan, acceptance by co-workers, and a friendship.

Objectives of Members

A person joins or remains a member of a group because he expects it to serve some function or objective for him. Groups or organizations often are used to solve man's economic, military, and other material problems, as explained in a previous chapter.

One might also join a group because of his need to be accepted and to prevent lone-liness and alienation. Religious, family, and other groups often serve these needs. Such groups also can provide support in time of trouble. They can give purpose and meaning to life by providing values, norms of behavior, and group allegiance.

Social, work, and other kinds of groups provide prestige, status, and recognition. Groups, by their very existence, give man an opportunity to satisfy his need to express his feelings and to communicate in other ways. A feeling of personal security often is gained from groups if they reduce a person's anxiety by providing support, protection, and a feeling of belonging. Sometimes a group serves a therapeutic function when it helps a person solve his inner problems.

The advantages of group membership can be both *intended* or *unintended.* Intended advantages are those that the person expected; unintended advantages were not ex-pected, and hence were not a basis for his membership. To illustrate the difference be-tween intended and unintended advantages, a person may join a group because he is lonely (intended advantage). He may get an unintended advantage, however, if the group provides something with which he can identify. It thus might have a powerful effect on his personality and life style.

Some studies have shown that persons relate more to groups than to their own per-sonal selves. For instance, some college students were asked to write twenty answers to the question, "Who am I?" They responded mainly with group-related terms such as "student," "Methodist," and "man," describing themselves as members of groups or social classes. Thus one's self-concept is largely derived from his group memberships. The ways one perceives or sees things also is greatly affected by his group experiences.

The family group is perhaps the prime determinant in a person's intellectual and emotional development. Through his family and play groups a young child learns the rules of life and comes to understand himself. He structures his personality by observing and reacting to important others in his life. He learns the words by which his culture identifies things and events, and he becomes aware of himself as a unique person. Man is a social being who takes not only his surface appearance but also much of his person-ality from his social environments. Groups play a vital part in his life by providing op-portunities for training, support, and emotional development.

Generally, a person wants to join groups he sees as coinciding with his interests, goals, and values. If he, according to his values, sees the group as having high status and success, he will tend to desire membership more. Ironically, if membership is difficult to attain, he often will work harder to get it.

Multigroup Membership

The typical person is a member of numerous groups—perhaps as many as fifty or more. It usually is easy to list thirty or more groups of which one is a member. Often the memberships of one's groups overlap; one might share membership in several groups with the same persons. This situation is illustrated in Figure 10-1. A small town or a neighborhood provides an excellent example of such overlapping memberships. Some of the same persons might be members of the same school, club, religious group, political group, and so forth. Membership in some groups is formal if formal applications, invitations, roster of members, officers, or minutes of meetings are used. On the other hand, informal groups do not use such procedures. In an informal group members come and go, and the group operates spontaneously, without established procedures.

NEGATIVE EFFECTS OF GROUPS

A group sometimes has detrimental effects. It may restrict, inhibit, or even smother a person. The pressure to conform in ideas and behavior may produce other negative con-

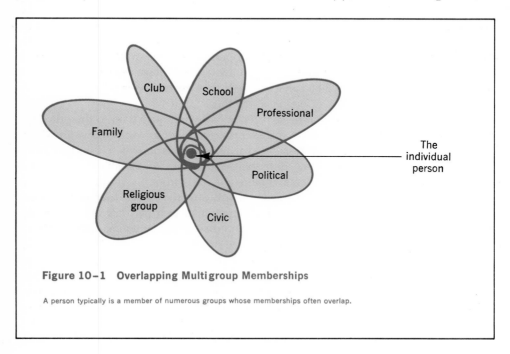

Figure 10–1   Overlapping Multigroup Memberships

A person typically is a member of numerous groups whose memberships often overlap.

sequences. For example, groups of workers often set unreasonably low production norms. Anyone producing more or working harder than the norm may be called a "rate buster," and be ostracized or otherwise severely punished. It takes a strong-willed person to resist group pressures. One wishes to belong, but he also needs to differentiate himself as an individual. Personal distress in attempting to solve this conflict can be great.

Groups also have been blamed as root causes of prejudice and other forms of unfair treatment. Members tend to view other members (in-group) in different ways from non-members (out-group). Attitudes, judgments, and perceptions tend to be distorted in favor of the in-group and against the out-group. Such distortions may be due to the need of persons to feel that they belong to the best groups. (On a deeper level this desire probably comes from the individual's need to feel important.) Many types of conflict and unfairness appear to spring from such group tendencies.

ATTITUDES AND BEHAVIOR

Groups are the major determinants of attitudes and behavior. Groups generally set ideologies, roles, and behavioral norms. Even those who rebel against the standards of a certain group usually conform closely to the group standards of their rebel group. Further, because persons tend to adopt group standards unconsciously, groups profoundly affect perception. That is, the very way one sees or understands events is greatly determined by his group experiences.

Selecting Groups

A person typically seeks to reinforce his attitudes and biases by selecting associates with whom he can agree. Upon joining a group, he tends to subordinate those personal interests that do not fit in with the group. An extreme example of this is a violent mob involving persons who as individuals would never engage in such acts. There is not only strength in numbers, but there also is a group psychology that moves persons to do things they never would do alone. How many college students would start a demonstration by themselves? How many "witches" would have been tried in Salem without a mob? How many radical movements would have much effect without a group devoted to the cause? Very few, if any.

A person usually has a wide range of interests; he seldom can satisfy them all within a single group. Therefore he joins a number of groups such as a social club, a professional association, a pollution-control society, until he finds expression for each of his interests.

Perception and Establishment of Norms

A classic experiment illustrated the effect of a group upon persons' perception. A darkroom with no visual standards by which a person could orient himself was used. In such a setting a person invariably perceives a fixed point of light as moving. The light appears to move back and forth slightly, though it does not. Test participants looked into a box in which they could not see anything except the apparently wavering point of light. After each of several observations through the peephole, each subject reported how much the light seemed to move. His report was not made known to others making and reporting similar observations. Each person's report came to center about a certain distance—for examples, 2 inches for one subject and 3 for another. Then the subjects were grouped in twos and threes and asked to give their estimates of movement, this time in the presence of fellow subjects. Group members did not consult one another to agree on a norm; they simply continued to give their own estimates and to hear the estimates of others. The previously wider individual estimates converged toward a new group estimate, or norm.

After the group norms had been established, the groups were broken up and each person was asked to record his judgment privately. Significantly, the individuals retained the group norm, and carried with them the estimate that had been established when together. This and other experiments showed that although members derive opinions from groups they often are unaware of the fact. The values and objectives of the individual usually become tangled and modified by the norms of the group. If a college freshman joins a group emphasizing high academic achievement, his grades probably will be higher. Or if his group scorns high grades, it will tend to pull his grades down. How much one studies, plays, sleeps, drinks, smokes, or works is vitally affected by the norms of his group.

The powerful effect of work norms was illustrated by the case of some auto workers:

> The five members of this United Auto Workers Local were charged by fellow workers with "working too hard," were fined and three of them suspended from the union for two years. These men were accused of working at speeds above a normal standard provided in a contract with the employer. . . . In August, their local ordered a slowdown to the standard rate because of a backlog of grievances involving work rules. Previously, workers had been earning extra wages by producing above the standard. The five were charged with ignoring the slowdown order, failing to follow the dictates of the majority, violating their membership pledges and setting themselves apart from fellow members. [3]

Almost everyone's level of work is affected by his group. The hated "rate-buster" ("curve-buster" in college) who works above group norms often must endure severe pressure to get him down to the group norm of work. Norms are established by a group as means of accomplishing its goals such as job security, avoiding working too hard, continued existence of the group, and so forth. Deviating members, who produce above or below the norm, tend to be rejected because they are seen as threats to the group. Conforming to norms likely increases cohesion within the group, but the group's norms can increase tension with outside persons or organizations if they do not agree with the norms.

Over time a group develops rather clear-cut behavioral norms or roles. These roles are patterns of expected and acceptable behavior for members. Conceptions of their roles

[3] *The Wall Street Journal,* Nov. 10, 1961, p. 2.

give the behavior expected from parents, children, students, professors, presidents, generals, servants, and so forth. Much education, training, and other effort is spent in learning roles.

Group Change, Decisions, and Problem Solving

Group change generally is easier to bring about than is change of individuals within the group. A group decision reduces inside and outside pressures that might be directed toward an individual if he were to go it alone. Further, group change will likely be longer lasting; this tendency also springs from the individual's desire to live up to group norms. With group standards the individual has more than personal discipline at work—he has group discipline too. The stronger the group bonds, the more deeply interwoven with group norms are the individual's attitudes. Applying these ideas, company training directors often avoid individual training, for it may be ineffective if the work involves a number of persons. Instead, they seek to have all affected persons attend a training session. Thus they try to establish a group norm rather than an individual one, which more likely would be ignored or sabotaged by the group. Group influence, then, is like weight— it is something like momentum or inertia. If the group remains the same, it is hard for the individual to change; and if the group changes, it is hard for the individual not to change.

Group decisions likely will be more effective if the affected individuals participate in making them. One will most readily accept ideas and decisions that he has had an active part in forming. He will support them because they are partly his. The fact that group discussion often produces deeper understanding than lecturing also illustrates the importance of personal involvement.

Groups have important problem-solving abilities. Groups can be valuable simply because they provide more ideas than an individual typically has. This is true because members have different abilities and outlooks. Group discussion often results in modification, refinement, and testing of ideas. Discussion also can produce many new ideas because group interaction stimulates new thoughts in each member. Groups may have better learning and recall, make fewer mistakes, and detect mistakes quicker. Group forecasting and judgment likely are more accurate. Group discussion also makes valuable contributions to communication among members. Group members show high enthusiasm for group goals, perhaps because they had a hand in setting those goals. The decisions that guide large and small organizations are to a great extent made by groups, frequently functioning as committees. In industry, government, education, and other organizations, billions of dollars are spent with the idea that group decisions often are better than those made by individuals. Groups certainly cannot fully replace individuals in decision making and problem solving, but they often are extremely valuable for these purposes.

Interaction in groups helps solve a basic problem of man—communicating with others. Also, communication among group members is necessary to accomplish group objectives. In formal groups much communication takes place in the formal channels. However, informal communication is important in formal as well as informal organizations.

Culture and Rational Behavior

As a group continues, more and more ideas, norms, rules, and procedures come into being and are changed, refined, and handed down. All this adds up to culture, which ties together, shapes, and refines values, art forms, dress styles, behavioral patterns, and many other standards to give a distinctive identity to a group. In addition, because of his identity with a group, group culture helps a person to orient and identify himself. He feels secure if he is satisfied with his position in a group he accepts and understands.

Culture, as long-established and accepted behavioral norms, even to a large extent defines rational behavior. Consider the case of K:

> All through childhood, K was extremely meditative, (he) usually preferred to be alone. He often had mysterious dreams and fits, during which he sometimes fainted. In late puberty, K experienced elaborate auditory and visual hallucinations, uttered incoherent words, and had recurrent spells of coma. He was frequently found running wildly through the country-side or eating the bark of trees and was known to throw himself with abandon into fire and water. On many occasions he wounded himself with knives or other weapons. K believed he could "talk to spirits" and "chase ghosts." He was certain of his power over all sorts of super-natural forces.[4]

According to most standards of behavior K certainly would be considered insane. But because K was a member of a primitive tribe of fishermen and reindeer herders in the Arctic wilderness of eastern Siberia, and because his behavior was normal—even desirable—in his culture, K's behavior was accepted as rational by his tribe. He even became a tribal leader. Thus, whether behavior is rational or not depends upon the culture, the situation, and the person. There is no universal standard of rationality.

COHESION AND DISRUPTION

A group has some forces that tend to make it stay together and other forces that tend to tear it apart, as illustrated in Figure 10-2. Cohesive forces are those in favor of member-ship; they are the rewards a group offers to its members. These rewards can be political, economic, social, or in other dimensions—anyway a person perceives he may gain from group membership.

Disruptive forces can be internal (within the group). Some internal disruptive forces are conflicts within persons that prevent them from being purely devoted to group goals. Indeed, these ambivalences probably are typical, for the gains of group membership usually are accompanied by certain costs. To get the benefit of a group a person may have to give time, money, effort, or endure the face that some group goals may conflict

---

[4]*State of Mind*, Ciba Pharmaceutical Co., Summit, N.J., 1957, p. 12.

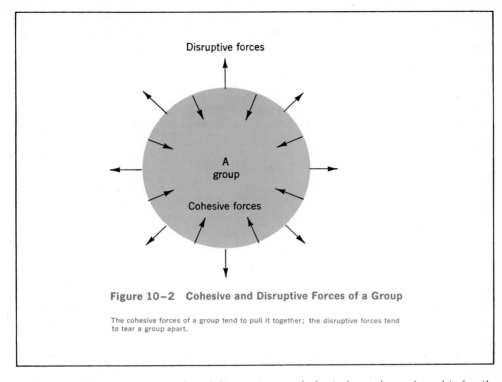

Figure 10–2   Cohesive and Disruptive Forces of a Group

The cohesive forces of a group tend to pull it together; the disruptive forces tend to tear a group apart.

with some of his own. Witness the adolescent's struggle for independence from his family group. He has powerful needs to make his own decisions, but he also may still be dependent—emotionally or otherwise—on his family. In another case, group benefits might be gained only by putting up with conflicts. For example, some management classes for a group of practicing engineers had to be discontinued simply because televised professional football games were started on the nights when the classes had been held. The conflicting objectives of members literally tore the group apart. Another form of internal disruptive forces are the personal disagreements and conflicts members often have with each other. These disagreements may be due to different expectations about group goals, activities, and behavior of members.

External disruptive forces are those that come from outside the group. A pot party may suffer from the knowledge that it might be raided by police. The same is true of a group of subversives that the government seeks to destroy. In another case, a political action group might be effectively destroyed by passage of a law that accomplished group goals. Or a business might attempt by lowering prices or improving service to run a rival out of business. The simple growing older of members of a teen-age group may disrupt the group, because of members' changing interests.

Members of highly cohesive groups tend to be relatively contented and relaxed. On the other hand, where the forces of dissension and disruption are relatively high, members tend to be anxious and insecure. This may be one way of understanding better the recent distress in many areas of American society. Regrettably, during these trying times there often has been a lack of general agreement on national (group) goals. To solve such problems, it frequently has been maintained that national leaders have intentionally involved their countries in war as a means of unifying them. For instance, it has been suggested that President Franklin D. Roosevelt chose to ignore persuasive evidence that the Japanese planned to bomb Pearl Harbor. He thought a war was inevitable, but he also saw one as a means of solving the severe internal national discords of the time.[5]

LEADERSHIP

Most groups have leaders who perform functions for the group such as defining the group, defining group objectives, setting the climate, controlling behavior, speaking for the group, and so forth. Or, in other words, the leader (manager) performs the managerial functions of creating, planning, organizing, motivating, communicating, and controlling. The leader of formal groups is formally appointed and recognized. Leaders of informal groups emerge, are not formally recognized, and may change without formal procedure.

Attempts often have been made to specify the qualities of a good leader. This is sometimes called the "attribute," or "boy scout," approach: a leader is loyal, brave, trustworthy, clean, and kind. Unfortunately this approach has little merit; it now is recognized that good leaders use a variety of techniques and styles. The qualities required for a good leader depend upon the specific group's objectives and values, the resources available, and the requirements of the environment. A withdrawn, unsociable, or self-absorbed person does not usually become a leader. However, in some cases even the shyest, most cynical, or most self-centered person may put forth extra effort to become a leader, especially if by so doing he reaches important personal goals. Successful leadership also depends upon the situation: a highly sophisticated union president once expressed amazement at his lack of authority on a picket line. He was accepted as leader when calm, deliberate discussion and negotiation were called for, but the group wanted an entirely different type of leader when emotions were high on the picket line.

The success of a leader from his group's viewpoint depends upon the extent to which he is able to lead the group so as to accomplish members' individual objectives, or needs. To illustrate, Figure 10-3 gives a comparison between weak and strong supervisors according to their reactions to employees' needs. To maintain his leadership position a strong supervisor also must emphasize accomplishing group goals.

INDUSTRIAL GROUPS

A study of work groups examined work records, held interviews, and observed 300 work groups in 30 plants in a variety of industries. Four general work-group types were identified with these characteristics:[6]

[5]Cf. George Morgenstern, *Pearl Harbor,* The Devin-Adair Company, Inc., New York, 1947, pp. 13–15; John T. Flynn, *The Roosevelt Myth,* rev. ed., The Devin-Adair Company, Inc., New York, 1956, pp. 171–174.

[6]Adapted from Leonard R. Sayles, *Behavior of Industrial Work Groups: Prediction and Control,* John Wiley & Sons, Inc., New York, 1958, pp. 7–40. (By permission.)

EMPLOYEE'S NEED	REACTION BY WEAK SUPERVISOR	REACTION BY STRONG SUPERVISOR
1 Need for approval	1a Governed strongly by this need himself b Reacts sternly or negatively against expression of need by subordinate	1a Recognizes that need exists b Is not bound by his own need for approval
2 Need for security: knowledge (knowing where he stands)	2a Ignores this need b Is so insecure— asks, "How can I tell you how you stand when I don't know how I stand?"	2a By his security lends security to subordinate b Is able to express feelings and tells employee where he stands
3 Need for security: limits (consistent discipline)	3 Is so afraid he won't be liked, cannot set limits	3a Is not concerned with approval of subordinate b Recognizes one of his primary functions is to direct—set limits
4 Need for recognition	4a Feels insecure. If he gives recognition, subordinate may surpass him b Again, own needs blind him to subordinate's needs	4a Understands this need b Gives credit where credit is due
5 Need for self-development	5a Fears competition with developing subordinates b Due to insecurity, keeps subordinates from growing	5a Helps subordinate grow b Can teach others c Can inspire confidence in others

Figure 10-3 *Comparison of Weak and Strong Supervisors according to Their Reaction to Employees' Needs.*

Strong supervisors focus on the needs of employees; weak ones do not.

SOURCE: Unknown.

1 *Apathetic groups* usually made up of low-skilled and low-paid jobs, not likely to challenge management or union decisions, grievances and pressure tactics rare, leadership not clearly defined or accepted, internal disunity and friction, evidence of suppressed discontent;

2 *Erratic groups* found chiefly where jobs are nearly identical and primarily worker controlled, large amount of worker interaction, group easily inflamed, poor pressure tactics and inconsistent behavior, quick conversion to good relationship with management, often highly centralized leadership, active in organizational phase of union;

3 *Strategic groups* hold better jobs than majority of two previous groups, high self-interest activity, heart of union and grievance activity within the respective plants, most jobs individual operations, skills identified with the ability of the individual worker to make decisions in performing his work, jobs relatively important to management and employees, high degree of internal unity, sustained union participation, relatively good production records over long run;

4 *Conservative groups* usually located at top rungs of promotional and status ladders of plant, self-assured and successful, restrained pressure for highly specific objectives (for example, if existing benefit or status threatened), individual operations, members widely distributed throughout plant, active-inactive cycles of union activity and use of grievance procedure. These and other types of groups require different managerial approaches to be most productive in a business organization.

SUMMARY

The dominant determinants of man's thinking, emotions, and activities in many, if not most situations, are his present and past group memberships. But it can be questioned whether groups really exist. Some hold that a group is no more than the individuals who belong to it. A more preferred view is that individuals are vitally important, but groups do exist because they can be identified and the important effects they have can be described.

Group membership may come through birth, application, invitation, and mutual consent. Persons seek membership because they view the group as being able to satisfy economic, social, and many other needs. Most persons are members of numerous formal and informal groups, often with overlapping memberships.

Groups can produce good or bad consequences, for they are composed of ordinary persons with all their strengths, weaknesses, triumphs, and problems.

A person usually selects groups that agree with his values. Once he becomes a member the group profoundly affects his perception, or the way he sees and understands things. The group exerts great pressure, subtly or otherwise, to conform to its norms of thinking and behavior. This pressure often is so powerful that it is a significant factor in personality development.

Typically group change is easier to bring about than individual change because of this tendency to conform. Because of their pooling of individual abilities and their tendency to stimulate members, groups often are effective decision makers and problem solvers. This ability is shown in the frequent use of committees. Through time, group norms create culture, often with varying concepts of rational behavior.

A group almost always has cohesive forces that tend to make it stay together, along with disruptive forces that work to pull it apart. The net stability of a group can be thought of as the degree to which cohesive forces exceed disruptive ones.

Group leaders have no universally common attributes. Almost any type of person can be an effective leader, depending upon the circumstances, persons involved, and group objectives. Many types of groups exist; four that have been identified in industry include apathetic, erratic, strategic, and conservative.

The study of human behavior in groups is indeed complex, and much remains to be learned. Fortunately, however, much knowledge already is available that can improve one's understanding of and participation in groups.

FOR REVIEW AND DISCUSSION

1 What is rational behavior? How do groups affect culture?

2 How do a person's attitudes and biases determine which groups he will join? How do the values of a group affect the values of an individual?

3 Describe the effect of groups on a person's self-concept, as explained in the text. Test this idea on three friends by noting their answers to the question, "Who am I?" (Write the question on a sheet of paper and hand it to each friend. In the question "I" refers to the person answering the question.)

4 Explain the statement: "One wishes to belong, but at the same time he also wishes to differentiate himself and to proclaim his individuality." Include some examples in your discussion to illustrate the problems involved.

5 How do groups affect a person's perception of reality? Illustrate your answer with an example from your own experience.

6 Suppose a person is a member of a work group and that the manager of the group wishes to make some changes that affect the group. Is it likely to be easier to change the group as a whole, or an individual member separately? Which is likely to be more permanent, changes by an individual member or by the whole group? Is a group decision likely to be more readily accepted by an individual if he participated in making the decision? Fully explain your answers.

7 Describe in your own words apathetic, erratic, strategic, and conservative groups. (These classifications are not necessarily restricted to industrial groups, but may also be found in other parts of society.) Give an example not in the text to illustrate each type.

8 In what ways are groups superior to individuals for problem solving?

9 Describe the qualities found in group leaders.

10 Explain the statement: "Every group member has forces that encourage him to quit the group. He must continually evaluate for himself which set of forces is greater." Include in your discussion some examples from your own experience.

11 Summarize the reasons for the positions or assumptions that groups do or do not exist. Which position seems best to you? Why?

12 What are the ways through which group membership is attained? Give a one sentence explanation of why a person joins or remains a member of a group. Explain with examples from your own experience the fact that many groups have overlapping memberships.

13 Explain how cohesive and disruptive forces affect group stability.

14 How can groups positively and negatively affect one's productivity? the whole group's productivity? Use examples from your experiences.

CASES

A Modern Chemicals had a large and complex organization. For years the policy of the company had been to select outstanding managers or other employees and to send them individually to outside educational and training programs. However, the company had seriously questioned the merit of this policy. According to one top executive: "The men come back from the programs all fired-up, but a month later they are right back in the same old rut. I wonder if we're getting our money's worth."

Mr. Goodrich, the president, was considering a proposal from his training director that would require all or none of a particular group or class of employees to attend any proposed training program.

> **1** Upon what bit of knowledge about individuals and groups is the training director basing his proposal?
>
> **2** Should Mr. Goodrich adopt the new policy proposed by the training director? What are the advantages and disadvantages of the proposal?

B Millard Certs had always been known as a highly individualistic person. For many years he had refused to accept government subsidies for the small farm on which he had lived all his life.

The Whizzer Bicycle Company had recently started a manufacturing facility in Newberg, a small town 5 miles from Millard's farm. With his new tractor Millard found that he could work his farm after hours and also hold a job with Whizzer. He was employed in the bicycle assembly department four weeks after the plant had started full production.

Millard, who believed he owed his best work to his new employer, worked very effectively and soon was assembling over fifty bicycles each day. The average for the other workers in the department was thirty.

On Friday of his first week John Barnes, who was also an assemblyman, said to Millard, "Look, Millard, you're working too hard. In this department we have all agreed that we will assemble thirty bicycles each day. If you're going to stay here, you had better get in line."

"John, nobody except the boss is going to tell me how to do my work."

"Well, this is your first and last warning. We mean what we say."

1 Is Millard or John likely to win the argument? Why?

2 What group purpose is served by the group's agreement to assemble only thirty bicycles per day? Why is it so difficult for the company to break up such an arrangement?

3 What methods might the group use to persuade Millard to come to terms?

C John and James Stevens were identical twins whose parents had been killed in an accident shortly after their birth. After the accident John was taken to live with his Aunt Susan and Uncle Raymond in the United States. Both Susan and Raymond were vigorous supporters of capitalism.

James, on the other hand, was taken by his Aunt Freda and Uncle Simon to live with them in Russia. Freda and Simon firmly believed that communism provided the best political and economic system.

The twins did not meet again until they were over twenty years old. They quickly got into a political discussion. John argued that capitalism was superior, and James just as loudly proclaimed that communism was better.

1 Were John's and James's political views arrived at purely by accident? Why?

2 What effect did environment and group experiences have on the development of each of the brothers' beliefs?

D The first day of class of a new semester Professor Ricks met his doctoral-level organization theory class in Hines Hall, Room 231. At the beginning of the class he announced that the class would move to a more comfortable seminar room, Library 151. He wrote the new room on the board and walked out to go to it, followed by his fourteen students.

In the foyer of the Library Building, while walking and chatting with several of the students, he looked back and saw a group of his students, absorbed in conversation, following Mr. Blandon, also one of the students in the class. Mr. Blandon led about eight students down the stairs into the basement of the building. Mr. Blandon and every student following him knew the Library Building intimately, including the fact that all rooms numbered 100 to 199 were on the first floor, not in the basement.

Several minutes later the wayward group showed up in Room 151. Professor Ricks said that they had just demonstrated a fundamental principle of leadership—that is, "a leader does not have to be right to be followed. He only needs to give others the impression that he knows what he is doing." A stimulating discussion of leadership in organizations followed.

1 Why do you think the students followed Mr. Blandon?

2 Do you agree with Professor Ricks that a leader does not necessarily have to be correct to be followed? Illustrate your answer with examples from your own experience.

FOR FURTHER STUDY

Additional sources can be found in the sources cited in the chapter.

Books

Chris Argyris: *Personnel Practice and Policy: The Changing Picture,* American Management Association, Personnel Series, no. 168, New York, 1956, pp. 3–11. "Research suggests very clearly that the first task we must undertake is to create that kind of leadership which . . . can help people become more independent, more active, and more responsible."

Articles

Dorwin Cartwright and Ronald Lippitt: "Group Dynamics and the Individual, " *International Journal of Group Psychotherapy,* January 1957, pp. 86–102. A valuable examination of the effects of individuals on groups and of groups on individuals.

Jerry S. Cloyd: "Patterns of Role Behavior in Informal Interaction," *Sociometry,* November 1964. Patterns of role behavior are a series of configurations abstracted from role structures of small groups. The patterns are simply contexts of associated expectations which cut across the allocation of behavior to individual roles or types of roles.

James S. Davie and A. Paul Hare: "Button-Down Collar Culture," *Human Organization,* vol. 14, 1956, pp. 13–20. A highly readable report of behavioral norms for a group of undergraduate Ivy League students.

Charles A. Kiesler: "Attraction to the Group and Conformity to Group Norms," *Journal of Personality,* December 1963. Attraction to the group decreases when the individual has a disconfirmed experience and varies directly with the level of acceptance of the individual by the group.

Irving Knickerbocker: "Leadership: A Conception and Some Implications," *Journal of Social Issues,* Summer 1948. A clear presentation of the role of and characteristics of leaders in all types of organizations.

Stanley Milgram: "Group Pressure and Action against a Person," *Journal of Abnormal and Social Psychology,* August 1964. Tests and demonstrations show that group influence can shape behavior in a domain that might have been thought highly resistible to such effects.

Edgar H. Schein: "Organizational Socialization and the Profession of Management," *Industrial Management Review,* Winter 1968. Organizational socialization is the process by which a new member learns and adapts to the values, norms, and required behavioral patterns of an organization.

Edward A. Shils and Morris Janowitz: "Cohesion and Disintegration in the Wehrmacht in World War II," *Public Opinion Quarterly,* Summer 1948. An interesting, penetrating analysis of social factors contributing to the solidarity of the German army in World War II.

Alvin Zander and Herman Medow: "Individual and Group Levels of Aspiration," *Human Relations,* February 1963. Selection of a level of aspiration for a group can be explained in terms ordinarily used for explaining the selection of a level of aspiration by an individual.

11
Interorganizational Behavior

Organizations are embedded in an environment of other organizations.
    WILLIAM M. EVAN

From time immemorial, relations between groups or organizations—expressed in war and peace, domination and slavery, conflict and harmony—have been vital human affairs. Modern society's problems of intergroup behavior or relationships seem more acute than ever. Indeed, sometimes one wonders if man will survive it all. Conflicts between governments; labor and management; and ethnic, religious, and other groups with different ideologies or ways of life are causes of grave misfortune for billions of persons.

In a more positive view, organizations interact for mutual benefit in countless instances and ways. It is easy to forget the benefits of organizational interaction if the problems of such interactions are overemphasized.

Regrettably, little analysis of interorganizational behavior has been done; organizational studies have tended to focus on problems within organizations. However, it is encouraging that in recent years increasing emphasis has been given to interorganizational relationships. Progress is sorely needed in this area, for every organization, no matter how weak or how powerful, depends on or interacts with others. No organization functions as a closed, independent system; all organizations are interdependent. The concern with pollution and other aspects of ecology has emphasized this interdependence, which likely will become greater as society becomes more complex. More effort, knowledge, and wisdom will be required to maintain satisfactory relationships among organizations.

Previous chapters in this part have examined the individual, relationships between persons, and individual-group relationships. The present chapter's unit of analysis is the relationship between two or more organizations. Even at this level of analysis it often is helpful to recall that, in the final analysis, it always is individuals who act and interact within organizations. Thus, the material already presented in this part is relevant in studying the interaction of organizations. The reader is requested to bear this previous material in mind when studying interorganizational behavior.

COMPLEXITY OF INTERACTION OF ORGANIZATIONS

As noted above, behavior in organizations can be studied on several levels. The unit of analysis can range from the individual to the relationships of organizations with each other. Organizational relationships range from simple to extremely complex ones.

Simple Organizational Interaction

Simple organizational interaction is the interrelationship that occurs when organizations that otherwise are unrelated deal with each other. In one type of simple interaction two (or more) informal (without a hierarchy) organizations have a relationship. For example, a group of men students living in a dormitory spontaneously decided to have a party. One of them called up a friend in a women's dormitory who provided dates for all the men. The relationship of these groups is shown in Figure 11-1a. Another type of simple interaction occurs when two companies, otherwise unrelated, deal with each other on a business matter. For example, Foster Products may purchase some floor wax from Real-Klean, Inc. Mr. Richeau, building custodian of Foster Products, simply stopped by Real-Klean's store, picked up the wax, and paid for it out of his petty cash fund. This transaction is shown as Figure 11-1b.

Complex Organizational Interaction

A complex interaction is one that is affected by additional organizational relationships. A typical complex interaction involves the organizational hierarchy of one or more of the participating organizations. Complex interactions may be vertical, horizontal, or diagonal. Examples of complex interactions are shown in Figure 11-2.

In Figure 11-2, interaction A, a vertical one, may have concerned the budget of the shown manufacturing department. The vertical organizational relationship probably

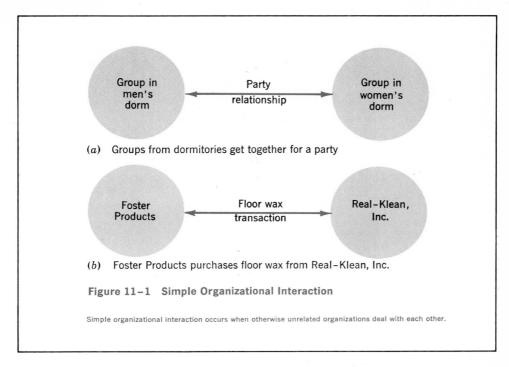

(a)   Groups from dormitories get together for a party

(b)   Foster Products purchases floor wax from Real–Klean, Inc.

Figure 11–1   Simple Organizational Interaction

Simple organizational interaction occurs when otherwise unrelated organizations deal with each other.

heavily influenced the interaction. Interaction B, the manufacturing department with a forging department, may have been about the manufacturing department needing to know a new, tricky forging process. These departments are on the same organizational level, which probably affected their relationship. Interaction C, the manufacturing department with the controller's office, may have concerned some excessive manufacturing costs the controller's office wished to bring under control. This interaction is a diagonal one, involving organizations on different levels that do not have a direct vertical relationship. Interactions A, B, and C also are personal ones for the participants; previous chapters in this part have analyzed some of these additional dimensions.

It is practically impossible to adequately describe the complexity of organizational interactions. Even within a complex organization many organizational interactions occur among component parts. There are organizations within organizations, within organizations, within organizations, and so on. All can interact with each other and with outside organizations. Because the interests of an organization tend to differ from the interests of another organization, problems of interaction are typical. This is true even among units of a large organization. A frequent consequence is suboptimization, where an organization in pursuing its interests may not maximize its contribution to the larger organization of which it is a part.

The above description of some of a manufacturing department's relationships barely scratched the surface of the countless dealings organizations have with each other. In

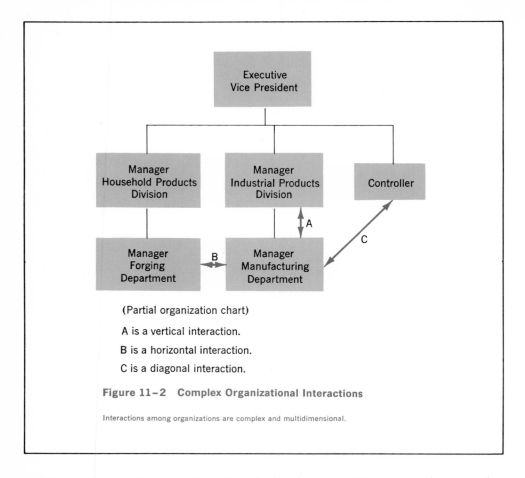

(Partial organization chart)

A is a vertical interaction.

B is a horizontal interaction.

C is a diagonal interaction.

Figure 11–2   Complex Organizational Interactions

Interactions among organizations are complex and multidimensional.

addition to the specific interactions described, a department interacts with many other organizations in the company in numerous other vertical, horizontal, and diagonal relationships. Also, this department may have many relationships with other organizations outside the company.

The example in Figure 11-2 involved a business organization, but similar countless, multidimensional organizational interactions occur among governmental, educational, social, and other kinds of organizations. Analyzing and improving these countless organizational contacts or interfaces provide a great challenge.

COOPERATION AND COMPETITION OF ORGANIZATIONS

The question often is asked: Is man inherently (naturally) cooperative or competitive? The best answer seems to be: he is both. This answer may be somewhat surprising in view of numerous attempts to label man as inherently good (which usually seems to mean cooperative) or bad (competitive). Yet the best evidence of biology, ecology, and the social sciences seems to indicate that man is likely to be cooperative in situations where he views cooperation to be to his advantage. Similarly, he tends to be competitive if he thinks competition will be advantageous.

A similar question can be asked about organizations: Are organizations inherently cooperative or competitive? Again the best answer seems to be: both. Some of the almost unlimited interactions of organizations are cooperative; others are competitive. And cooperation and competition for an organization can exist at the same time. For example, the basketball teams of Ivy and City Colleges may compete at a game, shown as interaction D of Figure 11-3. At the same game, Ivy's team may have interaction E, a cooperative one, with Ivy's band. At another level Ivy and City can be said to have a cooperative-competitive relationship, shown as interaction F. The colleges cooperate in having the game in such matters as time, place, and other conditions. Also, the colleges may cooperate as members of the same league, but their relationship may have competitive elements if they disagree about certain league policies.

More generally, perhaps almost all organizational relationships can be described as

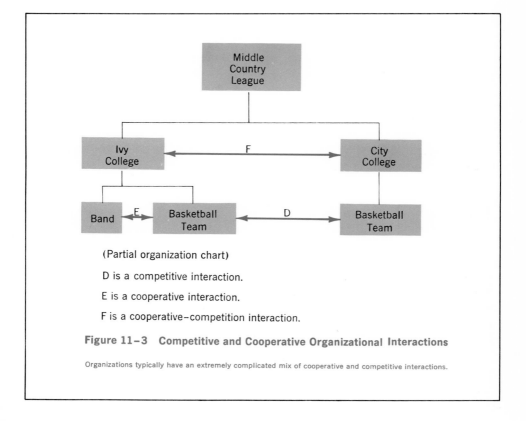

(Partial organization chart)

D is a competitive interaction.

E is a cooperative interaction.

F is a cooperative–competition interaction.

Figure 11–3   Competitive and Cooperative Organizational Interactions

Organizations typically have an extremely complicated mix of cooperative and competitive interactions.

cooperative-competitive ones. Even nations competing with each other in war typically cooperate on such matters as treatment of prisoners, limitation of too dangerous weapons, and so on. More friendly cooperative competition is seen among business firms that vigorously compete for larger market shares. At the same time they may cooperate (perhaps passively) in observing the same rules of operation—laws, ethics, and so on. The basketball teams mentioned above also may cooperate in many ways even though their basic interaction is competitive. They obey the game officials—sometimes reluctantly—share emergency medical facilities, if needed, and so forth.

A typical pattern is internal cooperation (within the organization) and external competition (with other organizations) of organizations. However, even this generalization often is not accurate, for within a basketball team competition exists among members for positions. In like manner, the divisions of General Motors Corporation compete with each other in many ways, while cooperating in others.

Thus, organizations have extremely complicated webs of cooperative competition or competitive cooperation in their interactions. Both cooperation and competition seem equally natural because elements of each are found in most organizational interactions. The interactions of nations with each other, states with nations, company divisions, a parent-teachers association with a school board, and businesses with each other give an almost infinite number of mixes of cooperation and competition.

Some cooperation is necessary to accomplish organizational goals. Not so clearly recognized is the fact that competition (perhaps at some other levels) can contribute to organizational goals (perhaps also at other levels). For example, competition may be a factor that causes an organization to renew itself. Also, competition among members or subunits may be a powerful motivator to work toward objectives of higher levels. Witness the numerous contests companies have for salesmen or divisions to get them to try to outdo each other. Competition in sports also is valuable because spectators enjoy watching it. And at least the winners gain prestige from it. Competition, like cooperation, can produce good or evil, depending upon its perceived effect upon its evaluator.

INCREASING COOPERATION OF ORGANIZATIONS

Increased cooperation of organizations generally produces gains in organizational productivity and effectiveness. Recalling a previously explained concept, the very essence of an organization is that persons interacting in the organization do so because they expect the organization to provide values they otherwise might not have. A parallel concept operates in regard to organizational cooperation. That is, when organizations engage in cooperative interaction, they have the potential of creating values. Vertical interaction—when a subunit of an organization interacts with a higher, larger unit of which the subunit is a part—can produce such values. Horizontal interaction—when an organization interacts with another on its level—also can produce values. Diagonal organizational interactions have the same potential. Indeed, just as for individual persons, all types of interactions of organizations have the potential for productivity.

Is Cooperation Desirable?

Although increased cooperation of organizations generally seems desirable, for some organizations at some times conflict or competition may be preferable. For example, subunits of a larger organization may benefit both the larger organization and themselves by competing with each other for higher productivity. The several campuses of a statewide university system could exhibit such healthy conflict. This sort of competition within broader cooperation potentially can benefit all participating organizations.

In another type of conflict, one organization gains at the expense of another. The winner may have more at the end of the conflict than before. For instance, at the end of a war the victorious nation may have increased its territory. The war could have been valuable to it if its gains were more than its costs. Similarly, in some respects a winning team may gain at the expense of the loser. Also, union-management relationships often seem to have such characteristics. This type of conflict with an outside organization often has the additional advantage of providing internal unity in each of the conflicting organizations. An adroit leader thus may encourage external conflict to solve internal problems of his organization.

Sometimes the advantages of conflict may be more subtle. One author, for instance, argued that society could benefit from riots, crowding in cities, and other conflicts that result in lower birth rates.[1] He argued that such population controls were needed if the older ones of war and disease no longer are sufficient. Conflict also can excite and interest members of an organization so much that the organization may be extraordinarily creative in solving its problems.

Thus, there are several reasons for conflict of organizations. First, conflict as competition can be a powerful motivator and incentive for creativity. Second, competition for limited land, money, markets, or other resources can produce conflict. Third, conflict can be enjoyable to watch and it can give prestige to the winner, as in competitive sports. Fourth, sometimes personal gain may result from promoting conflict. Hitler, who promoted World War II, may be an example of this. Fifth, the "we-feeling" of groups, that prejudices members in favor of their group and against outside groups, causes conflict of the groups.

Utopians often seem to argue that the most desirable condition of organizations (and individuals) is one of perfect harmony and cooperation. That line of reasoning collides head on with the fact that conflict often is to an organization's advantage. So long as there are advantages of conflict, it likely will exist. Whether conflict is desirable or not must be judged in terms of its results for the particular organization, situation, and persons concerned.

To summarize, competition or other forms of conflict often are functional for organizations and individuals. Granted this, the more generally desired objective is to increase cooperation of organizations. At least it seems desirable to make conflict more constructive. The remainder of this chapter assumes that increased cooperation is desirable,

[1]Robert Ardrey, "Control of Population," *Life*, Feb. 20, 1970, pp. 48–61.

and ways of achieving this goal are explored. However, as this material is studied, the advantages of conflict in numerous situations should be remembered.

Methods of Conflict Resolution

One of man's most persistent interests has been to find ways of reducing conflict—or increasing cooperation—of organizations. The assumption is that increasing organizational cooperation makes organizations more productive, or at least more pleasant.

Many measures to combat the problems of intergroup conflict have been proposed by social scientists, managers, politicians, and educators. Included are legal sanctions, creation of social and other contacts between members of conflicting groups, and the dissemination of correct information to break down false prejudices and unfavorable stereotypes. Other measures have appealed to ideals of fair play and brotherhood. Also, vigorous physical activity to reduce tensions, pent-up frustrations, and aggression has been used. Further measures have encouraged participation in community activities. Also, leaders of antagonistic groups have been brought together in the intimate atmosphere of the conference room. Measures such as improving communication, certain leadership approaches, and provision of superordinate goals are particularly relevant for managerial use.

Communication   An experiment studied communication between groups.[2] High- and low-status groups were established by favoring the "highs" and discriminating against the "lows." The effects of this treatment upon communications between the groups of the different status levels were observed. As the discrimination in favor of the high-status groups proceeded, the amount of communication the lows addressed to the highs increased. The study suggested the possibility that low-status persons may desire communication with higher-status persons as a substitute for belonging to a higher group.

Another study analyzed the direction—whether upward or downward—in which planted rumors were transmitted within an organization.[3] The findings suggested strong tendencies to communicate upward. This too was thought to indicate the value of communication as a substitute for mobility into higher levels. There also were indications of strong resistance by persons at higher levels to communicate with those of lower levels.

The two studies just cited suggested the broader theoretical focus for a third, more extensive study by Kelley.[4] In it the communication output of group members in high- and low-status positions was analyzed. Both the conditions of possible and no possible movement between levels were studied. The findings can be summarized:

[2]J. W. Thibaut, "An Experimental Study of the Cohesiveness of Underprivileged Groups," *Human Relations,* 1950, p. 252.

[3]K. Bach et al., "The Methodology of Rumor Transmission," *Human Relations,* 1950, pp. 307–312.

[4]H. H. Kelley, "Communications in Experimentally Created Hierarchies," *Human Relations,* 1951, pp. 39–56.

1 The more unpleasant a person's position in an organization, the more he desires to communicate his feelings about his work. This holds true whether the communication is directed at members on his own level or those of another level. Just talking apparently helps the occupant of an undesirable position relieve his feelings about it.

2 High-status persons tend to refrain from criticizing their jobs to lower-status persons and from expressing confusion about their work. In other words, there is a general tendency to withhold information which would lower a person's status in the eyes of others or which would make him appear incompetent in his high-status position.

3 The existence of a hierarchy produces restraint against criticism of persons at a higher level. Conversely, high status seems to give persons freedom to express whatever criticism they have of lower-status persons directly to the criticized persons.

4 Low-nonmobile and high-mobile conditions are relatively detrimental to the total group's cohesiveness. Apparently hostility results from a person's perceiving individuals at another level either as threats to his own desirable position or as occupants of a coveted but unattainable position.

The fourth finding may explain why recent moves toward equality in several dimensions of American society sometimes appear to produce more—not less—hostility. The hostility can be expected to continue until a new stable relationship among groups is reached. Also, some more recent studies have suggested that a low-status group may become more hostile to a higher group when the lower group gets closer to the higher group. Apparently, when groups are widely separated with little or no communication, there tends to be little overt hostility between them. But when they get closer and communicate more, greater hostility—at least temporarily—may exist.

Thus, communication, particularly if it is honest and complete, can improve relationships of organizations. Indeed, it is tautological that improvement cannot occur without communication. However, since communication can make a group more aware of its unfavorable position, it can increase conflict if it acts upon this new awareness. But, after the awareness has been gained, additional positively oriented communication often can produce final resolution of the conflict.

Leadership approaches   "There are three ways of settling differences: by domination, by compromise, or by integration."[5] Mary Parker Follett wrote this in a classic paper of 1933. Later Herbert Shepard paralleled Follett when he described suppression, bargaining, and problem solving as ways of solving conflict.[6] Figure 11-4 shows the bases and results of these three solutions to conflict.

Domination, or all-out war, occurs when one party of a dispute—through its rela-

[5]Mary Parker Follett, in Harold F. Merrill (ed.), *Classics in Management,* American Management Association, New York, 1960, p. 341. These leadership approaches are presented here as ways of resolving conflict between organizations. They are equally valid for resolving conflict between individuals and between an individual and an organization.

[6]Herbert Shepard, "Ways of Dealing with Conflict in Organizations" (motion picture film), University of California Extension Media Center, Berkeley, Calif., ca. 1965.

CONFLICT RESOLUTION APPROACH	BASIS	RESULT
Domination	Large power of one party; other party has little power	Victory of one party; submission of other
Compromise	Significant power held by each party	Each party gives up something valuable
Integration	Mutual desire to achieve completely satisfactory solution	Both parties completely satisfied

Figure 11-4 *Ways of Resolving Conflict*

Conflicts can be settled by domination, compromise, and integration.

tively great power—forces its solution on the other. It is a victory for the winning side. However, the solution is likely to be unsatisfactory for the losing side, which will await its turn to dominate, if it can. In a business organization domination occurs if the president orders the manager of the manufacturing department to implement a policy with which he does not agree. Frequently, domination manipulates and exploits individuals or groups.

Compromise, the second way, often is praised because of its advantages over domination. However, in compromise—often through a bargaining procedure—both sides give up something to secure a settlement. Both sides likely are less than totally satisfied with the solution. As Follett pointed out, domination gives one side what it wants; compromise pleases neither. Often compromise is used to determine how to divide a given "pie." A strike compromised by union and management often has this characteristic. The problem is that often little or no attention is given in a compromise to making a bigger or better pie.

The third way, integration, seeks a solution every side finds completely acceptable —where no sacrifice is made by anyone. Integration seeks to get out of the either-or trap of domination and the frequent static condition of compromise. Instead of both sides focusing on "my way instead of your way," a third way, completely satisfactory to all, is sought. A simple example of integration occurred in a business. The sales manager told the manufacturing manager that twice as much could be sold if he could reduce the price 20 percent, based on reduced costs of manufacturing; the manufacturing manager resisted, saying he could cut costs only by lowering quality. Both men discussed the matter at great length. Eventually they modified the product. The modification was just as good, but it could be produced for 30 percent less. They then had a solution better than the original for both departments. Thus, integration as a problem-solving objective often gives creative solutions that are favored by all. Frequently, integrative resolutions are breakthroughs to totally new solutions. Dramatic breakthroughs seldom, if ever, are achieved by domination or compromise.

Superordinate goals   A landmark study to define and analyze intergroup conflict was undertaken by Muzafer and Carolyn Sherif.[7] An important finding was the high effectiveness of superordinate goals in reducing intergroup friction. A later study by the Sherifs further tested the use of superordinate goals in group conflict.[8]

Groups were formed by the Sherifs, conditions conducive to conflict were introduced, and relations between them were studied. First, situations were introduced in which one group could achieve its goal only at the expense of another group. These situations included competitive events with desirable prizes for the winning group. Members of the group developed highly unfavorable and hostile attitudes toward the other group and its members. Social distance between the groups became so great that members of one group wanted nothing to do with members of another group.

At the same time intragroup solidarity and cooperation increased. This finding suggested that cooperation and democracy *within* groups do not necessarily lead to democracy and cooperation *among* groups if the interests of the groups conflict. For example, cooperation within a team may be at a peak at the same time there is great rivalry with other teams. Members are bound to each other, but they may have hostile feelings for members of rival teams.

Effect of contact   Social contact of members of antagonistic groups in activities that were satisfying to all them was used by the Sherifs in attempting to reduce the established intergroup conflict. Eating and watching movies together along with other entertainment activities where members were physically close together were used. These activities, which were satisfying to each group but did not involve interdependence and cooperation among groups for the attainment of goals, were not effective in reducing intergroup tension. On the contrary, contact between groups frequently resulted in name calling and even physical abuse.

Contact of group leaders also did not always reduce conflict. It was suggested that moves of leaders may be rejected by a group if the members think the moves are ill advised. The leader may even be subjected to severe criticism or loss of status in his group for trying to reduce conflict of his group with another group.

Perhaps the different ethnic groups who often live close together in large cities are examples of conflict where physical closeness exists. Just because groups live together does not mean they are willing to cooperate.

Effect of superordinate goals   After establishing the ineffectiveness, perhaps even the harm, of simple intergroup contacts, a series of superordinate goals was introduced. The situations were varied, but all had an essential feature—goals that could not be at-

---

[7]Muzafer Sherif and Carolyn W. Sherif, *Groups in Harmony and Tension,* Harper & Row, Publishers, Incorporated, New York, 1953.

[8]Muzafer Sherif and Carolyn W. Sherif, *An Outline of Social Psychology,* rev. ed., Harper & Row Publishers, Incorporated, New York, 1956, chap. 9.

tained by any group alone. Thus, it was necessary for groups to work together to accomplish these superordinate goals. Thereby interdependence among groups was created.

One problem involved obtaining necessary water for drinking, which could be obtained only by intergroup cooperation. Another problem involved getting food. Everyone was hungry, and food was at a distance. It could be obtained only if the groups cooperated by putting a truck in working order. The groups worked effectively together to reach these superordinate objectives.

Formerly hostile groups cooperated to reach superordinate goals. They carried on discussion and made combined decisions where needed. Working together on several superordinate goals gave more lasting reduction of intergroup conflict than cooperation on only one goal.

If cooperation was effective in accomplishing one superordinate goal, it was extended to related activities. The occasional member who preferred intergroup conflict found it more and more difficult to be heard in his primary group. Moreover, actions previously judged only in terms of intragroup values now were evaluated relative to other groups as well. Even the proprietary pride in a place, technique, or tool that is "ours" became modified in cooperation toward superordinate goals. Now the criterion became: How can we—even though we are members of different groups—best work together to accomplish superordinate goals. The larger group—made up of smaller groups—now became more important. This phenomenon can be witnessed in a nation where formerly competing political parties, ethnic groups, and economic interests work together to accomplish their superordinate goal of defeating an enemy nation.

Thus, the existence of superordinate goals is usually the most effective way of reducing intergroups conflict. Politicians, educators, and managers frequently put this idea into practice by providing superordinate goals for their organizations.

SUMMARY

Organizations interact with one another in countless instances in a complex society. These interactions are comparatively simple when they involve groups or organizations that otherwise are unrelated. In more complex fashion, larger groups have smaller groups within them that interact with each other, the larger organization, and outside groups. Vertical, horizontal, and diagonal relationships are involved in these complex, multidimensional interactions.

Both competitive and cooperative relationships of groups are typical. In a complex organization competition may exist between groups at certain levels at the same time cooperation exists at other levels. Most relationships contain elements of both competition and cooperation.

The advantages of cooperation often are well understood. Not so well appreciated are advantages of competition, including motivation, contributions to organizational viability, inherent interest in the competitive struggle, and so forth. Cooperation on broader levels is advantageous in most situations, but at lower levels competition may be desired. In competition one group sometimes gains at the expense of another. Frequently both gain from the competition.

Communication is necessary for cooperation of groups; increased cooperation requires effective communication. Yet, communication can increase conflict if it makes a group more aware of its grievances. Such awareness offers the opportunity for resolution of the conflict, however.

Contact of members of hostile groups sometimes reduces conflict of groups. However, contact may increase conflict, particularly if superordinate goals of the groups are absent. Very frequently, cooperation of groups is increased in the presence of superordinate goals. When groups work together in an interdependent relationship, lasting reduction of conflict can result. Communication and contact as means of increasing cooperation become much more effective in the context of superordinate goals. An effective leader often recognizes that he can make his groups more cooperative by providing superordinate goals. "Let's work together," he may say, "toward something we all want."

FOR REVIEW AND DISCUSSION

1 Explain simple and complex interactions of organizations. Include an example from your own experience of vertical, horizontal, and diagonal interactions.

2 Is competition more natural than cooperation? Explain your answer with examples from your own experience.

3 Explain, using examples, how competitive organizational relationships can exist within a generally cooperative broader relationship. Also show how cooperation can exist within a broader competitive relationship.

4 Explain, using examples, the advantages of competitive relationships of organizations.

5 Explain, using examples, three leadership approaches for resolving conflict.

6 Do high- and low-status groups communicate easily with each other? In your own words summarize Kelley's findings about communication between such groups.

7 How effective are communication, contact, and superordinate goals in reducing conflict of groups? Explain your answer.

8 What are superordinate goals? Is every organizational goal a superordinate goal? Explain.

9 Explain how pride in one's group can contribute to conflict among groups.

CASES

A Mr. Canzerio moved his woodworking plant to a small town to escape the high wages and union bosses of the city. He selected Coville because of its plentiful supply of inexpensive labor.

Most of the people who lived around Coville were descendants of immigrants from an Eastern European country. They were extremely clannish and suspicious of outsiders.

Shortly after opening his new plant Mr. Canzerio verbally reprimanded Mr. Stober before all the workers in the plant for not being more safety conscious. Fifteen minutes later there was no one in the plant—all the workers had left and gone home.

Later Mr. Canzerio found that Mr. Stober was one of Coville's leading citizens; he was an elder of the clan. Mr. Canzerio learned indirectly that he could not expect to start any work again in the plant until he had settled his differences with Mr. Stober.

    1 What are the special problems that Mr. Canzerio has in dealing with his new workers?

    2 How might Mr. Canzerio have prevented or reduced his problems?

    3 What action should Mr. Canzerio now take?

    B   Throughout its history, Junction City had been plagued by the spring floods of the Miles River. A levee had reduced the problem, but each year during high water a levee watch had to be maintained. When a break began in the levee, sandbags had to be thrown quickly over the leak if the town was to avoid a flood.

The population of the town consisted mainly of two distinct ethnic groups. There had been many cases of squabbles and conflict between the two groups. The only time the two groups worked effectively together was when a flood threatened.

    1 Why did the groups work well together in the flood season but not at other times?

    2 What measures would you take if you were the mayor of Junction City and wished to reduce tension between the groups?

    C   Peerless Foundry, Inc., had a policy that the company would not pay an employee for the first day he was away from work on sick leave. Normal sick pay began on the second day of absence. The company found that the policy was highly successful in reducing absenteeism.

There were twenty-seven workers in the casting department. Members of this department had been very close for many years. They loudly proclaimed that they were the best department in the company. Recently, they pooled their resources and bought a camp on a river for fishing and hunting. The camp was large enough for three families, and any member of the department could use it for himself or his family on a first-come, first-served reservation basis. Recently the president of the camping club, Jerry Noe, came to the production manager with a proposal.

"Mr. Donner, we can see why the company decided not to pay for the first day of sick leave. A lot of people had abused the old policy that paid from the very first day. But I am sure you will agree that this was not true of the casting department. We have never let anyone stay in the department who was taking advantage of his sick leave. Every man in our group pulls his weight."

"Yes, Jerry, I agree with everything you've said."

"What we want to do, Mr. Donner, is for one of us who is regularly off for the day to come in and work free for one of our bunch who gets sick. We'll work out the details. That way the company could go ahead and pay the sick man from the first day. It sure hurts to lose a day's pay when you're sick."

"Gee, I don't know, Jerry. I'll have to think about it."

1 What should Mr. Donner do? Why?

2 If Mr. Donner accepts Jerry's proposal, how will this affect the other parts of the organization?

3 If Mr. Donner rejects Jerry's proposal, what effect will this have on the members of the casting department?

D   Modern Company, which produced a wide variety of consumer and industrial products, employed almost 500,000 persons. The company was divided into twenty-three divisions, each headed by a vice-president.

Modern's policy was that all operating decisions were made at the divisional or lower levels, subject only to broad company policies and legal requirements. The president, Mr. Barr, and his headquarters staff tried to restrict themselves to setting broad policies, overall financial management, and evaluation of each division's performance.

Each division was a "profit center," and a division was evaluated primarily on the amount it contributed to the overall profit of the company. "We operate on the principle that insofar as possible each divisional vice-president is running his own company," said Mr. Barr. "Within broad limits he can do whatever he likes. We think he is the man who knows best how his division can contribute most to the welfare of Modern."

The base salary of each divisional vice-president was $35,000, which was extremely low when compared with positions of similar responsibility in other firms. However, Modern also had a bonus fund each year for the vice-presidents. The total amount in this fund was based on overall company profits for the year. The fund was divided among the divisional vice-presidents in proportion to the percentage each division contributed to "extra" company profits. Normal profit for each division was to be 10 percent of its capital investment. Anything above this 10 percent was considered to be "extra" profit, which was considered in determining bonuses. When a division had a successful year its vice-president might earn a bonus of more than $100,000. Vice-presidents earning no or low bonuses were encouraged to seek employment elsewhere. "We aren't running a welfare system here," Mr. Barr said. "We want above average profit performance from every vice-president. We think our bonus fund for them helps to get it."

1 Describe the competitive and cooperative patterns of interaction among Modern's organizations.

2 How did Modern's bonus fund for its divisional vice-presidents contribute to both competitive and cooperative organizational relationships in the company?

FOR FURTHER STUDY

Additional sources can be found in the sources cited in the chapter.

Books

Alex Bavelas and George Strauss: "Group Dynamics and Intergroup Relations," in *Money and Motivation,* William F. Whyte et al. (eds.): Harper & Brothers, New York, 1955. Changes in a factory caused intergroup conflict within the organization.

D. Cartwright and A. Zander (eds.): *Group Dynamics, Research and Theory,* Harper & Row, Publishers, Incorporated, New York, 1960. A democratic society derives its strength from the effective functioning of the multitude of groups which it contains.

James C. Coleman: *Psychology and Effective Behavior,* Scott, Foresman and Company, Glenview, Ill., 1969, chap. 9. Human groups have patterns of development, function, and interaction.

John P. Dean and Alex Rosen: *A Manual of Intergroup Relations,* The University of Chicago Press, Chicago, 1955. A new profession, emerging out of the need in our time for skillful mediation of intergroup relations in our society, is just developing.

Articles

"Auto Workers Hear the Drums Again," *Time,* Sept. 28, 1970. The confrontation of two strong organizations—automobile manufacturers and the union—is described.

James W. Julian, Doyle W. Bishop, and Fred E. Fielder: "Quasi-therapeutic Effects of Intergroup Competition," *Journal of Personality and Social Psychology,* March 1966. Intergroup competition can lead to improved work relations in the group, high self-esteem, lower anxiety, and greater satisfaction with conditions of group life.

Eugene Litwak and L. F. Hylton: "Inter-Organizational Analysis: A Hypothesis on Coordinating Agencies," *Administrative Science Quarterly,* March 1962. Interorganizational analysis requires unique perspectives and models that differ radically from those used in intraorganizational analysis.

A. K. Rice: "Individual Group and Intergroup Behavior," *Human Relations,* December 1969. The leader controls transactions between a group and other groups or the environment.

John A. Seiler: "Diagnosing Interdepartmental Conflict," *Harvard Business Review,* September–October 1963. Interdepartmental conflicts, if dealt with properly, can be made to stimulate productive competition within the organization.

Daniel A. Wren: "Interface and Interorganizational Coordination," *Academy of Management Journal,* March 1967. Organizations interact with each other at their contact point or interface.

III
Functions
of Management

12

The Functions of Managers— An Overview

"We're all seamen here, I should hope," said young Dick. "We're all fo'c'sle hands you mean," replied Long John Silver. "We can sail a course, but who's to set it?"
ROBERT LOUIS STEVENSON

The manager has the task of creating a true whole that is larger than the sum of its parts, a productive entity that turns out more than the sum of the resources put into it.
PETER F. DRUCKER

Organizations, either formal or informal, without managers probably will dissipate members' energies and other resources in random activity. Effective management, on the other hand, leads to purposeful, coordinated, goal-directed activity.

The crucial importance of management was recognized by a leading stockbroker with the comment: "Many experts view a company's management as *the* dominating element in evaluating the worth of the company." It is generally agreed that organizations with effective managers likely will be successful, whereas organizations with poor managers likely will fail.

MANAGEMENT IN FORMAL AND INFORMAL ORGANIZATIONS

Managers are important in informal organizations as well as formal organizations. The differences between the operations of formal and informal managers are in the areas of the style, or way, managerial functions are performed and the degree to which various managerial approaches are utilized. But the functions managers perform are the same in both types of organizations. Managers of informal organizations perform their functions informally while managers of formal organizations tend to act more formally. A distinguishing feature of formal organizations is that they include appointed managers in official positions.

Informal organizations, on the other hand, generally do not have officially recognized managers. But the managerial functions of creating, planning, organizing, motivating, communicating, and controlling are as vital to a kindergarten car pool as they are to the management of an industrial activity. True enough, the degree of application of each function may vary among formal and informal organizations, just as there is a difference in the application of managerial functions among formal organizations. Also, the style of management in informal organizations may be different from that found in formal organizations. Informal organizations tend to pass managerial functions around among the membership. Someone must create, plan, organize, motivate, communicate about, and control the Wednesday afternoon ladies' bridge club, an informal organization. By implicit (as compared to explicit in the formal organization) agreement, managerial functions for the bridge club may be passed around among the different members. One major criterion in the bridge club for determining who will be "manager" at a given time may be the location of the next session. Ordinarily, the hostess will perform most, if not all, of the managerial functions for a particular meeting.

Thus managerial functions are performed in all types of organizations, formal and informal. The analysis below emphasizes formal organizations because most students of management and organizations will apply their knowledge of managerial functions in formal organizations. However, the topics in this chapter are also relevant (perhaps, indirectly in many cases) to informal organizations.

THE WORK OF MANAGERS

The mix of work that managers perform varies according to the organizational level of the manager. This relationship is shown in Figure 12-1, where managers on higher levels tend to spend relatively more of their time performing managerial functions than do managers on lower levels in the organization.

UNIVERSALITY OF MANAGEMENT FUNCTIONS

Managerial functions are essentially the same regardless of the type of organization or the level of the manager in the organization. That is, a manager when creating, planning, organizing, motivating, communicating, and controlling does essentially the same work regardless of the objectives of his organization, his particular activity, or his rank in the organization. Koontz and O'Donnell put it very clearly: "Acting in their managerial capacity, presidents, department heads, foremen, supervisors, college deans, bishops, and

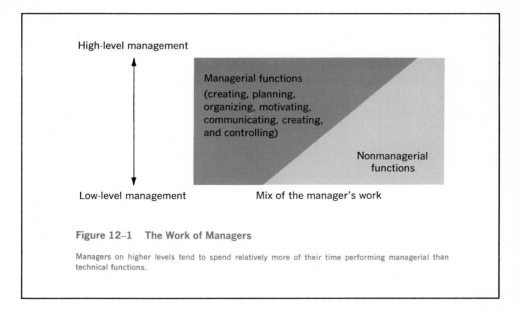

Figure 12–1   The Work of Managers

Managers on higher levels tend to spend relatively more of their time performing managerial than technical functions.

heads of government agencies all do the same thing."[1] Of course, the nonmanagerial skills required for various managerial posts vary from job to job. Because management functions are essentially the same wherever found, *the functions of management are considered to be universal.*

TRANSFERABILITY OF MANAGERIAL SKILLS

Because management functions are universal, they can be transferred from one organization to another, as experience has often shown. And the more "pure" the managerial job (that is, the "higher" it is and the fewer the nonmanagerial components involved in the job) the more transferable managers are into and out of their jobs. Thus, high-level managers are often transferred from job to job within an organization or even to entirely different organizations. A retired general officer may make an excellent president for a university or an industrial firm because the managerial skills in these presidential posts are almost the same as those the general may have demonstrated in his high-level military position. On the other hand, managers at relatively low organizational levels are not so easily transferred. For example, it is hard to imagine that a buyer in a department store could adequately perform in the post of a department head in a chemical manufacturing company, or vice versa. On the other hand, the president of the chemical firm perhaps

[1]Harold Koontz and Cyril O'Donnell, *Principles of Management,* 4th ed., McGraw-Hill Book Company, New York, 1968, p. 54.

could fairly easily exchange positions with the president of the department store. The department heads are not transferable to the same degree because of the differences in the nonmanagerial requirements of their jobs. The buyer needs to have an expert knowledge of clothing, while the department head in the chemical firm needs to be an expert chemist. But the *managerial functions* of both department heads are essentially the same. Both create, plan, organize, motivate, communicate, and control in performing their managerial duties.

SEQUENCE OF THE PERFORMANCE OF MANAGERIAL FUNCTIONS

For a particular organizational task, a manager ordinarily will perform the managerial functions in sequence: creating, planning, organizing, motivating, communicating, and controlling the human behavior in the organization, as shown in Figure 12-2. However, a manager will usually be simultaneously responsible for several organizational tasks. Therefore, if we studied the typical work day of a manager we probably would find him performing all six functions, perhaps several times during the day. We probably would find the manager and his organization involved in projects in various stages of completion. For some projects he would be in the creating stage; for others he would be planning, organizing, motivating, and communicating; and for still others, controlling.

ITERATIVE NATURE OF MANAGERIAL FUNCTIONS

Management functions have the quality of being iterative. That is, they are contained within each other. For example, creating, planning, organizing, motivating, communicating, and controlling all occur within the planning process. Similarly, in performing the organizing functions, planning, organizing, and the other functions would be involved. Thus for organizing we need to do creating, planning, organizing, motivating, communicating, and controlling. All six functions can be conceived as subfunctions of

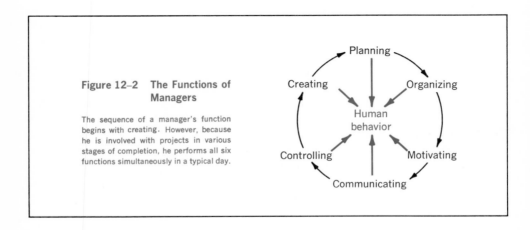

Figure 12-2   The Functions of Managers

The sequence of a manager's function begins with creating. However, because he is involved with projects in various stages of completion, he performs all six functions simultaneously in a typical day.

each other. The process of iteration could be continued to additional levels if desired. For example, within the subprocess of planning for the larger function of planning we may have creating, planning, organizing, motivating, communicating, and controlling. The iterative nature of managerial functions illustrates the extreme dynamism of the manager's role.

RELATIVE IMPORTANCE OF MANAGERIAL FUNCTIONS

The question of which management function is most important has often been raised. Each function has its champions, and excellent books emphasizing each are available.

But no one of the managerial functions is more important than the others. It is true that the mix of the functions will vary from task to task, but they are all important and necessary to some degree in the accomplishment of any organizational goal. The wise manager will implement each of the functions in whatever ways will best accomplish the goals of the organization.

SUMMARY

The job or functions of managers include creating, planning, organizing, motivating, communicating, and controlling to accomplish organizational objectives. These functions are performed in both informal and formal organizations.

Because of the similarity of managerial functions, a manager skilled in performing them can transfer his skills from one organization to another. However, higher-level managers are more transferable than lower managers because higher-level managers require less technical knowledge and more emphasis on managerial functions. But all six managerial functions are performed by all managers to some degree in every managerial job.

FOR REVIEW AND DISCUSSION

1 What are the six functions managers perform in organizations?

2 Are the six managerial functions performed in both: (a) the local chapter of the Great Books Discussion Club and (b) Foster Construction Company, which is building a large bridge? Explain your answer.

3 Describe what is likely to happen in an organization where no one performs the managerial functions.

4 Do foremen and presidents perform the same kind of work? Explain.

5 Explain the concept of universality of management functions.

6 Are managerial skills transferable? Explain. Why are higher-level managers more easily transferable than lower-level managers?

7 What is the usual sequence of performance of the managerial functions for a particular project? A manager may happen to perform all six functions, but in a completely different sequence during a typical work day. Explain how this can happen.

8 Explain what is meant when managerial functions are said to be iterative.

9 Ask a practicing manager to list the managerial functions he performs. Ask him to estimate the percentage of time that he spends on each of these functions. Compare this list with that given in the text. How do you account for the differences, if any?

CASES

A Arnold Hodge has recently been promoted to the position of sales manager of the eastern division of Alco Products, Inc. Before his promotion Arnold had spent twelve years as a highly successful salesman for the company. He seemed to have a knack for talking to people, and many of his clients thought of him as a close personal friend.

In his new job Arnold spent his time in hiring and firing salesmen, in setting up sales programs for his division, in reviewing the daily reports of his twenty salesmen, and in supervising the activities of his office staff. Sales in the eastern division had risen 10 per cent since Arnold had become manager, while no similar improvement had occurred in the other divisions.

One evening Arnold was talking to his friend Ray Bower about his new job. "It just seems like I never get anything done in the office. It's just a constant stream of other people's problems. I wish I were back on the road where I was doing some real work. I feel like all I'm doing in the office is pushing paper."

> **1** Why did Arnold feel that his selling job was more important than his managing job? Do you agree? Why?
>
> **2** Arnold had never studied anything about organizations and management. What information about the functions of management is needed so Arnold will have a better appreciation of his managerial job?

B Gordon Borth had spent twenty years in the supply corps of the army and had risen to the rank of major. Shortly after his retirement from the army Gordon decided that he was too young to quit working; he was only forty-one years old, and he thought he had many good years available for a second career.

Gordon went to see his old friend Lee Walters who was president of a fairly large manufacturing firm. "Yes, Gordon," said Lee, "we do have three openings in our managerial ranks; we need an executive vice-president, an office manager, and a machinist supervisor. But, I don't know—you've never had any experience in our business."

> **1** Compare Gordon's qualifications with the requirements of each of the three jobs. Which one(s), if any, do you think Gordon is qualified to accept? Fully explain your answer.

FOR FURTHER STUDY

Additional sources can be found in the sources cited in the chapter.

Book

Peter F. Drucker: *The Practice of Management,* Harper and Brothers, New York, 1954, chaps. 1 and 2. Drucker explains the role, contributions, and tasks of management in modern business organizations.

Articles

David W. Ewing: "The Knowledge of an Executive," *Harvard Business Review,* March–April 1964. The knowledge possessed by an executive can be usefully divided into methods, realities, and goals.

Fred E. Fiedler: "Leadership Experience and Leader Performance—Another Hypothesis Shot to Hell," *Organizational Behavior and Human Performance,* January 1970. More experienced leaders may be poorer than those with less experience.

Harold Koontz: "Challenges for Intellectual Leadership in Management," *California Management Review,* Winter 1965. "Management is an art whose intellectual needs are urgent, manifold, and socially important."

R. Alec Mackenzie: "The Management Process in 3-D," *Harvard Business Review,* November–December 1969. The process of management is effectively explained and illustrated.

Leroy G. Malouf, Jane S. Mouton, and Robert R. Blake: "A New Look at the Functions of Managing People," *Personnel Administration,* March–April 1965. This article relates the functions a manager performs to managerial style, with the goal being to describe the functions in terms of an effective style.

Joseph G. Phelan: "Problem-solving: Management's Prime Responsibility," *Personnel Administration,* January–February 1966. Modern organizations have built-in blocks to problem-solving efforts because they are too committed to repeat formulas of past successes.

Julius Rezler: "Managerial Functions in the Era of Automation," *Advanced Management Journal,* April 1964. Automation has been an instrumental factor in broadening and redefining managerial functions.

Seymour Tilles: "The Manager's Job: A Systems Approach," *Harvard Business Review,* January–February 1963, pp. 73–81. This article explains the systems point of view of the manager's role in organizations.

William H. Whyte, Jr.: "How Hard Do Executives Work?" *Fortune,* June 1956. This article describes the work and life of the modern business executive.

Section A
Creating

13
Concepts
of Creativity

A first rate soup is more creative than a second class painting.
ABRAHAM H. MASLOW

If several people were asked to define creativity, the terms given most frequently would probably include "discovery," "invention," "something new," "extending the boundaries of knowledge," etc. Most people would probably agree that creativity involves the application of a person's mental ability and curiosity to some area, with the creation or discovery of something new as a result. The discovery or invention may be a new theory, a new product, a new manufacturing process, a better accounting system, a book, a play, or any other new or improved thing.

Until recently, creative ability has been generally regarded with awe, mystification, confusion, and helplessness. It was thought of as a gift of the talented few, and nothing could be done for those persons not among the chosen. A person was considered as creative or not creative—there were no in-between degrees of creativity. The creative process was a phenomenon that even gifted persons could not explain—therefore there was very little reason why "normal" individuals should or could have been expected to understand this complex, rare, and valuable talent.

I never could believe that Providence had sent a few men
into the world, ready booted and spurred to ride, and millions
ready saddled and bridled to be ridden.
  RICHARD RUMBOLD

Recently, however, we have witnessed the emergence of a different point of view. Many people have come to recognize that whether it occurs in painting a picture; writing a poem or symphony; inventing a new jet-propulsion system, marketing technique, or wonder drug; or managing a creative organization; the creative process is a manifesta- tion of a fundamental ability—that of relating previously unrelated things.

Creativity in all fields seems to fall back on this ability—the ability to look at things with a fresh eye.

From the hay loft, a horse looks like a violin.
  LORD CHESTERFIELD

A hen is only an egg's way of making another egg.
  SAMUEL BUTLER

Genius in truth means little more than the
faculty of perceiving in an unhabitual way.
  WILLIAM JAMES

Creativity in any field, however, is stimulated less by gimmicks than by an inward motivation to contribute, by challenging objectives, by the organizational climate, and by the sense of far-reaching significance that a person derives from his work. The creative ability in all fields seems to be interrelated, and training in creativity can actually in- crease an individual's creative output. Furthermore, a definite pattern for the creative process is emerging. A knowledge of this process can expand our ability to perceive the vital relations between previously unrelated things.

THE CREATIVE PROCESS

The creative process may have several patterns: (1) logic, (2) idea linking, (3) problem solving, and (4) free association.

Logic

In the first pattern of the creative process, logical thinking, the person approaches nature with a hypothesis or theory which, through testing and verification, may lead to a conclu- sion. The manufacture of synthetic diamonds is an illustration: scientists observed that natural diamonds apparently developed from pure carbon under conditions of extremely high temperature and pressure. These scientists theorized that diamonds might be manu- factured if similar conditions could be set up in a laboratory. After much experimenta- tion the hypothesis was proved to be correct; synthetic diamonds were produced, and a large proportion of our industrial diamonds are now made synthetically.

Logic may be of two types—deductive and inductive. Deductive logic is used where an accepted general statement is applied to a specific case. For example: All persons have some creative ability; you are a person; therefore you have some creative ability. Inductive logic, on the other hand, draws a generalization based on specific observations: each individual that I have observed has some creative ability; therefore I can expect all persons to have some creative ability.

In practice it is usually difficult to say whether inductive or deductive logic was used to arrive at a conclusion. The two are often interwoven into a specific logical process. However, it is necessary only to know that logic is being used whenever one thing is assumed because another is true. If the statement is made that A is true (or untrue) and therefore B is true (or untrue), logic has been employed in creating B.

Idea Linking

A second pattern of the creative process may be called "idea linking." A person using this method forms links between many different ideas or pieces of information. Education, by increasing an individual's store of knowledge, may also increase the potential number of links. Therefore, a highly educated person probably will be more creative through the idea-linking pattern than a person with less education. However, life experiences other than formal education can contribute to the storehouse of information and thereby to creativity. Thus, an engineer may fairly easily design and build a bridge if he has either studied the theory of bridges (education) or worked previously with other bridges (experience).

However, education and experience, to the extent that they perpetuate old ideas or reinforce prior interests, can also inhibit the creative process. Many significant discoveries are being made by people who are not recognized experts in the field. This raises the question of whether or not some education and experience has been merely teaching students obsolete answers rather than encouraging them to raise questions and search for their own answers. Perhaps our fascination with old things is the reason that color film, jazz, aluminum aircraft propellers, and the Bessemer process for converting iron to steel all were invented by people outside the fields of primary interest for these products. Sir Henry Bessemer in speaking of his discovery said:

> I had an immense advantage over many others dealing with the problem inasmuch as I had no fixed ideas derived from long established practice to control and bias my mind, and did not suffer from the general belief that whatever is, is right.[1]

Problem Solving

A third pattern, the problem-solving approach, is one of the most widely understood and accepted ways of stimulating creativity and of describing the creative process. This ap-

---

[1]Quoted in W. I. B. Beveridge, *The Art of Scientific Investigation,* W. W. Norton & Company, Inc., New York, 1957, p. 2.

proach places a premium on defining "the problem" and assumes that once this problem is defined, solutions will be produced almost automatically.

> A problem well-defined is half solved.
> JOHN DEWEY

The problem-solving approach incorporates the following steps: (1) Obtain the facts; (2) identify the problem; (3) formulate alternative solutions; (4) select the best solution; and (5) put the selected solution into practice. We are all quite familiar with the problem-solving approach and we use it every time someone comes to us in a troubled state and we ask him first, "What's your problem?" Knowledge of the problem, we are sure, is often a valuable step toward solution. After identifying the problem we think of possible solutions, finally putting into practice the one that seems best.

Free Association

Free association is the fourth pattern that we may observe in the creative process. In contrast to idea linking which focuses upon rational, conscious thinking, free association emphasizes the value of the often irrational unconscious mind where ideas are supposedly able to fly about and mingle, free of censorship and restraint by logic and habit. The human mind is viewed as if it were an iceberg, the vast majority of which is below the level of consciousness.

Figure 13-1 illustrates this concept, showing a barrier that restricts the free flow of material between conscious and unconscious levels. Further, it includes a censor (an idea that Sigmund Freud, the founder of psychoanalysis, originated) who guards the "gate" connecting the conscious and the unconscious. The censor's primary concern is that ideas that are irrational, unacceptable, bizarre, stupid, irrelevant, frightening, etc., be prevented from passing to the conscious mind.

Proponents of the free association pattern contend that maximum creativity occurs when ideas are permitted to flow and be expressed without being censored by such statements and attitudes as, "That's stupid!" or "It won't work!" or "That's a crazy idea!" Lack of censorship by the person himself or by others will, it is hoped, stimulate the flow of good or workable ideas or thoughts as well as the "wild" ideas. Apparently, it is impossible to get one without the other.

The free association theory, therefore, holds that creativity is a product of the whole mind, unconscious as well as conscious, and that the unconscious may well be the richest storehouse for creativity.

One final word of caution regarding the free association view: Many persons seem to confuse the censoring of *ideas* and *thoughts* with the censoring of *actions*. We must remember that an idea or thought by itself, no matter how weird or crazy, is unlikely to hurt anyone. Only when bad ideas are converted to action is harm likely to be done. Some such actions are indeed harmful to other people or to organizations. Therefore, to

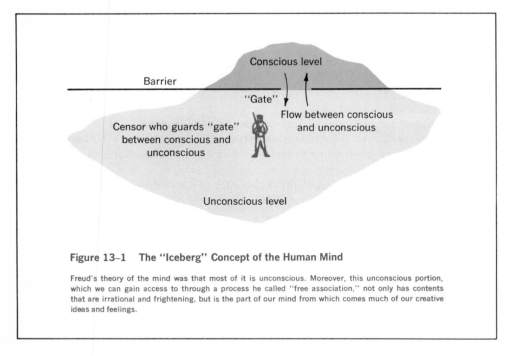

Figure 13–1 The "Iceberg" Concept of the Human Mind

Freud's theory of the mind was that most of it is unconscious. Moreover, this unconscious portion, which we can gain access to through a process he called "free association," not only has contents that are irrational and frightening, but is the part of our mind from which comes much of our creative ideas and feelings.

maintain discipline in an organization actions must to some degree be censored and controlled.

THE CREATIVE INDIVIDUAL

Creativity is a quality which is given many names—imagination, vision, ingenuity, inventiveness. Whatever the term, it is seldom that the ideal young man or woman walks through the door of a company office. Researchers have tried for years to find ways of sifting through applicants to find those who have more rather than less creative ability. In so doing, they have developed measurement techniques that can supplement the judgment of personnel managers, guidance counselors, and others who are concerned with identifying persons of unusual creative ability.

In the past, persons were too often assumed to be divided into only two classes—creative and noncreative. This assumption reduced the amount of creative talent available to an organization because most members were placed in the noncreative category. No originality was expected of the majority of members, and therefore little, if any, was received. Authorities today generally agree that rather than being restricted to a minority of people, creativity exists to some degree in almost everyone. However, some people have more ability than others; in fact, there is a rather wide range. In addition, any latent creativity that an individual does have is stimulated with varying degrees of ease, depending on the person. Finally, training in the creative process can actually increase a person's creative ability. The assumption that everyone in the **organization** has some degree of creativity is far more fruitful than to assume that creative **ability** is limited to a selected few.

Creativity Measurement Tests

Creativity tests compare the ability of one person with others, much as IQ tests do. They do not measure the absolute amount of creativity that any person possesses. However, the results of the measurements are encouraging and give a definite separation between the more creative and the less creative.

Although there have been other attempts and other types of tests devised, the battery of tests developed at the Institute of Personality Assessment and Research in Berkeley, California, is among the best.[2] Briefly, the parts of this test can be described as follows.

1 *Unusual uses test.* The person is asked to list six uses to which a common object can be put. Such an object might be a pencil eraser. The less often the answer has been given by others, the higher the score. One answer to the eraser question might be: "Remove grease spots from a radiator fan belt." This answer is given infrequently and receives a high score.

2 *Consequences test.* The person is asked to write down all the things he can think of that might happen if a stated change took place. Such a change might be this: "What would happen if suddenly everyone had x-ray eyes?" Again, the least obvious, most infrequent answers receive the highest score.

3 *Plot titles test.* The person is given two short stories and asked to make up as many titles as he can. More clever answers receive higher scores.

4 *Ink blot test.* The person is asked to interpret ten ink blots. The answers given are scored for infrequency of response, but they must make some sense. Bizarre answers which do not seem to be based on reality are not counted as positive indicators of creative ability.

5 *Anagrams test.* The person is given a test word like "abbreviation" and asked to make up as many words as possible, using these letters. The test is scored for infrequency. Answers given most infrequently indicate creative ability.

6 *Thematic apperception test.* The person is given pictures and asked to make up stories about them. Two raters working independently score for originality.

7 *Word rearrangement test.* The person is given a random list of words and asked to compose a story using as many of the words as possible. Originality receives a high score.

The several parts of the whole test are scored independently to avoid the possibility that a score on one test will prejudice the person scoring the other parts. All are free

[2]Frank Barron, "The Disposition toward Originality," *The Journal of Abnormal and Social Psychology,* November 1955, pp. 478–485.

response tests. The answers must be summoned by the person from within himself. Most people are better at one kind of test than another. The visually creative (measured by ink blot tests) are not necessarily verbally creative (measured by word tests) as well. However, those who do very well on one test usually have higher-than-average scores on most of the others.

The results of these tests have proved to be very useful in measuring the inventive abilities of individuals. They not only provide a separation between more creative and less creative persons, but they also tend to pinpoint talent in a certain area or areas. Such tests in whole or in part can be very useful to organizations in their counseling, hiring, training, and evaluation work.

Creative Personality Traits

The tests designed for measuring creativity have opened up another significant area of research. Persons at the two extremes of ability have been studied to see what, if any, personality traits seem to go along with creativity. Once the traits of highly creative people have been established, a manager is armed with another tool for helping in the proper selection, training, and evaluation of most creative members in his organization.

First, highly creative people tend to be unusually inquisitive and are generally somewhat dissatisfied with the *status quo*. For these people there is a continual conflict between order and new experience, between intellect and intuition (hunches), between conformity and independent thinking, and between complexity and simplicity.

Second, highly creative persons are usually intelligent, yet they are seldom stimulated by logic and rationality in all phases of their lives. In fact, asymmetry and disorder seem to be a challenge to most of them.

Third, highly creative persons are not psychological cripples; they usually have a broad, deep, and flexible awareness of themselves. They are both more primitive and more cultured, more destructive and more constructive, a bit madder and more sane than the average person. As a result they tend to be somewhat unconventional in thought and expression.

Fourth, highly creative persons seem to share certain other characteristics—purpose on a grand scale, dedication to work, freedom of expression, unconcern for dissent or contradiction, and a refusal to be hampered by custom or tradition.

Fifth, personal traits that indicate a relatively high creative ability include a high IQ, an enriched childhood environment, relative independence in setting one's own standards, good mental and physical health, and stamina.[3] These traits can be discovered through appropriate tests.

TYPES OF CREATORS AND CREATIVITY

We will consider four types of creativity: innovation, synthesis, extension, and duplication.

---

[3]William E. Scott, "The Creative Individual," *Academy of Management Journal,* September 1965, pp. 211–219.

Innovation

Our breakdown of creativity begins first with *innovation,* which many persons think of as the sum total rather than a type of creativity. Innovative creativity results in the generation of something new: a new idea, theory, or hypothesis; a new style of writing or painting; a new invention; or a new method of managing an organization.

Fantasy or dreaming often is involved in innovation. The mind may wander into areas of inquiry that have not been delved into before, producing a sharp break with traditional knowledge. For example, both Galileo's and Einstein's theories broke sharply with accepted theories. Because of the break with tradition the innovator may face serious difficulty in getting his idea accepted. It may be necessary to challenge tradition and to battle the vested interests in the *status quo.*

Synthesis

A second type of creativity may be called *synthesis.* It involves the ability to absorb and use ideas from several varied sources. A synthesizer may combine seemingly unrelated data or concepts into a valuable idea or product. The application of mathematics to business administration problems is an excellent example of creative synthesis in two fields of study.

Thus, the organization manager in performing his role as the leader of a group of people can be highly creative. He is, in fact, one of the primary users of synthesis, for he combines the highly varied talents of people and resources such as machines, materials, and money to create the product of the organization. Although he has not been generally recognized as such, a good manager in his role of a synthesizer actually may be one of our most creative people.

Extension

Extension, the third type of creativity in our analysis, is closely related to innovation and synthesis. *Extension* is at work when someone takes a basic innovation and increases its usefulness by enlarging its boundaries. Much research and development work is concerned with expanding a previously recognized discovery. From the broad outline or general framework established by innovation or synthesis, extension provides the details necessary for practical use.

A clear example of creative extension is found in the field of atomic physics. In 1905 Professor Einstein made the theoretical discovery (innovation) that tremendous quantities of energy could be produced by atomic reactions converting mass into energy. Einstein's innovation set the stage for an almost unbelievable amount of extension by those who created numerous practical applications of his basic discovery. Seven decades after the original discovery, extensions and practical applications continue to pour forth.

Another clear example of extension as a type of creativity may be found in the automobile industry. Each· year we witness the improvements on the basic automobile that was invented around the turn of the century.

Duplication

As strange as it may seem, it is appropriate to list *duplication,* or the copying of the success of others, as the fourth type of creativity. Although not creative in the innovative sense, duplication is certainly creative from the point of view of any organization into which it is brought, for it provides something new for that organization. A large proportion of progress is made because followers are quick to adopt the successful practices of leaders. It simply is neither feasible nor desirable for everyone to have to discover each new thing for himself.

He is wise who "stands on the shoulders" of those who have gone before, to the extent that such standing is to his advantage. Many individuals and organizations are adept in screening the products, methods, and procedures of others and in successfully adopting many of these things for their own use. In fact, for some organizations duplication may become almost a way of life. Consider the success of Japanese industry that has produced lower-cost imitations of products originated elsewhere.

Although patent and copyright laws tend to restrict duplication somewhat, the practice is much more prevalent than might be expected. In fact one view of the educational process is that to a large extent we are teaching students to duplicate successful experiences of others.

Combined Types of Creativity

Often it is difficult to say whether a particular discovery resulted from innovation, synthesis, extension, or duplication. The various types of creativity are frequently combined. One good example of this combination is in the discovery of the carbon dioxide–oxygen cycle.

About 300 years ago, an English chemist, John Mayow, became fascinated with the question of why breathing was necessary to stay alive. As an experiment, he set two stools in a shallow pan filled with water; on one stool he placed a lighted candle, on the other a mouse; then he covered each with a bell jar. The result was that both the candle flame and the mouse died. Burning and breathing took the same substance from the air, Mayow concluded. But what was this substance? He never found out.

One hundred years later Joseph Priestley, a minister in Leeds, England, discovered that burning objects and breathing animals produce the same substance—carbon dioxide. Further, he found that a candle burned brighter and a mouse in some ways was in better physical condition in oxygen than in air. He concluded that pure oxygen may be better to breathe than air.

The great French chemist Antoine Lavoisier heard of Priestley's experiments and thought they showed a close connection between breathing and burning. After experimenting with the melting of ice by burning charcoal and by the breathing of a guinea pig, Lavoisier concluded that respiration was indeed a form of combustion, although a very slow one.

The next question raised was: With all of this burning of oxygen what is the source of new oxygen? Eventually, scientists discovered that green plants take carbon dioxide from the air, retain the carbon, and return the oxygen to the air. Thus the discovery of the carbon–oxygen cycle involved several decades and numerous scientists. Was creativity evident? Definitely, but what type? The best answer is that several types were involved—innovation, synthesis, extension, and possibly even duplication. This example illustrates that in actual practice creativity can seldom be broken down into pure types, but must instead be regarded as an integrated process involving all four.

SUMMARY

Being creative is a natural expression of a healthy person. Some persons are more creative than others, but everyone has some creative ability.

The creative process may have several patterns including logic, idea linking problem solving, and free association.

Tests have been developed that can assist in identifying highly creative persons. Such persons tend to be inquisitive, intelligent, and hardworking.

Innovation often is thought of as the only type of creativity. However, synthesis, extension, and duplication also are important types of creativity. Frequently, all four types are combined in creating something. An organization can be creative in improving the ways it achieves its current objectives and in developing new and better objectives.

FOR REVIEW AND DISCUSSION

1 What is creativity? Why is it so important in an organization?

2 Describe the four patterns of the creative process. Give an example not in the text to illustrate each of the four patterns.

3 Are education and experience likely to increase a person's creative ability? Why?

4 What are the five steps in the problem-solving pattern?

5 For the free-association pattern, freedom from censorship and evaluation in the idea-producing stage is emphasized. Explain the reason for this.

6 Explain the iceberg concept of the human mind.

7 ". . . an idea or thought by itself, no matter how weird or crazy, is unlikely to hurt anyone." Do you agree or disagree? Why? What things, if any, that have been taught you in political, social, or religious areas affect your answer?

8 What is the purpose of creativity measurement tests?

9 Define and give an example not in the book of each of the four types of creativity.

10 Explain this statement: "It may be wiser to seek better things to do than constantly to try to do better the things an organization is already doing."

11 How might lack of experience in a field assist a person in making creative contributions to that field?

12 Does everyone have creative ability? Explain. Is it harder to get some persons to be creative than others? Explain.

CASES

A Foster Chemical, Inc., had a problem of quality control in one of its manufacturing departments. The product produced in this department required an extremely complex process.

At a supervisor's meeting Mr. Knowles, the plant manager, said: "We must lick this quality control problem. Jim [a chemical engineer], I want you to study this problem and give me a recommendation next Monday."

Jim replied: "Perhaps the men in the department could give me some ideas if I talk to them."

"No, Jim, that won't be necessary. Those men just work; they don't think. They wouldn't be able to give you any ideas."

> **1** Do you agree with Mr. Knowles that the men in the department could not help in solving the problem? Why?
>
> **2** What effect will Mr. Knowles's attitude likely have on solving the problem?

B Joe Lightwood, a recent nontechnical college graduate, reported for work in his new job with the telephone company. The company's first task for Joe was for him to attend the company's manager trainee course, but the course would not begin until the next week. The training director was faced with the problem of what to do with Joe for the week. His first thought was to assign readings about the company to occupy Joe for the week. But, on second thought, he decided to give Joe a special assignment.

Joe's special assignment was to diagnose and recommend solutions to the "wrong-number problem" in a nearby city that had been converted to an all-digit telephone-numbering system. Unknown to Joe the company considered the problem so serious that a team of company engineers had been working on the same problem for four months, without success.

On Friday afternoon Joe placed a neatly typed, well-written report on the training director's desk. Joe's report concluded that the wrong-number problem was caused by two factors. First, there were five mistakes in the dialing instructions in the new telephone directory. Any one of these could cause a wrong number. Second, Joe discovered that there was an antidigit league in the city. One of the league's members confessed that the league "was making a lot of wrong-number calls as a protest against the digit system."

Joe then recommended solutions that were accepted by the company and that resulted in a completely satisfactory solution to the problem. The training director checked with the engineering team and found that they had concentrated solely on technical aspects in trying to find a solution.

> **1** Did Joe have any advantage over the engineers in reaching the solution to this problem? Explain.
>
> **2** Should the training director have told Joe about the team of engineers working on the problem? Why?
>
> **3** Should special assignments be a part of each manager trainee's program? Why? Give advantages and disadvantages.

C Mr. Bales, the president of Bales, Inc., was continually talking to managers in other organizations about the approaches they used in managing their organization. After these conferences Mr. Bales often made favorable changes in his firm's operations.

    1 How might the conferences Mr. Bales had increase his creativity?

    2 Would you classify Mr. Bales's changes as innovation, extension, synthesis, duplication or possibly all four? Explain.

FOR FURTHER STUDY

Additional sources can be found in the sources cited in the chapter.

Books

Creativity: Key to Continuing Progress, AMA Bulletin No. 4, American Management Association, New York, 1960. Four excellent articles concerning creativity, its role in industry today, the proper climate for creative effort, and basic requirements for creativity's existence.

Eugene Raudsepp: *Managing Creative Scientists and Engineers,* The Macmillan Company, New York, 1963, parts 2 and 3. There are definite subtle environmental forces and psychological conditions that best match the inherent requirements of creative functioning.

Paul Smith (ed.): *Creativity,* Hastings House, Publishers, Inc., New York, 1959. "The world is discovering that creativity is important, and it has become Big Business. The true value of creativity is just now being realized."

E. Paul Torrance: *Rewarding Creative Thinking,* Prentice-Hall, Inc., Englewood Cliffs, N.J., 1965. "If we want to develop the creative thinking potential of today . . . it is reasonably certain that we must somehow learn to reward creative thinking."

Eugene K. Von Fange: *Professional Creativity,* Prentice-Hall, Inc., Englewood Cliffs, N.J., 1959. Every man has creative talent to some degree and, through proper use of his mental powers and resources, can perform creative work.

Articles

Robert A. Denther and Bernard Mackler: "Originality: Some Social and Personal Determinants," *Behavioral Science,* January 1964. A basic component of creativity is originality, and the social environment can affect the quantity and quality of original ideas.

Jerome E. Doppelt: "What Is Creativity? III: Definitions of Creativity," *Transactions of the New York Academy of Sciences,* no. 7, 1964. Creativity is one of the words in the English language which means many things to many people. To understand it better and to use it necessitates clarification of the definition of creativity.

William D. Hitt: "Toward a Two Factor Theory of Creativity," *Psychological Record,* January 1965. "Original thinking and logical reasoning are complementary aspects of creative thinking, and these two facets of behavior are mutually dependent forces which, when acting together, can produce creative ideas."

John F. Mee: "The Creative Thinking Process," *Indiana Business Review,* February 1956, pp. 3–7. A step-by-step description of the process of creativity.

"You and Creativity," *Kaiser Aluminum News,* vol. 25, no. 3, 1968. This issue contains several outstanding articles on creative persons and the creative process. Alternate source: Don Fabun: *Three Roads to Awareness,* Glencoe Press, Beverly Hills, Calif., 1970, pp. 41–80.

14
Stimulating Creativity in Organizations

First they tell you you're wrong, and they can prove it.
Then they tell you you're right, but it's not important.
Then they tell you it's important, but they've known it for
years.
   CHARLES F. KETTERING

Simply identifying or understanding creativity is quite a different matter from fostering it and putting it to effective use. Continued survival and prosperity demand that organizations today not only recognize creativity but encourage and utilize it as well. The organization that fails to develop its creative resources is soon forced out of the market place by competitors who have a better product, lower costs, better advertising, or a more imaginative and farseeing management.

Any new discovery takes time to assimilate and coordinate; consequently, a firm with initiative will experience some inefficiency. Too many organizations are lulled into a deadly sleep by the sweet drug of efficiency; and although they may be making full use of synthesis, extension, and duplication, they ignore innovation and lose sight of new objectives in the field. For example, a highly efficient buggy-whip manufacturer would command little prestige or profit today!

To remain healthy and productive, an organization must utilize all types of creativity. To do this a manager can arouse, stimulate, and reinforce the latent talent available to him.

This chapter discusses three major factors in organizational creativity: (1) characteristics of creative organizations, (2) creative techniques in organizations, and (3) the creative climate. Methods for spotting a highly creative individual already have been described; among the questions now discussed are:

How does one assess an organization's creative resources?
How does one deal with persons who are not highly creative?
How does one maintain the discipline and control needed without stifling creativity?
How does one use the pressure of group conformity constructively?

TRAITS OR CHARACTERISTICS OF CREATIVE ORGANIZATIONS

Social scientist Gary A. Steiner has raised the question of how to distinguish between a creative organization and one that produces for a creator.

> An organization can be an efficient instrument for the execution of ideas and yet not be in itself creative. For instance, a smooth military unit under a great strategist; a top-notch symphony orchestra under a creative baton; or in the same terms, a business that hums to the tune of a creative president.[1]

The question is essentially a rhetorical one, however, for the most talented manager, military strategist, or orchestra conductor is, after all, a part of his organization. If he is the most creative or even the only highly creative member of the group, then the organization itself is utilizing his talents in accomplishing its objectives, and is, therefore, creative. We are interested both in organizations that are generally creative and in organizations that express the creativity of their managers.

From another point of view, consider the highly competent engineer who performs poorly when he is promoted to manager. Perhaps in his technical work he was primarily concerned with extension and duplication, but he is incapable of the synthesis and innovation required by his new position. At any rate, if his creative ability is insufficient to carry the rest of the organization, or if he is unable to obtain enough creativity from the other members to supplement his own, then the whole organization fails to be creative.

The specific characteristics that contribute to an organization's creativity need to be identified. As a starting point, consider the overall "personality" of the organization. If a business has been outstanding in the areas of growth, product development, innovation, and problem solving, it may have the general image of being highly creative. Whether this personality is a result of a few individuals' influence or whether it is the result of all or a majority of the members' creative contributions is immaterial — the organization generally is viewed as creative. However, comparison of characteristics

[1]Gary A. Steiner, *The Creative Organization,* Graduate School of Business Administration, The University of Chicago, Chicago, 1962, p. 29.

of creative individuals and of creative organizations yields some highly significant insights.

Many of the characteristics found in *highly creative organizations* seem to match those of *highly creative individuals*. The comparison as outlined below by Steiner illustrates the similarity of characteristics.

Steiner's comparison between the characteristics of a highly creative organiza-

---

Characteristics of Creativity[2]

THE CREATIVE INDIVIDUAL:	THE CREATIVE ORGANIZATION:
Has conceptual fluency. Is able to produce a large number of ideas quickly.	Has idea men. Has open channels of communication. Has suggestion systems and idea units with no additional responsibilities. Encourages contact with outside sources.
Is original. Generates unusual ideas.	Hires a variety of personality types. Assigns nonspecialists to problems. Allows eccentricity.
Considers ideas on the basis of their merit, not their source. Is motivated by interest in problem itself; follows wherever it leads.	Has an objective, fact-founded approach. Evaluates ideas on their merits, not status of originator. Selects and promotes on merit only.
Suspends judgment; avoids early commitment. Spends considerable time in analysis, explanation.	Exhibits lack of financial, material commitment to present products, policies. Invests in basic research. Has flexible long-range planning. Experiments with new ideas and does not prejudge them on rational grounds. Gives everything a chance.
Is less authoritarian. Is flexible. Accepts own impulses. Undisciplined exploration.	More decentralized. Provides time and resources to absorb errors. Tolerates and expects taking risks. Is not run as a "tight ship." Employees have fun, have freedom to choose and pursue problems. Free to discuss ideas.
Has independence of judgment. Is less conformist. Is often deviant from accepted ideas. Sees self as different.	Is autonomous and independent. Has original and different objectives. Is not trying to follow the leader.
Has rich, bizarre fantasy life, and a clear view of reality.	Has enough security of routines. Allows creators to roam. Has separate units or occasions for generating versus evaluating ideas. Separates creative from productive functions.

---

[2] Adapted from *ibid.*, pp. 22–23.

tion and a highly creative individual tends to contradict the general belief that group creativity is necessarily dependent on a very few highly creative individuals, and that if an organization has few such individuals its only course is to recruit these rare people.

On the contrary, many organizations have creativity spread throughout their personnel, and a look at the characteristics of these generally creative organizations clearly shows that the organization's personality may reflect the personalities of many of its members rather than of a very few. Creativity characteristics permeate the organization from top to bottom, including areas of *personnel* (hires different types of persons); *objectives* (original and different); *structure* (more decentralized); *compensation* (selects and promotes on merit only); and internal *environment* (less talented employees provide stable environment that allows creators to roam).

A generally creative organization, then, develops its characteristics by utilizing and developing the abilities of all its members—those who are not, as well as those who are, highly creative.

PROGRAMS AND TECHNIQUES FOR DEVELOPING CREATIVITY

There is some difference of opinion as to whether a person's ability to exhibit creativity can be increased. Some authorities think that a truly significant increase can be achieved through creative training methods that help a person utilize his latent creative talents.[3]

Whether or not a person's innate creative ability can be increased is apparently a purely academic question with which organizations need not concern themselves. For even if training programs do fail to increase the innate creative abilities, they offer great potential in terms of making individuals more productive by helping them use their present level of creative ability more effectively. Few persons use more than a small fraction of their creative ability, but an understanding of the creative process and use of techniques designed to stimulate creativity can greatly increase creative output.

Operational Techniques

The aspect of the creative development movement that has attracted the most interest in business and educational circles is that of operational techniques—probably because the techniques themselves and their usefulness are easily demonstrable. An *operational technique* is a system, procedure, or method designed to enable an individual or group to produce a large quantity of new ideas in the hope that one or more may be productive. The chief value of such techniques is that they set up conditions which help overcome the many obstacles to originality.

Operational techniques rely on two basic rules which must be followed if positive results are to be obtained: (1) judgment or evaluation must be eliminated from the idea-producing stage; (2) all ideas, even the apparently impractical, must be considered.

[3] See Alex F. Osborn, *Your Creative Power*, Charles Scribner's Sons, New York, 1948.

These techniques can be grouped into four general categories: analytical, free association, forced relationship, and eclectic (combinations of the other three).

Analytic techniques   Analytic techniques rely on a thorough and logical attack on the problem and its various elements. The best known of such techniques are: (1) attribute listing, (2) the input-output technique, and (3) grid analysis.

1 Attribute listing was developed by one of the pioneer teachers of creative thinking, Professor Robert Crawford.[4] It is a very simple technique. The first step is to isolate the major characteristics or attributes of a product, an object, or an idea. Each major attribute (such as color, size, expense) is then considered in turn, and is changed in every conceivable way. There is no attempt made to limit the suggested changes.

As with all operational techniques, no idea is rejected, however fantastic it may seem. In fact, no evaluation or judgment is allowed until after all the ideas have been enumerated. Then, and only then, are they evaluated in the light of limitations imposed by the problem and the situation. Separating evaluation and judgment from creation gives ideas a better chance to come to the surface. The obstacles to new approaches, and a new way of thinking, are overcome.

Thoughts shut up want air,
And spoil, like boles [sic] unopen'd to the sun.
EDWIN YOUNG

2 The input-output technique was developed at General Electric Company and is widely used as a means of considering problems that involve the use of energy in one form or another. The first step in using this technique is to specify the desired end result, or *output.* Second, the available sources of energy, or *inputs,* are defined. Finally, every possible way of converting the available inputs to the desired output is explored.

It is often helpful to establish any limiting requirements or specifications which the final solution must meet. During the early stages, however, these limiting requirements may be detrimental to productivity because they may restrict the free flow of ideas.

3 Grid analysis was developed by Dr. Fritz Zwicky.[5] Basically, it consists of first defining the problem, then listing every conceivable theoretical solution, and finally evaluating each of the suggestions.

This method involves listing the major variables of a problem on both sides of a two-dimensional grid so that all possible combinations can be considered. For example, when the problem of how to design and construct a building is considered, the different kinds of material and the various types of construction are all listed both horizontally

[4]Robert P. Crawford, *The Techniques of Creative Thinking,* Hawthorn Books, Prentice-Hall, Inc., Englewood Cliffs, N.J., 1954.
[5]Calvin W. Taylor, *Creativity: Progress and Potential,* McGraw-Hill Book Company, New York, 1964, p. 134.

and vertically on a grid. Thousands of combinations of characteristics may appear for consideration. For example, in Figure 14-1 the checked block, J-4, gives the combination "prefabricated plastic." This block of the grid would be brainstormed to discover a number of ideas for the building suggested by prefabricated plastic. In turn, each of the other open blocks on the grid would be brainstormed. Finally, a solution would be derived from the large number of ideas presented.

Free association techniques This group of operational techniques places a very strong emphasis upon the free flow of thought. It permits and encourages each participant to offer any and all ideas that may come to mind, with no particular effort to guide the process. Three of the free association techniques are "brainstorming," the "Gordon technique," and the "Phillips 66 buzz session."

1 Brainstorming is a technique designed to maximize the flow of ideas in a group by eliminating any critical or even realistic impulses a member might have. These critical and appraisive functions are postponed by the group leader who, banging his gavel, rules out of order any member who begins to indulge in negative thinking. Thus,

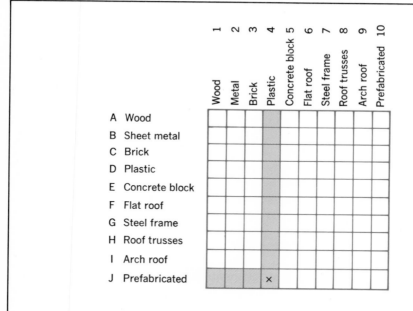

Figure 14–1   Grid Analysis Technique of Creativity

By using the grid system, all possible combinations of elements can be considered more easily and from these possibilities a solution derived.

attempts are made to eliminate major constraints on creativity; the principal objective is to get ideas out.

Brainstorming is a problem-solving conference method originated and made popular by Alex Osborn. It is perhaps the most widely and successfully used operational technique. Thousands of American businesses and other organizations have used it, and many have made it a regular feature of their operations. One report stated that brainstorming was known to be used by the armed services, 213 colleges, government bureaus in Washington, and almost all of the blue chip corporations.

The success and popularity of brainstorming are probably due to its effectiveness and the ease with which its rules may be learned. In fact, its wide popularity has led many people to believe that brainstorming is the ultimate answer to the problem of creativity. This is unfortunate because, as a result, other valuable techniques are often ignored.

A typical brainstorming session consists of a group of from six to twelve people sitting around a table and spontaneously producing ideas designed to solve a specific problem. Four basic rules generally are followed in conducting a brainstorming session: (1) judicial evaluation is ruled out; (2) "free wheeling" is welcomed (the wilder the idea, the better—it is easier to tone down than to think up); (3) quantity is encouraged; and (4) combination and improvement are sought. Brainstorming relies very heavily on the basic theory that harsh and critical judgment prevents most people from expressing unorthodox ideas, many of which may be valuable if allowed to develop. No attempt whatever is made to judge or evaluate their responses during the session. Evaluation takes place only after the brainstorming session has ended. The technique arouses enthusiasm, stimulates a competitive idea atmosphere among participants, and provides a good opportunity to improve, change, or build onto the ideas of others.

> *The sublime and the ridiculous are often so nearly related*
> *that it is difficult to class them separately. One step*
> *above the sublime makes the ridiculous, and one step*
> *above the ridiculous makes the sublime again.*
> *THOMAS PAINE*

> *It takes courage to be creative. Just as*
> *soon as you have a new idea, you are a*
> *minority of one.*
> *E. PAUL TORRENCE*

2 The Gordon technique, which also has aroused a great deal of interest, was developed by W. J. Gordon of the Arthur D. Little Company, a research and consulting firm in Cambridge, Massachusetts.[6] One of the unusual services offered by this firm is that of its invention design group which, for a fee, will invent a product to order, and

---

[6]William J. J. Gordon, "Operational Approach to Creativity," *Harvard Business Review*, November–December 1956, pp. 41–51.

which claims it has never failed. A new can opener, a new type of gas pump, and a new method of building construction are among successful inventions this group has created using the Gordon technique.

This technique is similar to brainstorming in that it is a group-conference method in which an unevaluated free-flowing discussion takes place. One basic difference between the two methods, however, is that in the Gordon technique no one except the group leader knows the exact nature of the problem under consideration. The principal reason for keeping the rest of the group members in the dark is to avoid arriving at a solution too soon. Members cannot begin to argue the merits of their solutions, for they do not know what the problem is. They continue to search for new ideas, having only a vague description of the area of the problem.

Proponents of the Gordon technique feel that a typical brainstorming session may only scratch the surface, for when specific solutions occur as soon as the session begins, most of them will tend to be superficial—more often a gimmick than a true innovation. And participants are likely to feel too quickly that they already have solved the problem.

The Gordon technique usually lasts about three hours with five to twelve participants. Gordon maintains that in an ordinary brainstorming session there is danger of a participant's becoming convinced that an idea (or ideas) he has proposed is the best solution to the problem. This satisfaction with his creative abilities may cause him to stop trying to produce additional ideas and instead devote his energies toward defending and selling his creation. This, of course, makes him a most ineffective participant. A Gordon session avoids this danger since there can be no "best" solution proposed for a problem that is never stated. The leader starts a general discussion in the area of the problem and guides it toward a more narrow discussion, but he never reveals the exact nature of the problem. For example, if the session dealt with the transportation problems of a large firm, the discussion subject might be "transporting things" or "moving things."

The success of the Gordon method relies very heavily on the leader. It requires great imagination and vision while a free-flowing discussion is evolving to relate the conversation to the actual problem.

3 The Phillips 66 buzz session, developed by Donald Phillips, is one means of utilizing the services of a larger group than is feasible for an ordinary brainstorming session. A large group is divided into a number of small groups of about five or six persons. Within each of the smaller groups, a chairman is appointed. If at all possible, the chairman is briefed beforehand to increase the group's chances of following a good brainstorming procedure.

Each group conducts its own session after the leader announces the problem. All groups attack the same problem, produce ideas, and evaluate them, selecting the one best idea or a limited number of the better ideas. The chairmen then present the ideas selected to all the other groups.

The Phillips 66 buzz session is a type of competitive brainstorming among small groups. Its success depends upon the leader's ability to organize the large group into smaller units very rapidly, and to brief them on the brainstorming method. The buzz session has generally the same advantages and disadvantages as brainstorming, but it does help the culling process and lighten the burden of final evaluation. One particular disadvantage is that in the process of evaluation the small group must rely on critical judgment quite early, and some good ideas may never come up for consideration.

Forced-relationship techniques   There are several operational techniques which rely upon the establishing of a forced relationship between two or more normally unrelated products or ideas, and which are therefore called forced-relationship techniques.

The forced relationship in most cases is established arbitrarily, often by mechanical means. Since this relationship probably never has been considered before, there is good opportunity for the stimulation of original ideas.

1 The catalogue technique is probably the simplest and most widely used forced-relationship technique. It consists merely of opening a catalogue or some other printed source of information and selecting at random an item, subject, picture, or even a single word. Then, a second item, subject, picture, or word is selected in the same fashion. These elements are then considered in combination, and the attempt is made to extract original ideas based upon the relationship.

Neither of the items is controlled; therefore the area in which ideas are needed must be extremely broad. This, of course, limits the use of the catalogue technique.

2 The listing technique consists of first listing a number of objects or ideas (usually several associated with one general subject). Every item is then given a number, and the first is considered in relation to each of the others to see whether or not any useful ideas can be developed. The second item is treated in the same manner, and this process continues until all the items on the list have been considered.

3 In the focused-object technique one of the elements is preselected with a definite purpose in mind. The fixed element may be a product, an idea, or a problem statement. The other object is chosen at random so that the forced, or unnatural, relationship is established. This relationship is then used as the basis for a chain of free associations from which new and original ideas can develop.

Eclectic approaches   Eclectic approaches, or approaches that use the best parts of many different techniques, have emerged as significant means of fostering creativity in organizations. For several years the State University of New York at Buffalo has offered a course on such approaches in its Creative Problem-solving Institute. This program covers a five-day period, and the faculty for the program includes many outstanding contributors to creativity. Participants come from varied backgrounds in many types of organizations. Gerald Nadler has also made significant contributions to creativity development in his work-design approach.[7] The author has provided an eclectic

[7] Gerald Nadler, *Work Design*, Richard D. Irwin, Inc., Homewood, Ill., 1963.

approach to creativity for several of the world's leading corporations through an "organizational-creativity"[8] one-day course.

Participation in Operational Techniques

Regular participation in group operational technique sessions develops an acute awareness of the importance of creativity and new ideas to the success of both the individual and the organization. Participation also develops the members' confidence in their own ability to produce ideas—ideas that are not only original, but often fruitful and valuable.

> Several scientific investigations . . . have shown that those who have taken such courses have acquired the ability to produce significantly more good ideas than [those] who have not had the benefit of such courses.[9]

Through participation in creativity sessions, an individual can realize his capabilities and is likely to be a more valuable member of the organization.

When members of lower levels of the organization are included, group sessions can provide a channel for communicating ideas to higher levels of management, where action may be taken upon them. The freedom from restraint in sessions of this type permits the lower-level employee to voice his ideas without fear of ridicule or censure. Group sessions with younger members of the organization also enable management to spot exceptional talent years before it might ordinarily be recognized. Both the opportunity to be heard and the opportunity to be discovered can have a beneficial effect on employee morale. Thus the program can serve as an aid to communication, which is as vital a function as creativity.

Although creative training programs are not universal cure-alls which will instantaneously propel an organization to the top of the heap, there are many benefits to be gained for both the individual and the organization. To recognize these benefits and to have an organization in which they can be utilized to the fullest, however, requires another element—one most important to organizational creativity—a creative climate.

THE CREATIVE CLIMATE

The discussion thus far has dealt with defining creativity, examining the creative process, comparing the highly creative individual and the creative organization, and developing creative abilities for the good of both individual and organization. These factors can go a long way toward increasing the vitality and effectiveness of organizations. However, the potential gains can be tremendously reduced or totally nullified by an atmosphere that stifles originality. The organization must foster a favorable climate for creativity to flourish. Such a climate requires creative management.

[8] Trade name applied for, U.S. Patent Office.
[9] Alex F. Osborn, "A Request for Information," Creative Problem-solving Institute, The State University of New York at Buffalo, Buffalo, N.Y., p. 2.

There is little doubt of the tremendous impact that environment has upon the behavior of individuals. Doubt remains in some corners about whether heredity or environment influences the person more, but there is practically no disagreement about the fact that environment is one of the major determinants of any individual's pattern of behavior.

Because individuals spend the majority of their adult waking hours in some type of organized activity, organizations are themselves a major factor in any person's environment. An organization's environment affects the behavior of all its members; even the most creative individuals find themselves impotent in an environment apathetic or hostile to new ideas.

According to a study at the University of Utah Conference on the Identification of Creative Scientific Talent, a scientist's creativity is the result of a fortunate combination of intellectual characteristics, personality factors, and a particular climate that is favorable to him. It was agreed that the climate of an organization could be *stimulating, supportive, neutral, hostile,* or *destructive* to the creative scientist. [10]

The Creative Manager

These findings are of paramount importance to a manager in his attempt to help mold his organization into a creative one. When combined with mental abilities, personality factors determine only the *potential* creative abilities of the individual in the organization. The climate or environment determines the utilization of that potential, and a manager must coordinate and direct and control his employees' behavior and activities toward the accomplishment of their objectives and the organizational objective.

In addition a manager must himself continually create an environment in which originality is encouraged rather than inhibited. He must consider it in his approach to motivation: in setting objectives, in motivating members to the accomplishment of their objectives, and in continually changing the organizational environment to allow the creative elements to flourish. This task requires a great deal of creative ability in management itself.

The A.C. Sparkplug Division of General Motors recognized the importance of management's influence on a person's creative productivity and devised a program entitled "supervising for creativity." The principles on which this program is based have been placed in three categories:

1   *The Supervisor-Employee Relationship.* First, the supervisor should strive to build up an atmosphere which encourages new ideas and changes. Secondly, he should design a positive approach, to stimulate and encourage creativity in each individual. He should give recognition for all new ideas and, further, commendation when deserved.

2   *Active Support of Creativity.* The supervisor should actively support the creative activities of his people. He should maintain effective communications with his department and other

[10] J. P. Guilford, "Intellectual Resources and Their Values as Seen by Scientists," in Calvin W. Taylor (ed.), *The Third* (1959) *University of Utah Research Conference on the Identification of Creative Scientific Talent,* University of Utah Press, Salt Lake City, Utah, 1959, pp. 128–149.

departments. A definite or formal procedure should be established for the fair and consistent consideration of all ideas conceived in the department.

3 *The Highly Creative Person.* The supervisor should permit the creative individual to work in an atmosphere where he can easily try out his ideas. The creative individual should be provided with an environment conducive to study and work. The assignment of work to the creative individual should be done very carefully. [11]

In any such program the manager must understand creativity and the creative process, and must be creative himself, not only as an individual in his own technical area but in his position of organizational influence.

Conformity versus Creativity

In setting up a creative climate one of management's greatest problems is in dealing with conformity versus creativity—the two are generally assumed to be diametrically opposed. It has been fairly well established that creativity relies very heavily on divergent thinking. This means the creative person sees things differently and proposes a change in the *status quo.* However slight the change may be, it is new, untested, and a source of uncertainty for the persons who are affected. People generally resist change because they are likely to perceive a threat to their vested interest. They prefer the security of the *status quo* and are inclined to reject a divergent opinion as a threat to themselves.

> The wisdom of mankind creeps slowly on,
> Subject to every doubt that can retard
> Or fling it back upon an earlier time.
>   *RICHARD HENRY HORNE*

> Every man takes the limits of his own field of vision for
> the limits of the world.
>   *ARTHUR SCHOPENHAUER*

> There is nothing more difficult to take in hand, more
> perilous to conduct, or more uncertain in its success, than
> to take the lead in the introduction of a new order of things.
>   *NICCOLO MACHIAVELLI*

Persons who deviate are frequently punished by the group; persons who conform are rewarded. Group pressures *can block* the expression of originality. However, it is also true that group pressures *can increase* the amount of creativity. Creativity can be one of the goals of a group; divergency can be one of the standards which is rewarded. In some organizations divergency is punished and suppressed; in other organizations divergency is prized and rewarded—these organizations gladly utilize it.

Conformity pressures are not necessarily detrimental. If there were no conformity,

---

[11] Walter J. Friess, "A Case History on Creativity in Industry," in Paul Smith (ed.), *Creativity: An Examination of the Creative Process,* Hastings House, Publishers, Inc., New York, 1959, p. 192. (By permission.)

traffic would snarl, production lines would erupt in chaos, and social machinery would collapse. Group pressures serve positive ends in sustaining the day-to-day operations of any organization—a specific corporation or the entire society. A proper balance between conformity and divergence is the crucial factor in organizational success. When creativity is accepted, assumed, and rewarded, groups can use their pressures to cause persons to conform to a norm of high creativity. Thus, organizations can encourage as well as discourage creativity.

Levels of Conformity

The various types of conformity become extremely important to organizations and management when it is recognized that the kind and amount (level) of conformity which occur depend on two sets of factors: individual and environmental.

Both factors can be greatly influenced by management. As we have seen, the individual can be affected by an understanding of the creative process and by programs designed to develop his creative abilities. The environment can be influenced toward creativity by creative management's shaping an environment that will reinforce and stimulate the originality of all members of the organization. Creativity *and* conformity, not creativity *versus* conformity must be the philosophy of creative management. Both are vitally important to every organization.

SUMMARY

Organizations usually have a great deal more creative talent than they are using effectively, since creativity is often stifled by pressures which work within both the individual and the organization. To remedy the situation, management can use tests to select highly creative individuals to staff organizations where needed. It can develop programs to bring out the latent creative abilities of some and to reinforce the abilities of others.

Management can also use groups to stimulate creativity in innumerable ways. Participation in decision making can be used to shift group goals to accomplish broader organizational objectives best. Groups can be formed in which creativity rather than conformity becomes a major goal. Procedures can be instilled to ensure a full hearing of minority opinions. Differences in status can be made less obvious; the place a member holds in the organizational hierarchy can be consciously eliminated as a factor in judging his contributions. Groups can bring together many different kinds of people; originality seems to flourish under these conditions. Groups may be made aware of the conformist pressures that they bring on individual members, and they can work to reduce these pressures. Experts in "creating creativity" can be used as consultants.

If managers can recognize the effect of such methods, then some of the ready reserve of creativity will begin to appear. These reserves can be far-reaching and can pay off tremendously for an organization that takes the time and effort to find, free, and develop them.

FOR REVIEW AND DISCUSSION

1 Why will a creative organization sometimes be inefficient in its operations?

2 What is the difference between a creative manager and a creative organization?

3 What are the more important characteristics of a creative individual? A creative organization?

4 Do creativity training programs increase the expression of creativity in an organization? Why?

5 What are the two basic rules for successfully using creativity operational techniques? Why is each important?

6 Explain the three analytical techniques given in the text.

7 Explain the three free association techniques given in the text.

8 Explain the three forced-relationship techniques given in the text.

9 What is meant by the creative climate of an organization? Why is it important? What is the manager's role in developing a creative climate?

10 Why do many members of an organization resist creativity?

11 How can group pressures be used to increase the expression of creativity? What role does a manager play in this?

12 Explain the statement: "A proper balance between conformity and divergence is the crucial factor for organizational success."

CASES

A Jason Morrow, plant manager, had no formal education beyond the eighth grade. He had started as an apprentice with the company and had been promoted through the ranks.

Mr. Morrow had always had trouble supervising the research and development department, which had always been responsible to the plant manager. After visiting the research and development department, Mr. Morrow went to his office and wrote a memo as follows to Mr. Cole, the manager of the research and development department.

"There is a lot of wasted time and effort in your department. I know enough about running a plant to know inefficiency when I see it. I suggest that you talk to Mertes [production manager] so that you can learn about how to run an efficient organization."

    1 Is Mr. Morrow justified in writing such a memo? Why?

    2 How would you respond if you were Mr. Cole?

    3 What changes in the organization of the company would help to solve this problem?

B Professor Justin had been invited to spend three weeks studying the organization of Friona Petroleum, Incorporated. On the last day of the visit Professor Justin was talking to Mr. Able, executive vice-president of the company.

Mr. Able: "Well, Professor Justin, what do you think of our organization, especially our managers? We are quite proud of the quality of our men."

Professor Justin: "Yes, Mr. Able, they certainly are impressive. However, I have been impressed by the similar characteristics of your men. They all seem to dress alike, act alike—perhaps even think alike."

Mr. Able: "Yes, we have worked hard to get a group that works well together."

1 How creative do you think such an organization will be?

2 What are the dangers inherent in such an organization?

3 What personnel hiring policy would you recommend for Friona?

C As a practice exercise, working either individually or in groups of four to eight members, discover as many uses as you can for the following objects: (*a*) a pencil, (*b*) a brick, (*c*) a paper clip, (*d*) a coin, and (*e*) a piece of paper.

As you proceed remember the principles of creativity given in this chapter and the preceding one. Spend approximately five to fifteen minutes on each object.

FOR FURTHER STUDY

Additional sources can be found in the sources cited in the chapter.

Book

Norman R. F. Maier and John J. Hayes: *Creative Management,* John Wiley & Sons, Inc., New York, 1962, chaps. 9–11. Creative management is properly introduced into an organization through face-to-face communication and group problem-solving and decision-making processes.

Articles

Larry Cummings: "Organizational Climates for Creativity," *Academy of Management Journal,* September 1965. This paper explores the organizational climate that best stimulates productive creativity.

M. R. Feinberg: "14 Suggestions for Managing Scientific Creativity," *Management Review,* December 1968. "The major challenge of the industrial research director is to manage truly creative efforts that meet the test of profitability."

William J. J. Gordon: "Operational Approach to Creativity," *Harvard Business Review,* November–December 1956. The difficulty with the creative process is that it is usually considered to be something personal. Operational creativity is a theory of how creative groups function, and its value lies in its making conscious, and thus performable at will and repeatable, a process that is usually left to chance.

Salvatore R. Maddi: "Motivational Aspects of Creativity," *Journal of Personality,* June 1965. "Motivation is probably the most important reason why people functioning creatively are not vulnerable to the snares of restrictive, evaluative environments and states of torment and frustration."

A. H. Maslow: "The Need for Creative People," *Personnel Administration,* May–June

1965. The majority of the approaches toward creativity have dealt with the creative product and not the creative process, the creative attitude, and the creative person. The inspiration phase of creativeness has been practically ignored.

George S. McIsaac: "How to Practice What We Preach in Making Business Changes," *Business Horizons,* Summer 1963, pp. 29–36. Ways to overcome organizational resistance to change are discussed.

Donald C. Pelz: "Conditions for Innovation," from "The Innovating Organization," a special supplement published by *Trans-Action,* January–February 1965. Decribes some simple procedures for stimulating creativity in an organization.

James Thompson: "How to Prevent Innovation," from "The Innovating Organization," a special supplement published by *Trans-Action,* January–February 1965. Some down-to-earth procedures for killing creativity in an organization are given.

Maneck S. Wadia: "The Administrative Function of Innovation," *International Review of Administrative Sciences,* no. 1, 1961, pp. 324–328. This article examines innovation as a function of management.

15

The Place of Creativity in Organizations

*Life is not long, and too much of it must not pass
in idle deliberation how it shall be spent.*
  SAMUEL JOHNSON

The great end of life is not knowledge but action.
  THOMAS HUXLEY

Many organizations, especially the largest and most progressive, have experimented with operational-creativity techniques. Few of them, however, have organized permanent formal programs with the objective of utilizing the creative abilities—both evident and potential—of all their employees. There are several reasons for this failure to take full advantage of available talent.

First of all, the study of creative thinking is controversial. Although it has its champions, it also has opponents—for example, those who feel that brainstorming is just another fad of little value. In many organizations, the mere mention of creativity or creative thinking can start a violent argument. Unfortunately, many ardent proponents of creative training too often use a superficial, gimmick-filled presentation and make exaggerated claims regarding its effectiveness. Creative training is sometimes presented as a sort of universal wonder drug that is capable of supplying all answers and solving all problems. Many businessmen and educators, realizing that creativity is not the "be all and end all" of management, are repulsed by such an approach and therefore may wrongly refuse to consider the subject at all.

Many programs have been poorly conceived, poorly organized, and poorly presented. Because of inadequate follow-up, many organizations have been unable to cope effectively with the ideas produced. Employees and managers often see time and money spent in creativity sessions that produce a multitude of ideas, but too often no one has been given the responsibility for processing them. The program is soon discontinued because concrete results are lacking. It is just as important to recognize the necessity for practical application of the ideas obtained as it is to know what operational methods produce creative thought.

The situation described above is indeed unfortunate, for besides offering solutions to some of the problems that the organization encounters, a creativity program can provide benefits in training, human relations, and communications, all of which are just as important as originality, if not more so. Creativity must be considered in proper perspective, for it is only one of the requirements for successful organizations.

Also, the structure of an organization seems limited in the amount of creativity or change it can endure without falling apart. Recent years—a period of extreme change—may have seen this limit approached on the national level in the United States. A balance between change and stability—a condition of stasis—must be struck if organizations are to be most effective. An organization that does not change surely will die. On the other hand, one that changes too fast, or changes merely for the sake of change, likewise will be ineffective.

CONVERTING IDEAS TO ACTION

A valuable idea is not automatically transformed into innovative action. Many new ideas are generated by persons—for example, staff experts—who do not have the authority or the responsibility for carrying them out. As a result there may be chronic complaints: the idea-producing group complains that the action-taking group pays no attention to their good ideas, and the action-taking group claims that they are too busy running the business to work with the new ideas.

> A fair idea put to use is better than a
> good idea kept on the polishing wheel.
>   ALEX F. OSBORN

The main problem often lies not in creating ideas but in producing the disciplined activity necessary to convert them to practical usefulness. Ideas are valuable only when responsible, disciplined persons convert them to action. "All in all, [creativity] is relatively abundant. It is its implementation that is more scarce."[1] Ideas are first produced in "hot-water" thought sessions, either individual or group, and they must be evaluated and implemented in the real world or "cold-water" thought sessions. Then, and only then,

[1]Theodore Levitt, "Creativity Is Not Enough," *Harvard Business Review*, May–June 1963, p. 73.

do they become likely candidates for practical use. Often persons who are talented in creating ideas are not qualified or responsible for their application.

Ideas can be evaluated according to three criteria:[2]

1 Can the organization make available the resources necessary to implement the idea? For example, if the suggested idea is to take a trip to Mars, the organization would need billions of dollars of resources available to put it into practice.

2 Will the environment within which the organization operates permit the idea to be carried out? For instance, a university administrator might not be able to fire an incompetent teacher because of tenure restrictions.

3 Will the idea, if utilized, be worth the cost? For example, a student group might want to spend the summer in Europe, but they would give up the plan if they concluded the cost was more than the worth of the trip.

If an idea survives the test of these three criteria, it is a candidate for practical application. Here the value of the organization's less creative persons who do principally routine work becomes apparent.

THE FUNCTION OF LESS CREATIVE PERSONS

One advantage of formal organizations is that they achieve order. With order comes discipline, controls, and efficiency in performing work. Production becomes routine and standardized. The economies of mass production can be realized. In such circumstances the place of the less creative persons who are willing to do routine, repetitive work is clear. They are responsible for the day-to-day carrying out of an innovative plan. For example, only a few persons are required for a relatively short time to design a new accounting system; in a large firm hundreds of persons may spend their full time for a number of years working with the system. Similarly, the players on a football team are expected to executive routinely plays designed by the coach. The players are even told how they are to run, block, and tackle. Some organizations, in fact, spend their total energies in carrying out the creative ideas of a single person.

Clearly, despite the advanced technology of our modern world, many less creative persons still make enormous contributions to organizations. What is needed is a balance of creativity with the established routines of successful practice.

WHEN IS CREATIVITY NEEDED IN ORGANIZATIONS?

Two types of thought patterns, analytic and creative, are required continually in maintaining effective organizations.

Analytic Thought

One of man's ways of bringing order and discipline to organizations is his power of *analytic thought,* or the application of the scientific-research method of problem solving.

[2]Cf. Charles H. Granger, "The Hierarchy of Objectives," *Harvard Business Review,* May–June 1964, p. 65.

It helps to convert the unknown to the familiar, to bring order out of disorder, or chaos. Motion and time study, job analysis, job descriptions, cost and financial accounting, market research, and standardization of procedures are all analytic techniques that can have powerful effects in making organizations more efficient. Analytic thought is structured, logical, and disciplined. It is a central feature of management thought.

Because analytic thought helps to bring discipline and order, it is usually extremely valuable, especially in the short run. However, over a period of time pure analytic thought often produces organizations that tend to become closed systems and isolate themselves from changes in the environment. Rationality, order, and protection of internal vested interests become values of high priority, and there is a tendency to strive for more and more efficiency with a current product, process, or service. As we have seen, such an attitude may fail to supply the creativity needed for survival.

Creative Thought

The second class of thought required in organizations is creative. Creative thought is relatively unstructured, undisciplined, and is often illogical. But creative thought supplies the new concepts needed in an organization.

Creative thought often has the effect of shattering the *status quo* and, consequently, is often resisted by members of the organization. But discovering something better than the organization presently has is the very purpose of creative thought. It involves an exploration of the unknown in attempting to discover what valuable ideas can be gained.

Creativity is essential for organizational prosperity, but there is a limit to the amount that each organization can use profitably. No business can cope with the disorder resulting from constant creativity by every member, department, or part of the organization. Most members are likely to spend the majority of their time and effort on routine work, accomplished in more or less standard ways. If routines are not followed, order, control, and discipline cannot be obtained.

THE PROGRESS OF IDEAS IN ORGANIZATIONS

The relationship of analytic and creative thought in a typical business can be seen by tracing the progress of a new thought in an organization. The progress of an idea follows three steps: inception, attainment, and renewal.

Idea Inception

The typical business is started when someone has an idea that he believes will result in a product or service that will be demanded. The idea must offer something that is better or that can be produced at lower cost than what is currently available. Creative thought is essential in the idea-inception stage.

A significant idea often spawns enormous organizational activity: for example, the ideas of Thomas Edison resulted in effective generation and use of electric power, those of Alexander Graham Bell produced the telephone, and the ideas of Charles Kettering are often credited with the development of an efficient gasoline internal combustion engine. Thus, creativity is an essential ingredient for getting any endeavor started.

Idea Attainment

Attainment is the second stage in the use of ideas in organizations. Ideas originate in the inception stage; they are converted to practice in the attainment stage. It is significant that in the inception stage, creative thought was paramount, but that in the attainment stage analytic thought predominates. Excessive creativity can be harmful in this stage because it may result in uncoordinated activity.

In the attainment stage, organizations become primarily concerned with delegation of authority, the structure of the organization, performance standards, cost control, quality control, and all the other things that are needed to operate efficiently. Analytic thought can result in an organization where the work of numerous persons, often hundreds of thousands, can be efficiently coordinated to use ideas to the organization's best advantage.

Persons who are strong in creativity are frequently weak in analytic abilities. This fact often causes organizational problems. For example, the typical small business was probably started by an individual skilled in the use of creative thought. These thought patterns were essential in the inception stage of the business, or else there would have been no business in the first place.

However, once the product or service is conceived, the next step is to discover ways of producing it in large numbers at a reasonable cost. Without the ability to produce or perform service competitively, the fledgling business will fail. Efficient production requires analytic thought for organizing and controlling necessary activities, and since, as we noted before, our chief executive's major asset may be in the creative realm, we often find firms with products or services of high potential that may fail to reach that potential for lack of good analytic thought. The organization may change leadership when it becomes apparent that those who originally conceived the services or products cannot manage the organization efficiently. At this point in the organization's life it may happen, indeed it may be desirable, that a leader skilled in the analytic organizational techniques accepts the leadership of the firm. Perhaps the firm should be sold if such a leader cannot be found.

Idea Renewal

A successful product or service will eventually be replaced by other innovations. However, the analytic managers required for idea development are often not proficient in providing ideas for renewal. As in our example of the buggy-whip manufacturer, the organization will find itself in the paradoxical position of performing more expertly and more inexpensively something for which there is less and less demand. If the organization is small with but a single line of production, it will die with the line.[3]

Resistance to new ideas on the part of those responsible for the idea-development stage often arises because the new ideas will replace products or services in which they are already expert. They may want to preserve their comparative advantage in the current technology. Their present comparative advantage may lie in such areas as buildings or equipment in place, technical knowledge, or market position.

Thus organization ordinarily requires both analytic and creative thought. Creative thought is required at the inception stage for each new idea. As the idea is attained, analytic thought takes precedence. Finally (see Figure 15-1), the circle is completed when creative thought is again required for organizational renewal since the previously developed ideas will eventually see the end of their useful lives.

The discussion has assumed so far that the members of the organization wish it to continue. Such is not always the case; for example, if the organization has completed its purpose it may be more desirable for the organization to die or fail rather than continue. This is a decision that the responsible members should make with the full knowledge that ordinarily the organization can, if desired, continue to live indefinitely, provided ideas for renewal are developed.

CREATIVITY FOR ANALYTIC OR ROUTINE WORK

Even within the restrictive boundaries of a disciplined and structured organization, there is opportunity for the expression of creativity by every member. Every single janitor,

[3]Peter Drucker clearly describes the distinctive problems of different-sized organizations. He also explains the problems an organization is likely to encounter in growing from one size to the next. See Peter Drucker, *The Practice of Management,* Harper & Row, Publishers, Incorporated, New York, 1954, pp. 227–252.

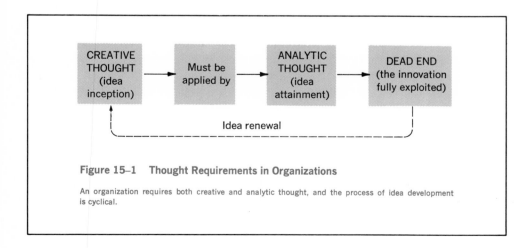

Figure 15–1   Thought Requirements in Organizations

An organization requires both creative and analytic thought, and the process of idea development is cyclical.

ditch digger, assembly-line worker, student, or professor can use his innate creative ability in some way to improve his work.

A general statement can be made about the place of creativity for different persons in organizations: Leaders with general responsibility have the obligation of using creativity to determine *what* things the organization will do, principally in the inception and renewal stages. In addition, almost everyone has the responsibility for using creativity in determining *how* to do things better.

It often is difficult to combine creativity with routine, standard operations. The desire to do something new flies in the face of efficiency on current projects. As a solution, many organizations have set up separate units charged with the primary responsibility for innovating. "Research and development departments" is a favorite name for these innovative units.

Innovative activities are often separated from operating activities physically, financially, and by responsibility. They normally are not managed by operating personnel because the desire of operating managers for standardization is frustrated by innovations. Moreover, research and development activities require a type of management different from the analytical approaches typically used in operating activities. In a large firm the research and development department is sometimes located in a separate city to emphasize the independence of innovation from operation.

SUMMARY

Every member of an organization can and probably wants to create. "Everyone has the motivation to create."[4] Creativity may be encouraged in an individual or a group by establishing an organizational climate that encourages full expression of abilities. Creativity can be obtained in hot-water thought sessions (individual or group) where persons give up standard solutions, preconceived habits, and the censoring of thoughts— where they seek a sort of "rational dream" that may have merit. However, no amount of creativity alone will ordinarily make a successful organization, for no organization can for long stand the strain of continual innovation in every area.

After ideas have been created, they are evaluated in the rational light of reality, sometimes called "cold-water thought sessions." Here judgments are made on whether the ideas are practical, economical, or otherwise feasible. Those ideas that pass the cold-water test are then candidates for attainment.

Ideas come to practical realization when the organization does the necessary work for effectively producing the new product or service. To do such work efficiently often requires a high degree of organizational skill, discipline, standardization, and control. During this disciplined period managers should keep in mind that the organization probably will eventually require new additions of creative thought.

Organizations are renewed when they again use creativity in inventing or discovering ideas, products, services, or technologies to replace older ones.

[4]A. H. Maslow, *Eupsychian Management,* Richard D. Irwin, Inc., Homewood, Ill., 1965, p. 8.

The place, importance, and use of creativity in organizations are clear: an organization works best with a neat balance of creative and analytic thought—creative thought for discovering unfamiliar ideas, and analytic thought for converting the unfamiliar ideas to familiar, practical attainments. Members should be encouraged to be creative, but at the same time their thoughts and activities should be directed in practical ways— such is the function of a manager. For encouraging creativity a useful motto may be: "It is better to do a better thing than merely a thing better."

FOR REVIEW AND DISCUSSION

1 What are some reasons why many organizations have not used creativity-producing techniques?

2 Describe the problem of implementation that still exists even if a good idea is available.

3 Describe the criteria that can be used to evaluate an idea. Give an example not in the text to illustrate each criterion.

4 Describe the role of less creative persons in an organization.

5 Describe analytic thought and explain its place in organizations.

6 Describe creative thought and explain its place in organizations.

7 Explain the step-by-step progress of an idea in an organization.

8 What problem is likely to exist in an organization with too much creativity? With too much stability?

9 Why is creativity absolutely necessary for organizational renewal?

10 Can creativity improve the performance of routine work? Explain.

11 Why are research and development departments often separated from the routine operations of a company?

12 Explain the difference between a hot-water and a cold-water thought session.

CASES

A   Mr. Phillips had founded and been for twenty-five years the president of Phillips Products, Inc., until his death five years ago. Mr. Phillips had been highly creative; he had provided not only the coordination but also the vision for his company. In the five years after Mr. Phillips' death the company steadily lost competitive position. Mr. Stores, the president during those five years, saw his job mainly as carrying on the highly successful policies of Mr. Phillips.

Mr. Snell has just been appointed president of the company. According to him: "One of our first jobs will be to develop the latent creative talent in our organization. There are many previously unused creative resources available just for the asking."

1 Compare the approach toward creativity of the three presidents.

2 What effect will Mr. Snell's statement have?

    3 What further steps should Mr. Snell take for creating creativity in his organization?

    B Mr. Hall, president of Eastern Instruments, was widely recognized as one of the most creative persons in his field. He had been responsible for developing a number of concepts that had eventually been highly successfully adapted by his competitors. On the other hand, Eastern Instruments had never been successful. Mr. Hall was very reluctant to put one of his ideas into production. "I'm just not satisfied," he said about one product. "I know that if I work at it another year, I'll get it perfect."

    During the year Mr. Hall was attempting to perfect his product, a competitor captured the market with a product inferior to the one Mr. Hall had already developed.

    1 What are the reasons for the lack of success of Eastern Instruments?

    2 What changes would you recommend to the board of directors of Eastern Instruments?

    C Jules Marsh was the janitor for a classroom building at the university. When Jules had been hired, Jack Hays, the foreman, spent two days instructing him. Mr. Hays had told Jules: "We have been keeping these buildings clean for many years, and I want to show you the very best way to do your work."

    Jules learned Mr. Hays's procedure and followed it for a number of months. One day, however, Jules thought of a new procedure for doing his work. He tried the new method and found that he could do his work with no more effort in seven hours instead of eight. The quality of the finished work was the same using either procedure. Jules was very careful to conceal his new method so that he could keep his extra hour for additional rest during his working day.

    1 Was Jules justified in concealing his new method?

    2 Was Jules a typical workman in that he was capable of developing a better way to do his job?

    3 What could the university do to make available to it improvements such as that discovered by Jules?

FOR FURTHER STUDY

Additional sources can be found in the sources cited in the chapter.

Book

Leonard R. Sayles: "Stability and Change in Organizations," *Managerial Behavior,* McGraw-Hill Book Company, New York, 1964, pp. 160–161, 201–206. The manager's job includes the attainment of both stability and change.

Articles

Robert Albanese: "Overcoming Resistance to Stability," *Business Horizons,* April 1970. An organization needs a balance of change and stability.

Theodore Levitt: "Creativity Is Not Enough," *Harvard Business Review,* May–June 1963. "A new idea can be creative in the abstract but destructive in actual operation, and often instead of helping a company it will even hinder it."

Jonathan A. Slesinger and Ernest Harburg: "Organizational Change and Executive Behavior," *Human Organizations,* Summer 1968. Organizational change is not insured by simply adopting a rational plan for change.

Section B
Planning

16

Planning

*The plan of action is, at one and the same time, the
result envisaged, the line of action to be followed, the
stages to go through and the methods to use.*
HENRI FAYOL

Planning is the second managerial function performed for a particular activity. Its successful accomplishment requires analysis of the data from the past, decision in the present, and an evaluation of the future.

PLANNING: AN OVERVIEW

Someone has said: "If you don't know where you're going, *any* road will get you there." Perhaps there is also truth in the thought: "If you don't know where you're going, *no* road will get you there." Whichever view is taken, it is clear that individual and organizational activity without a plan is likely to be ineffective.

From an organizational viewpoint planning is concerned with: (1) setting organizational goals or objectives and (2) determining the approach by which the goals and objectives are to be accomplished. Planning determines where the organization is going and the general approaches it will use to get there. For example, a company might accomplish the two steps of planning by: (1) deciding it will sell 1 million dollars' worth of a certain product in the next year and (2) deciding that it will produce the product itself (rather than buy it from another producer, for example).

Formulation of new goals or objectives is at the very heart of the steps that are necessary for organizations to have long lives. Planning is also a necessity for shorter-lived organizations for the most effective accomplishment of their immediate objectives. "Often an [organization] will drift along until someone defines what it is and where it should go."[1]

Purpose of Planning

Planning coordinates the activities of the organization toward defined and agreed upon objectives. The alternative is random behavior. Although there is some chance that activity can be coordinated without planning, the probability is very high (because of the almost infinite variability of persons and their objectives) that unplanned activity will be random, dysfunctional, and not directed toward organizational objectives. Figure 16-1 shows how the process of selecting and communicating an organizational goal can reduce random behavior and produce goal-directed, coordinated organizational behavior. If there were eight departments in the organization, the numbers in Figure 16-1 might

[1]"To Reorganize—Turn Bottom Up," *Business Week,* Apr. 10, 1965, p. 81.

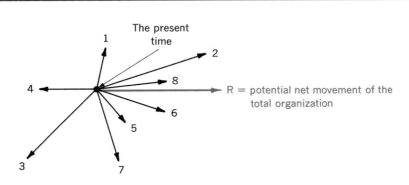

Figure 16–1   Potential Directions and Quantities of Movement of Eight Departments of an Organization, Each Department Acting Independently

Each number represents the goal of a different department in an organization. The dot represents the present moment. The black lines represent the different directions in which each of eight departments of a given organization would move if these departments were to act independently, the length of each line indicating the intensity of the desired movement. The brown line represents the resultant of these conflicting forces and is the direction in which the total organization actually moves into the future.

represent the separate, independent objectives of each respective department. The center dot represents the present time, and each arrow represents the potential direction and quantity of the respective departments' movements without a coordinating plan.

In Figure 16-1 the combined effect, or net movement, is shown as a resultant by the color line.[2] In other words, the net effect of the organization movement without a preconceived, conscious, deliberate plan is shown by the resultant. There is some agreement on the direction of movement by departments numbered 2, 8, 5, 6, and 7; but departments 1, 4 and 3 will tend to reduce the net effect of the other departments. Departments 2, 8, 5, 6 and 7 may have received some degree of coordination through "hit-and-miss" management methods. But this poor coordination may be due to a lack of conscious, deliberate, systematic planning.

In Figure 16-2 we diagram the same organization's potential movement after the successful adoption, communication, and acceptance of a coordinating plan.

The effect of the successful adoption of a coordinating plan, as shown in Figure 16-2, is to reorient the respective objectives of the several departments.

> If all the ideals animating the organization could be lined up so as to pull in the same straight line, the resultant would be a very powerful effort; but when these ideals pull in diverse directions, the resultant force may be insignificantly positive—may, in fact be negative.[3]

After successful planning, there is more general agreement about the desired direction

[2]As shown in chap. 3, for conceptual purposes, vector addition may be used but is not required to convey the basic concepts.

[3]Harrington Emerson, *The Twelve Principles of Efficiency,* The Engineering Magazine Company, New York, 1912, pp. 59–60. Reprinted in Harwood F. Merrill (ed.), *Classics in Management,* American Management Association, New York, 1960, pp. 179–180.

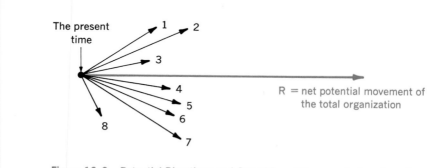

Figure 16–2   Potential Directions and Quantities of Movement of an Organization of Eight Departments Following a Coordinated Plan

Here we see a schematization of the potential and actual directions of the same organization as shown in Figure 16–1 after a coordinating plan has been adopted, communicated, and accepted. Each number represents the goal of a different department in an organization.

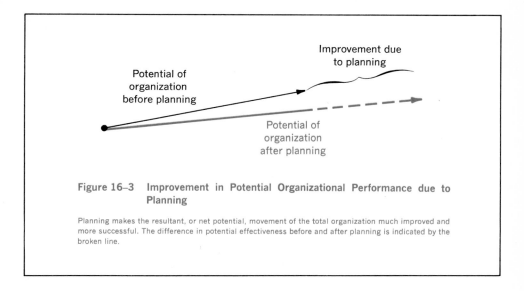

Figure 16–3   Improvement in Potential Organizational Performance due to
Planning

Planning makes the resultant, or net potential, movement of the total organization much improved and
more successful. The difference in potential effectiveness before and after planning is indicated by the
broken line.

of movement of the separate departments. Hence, the resultant, or net potential movement of the total organization, is much greater than before planning was implemented.
The difference is a net improvement in the potential effectiveness of the organization,
as shown in Figure 16-3.

Planning brings a higher degree of rationality and order into the organization than
would be present without planning. Without planning a manager is forced to *react* to
situations or problems. Planning permits a manager to *act* with initiative, and to *create*
situations to the organization's advantage. Many poorly managed organizations never
seem to get out of the vicious circle of being almost totally occupied with immediate,
crises problems. Such an approach to management is known as "fire fighting," or attempting to bring emergency situations under control. The organization that only fights
fires will soon be outdone by its competitors. An organization with a clearly defined
future goal likely will soon greatly outdistance a competitor which endlessly spends
its time fighting fires.

Planning helps a manager shape the future of his organization rather than let him
be caught in an endless trap of reacting only to current crises, or problems. Now we have
pinpointed a key feature of planning—*planning is concerned with the future*. Perhaps
the futuristic aspect of planning is why many managers refuse to do adequate planning.
Even with planning, the future remains unknown, and one always takes a risk in predicting or creating it. Many managers are apparently not willing to take that risk. But to
deal with the future is an important part of the manager's job.

Planning is concerned with the future—but the future encompasses a great span
of time. As a practical matter administrators often desire to know exactly how long into
the future they should plan. Unfortunately, there is no precise answer to this question.

However, some general guidelines have been formulated to assist the manager in resolving this difficulty.

The Commitment Principle

The implementation of a plan commits an organization to specific courses of action. Therefore, plans should cover a time period long enough to foresee, through a series of actions, the fulfillment of commitments made in the plan.[4] As elusive as this may be, it is about the only realistic standard available because the time period a plan should encompass is uniquely related to the problem it is designed to attack.

The decision of the United States to enter the "space race" entailed numerous commitments and initiated a complex planning effort that covered a long period of time. Even while man was entering a new frontier through suborbital flights, ambitious plans were being devised for lunar landings. The decision to explore space, which was made in the early sixties, committed the nation to a series of actions that would require more than a decade to accomplish. The decision of a sales manager to increase sales by 10 percent in the following year results in shorter commitments and plans of correspondingly smaller scope. The important point to recognize is that it is the nature of the decision, the particular problem under consideration, and the numerous other factors that determine the exact length of the commitment and time period of the plan.

Uncertainty is characteristic of the future. Some plans and commitments are easier to change than others. For this reason, it generally is accurate to say that the commitment period is inversely related to the ease with which a plan may be altered. This brings up the second guideline of good planning, flexibility.

Flexibility of Plans

Because one never knows exactly what the future holds, plans generally do not work out precisely as expected. "It is a bad plan that admits of no modification"[5]

In planning, one is aiming at a moving target. Ordinarily, before a given target (plan) is fulfilled, a revision is made in the old plan, or the old plan is scrapped altogether. In either case a new plan is created; a new target is set up. The dynamic nature of the planning process is shown in Figure 16-4.

In Figure 16-4, points A through F represent plans (for example, each could be a sales goal) for several points in time. At any time, the organization works toward the appropriate plan, but a new or revised plan may be put into effect before the old one is reached. It would then be foolish to continue to work toward an obsolete plan or goal. Efforts are directed toward a new plan whenever the new plan is developed. For example, at time point 1 in Figure 16-4 plan A became obsolete; the goal to be worked toward immediately became point B. Similarly, before B was reached, C took effect. Effective

---

[4]Harold Koontz and Cyril O'Donnell refer to this proposition as the "commitment principle" in their text *Principles of Management,* 4th ed., McGraw-Hill Book Company, New York, 1968, p. 224.

[5]Publilius Syrus, *Maxim 469* (ca. 42 B.C.), trans. Karius Lyman.

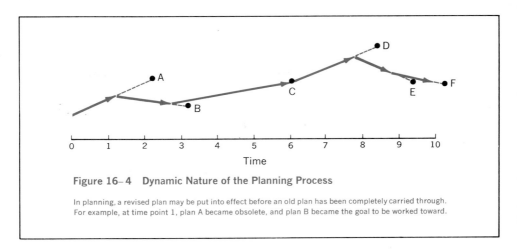

Figure 16– 4   Dynamic Nature of the Planning Process

In planning, a revised plan may be put into effect before an old plan has been completely carried through. For example, at time point 1, plan A became obsolete, and plan B became the goal to be worked toward.

management requires that plans be revised and the efforts of the organization be re-directed whenever a new plan will better serve the interests of the organization and its members.

Planning at Different Management Levels

All levels of management should be involved in planning, but like the other management functions, managers at higher levels in the organization probably spend more of their efforts planning than do lower-level managers. There is another important general rela-tionship of planning activities to organizational levels. Because lower levels tend to derive their plans from the plans of higher levels, higher-level plans must be set *before* lower-level plans are established. In other words, the higher one is in the organization structure, the farther into the future he must plan. This relationship is shown in Figure 16-5. The president may spend the majority of his planning activities on broad company objectives that are expected to develop five, ten, or even twenty years hence. A foreman,

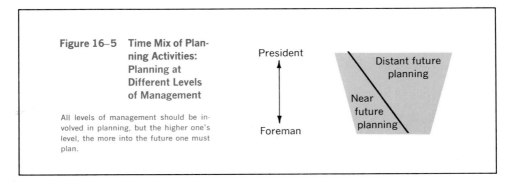

Figure 16–5   Time Mix of Plan-ning Activities: Planning at Different Levels of Management

All levels of management should be in-volved in planning, but the higher one's level, the more into the future one must plan.

on the other hand, is much more concerned with more immediate objectives, such as planning how to meet this month's production quota. Middle-management planning activities are between those of the foreman and the president.

TYPES OF PLANS

The plans used by the various levels of management may be classified in a number of ways. Generally, however, all plans derive from organizational goals and can be easily differentiated by the frequency with which they are used. From its objectives an organization develops standing plans and single-use plans.[6] Standing plans lead to the development of policies, procedures, and rules. Single-use plans produce programs, projects, and budgets. These relationships are shown in Figure 16-6. Plans also can be classified as strategic and administrative.

Standing Plans

Standing plans, those which are used again and again, include policies, procedures, and rules.

Policies   General statements that guide decision making are called policies. Policies define the boundaries within which decisions can be made, and they direct decisions toward the accomplishment of objectives. Once goals have been established, a top-level manager may now attempt to determine the numerous ways in which this goal could be

[6]The terms "standing plans" and "single-use plans" were developed by William H. Newman, *Administrative Action,* 2d ed., Prentice-Hall, Inc., Englewood Cliffs, N.J., 1963, pp. 29–54.

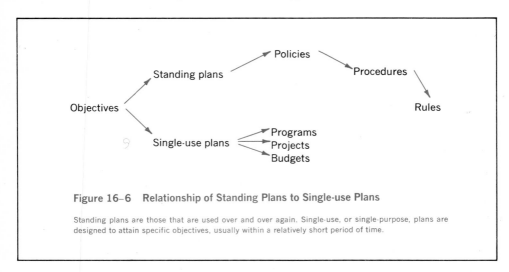

Figure 16–6   Relationship of Standing Plans to Single-use Plans

Standing plans are those that are used over and over again. Single-use, or single-purpose, plans are designed to attain specific objectives, usually within a relatively short period of time.

accomplished. He does not have to analyze all these possible alternatives and select the best one to use. In the progression from objectives to policies to procedures to rules, the limits become increasingly more narrow. Rules are specific statements of what should or should not be done. Thus a business organization would construct a hierarchy of objectives. It would also need a hierarchy of supporting policies throughout each of the broad operating areas—sales, procurement, manufacturing, personnel, and financial operations. Policies in each of these operational areas would be formulated. For example, in personnel, numerous policies would be established to provide consistent guides to action in the areas of securing, selecting, training, compensating of employees, working conditions, employee services, and industrial relations.

Procedures   The need for procedures arises when the organization wishes to achieve a high degree of regularity in a frequently recurring event. A procedure provides a narrower, more specific guide to action than a policy. For example: A major airline adopts as one of its *objectives* the securing of safety for its passengers. Since one of the contributing factors to air traffic safety is the proper functioning of all the equipment of the airplanes, the airline adopts a *policy* of preventive maintenance. A *procedure* for carrying out preventive maintenance is required. Such a procedure would spell out the series of steps that should be taken when conducting preventive-maintenance checks. The steps would be arranged in some predetermined best order. For example, the procedure for a preventive maintenance check on a piece of electronic equipment may start with a check of the fuses and then proceed step by step to the components that frequently become inoperative.

This step-by-step ordering of action can thus be performed by several individuals who need not be as skilled as the individuals establishing the procedure. Thus, in addition to the advantage of making sure the work is done, a good procedure can result in labor and time savings. An apprentice may carry out a simple procedure for preventive maintenance on electronic equipment and if he observes a malfunction at some step, he may take that piece of equipment out of the plane and replace it with a proper functioning piece of equipment. Then the malfunctioning equipment could be turned over to the others for repair.

Personnel hiring is an example where procedures may be used. Selection of a candidate depends on past training, experience, previous work records, health, present job, results of tests, and results of interviews. Establishing a hiring procedure ensures that all important points are covered. Each step eliminates some applicants. Thus, if the final step in an employment procedure is an interview by the top manager, this manager may be required to interview only three applicants instead of the fifteen that originally applied for the job.

Rules   Rules are specific statements of what may or may not be done. The only discretion left to the manager is whether or not to apply the rule. The development and communication of rules provide ways for informing the organizational members exactly what the boundaries of acceptable behavior are. "No smoking in the plant" is an example of a rule.

Single-use Plans

Single-use, or single-purpose, plans are designed to accomplish specific objectives— usually within a relatively short period of time. Budgets, programs, and projects are examples of single-use plans.

From an economic forecast a company estimates the general trend of economic conditions within its industry. This forecast becomes the basis for establishing single-use operating plans or budgets to be used to guide operations during the year. The overall budget might include the following components.

Sales budget showing anticipated sales in total and by districts, areas, and individual salesmen.

Advertising budget expressing the proposed advertising campaign and the estimated financial outlay required.

Production budget based on anticipated sales by time periods and existing inventory and minimum inventory balances. Gives expected starting and completion times for manufacturing the products, and anticipated costs can be prepared.

Raw materials budget based on production time requirements (established in the production budget) and current raw material inventory, reorder points, minimum balances, and time to get delivery on orders. This budget shows the materials needed by time periods, when to submit orders, and anticipated costs.

Personnel budget showing current manpower needs based on average normal turnover and production and sales demands. Included within this budget would be a schedule for vacation and military leaves as well as a schedule for hiring new personnel and training of personnel.

Equipment purchasing and maintenance budget would include the cost of new equipment necessary for production of anticipated sales and the costs of maintenance of all equipment.

Cost budget would estimate the costs by time periods and by operating departments for manufacturing, advertising, and distributing the products of this firm. It would also include both direct and overhead costs in total and by operating departments.

Cash-flow budget a time budget indicating the cash inflow and outflow of the firm. Planning a budget of this type in advance of actual operations makes it possible to make additional plans for cash shortages in advance of the occurrence.

Profit budget based on the anticipated volume of sales, selling prices, and costs, an anticipated profit budget could be constructed. This budget would serve as an operational plan as well as a control device for the entire organization. This budget should also be broken down by departments and by time periods so that it could be used as an operational plan and control device for operating departments.

All these budgets must be coordinated if the total organizational effort is to be a united one. Here again objectives play a unifying role—for each budget should be and can be related to the goals of the organization. Thus the organizational goals should provide the unifying framework for all the operational plans—both standing and single-use—and controls.

Programs and projects are also examples of single-use plans that are developed under the umbrella of organizational goals. The automatic replacement of typewriters within an organization after they reach a certain age is an example of a program. Expansion programs, training programs, and management-development programs are further examples.

Projects have some of the same characteristics as programs but they are usually part of some specific program. The inventory of existing typewriters is an example of a project. Building a new plant and marketing a new product are further examples of projects.

Strategic Plans

Strategic plans are concerned with broad matters that vitally affect development of an organization. Strategic planning pays special attention to relatively uncontrollable economic and technological environmental factors. Emphasis is placed upon predicting the future behavior of external variables and the formulation of alternative courses of action in light of expected events.

Consider, for instance, the planning of a firm's product line. Suppose a producer of television sets decides there is great opportunity in the production of specialized electronics for the space program and changes its product line accordingly. This strategic decision affects organizational development because a new set of organizational objectives must be formulated, with different growth potential.

A manager should do a lot of forecasting before such an important decision is made. He should predict federal government budget allocations for the space program. He should judge public attitudes toward the program. Decreasing interest in it would suggest a slowdown in the program. What effect will alternative uses for government funds— housing, welfare, education, and so forth—have on the program? Is he too late in entering the field? Each of these variables is largely uncontrollable by the individual firm, but the strategic planner must recognize their influence upon his organization. In such decisions, there is a special incentive for accuracy in the predictions. Once the decision is made, the organization is irrevocably committed to large expenditures. It may have to do the best it can and adapt to whatever situations materialize. A serious mistake in strategic planning can be disastrous. The perils are increased because of the uncontrollable nature of the relevant factors.

Strategic planning is especially complicated in many of today's highly technical industries that are subject to the "law of acceleration."[7] This "law" suggests that changes tend to occur at an increasing rate. Consider that it took man over 3,000 years to develop

[7] Townsend Hoopes, "The Corporate Planner (New Edition)," *Business Horizons*, no. 4, 1962, p. 59.

a mechanical means of flying. Yet less than 100 years later he set foot on the moon. Just think of the opportunities and challenges this sort of thing provides for strategic planners.

A key point to remember about strategic planning is that the process is subjective. When an administrator establishes the ultimate ends or objectives of his firm, he exercises managerial judgment, not scientific reasoning. There is no objective process by which he can conclude one organizational goal is better or worse than another without referencing his analysis to some other value or objective.

Administrative Plans

Stategic planning and organizational development are vitally important, but managers also must provide for growth and efficiency within overall objectives. Administrative planning is concerned with how a firm can optimize the use of its resources within strategic objectives. Strategic planning focuses on *what* the organization would do. Administrative planning focuses on *how* to accomplish those objectives.

Generally, administrative plans concern factors within the control of the organization. For instance, the television producer mentioned above with administrative plans would determine dollar investments and manpower needs for the product line alteration to space work.

Administrative planning is less subjective than strategic planning. For example, the evaluation of an administrative decision plan is primarily in terms of how well did it contribute to the established objectives of the organization. In most cases this question is more easily and objectively answered than the question of whether the goal itself is correct.

A number of techniques have been developed to assist with administrative planning. One of the most popular is Program Evaluation and Review Technique, or PERT. PERT belongs to a larger class of methods known as network analysis and is an outgrowth of scheduling work done in connection with the Polaris missile program.

To use PERT, the following steps must be taken.

1 Define the project objective.
2 List the activities required to complete the project.
3 Understand the relationship between the required activities.
4 Estimate the time required to complete each activity.

The successful utilization of PERT also requires that the project have a definite starting and completion date. In general, it has found its greatest application on "one-time crash programs" consisting of numerous subprocesses and where completion time is more important than cost.

To illustrate, assume that a group of students at a university decide in the Fall of 1971 that they would like to publish a student affairs journal known as SPEAK. It is to be student organized and managed. Also the editor is dedicated to having the first edition available no later than September 1972. To insure a logical approach to the problem, the organizers decide to apply program evaluation and review technique in their scheduling.

In Figure 16-7 the activities necessary prior to publication have been itemized, be-

ACTIVITY	TIME IN WEEKS			
	O_T	L_T	P_T	E_T
Conduct opinion poll	½	1	1½	1
Acquire administrative approval	1	2	3	2
Recruit staff	4	8	12	8
Train personnel	2	3	4	3
Solicit advertisements and contributions	4	6	14	7
Assemble student articles	2	6	10	6
Review articles	1	2	3	2
Select manuscripts	½	1	1½	1
Publication				

Figure 16-7   *Activities Required before the First Publication of SPEAK*
Estimates of time required to accomplish something can be optimistic, likely, and pessimistic. An estimated time is derived from a weighted average of these times.

ginning with an opinion poll to establish the need for the journal and continuing through the selection of articles to be published in the first edition. Note that three times are given beside each activity (in units of weeks). The first figure (O_T) is the optimistic time required for the activity, providing perfect conditions occur. The second figure (L_T) is the likely time, or the period most likely to occur, while the third figure (P_T) is a pessimistic time which assumes that the most unfavorable conditions possible materialize. The final figure (E_T) is the expected time or the weighted average of the other three periods, assuming that E_T is four times more likely than either of the other two possibilities. Therefore,

$$E_T = \frac{O_P + L_T(4) + P_T}{6}$$

Figure 16-8 provides a graphical representation of a simplified PERT network and illustrates that three distinct "paths" must be completed before publication can begin. Some information abstracted from the network chart appears as follows.

PATH	ESTIMATED TIMES	TOTAL	CRITICAL PATH	SLACK
ABCD	1 + 2 + 7	10.0	14.0	4.0
ABCEF	1 + 2 + 8 + 3	14.0	14.0	0.0
ABCGHI	1 + 2 + 6 + 2 + 1	12.0	14.0	2.0

Path ABCEF is the critical path, or the series of activities requiring the longest time

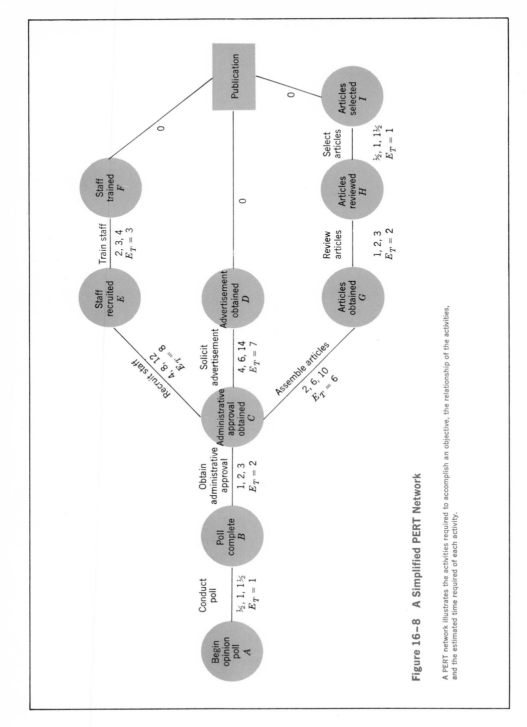

Figure 16–8 A Simplified PERT Network

A PERT network illustrates the activities required to accomplish an objective, the relationship of the activities, and the estimated time required of each activity.

to complete. This is the path that will result in the greatest trouble if complications develop along it. All the other routes have slack or spare time, which is obtained by subtracting from the time required along the critical path those times necessary for accomplishing the activities along the other routes.

Several simplifying assumptions have been made in this example, such as the implicit assertion that two activities along the same path do not take place simultaneously. In other words, it has been assumed that activities such as G are completed before others like H begin. In reality this may or may not be true.

PERT forces one to systematically analyze the problem under consideration. The editor of SPEAK knows now that if he desires to have the first edition out by the first of September, he had better begin work no later than 14 weeks prior to that date. Even then he is playing the odds, and would do well to allow himself a little extra time. Moreover, he now knows that he should concentrate especially upon soliciting advertisements and contributions, because he has little spare or slack time available for the other activities. Certainly, he is more knowledgeable and better prepared to proceed toward his objectives, because of having systematically planned his approach.

ORGANIZATIONAL PLANNING AND CONTROL STANDARDS

Planning provides control standards against which actual performance can be measured. If there is a significant deviation between actual and planned performance, corrective action can be taken. A clear example of the use of plans as control standards can be found in the single-use budgets discussed earlier. These budgets provide a basis for continuous control standards throughout the operating year. If actual performance does not correspond closely to planned, budgeted performance in some area (for example, production), then corrective action can be taken. Chapter 23 will explain controlling and its relationship to the planning function.

SUMMARY

If an organization is to remain healthy it must pursue realistic objectives. Planning is concerned with the establishment of organization objectives, and the general ways these objectives can be accomplished. The alternative to good planning usually is random, uncoordinated, wasteful activity. As a minimum, planning should cover the period for which resources have been committed. Effective plans are flexible, and adapt to changing conditions. Because they are more directly concerned with the long-range future of the organization, higher-level managers spend relatively more time planning than lower-level managers.

The types of plans include standing, single-use, strategic, and administrative. Standing plans are used for an indefinite period and include policies, procedures, and rules. Single-use plans, such as a yearly budget, cover only a particular period. Strategic plans concern the development of the organization in determining what the overall broad objectives will be. Administrative plans determine the best way to accomplish broader objectives. A number of techniques, such as PERT, are available to assist with planning. However, executive judgment in formulating plans remains important. This is particularly true in strategic planning, where the determination of the broad goals of the organization always involves values.

FOR REVIEW AND DISCUSSION

1 Explain the two purposes or functions of planning.

2 Explain the commitment principle.

3 What information must be available about a project if one is to employ the critical path technique, PERT?

4 Explain the difference between standing and single-use plans.

5 What is meant by the "law of acceleration"?

6 What is the relationship between organizational planning and control standards.

7 What is the relationship between the time mix of planning activities and the levels of organizational hierarchy.

8 Explain the difference between strategic and administrative planning.

9 Compare and contrast a policy and a rule.

10 Name at least five types of budgets, and explain the function of each.

11 What is likely to happen to an organization without effective planning? Fully explain your answer.

12 What kinds of projects are not well-suited to the use of PERT?

CASES

A   Mr. Compton, president of Mid-West, Inc., was known as a dynamic leader. As a managerial practice, Mr. Compton called a meeting of his managers at the end of each three months "to find out what we've done wrong." Each activity was discussed in detail and suggestions made as to how the work might have been done better. Other than for routine operational matters the managers had no contact with each other until the next quarterly review meeting.

Joe Wiggins confided: "I surely do dread those meetings. You're just a sitting duck. Before you get there you never know if you've done right or wrong."

    1 What is the basis for Joe's anxiety?

    2 What changes would likely improve the operations of Mid-West, Inc.?

B   The Effecto Lawn Mower Company was one of the oldest and most respected names in the industry. During the company's fifty-year history every effort had been made to produce the highest quality push mower. While other companies diversified into power mowers and associated equipment—some of which was of inferior quality—Effecto's president, Mr. Flag, stood firm in his commitment to produce only the finest quality manual mowers. Recently, Mr. Flag had become very worried as orders for his mowers fell to only a small fraction of former sales.

    1 In what ways has Mr. Flag been deficient in planning for his company?

2 Assuming Effecto has had no formal plans, draw up a list of types of plans the company should have. Explain your reason for each type on your list.

C   Pitt Foundry had grown in a few years to the point where it employed more than twenty persons. The operation was a "one-man show" with Mr. Pitt, the owner, still making all the decisions. Recently Mr. Pitt became ill with an ulcer after working eighty to ninety hours per week for several months. He recognized that he was overworked, but said there was no one to help him.

"My problem is," said Mr. Pitt, "that no one else knows what to do. If I let one of my men make a decision, it usually turns out wrong."

When asked about the company's future, Mr. Pitt said: "I don't have time to worry about that. I have enough trouble solving my real problems."

1 Would managerial planning improve the operation of Pitt Foundry?
2 Why do formal planning and controlling become increasingly more important for Pitt Foundry as it grows?
3 Do you agree with Mr. Pitt that only his present problems are real? Why?

FOR FURTHER STUDY

Additional sources can be found in the sources cited in the chapter.

Books

William Newman: *Administrative Action,* 2d ed., Prentice-Hall, Inc., Englewood Cliffs, N.J., 1963, part I. Planning presents two management problems: (1) what form should planning take, and (2) how should planning decisions be made.

Harold Koontz and Cyril O'Donnell: *Principles of Management,* 5th ed., McGraw-Hill Book Company, New York, 1972, part 2. A detailed study of the modern manager's planning function.

George R. Terry: *Principles of Management,* 5th ed., Richard D. Irwin, Inc., Homewood, Ill., 1968, part II. Several chapters describe the planning function in detail.

Articles

Theodore A. Anderson: "Coordinating Strategic and Operational Planning," *Business Horizons,* Summer 1965. Business managers must be aware of the many problems involved in achieving efficient interrelationships between strategic and operational planning.

George J. Berkwitt: "The 7 Deadly Sins of Management," *Dun's Review,* November 1969. Poor planning causes waste of millions of dollars.

James S. Hekimian and Henry Mintzberg: "The Planning Dilemma: There Is a Way Out," *Management Review,* May 1968. Adaptive, contingency, and real-time are explained as three types of planning.

Robert J. Mockler: "Theory and Practice of Planning (Keeping Informed)," *Harvard Busi-*

ness Review, March–April 1970. The state of the arts of planning is described. Planning trends for the 1970s are predicted.

Seymour Tilles: "How to Evaluate Corporate Strategy," *Harvard Business Review,* July–August 1963. A company's strategy is a vital ingredient in determining its future.

Jack O. Vance: "The Anatomy of a Corporate Strategy," *California Management Review,* Fall 1970. Corporations must increasingly deal with accelerated technological obsolescence of entire fields of products and services.

Andrew Vazsonyi: "Free for All: The History of the Rise and Fall of PERT," *Management Science,* April 1970. The fundamental ideas of PERT remain sound, but the technique has been oversold in the past.

Section C
Organizing

17
Organizing

*Structural relationships are not once and for all
prescriptions but are "rules of the game" which are
adaptable to changing situations and the changing desires
of the participants.*
      OGDEN H. HALL

Organizing is usually the next function performed after planning. Organizing is concerned with: (1) determining the specific activities that are necessary to accomplish the planned goals; (2) grouping the activities into a logical pattern, framework, or structure; and (3) assigning the activities to specific positions and people. Alvin Brown wrote: "[Organizing] defines the part which each member of an enterprise is expected to perform and the relations between such members, to the end that their concerted endeavor shall be most effective for the purpose of the enterprise."[1] Organizing determines the way by which the goals conceived in planning can be accomplished. Organizing can be viewed as a bridge connecting the conceptual ideas developed in creating and planning to the specific means for accomplishing these ideas.

[1]Alvin Brown, *Organization, a Formulation of Principle,* Hibbert Printing Company, New York, 1945.

An example of the organizing function in action can be observed in a football game. Suppose that the planning process determines that a basic objective is to win the game (we would surely hope so!) and that the general offensive plan will emphasize a passing attack. The organizing function is executed when the specific plays are selected, when particular personnel (passing specialists, maybe) are appointed, and when particular assignments (what the players do on each play) are made.

An organization chart can be a valuable aid in accomplishing the organizing function. An organization chart can assist in structuring authority and accountability relationships, activities, and communication channels. But organizing can often be accomplished effectively without an organization chart. Indeed, in some cases a chart may be more of a liability than an asset. Organizing is a function—a job—to be done. The organization chart, on the other hand, is a schematic model which may assist in describing or designing organizational relationships.

THE ORGANIZATION CHART

The traditional way of depicting the structure of organizations is to draw an organization chart. Typical examples of organization charts are shown in Figures 17-1 and 17-2.

An advantage of an organization chart is that it helps to define organizational relationships. Without a chart, many people might view the organization as "just a group of people, parts, or activities." The organization chart provides us with a picture of the structure. The chart is a means through which we can better understand the organization as a whole, the components of the organization, and the interrelationships among these different components.

An organization chart can be compared to a road map. The road map, which consists of a set of lines and other symbols on paper, is not the system of roads itself. Similarly, an organization chart is not the organization itself. Nevertheless, as in the case of the road map and the road system it represents, we can better understand and communicate many aspects of the organization with the benefit of a chart or diagram showing its important components and some relationships among these components. But one can not drive an automobile on the road map any more than the organization chart itself will accomplish organizational goals. However, both the map and the organization chart are means of helping us do things. A map helps to reach a destination. Similarly, an organization chart may assist in the accomplishment of organizational objectives.

Both the map and the organization chart are merely static models of dynamic processes. The map must be changed frequently to reflect changes in the road system. Similarly, an organization chart is not the organized process of human interaction. The organization chart is a schematic, static model or structure of that process. A model of a thing is not the thing itself, but a model may help us better understand the thing.

Organization structures are not ends in themselves, but rather means through which the attainment of other objectives can be obtained. In other words, the structure of an organization is not the same thing as the organization. The structure, depicted

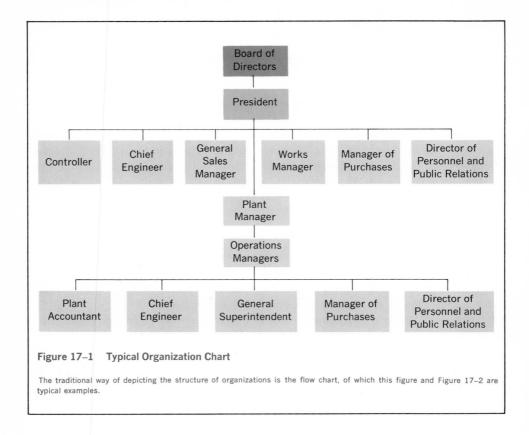

Figure 17–1   Typical Organization Chart

The traditional way of depicting the structure of organizations is the flow chart, of which this figure and Figure 17–2 are typical examples.

perhaps as a static model by a chart, is merely a characteristic of the organization. We can use the concepts and analysis of organization structures as valuable tools for attaining better organizational performance. The chart, a representation of the structure, serves as the basis for studying organization structures.

STRUCTURING AUTHORITY, POWER, ACCOUNTABILITY, AND RESPONSIBILITY RELATIONSHIPS

One purpose of an organization chart is to show the structure of authority, power, accountability, and responsibility in an organization. The organization chart can represent channels or conduits through which authority, power, and accountability flow. This concept is illustrated in Figure 17-3. Remember, however, that the typical organization chart shows these connecting links as simple lines rather than channels. In Figure 17-3, authority and power are shown as flowing downward through the organization structure, and accountability is shown as flowing upward through the organization structure.

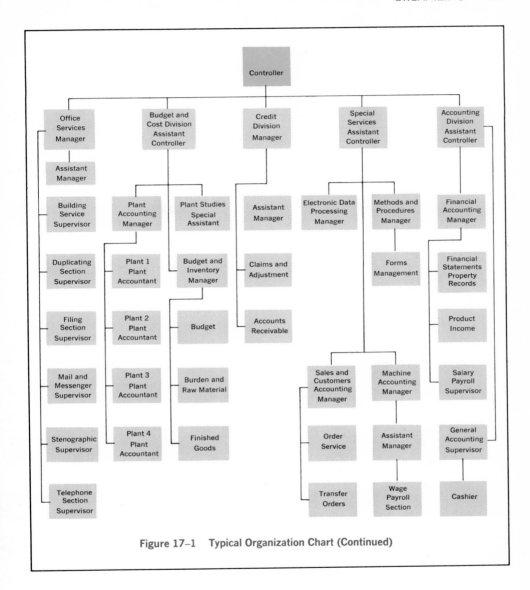

Figure 17–1   Typical Organization Chart (Continued)

Authority

Authority is one of the "glues" that holds an organization together.

Authority is the right to do something.

From an organizational viewpoint, *authority* is the right that a manager has to request or require a subordinate to do something to accomplish organization goals. For example,

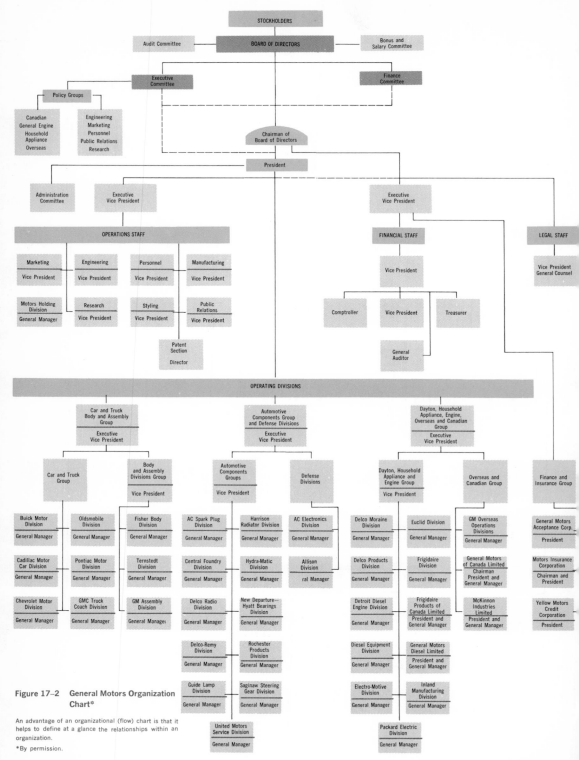

Figure 17–2   General Motors Organization Chart*

An advantage of an organizational (flow) chart is that it helps to define at a glance the relationships within an organization.

*By permission.

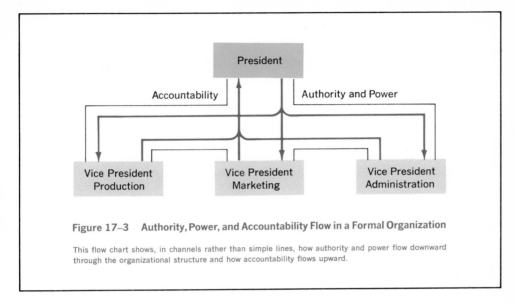

Figure 17–3   Authority, Power, and Accountability Flow in a Formal Organization

This flow chart shows, in channels rather than simple lines, how authority and power flow downward through the organizational structure and how accountability flows upward.

an instructor may have the authority (right) to ask a student to prepare a certain assignment for the next class. (Whether or not the student actually prepares the assignment is another question involving considerations of responsibility, power, or motivation.)

Managerial authority   Davis and Filley say: "Authority consists principally of the rights to decide and command."[2] In an organization the manager's authority consists of his right to such things as: (1) make decisions within the scope of his own authority, (2) assign tasks to subordinates, and (3) expect and require satisfactory performance from subordinates.

The manager has a right to do these things. He has a right to expect and even require satisfactory performance of subordinates, but he may not have the means available to enforce his right. Whether or not the manager can enforce his rights is a question of power, discussed later in this chapter.

Subjective nature of authority   One problem in achieving workable authority is that because authority is a right, in the last analysis one's concept of authority is based on subjective judgment factors. Moreover, the question of how much authority one should have tends to be heavily colored with moral and ethical considerations. For example, those who believed in the divine right of kings quite naturally felt that kings ought to have virtually unlimited authority (and power). On the other hand, exponents of democracy would feel that kings ought to have little or no authority. To some extent

[2]R. C. Davis and A. C. Filley, *Principles of Management,* Alexander Hamilton Institute, New York, 1963, p. 164.

almost everyone would disagree about how much authority a specific person or position ought to have.

Sources of authority   Authority (and its twin, power) can come either from above (supervisors) or below (subordinates). *Top-down authority* is passed along by a supervisor to a subordinate. The supervisor comes into possession of his authority either from higher supervisors or from "institutions" in the society. Examples of such institutions include private property, the divine right of kings (in former times), national sovereignty, the constitution of the nation or state, or individual sovereignty. Figure 17-4 shows how authority flows downward. Our example is a typical, corporate business organization.

Authority may also flow from subordinates to supervisors and institutions; authority of this type is called "bottom-up authority." Figure 17-5 shows that workers as well as all other organization members (all are citizens) may individually or as a group grant authority to supervisory levels. Note that bottom-up authority does not flow through the formal structure of the organization.

The upward flow of authority is shown by broken lines because it is not necessary that every individual at every level support every higher level. For example, a department head may not give bottom-up authority to the president, yet he may support the

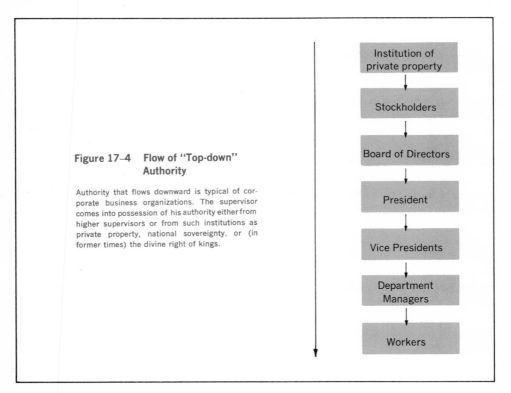

Figure 17–4   Flow of "Top-down" Authority

Authority that flows downward is typical of corporate business organizations. The supervisor comes into possession of his authority either from higher supervisors or from such institutions as private property, national sovereignty, or (in former times) the divine right of kings.

Institution of private property

Stockholders

Board of Directors

President

Vice Presidents

Department Managers

Workers

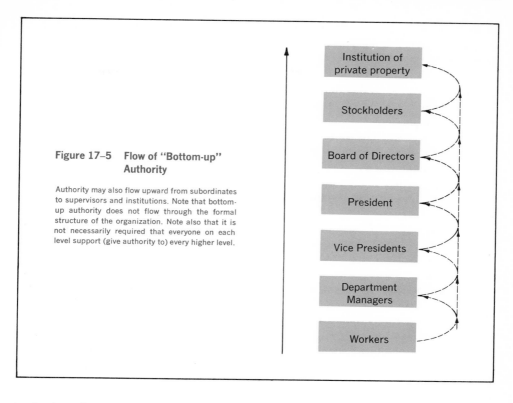

Figure 17–5   Flow of "Bottom-up" Authority

Authority may also flow upward from subordinates to supervisors and institutions. Note that bottom-up authority does not flow through the formal structure of the organization. Note also that it is not necessarily required that everyone on each level support (give authority to) every higher level.

institution of private property. The president may receive enough bottom-up authority from others or enough top-down authority to do his job. Hence, the president could exercise effective authority over a subordinate who individually does not give the president bottom-up authority. All that is required for the president to exercise effective authority is for him to receive enough general support, either from the top or the bottom.

Individuals are willing to grant authority to "higher" people or institutions because of: (1) fundamental beliefs, (2) rank, (3) personal qualities, (4) position, and (5) tradition. Each of these reasons will be illustrated with an example. For instance, referring to Figure 17-5, individuals at all levels might generally support the institution of private property because they might fundamentally *believe* that private property is one of the corner-stones of the society they desire. We have seen that total support by everyone is not required for the institution to be operative. All that is required is general support.

Rank may also be a reason for individuals to grant authority to higher levels. For example, a captain in the army is likely to ascribe a relatively large amount of authority to a colonel simply because the colonel outranks him. The captain might, for example, willingly follow an order of the colonel without investigating whether or not the colonel really possessed the authority to give the order.

One also may receive his authority because of his *personal qualities*. He may be admired for his intelligence, knowledge, wisdom, appearance, or interests. Because such qualities may be held in high esteem he may be given authority by those who approve such qualities.

Another important reason for bottom-up authority is the *position* one might hold. The President of the United States is likely to have a very large amount of authority simply because of the office he holds. To a large degree, presidential authority is independent of the particular person holding the office.

Finally, *tradition* (closely related, perhaps, to the other reasons) may be a reason why particular persons receive bottom-up authority. Several European monarchs, for example, continue to exert considerable influence in their countries even though they no longer have formal authority. But because kings and queens have traditionally possessed authority, the people still tend to respect their wishes.

Delegation of authority   Authority (and power) may be delegated. In organizations, *delegation of authority* refers to the process by which a supervisor gives a subordinate the authority to do his (the subordinate's) job. Without delegations of authority formal organizations could not exist. If there were no delegations, no one in the organization, except possibly the top official, would have the right to do anything; consequently, no organized accomplishment of organizational goals could take place. The process of delegating authority is constantly taking place in a large, formal organization.

How much authority may a manager delegate? The answer is that he can delegate to subordinates the right to do anything that he (the manager) has the right to do except those things he is specifically prohibited from delegating. There is one additional exception: The manager cannot totally delegate authority for performing the managerial functions of creating, planning, organizing, motivating, communicating, and controlling. To delegate total authority in these areas would mean that the manager gives up his role as a manager; this would probably lead to a breakdown in organizational performance.

There is a natural human tendency for managers to resist delegating adequate authority. A manager may fear that subordinates can possibly do undesirable things with the delegated authority for which the manager may be held responsible. Consequently, many managers tend to delegate as little authority as possible; often the amount delegated may not be sufficient for the subordinate to accomplish his assignments effectively.

The risk that managers take when they delegate authority is inherent in the managerial job. If all managers fully appreciated this fact perhaps they would be more inclined to delegate adequate authority. The manager who is unwilling to accept the risk of poor subordinate performance is really not qualified for a managerial position. The managerial position inevitably involves delegation of authority; delegation of authority inevitably involves risk; assuming risk, therefore, is an inevitable part of the manager's job.

Power

Power and authority are often confused, but we can clearly differentiate the two. We have already seen that *authority* is the right to do something. On the other hand, *power is the ability to do something.* In his role as a supervisor, a manager's power may be seen as his ability to cause subordinates to do what he wishes them to do. A manager's power may be measured in terms of his ability to: (1) give rewards, (2) promise rewards, (3) threaten to withdraw current rewards, (4) withdraw current rewards, (5) threaten punishment, and (6) punish.

Subjective nature of power   Power, like authority, is influenced by subjective factors, including ethical and moral considerations. Questions arise concerning how much power a certain person or position ought to have; these questions are similar to those already discussed about authority. In addition, because power may be thought of as the ability one has to influence another, the extent of power is determined in large part by the person being controlled. It may be more important what a person thinks his supervisor's power is than what it is in fact. A manager may take advantage of this phenomenon by bluffing, that is, by pretending that he has more power than he actually has. If the bluff succeeds the effect is exactly the same as if the bluffer actually possessed the power; he has *de facto* power. In like fashion, bluffing may also be present in authority determination and exercise.

Authority and power relationships   It is clear that a manager may have the authority (right) to do something, but he may lack the power (ability) to do it. On the other side of the coin, one may have the power to do something, but may lack the authority to do it. Either of these conditions represents an undesirable condition of instability in the organization. Failure to equate power and authority adequately at all levels will cause conflict in the organization. In extreme cases, this disequilibrium may lead to destruction of the organization, perhaps even to bloodshed. On a national scale, civil strife or war might result. And on the international level, nations may go to war with each other.

One of the most important jobs of managers at all levels is to provide their subordinates with equal authority and power. That is, the subordinates should, for organizational stability, have means (power) equal to their rights (authority) to do the things necessary to accomplish their part of the organization's objectives.

When power and authority for a given person or position are roughly equated, we have a condition we may call "legitimate power," or "workable authority." Achieving a state of workable authority at all levels in the organization is a goal toward which managers should strive. However, such a goal is much easier stated than attained.

Responsibility

Responsibility is closely related to authority and power.

Responsibility is the obligation to do something.

In organizations, *responsibility* is the duty that one has to perform his organizational tasks, functions, or assignments. Everyone in an organization has responsibilities because everyone has a job or function to perform. In formal organizations there is no other reason for organizational membership.

Impossibility of delegation of responsibility   Duties may be assigned to subordinates with appropriate delegation of authority. However, responsibility cannot be delegated. A supervisor's own responsibility is not in the least diminished when he delegates authority to a subordinate. In fact, delegation of authority could possibly *increase* the supervisor's responsibility because he is then responsible for personal supervision of the subordinate *in addition to* having the responsibility for seeing that the work of his organization is accomplished. In an extreme case—in a small organization, for example—the manager might have a choice of doing the work himself or delegating it to a subordinate(s). If the manager chooses to do the work himself, he obviously does not have to supervise the subordinate. In either event (whether the manager does the work himself or whether he gets a subordinate to do it) the manager retains complete responsibility for the accomplishment of the work. The spot on Lady Macbeth's hand would not be removed by any amount of rubbing or washing: "All the perfumes of Arabia will not sweeten this little hand."[3] Responsibility is like Lady Macbeth's spot; subordinates may be delegated authority and assigned tasks, but in the process the manager's own responsibility is not reduced one whit. No amount of delegating will reduce the manager's responsibility. "Often managers speak of delegating responsibility to their subordinates. In spite of this common remark, it must be stated that responsibility cannot be delegated or shifted to the subordinate."[4]

Source of responsibility   Responsibility is created *within* a person when he accepts an assignment together with an appropriate delegation of authority. It is not the act of delegating authority or assignment of tasks which creates responsibility. Rather, responsibility is "created" by the person within himself when he agrees to perform a task. If the person is not agreeable to the conditions of the assignment and is therefore unwilling to be responsible, he should reject the assignment. An unjustified rejection of an assignment, amounting to a refusal to be responsible, could lead to disciplinary action, even dismissal.

Flow of responsibility   Responsibility is largely retained within the person; for that reason it was not shown as "flowing" on Figure 17-3. Responsibility is primarily the person's obligation to himself to perform his tasks. However, a person's obligation to himself is not enough to ensure coordinated performance in organizations, particularly complex organizations. Therefore, accountability does flow upward through an organization.

[3]William Shakespeare, *Macbeth*, Act V, Scene 1.
[4]Theo Haimann, *Professional Management*, Houghton Mifflin Company, Boston, 1962, p. 56.

Accountability

In addition to his personal responsibility to himself, an organization member is account-able to higher authorities.

Accountability comes into being because the manager has a right to require an accounting for the authority delegated and tasks assigned to a subordinate. The sub-ordinate must answer to his manager concerning his (the subordinate's) stewardship of the authority granted him by the manager. As McFarland has put it: "Accountability refers to the fact that each person who is given authority . . . must recognize that the executive above him will judge the quality of his performance."[5] Davis and Filley agree: "Each [organization] member is obliged to report to his superior how well he has exercised his responsibility and the use of the authority delegated to him."[6]

Because, as we have seen, a manager cannot reduce his responsibilities by delegat-ing, it is clear that he also cannot reduce his accountability to higher authority through delegating. A manager is still accountable directly to his supervisor for authority he has delegated and for tasks he has assigned to subordinates.

Acceptance of Responsibility and Accountability

Because many people wish to avoid assuming duties or obligations, there is a tendency to minimize the responsibility they accept. They do not wish to account to a higher authority. This reluctance to be responsible and to account to someone is undoubtedly the cause of much organizational ineffectiveness and friction. Much labor-management strife may have been caused by the refusal of one or both sides to accept full responsi-bility for performing their assignments. Labor, for example, should accept its responsi-bility for providing needed work in the most efficient fashion. Management, on the other hand, should accept its responsibility to provide maximum possible satisfactions for workers, including human as well as economic factors. Both sides have often appeared to be more interested in getting a larger share of the given size "pie" (income of the organization). They should be more interested in accepting the responsibility to work together to create a larger pie. The responsibility for increasing the productivity of the organization should be a concern of every organizational member.

BALANCE OF AUTHORITY, POWER, RESPONSIBILITY, AND ACCOUNTABILITY

Authority, power, responsibility, and accountability at every point (for every position and person) in the organization must be balanced if a stable equilibrium is to be achieved and maintained. Consider the implications of an unbalance of these factors. Suppose

---

[5]Dalton E. McFarland, *Management: Principles and Practice,* 3d ed. The Macmillan Company, New York, 1970, p. 421.
[6]Davis and Filley, *op. cit.,* p. 168.

authority (or power) exceeds accountability (or responsibility). The extra authority and power may be used arbitrarily, capriciously, or without adequate consideration of the effect on others. This condition also may be unsatisfactory because people may fear the potential acts of the holder of excessive authority or power even if he never actually uses such authority or power. Thus, a benevolent-dictatorship form of government tends to be unstable. The problem is that the benevolence eventually may run out; besides, many people do not want others to make decisions for them, however good the intentions of the decision maker. The old maxim, "Power corrupts, and absolute power corrupts absolutely," has much validity.

It is also untenable to think of responsibility and accountability exceeding authority and power. If such were the case we would, in effect, be holding someone accountable for things he cannot change or control. The condition is unstable; the person will eventually object, and seek additional authority or power. Or he may seek to reduce his accountability and responsibility.

The principal authority-power–responsibility-accountability problem in organizations is that people at all levels may try to *maximize their own authority and power.* At the same time they may try to *minimize their own responsibility and accountability.* In a similar vein, managers may attempt to maximize the responsibility and accountability of subordinates while minimizing the amount of authority and power delegated to their subordinates. The natural result in an organization of individuals seeking what they often perceive to be their personal best interest is to produce *instability,* not stability, in the organization in terms of authority-power–responsibility-accountability relationships.

One of the most important tasks of the manager is to seek *continuously* some sort of acceptable balance between authority, power, responsibility, and accountability, both for himself and his subordinates. The organization chart or structure provides the manager with one of his most valuable tools in helping him structure these relationships. A manager may structure authority, power, responsibility, accountability in his organization through the processes of delegating, assigning tasks, and exacting accountability.

ORGANIZATION CHARTS AS IDENTIFICATION AIDS

Organization charts assist in the task of identifying and relating the various parts of organizations. The organization chart helps to provide answers to questions such as:

1 Who am I? (What is my position in the organization?)
2 What do I do? (What are my organizational tasks or functions?)
3 To whom am I accountable?
4 Who is accountable to me?
5 Who is he [or, for that matter, any other person(s) of interest in the organization]?
6 What does he do?
7 To whom is he accountable?

8 Who is accountable to him?

9 Etc.

The organization chart is a means of describing in generally understandable terms the functions and positions of organizational members. Members of an organization have a need to know their identity in the organization. With such knowledge they have a better chance of being involved in organizational relationships and in working coopera- tively toward organizational goals. Without a knowledge of his place in the organization, the individual is likely to behave in such a way that he does not help to accomplish organizational goals. Perhaps the member's failure to assist in accomplishing organi- zational goals may be attributed to his lack of understanding of his place and function in the organization.

To illustrate how an organization chart can assist in identifying and relating the various parts of an organization, we can study a typical organization chart, Smith Electronics Company, shown in Figure 17-6. Mr. Alton F. Vickers is president of the company as well as a member of the board of directors. Mr. Vickers is accountable to the board of directors. In turn each vice-president and the secretary-treasurer is accountable to Mr. Vickers. The chart also shows the area of responsibility for each person. For example, Mr. Vickers, president, is responsible for the overall management of the com- pany. Mr. Whitney, vice-president in charge of marketing, is responsible for all market- ing activities. In like fashion the chart describes the position and function of other members of the Smith Electronics Company. For the sake of simplicity some subordinate parts of the chart—for example, the production activity—are not shown in detail.

COMMUNICATION AND INFORMATION FLOW

Organization charts define and describe channels of communication or information flow within the organization. No coordinated, organized activity can occur without communication among units of the organization.

A complex organization has a vast quantity of information generated within itself and coming into it from outside. It is impossible, not to mention impracticable, for every member in the organization to accept and process every bit of information received. The organization defines channels through which information flows and through which formal communications are made in the organization. An organization chart presents a plan or system defining formal information flow and communication in the organization.

Information is one of the essential elements necessary for a manager to exercise authority and power. From another viewpoint, an emphasis on the importance of infor- mation and communication in organization helps us to understand that there is some truth in the old cliché, "The job makes the man." A position of importance ordinarily carries with it a preferential right to information not enjoyed by subordinates. With more and better information than others, a manager will make better decisions, other things (such as ability) being constant, than his colleagues. The job does help to make

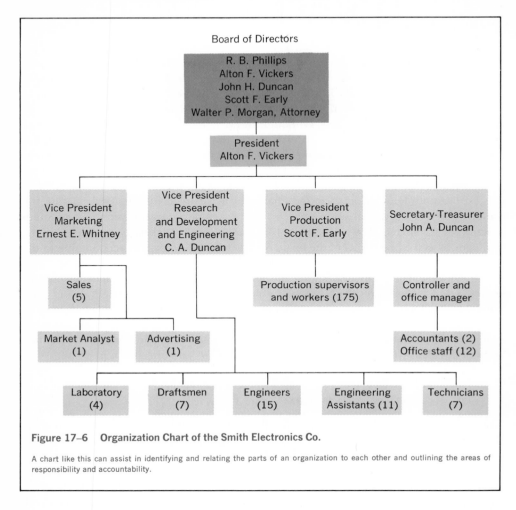

Figure 17–6   Organization Chart of the Smith Electronics Co.

A chart like this can assist in identifying and relating the parts of an organization to each other and outlining the areas of responsibility and accountability.

the man when it provides him with relatively superior information and gives him the opportunity to gain experience from observing the effect of his decisions.

This preferential access to information explains why a spot on a high-level committee may be so greatly valued. Also we can understand why being dropped from the list of those who receive carbon copies of important memoranda may be a disastrous omen for the person's future in the organization. There is an immediate loss of status plus a real loss in the ability to make quality decisions, simply because the person is no longer "in the know." This is one of the reasons why the president's secretary may be such an important person in the organization. Those friends to whom she might "leak" an important bit of information have a real advantage over others not so fortunate. High status also is enjoyed by those in the know.

STATUS AND RANK

Organization charts may be used to denote status or rank of organizational members. In military organizations one's rank can be determined from his uniform. However, most organizations do not have such a direct means of showing a person's rank. One organization partly shows a manager's rank by the number of pens he may have in the penholder on his desk. He must have a certain rank or higher to qualify for two pens. But such measures are not always adequate to communicate members' ranks. Consequently, the organization chart has emerged as a convenient means of showing a person's rank or status in the organization. Other things remaining constant, the higher one is in the organization hierarchy, structure, or chart, the higher his status or rank. This relationship tells us why almost everyone in the organization would like to be supervised by an official with the highest possible rank. For the higher the rank or status of one's supervisor, the higher one's own rank or status.

But position on the chart alone does not make for high rank or status. The authority, power, number of subordinates, etc., a person has also determine his status or rank. But position on the chart alone is undoubtedly very important in determining rank or status.

SYSTEM OF APPEALS

There will inevitably be many disagreements and problems within any formal, complex organization. Organization charts describe and define appropriate channels for appeals. The general rule is that problems which cannot be solved at lower levels are referred upward through the organization structure until the problem reaches an official with enough authority and power to solve the problem. The organization structure provides a well-defined, understood-in-advance means of handling organization problems or disagreements.

POOLED AUTHORITY

Although the organization chart certainly does have the advantage just described, in the typical organization there is an alternate, often better way of resolving conflicts. For example, a problem concerning product quality involving the production and marketing functions might be resolved quite satisfactorily by a conference of the marketing and production managers of the company. Neither manager has the authority to solve the problem alone. However, by combining or pooling their authority they may well be able to solve the problem together. Such a procedure eliminates the necessity for higher-level management to be involved in the problem, releasing higher management for other duties. Conferences and committees function in almost all formal organizations because through pooled authority, decisions can be made that would otherwise have to be made at higher levels. In some cases even the highest-level executive might not have sufficient authority and might feel the need for a conference to secure the agreements of others.

A good operating rule for an organization to follow is to solve the problem at the lowest possible level either individually or through pooled authority. Only those exceptional problems that cannot be resolved by such a procedure should be referred to higher levels.

CHARTS AS ORGANIZATIONAL DESIGN AIDS

In addition to being of value as descriptive portrayals of what presently exists, organization charts may also be of very significant value as design tools. Perhaps this is potentially the most valuable use of an organization chart. To use an organization chart as a design tool, *we simply view it as a statement of the relationships and activities we would like to have in the organization.* When changes are desired in the organization the chart is one of the best available ways of communicating the desired change.

The manager can structure the relationships and activities of an organization, by a simple process: (1) designing a chart to show desired relationships and activities, (2) communicating the chart and expected behavior to affected organization members, and (3) insisting that behavior conform to the organization plan as shown by the chart.

Through this simple process one can actually create an organization. Future developments may indicate the need for revisions in the organization structure, and revisions should be made when they will improve performance. The point is that in addition to serving as a passive description of an existing or past organization, the chart can be an extremely valuable tool in creating a desired organization.

If the organization chart is used to describe the desired organization, we should recognize that the actual behavior of members will tend from time to time to deviate from the chart. However, the chart then serves as a check point to help in getting behavior back on the right track. Otherwise, without the chart, organizational behavior might go further and further away from that which is desired. The chart serves as a connecting mechanism, tending to bring performance back to desired quality. The chart thus assists in giving meaning and direction to organizational behavior.

LIMITATION OF ORGANIZATION CHARTS

The most basic limitation of the organization chart is that the chart is but a static model of the highly complex, dynamic process of human interaction. The chart is like a snapshot—it is only a partially complete representation of a life process at a particular point in time. An organization is a dynamic process of human interaction. Thus, any chart must fall far short of any complete description of the organization. The chart is only a static model of the organization, not the organization itself.

SUMMARY

The relationships, activities, objectives, and communication flow in an organization are structured by the managerial function of organizing. Organizing sets up a structure of authority, power, accountability, responsibility, and information flow. Organizing gives meaning and identity to various parts of the organization. Often organization charts are useful in the organizing process. However, an organization chart is not the organization; the chart is merely a static model of the organization. The organization is the interaction and relationships among the members of the organization. Organizing can make these interactions and relationships more effective by reducing conflicts, by defining roles, and by producing a blueprint of the relationships in the organization.

FOR REVIEW AND DISCUSSION

1 Explain the three parts of the organizing process. Illustrate each part with an example.

2 Explain the difference between: (a) an organization, (b) the process of organizing, and (c) an organization chart.

3 Explain the statement: "An organization chart can help to structure an organization."

4 What is the difference between authority and power? Between responsibility and accountability?

5 Explain bottom-up power and authority.

6 Explain top-down power and authority.

7 Can the following be delegated: (a) authority, (b) power, (c) responsibility, and (d) accountability? Explain your answer in each case.

8 Discuss in detail the statement: "Authority, power, responsibility, and accountability must be balanced at every point in the organization."

9 Assume you are setting up a business organization. Explain the ways an organization chart might help you.

10 Explain the statement: "An organization chart is like a snapshot; it is a static model of a dynamic, living process."

11 "An organization chart can be used either as a description of what is or as a design tool." Discuss in detail.

CASES

A   King Products had two plants in Kingsport. One plant manufactured chemical products, and the other was a petroleum refinery. The plants were approximately 5 miles apart. The manager of the chemical plant, Mr. Rodney, reported to Mr. Adams, vice-president, chemical division. Mr. Hart, the refinery manager, reported to Mr. Boone, vice-president, refining. The offices of both Mr. Adams and Mr. Boone were in the company headquarters building in Chicago, and both reported directly to the president, Mr. Sears.

On August 12, Bob Johnson, fire chief of the chemical plant, received a call from John Turner, refinery fire chief.

"Bob," shouted Mr. Turner, "get your foam truck over here immediately! The cracking unit just blew up, and the fire may get out of control. Three bodies have already been found."

"I'm sorry, John. Mr. Rodney put out strict orders that our foam truck is not to leave the plant without his personal approval. He left yesterday for a technical meeting in Europe. I'm sorry."

John Turner slammed down the telephone, and Bob Johnson stepped outside to watch the rising smoke cloud in the eastern sky.

 1 Was Bob Johnson justified in refusing to send the foam truck? Why?

 2 What should John Turner do now?

 3 What managerial mistakes do you think have been made?

 B Douglas Fowler, sales manager of the Denver region, considered the performance of Robert Allen, one of his salesmen, to be unsatisfactory. On five separate occasions Mr. Fowler had talked with Mr. Allen about his problems, suggesting ways that Mr. Allen might improve his sales. During the last conference Mr. Fowler said, "Bob, I'm going to have to let you go if your sales are not up to quota this month."

Mr. Allen failed to meet his quota, and Mr. Fowler wrote him a letter informing him of his dismissal. Three days later Mr. Fowler received a call from Mr. Jones, general sales manager, "Doug, I want you to put Bob Allen back on the payroll immediately. You know he's the old man's nephew."

"O. K.," sighed Mr. Fowler, "I'll see that it's done."

 1 What are the authority-power–responsibility-accountability problems in this case?

 2 What effect will this situation have on the organization?

 C Carl Estes was appointed principal of Central High School shortly after the death of Mr. Beane, who had been principal at the school for twenty-three years.

During his first week at Central Mr. Estes prepared a list of seventeen major changes that he thought ought to be made. At his first faculty meeting Mr. Estes said: "We must make these changes immediately so that Central will get out of the dark ages." Mr. Estes pushed so hard for his changes that he received some rather violent reactions from his faculty.

Three weeks after Mr. Estes's appointment, Mrs. Cox, faculty representative, presented a petition signed by all members of the Central faculty to Mr. Farrow, the superintendent. The petition sought the immediate dismissal of Mr. Estes. After considering the petition, Mr. Farrow replaced Mr. Estes with Mr. Henry.

Mr. Henry's policy was to go slow on changes. However, three years after his appointment Mr. Henry successfully implemented the majority of the changes originally suggested by Mr. Estes.

 1 Why was Mr. Henry successful when Mr. Estes had not been?

 2 Do you think Mr. Farrow was correct in dismissing Mr. Estes?

FOR FURTHER STUDY

Additional sources can be found in the sources cited in the chapter.

Books

Ernest Dale: *Planning and Developing the Company Organization Structure,* American Management Association, New York, 1965. "Organization is a subject which needs to be treated not only with respect, because it is fundamental to company planning, but with realism, because it is of value only insofar as it is practical."

Paul M. Dauten (ed.), *Current Issues and Emerging Concepts in Management,* Houghton Mifflin Company, Boston, 1962, part IIIC. The principles and theories of organization set the foundation upon which formal organization is structured. It is a mistake to assume that organizational principles and theories are "just plain common sense."

Harold Koontz and Cyril O'Donnell: *Principles of Management,* 5th ed., McGraw-Hill Book Company, New York, 1972, part 3. A detailed study of a primary function of a manager, that of organizing.

George Terry: *Principles of Management,* 5th ed., Richard D. Irwin, Inc., Homewood, Ill., 1968, part III. "Organizing is the establishing of effective authority relationships among selected work, persons, and workplaces in order for the group to work together efficiently."

Articles

Keith Davis: "Group Behavior and the Organization Chart," *Advanced Management— Office Executive,* June 1962. "The social relations and interactions inherent in a group situation can exert a strong influence for good and bad in a company's operation. Since they cannot be abolished, all the manager can do is develop a mature understanding of them."

Robert J. House: "Role Conflict and Multiple Authority in Complex Organizations," *California Management Review,* Summer 1970. The problems of conflicting loyalties and directives in multiple authority organizations are examined.

J. A. Patton: "Make and Use an Organization Chart," *Business Management,* May 1963. "Organize people better and they will produce better. The fact of business life is the reason for a good organization chart."

Harold Stieglitz: "Organization Structures—What's Been Happening," *Conference Board Record,* June 1968. Patterns of corporate organization structures are examined.

Ross Webber: "The Roots of Organizational Stress," *Personnel,* September–October 1966. Organizational weaknesses are the main cause of dissension and stress that disrupt day-to-day operations.

Abraham Zaleznik: "Power and Politics in Organizational Life," *Harvard Business Review,* May–June 1970. Power is important in all political structures, including business firms.

Section D
Motivating

18
Motivation and the Need Hierarchy

Every man is in certain respects a. like all other men, b. like some other man, c. like no other man.
    CLYDE KLUCKHOHN AND HENRY A. MURRAY

The primary task of any manager or supervisor is that of maintaining an organization that functions effectively. To do so, he must see that his subordinates work efficiently and produce results that are beneficial to the organization. Since every action a manager takes in an organization stimulates a reaction in his employees, he has no choice of whether or not he motivates them, only of how he does it: will his action be effective, so that the subordinate works for the benefit of the organization—or ineffective, to the organization's detriment? It is this question—how to employ effective motivation—with which we are concerned in this section.

Motivation can be either positive or negative. Positive motivation, sometimes called "anxiety-reducing motivation," or the "carrot approach," offers something valuable to the person (pay, praise, the possibility of becoming a permanent employee) for acceptable performance. Negative motivation, often called the "stick approach," uses or threatens punishment (reprimands, threats of being fired, threats of demotion) if performance is unacceptable. Each type has its place in organizations, depending on the situation.[1]

Since motivation is closely intertwined with behavior, there are many diverse factors that affect it. The needs of the individual and the attitude of management are two of the most important. In our discussion, we shall take each of these separately, then attempt to work out a balance between them which will best serve organizational interests.

NEEDS, WANTS, AND GOALS

Individuals act because of certain driving forces within themselves represented by such words as "wants," "needs," and "fears." One person may want power; another, self-expression; a third may fear social ostracism or loss of his established position. Whatever the need or fear, behind every purposeful human act there is some desire—either conscious or unconscious—that prompts the person to act. It is in seeking to satisfy his needs that man spends his energies. Craving power, he may commit his effort, time, and other resources to becoming the president of a large corporation; craving status, he may try to buy his way into the "proper" social circles; fearing a threat to his established position from bright young management trainees, he may quash their ideas.

The central problem of motivation, as far as the manager of an organization is concerned, is how to induce a group of people, each having his own distinctive needs and personality, to work together toward the organization's objectives. He must convince members that to achieve their own objectives they must contribute positively to organizational objectives. This approach is practical and straightforward, and it would seem that it could be implemented rather easily. Unfortunately, this is not always the case. Successful implementation requires a deep understanding of the motivational processes relating individual needs to organizational objectives, a knowledge of the needs of the persons involved, and skill or finesse in the application of this knowledge.

Why does one person choose a particular action over the many alternatives that are available to him? Why do people continue a given action, even though other easier courses of action are open to them? The answers to these questions of direction and persistence of action are important in studying the behavior of persons interacting in organizations. A closer look at man's wants or needs is necessary: what are they, how do they evolve, and how does the individual organize them?

Needs are "the initiating and sustaining forces of behavior."[2] They have a direct influence on an individual, since they determine in part his thoughts and actions. A person's needs, working in conjunction with his emotions and other psychological functions, act as the motives that dictate his actions—his behavior. What an individual perceives as the real world about him, how he feels, what old thought patterns come into play,

---

[1]Mature, self-disciplined persons do not require external discipline from others, or the "stick." But it seems certain that our world is still populated by many persons who must depend upon others for their discipline. Cf. Douglas McGregor, *The Human Side of Enterprise,* McGraw-Hill Book Company, New York, 1960, p. 41.

[2]David Krech, Richard S. Crutchfield, and Egerton L. Ballachey, *The Individual in Society,* McGraw-Hill Book Company, New York, 1962, p. 69. Wants, needs, and desires, for our purposes, are taken to be the same.

his current activities—all these processes and many more are influenced by his needs and the means he uses to satisfy them.

It is almost an understatement to say that the wants-objectives-behavior relationship of an individual is extremely complex. The following generalizations indicate its complexity; nevertheless, the central ideas are not difficult to understand, and they can be applied to real-life situations.

First, *similar actions* may be related to *different wants.* For example, even a cursory examination of people's true reasons for joining an exclusive country club will uncover a number of different wants. Some members may have joined for privacy; others, for the status and prestige associated with membership; and still others, to further their business and professional interests.

Second, *different actions* may reflect *similar wants*—which is just another way of recognizing that there are many paths to the achievement of the same objectives. For example, children who wish to assert their independence from their parents do so in various ways—in their dress, their speech, or their choice of friends (often their friends are exactly opposite to those which their parents would prefer).

Third, although it reflects wants, *behavior is not determined by wants alone.* As discussed in Part II, environment, knowledge, perception (that which is believed or felt to be true), social norms, attitudes, and defense mechanisms all affect behavior. The desire for power, for instance, is often mitigated by the social norms governing acceptable means to gain power. In one society, physical strength and force may be acceptable; these same means may be totally unacceptable elsewhere.

Goals, or objectives, are the ends which provide satisfaction of human wants. The number of any individual's possible goals is probably greater than his wants, for several alternate goals can satisfy one want. Thus, one person satisfies a need for power by beating his wife and children, another by becoming president of his service club, and a third by belittling his subordinates. The particular goal chosen by an individual depends on four factors: (1) the cultural norms and values that are instilled in him as he is maturing; (2) his inherited biological capacities—mental and physical; (3) his backlog of personal experience and learning influences; and (4) mobility in his physical and social environment. The interaction of these four influences produces a framework within which a person can strive for the satisfaction of his needs.

For a particular individual, the dilemma posed by a large number of needs can often be resolved by a fusion of wants. In effect, one activity may solve several of his needs. Researchers have found that many overweight people continue to eat excessively because they have fused the satisfaction of a number of wants (love, security, and comfort) into the act of eating. Eating becomes a way of releasing the tension built up by the numerous unsatisfied wants.

Any individual's behavior is aimed at satisfying some set of needs at a given point in time. His particular means of achieving satisfaction are a direct reflection of his experiences of want fulfillment and frustration. If he is experiencing fulfillment of most of his wants, then the satisfaction of any particular one can be unimportant to him. However, in other cases if he is unsuccessful at satisfying only one, that need may come to dominate him. He will center on that want alone, substituting this goal for others. For example, a businessman who fails at achieving prestige, affiliation, or social status may make monetary gains his primary goal in life.

The wants-objectives-behavior chain indicates that any approach to understanding motivation should begin with a treatment of human wants or needs. A great deal of research has been conducted on the subject, but probably the first *general theory* of human motivation was developed by Professor A. H. Maslow.[3] Maslow's approach to wants or needs will be the starting point for our study of motivation.

MASLOW'S THEORY OF HUMAN MOTIVATION

Maslow advanced the following important propositions about human behavior:

1 *Man is a wanting being—he always wants, and he wants more.* But what he wants depends upon what he already has. As soon as one of man's needs is satisfied, another appears in its place. This process is unending. It continues from birth to death. Therefore, although a particular need may become satiated, needs in general cannot be.

2 *A satisfied need is not a motivator of behavior.* Only unsatisfied needs motivate behavior. To illustrate, consider your need for air. It affects your behavior only when you are deprived of or threatened with deprivation of it. Thus, only needs that have *not* been satisfied exert any considerable force on what an individual does.

Here we have a profoundly significant truth that is completely overlooked by supervisors who always attempt to keep employees happy. Such a goal is impossible and confuses morale with motivation. (A blue-chip company known to the author was profoundly shaken when it received a letter from a bright prospect to whom the company had offered employment. The man turned down the position because the company gave "too many fringe benefits." Ponder the implications of this!)

3 *Man's needs are arranged in a series of levels—a hierarchy of importance.* As soon as needs on a lower level are by and large fulfilled, those on the next higher level will emerge and demand satisfaction.

Thus, Maslow views an individual's motivation in terms of a predetermined order of needs, each with its own rank—not in terms of a simple, unorganized list of drives. Figure 18-1 illustrates this concept.

[3]See A. H. Maslow, "A Theory of Human Motivation," in I. L. Heckmann, Jr., and S. G. Huneryager (eds.), *Human Relations in Management,* South-Western Publishing Company, Cincinnati, 1960, pp. 122–144; A. H. Maslow, "A Preface to Motivational Theory," *Psychosomatic Medicine,* January 1943, pp. 85–99; and A. H. Maslow, *Motivation and Personality,* Harper & Row, Publishers, Incorporated, New York, 1954.

Other motivation theories are available. See, for example, H. A. Murray, *Explorations in Personality,* Oxford University Press, Fair Lawn, N.J., 1938, which lists a large number of human needs.

R. Likert provides a modified version of Maslow's hierachy in his study, "A Motivational Approach to a Modified Theory of Organization and Management," in M. Haire (ed.), *Modern Organization Theory,* John Wiley & Sons, Inc., New York, 1959, pp. 185–217.

We prefer Maslow's approach because of its general scope, directness, simplicity, and practicality; and it is this theory that forms the basic framework for the remainder of this chapter.

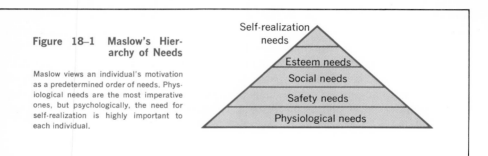

Figure 18–1   Maslow's Hierarchy of Needs

Maslow views an individual's motivation as a predetermined order of needs. Physiological needs are the most imperative ones, but psychologically, the need for self-realization is highly important to each individual.

Physiological Needs

At the lowest level of the hierarchy and at the starting point for motivation theory are the physiological needs. These are the needs which must be satisfied to maintain life. Oxygen, food, drink, elimination, rest, activity, and temperature regulation would be included on this level. Physiological needs have characteristics in common: (1) they are relatively independent of each other; (2) in many cases, they can be identified with a specific location in the body (for example, extreme hunger can be identified with the stomach); (3) in an affluent culture these needs are unusual rather than typical motivators; (4) finally, they must be met repeatedly within relatively short time periods to remain fulfilled. (The desire for food, for example, usually arises at least three times a day, although it is certainly not so intense as in someone who has been totally without food for several days.) In addition most of the physiological needs require some conscious provision for their future satisfaction.

Physiological needs take precedence over other needs when thwarted. Consequently, the human being who is lacking everything in life will probably be motivated by physiological needs. For a starving person, higher-level needs become temporarily nonexistent, or are pushed into the background; a person who is deprived of food, safety, companionship, and esteem will probably want food more strongly than everything else. All the abilities of a starving man may be directed toward hunger satisfaction. Faculties not useful for obtaining food are ignored. His conscious and unconscious acts become directed by hunger motivations—he thinks of food, wants food, dreams about food, and has fantasies about food.

When an individual is dominated by a certain need his whole philosophy of the future tends to reflect that need. For our starving man, Utopia is a place where food is plentiful; he feels that if he had enough food for the rest of his life he would not want anything else. Similarly, a drowning man wants only air; an overworked executive may yearn only for rest.

One way to keep higher levels of needs from merging is to keep individuals extremely and chronically hungry or thirsty, as was done in many prisoner of war camps during World War II and the Korean War. Similarly, a study of a seminomadic Bolivian

Indian group in a climate that made food storage impossible, revealed that art forms, folk tales, and mythology were poorly developed among these people. But such conditions are not typical in an affluent culture. As Maslow aptly puts it: "It is quite true that man lives by bread alone—when there is no bread. But what happens to man's desires when there *is* plenty of bread and when his belly is chronically filled?"[4]

Maslow's answer is that at once other, higher-level needs emerge to demand satisfaction, and the process continues "from belly to brains" through the satisfaction of needs at each level. This continuing emergence of new needs is what is meant by a hierarchy of needs.

Safety Needs

When physiological needs are reasonably (not necessarily completely) fulfilled, needs at the next higher level, safety needs, begin to dominate man's behavior. These needs (often called "security needs") are expressed in such desires as protection from physical danger (fire, accident, or criminal assault); the quest for economic security; preference for the familiar rather than the unfamiliar; and the desire for an orderly, predictable world. Safety needs also include the desire to know the limits or boundaries of acceptable or permissible behavior—that is, the desire for freedom within limits rather than unrestricted permissiveness. A person who does not have a firm knowledge of the boundaries of acceptable behavior for himself can feel intensely threatened. He is likely to try to discover such limits even if he sometimes has to behave in unacceptable ways. Supervisors (including parents) can provide for the safety needs of those in their organization by setting up and enforcing clear standards of behavior.

Man's feeling of safety is also threatened when he is dependent on someone else; he feels that he may be deprived of his security by the other person without warning and with little recourse. When an individual is in such a dependent relationship, his greatest need is for guarantees, for protection. Almost every industrial employee is dependent on his organization for order, for supervision, for decisions affecting his work, for continued employment. Thus, in industrial situations safety needs may be of considerable importance. Arbitrary or unpredictable actions, actions which create feelings of uncertainty (particularly regarding continued employment), favoritism, or discrimination on the part of his superior, can all be regarded as threats to work-life safety and therefore are powerful motivators of behavior at all organizational levels. Such behavior may or may not help in accomplishing organizational objectives.

Social Needs

When man's physiological needs and safety needs are relatively satisfied, social needs, the next level, become important motivators of his behavior. The individual wants to belong, to associate, to gain acceptance from his fellows, to give and receive friendship

---

[4]Maslow, "A Theory of Human Motivation," *op. cit.*, p. 126.

and affection. Deprived of these comforts, he will want them as intensely as a hungry man wants food. Although many managers today know these needs exist, they may wrongly see them as threats to the organization and act accordingly. Managers frequently have gone to considerable lengths to control and direct employees' relationships in ways that are opposed to the natural groupings of human beings. Therefore, when a manager assumes that informal groups always threaten his organization, and actively strives to break up existing groups, the individuals affected may become resistant, antagonistic, and uncooperative. These resistant actions are often consequences or symptoms, not causes, for the manager may have thwarted the satisfaction of social needs, and perhaps even safety needs.

Esteem Needs

Next in Maslow's hierarchy are esteem or egoistic needs—both for self-esteem and for the esteem of others. Self-esteem needs include those for self-confidence, achievement, competence, knowledge, self-respect, and for independence and freedom. The second group of esteem needs are those that relate to the individual's reputation, or the esteem of others: needs for status, recognition, importance or appreciation, and the deserved respect of his fellows. The competitive desire to excel—to surpass the performance of one's fellows—is an almost universal human trait. This major esteem need, properly utilized, can produce extremely high organizational performance. A manager's stimulation of these needs and their subsequent satisfaction by the employee lead to feelings of worth, capability, and of being useful and necessary in the world. Thwarting them results in feelings of inferiority, weakness, and helplessness.

Unlike some of the lower needs, esteem needs are rarely completely satisfied. In fact, they are apparently insatiable. Once they have become important to an individual, he seeks indefinitely for further satisfaction of them. Having won a game, a football team may strive still harder to win the next. Too often, the typical industrial organization offers few opportunities for the satisfaction of these needs at the lower levels of employment.

Self-realization Needs

At the apex of the hierarchy is the need for self-realization, or self-actualization. These are the individual's needs for realizing his own potentialities, for self-fulfillment, for continued self-development, for being creative in the broadest sense of that term. The specific form of these needs will vary almost infinitely from person to person, just as human personalities do. Advancing an important theory, becoming a star athlete, rearing healthy, well-balanced children, successfully managing a business, or being elected to a political office may be examples of the satisfaction of self-realization needs. Self-realization is necessarily a creative state, but it does not only involve creating poems, theories, novels, experiments, and paintings. It is, more broadly, creativeness in realizing to the fullest one's own potentialities, whatever they may be. It is a feeling of accomplishment and attainment and of being satisfied with the self.

Once a person has moved from a lower level of wants to a higher level, the lower-level wants assume a less important role. They may, of course, become temporarily dominant again as a result of deprivation. For example, during World War II conscientious objectors participating in an experiment on the effects of inadequate diet experienced dramatic changes in behavior. They became preoccupied with thoughts of food, sullen, and very quiet. Occasionally they would "blow up" over heretofore minor irritations and were unable to concentrate on any activity other than obtaining food.

As an individual moves up the ladder, his wants and goals increase in number and variety. This progression is illustrated in Figure 18-2. Notice that the peak of each level must be passed before the next level can begin to assume a dominant role. Also, as personal development or self-development takes place, the number and variety of wants increase. (This is especially evident in the esteem peak where all are simultaneously active.) The diagram illustrates another salient point of Maslow's thesis: the levels are interdependent and overlapping. Thus an individual's needs will tend to be partially satisfied in each area; for example, physiological needs do not disappear when safety needs emerge, they simply become less pressing. Needs do not have to be satiated or 100 percent satisfied before higher needs emerge—as Herbert Simon put it, they only have to be satisfied enough, or "satisficed."[5] That is, a sufficient, not necessarily a maximum or optimum, level of satisfaction is acceptable.

[5] Herbert A. Simon, *Administrative Behavior*, The Macmillan Company, New York, 1957, p. xxv.

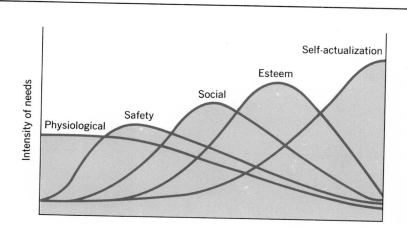

Figure 18–2   Level of Attainment or Personal Growth*

The peak of each level must be passed before the next level can begin to assume a dominant role. With self-development, the number and variety of wants increase. Note that in the esteem peak the different needs of an individual are simultaneously active.
*From David Krech, Richard S. Crutchfield, and Egerton L. Ballachey, *The Individual in Society* (McGraw-Hill Book Company, New York, 1962), p. 77. By permission.

The Individual and His Need Hierarchy

Maslow's theory of human needs must be regarded as having general, not specific, applicability. In general, as a healthy individual matures, creativeness, independence, autonomy, discretion, and personality expression all become increasingly important. However, because maturity implies a high level of adjustment to whatever conditions life presents, there are no totally mature people, only maturing ones. These conditions are constantly changing, and the adjustment must be a continuing process.

Maturity, then, is a dynamic, not a static concept, and individual behavior patterns depend on the need level to be satisfied, on the individual's personality makeup, and on various stimuli. In Figure 18-3, Maslow's basic theory has been modified to include the individual as a determining factor in motivation and behavior. Such a simplified model is grossly incomplete, however, and there are still further qualifications that must be added to make our concept more comprehensive. Some of these qualifications were recognized by Maslow; some have been added by other authorities.

First, the levels in the hierarchy are not rigidly fixed. The boundaries between them are hazy and overlapping as shown in Figure 18-2.

Second, because this is a general theory of needs, based on normal people, there are exceptions to the general ranking of the hierarchy. Some people apparently never develop above the first or second level; others (Michelangelo may have been a case in point) are so absorbed by higher-level needs that those on a lower level may go largely unnoticed. In addition, continued existence at low levels of attainment tends to deaden aspiration to higher levels. Consider, for example, persons in underdeveloped countries who may never hope for anything above bare subsistence. Also, needs that have been satisfied over long periods of time become undervalued in a person's mind. Compare the needs of two young executives: Mr. Smart who came from the wrong side of the tracks, completed high school and college by working days and going to school at night; and Mr. Prince who was born with a silver spoon in his mouth, and attended an Ivy League school. The need for business success that Mr. Smart may chronically overestimate may be chronically underestimated by Mr. Prince.

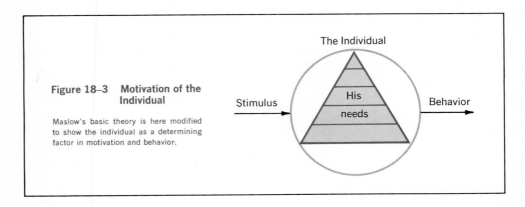

Figure 18–3   Motivation of the Individual

Maslow's basic theory is here modified to show the individual as a determining factor in motivation and behavior.

Third, a qualification, and one of the most important, is that the chain of causation may not always run from stimulus to individual needs to behavior. Although Maslow's thesis states that when a person is deprived of two needs he will want the more basic of the two, he may not act upon his desires: ideals, social standards, norms, and duty can influence him. For example, generally, an individual deprived of both self-esteem and companionship will seek companionship, the more basic of the two. But suppose the only companion available is a lower-status person. The person wanting companionship may then restrain himself because of his social standards.

Fourth, an act is seldom motivated by a single need; any act is more likely to be caused by several needs. Consequently, if it were possible to analyze a single act of an individual, we probably would find that all levels of needs contributed to it in varying degrees of intensity.

Fifth, the same need will not lead to the same response in all individuals: aggressiveness, shrewdness, discretion, and assertiveness are only four of many approaches that may be exhibited by candidates for the same political office. The difficulty an administrator faces is that of not being able to see people's needs directly; he sees only behavioral acts and, therefore, tends to judge needs by the behavior displayed. This approach is obviously open to error, for one can easily assume that certain types of behavior (for example, aggressiveness) always denote certain needs (for example, power). Such a conclusion will often be quite incorrect. An individual's acts may indicate the opposite of his needs if for some reason he is unable or unwilling to face and deal with those needs—a person who appears so secure as to be snobbish may actually be extremely shy and insecure.

Sixth, individuals may develop substitute goals if direct achievement of a need is blocked. Consider the case of a young wife who is unable to have children. There are a number of acceptable substitute goals: she may adopt children, engage in social work, become a teacher or a nurse. These substitute goals will not at first have the same intensity as her primary goal, but they can with time become primary goals as she experiences success in achieving them. The woman may come to desire social work in orphanages for the satisfaction of the job rather than as a vicarious means of achieving motherhood.

Finally, many of the goals which man strives for are remote, long-range goals that can be achieved only in a series of steps. The pursuit of long-range goals is one of the unique features of human behavior. What sustains a young premed student through eight to ten years of grueling work with low pay? What sustains a lawyer? A professor? A pharmacist? Or a skilled tradesman? Two things do. First, individuals set up intermediate goals to be accomplished en route to the final goal. The final goal can then be worked toward in a series of small steps which provide evidence of accomplishment, thereby reinforcing or sustaining the work. For a young doctor-to-be, these steps may be the completion of premed training, medical school, and then internship—and each of these can be subdivided into smaller attainments. Nothing succeeds like success and nothing fails like failure. Thus, it is very important for a football team to complete its first pass and to win its first game. Second, an individual is sustained in his step-by-step march toward a remote goal by his ideas and ideals of that goal. The young medical student may see himself as a leading surgeon, or the young student of law may think of himself as a famous lawyer. However wild these perceptions of his goal may be, they do serve as a sustaining force through the adversity he encounters on his way.

With so many variables to consider, it would seem almost impossible for a supervisor to accumulate, evaluate, and coordinate all of them for each of his subordinates. Fortunately, this task is not so difficult as it seems at first glance, for an individual's personality and the way he behaves are affected to a large degree by three interrelated factors: his personality, his culture and its historical influence, and his environment. Is the employee from Iran or from the United States (culture)? Is he highly educated and from a well-to-do family, or a high school dropout from a big-city slum area (again culture)? Does the present state of the economy make it easy or hard for him to get a job at this time (environment)? Is he currently employed as a machinist in an automobile factory, married, and living at home, or is he serving with the Marine Corps far from his family (again environment)? None of these factors taken alone will give much indication of the individual's probable reaction to different stimuli; but in combination, they can give his supervisor a reasonably accurate basis for some general assumptions of what will effectively motivate the person.

SUMMARY—NEEDS AND THE WORK SITUATION

What does our discussion of Maslow's theory of human needs have to do with motivation in a real-life work situation? Quite a lot. As Mason Haire put it:

> Everyone is constantly striving for need-satisfactions. It is part of the situation that, at work, the superior controls many of the means to need-satisfaction. By the proper use of his control of the means of need-satisfaction, he can provide or withhold rewards at appropriate times. When we remember the principle of the Law of Effect—that behavior which seems to be rewarded tends to be repeated, while that which seems not to lead to reward or seems to lead to punishment tends to be eliminated—it is clear that the superior has a great opportunity for shaping behavior. Indeed, whether he is conscious of it or not, the superior is bound to be constantly shaping the behavior of his subordinates by the way in which he utilizes the rewards that are at his disposal, and he will inevitably modify the behavior patterns of his work group thereby.[6]

Physiological needs are satisfied largely off the job by the money earned by working. This includes not only current income but the hope for improvements in future earnings as well. An individual's first need is to earn enough money on which to live, to achieve his desired standard of living now and in the future. But in an affluent society, the acceptable standard of living has gradually risen until it has taken on social aspects. A recent study indicated that people at all income levels thought their financial problems would be solved if their income were only 20 percent higher! Another study showed an income of $25,000 per year as being a dangerous level because of the difficulty that the family

---

[6]Mason Haire, *Psychology in Management*, 2d ed., McGraw-Hill Book Company, New York, 1964, pp. 22–23. (By permission.)

has in living within that income. Apparently, $25,000 per year allows and requires a teasing taste of luxury but is not adequate to provide real luxury. Thus current income, the knowledge of future income, and improvements in income are intertwined as satisfiers not only of physiological needs, but also of some safety and social needs.

The job itself may provide opportunities for the satisfaction of many social needs. The individual's work group can provide help, friendship, identification, status, and a feeling of participation and belonging. Further, the supervisor usually controls the treatment an individual will receive, the system of rewards and punishment, and the information on where an individual fits into the organization.

Some work may provide opportunities for the satisfaction of esteem and self-realization needs. Autonomy, accomplishment, and success in competition are examples of esteem-need satisfaction within the work situation. A company can also provide the opportunity for and the encouragement of individual growth within the framework of the organization. As Haire pointed out, organizations control the methods of satisfying on-the-job needs of their members. In the next chapter we will look further at the ways organizations, through their managers, can provide for the satisfaction of individual needs.

FOR REVIEW AND DISCUSSION

1 When does a manager motivate his employees?

2 Define and give illustrative examples of positive and negative motivation.

3 Give two examples not in the text to illustrate each of the following: (a) similar actions may be motivated by different wants and (b) different actions may be motivated by similar wants.

4 What factors other than wants or needs determine behavior?

5 Are man's needs ever completely satisfied? Discuss fully.

6 Describe the hierarchy of needs, giving examples not found in this book for each level.

7 Is the hierarchy of needs the same for all persons? Explain your answer, and include examples to illustrate your points.

8 Do you agree with the statement: "Needs are 'the initiating and sustaining forces of behavior'"? Explain your answer in detail.

9 Do you think it is possible for everyone to achieve self-actualization, or self-realization? Explain your answer.

10 Explain the effects of environment and culture on motivation.

11 How could Maslow's theory of human motivation be applied to solving a practical problem in motivation in an organization? What problems in applying the theory would you expect to encounter?

12 Evaluate the statement: "Everyone is constantly striving for need-satisfaction. It is a part of the situation that, at work, the supervisor controls many of the means of need-satisfaction."

13 Show by an example how a person's job might satisfy, at least in part, all five need levels.

CASES

A Army personnel stationed at Akut, a small, wind-swept base in the Aleutian Islands of the North Pacific, were far removed from the dangers of combat. Yet when a call came for volunteers for paratrooper training, which had a high casualty rate, nearly 60 percent of the men at Akut volunteered.

    1 What motivational factors would account for this?

    2 What motivational programs would you suggest to the Akut commander, who did not want to lose so many of his men?

B Professor Starks, a brilliant scientist, would often get so involved in one of his projects that he would go for two or three days without food, sleep, or companionship.

    1 What are the motivational factors that would cause Professor Starks to work in such a pattern?

    2 Do you think the Professor is normal? Why?

C After studying the personnel and work situation in an industrial plant, Dr. Holt, a management consultant, concluded that additional motivation of workers was needed. In his week at the plant, Dr. Holt had found that working conditions were good, employment was steady throughout the year, and the average pay was well above the community average.

    1 Recommend a motivational program for the plant.

    2 Dr. Holt has another week available to spend at this plant. What additional work would you suggest he do? Why?

FOR FURTHER STUDY

Additional sources can be found in the sources cited in the chapter.

Books

Mason Haire: *Psychology in Management,* 2d ed., McGraw-Hill Book Company, New York, 1964. "If management can understand the nature of the employees and know how to use this understanding in management practices and policies, then it can work toward control of one of the factors in the complex set of problems presented by a modern business organization."

K. B. Madsen: *Theories of Motivation,* Kent State University Press, Kent, Ohio, 1963. Twenty psychological theories of motivation are analyzed and compared. The presentation is on an advanced level.

Norman R. F. Maier: *Psychology in Industry,* 3d ed., Houghton Mifflin Company, Boston, 1965, chaps. 13 and 14. Applications of psychology and related sciences to industrial problems require considerations of many variables, ideas to be generated, and evaluating judgments to be made.

George Strauss and Leonard R. Sayles: *Personnel,* Prentice-Hall, Inc., Englewood Cliffs, N.J., 1960, part 2. The basic problem in motivation is creating a situation in which employees can satisfy their individual needs while at the same time working toward the goals of the organization.

Articles

L. L. Cummings and A. M. El Salmi: "Empirical Research on the Bases and Correlates of Managerial Motivation: A Review of the Literature," *Psychological Bulletin,* no. 2, 1968. A review of the literature that explains in detail the two basic streams of modern motivation thought–the need hierarchy and motivation hygiene concepts.

Judson Gooding: "Blue-collar Blues on the Assembly Line," *Fortune,* July 1970. Young auto workers find their jobs extremely unattractive and react in destructive ways.

Douglas T. Hall and Khalil E. Nougaim: "An Examination of Maslow's Need Hierarchy in an Organizational Setting," *Organizational Behavior and Human Performance,* February 1968. The relevance of Maslow's hierarchy was tested.

Frederick Herzberg: "The Motivation—Hygiene Concept and Problems in Manpower," *Personnel Administration,* January–February 1964. "Opportunities relating to job satisfaction are true motivators; removal of negative job factors, or those which make for dissatisfaction, only has preventive value."

Frederick Herzberg: "One More Time: How Do You Motivate Employees?" *Harvard Business Review,* January–February 1968. The only way to motivate an employee is to give him challenging work in which he can assume responsibility.

M. Scott Myers: "Who Are Your Motivated Workers?" *Harvard Business Review,* January–February 1964. Some workers can be motivated; some can not. A challenging job that gives a feeling of achievement, responsibility and growth, advancement and enjoyment should solve many motivation problems.

19

Managerial Assumptions and Their Effects

An organization of human effort is based on a concept
. . . of the nature of man. . . .
MASON HAIRE

To discover the effects of managerial methods on employees' behavior we must first examine the opposite extremes of current assumptions about employees. Second, the managerial attitudes and supervisory practices resulting from each extreme must be examined to see the various ways in which management has provided need-satisfying opportunities.

Douglas McGregor, late professor of management at Massachusetts Institute of Technology, stated that "the human side of enterprise is 'all of a piece,' [and] the assumptions management holds about controlling its human resources determine the whole character of the enterprise. [These assumptions] determine also the quality of its successive generations of management."[1] The control that McGregor wrote about

---

[1]Douglas McGregor, *The Human Side of Enterprise*, McGraw-Hill Book Company, New York, 1960, pp. vi–vii.

is how managers use the organizational resources at their command in satisfying members' wants.

McGregor presented two opposite sets of assumptions that he thought were implicit in most approaches to supervision. These two sets of assumptions, which he called "theory X" and "theory Y," can be regarded as the extremes or boundaries on a spectrum or range of assumptions. Within the boundaries provided by theories X and Y there exist any number of possible combinations of the two, and it is between the two extremes that valid operational theories can best be developed. To understand the possibilities within the spectrum, we must first study the two extremes.

THEORY X

The bulk of current managerial principles, according to McGregor, has been directly derived from the first set of assumptions, theory X. These assumptions are, to quote McGregor:

> 1   The average human being has an inherent dislike of work and will avoid it if he can.
> 2   Because of this human characteristic of dislike of work, most people must be coerced, controlled, directed [or] threatened with punishment to get them to put forth adequate effort toward the achievement of organizational objectives.
> 3   The average human being prefers to be directed, wishes to avoid responsibility, has relatively little ambition, [and] wants security above all. [2]

Theory X provides an explanation for some behavior patterns in industry. But are these inherent human traits or are they learned through man's experience in organizations?

Causes and Consequences of Theory X

Organizations, in striving toward their objectives, have been greatly influenced by the results of specialization, standardization, and mass production techniques. Skilled jobs have been subdivided into many smaller parts; individual performance on these minute tasks has been programmed; initiative and discretion have been reduced; conformity, obedience, and dependence have been demanded from organization members. Pressure, through the use of rewards and the threat of punishment, has been used to achieve these ends. In the process many individuals have come to feel alienated from their work. Pressure has bred counterpressure, and subordinates have reacted in ways detrimental to organizational efficiency. To achieve the desired behavior, management has had to impose still more restriction, a vicious cycle has been set up, and the assumptions of theory X seem to have been confirmed. Management has regarded employees as indolent, without ambition, and resistant to change and responsibility.

The assumptions of theory X, and the approaches to motivation and supervision which result from it, may indeed be what exists in many organizations. But theory X

---

[2]*Ibid.*, pp. 33–34. (Italics in the original. By permission.)

does not reflect man's inherent nature; rather, such behavior in man is in part the result of management philosophy and practice. McGregor himself regarded theory X as an extreme and as an unacceptable set of assumptions about human beings:

> To some extent industrial management recognizes that the human *adult* possesses capabilities for continued learning and growth. . . . In its *basic* conceptions of managing human resources, however, management appears to have concluded that the average human being is permanently arrested in his development in early adolescence. Theory X is built on the least common human denominator: the factory "hand" of the past. . . . conventional managerial strategies for the organization, direction, and control of the human resources of enterprise are admirably suited to the capacities and characteristics of the child rather than the adult.[3]

Nevertheless, because theory X and the conventional management approach founded upon it is prevalent in organizations today, it does serve as a meaningful boundary on the range of possible approaches. Possibly, many of the supposedly more humanitarian approaches tried in recent years did not achieve expected results because management did not change its fundamental notion about people, and the right methods based on wrong principles will sooner or later fail.

The Self-fulfilling Prophecy

At this point we are in a position to recognize and appreciate the practical implications of one of the most profound observations ever made about human behavior—the self-fulfilling prophecy. This phenomenon operates in four steps:

1 Something is assumed to be true.
2 Action is taken based on the assumption.
3 Reaction occurs to the original action.
4 The reaction is observed and is taken as verification of the original assumption.

Maslow tied the self-fulfilling prophecy to motivational theory in this way:

> The belief [is often held] that some people are sheep and some people are shepherds, that only a small proportion of the population is capable of self-rule, [and] independent judgment . . . while the larger proportion of the population is stupid, suggestible, and is fit only to be led and taken care of. The fact of the matter is that when people are led, and when decisions are made for them, they steadily become less and less capable of autonomy, of leading themselves, of making their own decisions. In other words, this belief is a self-fulfilling prophecy.[4]

Thus we come to the rather shocking realization that theory X may be true and may work simply because we believe it to be true and act as if it were true. "If men define situations as real, they are real in their consequences."[5]

[3] *Ibid.*, pp. 42–43. (Italics in the original. By permission.)
[4] A. H. Maslow, *Motivation and Personality*, Harper & Row, Publishers, Incorporated, New York, 1954, p. 358. (By permission.)
[5] W. I. Thomas, quoted in Robert K. Merton, *Social Theory and Social Structure*, The Free Press of Glencoe, New York, 1957, p. 421.

THEORY Y

The accumulation of knowledge about human behavior from many specialized fields has led to further research regarding the validity of conventional managerial assumptions. From these data, McGregor derived a new set of assumptions which he called "theory Y":

1 *The expenditure of physical and mental effort in work is as natural as play or rest.* The average human being does not inherently dislike work. Depending upon controllable conditions, work may be a source of satisfaction (and will be voluntarily performed) or a source of punishment (and will be avoided if possible).

2 *External control and the threat of punishment are not the only means for bringing about effort toward organizational objectives. Man will exercise self-direction and self-control in the service of objectives to which he is committed.*

3 *Commitment to objectives is a [result] of the rewards associated with their achievement.* The most significant of such rewards, e.g., the satisfaction of ego and self-actualization needs, can be direct products of effort directed toward organizational objectives.

4 *The average human being learns, under proper conditions not only to accept but to seek responsibility.* Avoidance of responsibility, lack of ambition, and emphasis on security are generally consequences of experience, not inherent human characteristics.

5 *The capacity to exercise a relatively high degree of imagination, ingenuity, and creativity in the solution of organizational problems is widely, not narrowly, distributed in the population.*

6 *Under conditions of modern industrial life, the intellectual potentialities of the average human being are only partially utilized.*[6]

These assumptions, McGregor felt, provide a better explanation of human nature and, therefore, indicated the need for a different managerial strategy in dealing with people.

Implications of Theory Y

Advocates of theory Y regard traditional organizational techniques as the cause of the ineffective behavior patterns listed in theory X. Theory Y advocates do not consider theory X behavior as showing natural human characteristics but, rather, patterns of behavior learned within organizations. According to theory Y, many managers should rearrange their assumptions, thinking, and methods so that organizational and individual goals are compatible. Management should adopt policies that promote on-the-job need satisfaction, individual development, and expression. Therefore, theory Y is not only a call for a new managerial philosophy regarding the nature of people, it is also a criticism of traditional managerial policy and action.

Limitations of Theory Y

Discussions of the nature of human behavior immediately following the publication of McGregor's theories tended to regard theory Y as the missing link in the much-sought-

---

[6]McGregor, *op. cit.*, pp. 47–48. (Italics in the original. By permission.)

after theory of motivation. Managers who were administering their operations along the lines of theory X were admonished to change to Y; for after all, theory Y argued, organizational members become dullards only because they are not given the opportunity to be otherwise. Articles in management journals, after-dinner speeches, and classroom lectures all called for managers to accept and adopt theory Y in their organizational relationships.

But the policies resulting from theory Y also can be criticized. One of the basic criticisms of theory Y applies to theory X as well. Neither is simply a cold, impersonal theorem, as it might seem at first glance. Each theory prescribes a course of action for management to follow, but implicit in these prescriptions are strong value judgments.

Is theory Y unreasonably idealistic?[7]   Theory Y bears all the values of its academic origins, emphasizing autonomy, self-direction, individual freedom, and inner direction. Although these conditions may be desirable for some people, others do not want and cannot handle them. Nevertheless, proponents of theory Y may impose their own value judgments and their will on other persons. And this may be done after the theory Y proponents have verbally chastised the theory X adherents for doing the same thing. Theory Y puts an extreme emphasis on self-actualization and freedom, implying that all people not only do desire but should desire them. But some persons are extremely uncomfortable with too much freedom. The desire for complete individual freedom is not a universal trait, nor is it necessarily compatible with organizational goals—in some cases it may be in direct opposition to them. In some new nations suddenly released from colonial control, virtual anarchy has occurred. The population, which had never experienced freedom, was often unprepared and could not make freedom work.

Several authorities have pointed out that complete freedom is not the answer. Erich Fromm, a noted psychoanalyst, has suggested that persons want freedom but only within defined limits.[8] George Strauss agreed, emphasizing that even persons who accept complete freedom in some areas demand restriction in many others.[9] Maslow, in further agreeing, stated that although gratification of basic needs is the main prerequisite for healthy growth, unbridled indulgence leads to such dangerous consequences as psychopathic personality, irresponsibility, and inability to bear stress.[10]

Accordingly, the answer is not to be found in complete and unlimited individual freedom, but in freedom within limits. And, like the intensity of all needs, the intensity of the need for clearly defined limits differs from individual to individual. Some persons may prefer broad, loosely defined limits; others, a highly defined situation. Perhaps one of the greatest problem causers of the past was the tendency to specify precisely defined narrow limits for all workers regardless of individual personalities. Although

[7]For a list and discussion of thirty-seven reasons why theory Y may be unrealistic, see Abraham H. Maslow, *Eupsychian Management,* Richard D. Irwin, Inc., and The Dorsey Press, Homewood, Ill., 1965, pp. 15–33.

[8]Erich Fromm, *The Sane Society,* Holt, Rinehart and Winston, Inc., New York, 1955, p. 318.

[9]George Strauss, "Some Notes on Power-equalization," in Harold J. Leavitt (ed.), *The Social Science of Organizations,* Prentice-Hall, Inc., Englewood Cliffs, N.J., 1963, p. 50.

[10]A. H. Maslow, *Toward a Psychology of Being,* D. Van Nostrand Company, Inc., Princeton, N.J., 1962, pp. 153–154.

forcing a truly self-actualized person to function in a low-skilled highly programmed job may result in inefficiency, we must realize that not everyone will be affected in this fashion. The selection and training procedures in organizations must take into account the almost infinite variability of persons' needs, including their needs for external discipline.

Theory Y and modern industry   A second criticism is that adherents of theory Y make a big issue of man's alienation from his work as a result of the industrial revolution, miniaturization of the job, simplification, standardization, and programmed work movements. Theory Y holds that as a result of the combined weight of these forces, industrial organizations have created a personality-organization conflict that is most often present in large-scale mass-production industries. These forces, says theory Y, have so reduced job satisfaction that individuals perform in irrational and dysfunctional ways.

Considering only mass production jobs for a moment, satisfaction may indeed be less in some jobs than it was a century ago, but work satisfaction undoubtedly has increased in many work situations in modern industry. Moreover, this individual-versus-organization conflict may be just one facet of a universal conflict between the individual and family, the individual and social organizations, the individual and work organizations, and the individual and society. If the conflict is inherently individual versus organization, all organizations, not just industrial ones, are liable, and theory X is not necessarily the cause.

Where individuals satisfy their needs   A third criticism of theory Y is that it may overemphasize the job as the primary place for need satisfaction. For many persons, the focus of their lives is off, not on, the job. With the tendency to shorten the work week, particularly for blue-collar workers, off-the-job need satisfaction may become increasingly important and the use of leisure time more of a problem.

Nevertheless, McGregor's contributions in developing theories X and Y are highly significant. By setting up the boundaries of a spectrum within which motivational theories can be developed, he accomplished the first task necessary for the development of a more complete operational theory of motivation. Now, it is possible not only to isolate the theme of each boundary condition but also to fill the space between them.

DEPENDENCE AND INDEPENDENCE IN ORGANIZATIONS

McGregor also provided a framework within which one of the previously unresolvable human-relations problems can be approached: the problem of dependence versus independence, domination versus freedom, control versus permissiveness. For, as we have seen, when stripped of value judgments, each theory emphasizes a different approach to employer-employee relationships: theory X emphasizes dependence, domination, and control; theory Y emphasizes independence, freedom, and permissiveness.

In any business firm the employees are, to some extent, dependent upon the organization for regular, continuous employment (job security), for increases in pay, for promotions, and often for status and prestige within their work group and the broader social community of which they are members. Fringe benefits, privileges, authority, feelings of accomplishment, and numerous other benefits are also dependent wholly or in part on the employee's work situation. Many of these aspects of dependence are quite healthy and normal. They are in fact counterbalanced by the employer's dependence on employees for the work they do. This mutual reliance may be called "interdependence" and may be quite appropriate.

Robert L. Katz argues that the conventional way of thinking about how an enterprise should be organized and administered actually encourages dependent relationships.[11] According to conventional organizational concepts, managers have the *right* to manage and employees have the *duty* to obey. Only *roles*, or *positions*, are important—the relationships between the unique, peculiar human beings who happen to be occupying those positions are unimportant. Power is a definable substance, residing at the top of an organization and is "distributed in successively diminishing amounts downward through a hierarchy of positions."[12] The holder of any position is viewed as having a predetermined and continuing right to exercise the power attached to his position. Thus, persons occupying superior positions are automatically empowered to direct subordinates. Subordinates, to receive rewards (income, prestige, or security), are thought of as being required to accept the direction of those in power. The power relationship is supposed to exist and continue between superior and subordinate regardless of the individuals that occupy the respective positions.

Dependence in Organizations

The conventional theory X organizational and motivational concepts discussed above get results—they reduce arbitrary, random individual action by organization members. Top executives can "shoulder their enormous responsibilities with some equanimity," and subordinates are provided with "greater certainty of superiors' expectations, assurances of justice, some protection from individual caprice, and the availability of authorized channels for expressing feelings and grievances."[13]

But the strengths provided by this traditional organizational concept have been purchased at a price. By emphasizing dependence in the work relationship, these procedures have sacrificed subordinates' initiative and creativity to "the search for certainty."[14] Consequently, the organization receives only "minimal effort and minimal creativity from its members";[15] managers fail to deal directly with the major problems at hand; organizational response to the market and environment is sluggish; mental growth and on-the-job need satisfaction are so limited that employees attempt to satisfy these needs off the job. Management, Katz feels, responds to this low performance by

[11]Robert L. Katz, "Management Assumptions and Organizational Consequences," in Paul R. Lawrence et al. (eds.), *Organizational Behavior and Administration*, The Dorsey Press, Homewood, Ill., 1961, pp. 734–746.

[12]*Ibid.*, p. 737.

[13]*Ibid.*, p. 741. (The quotations in this paragraph are all from this source.)

[14]*Ibid.*

[15]*Ibid.*

increasing pressure on subordinates, not by questioning its own policies. Other authorities agree:

> The trouble with conventional thinking is this: delegation of authority as the formal power to influence others inevitably creates a relationship of dependency between the superior and the subordinate. The subordinate is dependent on his superior for continued favor and for support to back him up if he runs into trouble in carrying out his actions. His conduct tends to be determined by the personal ties and sentiments he forms toward his superior. In effect, his behavior over the course of time becomes similar to that of his boss. Differences are not encouraged, often not tolerated. . . . The moral order comes to rest on power alone. If one has the authority, his actions come to be thought of as right. . . . To meet resistance, superior authority brings more power to bear, which in turn causes more resistance. [16]

Although no competent organizational theorist questions the need for some certainty and order within an organization, many doubt that encouraging the excessively dependent relationships inherent in many work situations is the best way to achieve high productivity. Extreme dependent relationships result in a loss of self; people tend to become like mechanical zombies following the lead of their dominators. Organizational members refuse to get involved in anything controversial and merely "do time" on the job. Although dependence provides order and certainty for the organization, it also does so for those individuals who adopt a safe behavior pattern. Thus, when the emphasis is placed on dependency relationship, the employee's chief interest is to do only and exactly what he has been told; to do more would be dangerous.

Independence in Organizations

Theory Y, in contrast, represents a complete shift in emphasis—from domination to permissiveness, from dependence to independence. It emphasizes the individual's need for self-determination, self-regulation, and self-respect. This view is advanced on the grounds that in our culture, lower-level safety and security needs have largely been satisfied and are therefore no longer motivators. Accordingly, the dependency relationships inherent in work situations are deemphasized, and new independent work relationships are sought. Job enlargement, consultative planning, general supervision, and junior boards of directors are some of the approaches that are encouraged. Work is reoriented so that jobs become almost independent; that is, each task can be treated almost as if it were being done by a subcontractor—the worker.

Some authorities—Maslow, for example—presumably would have characterized those people who fit the assumptions of theory Y as self-actualizing. Apparently, he regarded the self-actualizing person as the ideal of mental health, an ideal toward which he preferred to see individuals develop. Thus, in his view (and that of some other author-

---

[16]Bennett E. Kline and Norman H. Martin, "The Problem of Freedom," in W. Lloyd Warner and Norman H. Martin (eds.), *Industrial Man: Businessmen and Business Organizations*, Harper & Row, Publishers, Incorporated, New York, 1959, pp. 50–54. (By permission.)

ities) putting theory Y into widespread practice would be a major step toward better mental health for the entire population.

Other social scientists have welcomed this shift in emphasis as an extension of individual freedom into the work environment. They believe that heretofore our social and political system has stressed freedom, while our employing institutions have emphasized authority, direction, and control. This viewpoint is supported by some businessmen; witness this statement by General Robert E. Wood, former chairman of the board of Sears, Roebuck, and Company:

> We complain about government in business, we stress the advantages of the free enterprise system, we complain about the totalitarian state, but in our industrial organization, in our striving for efficiency we have created more or less of a totalitarian system in industry, particularly in large industry. The problem of retaining our efficiency and discipline in these large organizations and yet allowing our people to express themselves, to exercise initiative and to have some voice in the affairs of the organization is the greatest problem for large industrial organizations to solve. [17]

The typical business executive apparently does not see his organization as having these responsibilities. He regards his organization as beneficial to both employers and employees. After all, he says, the employee who dislikes the behavior of a firm can always quit and shop for a more suitable job. But the point is debatable:

> It appears to many millions of Americans that, while they live in a free society, earning and using their incomes in a free economic system, they spend most of their working hours in authoritarian institutions playing the role of the managed. The employing institutions do not match the system in their use of freedom. Being managed, it seems, is not the same as exercising freedom. [18]

By encouraging independence, theory Y proponents expect to stimulate initiative, contribution, involvement, and creativity of organizational members. They expect to prevent the command hierarchy from institutionalizing ignorance, minimum acceptable performance, and apathy. The lure of individual freedom becomes the motivational tool or technique employed. Each person is encouraged to be self-motivated and self-disciplined in pursuing his individual goals. The organization ceases to be a benefit provider and becomes an opportunity provider. It becomes an important means through which the employee can pursue his goals, and since organizational goals are compatible with individual goals, in his pursuit he contributes to organizational achievement.

WHICH THEORY IS BEST?

Obviously, all people are not alike, and to take the extreme position that one or the other of these theories works best in *all* situations is therefore a fallacious assumption. Although many managers when exposed to these two theories immediately recognize this fact, others fall into the "either-or" trap. Such a choice is not necessary or even desirable.

[17] Quoted in Kline and Martin, *op. cit.,* p. 503. (By permission.)
[18] *Ibid.,* p. 501.

Generally, the situation in which theory X works best is exactly opposite to the one where Y works best. Management by directives—theory X—apparently works best when the job itself does not offer intrinsic job satisfaction, and with people who must satisfy many of their higher-level needs *off* rather than *on* the job. Studies of job satisfaction by occupational groupings indicate that such conditions exist in the unskilled and semi-skilled occupational levels. In those cases where jobs offer intrinsic satisfaction and in those where individuals can satisfy some of their higher-level needs on the job, theory Y may work best. In general, these jobs (mathematicians, physicists, doctors, lawyers, or professors) would be ranked near the top of the occupational ladder.

Theory X works better where output can be measured objectively—for example, in the production department of a manufacturing firm or for a salesman on quota. In teaching, engineering, or research and development where output is difficult to measure, theory Y may work best. Theory X implies the use of the stick (to punish if the job is not done as expected), but the stick usually can be applied judiciously only when there is advance agreement of the expected and required output. For example, if a manager expects a laborer to dig 30 feet of a ditch per day but does not tell him so, it would be difficult to discipline the laborer effectively for digging only 20 feet per day since he was not told what was expected of him.

Theory X may also be indicated in emergency conditions. If the captain commands, "Charge and take that hill!" he does not wait to see if the private is self-actuated. In some cases the private might be shot for disobeying orders if he refused to join the charge.

Both theories X and Y can be used effectively in the same company. The author has observed this coexistence of theories X and Y in several large firms. However, it can provide a potential source of friction if either group of supervisors tries to sell its views to the other as the ultimate approach to supervision. The two groups often fail to realize that what works best for one type of work or group of workers may not work best for another.

The dependence-independence controversy has often seemingly forced an either-or choice between the two theories. Again, no such choice is necessary—they are not mutually exclusive (except in their extreme forms). The central problem is to determine the role and the blend between the two—what we might call "interdependence."

Mason Haire has recognized and treated this problem of balance most clearly by tracing briefly the development of a child.[19] An infant is born with a complete set of physical needs, but is unable to satisfy them for himself. He is totally dependent on someone else for survival. This complete dependence on someone else is in many ways comfortable. But the child soon learns that complete dependency means that he is also at the mercy of some other person—not only does he become frustrated, but also his existence is threatened. Two contradictory groups of drives grow up simultaneously—dependence and independence. Further development of the individual results in a growing awareness of self, which strengthens both sets of drives. Similarly, when a worker first

---

[19]Mason Haire, *Psychology in Management,* 2d ed., McGraw-Hill Book Company, New York, 1964, pp. 48–51, 65–86.

enters his job, he is dependent on his superiors at work for need satisfaction. If the organization exploits this dependence, he may become the passively acquiescent "yes man" who does only what he is told, nothing more. On the other hand, if independence is overemphasized, internal order and coordinated behavior may be made difficult. However, there is evidence indicating that the organizational environment is not the only factor affecting the balance—personality is also a factor. Just as in Maslow's theory, the individual is a decisive element in organizational policy. For example, M. Scott Myers in several years of research at Texas Instruments concluded that personality may help determine whether a person is a "maintenance seeker" or a "motivation seeker."[20] The first type realizes little satisfaction from accomplishment, while the latter gains considerable gratification.

Another researcher, Chris Argyris, apparently accepts the idea that the proper balance between dependence and independence depends partially on the personality of the individual, for Argyris constructs a model of two archetypes.[21] One is the domination-emphasizing firm, and the second is the individual who is enthralled with independence. He questions the result of placing this independence-seeking individual in an organization which emphasizes dependent relationships; frustration, conflict, a narrow viewpoint, and too much of a tendency to form informal organizations are potentially among the undesirable consequences. Similarly, a person with insufficient self-discipline could be a disastrous influence in an organization emphasizing independence and theory Y.

In the same vein Kurt Lewin has found that the experience of success or failure does not depend upon the achievement per se, but rather upon the relation between the achievement and the person's expectations or level of aspiration.[22] Thus individuals measure their own success or failure not in terms of absolute success but in terms of their momentary level of aspiration. But the level of aspirations varies directly with past successes and failures and with the achievements of their competitors. Past successes raise expectations, whereas past failures lower them, but one cannot create strong feelings either way by assigning easy tasks. In the person's eyes, significant success and failure occur only if the difficulty of the task lies close to the upper limit of achievement, that is, if there is a chance for either success or failure to occur in the task and if it is equal to or more difficult than tasks already completed by his coworkers.

J. W. Atkinson suggested that there are two different motivational influences: (a) the desire to achieve success and (b) the desire to avoid failure; and the strengths of these influences vary among individuals.[23] Thus whether or not a man will take a risk depends

[20]M. Scott Myers, "Who Are Your Motivated Workers?" *Harvard Business Review,* pp. 73–88, January–February 1964.

[21]Chris Argyris, *Understanding Organizational Behavior,* The Dorsey Press, Homewood, Ill., 1960, pp. 12–25.

[22]Kurt Lewin, "Psychology of Success and Failure," in Timothy W. Costello and Sheldon S. Zalkind (eds.), *Psychology in Administration: A Research Orientation,* Prentice-Hall, Inc., Englewood Cliffs, N.J., 1963, pp. 67–78.

[23]J. W. Atkinson, "Motivational Determinants of Risk-taking Behavior," *Psychological Review,* pp. 359–372, November 1957.

on the strengths of his personal needs for success or for avoidance of failure—which in turn are largely culturally determined by past experience.

Therefore it is no longer sufficient to take Maslow's need hierarchy as permanently fixed for a *particular* individual. Although the general need hierarchy provides the general structure of needs, no person will fit that pattern precisely.

Figure 19-1 shows the major factors which contribute to the development of the hierarchy of needs for a particular individual. As the diagram indicates, these factors are dynamic and mutually interacting—each acts on the individual's need hierarchy and on all the others.

MANAGEMENT BY RESULTS

We are interested in the individual's behavior that contributes to productivity in the organization. The standard for acceptable behavior in the interdependence concept is that behavior, which primarily seeks to satisfy individual objectives, be compatible with and help to accomplish organizational objectives. If it is and does, rewards can reinforce this behavior. If not, the organization has three alternatives. First, it can use discipline

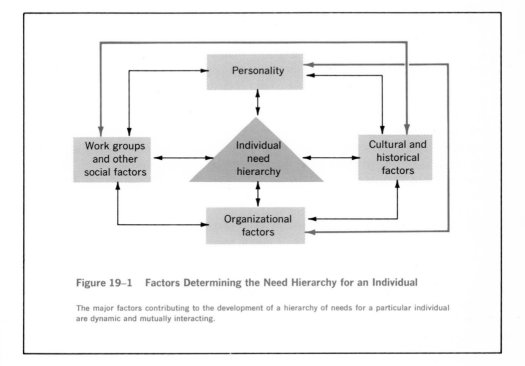

Figure 19–1   Factors Determining the Need Hierarchy for an Individual

The major factors contributing to the development of a hierarchy of needs for a particular individual are dynamic and mutually interacting.

to seek to produce the desired behavior. Second, it can reevaluate the stimulus (motivation) originally used. The motivation may not be the proper one for the individual involved. If such is the case, other approaches to stimulating desired behavior can be tried. Finally, if the particular individual is incompatible with the organization, terminating his membership may be the best solution.

There are persons who prefer dependence or independence because of their particular personalities. There are many others who have learned to prefer one to the other because of prior experiences. But the majority of individuals apparently do not want one to the exclusion of the other—they want some blending of the two. The average employee desires freedom to act, but he wants clearly defined limits which are known to both him and his employer. The granting of freedom is evidence of the supervisor's confidence, which creates a sense of responsibility in the subordinate and allows a greater chance for individual growth, creativity, and innovation. The interdependence approach may be termed "supervision by results."

Management by results means that instead of telling subordinates exactly how to do their work, supervisors delegate authority and give the subordinate definite assignments of results or goals to be achieved. The subordinate is allowed to decide, *within the limits of the assignment and the policies of the organization,* how best to achieve these results. The supervisor can then measure performance in terms of the employee's accomplishment instead of by his ability to carry out a specific set of orders about how to do his work. It is assumed that the employee knows more than the manager about how to do his job; or, alternatively, that the employee can best take the initiative in discovering from others, reading, training, or research how best to perform his assigned objectives. A relatively large amount of security is provided by the limits of company policy, and the employee is not thrown completely on his own self-discipline as he is in theory Y. Also, the employee is free to seek the expert advice of the manager when the manager has a contribution to make to the question of how to do the work.

As an approach to supervision, management by results has a number of advantages over directive management of procedures. First, it requires the employee to use his own imagination and creativity in determining how assignments are to be carried out. This freedom to make decisions creates a sense of independence and causes the employee to feel that he is participating more in his work.

Second, the employee's knowledge that his independent performance will be evaluated in terms of results provides him with an incentive to achieve the goal. Coming up short of the goal is poor performance; it is not necessary for anyone to make a value judgment that his performance is poor. The supervisor can better evaluate effectiveness and discuss any shortcomings since the subordinate already knows that his performance did not measure up.

Third, management by results provides a continuous training program for future managers. Subordinates learn by example (their supervisor's) and by doing (making decisions). As they move up the organizational ladder, the range for decisions becomes broader and the decisions become more complex. Promoting employees on the basis of their performance and success in goal accomplishment allows them to work toward whatever result is most important to them and the organization at a particular time.

SUMMARY

⸢Motivation in organizations is concerned with discovering the stimuli that a manager can use to achieve productive behavior in organizations⸥ But motivation is in the final analysis a purely individual thing that must be geared to fit each particular person and situation. However, a knowledge of the general characteristics of persons is necessary, and Maslow's need hierarchy helps in understanding the general nature of wants for individuals. McGregor's theory X and theory Y provide guidelines for assumptions about the nature of people's needs in contemporary organizations.

Until recently an organization was forced to choose between a dependence-fostering or an independence-fostering philosophy of operation. Apparently, most employees do not wish to choose between these two alternatives. Their most honest answer to the question, "Do you prefer direction or freedom?" would be an emphatic, "I want some of both!" The balance or mixture for the individual depends on his needs and personality, and the central objective for managers is to find the proper one for each individual and group within his organization.

FOR REVIEW AND DISCUSSION

1 Summarize and evaluate theory X.

2 Summarize and evaluate theory Y.

3 Explain how both theory X and theory Y could be confirmed through the action of self-fulfilling prophecy.

4 Illustrate the self-fulfilling prophecy in action with three examples not drawn from the text.

5 Explain the following types of relationships in organizations: (a) dependence, (b) independence, (c) interdependence.

6 Summarize and evaluate management by results.

7 Explain the place of the following in motivating an employee: (a) personality of the employee, (b) personality of the manager, (c) the environment, (d) attitudes of the manager, (e) type of work, (f) permanency of work or of the worker's membership in the organization.

8 Explain additional factors other than those listed in the preceding question that will be important in effective motivation.

9 Write a short paper supporting one of the following approaches to supervision (select the one assigned to you by your instructor): (a) theory X, (b) theory Y, (c) management by results.

10 Explain and evaluate the statement: "Theory Y is unreasonably idealistic."

11 What pattern of supervision would you use for each of the following classes of workers? Explain your answer in each case: (a) typists, (b) ditch diggers, (c) research scientists, (d) teachers, (e) engineering draftsmen, (f) migratory farm workers, (g) assembly-line workers in an automobile plant, (h) women assembly-line workers in an electronics plant, (i) janitors.

CASES

A   John Mikal was foreman of a large timber-cutting crew. Absenteeism and labor turnover had always been high for this work in the area. Mr. Mikal said that unless he closely supervised his employees, the production rate of his crew would soon fall to a totally unacceptable level. Mr. Mikal often threatened his men; he also frequently fired men if he thought their work was below standard. The men in the crew hated and feared Mr. Mikal, but the crew often cut more timber than any other crew in the company.

    1 What do you think of Mr. Mikal's approach to supervision?

    2 What suggestions to improve his supervision would you make to Mr. Mikal? Why do you think your suggestions would help?

B   Professor Carnes, head of his department, had never criticized the work of any of his faculty members. He always was helpful when a faculty member asked him for assistance, but he had never suggested what work his faculty members should do other than meet their classes. Professor Carnes said that he wanted his department to become one of the very best.

    1 Do you think Professor Carnes's methods of supervision are likely to make his department "one of the very best"?

    2 How might Professor Carnes improve his supervisory techniques?

C   "Men," said Abe Stinson, the general sales manager, at the annual sales meeting, "we must beat last year's sales by at least 20 percent. I'm leaving it up to each of you divisional sales managers to determine exactly how you will do the job in your division. Let me have your plans for review by next Friday. Any questions?"

There were no questions and the meeting was dismissed.

    1 Evaluate Mr. Stinson's approach to motivation.

    2 Would you suggest that each divisional sales manager use a similar approach at his divisional sales meeting? Why?

FOR FURTHER STUDY

Additional sources can be found in the sources cited in the chapter.

Articles

Chris Argyris: "We Must Make Work Worthwhile," *Life,* May 5, 1967, pp. 56–68. "The fundamental structure of industry and management often creates conflict and undermines the real needs of employees."

Frank Friedlander and Eugene Walton: "Positive and Negative Motivation Toward Work," *Administrative Science Quarterly,* September 1964. Much of the confusion concerning job motivations result from a failure to distinguish between positive and negative motivation.

Charles D. McDermid: "How Money Motivates Men," *Business Horizons,* Winter 1960, pp. 93–100. McDermid shows how money can contribute to every level of human need satisfaction.

Douglas McGregor: "Conditions of Effective Leadership in the Industrial Organization," *Journal of Consulting Psychology,* March–April 1944, pp. 55–63. A splendid analysis of dependency and independency needs of employees. Enlightened viewpoints for managers are suggested.

Douglas M. McGregor: "The Human Side of Enterprise," *Management Review,* November 1957. In this classic article McGregor describes his famous theories X and Y and how they relate to the satisfaction of human needs in organizations.

M. Scott Myers: "Who Are Your Motivated Workers?" *Harvard Business Review,* January–February 1964. Some persons seek only maintenance from an organization, and others seek self-expression.

John J. Morse and Jay W. Lorsch: "Beyond Theory Y," *Harvard Business Review,* May–June 1970. "Competence motivation" related to each employee aims to integrate organization, task, and individual.

"Reward and Punishment," *Kaiser Aluminum News,* no. 2, 1968, pp. 22–26. Alternate source: Don Fabun: *Three Roads to Awareness,* Glencoe Press, Beverly Hills, Calif., 1970, pp. 1–40. "Human motivational systems are based on the belief that, through the offer of rewards and the threat of punishment, individuals can be led to expend their energy in a desired direction."

Charles R. Walker and Robert H. Guest: "The Man on the Assembly Line," *Harvard Business Review,* May–June 1952. Analyzes the benefits and disadvantages of mass production and its effect upon workers.

Marvin R. Weisbord: "What, Not Again: Manage People Better?" *Think,* January–February 1970. McGregor's Theory Y should be practiced by managers.

20
Managerial Applications of Motivation

*Management must develop as broad a horizon as possible
for every position, with guide posts along the way rather
than rigid fences that hem the individual into a
completely preplanned . . . existence.*
EDWARD C. SCHLEH

In our study of motivation we have discussed individual needs and managerial practices that affect behavior. The remaining problem is that of developing a workable
approach to the two which will have general applicability in organizations. As suggested in the previous chapter a mutual dependence or interdependence[1] between
employers and employees is likely to stimulate an approach that emphasizes high
productivity. There are three major steps in this approach: (1) defining acceptable
boundaries of employees' actions, (2) granting the freedom to act within these boundaries, and (3) supervising by results.

Accomplishing the above steps requires: (1) a realistic attitude of managers toward

---

[1]Interdependence was suggested by Douglas McGregor, *The Human Side of Enterprise,* McGraw-Hill
Book Company, New York, 1960, pp. 26–27. See also Victor A. Thompson, *Modern Organization,* Alfred A.
Knopf, Inc., New York, 1961, p. 29.

employees (see the two previous chapters), (2) a comprehensive system of rules or discipline, (3) the maintenance of an adequate system of communication (see the following three chapters), (4) an objective follow-up pattern, and (5) a realistic organizational atmosphere (see Part I and the two previous chapters).[2]

REALISTIC ATTITUDE

If our arrangement is to be workable, both managers and employees must be aware of its effects. Within the interdependence framework, when a manager grants an employee the freedom to decide and act within clearly defined limits, he does not reduce any of his own responsibilities for achieving results. He does, however, relinquish a large degree of detailed control over his men. Employees assume the task of determining their own goals, procedures, and methods. They become their own taskmakers to a great extent, and they are free to question, dream, break tradition, experiment, and seek new knowledge or find it by accident. Of course, they are not free to overlook organizational goals, fabricate or distort information, exceed their authority, violate organizational policies, or violate the rights of others. As the employee becomes more

[2] Bennett E. Kline and Norman H. Martin, "The Problem of Freedom," in W. L. Warner and Norman H. Martin (eds.), *Industrial Man,* Harper & Row, Publishers, Incorporated, New York, 1959, pp. 506–514.

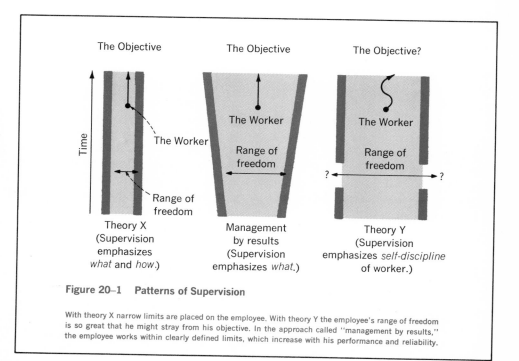

Figure 20–1   Patterns of Supervision

With theory X narrow limits are placed on the employee. With theory Y the employee's range of freedom is so great that he might stray from his objective. In the approach called "management by results," the employee works within clearly defined limits, which increase with his performance and reliability.

competent through attaining each new goal, his manager should become more demand-ing in setting new goals.

Three patterns of supervision are shown in Figure 20-1. Theory X supervision sets extremely narrow limits of freedom for the employee. In this approach the manager instructs the employee in detail what is desired and how the work will be performed. Employee initiative is not emphasized because the manager tells him both what to do and how to do it.

On the opposite extreme, theory Y supervision gives a wide range of freedom to the employee—so wide that the limits of acceptable behavior are often unknown to him. Theory Y assumes that the employee is self-disciplined and that he will adjust his ac-tivities to work toward the organization's objective. With such excessive freedom the employee is likely to wander and not work effectively toward his objective.

Again referring to Figure 20-1, the third approach to supervision is management by results. In this approach the manager gives wide freedom to the employee, but *within clearly defined limits*. Supervision is principally in terms of what results are expected of the employee, rather than how the work will be done. The initiative for determining how to do the job rests in large part with the employee, but monetary and behavioral limits are made clear. As the worker becomes more reliable his range of freedom will be increased.

Granting freedom to act within clearly defined boundaries is evidence of a man-ager's confidence in his employee—the range of the boundaries indicates the degree of confidence. Extremely narrow boundaries (theiry X) result in little if any freedom, but extremely broad limits (theory Y) may result in lack of effective discipline. Being granted an appropriate amount of freedom results in the employee's responding to the trust and confidence placed in him by developing a sense of responsibility and individ-uality. He feels a sense of pride in accomplishing the desired results and in determining the details of achieving these results. The employee need no longer feel that he is a means to an end, a cog in an impersonal wheel. His acceptance of responsibility means there is less need for close control, direction, and discipline, and the manager's role becomes more that of a leader than a manipulator. His time is focused on defining limits, assigning tasks, evaluating results, using results to instruct, and rewarding good performance instead of on close, detailed scrutiny of the precise methods used in doing the work. Nevertheless, a system of rules is important for defining the outer limits of acceptable behavior.

SYSTEM OF RULES

The two major facets of organizational discipline are the development of a system of rules and the administration of that system. The general function of a system of rules is to ensure efficient organizational effort—to reduce random, undirected individual effort. Ideally, the organization's objectives provide standards, boundaries, or limits by which the individual's behavior can be evaluated, and the resulting rules help to de-fine the limits within which freedom of action is permissible.

Many organizations have rules directly concerned with the behavior of personnel. Behavioral rules commonly state what members must or must not do and the punishment or penalty for disobeying. Prescribed penalties are designed to fit the seriousness of the offense; excessive absenteeism would call for a type and degree of punishment quite different from that for theft. Repeated offenses of the same type increase the severity of the punishment. For example, a single unwarranted absence might result in minimum punishment; but several such offenses in a given time period will probably incur increasingly heavier punishment and, finally, the loss of the offender's job.

Employees are rarely discharged for a first offense of a minor nature. Major offenses, such as theft, fighting, or drinking on the job, may result in major penalties for the first offense. Organizations generally have come to accept the idea of major and minor offenses and of a sequence of penalties or progressive discipline for repeated minor offenses within a given time period.

Types of Organizational Discipline

Many organizations are meticulous in developing rules of discipline. Ordinarily the sequence of penalties under progressive discipline is as follows: First, a clear oral warning is given that any repetition of the offense will call for more severe discipline; second, written warnings may be issued and are made part of the employee's personnel record to be presented as evidence if offenses continue; third, as the next level of severity, disciplinary layoffs for a limited time with loss of pay may be imposed; and finally discharge, the ultimate penalty, may be ordered.[3] Demotion is seldom used as a disciplinary measure because it humiliates the employee, and the organization cannot then make full use of his skill. Companies that follow policies consistent with theory X are faced with the problem of devising an extensive and detailed set of rules. These organizations may even attempt to devise rules to apply to all possible situations. Such extensive sets of rules are difficult to develop and administer; they narrow the employee's range of freedom; and, typically, the lists get longer and more complex as the organization matures. Because many such rules become unenforceable, employees may feel that the administration of these rules is capricious and arbitrary: the boss may enforce the no-smoking rules this week, last week it was coffee breaks, and who knows what it will be next? Theory Y organizations, with their deemphasis of detailed rules, may go to the extreme in the other direction and leave employees without any sense of guidance or direction. Disorganized effort often results.

The interdependence approach to discipline avoids these extremes — it is an attempt to allow maximum elbow room for each individual and at the same time increase coordinated and efficient action. Rules are recognized as necessary, but they are not regarded as ends in themselves. Rather, the relationship of rules to the objectives of the organization becomes the point of emphasis. The primary question asked in the development of any new rule is: "How does this rule contribute to the successful attainment

---

[3]However, one major company known to the author adopted the additional penalty of criminal prosecution of employees and managers who committed fraud against the firm.

of organizational objectives?" If there is no positive contribution, the rule should be eliminated on the grounds that it is an unneccessary restriction on the freedom to act.

Effective Discipline

The purpose of discipline is to assist in obtaining organizational objectives by guiding members' behavior. Discipline should not be used for the purpose of getting even with the employee; it should be corrective rather than punitive and should encourage employees to learn from their mistakes. Effective discipline modifies the old saying, "Experience is the best teacher," to read "Experience is the best teacher—if you learn from it."

Discipline that teaches is something that we have experienced throughout our lives. In fact a valuable rule of discipline can be illustrated by a person's first experience with a hot stove. When you touch a hot stove your discipline is *immediate*—there is no question of cause and effect; you had *warning*—the feel of the heat from the stove; the discipline was *consistent*—every time you touched the stove you were burned; and the discipline is *impersonal*—anyone touching the stove is burned, no matter who he is. The "hot-stove rule" makes the act committed and the discipline incurred seem almost one.[4] You are disciplined because you have committed a certain act—not because you are bad. The discipline is directed against the act—not against the person. Immediacy, forewarning, consistency, and impersonality are as effective in organizational discipline as they are when a person touches a hot stove.

Immediacy   The sooner the discipline follows the offense, the more likely it is to be associated with the offense rather than with the person imposing the discipline. Prompt disciplinary action has more impact. Investigations, where required, should be made speedily.

Forewarning   There should be clear knowledge of those offenses that lead to discipline and of the severity of discipline imposed for each. Unexpected discipline is almost always considered unjust and is met with resentment. If an organization wishes to begin strict enforcement of a heretofore poorly enforced rule, then it should issue a warning of the change in policy.

Consistency   If rule enforcement is consistent, an employee is far more likely to accept discipline without cries that someone is discriminating against him. Consistent administration of discipline helps to set well-defined limits. As we have seen, an individual wants to know the limits of permissible behavior, and one way to establish these limits clearly and dramatically is to punish consistently those who exceed the limits. Consistent discipline also provides stability and certainty in the work environment when an employee knows that rules will be enforced.

[4]See George Strauss and Leonard R. Sayles, *Personnel,* Prentice-Hall, Inc., Englewood Cliffs, N.J., 1960, pp. 288–298.

Impersonality   Impersonality minimizes the resentfulness and aggressiveness of a person being disciplined. He realizes that it is not he the person but the particular act he has committed that invites punishment. As we noted before, management by results is of great help here, since the employee knows his performance is below standard before he talks to his superior. An apology for disciplinary action injects personal feelings into the situation and causes the offender to feel that the apologetic supervisor does not accept the company standard.

COMMUNICATION

How much does an employee need to know? If interdependence is desired, he should be provided with enough information to extend his horizons beyond the confines of his particular job. He must know something of the organization's overall objectives, the purposes and activities of major departments, and the results expected of him and his associates.

Nearly every aspect of manager-employee relationships involves communication. Communication is particularly important in the areas of defining limits, granting freedom to act, and supervising by results. But the supervisor must guard against the assumption that simply telling his subordinates something is enough to ensure successful communication. As we will see in the following section on communication the supervisor must be sure through "feedback" from the employee that the employee understands what is expected of him.

PATTERNS OF SUPERVISION

Theory X Supervision

Managers in theory X supervision have the responsibility for all steps other than the actual performance of tasks. The person most directly involved in the work, the employee, participates inadequately. Theory X organizations assume that management should think out all the necessary plans and alternatives, devise the best procedure for accomplishing a task, and write rules to see that the task is done in the prescribed fashion. When these steps are carried out properly, the work usually will be accomplished. The emphasis is placed on employees following prescribed procedures, and the burden of the follow-up is placed on the manager. If the results are not as planned, it is presumed that the procedures are not being followed properly. Discipline for its own sake and conformity-producing techniques are often encouraged. Adherence to rules may become an end in itself, displacing the original goals. Emphasis on rules as ends in themselves can cause organizational *rigor mortis* to set in; formalized procedures may be adhered to at all costs—even if they interfere with the achievement of the organization's objectives. Technique and red tape rule the flow of work. In a complex organizational structure, the lower the level of authority, the more bureaucratic and arbitrary the official. At the foreman level, everything may have to be done by the book.

Potentials of theory X supervision When management is successful in operating the theory X pattern, stated objectives will usually be accomplished. Theory X, if the enforcement of rules is effective enough, does indeed set minimum acceptable levels—floors—of performance. Unfortunately, minimum acceptable performance tends to become at the same time a floor *and* a ceiling. Under theory X persons rarely, if ever, develop or perform anywhere near their potential. "... Theory X ... will fail to *discover,* let alone utilize, the potentialities of the average human being."[5] They simply do their prescribed task; often they are not even expected to do more.

> The ... worker makes no decisions, follows orders so detailed as to preclude any freedom of action, and is cut off from communication with anyone higher than the foreman. Consequently, he may have little or no pride in his work and no sense of being an important part of the company hiring him. And he may work no harder than he has to.[6]

Theory X thus tends to become self-limiting, a tendency which clearly can have disastrous long-run consequences for the organization.

(In summary, theory X, if it is enforced, can result in prescribed performance, but it fails to challenge workers to their full potential and is therefore self-limiting.) It has the undesirable quality of limiting productivity over a longer period even though it is designed as a method for increasing organizational productivity.

Theory Y Supervision

Theory Y supervision is based on the assumptions that a worker is self-disciplined and that he will work toward organizational objectives when he is committed to them. Because, under theory Y, workers are self-disciplined and self-controlled, the manager's principal task is to create a work environment where the worker can express his full productive potential.

Theory Y has proved successful in many business organizations. Lincoln Electric Company has carried it to the point where each employee is very much like a subcontractor. Workers are responsible for their own raw materials, including the ordering and controlling of supplies. Workers are also responsible for the quantity and quality of their own output.

Potentials of theory Y supervision For ideally mature, self-disciplined persons working under ideal conditions, theory Y unquestionably offers the greatest potential of both organizational productivity and human development of any pattern of supervision; and in the long run it seems quite possible that theory Y will prove itself more valuable. (See the self-fulfilling prophecy described in the previous chapter.) Unfortunately the full potentials of theory Y are not likely to be attainable for several generations, if ever. The world presently contains billions of persons who require external

---

[5]McGregor, *op. cit.,* p. 43. (Emphasis added.)
[6]Lee Berton, "More Companies Give Blue-collar Employees Greater Responsibility," *Wall Street Journal,* March 14, 1966, p. 1. (By permission.)

discipline from a supervisor before they will work efficiently toward organizational objectives.

Thus, theory Y offers a long-run potential that may be an ideal pattern of supervision. For the present, however, we must supervise workers mainly as we find them (requiring some external discipline). The long-run potential of theory Y must be tempered by the short-run requirement of supervising to reach more current organizational objectives effectively with employees who are not now and perhaps never will be as mature as we might like.

Management by Results

We have seen the harmful effects of overemphasis on procedure (theory X). And we have seen that extremely loose supervision—theory Y—may be unreasonably idealistic. To overcome both objections, management by results places the emphasis where it should be—on results.

(Management by results gives the employee the objective of a project, the decision-making data he needs, the limits within which he is to operate, and the freedom to operate within these limits.) Management by results assumes that the employee has been properly selected and trained, and that he is informed that he will be responsible for achieving the desired results.[7]

Management by results places the manager-employee relationship on a more direct, less complex basis than theory X. Any judgment of whether or not a job has been done well can be made in terms of planned versus actual results. Evaluations of success can be made in an objective, unemotional way. Deviations of results from plans bring up the question of whether or not goals are realistic, as well as disclose different routes which can be taken to attain the goals. No one is prescribing detailed procedures to follow, no one is looking over the employee's shoulder, but his actions are goal directed. Both manager and employee are concerned that the employee receive the education and training needed for his job. The employee is largely self-motivated and self-disciplined in the details of his job, and if disciplinary action is called for from the supervisor, the employee knows why—he has not achieved the results required within the broad limits that govern his action.

Objective, results-oriented follow-up is more efficient because it frees management of concern for detailed plans and procedures, thereby releasing managerial talent for more important tasks. It may also increase management's work load and responsibility, but in areas which management should be working—realistic determination of objectives, for example.

Potentials of management by results   The management-by-results approach includes necessary external discipline and control over the employee. Thus it may be highly effective in the short run. Further, in the longer run, management by results

[7]Cf. Edward C. Schleh, *Management by Results,* McGraw-Hill Book Company, New York, 1961.

e same virtually unlimited potentials as theory Y. In fact the long-run benefits of self-discipline and control may actually be realized more quickly with management by results than by theory Y. One learns self-discipline by living in an environment of gradually decreasing external discipline. Management by results offers this gradual decrease; theory Y implies immediate freedom that may be more than the individual is prepared to handle. And too much freedom can lead to virtual chaos. Individual development thus may proceed faster in a stable environment of gradually decreasing external discipline (management by results) than in an environment of chaos caused by excessive freedom too soon (theory Y). This approach develops a large measure of self-reliance, self-confidence, and a personal capacity to grow and develop. At the same time it emphasizes the necessity of accomplishing present goals.

REALISTIC ATMOSPHERE

In setting up an effective organization, we are concerned with the consistent application of the interdependence concept throughout the entire organization, not just in upper managerial ranks. Interdependence must become part of the philosophy and practice of the entire organization. Foremen as well as presidents must supervise primarily by results, giving members at all levels the responsibility and opportunity to contribute the maximum to organizational objectives. Such an atmosphere cannot be created with a quick do-it-yourself kit. A realistic atmosphere stems from a philosophy of management—a philosophy that recognizes that organizations exist to accomplish personal as well as organizational objectives, and that recognizes the mutual interdependence of managers and employees.

When the organization accepts the philosophy of defining objectives realistically, spelling out prescribed limits of behavior, and evaluating performance by results, there will be less top-to-bottom pressure to conform and more opportunity for unrestrained organizational performance.

THE IMPORTANCE OF MOTIVATION

The central place that motivation has in determining an organization's productivity has been shown by Robert A. Sutermeister, who expressed his basic ideas in a diagram adapted here in Figure 20-2. Sutermeister explained the use of the diagram as follows:

1 The diagram consists of a series of concentric circles, each divided into segments. No attempt has been made to have the size of each segment reflect its relative importance; the importance of each segment would probably be different for each organization studied.
2 The factors in each segment of each circle are deemed to affect or determine the factors in the corresponding segment of the next smaller circle.
3 The factors in each segment of each circle frequently affect and are affected by factors in some other segments of the same circle.
4 The factors in each segment of each circle may also affect factors in segments elsewhere in the diagram.

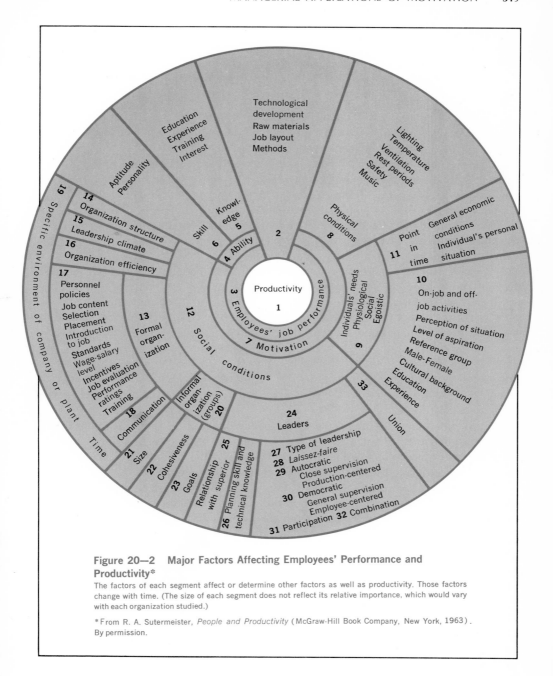

Figure 20—2   Major Factors Affecting Employees' Performance and Productivity*

The factors of each segment affect or determine other factors as well as productivity. Those factors change with time. (The size of each segment does not reflect its relative importance, which would vary with each organization studied.)

*From R. A. Sutermeister, *People and Productivity* (McGraw-Hill Book Company, New York, 1963). By permission.

5 All the factors in the diagram are subject to change with time. The special importance of time in affecting individuals' needs and formal organization is indicated.[8]

SUMMARY

In motivation, managers are faced with complex and interrelated problems. Managers must provide for an orderly hierarchy of responsibility and authority and logical, rationally planned distribution of work in order to meet organizational objectives. From the standpoint of the individual, organizations provide channels through which personal goals can be achieved and a set of boundaries within which actions can take place. Hopefully, these boundaries are general enough to allow some freedom of action. Theory X emphasizes following prescribed procedure at the expense of individual freedom. Theory Y does just the opposite in emphasizing the individual at the expense of organizational discipline. But individual and organizational objectives can be integrated by emphasizing their mutual interdependence. This management-by-results pattern of supervision uses the best features of both theory X and theory Y.

Before a manager can positively motivate different people in different situations he must understand the motivational process. Maslow's need hierarchy, McGregor's theories X and Y, and management by results are all aids to such understanding. However, use of any one of theory X, theory Y, or management by results must be adapted to the specific situation at hand. None of the three can be applied successfully to everyone in every organization, simply because not all individuals can be fitted into any one slot. No single type of motivation can be universally appropriate—the kind which is successful with assembly-line operators can hardly be expected to work with research scientists. For maximum productivity, each person requires motivation tailored specifically to his own personality.

For theory X jobs, the proper personnel policy might be to select people who are seeking extreme forms of security. The opposite approach could be used for less highly programmed or more creative theory Y jobs. However, the majority of organizational members will probably work best with management by results.

The achievement of positive motivation in organizations depends not only on understanding the concepts of motivation but also on accepting the commitments required and in actually living effective motivation within the organization.

FOR REVIEW AND DISCUSSION

1 What is meant when employers and employees are said to be interdependent?
2 What are the essential characteristics of management by results?
3 What are the purposes of a system of behavioral rules in an organization?
4 What is the purpose of discipline in organizations?

[8]Robert A. Sutermeister, *People and Productivity,* McGraw-Hill Book Company, New York, 1963, p. 3. (By permission.)

5 Explain the hot-stove approach to discipline, giving an example to illustrate each of the four major points.

6 Explain the statement: "Discipline is directed against the act—not against the person."

7 Explain the statement: "Under theory X persons rarely, if ever, develop or perform anywhere near their potential." Do you agree? Why?

8 What are the ultimate potentials of theory Y? What things might keep this potential from being achieved?

9 What are the potentials of management by results?

10 Do you agree with the text and with Sutermeister that motivation occupies a central place in the study of organizations and management? Explain your answer.

11 Five requirements are needed to make an interdependency approach to super-vision effective. What are they and why are they required?

CASES

A You are the sole owner of a chain of quick-service, convenience grocery stores. You suspect that some of your employees are stealing, so you require every employee to take a lie-detector test or be fired. The results show that: (a) every employee stole some merchandise during the past year; (b) 20 percent of the employees stole between $10 and $50 during the year; and (c) 4 percent stole over $2,000 each during the year.

1 What would you do? Why?

2 What policies would you set up to prevent this problem in the future?

B Captain Blake, the company commander, shouted, "Charge, take the hill!" After running for a few feet, the captain turned around and saw Private Matthews running away from the battle.

1 What should the captain do about Matthews?

2 What effect will your answer have on the remainder of the members of the unit?

C Rex Moore, general foreman, went to the washroom and found Tom Scale, a machine operator, asleep on a bench. Without waking Tom, Rex stuffed a dismissal notice in his pocket.

When Rex returned to the plant, he found that the maintenance crew had Tom's machine down for repairs. The maintenance foreman had told Tom "only to get lost for a couple of hours."

1 What do you think of the way this situation was handled?

2 What suggestions for improvement would you make?

D At Acme the penalty for clocking someone else out was an automatic two-week suspension. As Jane McDougal passed through the line she saw that Mary Foster, her friend, had left without clocking out. Mary had received an emergency call fifteen minutes earlier. Jane clocked Mary out, and was seen in the act by the foreman. The foreman told her she was suspended for two weeks. He refused to discuss the matter.

1 Do you think the foreman was correct? Why?

2 What should Jane have done? Why?

E   J. K. Lasser, purchasing agent, heard from a salesman that his secretary was "selling" his appointment time to salesmen for gifts of liquor, candy, flowers, etc. According to the salesman, the fee had been getting larger recently. "We have to pay it because we can't afford to lose your account."

Mr. Lasser called the personnel officer and asked him to transfer his secretary to a new job "for personal reasons."

1 Evaluate Mr. Lasser's action.

2 How should the situation have been handled?

FOR FURTHER STUDY

Additional sources can be found in the sources cited in the chapter.

Book

Edward C. Schleh: *Management by Results,* McGraw-Hill Book Company, Inc., New York, 1961. An effective managerial approach focuses on the results that are expected from each person in the organization.

Articles

Judson Gooding: "It Pays to Wake Up the Blue-collar Worker," *Fortune,* September 1970. New theories of job enrichment are boosting morale, productivity, and profits in pioneering plants.

Harry Levinson: "Management by Whose Objectives?" *Harvard Business Review,* July–August 1970. Management by objectives raises great psychological problems in performance appraisal.

Rensis Likert: "A Motivational Approach to a Modified Theory of Organization and Management," in Mason Haire (ed.), *Modern Organization Theory,* John Wiley & Sons, Inc., New York, 1959. "Management will make full use of the potential capacities of its human resources only when each person in an organization is a member of one or more well-knit, effectively functioning work groups that have high skills of interaction and high performance goals."

N. R. F. Maier: "Discipline in the Industrial Setting," *Personnel Journal,* no. 4, 1965. "Discipline is necessary in industry in its function as a deterrent; and if it can be administered without accomplishing certain undesirable effects, such as frustration and depression, then it becomes an invaluable and excellent technique."

George V. Moser: "Rules and Discipline," *Management Record,* no. 5, 1961. Modern management is attempting to make rules and discipline more reasonable, in an effort to encourage self-discipline and voluntary compliance with rules and regulations.

M. Scott Myers: "Conditions for Manager Motivation," *Harvard Business Review*, January–February 1966. A manager's style of supervision is largely an expression of
his personality characteristics. This style greatly influences the satisfactions members get from the organization.

Vance Packard: "A Chance for Everyone to Grow," *Reader's Digest*, November 1963.
A report of improved productivity and morale resulting from the experience of
several firms that enlarged the scope of employees' jobs.

Henry L. Tosi and Stephen J. Carroll: "Some Factors Affecting the Success of 'Management by Objectives'," *The Journal of Management Studies*, May 1970. To be effective management by objectives must be individually designed and worked through
for each employee.

Henry L. Tosi, John R. Rizzo, and Stephen J. Carroll: "Setting Goals in Management
by Objectives," *California Management Review*, Summer 1970. The stress involved
in implementing an effective management by objectives program is explained.

SectionE
Communicating

21
Concepts of
Communication

Communication . . . is so fundamental . . . that without
it an organization could not exist.
    I. L. HECKMAN, JR. and
    S. G. HUNERYAGER

Man has a special ability that helps him bring order out of chaos, better understand his surroundings, interact with others to accomplish compatible objectives, and profit from the knowledge of others, both living and dead. This ability is man's capacity to communicate at a high level. Many lower forms of life communicate in crude ways. Also, systems involving computers and other mechanisms even extend communications to the non-living world. Yet man alone possesses his high capacity to communicate and—equally significant—to learn so much from it.

THE IMPORTANCE OF COMMUNICATION

Communication is so interwoven in man's daily life that few persons realize how much time is devoted to it. A study showed that an average American spends approximately 70 percent of his active hours communicating verbally—listening, speaking, reading, or writing, in that order. This amounts to ten or eleven hours a day.[1] These verbal forms, however, are not the only methods persons have for communicating. Expressions, movements, gestures, colors—any efforts to produce meaning—all are forms of communication.

The diversity of communication problems is even greater than the number of ways to communicate. Many problems are immediately obvious—the tourist struggling in a foreign tongue, the union leader deadlocked with management, teachers unable to explain concepts to students, and so on. Other communication problems are not so clear cut—for example, differing political views, conflicts of the so-called generation gap, misunderstandings between legislators from different areas.

Perhaps it is true, as someone has suggested, that at the heart of all the world's problems—at least of men with each other—is man's inability to communicate as well as he thinks he is communicating. Maybe the basic and pervasive nature of communication has dulled man's ability to see his communication problems.

Only since the early 1900s have any real efforts been devoted to studying communication, seeking to understand what it is, how it is done, and how to improve it. Communication has proved to be a necessary key to understanding persons in today's complex world. Without it man would exist on a very primitive level; complex organizations would be impossible.

A study was made where human and chimpanzee babies were raised together. The chimps advanced faster than the human babies in many respects, up to a certain point. When the children were taught a language and the chimps were taught only simple commands, the children rapidly outdistanced the chimps. The chimps, lacking the mental capacity for language communication, stayed at the level of three-year-old children. Without communication to bring him accumulated knowledge, man could advance little further than the chimps.

Similar effects were seen in a child of about six who had been raised alone with a deaf mother. When discovered, the girl showed signs of being mentally retarded and un-educable. Unable to communicate with language, she had been able to perform only simple acts such as eating, dressing, sleeping, and sitting. However, intensive training stressing the use of language brought the child to normal levels by the age of eight and a half.

The remainder of this chapter and the one following seek to provide a fundamental understanding of the communication process. Communication is the cohesive bond between members of an organization. A better understanding of it can improve organizations.

THE PROCESS OF REALITY

Scientists agree that everything in the world is made up of atomic structures in varying degrees of complexity, the structures themselves being composed of some form of

---

[1]David K. Berlo, *The Process of Communication*, Holt, Rinehart and Winston, Inc., New York, 1960, p. 1.

energy. The world is a mad dance of electrons; much of it exists beyond the perception of ordinary senses. Even the most powerful electronic microscopes cannot see into this primary world of energy, but scientists know it exists. The world is not static and permanent because everything constantly changes. The objects that people think of as comprising the world around them are merely perceptible parts of the events of a process. Further, every perceptual experience is an abstraction, for a perception is limited to the stimulation possibilities of the human nervous system. For instance, there are sounds above and below the normal range of human ears, sights on different wavelengths than the light man's eyes can see, feelings that one's skin cannot perceive, and odors and tastes impossible for one's senses to detect. Thus, the boundaries of an individual's world are dependent upon his set of senses and how well they function.

This concept of a changing world leads to the conclusion that persons live in at least three different worlds, identified by Alfred Korzybski:[2]

1 The world of events—the energy world that scientists describe but is beyond present human abilities to observe.
2 The world of objects—the microscopic and perceivable world that human senses and scientific instruments indicate is there.
3 The world of symbols—the world of words, labels, inferences, etc., that comprises communication about the second world.

If the world is in process, then meanings are in process. Language and communications need to reflect the changing nature of both the world and meanings. Accuracy of communication is hindered or limited by the process nature of the world, and the inability of communication systems to totally describe this process.

LANGUAGE

The most obvious way man communicates is with language. Gestures, facial expressions, body positions, signals, art forms, music, and any other thing a person perceives often are important means of communication. In organizations, however, the most frequent and important way members communicate is with language. A language usually is thought of as consisting of words. More broadly, computer languages, systems of mathematical notation, and other systems of symbols also can be described as languages. The sections below emphasize traditional word forms in the analysis of language in communication, because words are so important in organizational communication. The general concepts of abstracting, symbols, language inflexibility, meaning, and so forth also apply to nonword languages as well, however.

Abstracting

Everyone abstracts; it is a necessary activity to come up with any meaning. Stated simply, when anything is deleted or left out, then abstracting has occurred. Abstracting is easily

---

[2]Adapted from Alfred Korzybski, *Science and Sanity: An Introduction to Non-Aristotelian Systems and General Semantics*, 3d ed., The International Non-Aristotelian Library Publishers Company, Lakeville, Conn., 1948. Korzybski provided the theoretical framework for most of this chapter.

recognized in one's views of reality. The energy world of events described by scientists is abstracted through one's five senses (touch, taste, smell, sight, and hearing) to give an impression of something out there existing. The relatively limited amount of information supplied to the central nervous system also falls prey to the abstracting process as one mentally leaves out parts of the millions of bits of information coming in through the senses. When the mind forms a concept, its "picture" is narrower than the world of objects that stimulated the picture.

Consider what happens when someone with a hammer strikes his finger instead of the nail. The nerves in the injured finger send millions of impulses to the brain, which considers the total picture instead of each impulse separately, and this is abstracting. In fact, immediately after the impact, the person may abstract all the things in his world except one very definite object—his swelling finger. He will be completely unaware of anything else; and even the influence of this object will be an abstraction, for he will consider it a whole rather than many parts.

In another vein, modern art provides an excellent example of the abstracting process. Imagine a modern painting consisting of bursts of colors, similar to exploding fireworks against a midnight blue sky. The colors are brilliant splashes of red, orange, gold, yellow, and blue in many shades. The title of this composition is "Spring Field." How, many people may ask, can this conglomeration be a spring field? If the artist used the process of abstraction, the answer can be relatively simple. If one looks through squinted eyes at a field full of brilliant spring flowers on a sunny day, the view becomes a panorama of color splashes without specific detail. The squinting abstracts the view by cutting out the details—the weeds, a cow grazing, and whatever else might have been present in the object world. Like the abstract artist, all observers ignore many details and recognize only some that seem to apply and give representative meaning to a particular situation or moment.

Returning to the person with the sore finger, still higher levels of abstraction can be described. Moments after impact, he may voice his feelings, perhaps first to the hammer and then to someone helping him apply first aid. When he describes how his finger feels, he has abstracted four times: first, when his senses considered only part of the many influences around him and only part of the stimuli of the hammer; second, when his senses received the impact and he constructed a total picture of the hit in his mind; third, when his mind reacted and created feelings which could not be fully described, only felt; and fourth, when he tried to explain his pain to a friend by using words to represent his feelings.

Thus, communication about reality is not the same as the reality itself. Even the most accurate statements only approach, but never reach, a perfect description. Abstracting leaves out details and characteristics at each level.

The abstracting process, by leaving out details, permits classification. Hayakawa provided a classic example by abstractly classifying a cow on an abstraction ladder, shown as Figure 21-1. The cow, Bessie, is uniquely herself, and differs from all other objects in the same classifications. This uniqueness is an important point—objects or persons included under a classification differ from one another. For more accuracy, they must not be treated as similar in all respects. Awareness that abstracting enters all state-

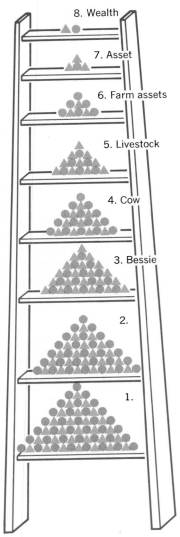

8. Wealth

7. Asset

6. Farm assets

5. Livestock

4. Cow

3. Bessie

2.

1.

8. The word "wealth" is at an extremely high level of abstraction, omitting *almost* all reference to the characteristics of Bessie.

7. When Bessie is referred to as an "asset," still more of her characteristics are left out.

6. When Bessie is included among "farm assets," reference is made only to what she has in common with all other salable items on the farm.

5. When Bessie is referred to as "livestock," only those characteristics she has in common with pigs, chickens, goats, etc., are referred to.

4. The word "cow" stands for the characteristics we have abstracted as common to cow_1, cow_2, cow_3 . . . cow_n. Characteristics peculiar to specific cows are left out.

3. The word "Bessie" (cow_1) is the *name* we give to the object of perception of level 2. The name *is not* the object: it merely *stands for* the object and omits reference to many of the characteristics of the object.

2. The cow we perceive is not the word, but the object of experience, that which our nervous system abstracts (selects) from the totality that constitutes the process-cow. Many of the characteristics of the process-cow are left out.

1. The cow known to science ultimately consists of atoms, electrons, etc., according to present-day scientific inference. Characteristics (represented by circles [and triangles]) are infinite at this level and ever-changing. This is the *process level*.

Figure 21–1   Abstraction Ladder*

Start reading from the bottom up.

*Illustration redrawn and text reprinted from "Abstraction Ladder" in *Language in Thought and Action*, 2d edition, by S. I. Hayakawa. Copyright 1941, 1949, © 1963, 1964, by Harcourt, Brace & World, Inc., and reproduced with their permission.

ments and evaluations can reduce mistakes that occur if abstractions are seen as absolute reality. These limitations of classifications are important. However, classifications are extremely valuable in communication because they allow much information to be transmitted quickly.

Inferences

Inferences, additional levels of abstracting, occurred in the above example if the friend of the man with the injured finger made comments about the injury. The friend might make inferences about the injury, using the words and expressions of the injured one as a basis for his comments. And the process need not stop here; inferences can be made from the inferences that were originally based on words, and then inferences made from the inferences about inferences about inferences, and so on. These additional levels of abstracting—inferences—can continue without limit. Because each level is further removed from reality, they become less and less accurate.

When a person makes a statement about a previous statement, the second statement is an inferential statement because it is not based on direct observation. Successive statements abstract further and further from reality and move to ever higher levels of inference. Given the same initial set of stimuli, it is entirely possible (even likely) that two people will ultimately come to different conclusions if very much abstracting occurs. The variables which each person chooses to leave in his thoughts depend only upon that person and his unique thinking. The resulting problem is summed up by Weinberg:

> They [inferential statements] have widely varying degrees of probability of being correct because they are not linked directly to observation but represent a jump into the unknown which may or may not take off from verifiable observation. . . . There is nothing wrong with making inferences. . . . The misevaluation arises when we act as if our inferential knowledge was factual knowledge.[3]

Thus inferential statements provide unlimited opportunities for communication (and thinking) mistakes. Such mistakes can be reduced by being aware that abstracting and inferences always produce a distorted version of reality.

Words Are Symbols

Words are not the same as any object they represent. Words are but symbols of the object. The importance of understanding this aspect of communications cannot be overstated. Time and time again people treat words as if they have some natural inherent meaning. Yet, as the discussion of abstracting showed, words merely represent things; and they represent them imperfectly, incompletely (for some of the characteristics have been necessarily left out). Words are applied to objects only after several steps of abstracting. Certainly, then, the word cannot be the event, which would be necessary if

[3]Harry L. Weinberg, *Levels of Knowing and Existence*, Harper & Row, Publishers, Incorporated, New York, 1959, pp. 32–33. (By permission.)

the word had meaning in itself. A pinch on the arm, for instance, may provoke one to utter words. These words are not the same things as the sensations felt at the nonverbal level.

A simple device to illustrate how a word only represents something in a nonverbal world is the "triangle of reference" developed by Ogden and Richards.[4] This triangle, shown as Figure 21-2, has two solid sides and one broken side to represent the relationships which exist between objects and words that represent them. At one corner is the object to which a word refers. The other corners represent the thought and the word or symbol that refers to the object. The solid lines represent: (1) the relationship between the object and the thought and (2) the relationship between the thought and the word (symbol) uttered to represent the object. The relationship between the word and the object is represented by the broken line because this is an indirect relationship. The important point is that a word is only a symbol for something.

In broader terms, the object is considered as any concept that exists for the persons communicating. Concepts are much more encompassing than physical things. For example, people can communicate about mermaids, which exist only in mythical literature, and this communication can be as accurate as a communication about turtles, which actually exist. Once a person forms a concept about something and attaches words to this concept, then he can communicate symbolically about the concept by using the words. The areas of logic and mathematics offer additional examples where communication occurs with precision, but no physical thing exists. And the present book is devoted to communicating concepts about management and organizations from the author to the reader. Words are indispensable for this. Effective communication requires that the persons involved use words to which they attach similar meanings.

When many words with generally accepted meanings are used by a group of persons, they have a language. Languages are the main media for expressing thoughts, feelings, and knowledge. To communicate perfectly a language would have to exactly describe the world it represents, yet languages usually lack the complexity and dynamics of

[4]C. K. Ogden and I. A. Richards, *The Meaning of Meaning,* 8th ed., Harcourt, Brace & World, Inc., New York, 1947.

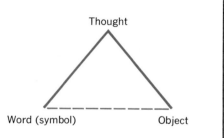

Figure 21–2   Triangle of Reference

A word means what we want it to mean. This single diagram shows that there is a direct relationship between an object and the thought of that object (solid line) and a direct relationship between that thought and the word that expresses it (solid line). The word, then, which is either a written or spoken symbol, bears an indirect relationship to the object (broken line).

the things they try to describe. At best, any language is related to reality only as a map is related to a territory it represents. Thus, Korzybski concluded that:

> The only usefulness of a map or a language depends on the *similarity of structure* between the empirical world (the real world) and the map-languages. If the structure is not similar, then the traveler or speaker is led astray. . . . If the structures are *similar,* then the empirical world becomes "rational" to a potentially rational being, which means no more than that verbal, or map-predicted characteristics . . . are applicable to the empirical world. [5]

The symbolic nature of words and languages was summarized by Korzybski in these three premises: [6]

1 Words which make up our store of knowledge are not the things they represent. *(A map is not the territory.)*
2 Words can never say everything about anything, for there are always certain characteristics about anything which cannot be included in or described by words. *(A map does not represent all of a territory.)*
3 Thus, an ideal map would have to include a map of the map of the map, and so on. With language it is possible to speak words about words, words about words about words, etc., to an infinite level of abstraction. *(A map is self-reflexive.)*

More Facts Than Words

A language may have hundreds of thousands of words, but even this large number is inadequate to perfectly describe everything. There is practically infinite variety in reality; hence, to totally describe it would require almost an infinite supply of words. Unfortunately, human languages do not meet these exacting requirements. Wendell Johnson wrote:

> The structure of our language . . . is much less highly differentiated [than reality and thinking]. Even though the English tongue, for example, contains many thousands of words and many of these have more than one recognized dictionary meaning, yet we are far from having one word for each fact. Each word, and even each dictionary meaning of each word, must do heavy duty, representing a great number and variety of facts. [7]

There are simply more things in more degrees than there are words to use in communicating about them. This deficiency inevitably produces inaccuracy in communication.

Language Inflexibility

The relative inflexibility of language compared with the more flexible, changing reality is another limitation to communication. When words are invented to represent some-

---

[5]Korzybski, *op. cit.,* p. 61.
[6]Adapted from *ibid.*
[7]Wendell Johnson, "The World of Words," in Harold E. Briggs (ed.), *Language . . . Man . . . Society: Readings in Communications,* Holt, Rinehart and Winston, Inc., New York, 1949, p. 68.

thing, they often remain static while the reality-event continues to change. For example, the word "automobile" does not now represent the thing that it represented at its inception; yet a person using or hearing the word automobile is probably not aware of the imprecision of the word. With words necessity is the mother of invention, as illustrated in cases when new terms must be coined to explain a new event. For example, the space age brought need for words to communicate about feats that had previously existed only in fiction and comic strips. Thus, miscommunication may occur from the use of old words and terms. The language may inadequately portray the present reality.

Another problem in language communication is the frequent confusion of two or more levels of abstraction. For instance, the object level may be confused with the word level. The use of the word "is" accounts for much of this problem. One might say, for example, "John Brown is a student," and tend to forget that John Brown may also be classified as many other things—a tennis player, a Methodist, a good dancer, a basketball fan, a collector of folk music, etc. Therefore, when it is said that someone *is* or something *is,* many other qualities and characteristics are being abstracted. The object level is being identified with the word level. This form of statement ignores the fact that people determine the label-name for something—pigs are not called "pigs" because they are dirty animals. They are called pigs because that is the symbolic word which people have chosen to represent such animals.

Language can lead into another trap when a certain choice of words implies that the objects, persons, or events in truth possess the particular qualities which the speaker uses to label them. Someone who *is* unpleasant, a movie that *is* amusing, or a football game that *is* exciting to one person may be just the opposite to another. Therefore qualities are products of relations between the observer and what is observed; there is not any described quality that exists in a pure state in reality. This is true because less than perfect symbols are used to describe reality. Language forms and words that imply that qualities exist in persons, objects, and actions are relative to the individual doing the observing; the descriptions may differ considerably among several observers.

Still another problem area in language is the two-valued orientation system found in Indo-European–based languages. Such languages give two values generally, or possibly three in some cases. The "is" problem in communication may have its origin in Aristotelian logic, which may lead one to the position that if something is one thing it therefore is not another thing. More accurately, a thing or person is many things. The polarized, two-valued orientation creates a tendency to think of things as black or white, good or bad, just or unjust, right or wrong, true or untrue. In contrast, reality tends to exist in terms of a spectrum between absolutes—things are rarely, if ever, black or white; instead they are more often some shade of gray. Reality is infinitely differentiated, so there are infinite shades between the extremes of anything. Some languages, such as Chinese, have more varieties of degrees; but even they suffer from not having enough words to describe every degree of variation.

The inability to pinpoint the specific quality of anything should signal one to think in terms of probability or degree. Often one should be less dogmatic in statements and evaluations, to be fair with oneself and with others. The limitations of language and the necessity to abstract make it impossible to have totally accurate communication.

Experience, Language, and Meaning

One of the myths in communication is that words have a natural, proper, inherent meaning. Although the most common words convey different meanings to different persons, many persons still persist in the belief that if they are very careful in choosing their words, they will be able to find and use the one "right" word for their purpose. Laboring under this myth, a person often simply cannot understand why others apparently do not understand.

At least two persons are required for interpersonal communication, and all involved persons must be considered with respect to meaning. Thus, even though Jim may have chosen his words very carefully as he tries to communicate with John, the reaction of John to the communication is not necessarily what Jim intended. This point is considered by Ogden and Richards:

> Normally, whenever we hear anything said we spring spontaneously to an immediate conclusion, namely that the speaker is referring to what we should be referring to whenever speaking the words ourselves. In some cases this interpretation may be correct. . . . But in most discussions which attempt greater subtleties than could be handled in a gesture language, this will not be so.[8]

If, then, a communication has different meanings for the speaker or writer and the listener or reader, misunderstanding, rather than communication, will result. In fact, the main product of many communications is misunderstanding.

Misunderstanding occurs when persons engaged in communication have dissimilar background experiences with the particular symbols being used. The degree of complementary experience with symbols, then, will determine to some extent how successful any communication is. If one person tries to communicate with another by using words that both have been conditioned to associate with certain meanings in the past, then communication will be possible with a fairly high degree of accuracy. Different meanings associated with words produce miscommunication. For example, most Americans would think a service station attendant might be crazy if he asked them whether or not he should check their "bonnet," for Americans think of a woman's headpiece when they hear bonnet. However, persons in England refer to the hood of an automobile as a bonnet.

Another example of confusion that results from a lack of complementary experiences is found in the song about Yankee Doodle Dandy. It does not make much sense to Americans to say that Yankee Doodle stuck a feather in his hat and called it "macaroni." But it does make sense to Italians who have a pleased reaction when they hear the word macaroni, or to one who knows the military braid and trappings on uniforms were referred to as macaroni by the British soldiers at the time of the American Revolutionary War, at which time the song was written.

The ultimate level of complexity is reached when two persons try to communicate with symbols that have no external, verifiable checkpoints, such as "love," "hate," "honesty," "democracy," "fair," "just," "horrible," "evil," and "moral." These conditions

---

[8]Ogden and Richards, *op. cit.,* p. 15.

do not exist in any pure form in the real world; they exist nebulously and only within the minds of individuals. When subjective considerations are combined with undefinable concepts, then a communication has a much greater chance of being misunderstood.

Both parties, then, must have been conditioned similarly to the symbols used, or communications will either fail completely (two people who speak a different language) or be deficient. (One person's concept of love may differ considerably from another's.) Full or perfect communication is impossible because no two persons have exactly the same experiences; inferences or interpretations occur in every communication.

THE ENVIRONMENT OF COMMUNICATION

A communication also is affected by the environment within which it occurs. The components of the environment may be classified as physical, psychological, and verbal. The physical place where words are expressed, the time of their expression, and the surrounding activities make up the physical environment. The experiences of the communicators, the prevailing mental and physical conditions, and the psychology of the participants determine the psychological environment. The verbal environment are the surrounding word symbols being used. The following remarks show the importance of environment:

> A statement, spoken in real life, is never detached from the situation in which it is uttered. For each verbal statement by a human being has the aim and function of expressing some thought or feeling actual at that moment and in that situation, and necessary for some reason or another to be made known to another person or persons—in order either to serve purposes of common action, or to establish purely social communion, or else to deliver the speaker of violent feelings or passions. Without some imperative stimulus of the moment, there can be no spoken statement. In each case, therefore, utterance and situation are bound up inextricably with each other and the context of the situation is indispensable for the understanding of words. Exactly as in the reality of spoken and written languages, a word without linguistic context is a mere figment and stands for nothing by itself, so in the reality of a spoken living tongue, the utterance has no meaning except in the context of the situation.[9]

Therefore, if communication is to be successful, the physical, psychological, and verbal context, setting, or environment of the communication must be considered. The same words have different meanings in different situations. For example, the phrase "I'm going to give you a bath" can have many meanings depending upon the context. It could be used by a mother preparing to bathe her small child. Or the phrase, if used at a riotous party, could mean that someone is going to get thrown fully clothed into the swimming pool. Or to a gangster the phrase could be a threat to drown someone. It is always helpful to "read between the lines" to determine what the particular meaning of a message is within the unique environment.

[9]Bronislaw Malinowski, "The Problem of Meaning in Primitive Languages," in Ogden and Richards, *op. cit.*, supp. I, p. 307.

SUMMARY

The purpose of communication is to transmit meaning from one person to another. Good communication is an essential element of a successful organization because no coordinated interaction can occur without it. Thus, communication is an indispensable element in modern life. Many persons spend the majority of their time in verbal, written, or other forms of communication.

Reality is a process—it is everchanging. Unfortunately, the words used to describe reality fall short of perfect description. This is true because a word or statement is merely a symbol of an event; it is not the event itself.

Languages, the most important form of communication in organizations, have several characteristics that limit their accuracy in communication. For one thing, because reality is so complicated, abstracting—which leaves out details of things—is necessary. Also, each person makes unique inferences in each communication. And miscommunication is caused by the fact that words are merely symbols and that there are more different events than words to describe them. In addition, although events change, languages tend to lag—thus, languages tend to be out-of-date.

The meaning one perceives in a communication depends upon his experiences, the meaning he attaches to the symbols received, and the environment of the communication. With all the limitations involved, it seems doubtful if perfect communication ever exists. However, awareness of the problems and factors involved can contribute to better communication.

FOR REVIEW AND DISCUSSION

1 Could an organization exist without words? Without communication? Explain your answer.

2 Give three examples of communication problems from your own recent experience. Explain the cause of the problem in each case.

3 Consider the statement: ". . . the heart of all the world's problems lies basically with man's inability to communicate as well as he thinks he is communicating." Do you agree or disagree with this statement? Explain your answer.

4 "Communication makes interaction possible by providing some exchange of information and meaning." Explain this statement in detail.

5 Explain in your own words the three fundamental communication premises of Korzybski.

6 Explain the three worlds in which we live.

7 Explain the process of abstracting. Is abstracting necessary for every communication event? Explain.

8 Construct a ladder of abstraction for each of the following: (a) gold ore, (b) a man, (c) a cat, (d) a rose.

9 Explain the problem of inferential statements in communication.

10 Do words have a natural, inherent meaning? Explain.

11 Explain how similar experiences can improve communication.

12 If a symbol is not meaningful in itself, then why can we communicate with symbols?

CASES

A On Monday Professor Grayson announced to his class: "I will be out of town from Tuesday until Friday. There will be no classes while I'm gone."

On Tuesday 20 percent of the members came to class, but Professor Grayson failed to appear. On Friday 40 percent came along and the professor was also present. Professor Grayson, angered by the poor attendance, said, "Students not present today will receive double cuts."

    1 What communication problems are illustrated by this case?

    2 What could the students have done to prevent the problems?

    3 What could Professor Grayson have done to prevent the problems?

B Captain Eldridge, inspecting the motor-pool office, said, "You fellows had better clean up around here!"

After the captain left Sergeant Todd cleaned off his desk for the first time in months, Corporal Snider went home and took a bath, and Private Merill remarked, "Guess the captain's pretty upset by my profanity."

    1 How effective was Captain Eldridge in communicating his message?

    2 How might the captain have improved his communication?

C "Men," said Mr. Yale, the plant manager, "this new cost control system will solve our problems of high cost. I want every man here to help make this system work."

"But, Mr. Yale," said Bert Brown, one of the company's best foremen, "I have a list of twenty-one changes that have to be made in that system before it will work right for us."

"Brown," replied Mr. Yale, "either you are for me or against me on this cost problem. I am not going to argue about the system. My consultants have told me that this system worked with another company."

"But, Mr. Yale, let's get the bugs out of the system before we install it."

"Brown, obviously you are against my system." Addressing the entire group, Mr. Yale asked, "Are there any questions?"

There were no questions and the meeting was adjourned.

    1 What communication problems are shown by this case?

    2 How might each of these problems have been prevented or reduced?

    3 What are the fallacies in Mr. Yale's approach?

FOR FURTHER STUDY

Additional sources can be found in the sources cited in the chapter.

Books

Stuart Chase: *Power of Words,* Harcourt, Brace & World, Inc., New York, 1954. Communication by means of language is man's distinctive activity.

Don Fabun: *Three Roads to Awareness,* Glencoe Press, Beverly Hills, Calif., 1970, part 3. Alternate source: "Communications: The Transfer of Meaning," *Kaiser Aluminum News,* 1965. A splendid, highly readable overview of communication.

S. I. Hayakawa: *Language in Thought and Action,* 2d ed., Harcourt, Brace & World, Inc., New York, 1964. Language can be studied through the methods of modern semantics.

I. L. Heckmann, Jr. and S. G. Huneryager: *Human Relations in Management,* South-Western Publishing Company, Incorporated, Cincinnati, 1967, pp. 505–520. Topics include why and how persons communicate, formal and informal communication, and barriers to communication.

Raymond V. Lesikar: *Business Communication,* Richard D. Irwin, Inc., Homewood, Ill., 1972, part I. An outstanding explanation of communication theory relevant to organizations.

Lee Thayer: *Communication and Communication Systems,* Richard D. Irwin, Inc., Homewood, Ill., 1968. A comprehensive text.

Articles

Stuart Chase: "Executive Communications: Breaking the Semantics Barrier," *Management Review,* April 1957. An interesting and penetrating analysis of semantics problems in communication.

William V. Haney: "Serial Communication of Information in Organizations," *ETC: A Review of General Semantics,* March 1964. A great deal of organization communication consists of serial transmissions.

Glen E. Haydon: "Don't Stand There Talking . . . Communicate!" *Supervision,* January 1968. A manager should attempt to perceive the other person's outlook to improve communication.

Wendell Johnson: "The Fateful Process of Mr. A. Talking to Mr. B.," *Harvard Business Review,* January–February 1953. "The ability to respond to and with symbols may be the single most important attribute of great administrators. . . ."

22
Organizational Communication

To be a manager is to be a communicator—
the person and the function are inextricably interwoven.
     MORRIS E. MASSEY

Communication is basic to an organization's existence. A manager spends up to 95 percent of his time communicating to coordinate human and physical elements of the organization into an efficient and effective working unit. When communication fails, organized activity also fails; uncoordinated or no activity prevails.

Chester I. Barnard stated that the first executive function is to develop and maintain a system of communication.[1] Pertinent information—facts, feelings, ideas—must be communicated before meaningful organizational decisions can be made. And it must continue if the objectives of the organization are to be reached efficiently.

A MODEL OF THE COMMUNICATION PROCESS

Communication is a dynamic process, just as is the meaning or reality it seeks to describe. An early, elementary model of the communication process was presented by Aristotle.[2]

[1]Chester I. Barnard, *The Functions of the Executive,* Harvard University Press, Cambridge, Mass., 1960, p. 226.
[2]See W. D. Ross (ed.), *The Works of Aristotle,* vol. 11, Oxford University Press, Fair Lawn, N.J., 1946, p. 14.

In Aristotle's model there are three main ingredients in a communication event—the speaker, the speech, and the audience. Modern models are more complex, but they are similar. The Shannon-Weaver model, developed in 1947 as a model in electronic communication, had been adapted very successfully by behavioral scientists to explain human communication.[3] Shannon and Weaver set up five ingredients in communication: (1) a source, (2) a transmitter, (3) a signal, (4) a receiver, and (5) a destination. The source is the speaker, the signal is the speech, and the destination is the listener. The numerous models that have been developed vary most in the inclusion of one or two components, in terminology, or in point of view.

The model discussed here includes nine components and is adapted from one by David K. Berlo.[4] The components are: (1) source, (2) encoder, (3) message, (4) channel, (5) receiver, (6) decoder, (7) meaning, (8) feedback, and (9) noise. The model, shown as Figure 22-1, describes any communication system—a television network, a college classroom, and two persons conversing.

Source and Encoder

Communication requires a source who has some thought, need, idea, or information to transmit. He translates his mental perceptions into a code that represents the meaning he wishes to transmit. Language is the most popular code used to express such mental perceptions. Encoding involves the motor functions of the body. Vocal mechanisms produce sound, muscles produce gestures and other movements, hands write or draw, and so on.

Thus, the source often is an encoder of the original message; they are discussed together here for that reason. However, an additional encoder separate from the source also often exists, as shown in Figure 22-1. For example, a military message might be encoded into a secret code. Or a business message might be encoded into computer language. Several factors affect the source and encoder, including communication skills, attitudes, experience and knowledge, and environmental and sociocultural elements.

Communication skills   To be effective, it is important that the source encoder have good communication skills in the medium. If the message is verbal, good pronunciation, vocabulary, and also syntax are important. Written messages also benefit from good spelling. Skill in drawing, gestures, and facial expressions can be important.

Attitudes   The source-encoder has attitudes based on his entire personality that affect his communications. His feelings about himself often cause him to structure his communication a particular way. A shy person makes guarded statements. For example, an uncertain salesman might say to a prospective customer, "Do you want to buy some of

---

[3]Claude Shannon and Warren Weaver, *The Mathematical Theory of Communication*, The University of Illinois Press, Urbana, 1949, p. 5.

[4]David K. Berlo, *The Process of Communication*, Holt, Rinehart, and Winston, Inc., New York, 1960, pp. 23–38.

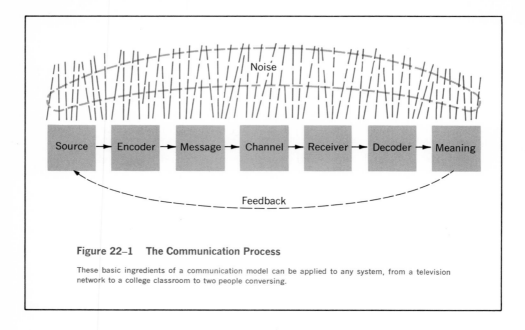

Figure 22–1   The Communication Process

These basic ingredients of a communication model can be applied to any system, from a television network to a college classroom to two people conversing.

my product?" A more assertive person might say, "I'd like to explain the benefits of my product to you." Also, many persons have very definite attitudes toward such topics as religion, moral standards, politics, government, their jobs, and so on. Typically, such attitudes will be reflected in one's communications. What is not said often is more important in revealing attitudes than what is said.

Experience and knowledge   It is difficult to communicate accurately about something one has not experienced. For example, mentioning the word "horse" probably provokes the image of a specific horse from the receiver-encoder's memory. But what of "horsefeathers"? A horse covered with feathers? Perhaps, for the word "horsefeathers" is a symbol that points to two familiar images—horses and feathers; but not necessarily, for this symbol could stand for anything and, therefore, it would be difficult, if not impossible, to provoke a desired thought by using it unless it is related to a past experience. On the other hand, if one has intimate knowledge or experience with something, he probably can communicate well about it.

Environmental and sociocultural elements   Everyone's communications reflect his environmental and sociocultural situations. For instance, one who perceives his environment as threatening might talk in a high voice that expresses his fear. Or, he may verbally lash out at threatening elements in his environment to try to remove their threat. Everyone lives certain roles, occupies certain positions, commands certain status and prestige, performs certain functions, and otherwise lives within certain restrictions. These and other elements in his environment and cultural background are reflected in his communications.

Message

The source encodes his meaning into a message that can be transmitted. The message is the source-encoder's physical product—spoken words, printed words, a graphic drawing, an expression of the face, a gesture of the arm.

Message codes have structures that determine how the symbols will be arranged. For example, languages have a general order for the elements of sentences. Music is a message sent in certain codes. When one says he does not understand certain types of music (classical, jazz) he means he does not understand the musical code or its meaning. The message represents the meaning the source is trying to convey, and it determines to a high degree the meaning the receiver will obtain. The message must be understandable to both source and receiver. Otherwise, fidelity will be low or noise will be high for the communication.

Channel

The channel is the link that connects the source and the receiver. The five senses are communication channels. Sight and sound are the dominant ones, although a punch in the nose may effectively communicate through the touch channel. Taste and smell also can be channels. Other examples of channels are a telephone system linking two persons talking. The air also is a channel when it carries sound waves. And a person lost on a desert island may use a floating bottle as a channel to carry a note.

Receiver, Decoder, and Meaning

A successful communication is received by the intended person who decodes it and attaches meaning to it. In complex communication systems, such as military ones using secret codes, a decoder may exist in addition to the receiver. In such complex systems the receiver still decodes and forms his own meaning of the message although the message may have been previously decoded in other ways.

Whether or not the receiver attaches the intended meaning to the message depends on many factors. One requirement for accurate communication is that the source and the receiver both understand the symbols being used. Further, they must attach similar meanings to the symbols. Like the source, the receiver's understanding of a communication also will depend upon his communication skills, attitudes, experience and knowledge, and environmental and sociocultural elements. Communication oriented toward the receiver has a greater probability for success than communication structured entirely from the source's perspective. For instance, a good teacher puts things in terms meaningful to his students. He may use different terms in discussions of the same topics in his professional society.

Feedback

After he decodes and interprets a message, a receiver becomes a source. That is, now he has a purpose (to respond to the original source's message) and he must encode a message and send it, over some channel, back to the other person. This is feedback, another vital element in communication. Feedback, or response, enables the source to know whether or not his message has been received and interpreted correctly. Feedback may cause the original source to modify future communication according to the way in which the source perceives the reaction of the receiver.

Noise

Noise, the ninth element in the model, is anything that reduces the accuracy or fidelity of communication. It hangs like an umbrella over the system and can be present in all of the other elements. A source creates noise if he is unable to understand or describe something. The encoding process contains noise if the meaning is not adequately represented by symbols. The message is subject to transcription or other mistakes. The channel may contain static or other noises that prevent the message from getting through accurately. The receiver may decode the message incorrectly or may attach a wrong meaning to it.

With all these possibilities for miscommunication, it sometimes seems a wonder that persons can communicate at all. But they do communicate, frequently with high accuracy. The important point is to realize the numerous opportunities for miscommunication, and to take them into account in all communications.

To explain the model further, suppose that Smith, a manager, is sitting in his office on Friday morning with Jackson, one of his foremen. Smith has noticed in Thursday's report on shipments that a special order did not leave the plant on Thursday as scheduled. Since Jackson is in charge of the shipping-room crew, Smith, as a *source,* has a purpose in talking to Jackson—he wants to know why the shipment was delayed. So he *encodes* a *message* and transmits it along a *channel* (the air) to Jackson: "What is delaying you on the special order to Texas?"

The foreman *receives* the message with his hearing mechanisms and *decodes* it into impulses that travel through his nervous system to his mind where he thinks about the *meaning* of Smith's question. Understanding the code (the English language) and reacting to his own personal interpretation and perception of the meaning of the message, Jackson, as *feedback,* encodes the following message: "It's not my fault." He has a purpose (to answer Smith and defend himself), he becomes a source, encodes a message, and orders his speech mechanism to transmit the message via a sound-wave channel to Smith. Thus, Jackson is first a receiver, then a source; while Smith acts in the reverse sequence. Jackson's message (and probably his facial expressions and body movements) serves as feedback to Smith, who can then construct another message in light of how he perceives the present situation: Jackson's response seems evasive, and Smith still does not know the answer to his question. Smith may not have had a clear concept of his purpose—whether to blame Jackson or to find out more facts. Possibly Smith, as a supervisor, had a condescending manner which affected the encoding and the transmission. Or, fatigue from a party the night before could have affected his encoding—or Jackson's decoding. The noise of a passing truck could have affected the channel (air) and prevented Jackson from decoding correctly or answering appropriately. If Smith and Jackson are of different nationalities, then their divergent cultural backgrounds might cause miscommunications. The simplest communication is filled with numerous chances for misunderstanding.

ORGANIZATIONS AS COMMUNICATION SYSTEMS

The model of the communication process just described was portrayed principally in terms of two persons communicating. Much of the communication in organizations can be expressed in such person-to-person terms. However, the model is equally valid in explaining other types of communication in organizations, including person to organization and organization to organization communications. The model fits even nonhuman communication as, for example, an automatic control system in a plant. For instance, an electric power-generating plant might have sensors (sources) that monitor parts of the plant. The sensors convert (encode) observed values into electric signals (messages). These signals are sent over wires (channels) to a computer (receiver) that compares (decodes) observed with desired values and decides (meaning) if corrections are required. If so, signals (feedback) are sent to appropriate correction units. Noise can be anywhere in the system.

In a complex organization, each subunit bases its activities on communications from other sources. Information may originate either internally (from another part of the total system) or externally (from a part of the environment surrounding the total system). Management's concern with communications lies often with the internal inputs of information passing between persons and subunits comprising the organization. However, inputs of information from the external environment may also be very important. Information about changing laws affecting the organization, actions of competition, or shifts in society's norms greatly affects the organization's activities. Because managers have greater control over internally produced inputs, it is easier to be sure that they contribute to the productivity of the organization.

Persons can be viewed as systems of interrelated biological and psychological subsystems, all combined to produce a functioning human (the total system). In a similar way, organizations can be seen as a set of subsystems that form a total complex of interrelated parts. Thus, locomotives, cars, tracks, switches, signals, and persons form a railroad system. Students, teachers, textbooks, administrators, buildings, and libraries form an educational system. Production units, marketing units, financial units, and administrative units form a manufacturing system, and so on.

Every total system must have interaction or cohesiveness between its subsystems if the total complex is to accomplish its objective. Acting as a binder, communication provides information that simultaneously guides both the smallest subunits and the entire complex toward organizational goal accomplishment. This view was described by Bavels and Barrett:

> It is entirely possible to view an organization as an elaborate system for gathering, evaluating, recombining, and disseminating information. . . . Communication is not a secondary or derived aspect of organization—a "helper" of the other and presumably more basic functions. Rather, it is the essence of organized activity and the basic process out of which all other functions derive. [5]

The purposes or functions of communication in an organization have been classified into five broad areas by Thayer:

1 *Becoming informed, or informing others.* This is the basic purpose of routine, day-to-day communication events. Communication provides a means of affirming the joint purposes of organizational members so that all the members will work toward compatible objectives. When decisions have been made, they will be implemented and reflected in organization operations only after members involved have been informed.

2 *Evaluating one's own inputs, or another's outputs, or some ideological scheme.* The dynamic nature of a functioning organization demands that constant evaluation be made of the activities in order that progress toward the desired objectives can be evaluated. Thus, the complete communication process is necessary, with feedback being particularly important. Feedback of the effect of one's own decisions, others' decisions and actions, and evaluation of alternate proposals help keep the organization on the right track. Evaluation involves many recurring communications within a complex organization. Detailed plans, budgets, and formal reports, all aid in the evaluation of internal and external factors affecting the organization.

3 *Directing others or being directed or instructed.* A manager's function of directing the combinations of men and materials toward goals requires that communication occur between the responsible manager and the human and physical resources within his authority. Job training depends upon communication. Delegation of authority cannot occur without communication.

4 *Influencing others or being influenced.* Motivation must be present as one of the elemental forces in providing for a dynamic organization. Any motivational forces not inherent in an individual are provided and then stimulated through communication. The balance between efficiency and inefficiency lies with the ability to persuade or influence.

5 *Several incidental, neutral functions.* Many communications within organizational contexts have no direct connection with accomplishment of the objectives of the organization. However, as auxiliary or contributing communications, they may contribute indirectly to organizational objectives and directly to satisfaction of individual

[5] Alex Bavels and Dermot Barrett, "An Experimental Approach to Organizational Communication," *Personnel,* March 1951, p. 368.

needs that are compatible with organizational goals. Providing social contact within the organization is an example.[6]

The incidental purposes of communication in an organization show that there is something more than the direct authority relationships often implied in an organization chart. Also, if communication flowed only downward the system would be incomplete. Some upward feedback must occur for management's control function to be performed.

In a complex total system, then, the subunits do not function autonomously but in relationship to other units and to the system as a whole. Without coordinating communication, a group of smaller units of a larger organization would in effect be no organization, for there would be no binding cooperative activity, except by chance. But with good communication, the subunits can function in coordination with the total system. A worker in a factory processes information from co-workers, supervisors, the company news organs, and his own feelings. Through the same process of information evaluation the activities of subunits larger than a single person can be coordinated.

All organizations have communication networks—paths of inputs that form intricate circuits of communication. An organizational communication network is analogous to a telephone system: information flows in certain restricted patterns or paths through the entire system. Certain units act as the sources, encoders, channels, decoders, receivers, and feedback loops described above in the communication model. Herein, then, lies a point of view for management with respect to communication—the entire organization functions as a complex information-processing network.

To illustrate, consider the way a newspaper functions as a communication network. Staff reporters observe news events (sources). They form ideas (decode) and write copy (message). These are sent to editorial desks (receivers). The messages are evaluated (decoded) and decisions are made (meaning) as to whether and in what form to publish them.

Some members work only on specialized messages (sports, society, or political news); others work more general beats. Certain workers determine message structure alone, while others determine only what is to be encoded. The editor decides the merit of the news and whether or not to produce messages in the paper. Thus, he starts a new communication process. Encoding and channeling functions become specialized with rewrite men, proofreaders, linotype operators, pressmen, and delivery boys who carry the paper to reader-receivers. Each person in the newspaper organization serves as a point for communication analysis by assuming one or more of the roles of the communication process.

The communication used by organizations basically travels through two types of networks—a formal network related to the formal organizational relationships and an informal network determined by the undefined relationships that develop among individuals making up the organization. A look at these two networks highlights additional implications about communication for management.

[6]Lee O. Thayer, *Administrative Communication*, Richard D. Irwin, Inc., Homewood, Ill., 1961, p. 283.

FORMAL ORGANIZATIONAL COMMUNICATION

The formal organization molds the communication process along certain lines, thus affecting the behavior of organizational units. If an individual were functioning in a non-organized environment, he would behave differently than if he were functioning within a military organization (imagine a private in an informal bull session with a general). Or, think of an educational system (everyone cannot ask questions if there are 150 students in a classroom), or a large manufacturing plant (all two thousand employees cannot talk over their personal problems with the president).

Organizational structures establish definitions for relationships and behavior that are mirrored in communication events involving the individual members of the organization as they interact. Without the structure of the organization, the relationship between a foreman and his work group, a vice-president and his division and other divisions, or an officer and his staff would probably be entirely different. For example, a union leader in a company usually does not belong to any management group; management men often participate in certain civic duties.

The defined relationships for communication within an organization may be partially determined by the formal organization chart. This chart describes the official lines of authority, power, responsibility, and accountability of the organization. These relationships, typical of organized activity, all involve communication. For instance, the exercise of authority may be viewed as a downward flow of information from a supervisor to a member that gives the member the right to take action, or perhaps to delegate others to take action. In the same vein, accountability is fixed through a flow of information that charges a subordinate to answer for his performance. Both authority and accountability frequently are defined by the use of stated policies and procedures.

The manager-employee relationships defined by the formal organizational structure are often complicated. A person often does not communicate with his supervisor in the same way he does with a person of equal standing or with his subordinate. Individuals subordinate to another are dependent upon that person to some degree, in some cases to a very high degree. For example, an individual's career may depend upon his supervisor; therefore, a subordinate will tend to try, consciously or unconsciously, to control as many factors as possible governing the supervisory judgment about himself. He will tend to transmit the required information, as well as favorably impress the superior: the anticipated pay raise or promotion may depend on it. Consequently, the subordinate's upward communication often involves subtle adaptations.

The higher up in the organization information travels, the more abstract it tends to become. To conserve time, certain information must necessarily be deleted or played down. In the selection of information for transmission, bias easily creeps in. Further, persons generally want to hear favorable reports. The net effect often is the transmission of "rosy" information. This problem was noted by Peter Drucker:

> People familiar with large organizations—executives, administrators, consultants—have known all along that keeping top management informed is the most elusive administrative

problem of the big corporation (and not of the business enterprise alone). To be usable at the top, information has to be so formalized and abstracted as to lose substantive meaning.[7]

Many persons think managers are generally well informed and members well understand their managers' positions. But research studies have shown startling evidence to the contrary.

One such study considered fifty-eight manager-employee pairs and found far from perfect agreement about organizational subjects of common interest. On the rather standard topic of job duties, 15 percent of the pairs agreed on less than half of the points describing the employee's job. Of more significance, in the area of "obstacles in the way of subordinate's performance," 38.4 percent showed almost no agreement, and 68.2 percent showed agreement on less than half of the points. The findings of this and other studies are indicative of the error potential in manager-employee communications. These weaknesses are pinpointed in the study's conclusions:

> Thus, the findings in general provide empirical evidence that substantial communication problems exist at high management levels in organizations—problems which one can expect to be reflected in poorer organizational efficiency and distortion of organizational goals at lower levels in the hierarchy.[8]

From such studies, the problems of organizational communication can be seen. Just because two persons in an organization go through the act of trying to communicate does not necessarily mean that they have actually communicated.

INFORMAL ORGANIZATIONAL COMMUNICATION

The futility of relying solely on formal communications to accomplish the interactions that are necessary for the life of the organization has often been recognized by alert managers. The formal network is often relatively static, while the organization it seeks to activate is dynamic and must react quickly to changing situations. Consequently, the informal network of communication comes into frequent play in every organization.

A typical informal communication network involves members within the same level of an organization. For example, direct communication is often needed rapidly among the production supervisors, or among the organization's officers, members of a work group, or between two staff heads.

To satisfy personal needs, members of an organization establish informal communication relationships that may or may not resemble the formal organization chart. These unstated links may provide a means of satisfying the human needs not fulfilled by pay checks, fringe benefits, or the general profit and service objectives of the organization.

[7] Peter F. Drucker, "Big Business and the National Purpose," *Harvard Business Review,* March–April 1962, p. 55.

[8] Norman R. F. Maier et al., *Superior-Subordinate Communication in Management,* American Management Association, 1961.

Often a foreman is leader of his work group in name only; the members of the group may have their own informal leader who actually controls the group. To really understand the dynamics of an organization, one must understand the informal units that occur within the formal organization groups.

The formal communication network is often inadequate or too slow. In such cases, the informal communication networks—often called the "grapevine"—spring into action to meet the needs of people.[9] These flexible channels can carry information with amazing speed and accuracy (as many managers have discovered to their shock). In fact, research studies have shown that approximately three-fourths of the information transmitted informally is very accurate, with the accuracy going even higher for noncontroversial organizational news.[10] The grapevine as an informal communication channel often has been looked upon by managers as something undesirable. However, a more realistic view is that it is a vital part of a dynamic organization. Unfortunately, these informal communication networks can also carry completely inaccurate information which harms rather than helps. From water cooler to mail desk to lounge to supply room to another secretary to others, on and on the information flows; by the time a communication completes its complex journey it may be completely distorted.

The grapevine seems to work in clusters of people. Thus, when one person has some information of interest to his own informal group, he passes it on to them. One member of the group may be a member of another informal group and he will pass it on to them.

The grapevine can be a very beneficial, rapid problem solver in an organization. It has been labeled "automatic horizontal communication."[11] Such communication occurs informally and decisions are made among persons on the same organizational level. Thus high-level management need not concern itself with as many problems. Furthermore, this allows ordinary formal channels to be kept open for more critical communication problems. Another positive aspect of such informal communication is that persons are involved, either directly or indirectly. Thus the decision often is made jointly rather than by one person. In addition, accuracy of decisions is likely to improve if informal communication flows among all concerned. Informal networks, with their inherent flexibility and speed, add much to communication throughout the organization.

SUMMARY

Good communication is necessary for all successful organizational activity. Communication is particularly significant for a manager who likely spends the majority of his working time in some kind of communication activity.

The communication process can be described by a model with several components. These components include a source who wishes to create a desired meaning in the mind

[9]Keith Davis, *Human Relations at Work,* McGraw-Hill Book Company, New York, 1967, pp. 222 ff.

[10]*Ibid.,* p. 224.

[11]Joseph L. Massie, "Automatic Horizontal Communication in Management," *Academy of Management Journal,* August 1960, p. 88.

of another. The meaning is encoded into a message, or set of symbols that represent the meaning. The message is sent along a channel to the receiver, who decodes the message and attaches meaning to it. The receiver responds to the source with feedback. Noise can be present in all parts of the system.

This model can describe the communication process of two persons talking. It also can describe any other communication system such as an automatic control system, a publication, or an organization. Organizations have particular characteristics that affect communication in them. These include the formal organization structure that sets up certain authority, power, accountability, and responsibility relationships. Within a formal organization an informal communication system—called a "grapevine"—has important effects.

The problems of exchanging meanings in organizations are complex. Members bring with them complex packages of skills, attitudes, experience, knowledge, values, and social and cultural factors. All affect the communication process.

Even the simplest communication is prone to almost limitless possibilities for error. Understanding the communication process can enable a manager to improve it, and thus improve his organization's performance.

FOR REVIEW AND DISCUSSION

1 Explain the concept of process. What problems occur in describing communication as a process?

2 Explain each of the nine parts of the model of the communication process given in this chapter. Which of these nine elements has the potential for miscommunication? Give the reasons why in each case.

3 Show how each of the following affects the quality of communication: (a) communication skills, (b) attitudes, (c) knowledge level, (d) sociocultural systems and environment.

4 Could the following be an effective message? Zferzhmn ekrop tp. Explain your answer.

5 Could a person who had never been to Iran communicate effectively about Iran with another person who had never been there? Give an explanation for your answer.

6 Explain the statement: "Language is the most widespread code used to express mental perceptions."

7 Give three examples of nonverbal communication from your own recent experience. What meaning was communicated in each case?

8 Explain the fallacy in the statement: "Good communication is sure to occur when one sends a clear message."

9 Students from other countries often find that their major difficulty is communicating. Using the model of the communication process, describe the specific areas or reasons for this difficulty.

10 What is the role of feedback in the communication process? Explain why good listening is so important for effective, dynamic communication.

11 What things necessary for an organization to function are provided by communication?

12 Explain the difference between internal and external organizational communication.

13 "By controlling the information flow in an organization a manager can acquire a great deal of power." Do you agree or disagree with this statement? Why?

14 What similar features as communication systems do a person and an organization have?

15 Explain the statement: "One use of an organization chart is to structure the communications in the organization."

16 Thayer has written that communication serves five basic functions in organizations. Give an example not in the text to illustrate each function.

17 What special problems in keeping informed about their organization do top managers have? Suggest several ways of reducing these problems.

18 Can members of an organization work effectively together if communication is poor? Why?

19 What are the advantages and disadvantages of informal communication channels?

20 If you were a manager, which approach would you take toward the grapevine? Would you (a) eliminate it, (b) ignore it, (c) try to keep it under control, (d) use it, or (e) utilize some other approach? Explain your answer.

CASES

A Major Hill, C squadron commander, had received the following order: "Bomb top of largest hill in fox sector immediately. Urgent."

Leaping into their planes the pilots of C squadron took off and quickly accomplished their mission. Flying back to the air base, Major Hill heard the following report on his radio: "Colonel commanding troops in box sector reports 146 of his men killed or injured by bombs from airplanes with friendly markings." Major Hill had a sinking feeling in his stomach.

    1 What was the basis of Major Hill's concern?

    2 List the places where miscommunication may have occurred.

    3 How could this situation have been prevented?

B During World War II the Army required 1,000 spare pistons for a certain motorcycle model. Seven months after the order was placed the parts arrived. However, instead of 1,000 there were 1 million units, a 250-year supply.

    1 Describe several things that could have caused this problem.

    2 Assume you are the inspector general, and that this case has been brought to your attention. What would you do?

C Mr. Randolph, a traveling salesman, was in the habit of calling his home every night. On March 17, the following event took place.

Mr. Randolph: "Operator, I would like to place a collect call. I want 719-743-1431."

Operator: "What is your name and number?"

Mr. Randolph: "Jenkins, 864-9417."

Operator (to person answering phone): "I have a collect call for anyone from Mr. Jenkins. Will you accept the charges?"

"No."

Both parties hung up. At the end of the month Mr. Randolph's phone bill included a charge for this call.

    1 Was the charge justified? Why?

    2 Suggest several ways of reducing or preventing this problem.

  D The board of directors of Acme Company voted to close its Jonesboro plant because it had decided to no longer produce the products made in this plant. All employees at Jonesboro were to be offered attractive jobs in other parts of the organization. After the meeting of the board at which these decisions were made, the following conversations took place.

Miss Snipe (the board's secretary) to Mrs. Toler (secretary to Mr. Fisch, vice-president of production) in the ladies' lounge: "Don't tell a soul, but the Jonesboro plant has had it. Sure do feel sorry for those people."

When Mrs. Toler returned to her desk, she called her friend, Mrs. Mary Jackson (secretary in the personnel department). "Mary, it's a big secret and I can't tell you where I heard it, but I know for a fact that Jonesboro is closing. Everybody's going to be looking for a job."

Mary then went in to see her supervisor, Mr. Tanhill, the personnel manager. "Mr. Tanhill, I have it on the best authority that Jonesboro is finally going to be closed and that all the employees there are to be dismissed. Shall I begin preparing the discharge papers?"

Mr. Tanhill replied, "Sure."

    1 Why has Mr. Tanhill made the wrong decision?

    2 How can miscommunication like this be prevented?

  E Mid-continent Specialties, Inc., had a management group consisting of the president and five vice-presidents. It had always been the habit of this group to send a carbon copy of correspondence between two members of the group to the other four.

Recently Ed Dalton, vice-president of production, has not gotten along well with Robert Melton, vice-president of finance. Mr. Dalton has told his secretary, "It will no longer be necessary to send Mr. Melton a copy of my letters to the other members of the management team."

    1 What effect do you think this action will have on Mr. Melton? On Mr. Dalton? On the management team?

    2 Why can such action be extremely serious in such an organization?

  F Mr. Bennett, a multimillionaire, controlled a number of large business organizations. No major policy decision could be made in any of the companies without Mr. Bennett's personal approval.

In recent years Mr. Bennett had become more and more seclusive. The presidents of his companies could never reach him directly; they were forced to leave a message with

Mr. Bennett's answering service. Often several weeks passed before Mr. Bennett returned a call.

    1 What effects do you think Mr. Bennett's actions will have on his companies?

    2 What advice do you have for Mr. Bennett? For his presidents? Give your reasons for your answers.

FOR FURTHER STUDY

Additional sources can be found in the sources cited in the chapter.

Books

Keith Davis: *Human Relations at Work,* McGraw-Hill Book Company, New York, 1967, chaps. 19 and 20. A very lucid explanation of communication with individuals and groups in organizations.

Willard V. Merrihue: *Managing by Communication,* McGraw-Hill Book Company, New York, 1960. The role and potential of communication as a management tool must be reexamined in the light of a series of rapid changes in American business: technological progress, influence of unions, etc.

Robert Newcomb and Mary Sammons: *Employee Communications in Action,* Harper & Row, Publishers, Incorporated, New York, 1961. "The growth and increasing complexity of our economy makes communication with employees a real and urgent need. Many industrial and business managements have come to recognize this, and the evidence grows that they are doing something about it."

Earl G. Planty and William Machaver: "Stimulating Upward Communication," in M. Joseph Dooher and Vivenne Marquis (eds.), *Effective Communication on the Job,* American Management Association, New York, 1956, pp. 141–157. There are barriers to upward communication, but they can be reduced with proper methods.

Articles

Jack R. Gibb: "Communication and Productivity," *Personnel Administration,* January–February 1964. Two alternative views of the communicative process can be taken: a persuasion approach, calling for communication improvement; and the problem-solving approach, attributing communication problems to poor line management.

M. F. Hall: "Communication within Organizations," *Journal of Management Studies,* February 1965. Symbols are used to communicate in organizations to make decisions and to modify attitudes.

Schuyler D. Hoslett: "Barriers to Communication," *Personnel,* September 1951. Describes barriers to communication in hierarchical organizations and suggests ways of improving these communications.

Donald L. Kirkpatrick: "Development and Validation of a Communication Inventory for

Supervisors," *Journal of Communication,* December 1968. Approaches, facts, and principles about communication that are useful to managers are presented.

Robert N. McMurry: "Clear Communications for Chief Executives," *Harvard Business Review,* March–April 1965. Good communications start at the top.

F. J. Roethlisberger: "The Administrator's Skill: Communication," *Harvard Business Review,* November 1953. A splendid paper showing through examples how distortions in communication cause organizational problems.

Section F
Controlling

23
Controlling

The modern concept of control . . . provides a historical record of what has happened . . . , why it has happened, and provides data that enable the . . . executive . . . to take corrective steps. . . .
   ERNEST DALE

The management process is completed when controlling has been accomplished. Controlling is concerned with: (1) comparing events with plans and (2) making necessary corrections where events have deviated from plans.

Controlling is the process by which management sees if what did happen was what was supposed to happen. If not, necessary adjustments are made. Moore sharply describes the controlling function: "There's many a slip between giving work assignments to men and carrying them out. Get reports of what is being done, compare it with what ought to be done, and do something about it if the two aren't the same."[1] Controlling is the checking-up part of the manager's job. The controlling function is illustrated in Figure 23-1, where actual performance is compared with desired, planned performance. The

[1]Franklin G. Moore, *Management: Organization and Practice,* Harper & Row, Publishers, Incorporated, New York, 1964, p. 122.

**Figure 23-1   The Controlling
Function in
Management**

Controlling is the part of the manager's job
in which he checks up on assignments, sees
what is being done, compares it with what
ought to be done, and does something about
it if the two are not the same. The broken
line indicates the degree of deviation to be
measured and corrected by controlling.

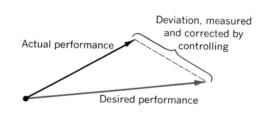

deviation, if any, is determined and appropriate corrective measures are designed in
the controlling function.

Planning is clearly a prerequisite for effective controlling. It is utterly foolish to think
that controlling could be accomplished without planning; without planning there is no
predetermined understanding of desired performance. This is one of the most common
problem areas of managers. Often managers attempt to control an organization without
adequate planning. This usually cannot be done, because who is to say whether or not
the performance is satisfactory if no desired performance standards have been agreed
upon in the planning process? If managers attempt to control using after-the-fact desired-
performance levels, these after-the-fact expectations if higher than actual performance
will surely run a high risk of causing resentment from organization members. After-the-
fact expectations are likely to be viewed as arbitrary and capricious.

The major purpose of accounting is providing the data to assist in controlling businesses and other economic enterprises. For example, sales and production budgets provide statements of desired performance. Accountants collect data derived from actual
operations, and these data are then compared with the appropriate budgets. Corrective
action is taken where indicated.

A football game can be used to illustrate the controlling function. For instance,
motion picture films are often made of important games. These films are examined at
great length to evaluate such things as overall game strategy and to collect a wide variety
of statistical data. Individual players may even receive a numerical score for their game
performance.

On another level, the police department of a typical city may be viewed as primarily
serving a controlling function. For example, traffic patrolmen observe behavior of drivers
and issue traffic citations to those who violate traffic regulations. Our penal system
is designed to give a potential offender an incentive not to commit an offense. If a law
has already been broken, the penal system supposedly corrects the matter when it requires the offender to "pay his debt to society."

Two factors create the need for controlling. First, individual and organizational objectives usually are different. Consequently, controlling is needed to insure that members

work toward organizational objectives. The alternative is random or uncoordinated activity. Second, controlling is necessary because there is a delay between the time when objectives are formulated and when they are accomplished. During this interval unforeseen conditions may cause a deviation between actual and desired performance.

For example, consider a case where the objective of a business is profit and the objective of a worker is income. These objectives are not identical but they can be compatible. Suppose the worker is paid so much for each piece he produces. He may work so fast to increase his income that he produces inferior goods that threaten the reputation of the firm. Controlling can require him to maintain acceptable quality, perhaps by working slower and more carefully. Another worker may have as an objective unrealistically high quality to satisfy his excessively high pride of workmanship. Controlling may require him to work faster to produce an acceptable quantity of goods.

Variations caused by unpredicted factors require a different type of controlling than the restraining and stimulating of individuals as described above. The only possible controlling often is to adapt to the changed conditions. For instance, a firm may have made its sales forecast before an economic recession. In the recession it may have to drastically change many of its activities in response to reduced sales.

Regardless of the way it is done, controlling is an adaptive, dynamic process. Objectives continually change, and controlling must adapt the organization to meet them.

If controlling anticipates deviations, it can be preventive. Preventive controlling is illustrated by the student who, at midterm, recognizes more study will be required to prevent disaster in the course. He then sets up a schedule for the additional studying. On the other hand, corrective controlling acts upon variations from desired performance only after they occur. On the part of the university, corrective controlling occurs when a student is required to repeat a course due to unsatisfactory performance. Preventive controlling is preferable to corrective controlling in most cases because the costs of achieving corrections is lower. Preventive controlling makes changes in the process as the need occurs. Corrective controlling requires that the process be repeated.

MEASUREMENT

Effective controlling requires measurement or evaluation. For some operations numerical measurement is possible. For instance, suppose the desired daily performance of a manufacturing department was to produce 100 units at a cost of not more than $20 per unit. The accounting (controlling) system revealed that actual production was 90 units at a unit cost of $21. The deviations of 10 units and $1 unit costs thus can be fairly easily measured.

In many activities measurement is extremely difficult. How can you quantitatively measure the productivity of a teacher, minister, politician, engineer, or secretary? Some facets of their work can be measured, but other aspects—often the most important— must be evaluated by subjective opinion. Controlling such work is a much more difficult task than controlling activities where output can be objectively measured.

CHARACTERISTICS OF EFFECTIVE CONTROL SYSTEMS

Control systems should be understandable, follow organizational patterns, register devia-tions quickly, remain flexible, point to corrective action, and be economical.

If controls are to be meaningful, the individuals involved must understand what they are attempting to accomplish and how each person relates to the objectives at hand. Likewise, if the correction of deviations is to be timely, standards must be developed for and related to specific positions in the organization structure. If not, managers cannot possibly know where to apply their corrective action. For instance, if specific profit ob-jectives are not established and communicated to operating divisions, administrators cannot possibly pinpoint profitability problems.

Time also is important in the controlling process. For one thing, a great virtue of controlling is that it can be a learning experience. When deviations are quickly detected, corrective action can be prompt. Everyone can learn from the experience, which would not be as likely if controlling occurs much later. If controlling is prompt, the situation is still familiar to the participants. Time also may be important because the standards them-selves may be incorrect. And the sooner improper standards are detected, the sooner they can be corrected.

Flexibility in the entire controlling process is important to adapt to changing con-ditions and to improve the operations of the organization. And the best controls point to the location cause of deviations, thus suggesting corrective actions.

Finally, costs are important in performing all management functions. Controlling often is used to keep costs at an acceptable level; hence it makes no sense to spend more on controlling than can be received in benefits from it.

HUMAN FACTORS IN CONTROLLING

For many members, controls are the means by which an organization determines the re-wards and punishments it will dispense. Thus controlling has emotional and motiva-tional implications with implied functional and dysfunctional consequences.

Often controls are seen as restraints. And man seems to have an inherent tendency to resist restraints. Unfortunately, however, persons often revolt from controls simply because they do not understand them. For example, sometimes young persons rebel against society before they understand that certain standards of conduct are required by society so that order may be provided for all. Workers, at times, disregard safety regu-lations without realizing that they are necessary for the protection of everyone against industrial accidents.

A too limited perspective also can cause problems. For instance, the foreman of a department may concentrate solely upon the objectives of his subunit while ignoring completely the broader objectives of the organization. In extreme cases this may lead to falsification of production records which are designed to ascertain how well each department is contributing to organizational goals. In fact, there are numerous accounts of employees becoming so obsessed with the accomplishment of limited objectives, that they neglect more important broader ones. Granick, for instance, described various examples of how Soviet management attaches so much recognition to breaking production records that workers are tempted to neglect proper maintenance, thus causing frequent breakdowns in future periods which result in lower total production.[2]

Several steps can be taken to make controlling more attractive and effective. First, it can be recognized that impersonal, quantitative standards do not take into account the individual differences of persons. This problem can be at least partially overcome if the standards are administered in ways that take into account the feelings and uniqueness of each person. Machines and other physical assets are expected to need individual attention. Surely the human assets of the organization are entitled to at least as much consideration. A patient, considerate approach can go far toward efficient meshing of persons, standards, and the objectives of the organization.

Second, forms of participative goal-setting emphasizing increasing self-control can be employed. With such procedures, members frequently set higher performance standards for themselves than would have been set by management alone. Everyone likes to consider himself an expert on his job. Participation in setting goals and standards recognizes individual competence and dignity. Where appropriate, the conflict between management and workers can be reduced by participative measures. They work more as one team, rather than two groups in a never-ending struggle.

PHASES OF CONTROLLING

Three phases of controlling have been identified: (1) the legislative phase, concerned with basic decision making; (2) the administrative phase, concerned with the day-to-day expediting of legislative decisions; and (3) the sanctions phase, concerned with enforcement.[3] Accomplishing these phases requires using other management functions, thus illustrating their iterative nature. For instance, legislation involves the formulation of organizational objectives and the rules and regulations to be used in accomplishing them. The administrative phase may use organizing, motivating, and communicating in expediting the decisions made in the legislative phase. Finally, sanctions often call for the best leadership and motivational work.

University policies, for example, usually are established through a legislative process involving the board of trustees or similar governing body. From these policies individual college and departmental objectives are formulated. To accomplish these objectives, deans, department chairmen, and faculty members are organized. They communicate about what each individual is accountable for doing and the progress being made. Sanctions are provided to assure adequate performance. The absence of an adequate control system in a university, as in any other organization, is an invitation to disaster.

---

[2]David Granick, *Management of the Industrial Firm in U.S.S.R.*, Columbia University Press, New York, 1954.

[3]Arnold S. Tannenbaum, "The Concept of Organizational Control," *Journal of Social Issues*, 1956, p. 53.

CONTROLLING AND CREATIVITY

Caution must be exercised in seeking conformity and applying sanctions, for when pressures for conformity become too great creativity may suffer too much. This problem has been described as a paradox: How can an organization continually innovate and renew itself through creativity and at the same time maintain the order necessary for efficient operations?[4] No easy answer is available for this question. Controlling is designed to assist in requiring actual performance to conform to desired standards. But, innovation requires experimentation with new processes and different procedures. Therefore, there must be some provision made to ensure that creative potential is not suppressed.

There is a thin line between effective and oppressive control. The major difference between the two is a matter of attitude and relates almost entirely to the manner in which controlling is approached. If individuals understand the need for order yet appreciate the essential character of creativity and are properly rewarded for displaying it, proper attitudes will likely follow.

VALUE OF REPORTS

Controlling tends to be more effective if reports of organizational performance are provided frequently to managers. Unacceptable performance can be corrected promptly. Also, good reports on performance tend to be self-reinforcing. That is, they provide incentive for continued good performance or for even better future performance.

Good reports also greatly assist a manager in making decisions. For instance, the personnel director of a large corporation does not have the time to constantly evaluate employee morale. But he can select some general indicator such as labor turnover as an indication of morale. When more workers begin to resign their positions than would normally be expected, a warning is given that trouble is developing and he can act accordingly. As long as turnover is in line with past trends he can concentrate his efforts on other things.

This approach allows the personnel director to practice management by exception. In other words, it affords him an opportunity to concentrate upon exceptional or particularly troublesome cases. Those areas that are not obviously outside desired performance standards are assumed to be working properly.

SUMMARY

Controlling (1) compares events with plans and (2) makes necessary corrections where events have deviated from plans. Controlling is the process by which management sees if what did happen was what was supposed to happen. If not, necessary adjustments are made.

Controlling is a dynamic process which involves action which is either restraining,

---

[4]Lyman K. Randall, "Organizational Paradox," *Harvard Business Review,* 1965, p. 87.

stimulating, or adaptive. It may anticipate deviations and prevent them from developing or act upon the variations after they take place.

Some type of measurement is an essential part of the process. However, the very idea of evaluation and measurement has an emotional meaning to man because it implies restraint. Thus, a number of difficulties may develop with respect to the human factor. To overcome these, management must utilize the best leadership and motivational approaches.

Controlling requires the effective use of the other managerial functions. Planning is necessary to establish the standards against which actual performance can be measured. Likewise, communicating, motivating, and organizing are essential to the expediting of established plans. And, of course, creating is required to assure that controls are developed and implemented in a fashion which will not be needlessly oppressive.

The management process is completed when controlling has been accomplished. It is the climax of the manager's job and the process by which he judges the success of his and his organization's efforts.

FOR REVIEW AND DISCUSSION

1 Describe the steps in the controlling process.

2 What is the relationship between planning and controlling?

3 Why is measurement so important in the controlling process? Describe some of the problems of measurement of an organization's performance.

4 Describe the characteristics of an effective control system.

5 Explain the human problems involved in the controlling process.

6 Explain the legislative, administrative, and sanctions phases of the controlling process.

7 How can controlling cause a problem for organizational creativity?

8 Explain the value of control reports to management.

9 Why is controlling necessary for the proper functioning of organization? What two things bring about the need for controlling?

CASES

A   Dr. Johnson, Dean of the School of Business Administration at City University, is developing a method to improve the "productivity" of faculty members. He has divided the areas of improvement into three general categories: teaching, research, and community service. At the present time he plans to "weight" the various categories by some factor and derive a productivity index based on the individual professor's activities during the school year. This index will then be used as the criterion for salary increases and promotions.

> **1** What do you think of the proposed system? Why? What weights would you assign to Dean Johnson's three categories of work?
>
> **2** What difficulties is he likely to encounter with this control device?

3 How can he reduce the problems that are likely to develop?

B   Mr. Ed Wilson, a respected member of the community, had been treasurer of the Highlands Savings and Loan Association for twenty years. Because of Mr. Wilson's reputation the board of directors had not thought it necessary to audit his accounts each year.

Yesterday the following news item appeared in the local paper: "Ed Wilson, long-time executive of Highlands Savings and Loan Association, has been booked on a charge of embezzling $20,000 from the association. According to preliminary reports the shortages occurred over a number of years."

> **1** What managerial principle has been violated? How might the problem have been prevented?
>
> **2** Did the failure of the Board to require regular audits contribute to the problem?

C   Recently Mr. Gross, Treasurer of Yazoo Manufacturing Corporation, spent $10,000 of company funds tracking down a shortage of $3,000 in his office accounts. He finally discovered that Miss Sterling, a payroll accountant, had embezzled the $3,000. He fired Miss Sterling, but was unable to recover the funds from her.

> **1** Was Mr. Gross justified in spending the $10,000 to discover the source of the shortage of $3,000? Why?
>
> **2** Can Mr. Gross (or any other manager) ever be sure that he is spending exactly the right amount on maintaining his control system? Why?

FOR FURTHER STUDY

Additional sources can be found in the sources cited in the chapter.

Books

Ernest Dale: *Management: Theory and Practice,* 2d ed., McGraw-Hill Book Company, New York, 1969, chap. 20. This chapter is a basic explanation of managerial control of an organization.

William Travers Jerome, III: *Executive Control—The Catalyst,* John Wiley & Sons, Inc., New York, 1961, pp. 31–34. Many different types of control can be used for different purposes.

Harold Koontz and Cyril O'Donnell: *Principles of Management,* 5th ed., McGraw-Hill Book Company, New York, 1972, part 6. A detailed study of the modern manager's controlling function.

William H. Newman: *Administrative Action,* 2d ed., Prentice-Hall, Inc., Englewood Cliffs, N.J., 1963, part V. These chapters describe the essential steps in controlling, budgetary control, and overall control structure.

George R. Terry: *Principles of Management,* 5th ed., Richard D. Irwin, Inc., Homewood, Ill., 1968, part V. Control, a major part of the entire concept of management, determines what progress is being accomplished.

Articles

Ernest I. Hanson: "The Budgetary Control Function," *The Accounting Review*, April 1966, pp. 239–243. Budgets are important means of achieving control of organizations.

Herbert G. Hicks and Friedhelm Goronzy: "Notes on the Nature of Standards," *Academy of Management Journal*, December 1966. Productivity standards are relative and must change with evolving technologies.

Harold Koontz: "Management Control: A Suggested Formulation of Principles," *California Management Review*, Winter 1959. Control principles are stated in the areas of the nature and purpose of control, the structure of control, and the process of control.

James L. Peirce: "The Planning and Control Concept," *The Controller*, September 1954. A clear statement of the meaning and practice of planning and controlling in modern business.

Douglas S. Sherwin: "The Meaning of Control," *Dun's Review and Modern Industry*, January 1956. "Control is action which adjusts operations to predetermined standards, and its basis is information in the hands of managers."

IV
Management Thought and Practice

24
Management Thought in Perspective

The roots of the emerging profession of management go deep, just as do those of such other, older professions as theology, law, medicine, and education.
LAWRENCE A. APPLEY

The present position of management thought is best understood in the light of its historical development.[1] The development of management theory occurred in four rather distinct time periods. We can label each of these periods according to the dominant new thought introduced during the period. However, each prior period's thought was carried forward and influenced following periods.

PERIOD I—PRESCIENTIFIC MANAGEMENT (PRIOR TO 1880)

Period I might be called the "prescientific-management period." Period I includes the time from the beginning of man's cooperative efforts to the start of his attempts in about 1880 to approach the study of management scientifically.

---

[1]A major part of this section is an adaptation of a portion of: Mother Mary Maurita Sengelaub, R.S.M., Thomas R. O'Donovan, and Arthur X. Deegan, *Fundamentals of Management,* The Religious Sisters of Mercy, Detroit, Mich., 1964. (By permission.)

Background Factors

In the prescientific-management period, workers were almost completely dominated by their supervisors, a relationship based on social caste systems of autocracy. The ancient Egyptians built their pyramids during this period. The whip and the ball and chain were effective ways of getting things done through people. In the society of the Roman Empire the fact of being a citizen of Rome separated the managers from all other men (viewed as barbarians), and armies such as the Roman legion were effective in carrying out the wishes of those in power. This period witnessed the development of the Roman Catholic Church, whose central-control type of government–management remains almost the same today as in the days of the first Pope. The feudal system, where land-owners needed no other principles to guide their management of the serfs but their hereditary title, was an important feature of the prescientific-management period. This was a period of enormous extremes: the lord and the peasant, the emperor and the slave, the king and the footman, the haves and the have-nots.

Management Theory

In the environment of the prescientific-management period it was not necessary to study any organized body of management concepts. One needed only to be in a position of authority, for authority meant power and control in the social and economic systems of the period. Men were content with their lot, or else they could do little about it. They were born into their place in life, knew nothing of the world beyond it, aspired to nothing except continuing in it. It was a time when everything took ages to accomplish. It required centuries to build cathedrals or pyramids.

In period I, groups of craftsmen who preferred the same type of work formed guilds. These guilds were the forerunners of modern trade unions. However, these guilds were of minor consequence in the social system in which they were buried. Their influence was not felt beyond the limits of the village in which they were suffered to exist. The struggle to survive was a primary concern.

It was not until men began to think beyond the realm of their immediate situation, to envision hopes of seeing in their day improvements in communication or production, that it was necessary to begin to think about effective management. This search for better management began to happen after the settlement of the New World; the Dark Ages were over.

Period I closed as a pair of Frenchmen named Voltaire and Rousseau were populariz-ing the cry for fraternity, liberty, and equality, and calling for a revolution in the field of politics, enlightenment in the field of intellectual thought, and a renaissance in the field of art; and an American named Franklin was writing about "taxation without representa-tion." Organizations such as political bodies (the Roman senate), military units (the Napoleonic army), the Church hierarchies (Roman Catholic Church), and others of period I provided little assistance in the development of management concepts. These organiza-tions certainly practiced certain functions of management, and they originated some of the same principles we find used today. But no coherent body of management thought was developed in period I. The blunt exercise of power and authority sums up management and organizational thought for period I.

PERIOD II—SCIENTIFIC MANAGEMENT (1880–1930)

The second period in the development of management thought can be labeled the "scientific-management period." The time period involved ranged roughly from 1880 to 1930.

Background Factors

Period II saw the rise of the business baron and the industrial revolution. The concept of a wage (rather than a subsistence allowance) being paid for work was recognized. The doctrine of private property became a dominant theme.

Management Theory

Industrialization can be described as the process whereby a nation learns to create more material things through the efforts of fewer workers. The emphasis in period II was on methods of production. A search was made for ways to obtain more efficiency, remedy inequities, and prevent waste. As the United States became overrun by the industrial revolution and standardization of production through the assembly-line technique, management literature centered on industrial technology as the focal point of good organization.

The foremost exponent of this approach was the "father of scientific management," Frederick W. Taylor. Based on first-hand studies of manufacturing practices at the shop level, he promulgated a series of principles in his work, *Scientific Management,* excoriating managers for their arbitrary approach to their responsibilities and workers for their apparent lackadaisical attitude to work norms. Taylor recommended making management a science, resting on "well recognized, clearly defined and fixed principles, instead of depending on more or less hazy ideas."[2]

By maximizing the productive efficiency of each worker, scientific management would also maximize the earnings of workers and employers. The aim was to use all available resources and knowledge of the universe in order to realize definite ideals. As Taylor put it:

> It becomes the duty of those on the management's side to deliberately study the character, the nature, and the performance of each workman with a view to finding out his limitations on the one hand, but even more important, his possibilities for development on the other hand; and then as deliberately and systematically to train and help and teach this workman,

[2]F. W. Taylor, "Shop Management," reprinted in *Scientific Management,* Harper & Row, Publishers, Incorporated, New York, 1947, p. 63.

giving him, wherever possible, those opportunities for advancement which will finally enable him to do the highest and most interesting and most profitable class of work for which his natural abilities fit him, and which are open to him in the particular company in which he is employed.[3]

Taylor then gave his famous four principles of scientific management:

First, the development of the science, i.e., the gathering in on the part of those on the management's side of all knowledge which in the past has been kept in the heads of the workmen; second, the scientific selection and progressive development of the workmen; third, the bringing of the science and the scientifically selected and trained men together; and fourth, the constant and intimate cooperation which always occurs between the men on the management's side and the worker.[4]

Because Taylor's work was shop-oriented, including many studies of ways to increase output at the level of the individual worker, he was criticized as being a mere, glorified "time-study analyst." In fact, this criticism was so widespread that he was called before a special United States House committee investigating the principles of the scientific-management school. Before this committee he defended his ideas as:

. . . not a piecework system, not a bonus system, not time-study. . . . The great revolution that takes place in the mental attitude of the two parties under scientific management is that both sides take their eyes off the division of the surplus as the all-important matter, and together turn their attention toward increasing the size of the surplus until this surplus becomes so large . . . that there is ample room for a large increase in profits for the manufacturer. [Increased output would be so large that all frictions between employers and workers would be eliminated. This approach would presumably also make collective bargaining unnecessary.]
    Under scientific management arbitrary power, arbitrary decision ceases; and every single subject, large and small, becomes the question for scientific investigation, for reduction to law.[5]

Taylor thus eliminated the personal exercise of authority. Managers became subject to rules and discipline as much as the workers. It was the task of management to place the right worker in any given job, but according to scientific selection, eliminating guesswork. Arbitrary judgments of both workers and managers gave place to the science of each task and both sides' willingness to abide by the laws.

Some authorities have suggested that Taylor's contribution has been somewhat overemphasized. First, the originality of his ideas has become suspect.[6] Further, business managers have opposed the idea of replacing judgment and executive decision with pre-fabricated techniques. Many would have nothing to do with his "mental revolution."[7] On the whole, managers have accepted many of his techniques, but have accused him

---

[3]F. W. Taylor, "Taylor's Testimony before the Special House Committee," reprinted in *Scientific Management, ibid.,* p. 42.
    [4]*Ibid.,* p. 48.
    [5]*Ibid.,* pp. 26–33.
    [6]See J. H. Hoagland, "Management before Frederick Taylor," *Proceedings of the Academy of Management,* 1956, pp. 15–24.
    [7]Robert Franklin Hoxie, *Scientific Management and Labor,* Appleton-Century-Crofts, Inc., New York, 1915.

of unwarranted interference in the domain of managerial prerogatives. Nevertheless, Taylor remains as the principal figure associated with the scientific management movement.

Others who contributed to scientific management include Henri Fayol, who popularized the universality of management principles,[8] and Edward D. Jones, who stressed the trusteeship role of management.[9] Frank and Lillian Gilbreth made very significant contributions in the fields of motion and time study, and they sought to improve the welfare of the workers.[10] Henry L. Gantt studied the habits in industry,[11] and Harrington Emerson championed standardization.[12]

All these contributions furthered the cause of scientific management, trying to find compatibility between management and workers.

> The mutuality of interests objective, based heavily on the economic motives of employers, was to result from ever increasing productivity and wider, more equitable distribution of an economic surplus. The pioneers felt that if this more immediate goal could be accomplished, the more ultimate necessity of human collaboration in industry would be forthcoming.[13]

To summarize, period II saw great advances in management practice by the application of empirical studies to determine faster and better methods of production. But the approach of scientific management tended to become one-sided. Stress was given to changes in methods for the sole purpose of improving production with little thought to the effect on the worker, or even his well-being. Workers were assumed to be more or less standardized units of production, concerned solely about pay.

Taylor and others of his period stressed the need for more cooperation between management and workers. But most advances of period II were in technology, not in human areas. Abuses were prevalent because technological advances were not matched by social advances. Bendix summed the problems of scientific management: "As the art of manufacture improves, the artisan recedes; as the masses are lowered, the masters are raised; and no human bond exists between employers and employed."[14]

By the end of the scientific-management period the worker had been reduced to the role of an impersonal cog in the machine of production. His job became more and more narrowly specialized until he had little appreciation for his contribution to the total product. Naturally, the worker had very little, if any, involvement and pride in his job. Although very significant technological advances were made in period II, the serious weakness of the scientific approach to management was that it dehumanized the or-

---

[8]Henri Fayol, *General and Industrial Administration*, Sir Isaac Pitman & Sons, Ltd., London, 1949.

[9]Edward D. Jones, *Industrial Leadership and Executive Ability*, The Engineering Magazine Company, New York, 1920.

[10]L. M. Gilbreth, *The Psychology of Management*, The Macmillan Company, New York, 1914.

[11]Henry L. Gantt, *Work, Wages and Profits*, The Engineering Magazine Company, New York, 1916.

[12]Harrington Emerson, *The Twelve Principles of Efficiency*, The Engineering Magazine Company, New York, 1913.

[13]William G. Scott, *The Social Ethic in Management Literature*, Georgia State College of Business Administration, Atlanta, Ga., 1959, p. 18. (By permission.)

[14]Reinhard Bendix, *Work and Authority in Industry*, John Wiley & Sons, Inc., New York, 1956, p. xviii.

ganizational member. He was assumed to be without emotion and capable of being scientifically manipulated, just like machines. The worker was seen simply as a factor of production like a machine. He was assumed to be a wage-maximizing "thing." At the end of the scientific-management period, about 1930, the time was indeed ripe for an emphasis on the human factors involved in management.

PERIOD III—HUMAN RELATIONS (1930–1950)

The third major period in the development of management thought emphasized human relationships in organizations. Beginning about 1930, period III extended to approximately 1950.

Background Factors

To a large extent period III represented a reaction to the dehumanizing aspects of scientific management. During this period concepts of the worker advanced from an unfeeling, unidentified human unit on an assembly line to a person of emotions and worth. In management literature the "man problem" became as important as the "machine problem" or the "sales problem."

In 1923, Oliver Sheldon began to bridge the gap between scientific management and human relations.[15] Sheldon called for professional management to deal with the labor and social problems of business organizations on a par with the technical problems of production. Thus Sheldon heralded the emergence of the human relations movement that was to be a dominant theme of management thought in the 1930s.

Management Theory

Perhaps the most important contributions made to management theory during period III came from Elton Mayo, especially his experiments at the Hawthorne plant of Western Electric Company. These experiments have become widely known as the "Hawthorne experiments." Mayo revealed that an organization was more than a formal structure or arrangement of functions. Mayo wrote: "[An organization] is a social system, a system of cliques, grapevines, informal status systems, rituals and a mixture of logical, non-logical and illogical behavior."[16]

According to Mayo, effective management involved leading men, not manipulating robots. Therefore, higher productivity was not necessarily achieved by positive financial incentives or improved physical working conditions. Indeed Mayo's experiments demonstrated that neither deterioration nor improvement in physical working conditions necessarily had significant effect on productivity. Mayo felt that social demands within the group resulted in the more or less tacit agreement of workers on the standards of work performance.

---

[15]Oliver Sheldon, *The Philosophy of Management*, Sir Isaac Pitman & Sons, Ltd., London, 1923.
[16]Quoted in Scott, *op. cit.*, p. 29.

Taylor presented the worker as a wage-maximizing individual in isolation, whose aptitude for work counts, not his relation to fellow workers. Mayo, on the other hand, insisted that the worker acts in natural solidarity with his fellows. He is not necessarily responsive only to economic incentives, but is also a product of personal sentiments and emotional involvements. He is often nonlogical in his thinking, with one overriding motive: the desire to stand well with his fellows.

Mayo's advice was to approach the management problem from the perspective of whatever knowledge of human nature we have. He recommended the use of all social-science disciplines focused upon understanding and solving conflicts within the industrial system. In turn, he believed, a successful human relations approach would create organizational harmony, higher employee satisfaction, and greater operational efficiency.

The human relations movement quickly attracted wide attention in both academic and industrial circles. Many firms significantly revised their approach to management to increase emphasis on the human factor.

However, many of the "human relationists" seem to have carried the movement too far. For instance, some apparently equated morale in the organization with high productivity. Morale is an elusive quality that describes a person's satisfaction with his membership in the organization.

Productivity is in fact related to motivation (both anxiety-producing as well as anxiety-reducing) and many other factors such as discipline and control. In the total mix of these many factors, morale may be relatively insignificant, or at least morale is often obscured by other factors. In any event organizations may have: (1) high morale and high productivity, (2) high morale and low productivity, (3) low morale and high productivity, and (4) low morale and low productivity. No significant relationship appears to exist between morale and productivity.[17]

Our conclusion is that morale is not a very meaningful concept of management thought and that some advocates of the human relations approach extended human relations concepts too far when they claimed that morale and productivity are necessarily directly related.

So we see that, exactly as in the scientific-management movement, some abused the human relations movement when they carried the basic concepts beyond an appropriate limit. Nevertheless, the human relations movement made extremely significant contributions to management thought by highlighting human and social factors in organizations.

While the human relations approach developed, classical management theorists continued the work they had begun in period II. By the late 1940s the classicists had greatly refined their ideas. Col. Lyndall Urwick, a noted British management consultant

---

[17]See Rensis Likert, *New Patterns of Management*, McGraw-Hill Book Company, New York, 1961, pp. 15–35; Harold Koontz and Cyril O'Donnell, *Principles of Management*, 4th ed., McGraw-Hill Book Company, New York, 1968, pp. 585–588; Philip B. Applewhite, *Organizational Behavior*, Prentice-Hall, Inc., Englewood Cliffs, N.J., 1965, pp. 6–31; Daniel Katz, Nathan Maccoby, Gerald Gurin, and Lucretia G. Floor, *Productivity, Supervision, and Morale among Railroad Workers*, Survey Research Center, Ann Arbor, Mich., 1959.

and author, did outstanding work perfecting management principles.[18] These principles were particularly applicable to organizational structures, authority and responsibility relationships, and other concepts of formal organization.

PERIOD IV—REFINEMENT, EXTENSION, AND SYNTHESIS (1950–PRESENT)

Our fourth period in the development of management thought began about 1950 and extends to the present time. Period IV has been characterized by processes of refinement, extension, and synthesis of management thought. During period IV scientific management has been brought to a high state of refinement in such areas as industrial engineering, motion and time study, and operations research. Paralleling the growth of scientific management have been advances in the human relations approach. Personnel

[18] See particularly Lyndall Urwick, *Notes on the Theory of Organization,* American Management Association, New York, 1952; and L. Urwick, *The Elements of Administration,* Sir Isaac Pitman & Sons, Ltd., London, 1943.

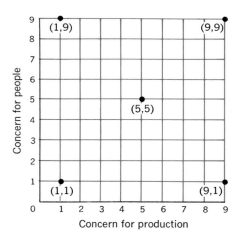

(1,1) Impoverished Management
Effective production is unobtainable because people are lazy, apathetic, and indifferent. Sound and mature relationships are difficult to achieve. Conflict is inevitable.

(9,1) Task Management
Men are a commodity just as machines. A manager's responsibility is to plan, direct, and control the work of those subordinate to him.

(1,9) Country Club Management
Production is incidental to lack of conflict and "good fellowship."

(5,5) Dampened Pendulum
(Middle of the road) Push for production but don't go all out. Give some but not all. "Be fair and firm."

(9,9) Team Management
Production is from integration of task and human requirements.

Figure 24–1   The Managerial Grid*

The most effective managers are people and production oriented. On this grid the better managers are described by points toward the top and right. Point 9,9 would indicate the best management: the integration of task and human requirements.

*From Robert R. Blake, Jane Srygley Mouton, and Alvin C. Bidwell, "Managerial Grid," *Advanced Management-Office Executive,* September, 1962, p. 13. By permission.

management, industrial relations, and other areas continue to emphasize the human relations approach.

During period IV it has become widely recognized that both scientific management and human relations have much to offer. And we now know that these two approaches are not necessarily opposed. Blake and Mouton have shown, for example, that the most effective managers are neither "people" (human relations) oriented nor "production" (scientific-management) oriented. Rather the best managers are people- *and* production-oriented. [19] Blake and Mouton have developed tests which place a manager on a "managerial grid." The managerial grid describes the manager's approach to his job. Better managers are described by points toward the top *and* right side of the grid, as shown in Figure 24-1.

The managerial grid suggests that a manager's score might be obtained by combining his people and production scores. A low score in either area is a good indicator of a poor approach to management.

In period IV, another stream of advances in management and organization thought has come from behavioral scientists and organization theorists who have suggested that best results can be obtained by building theories of management and organization based on the findings of the behavioral sciences. Relevant behavioral sciences include psychology, sociology, psychiatry, economics, cultural anthropology, and philosophy. Elaborate attempts have also been made to construct mathematical and schematic models of organizational processes. Those readers who wish to study further in organization theory will find a wealth of literature available.

Currently, there are several schools of organizational and management thought. The following section gives a summary of the important features of each school.

SCHOOLS OF MANAGEMENT AND ORGANIZATIONAL THOUGHT [20]

Modern-day students of organizations and management have approached the subject from several viewpoints. Each of these views has some merit, because each helps toward a better understanding of some facet of organizations and management. There is no particular order of precedence for the schools and some tend to overlap with others. However, by studying the different viewpoints of the several schools, we will be in a better position to understand the total process of organizations.

The Traditional School

The point of view of the traditional school is that management can be thought of as the process of getting things done through people in organized groups. Henri Fayol, a Frenchman, was one of the originators of this school. [21]

[19] Robert Rogers Blake and Jane S. Mouton, *Group Dynamics: Key to Decision Making,* Gulf Publishing Company, Houston, 1961, pp. 27–38.

[20] Harold Koontz, "The Management Theory Jungle," *Journal of the Academy of Management,* December 1961, identified several of these schools.

[21] Henri Fayol, *General and Industrial Management,* trans. Constance Storrs, Sir Isaac Pitman & Sons, Ltd., London, 1949.

Some of the fundamental characteristics of the process of management school are:

1 The functions of management, such as creating, planning, organizing, motivating, communicating, and controlling, are defined, emphasized, and studied.

2 Principles or fundamental truths about organizations and management are thought of as being important for clarifying the study of management and for improving managerial practice.

3 Principles of management should be the starting point for research and should yield the most useful management theory.

4 The process of management is an art which is concerned with the application of management principles.

5 Management is universal since good management principles have some applicability to all organizations.

Many principles of management are found throughout this book although they are not always designated as such. Thus, this book has incorporated many of the findings of the traditional school. The traditional school has greatly influenced—perhaps dominated— managerial thought, and outstanding examples of reference material in this school are widely available.

The Empirical School

The empirical school stresses experience as a factor of managerial performance and deemphasizes the theoretical aspects of the subject. This school holds that experience is the only way a manager can develop, and that it is the transfer of experience from the practitioner to the student that constitutes the most valid way of learning management. The view is taken that by studying the successes and mistakes of others and by having his own experiences, one can develop a general frame of reference on which to rely in managerial situations.

The empirical school shares an underlying premise with the traditional school. Both stress the generalizations or truths necessary for the successful practice of management. The traditional school holds that these generalizations can be codified and taught through written theory; the empirical school holds that the truths must be learned through experience. [22]

The Human Relations School

A basic thesis of the human relations school is that organizations always involve inter-relationships among members. The manager's role is seen as being heavily concerned with improving the relationships among organizational members. Leading and super-vising are seen as primary functions of the manager. The human relations school leans heavily on the findings of social sciences such as psychology and sociology.

---

[22]For a book describing outstanding practitioners of the empirical approach, see Ernest Dale, *The Great Organizers,* McGraw-Hill Book Company, New York, 1960.

The human relations school points to the importance of the individual's social and psychological needs, motivation, and informal relationships in organizations. Critics of this school complain that the school emphasizes "people without organizations."

It is clear that leading and supervising are only some parts of the managerial job, but they are certainly important components. Many aspects of the human relations school have been discussed earlier in this chapter where we have seen that the human relations approach defines an entire era in management thinking. Recent years have witnessed a revival of interest in human relations. Many outstanding books about human problems of organizations are available.

The Decision-theory School

The rationality of decisions and analysis of the process of making decisions are areas of primary interest to the decision-theory school. This view emphasizes the critical nature of decisions in an organization. Economics, value analysis, and information-transmittal processes are among the areas that are applied by decision theorists to arrive at the optimum decision. Decision theorists hold that the progress of an organization is determined by the cumulative effect of thousands of decisions made by managers at all levels. Therefore decisions are of crucial importance and ought to be the basis for theory and study.

The Mathematical School

Closely related to the decision-theory school is the mathematical school. The mathematical school takes the view that management can best be approached with the assistance of models and mathematics. The argument is made that if management involves a rational and logical pattern, the pattern can best be expressed through the use of mathematics, which is also logically based. The mathematical school holds that if the management functions of creating, planning, organizing, motivating, communicating, and controlling are logically based, it should be possible to express them in mathematical terms.

The emerging field of operations research combines the views of the decision-theory and mathematical schools.

The Formalism School

A basic assumption of the formalism school is that organizational members will perform their jobs best when jobs are clearly defined and structured. Thus, members will know what is expected of them and will work to fulfill these expectations. Heavy reliance is placed on the organization chart as a definition of organizational relationships. Formal channels of command and information flow are emphasized. Job descriptions also are used as aids in improving performance. Everyone in the organization reports to only one supervisor, as defined by the formal structure.

The formalism school has contributed much of what is known as "classical management thought." Topics of primary concern to this school include hierarchy of objectives, formal authority and responsibility relationships, unity of command, and span of control. Critics of this school complain that this approach amounts to "organizations without people."

As might be expected, formalism tends to create organizations which may be described as stiff, rigid, and inflexible. Some authorities feel that formalism tends to kill initiative and creativity within the organization. However, advocates of the formalism approach hold that it creates organizations which are stable, orderly, and rational.

The Spontaneity School

Group coordination and effective organizational behavior will automatically emerge around the "natural" leader, claim the advocates of the spontaneity approach to management. Formal structures, policies, procedures, and control ought to be minimized. This group stresses the importance of the informal, emergent organization. In fact, some members of this school believe that the formal organization ought to be designed as an official recognition of the informal—the real—organization.

Some students of management hold that there may be no conflict of the spontaneity and formalism approaches if neither is taken to an extreme. These observers claim that an acceptable degree of spontaneity can be obtained within a relatively flexible formal structure. Perhaps a judicious mix of the two approaches is best.

The Participative School

The participative school holds that organizational members will perform best when they are given an opportunity to participate in making organizational decisions which will affect them.

Because the participative school focuses on participation in decision making, the approach is seen in both formal and informal organizations. In formal organizations, participation is realized when an official consults with members through conferences, committees, etc. The participative school deemphasizes the naked exercise of blunt power by organizational officials.

The participative school of management believes that "several heads are better than one" for decision making. Members of this school feel that there is a large, often untapped, reservoir of talent, ideas, knowledge, and skills among organization members that will be realized only when members become actively involved in the organization through participation in decision making.

The Challenge-and-response School

Closely allied to the participative school is the challenge-and-response school of thought. The challenge-and-response approach advocates that members will respond with good performance when they are motivated through appropriate challenges. The belief is held that there is satisfaction to be gained through achieving a worthwhile goal.

Challenge-and-response advocates hold that workers should be given maximum latitude and freedom in performing their tasks. The emphasis should be on results rather than the detailed procedures that were used in accomplishing the results.

An application of the challenge-and-response approach is job enlargement. That is, in job enlargement, workers are given the responsibility for accomplishing as much as possible of the total finished products or service. In some job-enlargement applications, workers are held accountable for material purchase or quality control of their product.

The Directive School

A basic feature of the directive school of thought is that people want and need to be told what to do. Further, management is in a better position to make decisions than workers. Additional emphasis is placed on rights, power, authority, and the organization structure by this group. In a sense the directive school seems to equate power with knowledge; because one has the power, implies the school, he is an expert. The directive school is opposed in philosphy to the participative school.

The Checks-and-balances School

There is a rather prevalent belief that power corrupts, and that those in power will seek to increase their power unless some sort of safeguard is set up. People are not to be trusted; hence, some kind of limitation in the form of checks and balances on their behavior is necessary. Inspectors are required to control quality in industry, three branches of the United States government are necessary to prevent abuses, and unions are necessary to keep management in line; these are some possible examples of the checks-and-balances philosphy in action. The basic belief of the checks-and-balances school is that some form of control is necessary to check up on or even to limit the behavior of people in organizations.

Other Schools

Several other approaches to management are sometimes mentioned. For example, the paternalistic school sees management as being responsible for taking care of workers and even making decisions for them that involve their personal, off-the-job lives. Sophisticated forms of paternalism remain in most large organizations as exemplified by a wide variety of fringe benefits and security measures offered to workers by the organization.

Laissez faire describes still another approach to management. This view holds that managers should exercise as little supervisory control, or restraint, as possible over workers.

The social-systems school views an organization as a complex social system. Roles, cultural interrelationships, and group processes of behavior are seen as important by this school. The field of sociology has contributed much of the research and theory of this school.

Other approaches to management and leadership are described by words such as "democratic," "autocratic," "personal," and "nonpersonal." These approaches to management cover a very wide range of possible views.

Evaluation of the Different Schools

The question of which school of management thought is best is often raised. The answer is simple—no one of the schools is inherently best. But all of the schools of thought have some validity for managers. What is needed is an approach to management that will incorporate the views of every school, where the concepts of each school are valid.

Those who claim that their particular school of management thought is the meaningful view of management are perhaps like the six blind men in an old folk tale from the land of India. The six men were drawn into a fight among themselves when they disagreed upon the description of an elephant. The first blind man, touching only the broad side of the elephant, claimed the elephant was a wall. The second blind man felt the elephant's trunk and asserted that the elephant was like a snake. The third blind man, who felt the elephant's tusk, thought the elephant was a spear. Feeling only a leg of the elephant, the fourth blind man believed the elephant to be a tree. A fifth blind man thought the elephant was a fan, since he felt only the elephant's ear. Finally, the sixth blind man thought surely that the elephant must be a rope, because he felt only the elephant's tail. Happily, the fight was resolved when the Rajah pointed out that each blind man knew only a part of the elephant. In similar fashion, much of the controversy about the relative merits of the different schools of management thought disappears when it is realized that each school represents one view or aspect of the broader, dynamic process of organizations.

THE PROCESS-OF-ORGANIZATIONS APPROACH AND SUMMARY

The point of view taken in this book is that the process of management is a part of the larger concept of the process of organizations. When the broad process-of-organizations view is taken, then the several so-called schools of management are recognized as valid and variable approaches or techniques available to the manager. He is free to select the best approach for himself and his particular organization, depending on the goals of his particular organization, the specific conditions existing, and the particular place and time. One who takes the process-of-organizations view does not consider the several schools of thought as being necessarily contradictory or mutually exclusive. Rather, in the process-of-organizations view the manager recognizes the infinite complexity of people and their organizations, and he realizes that anxiety-producing as well as anxiety-reducing motivations can produce effective organizational performance. Further, the manager who sees organizations as complex, broad processes will realize that organizational performance is determined by many things including the style of management, attitudes, incentives, the organization structure, and control and discipline systems.

Performance is not, as some of the schools of thought seem to indicate, due to any single one or kind of these variables. The total mix of many variables determines the end result of organizational performance. The most effective manager is not one who totally subscribes slavishly to any one of the schools. Rather the effective manager is one who achieves a workable, judicious mixture of all the approaches and techniques of management.

FOR REVIEW AND DISCUSSION

1 Describe the important characteristics of each of the four periods of management thought.

2 Who is recognized as the father of scientific management? What is meant by scientific management? What weakness in scientific management led to the emphasis on human relations?

3 What were the results of the Hawthorne experiments?

4 What is the relationship of morale and productivity?

5 In your own words describe each of the following points on the managerial grid in Figure 24-1 (the number on the horizontal axis is given first: (1,9); (1,1); (5,5); (9,9); and (9,1). Give an example from your own experience of someone you have observed in a managerial position that fits each of these points.

6 Describe the principal characteristics of the following schools of management thought: (*a*) traditional, (*b*) empirical, (*c*) human relations, (*d*) decision theory, (*e*) mathematical, (*f*) formalism, (*g*) spontaneity, (*h*) participative, (*i*) challenge-and-response, (*j*) directive, (*k*) checks-and-balances, and (*l*) the process-of-organizations.

7 From the list given in the previous question select the three schools (first, second, and third choice) that you think contribute most to your understanding of organizations and management. Give the reasons for your choices. (You may also include the schools described under "other schools" in the text, if you wish.)

CASES

A Efferson Associates, industrial efficiency consultants, had been retained to study the work methods of Striker Products Co., a large fabricator of aluminum doors and windows. The consultants planned to do a motion-and-time study of each production job. For their pilot study in the plant the consultants planned to study a punch-press operation.

When the consultants tried to start their pilot study, every man in the plant shut down his machine and walked out. Frank May, the shop steward (union representative), went to the office of Mr. Brown, the production manager, and handed him the following statement:

"We, the production employees of Striker Products, represented by Local 1077, refuse to work in a sweat shop. The present plan of management to make a scientific study of the plant is nothing more than an old-fashioned speedup. We will not be a party to throwing some of our members out of work by permitting other of our members to break their backs trying to reach arbitrary work standards. The proposed motion-and-time study cannot succeed because it would reduce all our members to nothing more than machines. We demand that the program be eliminated before we will resume work."

Mr. Brown was deeply concerned about the effects of the work stoppage; yet he felt that management must retain the right to make decisions.

    1 What action should Mr. Brown take?

    2 What caused the resentment of the workers to the motion-and-time study?

    3 Do you agree that the results of such a study could, in effect, turn the workers into machines?

B   One morning Professor Cox, who taught organizations and management at the university, received a call from Frank Pyle, a former student. Frank had graduated three years earlier, and since that time Professor Cox had heard nothing from him.

"Professor Cox, I've gone up in the world since you last saw me. I've just been promoted to state commercial manager for the telephone company. And I want to tell you that what I learned in your classes is primarily responsible for my promotions.

"The reason I'm calling is that, unlike me, a lot of my managers have not had the benefit of taking any management courses. I want to set up a course to teach them what I know, and I want you to help me organize such a course. It's going to be difficult, however, because my managers range all the way from twenty-seven to fifty-seven years old. And some of them will think that the course is a waste of time. The older men think that the only way to learn is by experience. I want to use your book as a text."

"Sure, Frank, when do you want to get together?"

    1 What school of management thought did the older men belong to?

    2 Do you think Frank's career was helped as much as he claimed by his experiences in management courses? What kinds of things might Frank have learned that turned out so valuable for him?

    3 How does Professor Cox's textbook represent experience?

C   Fred Jones was one of the most popular managers in the Allison Company. Fred had a strictly observed open-door policy for his employees. Any employee could talk to Fred at any length about his problems; Fred often spent several hours each day in helping to solve the personal problems of his subordinates. Fred had never reprimanded or discharged anyone.

Once one of Fred's subordinates was overheard to say: "Fred's the best supervisor there is. I like working for him better than anyone in the world. He really takes an interest in his people." This feeling was shared by all Fred's subordinates.

Recently Gordon King, Fred's supervisor, has been considering removing Fred from his supervisory position. According to Gordon, the production of Fred's department was lower than other comparable departments, costs were excessive, and quality was poor. Gordon was reluctant to discharge Fred because of his popularity.

    1 Was Fred people- or production-oriented? Explain your answer.

    2 What action should Gordon take? What effect will this action have on the organization?

FOR FURTHER STUDY

Additional sources can be found in the sources cited in the chapter.

Books

Claude S. George, Jr.: *The History of Management Thought,* Prentice-Hall, Inc., Englewood Cliffs, N.J., 1968. This book traces management theory from prehistoric times to the present.

Harwood F. Merrill (ed.): *Classics in Management,* American Management Association, New York, 1960. This is a selection of works that have influenced the development of management thought.

L. Urwick: *The Golden Book of Management,* Newman Neame, Ltd., London, 1956. A collection of personal histories and contributions of the pioneers in management.

Articles

J. Boddewyn: "Frederick Winslow Taylor Revisited," *Journal of the Academy of Management,* August 1961. A review and critique of Taylor's contributions.

William C. Frederick: "The Next Development in Management: A General Theory," *Journal of the Academy of Management,* September 1963. At the present, there is not a general theory of management, and therefore no general agreement about what management is. An evolving theory will be composed of five parts: classical management principles, human relations, decision theory, behavioral science, and business responsibility.

Edmund R. Gray and Hyler J. Bracey: "Russell Robb: Management Pioneer," *S.A.M. Advanced Management Journal,* April 1970. Robb contributed significantly to management thought, but his contributions have not been widely appreciated.

Harold Koontz: "The Management Theory Jungle," *Academy of Management Journal,* December 1961. There are several schools of management thought (or approaches to the study of management).

B. A. Leerburger, Jr.: "Scientific Management: Story of a Revolution," *Factory,* October 1960. A summary of the life and work of Frederick W. Taylor.

John F. Mee: "Pioneers of Management," *Advanced Management-Office Executive,* October 1962. "The history of management thought indicates that all progress in management has been related to the intellectual discoveries of basic concepts and their conceptual relationships."

William G. Scott: "Organization Theory: An Overview and an Appraisal," *Journal of the Academy of Management,* April 1961. This is a classic paper defining the field of organization theory and explaining its relationship to other approaches to the study of organizations and management.

George Strauss: "Human Relations—1968 Style," *Industrial Relations,* May 1968. A critical review of recent contributions to human relations theory.

25
Management Concepts

. . . concepts [of management] have been widely accepted and applied—their validity rests in verifiable current management practice.
ELMORE PETERSEN, E. GROSVENOR PLOWMAN, AND JOSEPH M. TRICKETT

To perform the functions of management effectively a manager needs to have a tool kit of organizational concepts and principles for his use. Fortunately, a valuable body of concepts is at hand, ready to assist a manager. This chapter summarizes the most valuable and useful concepts available to a manager. These concepts are part of the language of management. Knowledge of the concepts gives managers more efficient means of communicating with other managers or organizational members. In addition, these concepts provide valuable insights into "how to get things done" in organizations.

ROLE OF MANAGEMENT

A large portion of the study of management is devoted to learning the manager's role. In brief, a *role* may be defined as an expected behavior pattern.

In our culture there is general agreement on the role of a fireman, a salesman, a banker, or a mother. Similarly, there is general agreement on the role that a manager is expected to perform in an organization, which includes such functions as creating, planning, organizing, motivating, communicating, and controlling. Other work or ways of behaving that are often seen as parts of the manager's role include setting an example for others to follow, representing the organization to outsiders (by making speeches, for example), being fair when arbitrating differences among employees, and having a clear understanding of the objectives of the organization.

The role of a typical manager can be compared in many respects to that of the conductor of an orchestra. (Of course, the conductor is a manager also—of the orchestra.)

1 The conductor plays no music, but is usually the most important member of an orchestra. In a similar vein, a manager in many cases will not directly perform the output work of the organization. Nevertheless, by effectively creating, planning, organizing, motivating, communicating, and controlling the work of others, the manager can in large part determine the effectiveness of the organization.

2 Both the conductor and the manager can learn a great deal through study and practice in their respective fields.

3 It is not required that the conductor be an expert performing musician. Likewise, a manager can perform his organizational tasks effectively without necessarily being expert in the technical work of the organization.

Thus we see that some rather clear expectations of the role of a manager have developed. Merely knowing that there is such a concept as the role of a manager will increase the manager's awareness of his job. Effectively implementing the elements of his role will make him still more proficient as a manager.

LINE AND STAFF

Perhaps the single most widely used concept of management is the concept of line and staff. Moreover, misunderstanding about line and staff is one of the major sources of friction in organizations. As Koontz and O'Donnell say: "there is probably no [other] area of management which causes more difficulties, more friction, and more loss of time and effectiveness."[1] In fact, problems in line and staff relationships have been so important that serious suggestions have been made that the entire concept of line and staff be discarded.[2] Those who would discard line and staff suggest that an organization could better be based on the tasks of functional responsibilities of members. Still, regardless of the problems, line and staff remains a popular managerial and organizational concept, and it is important that the student understand fundamental features of line and staff.

Much of the confusion regarding line and staff springs from conflicting definitions

[1]Harold Koontz and Cyril O'Donnell, *Principles of Management*, 4th ed., McGraw-Hill Book Company, New York, 1968, p. 291.

[2]See, for example, G. G. Fisch, "Line-Staff Is Obsolete," *Harvard Business Review*, September–October 1961, pp. 67–79.

of them. One definition is related to the functions one performs in the organization, while a second, completely different definition has to do with organizational authority relationships. Failure to differentiate clearly between these two definitions is responsible for many of the problems in the areas of line and staff.[3] We will now look at both the functions and authority-relationships viewpoints of line and staff.

Line and Staff as Functions

One of the viewpoints of line and staff is that they denote different functions within the enterprise: Line officials are those who have direct responsibility for accomplishing the objectives of the enterprise. To determine whether particular positions are line or staff from this viewpoint, one should look at the organization as a whole, or as an outsider sees it. Officials in the direct chain of command over workers who directly accomplish the objectives of the enterprise are regarded as *line*. Every other official is *staff*. For example, if we assume that the objectives of the organization shown in Figure 25-1 are "to produce and sell goods," then the president, production manager, and sales manager are line officials. The controller, research and development manager, and legal counsel are staff officials. Such is the meaning of line and staff when they are viewed as delineating functions.

Line and Staff as Authority Relationships

The other approach to line and staff is that they refer to authority relationships. In this approach, line officials are viewed as those having relatively unlimited authority over those to whom directions are given. Staff persons have authority which is restricted to their functional area. The key to determining whether one is line or staff from his authority is to take the viewpoint of one receiving directions. From this viewpoint, if the direction given springs from relatively unrestricted authority, the director is line. If his authority is restricted to a specific functional area, he is staff. For example, again referring to Figure 25-1, the subordinates of the controller would view him as a line official. The production manager who receives instructions from the controller relative to accounting practices views the controller as functional staff.

Other Problems in Line and Staff

An unfortunate result of the line-and-staff concept is that it appears to set up status problems in organizations. Line members are viewed as important, first-class members because they directly accomplish the objectives of the enterprise. On the other hand, staff members are often seen as being subsidiary, "overhead," second-class members of the organization. And second-class members always want to become first-class members.

---

[3]See Herbert G. Hicks, "The Meaning of Line and Staff," *The Southwestern Social Science Quarterly*, June 1962, pp. 19–21. The present section is based largely on this article by permission.

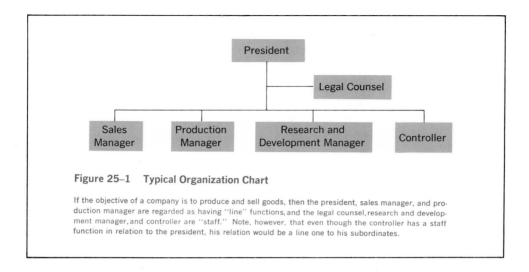

Figure 25-1   Typical Organization Chart

If the objective of a company is to produce and sell goods, then the president, sales manager, and production manager are regarded as having "line" functions, and the legal counsel, research and development manager, and controller are "staff." Note, however, that even though the controller has a staff
function in relation to the president, his relation would be a line one to his subordinates.

Staff members also object, often vigorously, to the implication that they are not as important members of the organization as are the line officials. In reality, one's worth to
an organization is certainly not determined by whether he is line or staff. Rather, his
worth is measured in terms of his net contribution to the organization. And a basic cause
of the friction is that the staff's contribution is often indirect and difficult, if not impossible, to measure. On the other hand, line's contribution is direct and more easily measured. Status problems between line and staff represent a serious disadvantage of the
line-and-staff concept.

Types of Staff

There are several different types of staff members, depending upon their particular position or function in organizations. The types of staff include personal, specialized, and
general.

Personal staff   A personal staff member assists a manager in managing his organization through advice, assistance, or service. Some titles used to define personal staff positions include staff assistant, assistant (manager), executive assistant, administrative
assistant, and assistant to (manager).

Specialized staff   Expert assistance in the staff member's area of specialization is
provided to a manager by specialized staff. Often a member of the specialized staff
knows more about his area than anyone else in the organization.

General staff   Top-management levels of organization often include general staff
members. Usually a member of a general staff is responsible for accomplishing a function

of the organization. The Army, for instance, has employed the general-staff concept by having general officers in charge of the separate functions of supply, personnel, intelligence, and operations.

Line and Staff in Perspective

There is significant confusion in many organizations about the meaning of line and staff. Moreover, the use of line-and-staff concepts seems to create problems of status and conflicts in the organization. Nevertheless, line-and-staff concepts are an important part of the vocabulary of management. When used effectively they can assist in structuring the tasks and relationships of an organization.

CENTRALIZATION AND DECENTRALIZATION

Centralization and *decentralization* refer to the degree of delegation of duties, power, and authority to lower levels of an organization. Centralization or decentralization may also be thought of as describing the effective level of decision making for the particular subject area under consideration. The two terms can be thought of as describing positions toward the ends of a spectrum defining the degree to which duties, power, and authority are delegated to lower organizational levels, as shown in Figure 25-2. A particular organization may fall at any point on the spectrum. Organizations that to a high degree delegate duties, power, and authority to lower levels would be placed toward the extreme left of the spectrum. Organizations where top management retains most power, duties, and authority would be placed toward the extreme right of the spectrum. Most organizations would be placed somewhere between these two extreme positions. Probably no organization is completely centralized or decentralized. Complete centralization would mean that subordinates have no duties, power, or authority; obviously such an organization could not exist because as an organization it could accomplish nothing. Only individual, disorganized behavior would be obtained. Complete de-

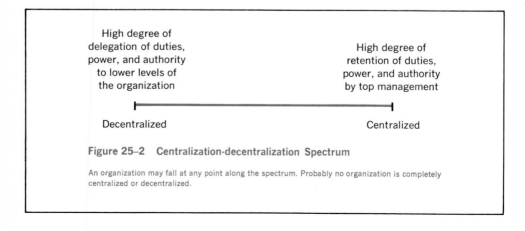

High degree of
delegation of duties,
power, and authority
to lower levels of
the organization

High degree of
retention of duties,
power, and authority
by top management

Decentralized

Centralized

Figure 25–2   Centralization-decentralization Spectrum

An organization may fall at any point along the spectrum. Probably no organization is completely centralized or decentralized.

centralization is also untenable since it would mean a complete lack of coordinated, organized activity. So, in centralization or decentralization we must talk about more or less, rather than absolutes.

More decentralization is desirable when the organization wishes to gain the beneficial effects of improved member participation through greater involvement in decisions and the implementation of projects. Decentralization also has the advantage of providing a less complex and less costly organizational control system.

More centralization is desirable when top management wishes to exercise more direct control over organizational activities. Centralization also helps to provide greater uniformity of actions or integration of efforts in the organization.

Statements of organizational policies issued by top management are desirable because they help to achieve some benefits of both centralization and decentralization. A policy statement permits top management some degree of broad administrative control while permitting lower levels to make decisions within the broad framework of the policy.

One method for implementing decentralization in a large organization is to establish autonomous divisions within the larger organization. Such autonomous organizational units are often run very much as if they were separate, independent organizations. Dividing a large organization into smaller, relatively independent units is called "federal decentralization." Federal decentralization usually implies that the decentralized unit will have a complete staff for research and development, accounting, or other necessary functions. Federally decentralized units are often set up in business organizations as profit centers. That is, in federal decentralization, the principal interest of the larger organization is whether or not the subunit contributes a profit. The interest of the larger unit is not primarily in the detailed operations of the subunit.

Historically, as organizations became larger and more complex, there was often a tendency toward greater decentralization. However, in recent years this trend may have been slowed and perhaps reversed. Spectacular advances have been made in electronic data processing and other information systems, permitting better and larger quantities of more timely information needed for effective decisions to be placed in the hands of top executives. In fact many organizations are able, with the assistance of modern information technologies, to operate with fewer middle managers. Previously, middle managers often served information-collecting and routine decision-making functions. These tasks are now often accomplished more effectively with automatic equipment.

The growth and power of labor unions have also contributed to greater centralization in large business organizations. With a strong union present, labor bargaining and industrial relations must be handled centrally by the firm to ensure uniformity throughout the organization. By bargaining centrally a firm is also able to present a more powerful face in the bargaining process than would be the case if each subunit of the firm bargained alone with a powerful union.

It appears likely that the future will see a continued trend toward more centralization in large organizations. Further improvements in automatic data processing and transmittal are likely. Furthermore, progressive automation of manufacturing processes will also probably push decision making further up the organizational ladder. Automation, by reducing the number of people required to produce a given product, reduces the complexity of the organization, thereby permitting decisions to be made at higher levels.

Neither centralization nor decentralization is necessarily a desirable organization goal. What is probably best is a judicious mixture of both that will best accomplish the organization's objectives.

COMMITTEES

A highly popular and prevalent organizational form is the committee.

A committee is a group of people who meet by plan to discuss or make a decision for a particular subject.

Because a committee meets by plan, we do not include groups which occur spontaneously or informally in the definition of a committee.

Like many other managerial concepts, committees can best be studied in terms of their advantages and disadvantages. Although such statements are common, one who is for or against committees really displays a lack of understanding of their nature. A manager taking such a short-sighted view will probably not make the most effective use of the committee in helping to attain organizational goals. In a particular case the relative advantages and disadvantages of committees must be weighed to determine whether or not the use of a committee will assist in achieving desired organizational performance and, if so, how a committee can be used to best advantage.

Advantages of Committees

Committees have many potential advantages to the organization that employs them. Some of the more common and important advantages of committees are:

1 *Creating.* Through brainstorming and other group-creativity activities, committees can produce creative ideas valuable to practically every organizational function.

2 *Communicating.* A committee can be an excellent means of transmitting information and ideas to interested organizational members.

3 *Motivating.* By participating in discussions or decisions in a committee, a member will likely be more highly motivated to accept a situation or implement a decision than he would be if he did not involve himself in the subject matter through participation in committee deliberations.

4 *Democratizing.* Where desired, a committee can be used to reduce the "tyranny of an executive" and to permit greater member participation in decision making. The United States Congress is a committee that attempts to accomplish such a purpose. A committee can thus serve as a balance to the formal, executive-authority structure of the organization.

5 *Consolidating power and authority.* Often individual members do not have sufficient power and authority to make or implement a particular decision. A committee can then be an excellent means of collecting and combining the authority and power of several individual members. The combined or consolidated power and authority of the whole committee may thus be sufficient to make or implement a desired decision. Suppose a problem in a manufacturing firm involved both sales and production functions. Neither the sales manager nor the production manager could alone make the necessary decision, but a good solution might be made at a committee meeting attended by these two officers. Additional persons who give effective information and counsel might also be included in the committee membership. In combining the efforts of several responsible officials, a committee is often known as a "plural executive."

6 *Combining abilities.* Committees often serve a valuable function by providing a means whereby the knowledge and abilities of several persons can be brought to bear on a problem. "Several heads may be better than one." A committee will often make decisions of better quality than an individual might make.

7 *Avoiding action.* Where an executive wishes to avoid action on a specific problem he may assign it to a committee. With adroit leadership the committee might quite easily get bogged down in interminable debate and indecision. The chairman might also delay action by not scheduling meetings, and by injecting "red-herring" issues into the discussion.

8 *Blurring responsibility.* In some circumstances it is desirable that a committee take responsibility for actions for which individuals do not wish to be responsible. In many law trials, for example, a jury renders a verdict because it is believed that the decision is too important to be entrusted to an individual. Another example of the use of blurred responsibility may be found in universities where committees invariably judge whether or not a graduate student will receive a degree. Most persons feel that the responsibility for overseeing a graduate student's program is far too great for an individual faculty member. So a committee, a formless creation, shoulders the blame in case the student's program is terminated.

9 *Coordinating.* A committee can perform as an excellent coordinating device. It can bring together for agreement on a course of action all parties who will be involved in accomplishing an activity.

10 *Advising.* A manager may wish advice and counsel before making a decision. For this purpose he may convene a committee to provide needed advice and counsel.

11 *Representing.* A committee can provide a forum for all sides of a question to be given a hearing before a decision is made. Also, the committee may often be a meeting ground where differences are resolved and compromises are reached.

Disadvantages of Committees

A number of disadvantages are also inherent in committee organization and operation. Some of the more significant disadvantages are:

1 *Cost.* Because a committee consumes the time of several persons the cost of the members' time can quickly mount up. For example, a one-hour meeting of six $25,000-per-year managers will cost approximately $100 for only the time of the members during the meeting. Time and expenses of travel, preparation, and other matters can quickly run the cost of such a meeting much higher.

2 *Least denominator.* It often happens that a committee decision is "watered down," and is not the best from anyone's viewpoint. Possibly nobody is happy with a committee decision. At least the decision maker would presumably be happy with a decision made by himself.

3 *Indecision.* Because of conflicting viewpoints of members or poor leadership a committee is sometimes unable to reach a needed decision.

4 *Split accountability.* It often is very difficult to enforce effective accountability against a committee. Members may hide behind the façade of the committee and may avoid personal responsibility by claiming: "It was not my decision; the decision was made by a committee."

5 *Tyranny of minority.* Since committees usually seek a consensus or unanimous agreement, it is easily possible for a minority of the committee to thwart committee action by refusing to accept the majority viewpoint.

6 *Self-perpetuation.* Committees are usually formed for a specific purpose. It often happens, however, that a committee continues to meet long after it has ceased to serve a useful purpose. The tendency to perpetuate themselves is particularly noticeable in committees which have assembled their own staffs of secretaries, research assistants, or attorneys.

By using committees where they are helpful and by careful concern for their disadvantages, a manager can often use committees effectively to assist in accomplishing organizational objectives. "The problems with committees are not so much how to eliminate them as it is how to use them properly."[4] Maximum utilization of committees requires an intimate knowledge of the complexities of committees plus strong and adroit leadership.

SPAN OF MANAGEMENT

There is a limit to the number of persons and activities that a manager can effectively manage. This limitation is expressed by the span-of-management concept. A manager's

[4]*The Wisconsin Productivity Letter*, School of Commerce, Madison, Wis., January 1965, p. 2.

span of management is a statement of the limitation of the number of people or activities that he can properly manage.

A manager's ability to manage a large number of subordinates or activities is limited by his time, knowledge, energy, personality, interests, and other abilities. In addition, as organizations grow, they rapidly become more complex. The number and complexity of organizational relationships increase much faster than the overall rate of growth.

Graicunas' Theory of Organizational Relationships

A French writer, V. A. Graicunas, demonstrated that the number of possible organizational relationships increases geometrically as the number of members increases linearly. Graicunas developed a mathematical formula for determining the number of possible relationships in an organization under certain assumptions.[5] Graicunas, for example, considered that a supervisor, A, would be concerned with certain relationships for two subordinates, B and C. The types of relationships Graicunas included in his formulation were:

1 A's own relationship with B.
2 A's own relationship with C.
3 A's relationship in supervising the group BC, with B leader.
4 A's relationship in supervising the group BC, with C leader.
5 A's relationship in supervising B's relationship to C.
6 A's relationship in supervising C's relationship to B.

Some critics have suggested that Graicunas was "splitting hairs" in describing the possible number of relationships. Perhaps so, but it should be noted that there are several other possible types of relationships which Graicunas did not include—such as the relationship of B and C with outside persons. In any event, if Graicunas' choice of relationships is accepted we see that an increase in the number of subordinates causes a truly amazing increase in the possible relationships. Figure 25-3 gives the number of possible relationships for selected numbers of subordinates according to Graicunas' formula. Thus, we see an almost explosive growth in the number of possible relationships with an increase in the number of subordinates.

There are three major limitations to Graicunas' approach. First, Graicunas' formula gives the number of *possible* relationships, not the number that actually exist. Second, Graicunas assumed that all relationships occur with equal *frequency*. Third, Graicunas assumed that every relationship is equal in *intensity*. Obviously, real-life organizational relationships will vary considerably from these assumptions. In spite of these substantial

---

[5]V. A. Graicunas, "Relationship in Organization," *Papers on the Science of Administration*, Institute of Public Administration, New York, 1937, pp. 181–187. Graicunas' formula is:

$$N = n\left(\frac{2^n}{2} + n - 1\right)$$

where N is the total number of relationships and n is the number of subordinates.

	Number of subordinates	Number of relationships
	n	N
	1	1
	2	6
Figure 25–3 Total Number of	3	18
Possible Rela-	4	44
tionships Accord-	5	100
ing to Graicunas'	6	222
Formula	7	490
	8	1,080
If we accept Graicunas' choice of rela-	9	2,376
tionships, we find that an increase in the	10	5,210
number of subordinates causes an amaz-	11	11,374
ingly great increase in possible relation-	12	24,708
ships.		

limitations, Graicunas' theory does have value in demonstrating the rapidly increasing complexity which occurs with organizational growth.

The Correct Span of Management

Recognition of the personal limitations of managers and the complexity of larger organizations has raised questions about exactly how many subordinates a supervisor ought to have. The Bible gives us an early example of one solution to a particular problem. Jethro, who thought that Moses ought not try to deal directly with all his people in all matters, said to Moses:

> The thing that thou doest is not good. Thou wilt surely wear away, both thou, and this people that is with thee; for this thing is too heavy for thee; thou art not able to perform it alone. . . . thou shalt provide . . . rulers of hundreds, rulers of fifties, and rulers of tens. And let them judge the people at all seasons; and it shall be, that every great matter they shall bring unto thee, but every small matter they shall judge; so shall it be easier for thyself, and they shall bear the burden with thee.[6]

The above passage implies that Jethro suggested that third-line supervisors have two subordinates, second-line have five, and first-line have ten.

Some writers from the traditional school of management have suggested that the best number of subordinates for a manager to have ought to be from three to seven. Some authorities have even been more specific in their recommendations. For example, according to one military general: "The ideal number of subordinates for all superiors appears to be four."[7]

[6]Exodus 18:17–22.
[7]Gen. Sir Ian Hamilton, *The Soul and Body of an Army,* Edward Arnold Ltd., London, 1921, p. 229.

At the opposite extreme, some organizations have employed extremely large spans of management. The Roman Catholic Church has about 750 bishops plus a large number of other church officials directly responsible to the Pope. An appliance-repair department of a large department store has had 125 service men reporting to one supervisor. Approximately 200 research personnel have answered to a single manager in the General Electric Company. Sears, Roebuck and Company has been noted for its wide management spans. A teacher often has 30 students in his class. Such examples are fairly numerous.

Advantages and disadvantages of narrow spans of management   Some advantages of a narrow span of management (few subordinates) are:

1 It offers tight control and close supervision.

2 The manager has time to think of future matters since he is not burdened with an excessive number of present problems.

3 Managers can better manage fewer and more specialized people and activities. Thus, managers of lower quality can perform effectively.

Disadvantages of a narrow span of management include:

1 The additional costs of more managers and their staffs.

2 The added complexity of communication and coordination problems in the organization when a large number of managers are involved.

Advantages and disadvantages of wide spans of management   A wide span of management has certain advantages:

1 Because the manager is literally unable to exercise close supervision, subordinates are forced to make more decisions on their own. Some authorities think that such a policy leads to faster and greater maturity of subordinates. The emphasis with a wide span must be on the results accomplished, not how well the boss's orders are followed.

2 There are reduced costs for fewer managers and their staffs.

3 There are reduced problems of communication and coordination in the organization.

A wide span of management also has certain disadvantages:

1 The manager is unable to exercise direct control and supervision. (As we have seen, this may actually be an advantage from the viewpoint of developing personnel, discussed above.)

2 In general, higher-quality and more costly people are needed in the organization because they must have larger jobs and act more independently.

So the question of how many subordinates a manager ought to have obviously has no universal, simple answer. The best solution in a particular case will be an optimum balance of the advantages and disadvantages for the particular situation. The best span of management will vary from one subordinate to several hundred subordinates, depending upon the particular circumstances.

MANAGEMENT AS A PROFESSION

The question often has been raised whether management is or is not a profession. To answer this question it is necessary to have a clear understanding of the essential elements of a profession. A profession traditionally has had the following five characteristics:

1 A body of knowledge.

2 Formal teaching of that knowledge.

3 An association of members that speaks for the profession on professional matters. (Membership in this association is often prerequisite to being a member of the profession.)

4 Ethical standards of conduct enforced by the profession itself.

5 Remuneration highly influenced by concepts of service and "fair play."

Law and medicine immediately come to mind as professions, because they meet the conditions listed above.

There is a large and fairly specific body of knowledge about organizations and management. Much information and many techniques, principles, and skills about the managerial job can be taught. Further, the process of management can be thought of as a distinct, separate, identifiable activity involving such functions as creating, planning, organizing, motivating, communicating, and controlling. As such, the managerial job is different from any other type of work. Moreover, the work of the manager is similar no matter what his organization or his position in his organization. With all these considerations it is apparent that management satisfies the first criterion for being a profession, because it does indeed have an underlying body of knowledge.

The field of management may be considered a profession from the viewpoint of the second criterion because there is certainly a vigorous program of formal education for management in existence. Specialized undergraduate- and graduate-degree programs are offered in almost all major universities. Business education is accepted by the society because holders of both undergraduate and graduate degrees in business administration are among the top income earners of all college graduates.[8] A wide variety of supervisory training, specialized short courses, and executive-development programs are enthusiastically attended and received throughout the country. Some sort of advanced training in management is considered highly desirable, if not essential, for promotion to responsible managerial positions in many firms. So, without doubt, there is widespread formal teaching of the subject matter of the field of management.

---

[8]See, for example, Herbert G. Hicks, "Are Undergraduate Business Administration Schools Doing Their Job?" *Collegiate News and Views*, December 1964. This article showed that holders of a bachelor's degree in business administration earn more in their careers than practically any other class of undergraduate-degree holders.

There are many professional organizations in the field of management. These include the American Management Association, the Society for the Advancement of Management, the Academy of Management, and perhaps a hundred others. However, there is no organization which speaks authoritatively for the entire field nor is membership in any organization required to practice management. Further, there are no widely accepted or enforced standards of management, other than legal requirements enforced by the governmental agencies. No significant changes are foreseen in this area. Many authorities claim that none are desired since enforced membership and standards would unreasonably restrict freedom to practice management in a society emphasizing economic competition and individual freedom. Management definitely does not satisfy the third and fourth characteristics of a profession since it is not organized professionally into associations that enforce membership and performance standards.

Lastly, the pay of managers is generally based on their contributions to their organizations rather than on a fee schedule. Further, managers are certainly responsible to stockholders, customers, the general public, and employees for the effective accomplishment of the organization's objectives, considering the rights of all affected persons. This stewardship responsibility is seen clearly in large corporations with widespread stock ownership. In these corporations there is a separation of ownership and management, and the management usually has effective power in the organization. Stockholders in large corporations are able usually to remove the management from office only when the management is grossly unsatisfactory. Even then a major effort is required to assemble enough votes from stockholders to take action against an incumbent management. In any event the scheme of pay and the relationships of the manager to his work are generally different from that observed in professions such as medicine and law.

Thus management does have some of the characteristics of a profession since it has a body of knowledge which is formally taught. However, a professional organization to enforce standards and membership is not present in the field of management. Finally, the method of payment for managerial services varies widely, but it does not approximate the plan of recognized professions. Although management does in some respects qualify as a profession, it does not have certain features which generally characterize recognized professions.

SUMMARY

A large body of managerial concepts is available to assist managers in performing their functions. These concepts include the designation of organizational units as line and staff. Line units are those that directly accomplish the objectives of the enterprise or that have general authority. All others are staff units.

Management is highly centralized when top managers delegate little power and authority. On the other hand, decentralized management delegates power and authority in large measure to subordinates.

Committees are found in almost all complex organizations. Committees are neither all good nor all bad, but they do have advantages and disadvantages. Each situation must be individually evaluated to determine if a committee can be used effectively.

A manager has a limit to the number of subordinates he can effectively manage. This limit is not rigid, however; it will depend upon the manager's ability, the particular employees he supervises, and the type of work.

The field of management has some characteristics that are not usually associated with a profession. However, the field also has some qualities that are clearly professional. The development and use of management concepts is a good example of the professional nature of the field.

FOR REVIEW AND DISCUSSION

1 What is a role? What are some of the features of a manager's role in an organization?

2 Define line and staff both as functions and as authority relationships. Why has the author suggested that consideration be given to discarding these concepts?

3 Define personal, specialized, and general staff. Illustrate each with an example.

4 Define centralization and decentralization. Why could neither exist in pure form? What is federal decentralization? Give an example not in the text of an organization that illustrates federal decentralization?

5 What is a committee? Explain in your own words the advantages and disadvantages of committees. Try to include some advantages and disadvantages in addition to those given in the text. Give an example, either real-life or hypothetical, not in the text to illustrate each advantage and disadvantage.

6 What is the span of management? What is the correct span of management? Explain the advantages and disadvantages of narrow and wide spans of management.

7 Explain and evaluate Graicunas' theory of organizational relationships.

8 In what ways is management a profession? In what ways is it not?

CASES

A   Ajax Manufacturing Corporation had a complex line-and-staff organization. Recently, Ned Forrester, who had spent his entire career in the production department, was elected president of the company. Shortly after assuming the presidency, Mr. Forrester wrote the following memorandum.

November 12

From: N. J. Forrester, President
To: All Vice-presidents
Re: Line and Staff Relationships

Since I have been in this company there has always been friction between line and staff. I want this to stop.

The purpose of our staff people is to advise and assist our line managers. If that advice is worth anything, our line managers ought to be willing to pay for it.

I propose that our staff departments be set up on a consulting basis. They are to bill the line departments for any work done at a mutually agreed-upon price. The entire budget of the staff departments will consist of money earned in this fashion. No line manager will be charged for any staff services he does not desire. As usual, line departments will be evaluated upon their profitability, after deduction of funds paid to staff departments.

I shall appreciate your prompt cooperation in implementing this policy.

N. J. F.

The memo from President Forrester represented a radical change because the budgets of staff departments had previously been determined each year by the president. Visibly upset by the president's memo, Jack Worthy, administrative vice-president, replied as follows:

November 19

From: J. P. Worthy, Administrative Vice-president
To: N. J. Forrester, President
Re: Line and Staff Relationships

Your proposal of November 12 would effectively wreck the accounting, production-control, industrial relations, public relations, and other staff departments for which I am responsible.

We do give advice to line functions, but we are also responsible for checking on, and in some ways supervising, the line. Most line managers would be glad to have us out of their hair; they certainly would not "hire" us, as suggested in your memo. I urge that you immediately withdraw your recommendation to put us on consulting basis.

J. P. W.

1 Should Mr. Forrester proceed with his "internal-consultant plan" for his staff departments? What are the advantages and disadvantages of the proposal?

2 Do you agree with Mr. Worthy that the proposal would wreck the staff departments? Explain your answer.

3 What effect do you think Mr. Forrester's memo will have on the organization, even if he withdraws the proposal? Is it likely to reduce the friction between line and staff that has always existed in the company?

B Hill, Inc., had for many years had an employee's representative committee. The committee consisted of four men elected by the workers of the plant plus Mr. Bales, the plant manager. A meeting of the committee was held the first Monday of each month in the office of Mr. Bales.

During the first several years of its existence the meetings of the employee's representative committee had often been stormy. Company-labor relations in those years were strained; an annual strike seemed to be the only way of clearing the air between the two sides.

Later, when the workers found that Mr. Bales was seriously interested in working with the committee, they began to submit their proposals and grievances to him through the committee. During this period the agenda of the committee was often long, and meetings frequently ran into the night. However, over the years, relations between the workers and the company gradually improved. The committee was generally credited with bringing about most of the improvements.

Recently, Mr. Bales has seriously considered disbanding the committee. "There just aren't any problems like there used to be," he said. "Why, last Monday we all sat around and mostly chewed the fat for two hours. It was a lot of fun, but I wonder if we should spend company time discussing whether or not we should buy tables for the men to play cards on at lunch. Everybody seemed satisfied when I told them no, but that I had no objection to the men buying their own tables. On the other hand, maybe the committee is still a good thing. Just knowing it's there may make it worthwhile."

1 Do you think Mr. Bales should disband the employee's representative committee? Explain your answer.

2 How did the committee serve the company and workers in its early years? How does it presently serve them? What are its present disadvantages?

C   Royce, Peterson & Company was one of the country's leading retail firms. The company had over 300 department stores in the country's largest cities, and it enjoyed a vigorous mail-order business.

Employee relations were excellent, and the company had for many years paid its employees extremely well. It was not unusual for a good salesman to retire with over $50,000 worth of stock in the company, acquired through a complex profit-sharing plan. In addition, whenever possible, employees were paid in large part through commissions on sales. This particularly applied to salesmen, department managers, store managers, and executive officers.

The average number of employees supervised by each manager was over twenty. Franklin Morse, a store manager, had this to say: "The company policy has always been to permit, or even make, a man stand on his own two feet. With so many people to look out for, a manager can't spend time sticking his nose into his subordinates' business. Of course, it's kind of dog-eat-dog in this outfit. If you can't make the grade you've had it, because your manager's pay depends on how well you do."

1 Does Royce, Peterson & Company have wide or narrow spans of management? What are the advantages and disadvantages of its approach? How do other organizational practices of the company relate to its span of management policy?

2 A recent military manual on organizations contained the statement that: "the correct number of subordinates ranges between three and seven." What would be the effects in Royce, Peterson & Company if it adopted the advice of the military manual?

FOR FURTHER STUDY

Additional sources can be found in the sources cited in the chapter.

Articles

Louis A. Allen: "Making Better Use of Committees," *Management Record,* December 1965, pp. 466–469, 493. Allen explains what committees are and gives the advantages and disadvantages.

Louis A. Allen: "The Line-Staff Relationship," *Management Record,* September 1955. A clear, simple explanation of line and staff organization.

Kenneth R. Andrews: "Toward Professionalism in Business Management," *Harvard Business Review,* March–April 1969. This article describes ways business is becoming more professional and how it can serve society better.

John K. Baker and Robert H. Schaffer: "Making Staff Consulting More Effective," *Harvard Business Review,* January–February 1969. Several ideas for making more effective use of staff experts are presented.

Melville Dalton: "Conflicts between Line and Staff Officers," *American Sociological Review,* June 1950. An analysis of the causes of conflict between line and staff.

G. G. Fisch: "Line-Staff Is Obsolete," *Harvard Business Review,* September–October 1961. "Line-staff is obsolete . . . and should be replaced by the functional-teamwork concept."

Gary R. Gemmill: "How Managers Use Staff Advice," *Personnel,* September–October 1968. If line and staff would support each other line-staff cooperation would become as common a term as line-staff conflict.

"Management: Its Meaning and Implications," *New York Times,* Sept. 15, 1963, sec. 11, pp. 7–8. This article clearly defines the role and professional aspects of management.

Gerry E. Morse: "Pendulum of Management Control," *Harvard Business Review,* May–June 1965. A trend is developing toward centralization of management.

Robert E. Thompson: "Span of Control: Conceptions and Misconceptions," *Business Horizons,* Summer 1964. "In span of control considerations, we are concerned essentially with a manager's work load. Span of control should therefore embrace the number of individuals who report directly to the manager and who require significant planning and control efforts on his part."

26
Selected Principles of Management

Principles are . . . fundamental truths applicable to a given set of circumstances and having value in predicting results.
HAROLD KOONTZ AND CYRIL O'DONNELL

A number of principles of management have been developed to aid managers in performing their functions. The purpose of this chapter is to present a short summary of the most useful and widely known principles of management. These principles of management have been developed primarily by members of the traditional school of organizational and management thought.

NATURE OF MANAGEMENT PRINCIPLES

Principles of management are guides for managerial action.

A management principle is a statement of a general truth about organizations or management. Principles of management may be thought of as the laws or fundamental truths of organizations and management. As such, they are more specific than management concepts, which are designed primarily to provide better definitions and understanding of organizational and management process. Concepts do not usually suggest particular courses of action, since the proper action depends upon pertinent circumstances. Principles, on the other hand, usually *prescribe* a particular course of managerial action.

Inherent in a principle of management is the implication that if the principle is followed, improved organizational performance likely will result. Similarly, a management principle implies that if the principle is not followed organizational performance probably will suffer.

Although management principles are generally valid we must recognize that they sometimes fail to indicate the best course of managerial action. Principles of management, because they have to do with human behavior, are not so exact or infallible as principles of the physical sciences.

The list of principles in this chapter is not exhaustive. Moreover, many so-called principles of management have been criticized as being little more than casual observations about organizations and management. In addition, some writers have complained that most principles of management have serious defects because of conflicts, inconsistencies, and lack of empirical verification.[1] Nevertheless, principles of management are important features of management thought.

VALIDITY OF MANAGEMENT PRINCIPLES

Proper use of management principles probably will improve organizational performance. In other words, a manager who correctly employs available principles has a relatively high likelihood of realizing effective or improved organizational performance. On the other hand, the manager who fails to take advantage of accumulated knowledge about organizations and management, as expressed in statements of principles, will be at a disadvantage when compared with a manager who is expert in applying management principles. The uninformed manager, if he is successful, must overcome his deficiencies through excellence in other areas.

Management principles should be viewed as being valid for *most* organizations under *most* circumstances. Principles in the field of management organizations are not comparable to principles in fields such as the physical sciences. In the physical sciences, for all practical purposes, principles are almost always valid. But even in the physical sciences, principles are often not universally meaningful. For example, it was thought for many years that the laws of motion developed by Sir Isaac Newton were "the last word." However, Einstein later showed that Newton's laws were not valid for describing some important motions of bodies moving through space.

But it is not necessary that a principle be valid for every conceivable circumstance, every time. It is quite enough that a principle be valid *most* of the time, and for *most* circumstances. Because the principles described in the chapter satisfy the condition of

---

[1]For example, Herbert A. Simon, *Administrative Behavior*, 2d ed., The Macmillan Company, New York, 1957.

being valid most of the time they are valuable aids for managerial use. It remains the manager's job to use his judgment in determining *when* to apply a certain principle. And the odds are in his favor when he includes pertinent principles of organizations in his managerial tool kit.

FAYOL'S GENERAL PRINCIPLES OF MANAGEMENT

The first principles of management were offered by Henri Fayol, a French industrialist, in 1916. Unfortunately, no English translation of Fayol's work was available in the United States until 1937,[2] and it was 1949 before Fayol's works appeared in book form in English and received wide circulation in the United States.[3] Thus, Fayol's pioneering work was not available to authors in the United States for many years. And authors in the United States during the period 1920–1950 did the fundamental work in developing principles of management.

Pointing out that the list was not exhaustive, Fayol offered fourteen principles of management which he had found useful in his career as an executive, which included the position of managing director for many years of a large mining and steel complex. Here is a summary of each of Fayol's principles:

1 *Division of work.* Economists call this principle "specialization." Division of work promotes efficiency because it permits an organizational member to work in a limited area, reducing the scope of the job. Division of work permits all types of work to be performed more effectively with greater knowledge and skill because the tasks are more familiar.

2 *Authority and responsibility.* Authority and responsibility go together. The right and power to give orders is balanced by the responsibility for performing necessary functions.

3 *Discipline.* Fayol saw discipline in terms of "obedience, application, energy, and respect." Penalties for poor performance should be coupled with competent and fair supervision.

4 *Unity of command.* A subordinate should take orders from only one superior. Here is one of the most popular of Fayol's principles. Fayol claimed that if the unity of command is violated: "authority is undermined, discipline is in jeopardy, order disturbed and stability threatened."

5 *Unity of direction.* Fayol wrote that each organizational objective ought to have only one head and one plan.

---

[2]Luther Gulick and L. Urwick, *Papers on the Science of Administration,* Columbia University Press, New York, 1937.
[3]Henri Fayol, *General and Industrial Management,* Sir Isaac Pitman & Sons, Ltd., London, 1949.

6 *Subordination of individual interest to general interest.* The interests of the organization ought to come before the interests of the individual.[4]

7 *Remuneration of personnel.* Pay should be fair. Time, job, piece rates, bonuses, profit sharing, and other methods should be used to arrive at the best scheme of payment.

8 *Centralization.* There should be one central point in the organization which exercises overall directional control of all the parts. In larger organizations some decentralization is necessary. Decentralization means that certain decisions are delegated to lower levels.

9 *Scalar chain.* There is an unbroken chain, or scale, of supervisors from the bottom to the top of the organization. This chain describes the flow of authority. However, quicker action is accomplished in many cases by direct communication of lower-level officials. Fayol used a diagram similar to the one in Figure 26-1 to illustrate this point. Fayol said that officials F and P, for example, might confer and reach a decision without the necessity of going all the way up and down the chain of command.

10 *Order.* "A place for everyone and everyone in his place." An organization ought to be based on an orderly, rationally thought-out plan.

11 *Equity.* Kindliness and justice on the part of managers will evoke loyalty and devotion from employees.

[4]As we have seen earlier in this book it is necessary only that the interests of the organization and the individual be *compatible*. It is not necessarily required for organizational efficiency that the individual *subordinate* himself to the organization. In fact, as many students of human behavior have observed in recent years a serious dilemma of modern man is that he has submerged himself in organizations, thereby losing much of his individual self and freedom. See Amitai Etzioni, *Modern Organization,* Prentice-Hall, Inc., Englewood Cliffs, N.J., 1964, pp. 5–19. While it might certainly promote short-run efficiency, it is our opinion that this principle has serious deficiencies. Making organizational and individual objectives compatible seems to be much preferred to the concept of subordinating individual objectives to the organization. In any event, appropriate discipline is necessary for organizational effectiveness.

Figure 26–1   The Scalar Chain

An unbroken chain, or scale, describes the flow of authority, but in many cases quicker action is achieved by direct communication at lower levels. In this figure, officials F and P might reach a decision without going up and down the chain of command.

Sample chain of supervisors

A
B   L
C   M
D   N
E   O
F — — — — — — — P
G   Q

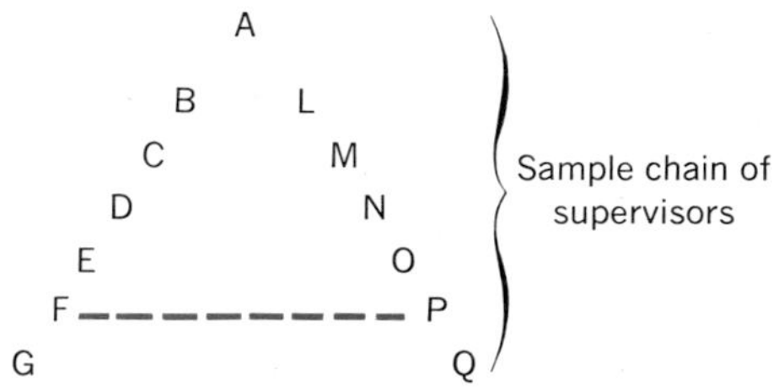

12 *Stability or tenure of personnel.* Efficiency will be promoted by a stable work force.

13 *Initiative.* To ensure success, plans should be well formulated before they are executed.

14 *Esprit de corps.* Fayol said that in union there is strength. The organization ought to function as a team, and every team member should work to best accomplish organizational goods. Fayol emphasized the importance of good communication in achieving teamwork.

OTHER PRINCIPLES OF MANAGEMENT

Harmony of Objective

This principle holds that the most effective organizational performance is attained when all persons or units of the organization work toward an objective that is harmonious. The principle is closely related to compatibility of objectives as discussed in Part I of this book.

Universality of Management

The functions of management are essentially the same regardless of the tasks of the organization or the level of management. It follows that managerial skills are transferable from one organization to another.

Primacy of Objectives and Planning

Formulation of objectives is a prerequisite step if the organization is to accomplish its goals in an orderly, rational manner. Planning is the process by which objectives are formulated and approaches are selected for accomplishing objectives. First, ideas, concepts, products or services are conceived or created. Planning must precede organizing, motivating, communicating, and controlling in the sequence of managerial functions. Therefore, objectives and planning are primary concepts for rational management.

Control by Exception

Management supervision and correction control are concentrated on the exceptional activities which are *not* operating according to plan. Activities performing as planned are handled routinely by subordinates.

Decision by Exception

A manager should make decisions on all matters which come to his attention *except* those for which he does not have sufficient authority. Matters for which the manager does not have sufficient authority are decided upon by committees or higher management.

Equality of Authority, Power, Responsibility, and Accountability

Stability in the organization requires that authority, power, responsibility, and accountability be balanced. If any of these factors is out of balance with respect to the others, the organization will be under pressure to restore the balances. Continued imbalance will cause resentment, hostility, friction, and strife. Serious imbalance can threaten the continued existence of the organization.

Coordination

The *principle of coordination* explains that effective organizational performance is achieved when all persons and resources are synchronized, balanced, and given direction. Without coordination, nonproductive random activity will result. Thus, one of the primary duties of the manager is to achieve coordination in the organization.

SUMMARY

The fields of organizations and management are clearly a long way from being codified by a simple, relatively short list of principles. Nevertheless, a number of management principles have been developed that suggest appropriate action for many managerial problems.

FOR REVIEW AND DISCUSSION

1 Define a principle of management. Explain why principles of management have been developed. Why have some writers criticized the principles of management approach?

2 Explain in your own words the statement: "It is quite enough that a principle be valid *most* of the time, for *most* circumstances."

3 In your own words, describe each of the following principles of management. For each principle give an example to show how an organization has used or might use that principle: (a) division of work; (b) authority and responsibility; (c) discipline; (d) unity of command; (e) unity of direction; (f) subordination of individual interest to general interest; (g) remuneration of personnel; (h) centralization; (i) scalar chain; (j) order; (k) equity; (l) stability or tenure of personnel; (m) initiative; (n) *esprit de corps*; (o) harmony of objective; (p) universality of management; (q) primacy of objectives and planning; (r) control by exception; (s) decision by exception; (t) equality of authority, power, responsibility, and accountability; and (u) coordination.

4 Explain why Fayol has been considered a universalist.

CASES

A Lieutenant Colonel Cole was in charge of aircraft maintenance at Foley Air Force Base, a large pilot-training base in the Southwest. The base was commanded by Col. R. L. Casper, to whom Colonel Cole reported directly. Foley AFB was part of the 17th Air Force, commanded by Maj. Gen. L. O. Pettit.

Each year the aircraft-maintenance activities at Foley were inspected by representatives of Col. P. J. Massey, who was in charge of the aircraft-maintenance staff office of the 17th Air Force. After their study of the activities at Foley and other bases within the 17th Air Force, the inspectors prepared a list of matters that were not satisfactory. Before leaving the base, the list was discussed by the inspectors and the base officer in charge of that activity.

On August 13 the inspectors made a surprise visit to Foley as a follow-up to the annual inspection they had completed June 1. They checked each item on their list of discrepancies of June 1 and found that no corrective action had been taken on most. The inspecting officers then returned to their office at the 17th Air Force Headquarters.

On August 20 the following letter arrived at Foley.

HEADQUARTERS 17th AIR FORCE

15 August

Col. R. L. Casper, Commander
Foley Air Force Base
Re: Aircraft-maintenance Inspection

On 1 June my representatives inspected your aircraft-maintenance activities. Discrepancies were duly discussed with Lieutenant Colonel Cole, your aircraft-maintenance officer. A follow-up inspection on 13 August showed that no action had been taken on most of the noted discrepancies.

Comments of my staff officers have the same effect that they would have if they came from my own mouth.

You will reply by endorsement before 1 September, giving the measures you have taken to correct this serious breach of military discipline.

L. O. Pettit, Maj. Gen.
Commander

1 Draw an organization chart showing the pertinent features of this organization.

2 Explain in detail the principle of management that is involved in this case.

3 What effect do you think the general's letter will have on the people at Foley? What should Colonel Casper say in his reply?

B There is a saying that "the sergeants are the backbone of the military." In any event many young officers have found that the quickest way to get something done is to establish a close working relationship with their top enlisted men.

Much of the work done in a military organization requires the cooperation of several units. Observations have shown that to achieve coordination, sergeants usually work with sergeants of other units, captains contact other captains, colonels talk to other colonels, and so on.

   1 Explain the principle of management that is illustrated here.
   2 What are the advantages and disadvantages of persons in one unit working with those of equal rank in another unit, when coordination is necessary?
   3 What would be the alternative if this cross-unit, rank-to-rank contact were not permitted?

   C   The following paragraphs are found in the organization manual of Perry Industries, Inc.

A policy of the company is that decisions should be made at the lowest possible level. When a manager thinks he cannot properly make a decision on a matter that comes before him, he should first check and see if the problem could better be handled by another department. If so, the matter should be directly referred to that department.

Second, for problems that he thinks he cannot solve adequately, alone, each manager should confer with other affected managers of similar rank in an effort to reach a solution.

Only after the two approaches described above have been exhausted should the problem be referred to higher authority.

   1 What principle(s) of management is illustrated by this policy of Perry Industries, Inc.?
   2 What effects would this policy have on the operations of the company?

FOR FURTHER STUDY

Additional sources can be found in the sources cited in the chapter.

Books

Henri Fayol: "General Principles of Management," *General and Industrial Management,* trans. Constance Starrs, Sir Isaac Pitman & Sons, Ltd., London, 1949, pp. 19–42. This book originally was published in French in 1916. It contains the original codification of management principles. It remains one of the best.

Luther Gulick and L. Urwick: *Papers on the Science of Administration,* Institute of Public Administration, New York, 1937. A fine collection of papers on administration and its place in society.

S. Avery Raube: "Principles of Good Organization," *Company Organization Charts,* National Industrial Conference Board, 1954. Twelve principles of good organization and the benefits therefrom are explained.

Herbert A. Simon: *Administrative Behavior,* 2d ed., The Macmillan Company, New York, 1961, chap. II. A stinging criticism of some management principles.

George R. Terry: *Principles of Management,* 5th ed., Richard D. Irwin, Inc., Homewood, Ill., 1968. A basic principles of management text.

Articles

Alan C. Filley: "Common Misconceptions in Business Management," *Business Horizons,* Fall 1964. "The businessman and the academician should cooperate in developing a body of knowledge that is acceptable to both."

Paul Pigors and Charles A. Myers: "Patterns of Management," *Industrial Management Review,* Spring 1964. Whatever the actual pattern of management, if there indeed is one, the essence of good management is getting effective results with the co-operation of other people. The philosophy or pattern of management present in an organization has a profound effect on those results.

T. E. Stephenson: "The Longevity of Classical Theory," *Management International Review,* no. 6, 1968. Classical principles of management continue to serve the needs of practicing managers.

L. F. Urwick: "'Organization and Theories about the Nature of Man," *Academy of Management Journal,* March 1967. A vigorous defense of the contributions of classical management theory.

Maneck S. Wadia: "A Reappraisal of Management Principles," *Advanced Management Journal,* April 1966. Principles are broad generalizations, which do not reveal anything about particular situations. Therefore, principles should be general guides, and the degree of their applicability should depend upon the conditions under which they are applied.

27
Wasteful Organizational Practices

Administrative man satisfices—looks for a course of
action that is satisfactory or "good enough."
    HERBERT A. SIMON

An organizational practice is wasteful if it fails to help accomplish organizational objectives. Wasteful practices may occur slowly, silently, without warning, and are often extremely difficult to recognize. Hence, they may be difficult to control. To curb wasteful practices a manager must have a clear understanding of their nature and causes. He also needs to have available remedies by which wasteful practices can be controlled or eliminated.

A basic cause of wasteful practices in organizations is that individuals may pursue their own personal objectives without at the same time contributing to objectives of the organization. This tendency to work toward individual objectives without adequate reference to organizational objectives has been termed "bureaupathology."[1] This disease becomes potentially serious when organizations are large, complex, and impersonal.

---

[1]Victor A. Thompson, *Modern Organizations*, Alfred A. Knopf, Inc., New York, 1961, p. 153.

PARKINSON'S LAWS

The problem of wasteful organizational practices was presented succinctly by Professor C. Northcote Parkinson. In his delightful book, Parkinson wrote: "Work expands so as to fill the time available for its completion."[2] This statement is illustrated by the student who works on (or, perhaps, mostly worries about) a term paper right up to the minute it is due. Many bricklayers busily occupy themselves laying their self-imposed limit of 400 bricks per day, although it has been shown conclusively that twice this quota can be laid without difficulty by a skilled workman. And who can imagine an organizational staff member or manager saying that he or his organization can accomplish more work without additional money or other resources? Such an admission amounts to organizational heresy, because it implies that the person or his organization unit now has more resources than work. A reduction in size might cause the manager or his organization to lose status. Perhaps the manager would suffer a cut in pay; certainly, he is hardly likely to receive a raise in the event that his organizational budget or activity is reduced.

Expanding this line of thought, Parkinson proposed that wasteful organizational practices are caused by two factors: First, an official wants to increase the number of subordinates he manages rather than create rival organizational members. This thought is expressed as the "law of multiplication of subordinates." Second, members of organizations make work for each other. The second factor is called the "law of multiplication of work."[3] To illustrate his laws Parkinson wrote about the trials and tribulations of a bureaucrat performing a typical day's work in a typical bureaucratic organization.[4]

The Law of Multiplication of Subordinates

To comprehend Factor I, we must picture a civil servant called A who finds himself overworked. Whether this overwork is real or imaginary is immaterial; but we should observe, in passing, that A's sensation (or illusion) might easily result from his own decreasing energy—a normal symptom of middle-age. For this real or imagined overwork there are, broadly speaking, three possible remedies:

1 He may resign.

2 He may ask to halve the work with a colleague called B.

3 He may demand the assistance of two subordinates to be called C and D. There is probably no instance in civil service history of A choosing any but the third alternative. By resignation he would lose his pension rights. By having B appointed, on his own level in the hierarchy, he would merely bring in a rival for promotion to W's vacancy when W (at long last) retires. So A would rather have C and D, junior men, below him. They will add to his consequence; and, by dividing the work into two categories, as between C and D, he will have the merit of being the only man who comprehends them both.

It is essential to realize, at this point, that C and D are, as it were, inseparable. To ap-

---

[2]C. Northcote Parkinson, *Parkinson's Law,* Houghton Mifflin Company, Boston, 1957, p. 2. (By permission.)
[3]*Ibid.,* p. 4.
[4]We wish to make it clear that bureaupathology can be found in business as well as governmental organizations. Any organization that is large, complex, and impersonal is likely to have the disease.

point C alone would have been impossible. Why? Because C, if by himself, would divide the work with A and so assume almost the equal status which has been refused in the first instance to B; a status the more emphasized if C is A's only possible successor. Subordinates must thus number two or more, each being kept in order by fear of the other's promotion. When C complains in turn of being overworked (as he certainly will) A will, with the concurrence of C, advise the appointment of two assistants to help C. But he can then avert internal friction only by advising the appointment of two more assistants to help D, whose position is much the same. With this recruitment of E, F, G and H, the promotion of A is now practically certain.

The Law of Multiplication of Work

Seven officials are now doing what one did before. This is where Factor II comes into operation. For these seven make so much work for each other that all are fully occupied and A is actually working harder than ever. An incoming document may well come before each of them in turn. Official E decides that it falls within the province of F, who places a draft reply before C, who amends it drastically before consulting D, who asks G to deal with it. But G goes on leave at this point, handing the file over to H, who drafts a minute, which is signed by D and returned to C, who revises his draft accordingly and lays the new version before A.

What does A do? He would have every excuse for signing the thing unread, for he has many other matters on his mind. Knowing now that he is to succeed W next year, he has to decide whether C or D should succeed to his own office. He had to agree to G going on leave, although not yet strictly entitled to it. He is worried whether H should not have gone instead, for reasons of health. He has looked pale recently—partly but not solely because of his domestic troubles. Then there is the business of F's special increment of salary for the period of the conference, and E's application for transfer to the Ministry of Pensions. A has heard that D is in love with a married typist and that G and F are no longer on speaking terms—no one seems to know why. So A might be tempted to sign C's draft and have done with it.

But A is a conscientious man. Beset as he is with problems created by his colleagues for themselves and for him—created by the mere fact of these officials' existence—he is not the man to shirk his duty. He reads through the draft with care, deletes the fussy paragraphs added by C and H and restores the thing back to the form preferred in the first instance by the able (if quarrelsome) F. He corrects the English—none of these young men can write grammatically—and finally produces the same reply he would have written if officials C to H had never been born. Far more people have taken far longer to produce the same result. No one has been idle. All have done their best. And it is late in the evening before A finally quits his office and begins the return journey to Ealing. The last of the office lights are being turned off in the gathering dusk which marks the end of another day's administrative toil. Among the last to leave, A reflects, with bowed shoulders and a wry smile, that late hours, like grey hairs, are among the penalties of success.[5]

Parkinson thus threw a spotlight on the cancer of wasteful organizational practices.

Parkinson supported his argument with empirical evidence.[6] He found, for example, that between 1914 and 1928 the number of officers and men in the British Royal Navy

---

[5]C. Northcote Parkinson, *op. cit.*, pp. 4–7. (Reprinted by permission of the publisher, Houghton Mifflin Company.)

[6]*Ibid.*, pp. 7–12.

decreased from 146,000 to 100,000. During the same period, the number of capital ships decreased from 62 to 20. Yet the number of officials in the British Admiralty Headquarters in Whitehall increased during this period at the average annual rate of 5.6 percent. As a second example, Parkinson cited the British Colonial Office.[7] British colonial territories shrank drastically in the period from 1935 to 1954, yet colonial-office officials grew in number from 372 in 1935 to 450 in 1939; 1,139 in 1947; and 1,661 in 1954—a steady increase at the average annual rate of 5.9 percent. Thus, Parkinson concluded that the size of administrative staffs tends to grow at the average rate of 5.75 percent per year, regardless of the fact that the work-load output of the organization may actually be decreasing.

Parkinson did not take into account the complexities of advancing technologies. Nor did he consider that some of the increase in staff may be justified because of real contributions they make to the objectives of the organization and to those the organization serves. In any event, Parkinson's laws are potent arguments for the proposition that organizations tend to grow in wasteful ways.

THE ORGANIZATIONAL MULTIPLIER[8]

An organizational multiplier, similar to economic multipliers, is at work in organizations. The multiplier stems from the natural tendency among individuals within organizations to try to act in ways which maximize their own welfare. And maximization of the individuals' welfare is not necessarily synonymous with that of the organization. Ramifications of these individual acts, though frequently unrecognized by the persons directly involved, bear significantly on the organization's ability to attain its goal with a high degree of efficiency. Thus an understanding of the organizational multiplier can be critical to the successful management of any organization.

Economic Multipliers

For several decades macroeconomists have theorized that a multiplier principle is operative in the monetary and fiscal structure of the economy. The theory is that expenditures in the investment sector of the company trigger additional spending in the consumption sector. One circular effect of this combined spending, so it is argued, is to raise the level of national income. An increase in national income causes an increase in the tax take of the federal government and an increase in employment.[9]

[7] Ibid.

[8] This section is an adaptation of Herbert G. Hicks and Benjamin B. Graves, "Is There an Organizational Multiplier?" *Academy of Management Journal,* March 1963, pp. 70–78. (By permission.)

[9] *National income* is defined as the sum of investment and consumption spending. Assume that $y =$ national income, $I =$ investment spending, $C =$ consumption spending, MPC = the national marginal propensity to consume, and $K =$ the multiplier. One economic multiplier is derived as follows:

If

$$K = \frac{\text{change in national income}}{\text{change in investment}} = \frac{\Delta y}{\Delta I} \tag{1}$$

An Organizational Multiplier

The specific proposition here is that a multiplier somewhat analogous to economic multipliers is operative in organizations. The basic point in the case of organizations is that an addition or reduction of personnel in one place in the organization may result in a long series of changes in other parts of the organization.[10] *The organization multiplier, then, is that factor by which a primary change in a particular sector of the organization is multiplied to determine the total change in the whole organization.* Support for the general thesis can be found in the work of Professor C. Northcote Parkinson, discussed earlier in this chapter.

The Organizational Multiplier at Work

To illustrate the workings of the multiplier, let us take a hypothetical case on a military base where the command has determined, after many hours of study, that a nine-hole golf course would help to maintain the morale of the people on the base.[11] First, we will make several assumptions:

The land for the golf course is available and can be used without additional capital expenditures for land acquisition.

The basic facilities required for the course, such as fairways, greens, and clubhouses, have been completed by external contractors and do not affect the size of the base organization.

At the time of the completion of the golf course, the base organization is operating at a level of peak efficiency, and there is no slack (resources not fully utilized) in the organization.[12] Thus the organization is in an equilibrium condition.

At this stage of the analysis, then, the situation stands with a completed golf course, but with no persons assigned to operate or maintain it. If it is assumed that five men are required to maintain the course, we must add this number to the base organization.

Then

$$\Delta y = K \Delta I \tag{2}$$

And

$$\Delta y = \Delta I + \Delta C \tag{3}$$

Therefore

$$K = \frac{\Delta y}{\Delta y - \Delta C} \tag{4}$$

Then

$$K = \frac{\Delta y / \Delta y}{\Delta y / \Delta y - \Delta C / \Delta y} = \frac{1}{1 - \Delta C / \Delta y} = \frac{1}{1 - MPC} \tag{5}$$

NOTE: Since MPC is always less than unity, K is therefore always greater than unity.

[10] We are primarily concerned here with organizations in the medium- and larger-size categories.

[11] Although the case here is purely hypothetical, an actual case which approximates this situation has come to the attention of the author.

[12] For a discussion of organizational slack, see James G. March and Herbert A. Simon, *Organizations,* John Wiley & Sons, Inc., New York, 1959, pp. 126, 149, 187.

These five men thus represent the first stage in a potentially large number of additions to organizational personnel.

With the addition of five persons to the golf course, we may normally expect an addition in the number of dependents who must either live on the base or be furnished housing and other facilities in adjacent areas. It is reasonable to assume an additional three people, a wife and two children, in the families of each of the original five. Thus our initial change of five persons has resulted in the addition of fifteen other persons who must be provided with housing and support facilities. *The total growth on or around the base has now reached twenty. This is the second stage of the multiplier.*

Does the growth process stop here? The answer is an emphatic no! The addition of twenty people at the first and second stages will surely result in expansion of facilities and increase in personnel in such service activities as the base exchange, theater, personnel office, payroll office, dining halls, and hobby shop. The multiplying process continues until perhaps every service department has increased its staff and facilities in order to take care of the original increment of five men and fifteen dependents associated with the golf course. *In this third stage more service personnel are added.*

Has the growth now ceased? Again the answer is probably no. Feedback among the various service functions may initiate a new series of multiplying actions entirely distinct from the original golf-course personnel. For example, the base exchange tends to grow as a result of the additions to the personnel office. And the personnel office grows because of additions to the base exchange. *So as the feedback process continues, a fourth stage of action by the multiplier enters the picture.*

It would be a relief to suggest that the process is now complete, but the malignant nature of the multiplier does not permit this. It is entirely possible that the rounds of increases in personnel and their dependents created in the second, third, and fourth stages have reached the point where the original nine-hole golf course has become inadequate! *If a decision is thereby justified to expand the course into an eighteen-hole layout, the multiplying process could start all over again, thereby creating a fifth stage of action for the multiplier.* Actually the total number of incremental changes created by the five stages may be very large, but the number of people added approaches a limit. In this hypothetical case, it might be assumed that this limit is forty. If the limit is forty, divided by five (the number of men in the initial addition), the result is eight (the multiplier in this case).

When the extreme effect of the multiplier is encountered, it is possible to have an organization constantly growing, but literally feeding on itself and contributing little to the primary objectives which justified its original establishment. This case— never experienced, it is hoped—is a condition where everyone in the organization is working for the other members of the organization with little, if any, external output. Such extreme cases, it is hoped, are rare, but in recent investigations there have been reported instances in which fund-raising organizations have absorbed internally 90 percent of the moneys collected. Similarly, there have been cases where investment bankers and brokerage firms have sold barely enough of a client's issue of stock to cover their own fees and commissions.

It is quite possible that every individual in such organizations has been working honestly, diligently, and performing his particular task in an efficient manner. But such a condition would raise a serious question about whether or not the organization ought to exist in the first place.

Mathematical Expression of the Multiplier

The sum of the changes in the organizational multiplier approaches a limit but never quite reaches it. If forty were the limit, as suggested in the hypothetical case of the military base, the multiplier would be the factor eight. This means that the addition of the original five men required to operate and maintain the golf course would eventually result in forty people being supported directly or indirectly by the base. The multiplier can be expressed mathematically as follows:

If

X = multiplier
A = service function where first addition is made
B = second service function
C = third service function
N = nth service function
ΔA = change in A
$\Delta B_{\Delta A}$ = change in B as a result of ΔA
$X\Delta A$ = total change in organizational personnel resulting from ΔA

Then

$$X\Delta A = \Delta A + \Delta B_{\Delta A} + \Delta C_{\Delta A} + \Delta A_{\Delta B} \cdots + \Delta A_{\Delta N}$$
$$+ \Delta B_{\Delta N} + \Delta C_{\Delta N} \cdots + \Delta N_{\Delta A} \cdots \Delta N \qquad (1)$$

Or

$$X = 1 +$$
$$\frac{\Delta B_{\Delta A} + \Delta C_{\Delta A} + \Delta A_{\Delta B} \cdots + \Delta A_{\Delta N} + \Delta B_{\Delta N} + \Delta C_{\Delta N} \cdots + \Delta N_{\Delta A} \cdots \Delta N}{\Delta A} \qquad (2)$$

Equation 2 states that the multiplier equals 1 plus the quotient of the sum of all the changes (except the first) divided by the value of the first change. In a large organization a number of changes would take place provided the initial change is substantial. Small organizations might have a short-run multiplier as low as one; additional work is performed in this case by service activities with slack.[13] A large number of changes actually could take place. So, if all changes were considered, there would be a large number of terms in the equation. For this reason, only sample terms are given. But if

---

[13] It might be noted that even in small organizations the pressures toward a multiplying effect would be cumulative. Enough primary changes would eventually cause secondary changes and hence, in the long run, would push the numerical value of the multiplier above unity.

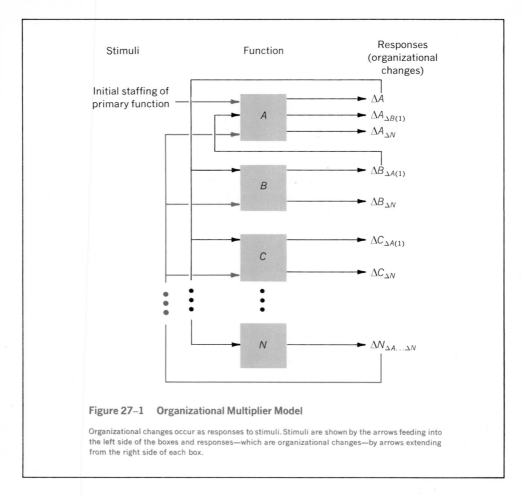

Figure 27–1   Organizational Multiplier Model

Organizational changes occur as responses to stimuli. Stimuli are shown by the arrows feeding into the left side of the boxes and responses—which are organizational changes—by arrows extending from the right side of each box.

any build-up or increase in personnel is experienced in the secondary stages, the equation clearly shows that the value of the multiplier must always be greater than one.

A schematic model of a portion of the organization changes created by the action of the multiplier, shown in Figure 27-1, indicates that organizational changes occur as responses from the application of stimuli to various functions in the organization. Sample functions are represented by the boxes A, B, C, . . . N. Stimuli are depicted by arrows feeding into the left side of each box, and responses (organizational changes), by arrows extending from the right side of each box. Figure 27-1 is analogous to the equation given above.

Some General Observations about the Multiplier

The extent of multiplication is likely to be determined by underlying factors in the organization. These factors include its nature, size, age, growth status, and external environment. Perhaps the multiplier:

1 Is most easily demonstrated under conditions of growth in the organization. On the other hand, during periods of stability, even when it is reducing its number of personnel, the organization may experience a multiplying effect.

2 Is especially significant in those organizations that have a number of service functions. Modern military and governmental establishments and the mass of the larger business, social, educational, religious, charitable, professional, and fraternal organizations are some examples. As construed here, service functions are those which contribute indirectly to the ability of the organization to fulfill its primary objectives.

3 Is more readily apparent in the nonprofit organizations, especially those supported by public funds.[14] This follows from the simple fact that these organizations lack the necessity to make a profit, which may act as a deterrent to the multiplying tendency in the business firm. The profit incentive, however, does not grant the organization an immunity from the effects of the multiplier.

4 Is affected by the size of the organization. The small organization is normally restricted by the availability of funds and space, factors which tend to deter the activation of the multiplier. Close observation and control by the owner-manager also minimize the effect. For example, the hiring or firing of one person in a small organization can be an event of special significance; in the larger organization, it could go virtually unnoticed.[15]

5 Is often overlooked. *The specific tendency is to ignore costs associated with the second, third, fourth, and fifth stages in the action of the multiplier.* It would be interesting, for example, to know the cumulative effects of the costs associated with the operation of executive dining rooms which frequently accommodate as few as eight or ten persons in some modern business organizations. If the action of the multiplier were fully recognized in the case of the hypothetical golf course, the command on the base might shudder at the thought of the ultimate effect on its organizational structure. It is probable that the management, in this case the base command, would consider only the costs associated with the five men deemed necessary to operate the course.[16] The organization may fail to give adequate consideration to the costs resulting from the secondary additions or, in other words, to the effect of the organizational multiplier. Had such costs been considered—and they are appropriate—the task of justifying the golf course would have been much more difficult. This "natural bias," then, almost surely raises the numerical value of the multiplier.

[14]"Nonprofit" should not be confused with "noneconomic." Some organizations seek profit; many more are economic if they seek to optimize the use of scarce resources.

[15]Additions and releases of personnel in small organizations create a condition often described as "lumpiness." In other words, one person in ten could represent a 10 percent change in work force, but one in one thousand would be only 0.1 of 1 percent. In the small organization the change is more apparent, and thus the management is more restrictive to the multiplying tendency.

[16]The ordeals of congressional appropriations and Defense Department approvals were disposed of in the basic assumptions. Thus the base command would consider costs associated with the construction of the course as "sunken" and no longer relevant.

Findings in certain studies have suggested that companies in the small- and medium-size range tend to produce higher returns on their stockholders' investment than the largest firms.[17] Perhaps the multiplier has created conditions of slack and senility in the larger organizations. Such situations may also support the economists' thesis that "diseconomies of scale" are typical of a large and unwieldy organization. Even profit-making organizations tend to feed on themselves, and much of their human energy is dissipated internally rather than in an increased output of the goods and services. In the long run the stern reality of competition may force a reduction in the size of the multiplier in the business firm, but this is a risky conclusion.[18] Except for the limited effectiveness of budget controls, even this brake does not exist in the nonprofit organizations.

Eventually the question arises as to what a management can do when the multiplier has reached significant proportions. The effect of the multiplier can be reduced or minimized by a two-step process; namely, a proper diagnosis of its existence and the application of an extensive and continuous program designed to eliminate slack and submarginal functions from the organization. This diagnosis includes a specific recognition of all the relevant costs associated with a change in the organizations, including those costs occurring in the secondary stages caused by the action of the multiplier.

A final question concerns the level in the organization which can be expected to diagnose the multiplying disease and suggest a remedy. It is doubtful if individuals below the level of top management in the organization can examine this condition on a rational basis and successfully initiate a corrective program. The reason underlying this doubt is simple. It is often the lower-level managers who have confused their own needs and desires with those of the organization, thus allowing the conditions to develop in the first place. Effective remedies must be instituted and prosecuted at the uppermost levels of management. To get the job done, it may even be necessary to bring in external reinforcements.

REASONS FOR WASTEFUL ORGANIZATIONAL PRACTICES

Wasteful organizational practices do not just happen. There are a number of reasons that motivate these practices.

Personal Limitations and Satisficing Behavior

The personal limitations of managers and other organization members are a principal reason for wasteful organization practices. In a complex organization it simply is impossible for one to know every detail about every activity. Consequently, almost every decision is made with some degree of uncertainty and without complete knowledge. Under

---

[17] See especially Rudolph L. Weisman, *Small Business and Venture Capital*, Harper & Row, Publishers, Incorporated, New York, 1945, p. 15.

[18] In his *Tract on Monetary Reform*, Lord Keynes succinctly pointed out that "in the long run we are all dead," emphasizing that one can get small comfort from long-run solutions. Business operates largely in the short run and may, therefore, be operating with a very high organizational multiplier.

such conditions it is practically impossible for an organization to operate with perfect efficiency. As Herbert Simon put it: "Human beings . . . *satisfice* because they have not the wits to *maximize.*"[19] Simon's comment is perhaps one of the most penetrating observations ever written about behavior in organizations. Persons do not, as a rule, do things perfectly, or at the maximum. Rather, persons tend to make satisfactory decisions, considering all the factors—often conflicting—which bear upon them.

Another way of viewing satisficing behavior is to remind ourselves that we seldom, if ever, really do our very best. It is often easier to do a satisfactory job. Perhaps there is much truth in the comment of the farmer who ignored some new advice of a county agent. According to the farmer: "I'm not farming as well now as I know how. What good is your advice going to do for me?" Certainly, persons are limited in their ability and desire to perform at the maximum or to make perfect organizational decisions. These considerations almost inevitably lead to a condition where resources are used at less than peak efficiency.

Lumpiness of Resources

Many resources needed by an organization often cannot be obtained in exactly the quantity required. Because resources are not infinitely divisible, they are referred to as "lumpy." For example, if seven-eighths of the time of an accountant were required, an organization would probably employ an accountant full-time. One-eighth of the accountant's time is possibly wasted because the accountant as a resource is lumpy. The organization may keep the accountant occupied with "busy-work" for the extra one-eighth of his time. However, it is obvious that such a procedure still represents a waste because the busy-work may be totally unproductive or probably could be done by a less-expensive employee. Employment of part-time personnel or other resources helps to reduce the effects of lumpiness of resources, but is not totally effective.

The more rigid the organization the more it is likely to suffer the effects of lumpiness of resources. Flexible organizations will transfer persons internally on a part-time basis.

Resources other than human are equally susceptible to this type of inefficiency. An expensive machine, for instance, that is only partially utilized contributes its share of extra costs to the organization.

Uneven Demand

A constant problem for a manager is to decide the capacity of the organization. At times more products or services are demanded from organizations than at other times. Moreover, it takes time, often several years, to "tool-up" to produce products or services. In addition it is quite impossible to predict exactly the level of future demand. For these reasons organizations are typically in the position of having too few or too many resources for the present demand. Inefficiencies are thus present; demand is unfilled, the

---

[19] Herbert A. Simon, *Administrative Behavior,* 2d ed., The Macmillan Company, New York, 1957, p. xxiv.

organization is overworked, or the organization may have idle resources on hand.

Perhaps a manager will lean toward providing more than the optimum level of resources. It is, no doubt, more comfortable for the manager to have available extra resources to take care of peak demand. (They can be easily occupied with busy-work at other times.) When a peak load of work comes, relatively little effort is then required to take care of it. It is perfectly legitimate to tool-up for some degree of uneven work. But if more than the optimum level of resources are used, wasteful organizational practices occur.

Empire Building

Higher pay, status, and power tend to go to managers of larger organizations. Consequently, managers often try to build up the size of their organization. This tendency is called "empire building."

Empire building is entirely justified if the larger organization provides additional desired products or services. However, managers also may be motivated by the increased pay, status, and power that tend to follow increases in the size of the organization. If managers follow these motivations, wasteful organization practices result. Empire building has been recognized for many years as a serious, wasteful organizational practice.

Insurance

A manager may be concerned that his organization's budget may be cut. Often these cuts are effective "across the board" for the entire organization. For example, the budget of every department may be cut 5 percent.

The only way a manager can protect himself and his organization from such arbitrary cuts is to build some insurance into his organization. That is, during "fat" times he may add extra personnel, so that when the cut comes he is prepared. He simply slices off the required 5 percent of personnel or other resources that were not needed in the first place. Large, complex organizations are best able to hide this type of behavior.

Time Lag

There is often a significant lag between the time a decision is made and the time it is implemented. Some of the necessary resources are likely to be ready before others. Hence, the resources which are ready first will have to wait. Often they are idle during the wait. The idle resources represent another wasteful organizational practice.

Communications

As we have seen in the chapters on communication in this book, communication is practically always something less than 100 percent effective. When communications fall short of perfection there will be resulting inefficiencies in the organization. Waste is then found in the utilization of resources because of the imperfectness of communication.

Nationalism

Like nations, organizations like to be independent or autonomous. Such a tendency is called "nationalism." The problem of nationalism is that it requires that the organization have a relatively large number of specialized staff and service activities. For example, in recent years many business organizations have felt compelled to purchase or lease expensive electronic data-processing equipment even when the work, in many cases, could be performed less expensively through other means. In many cases it would be cheaper to rent time on some other organization's computer or even do the work with older methods. But it has been, in part, a prestige factor for the organization to have its own computer. When nationalism results in ineffective use of resources, wasteful organizational practices are present.

Habit

Many things are done in organizations through the force of habit, or because "that's the way we've always done it." Rigid policies, procedures, and rules obviously aggravate this problem. There is a tendency to believe that "whatever is, is right." Such views lead to waste in organizational resources.

Conflicts in Objectives

Perhaps much of the problem of wasteful organizational practices is caused by residual conflicts in objectives. Individuals rarely have exactly the same objectives as the organization or other members. Therefore, efficiency will likely suffer because of conflicts in objectives.

SUMMARY—REDUCING AND CONTROLLING WASTEFUL ORGANIZATIONAL PRACTICES

Some activities in organizations do not contribute to organizational objectives; these practices are wasteful. Wasteful organizational practices can be reduced and controlled. The first step is to recognize that there is a tendency for the organization to grow in wasteful ways—ways which do not help to accomplish organizational objectives. Also, it is necessary to understand the basic reasons for wasteful organizational growth, if the wasteful growth is to be reduced and controlled.

Competition may be a powerful force in reducing wasteful organizational practices. For example, during World War II most of the large oil companies stockpiled thousands of employees. After the war the problem of excess employees was compounded when automation reduced the work force needed by the companies. But it was not until the advent of the compact car in the early 1960s that the oil companies really did much about the problem. The compact car used less gasoline. This fact caused an overall leveling of the demand for gasoline and other oil products. Coupled with adequate supplies, the leveled demand caused significant declines in gasoline prices. Finally, the oil companies began their "agonizing reappraisal" and laid off thousands of employees, many that had not been needed for years. We wonder when, if ever, these companies would have removed the "dead wood" if competition had not forced their hand. Similar examples could probably be found in almost every other type of organization.

Wasteful organizational practices can be reduced and controlled by an internalization of organizational objectives by its members. *Internalization* of organizational objectives means that members understand and accept organizational objectives. They then work toward these organizational objectives because they see such work as means by which they can accomplish their own, personal objectives. If individual and organizational objectives were perfectly compatible and internalized, it is doubtful that signficant wasteful organizational practices would occur. Such perfection is clearly impossible to reach, but it is certainly a reasonable goal toward which to work.

FOR REVIEW AND DISCUSSION

1 Explain and give an example of a wasteful organizational practice.

2 Explain Parkinson's statement on the expansion of work. Explain in your own words the two laws quoted from Parkinson.

3 Define the organizational multiplier. Show how the multiplier works by describing several stages of organizational growth. Explain why the multiplier is always greater than one.

4 Explain the statement: "The organization may fail to give adequate consideration to the costs resulting from secondary additions or, in other words, to the effect of the organizational multiplier."

5 Explain each of the following causes of wasteful organizational practices. Include in your discussion for each an illustrative example: (a) satisficing behavior, (b) lumpiness of resources, (c) uneven demand, (d) empire building, (e) insurance, (f) time lag, (g) communications, (h) nationalism, (i) habit, and (j) conflicts in objectives.

6 How does competition help to control wasteful organizational practices?

7 Explain how an internalization of objectives would help to reduce wasteful organizational practices. Do you agree with the statement: "A basic cause of wasteful organizational practices is that individuals may pursue their individual objectives without at the same time contributing to objectives of the organization"? Explain your answer.

8 What is the special reason why wasteful organizational practices are more likely to occur in governmental than business organizations?

9 Make a list of suggestions for a manager who is interested in reducing wasteful organizational practices.

CASES

A   Dan Pierce, division manager of Belmont Industries, was considering the feasibility of hiring a commercial artist for his division. He estimated that there was $350 worth of art work to be done each month. Miss Lark, who was qualified for the job, could be hired for a salary of $340 each month. Based on these data Mr. Pierce started processing the paper work to hire Miss Lark.

    1 Do you agree with Mr. Pierce's decision? Explain your answer.

    2 What additional data would you like to have to assist you in making a better decision?

    3 Explain how hiring Miss Lark might be justified from Mr. Pierce's viewpoint, but not from the overall viewpoint of the president of Belmont Industries.

    B   Blayton Fox had the reputation of being a very easy-going manager. The employees in his department were late an average of ten minutes each morning in arriving at work. Mr. Fox never said anything about this to his employees because he felt his criticisms would hurt morale.

Thomas Block, another department manager of the same company, had for years had a strict policy against tardiness. He required that any employee in his department who was late even one minute would be required to write a letter to him setting forth his reasons for not being at work on time. In the past four years incidents of tardiness have occurred only four times in Mr. Block's department.

    1 Which manager had the better policy? Explain your answer.

    2 Explain the particular bit of information (discussed in this chapter) about human behavior in organizations that supports Mr. Block's approach.

    C   Jack Fraser, a department manager of Aircraft Industries, Inc., was known as a very frugal and honest manager. He took pains to see that his department always operated at peak efficiency; if one of his workers became surplus to his needs, he requested that the worker be transferred to another department.

The policy of the other department managers was to demand more and more workers and other resources. In slack times they did not reduce their force as Mr. Fraser did; they simply "made work" for their surplus employees. Mr. Fraser observed that the size of other departments tended to grow continually, while the size of his department remained relatively constant.

On June 10, Mr. Fraser and all other managers received a memo from the president's office which stated: "In an effort to improve the efficiency of our organization, I am asking that all managers reduce their costs by 10 percent. Please supply me with your proposal for complying with this request by June 30."

Mr. Fraser wondered what his response should be to the president's request.

    1 How do you think Mr. Fraser should respond to the president's request? Give the reasons for your answer.

    2 Is the president's request reasonable? Support your answer with points covered in the text.

    3 What recommendations would you make to Mr. Fraser about the future management of his department?

FOR FURTHER STUDY

Additional sources can be found in the sources cited in the chapter.

Books

Rocco Carzo, Jr. and John Y. Yanouzas: *Formal Organization,* Richard D. Irwin, Homewood, Ill., 1967, pp. 118–129. Formal organizations have characteristics that cause unintended consequences of actions.

Lawrence J. Peter and Raymond Hull: *The Peter Principle,* William Morrow & Company, Inc., New York, 1969. Alternate source of a portion of this book: "The Peter Principle," *Management Review,* February 1969. Every employee of an organization tends to rise to his level of incompetence.

William G. Scott: *Organization Theory,* Richard D. Irwin, Homewood, Ill., 1967, pp. 253–256. Organizations have characteristics that cause them to behave in wasteful ways.

Victor A. Thompson: *Modern Organization,* Alfred A. Knopf, Inc., New York, 1961, chap. 8. A penetrating analysis of ten ways of pursuing personal objectives in a formal organization that fail to contribute to the accomplishment of organizational objectives.

Robert Townsend: *Up the Organization,* Alfred A. Knopf, Inc., New York, 1970. "How to stop the corporation from stifling people and strangling profits."

Articles

"America the Inefficient," *Time,* Mar. 23, 1970. Inefficiency pervades many aspects of American society.

Leland E. Dake: "Why Some Growth Companies Are Faltering," *Business Horizons,* Spring 1965. "A growth company falters because the strains of growth create management problems that are too great for the available human resources, and these in turn aggravate management weaknesses that would produce less serious consequences in a more stable and slow moving situation."

Louis Fried: "Games Managers Play," *Management Review,* September 1968. Managers often play destructive games with each other.

C. Northcote Parkinson: "Parkinson on Paperwork," *Administrative Management,* April 1966. Parkinson explains how organizations often continue to exist, even if they no longer are needed.

28
Management of Bureaucratic Organizations

. . . once formed, organizations acquire their own needs,
these sometimes becoming the masters of the
organization.
   AMITAI ETZIONI

A bureaucracy exists when officials of an organization are separated from the actual work. The German sociologist, Max Weber, was the first to give a systematic theory of bureaucratic organization. His views remain important because of his enormous influence on social scientists, and because of the continuing validity of much of his analysis. Weber's interest in organizations centered around the following questions: What are bureaucracies? What are their characteristics? Why and how do bureaucracies grow? What are the accompanying social changes? How efficient are bureaucracies, compared with other forms of organization structure and administration in achieving their goals?[1]

[1]See Max Weber, *The Theory of Social and Economic Organization,* trans. A. M. Henderson and Talcott Parsons, Oxford University Press, Fair Lawn, N.J., 1947. Also H. H. Gerth and C. Wright Mills, *From Max Weber,* Oxford University Press, Fair Lawn, N.J., 1946.

TYPES OF LEADERSHIP IN ORGANIZATIONS

Weber identified three grounds on which legitimate authority could be based: (1) the leader-oriented, (2) the patriarchal, and (3) the bureaucratic organization.[2] Each type has its own kind of organizational administration.

Leader-oriented Organization

In the leader-oriented organization the organizational hierarchy consists of the followers and a leader to whom the followers assign some special strength or unusual power. If followers lose faith in the leader's leadership capacity, or if his alleged unusual powers fail, then his leadership position may fall. Decision making is centralized in the leader; delegation of authority is strictly limited. Personal devotion and obedience to the leader become the criteria for appointment to an administrative staff—special qualifications, training, or professional competency are considerations of secondary importance. The administration of this organization has little orientation to rules and regulations; irrational decisions may be the rule rather than the exception. Office holding (and job holding) depends entirely on the decisions of the leader, and this extreme dependency on the leader makes all followers extremely sensitive to the leader's actions and desires; his wishes are taken as commands. The leader is *the* management of the organization; he considers unquestioned faith in his authority as absolutely necessary.

Patriarchal Leadership

In the second type, the patriarchal—or traditional—organization administration, authority is based on the traditional view of rank or station in the society under consideration—a "lord–subject" relationship. Decisions and commands are bound by precedent. Tradition is glorified. Within boundaries the lord can rule as his whim moves him. Who a person is and who his family was become criteria for work assignments.

Bureaucracy

A bureaucracy was the third type of organization discussed by Weber. In a bureaucracy the entire organizational structure as well as management techniques are largely determined without reference to specific leaders or power holders.

Jurisdictional areas of activity within the organization are designated. For example, a business organization may be subdivided into the areas of production, finance, marketing, and personnel. Duties of these areas are determined. Authority to carry out these duties is granted to the office in charge of each, and rules and regulations are established

[2] The discussion of these types is adapted from Max Weber, "The Three Types of Legitimate Rule," trans. Hans Gerth, in Amitai Etzioni (ed.), *Complex Organizations,* Holt, Rinehart and Winston, Inc., New York, 1961, pp. 4–14; and from Robert Dubin, *The World of Work,* Prentice-Hall, Inc., Englewood Cliffs, N.J., 1958, pp. 370–376.

to assure the regular and continuous fulfillment of assigned duties. Personal obedience is not owed to anyone. But obedience is owed to established rules and regulations. The process of determining jurisdictional areas is extended throughout the organization. A hierarchy results, with levels of graded authority and firmly ordered superior-subordinate relationships. Decisions may be appealed to higher authority levels.

Management of bureaucracies is largely based on the documents of the organization preserved in the files. This dependency on the files gives rise to all sorts of staff officials who concentrate on record keeping.

Thorough and expert training is required of a person filling an office. The terms of employment of these officials are contractual, and salary is based on the rank of the office, not on the amount of work or the individual office holder's productivity. The official business of the organization is to receive first priority. And management of bureaucratic organizations tends to follow the governing regulations of the organization—policies, procedures, and rules. Learning these rules represents part of the technical training.

A VIEW OF BUREAUCRATIC ORGANIZATIONS

Bureaucracies, as defined by Weber, are generally characterized as:

1 *Specialized.* There is a high degree of specialization of labor. Ability, not personal loyalty, is the condition for employment.

2 *Rational.* Official jurisdictional areas of the organization are rationally determined; offices within these areas are clearly defined; a hierarchy of authority is established; duties and measures of performance are established. Positions are described in detail, in writing, as to duties, responsibility, authority, and place in the hierarchy.

3 *Professional.* Offices are filled by full-time appointed officials. Employment is granted and performance is measured by formal, impersonal procedures. Officials are expected to perform in their offices within the impersonal rules of the organization. The organizational structure exists prior to filling its positions with people. Variation of personality is not admissible in measuring performance. Emphasis is on ability to perform, not on position in a social register.

4 *Impersonal.* Authority is impersonal; it is dependent on organizational regulations, and the amount of authority one has corresponds to the hierarchical rank of his office. Thus, acceptance of authority and acceptance of the person are not necessarily identical. The military service offers an excellent example of authority resting with rank and positions rather than persons.

5 *Autonomous.* Officials, because of their technical competence, are autonomous within their sphere of competence. Because they are the recognized experts within their area of competence, their decisions within this area are rarely questioned.

6 *Stable.* Successful accomplishment of assigned duties is encouraged by the rewards of stable careers, regular salary, expectation of promotion, increasing authority, salary increases, tenure, security, and guaranteed income after retirement.

When the bureaucratic organization is compared with the other types, we see that in some respects bureaucratic organizations have the potential for superior achievement of organizational goals. A bureaucracy frees the organization from the past and provides for delegation of authority. Power is no longer solely vested in a single individual. The bureaucracy also provides for the perpetuation of the organization through a line of succession and an orderly transfer of power. Weber was so impressed with the potential accomplishments of the bureaucracy that he came to regard it as the ideal type toward which the other organizational forms will tend to evolve.

DYSFUNCTIONAL BUREAUCRATIC BEHAVIOR

The same organizational and management techniques that make a bureaucracy potentially superior to leader-oriented and traditional organizations can be and often are used in ways contrary to organizational efficiency. Weber recognized that the bureaucratic apparatus may produce obstacles to efficiency, but he did not discuss these obstacles fully. The very factors which provide bureaucracies with their strength can be used in ways that will greatly reduce the advantages of the bureaucracy. Such dysfunctional organizational behavior is the subject of the remainder of this chapter.

Some behavior in bureaucracies is neutral if it does not help or hinder accomplishment of organizational objectives. Some behavior is negative; it actually tends to hinder organizational goal accomplishment. Both neutral and negative organizational behavior may be described as dysfunctional, because both do not function in ways that contribute to organizational goals. For the remainder of this chapter we investigate the ways in which members of bureaucratic organizations may behave dysfunctionally.

Avoiding Responsibility

When duties, regulations, procedures, and authority of jobs and offices are carefully described, then it would appear that accountability and responsibility could be determined easily. In a great many cases this is true. However, in bureaucratic organizations responsibility often can be avoided very easily by using bureaucratic techniques originally designed to produce efficiency. The letter of regulations rather than their spirit or intent may become the basis for decision making. Bureaucratic red tape and "the run around" may prevail. Minor officials may deny the right of appeal by hiding behind rules and regulations. Statements like "but the rules say this, and I can't do anything about it" may become commonplace. The slogan "don't stick your neck out" may become the operating philosophy of the managerial hierarchy.

The buck-passer   The first column in Figure 28-1 shows four management functions. The second column contains the typical situations in which there is a need for making

Management functions	Need for making command decision	Bases of decision	Ways of avoiding responsibility— (buck passing to:)
Directing	Existing operating problem	"The Book"	Higher or lower authorities
Coordinating	Departmental conflict	Existing power structure	Past history: "It has always been done that way."
Controlling	Questioning of control information	Right to exercise control function	Top decision makers
Innovating	New ideas	Custom	Past history: "Past methods or designs work."

Figure 28–1   Nonresponsible Bureaucratic Behavior Leads to Avoiding Responsibility*

Buck passing varies in method with the kind of work involved. Buck passing is one of the commonest ways to avoid responsibility and management decision making.
*From Robert Dubin, *The World of Work* (Prentice-Hall, Inc., Englewood Cliffs, N.J., 1958), p. 382. By permission.

decisions. The third column gives the basis on which responsibility is avoided. The last column gives the way in which responsibility is avoided. For example, a lower-level supervisor directing a large group of workers may when faced with an operating problem avoid his responsibility by making his decision according to "the book." That is, he may refer to the established policies and rules of the organization. His emphasis may be on the letter, not the intent, of the policies and rules. The supervisor willingly limits his discretion more than that intended by the rules so that he can protect himself in a secure position. Or a supervisor enforcing an unpopular rule can blame higher management for the establishment of the rule that he must enforce. At the same time strict enforcement of the rule for all his subordinates serves to protect the supervisor from charges of favoritism by these subordinates. Or a middle management supervisor may "pass the buck" of a bad decision to one of his subordinates, arguing that "I must back him, even if he is wrong."

Similarly, when a departmental conflict creates the need for a coordinating decision, a nonresponsible bureaucrat can avoid responsibility by basing his decision on the existing power structure, and his justification on the basis of past history. For example, in a manufacturing organization, the production and sales departments often disagree over product design. Sales wants a design that is easily sold, and production wants a design that could be produced economically. A manager who wishes to avoid responsibility in such a case can do so simply by siding with the stronger of the two departments. It is safer for the nonresponsible bureaucrat not to break with precedent.

Further, if a nonresponsible bureaucrat has one of his control (for example, cost control) decisions questioned, he can avoid responsibility for that decision by questioning the reliability, accuracy, and timeliness of the control data provided him. Such an inquisition can place the disagreeing departments on the defensive, and place top management in a position of having to correct the interdepartmental bickering. The original problem may be lost behind this smoke screen of bureaucratic squabbling.

Finally, innovation may be stymied by a nonresponsible bureaucrat seeking to avoid responsibility by his use of custom and past procedure. New ideas, new ways of doing things are arbitrarily rejected because "this is the way that we have always done things." If this is the prevailing management attitude, then new goals will probably never be developed.

The ostrich   One further way in which responsibility for decision making can be avoided in a bureaucracy is to refuse to face a problem. This type of management wants to "keep the lid on." It may regard the admission of the existence of problems as a sign of weakness. Managers of this type seem to live by the axiom, "Ignore it and it will go away." This behavior is dysfunctional because it permits small, relatively unimportant problems to fester and erupt into major crises. Thus a manager with this outlook may simply be involved in a cycle that defeats his original intentions. To avoid making problem-solving decisions, he ignores the problems. This type of manager buys time, but he may have to pay for it in the long run by creating major crises.

The climber   There is a related type of manager who uses the ignoring-the-problem technique with full knowledge of its consequences. We may call him "the climber." He knows full well that he can buy time by ignoring problems. This is exactly what he wants to do. For example, suppose he takes over the supervision of a troublesome department. By keeping the lid on the problems long enough, he begins to make it look as if his department were running smoothly. More importantly, he "looks good" as a manager. Thus, his chances of being promoted are increased. His task is to keep the lid on long enough until he can be promoted to another job. The crisis may erupt around his successor. Such an occurrence would confirm that the climber was a good manager. Top management may say, "After we promoted him to a new job, we found the new man could not handle that department."

The above are some ways a bureaucrat can avoid assuming responsibility despite the bureaucratic emphasis on pinpointing responsibility.

Spreading Responsibility

If an organization is faced with a general problem requiring expert opinion, the expert opinion likely can be obtained only from several sources. For example, in drawing up a long-range plan for future steel output, opinions on future markets, population centers, products, transportation, raw materials, and financial strength must be solicited. This need for expert opinion from many sources has led to what has been called "the bureaucratic process of conference, consultation and compromise."[3] Instead of a single office being charged with the responsibility for a complete task, as Weber apparently visualized, the task is assigned to a committee. Who assumes responsibility? Why, the committee, of course! But notice what happens to the concept of responsibility in the process. When responsibility for a task is assigned to a particular office, the incumbent takes that assignment as personal. But responsibility assigned to a committee is impersonal—each member feels that he can hide behind this impersonal body, for after all, all decisions were reached by compromise. A manager interested in avoiding responsibility soon learns that in numbers there is anonymity. Thus, the use of committees in bureaucratic organization is a means of spreading responsibility, often to the point where no effective responsibility exists. Poor performance often results. As one wag said, commenting on committee decisions: A camel is a horse designed by a committee.

Hoarding Authority

The bureaucrat who hoards authority attempts to gather to himself as much authority as possible. Typically, this type of bureaucrat sees himself as an infallible decision maker who is always eager to prove his competence and ability. As a result, he is often contemptuous of the decision-making ability of others, including subordinates. There appear to be two common conditions in which the hoarding of authority occurs:"filling the gap" and "empire building."

Filling the gap   Filling the gap occurs when some other executive is avoiding responsibility—perhaps even avoiding key organizational decisions. This avoidance of responsibility leaves an organizational void. Yet decisions must be made. When a void occurs, filling the gap is possible. The gap-filler may clearly recognize the void and be convinced that he is fully capable of filling it. Without official organizational authority, he steps in and fills the void. The important thing is that to fill the gap one must go beyond the boundaries of legitimately assigned authority. One must go far out on a limb. In such a vulnerable position, an executive must perform with superior competence or he will be removed. Realizing his vulnerability he may refuse to delegate. He may refuse to have any original thinkers in his department, and he may cultivate "yes men." He may overwork himself so that he will appear to be devoted excessively to his position. Be-

[3] William Miller, "The Business Elite in Business Bureaucracies," in W. L. Warner and N. H. Martin (eds.), *Industrial Man,* Harper & Row, Publishers, Incorporated, New York, 1959, pp. 109–129.

cause of his insistence on doing everything himself, he may become an organizational bottleneck. In the long run the organization suffers.

Empire building   The second type of responsibility hoarder is the empire builder. He clearly recognizes the importance of an office. He values the status, power, and pay of a substantial position. The amount of status, power, and pay may be measured by the number of subordinates reporting to him. Thus, one way of increasing his status, power, and pay is to enlarge his office. Being promoted is another way of achieving the same things. By adding more people, more space, and more physical facilities, an empire may be built. Make-work projects become prevalent.

Delay of Decisions

Modern organizations are highly interdependent; a delay in one place will have a cumulative effect elsewhere. Thus, large-scale organizations, particularly large-scale industrial organizations, place a high premium on timely decisions. In fact, a bad decision made on time may be better than a good decision made too late. For while the bad decision can often be reversed at low cost, the time lost waiting for a good decision in these areas can never be regained. Thus a problem of bureaucracies is that the complexity of the decision-making process makes it virtually impossible to get quick decisions. Smaller, less complex organizations may fill the void. In fact, many small businesses exist simply because they can make decisions faster than larger businesses.

Formalism and Ritualism

In a bureaucracy, reliability and conformity of behavior are valued. Merton pointed out that when a bureaucracy adheres to formalized rules, regulations, and procedures for a long time, the eventual result is that the rules become more important than achievement of organizational goals. Merton attributes this to the development of the bureaucracy.
The decay of a bureaucracy can be seen in four steps:

1 An efficient bureaucracy requires predictable responses and obedience to rules.
2 Obedience to rules eventually tends to convert them into absolutes. Rules are no longer seen as means to the accomplishment of organizational objectives. Obeying the rule becomes an end in itself.
3 Special problems not covered by the rules are not adequately dealt with.
4 Thus the rules which were designed to promote efficiency eventually become obstacles to that efficiency.[4]

Adherence to rules becomes a value in and of itself. The bureaucrat no longer sees rules merely as means to ends. Formalism and ritualism ensue. Technicalism and red tape result. The bureaucratic virtuoso, who never forgets a single rule, emerges. Rules must

[4]Cf. Robert K. Merton, "Bureaucratic Structure and Personality," in Amitai Etzioni (ed.), *Complex Organizations, op. cit.,* p. 54.

be strictly enforced to maintain personal security. Timidity, conservatism, and technicism become the operating guides for the bureaucrat. There is a petty insistence on the privileges of power and status.

Bureaucratic Sabotage

Sabotage within the bureaucratic hierarchy is more subtle than the wrench or sand in the gears that sometimes occurs in an industrial plant. But it can be just as effective in hurting performance.

Bureaucratic sabotage works within the framework of the established rules and regulations of the bureaucracy. Its most common form is the sabotage of a superior by his subordinates in either one of two ways. The subordinates may either withhold essential

---

Interdepartmental warfare*

1. Types	a. Cold war — avoid other departments — distorted, delayed or inadequate communications b. Cold war may escalate into open hostility. Warfare may spill over into other departments, resulting in alliances. c. Open hostility — follow the book to the extreme, red tape — bickering and arguing — gossiping — retain projects affecting enemy departments until the very last minute in order to create chaos for the enemy
2. Causes	a. No commonly accepted objective among the departments of a bureaucracy b. Communications breakdown c. Misunderstanding of rules and regulations d. Tactlessness e. Personality conflicts f. Power struggles g. Other
3. Objectives	a. Vengeance—"Teach them a lesson" b. Favorable recognition from superiors by making the enemy department look bad
4. Results	a. Reduced coordination and efficiency b. Damage toward the accomplishment of overall objectives c. Unity within departments against the enemy but increased pressure due to hostility between departments d. Time spent in both work and warfare creates a need for more employees. As a result, wasteful organizational growth and increased costs

---

* Contributed by John E. Bowen, Captain, United States Air Force.

information or they may flood their superior with so much information that he cannot possibly use all of it.

Another form of bureaucratic sabotage is illustrated by the following thought: If one wants to sabotage his supervisor, the best way to do it is to do exactly what the supervisor directs, and nothing more. Eventually such an approach is bound to make the superior look bad because:

1 The supervisor cannot possibly tell the subordinate everything to do. So the subordinate will not be effectively occupied much of the time.

2 Sooner or later the supervisor will make a mistake and give the subordinate an order that is incorrect. Although the subordinate knows of the mistake, it is the supervisor who is responsible because the subordinate merely followed orders (highly approved behavior in a bureaucracy).

In this case it is unlikely that the subordinate will be penalized for lack of initiative, for initiative is not highly valued in a bureaucracy. Adherence to instructions likely is more highly valued.

Stalemate

A bureaucracy may produce a stalemate among departments, where it is easier to do nothing rather than to make steps in the direction of progress. Consider, for example, two university departments, A and B. Department A supervises a certain curriculum, and has correctly decided that a certain course taught by department B should be dropped from the curriculum. Department B jealously wishes to keep the course in the curriculum. It may well be true that department B has the votes or other power required to block the change. Thus, department A would be stalemated into keeping the unneeded course, perhaps for many years.

The net result of such undesirable statemates is a tendency of the organization to become obsolete because it does not adapt fast enough to changing demands and environments. Unfortunately, these stalemates are frequently found in bureaucratic organizations.

VOCATIONAL ASPECTS OF BUREAUCRACIES

Regarding the vocational aspects of bureaucracies, Merton wrote:

> Most bureaucratic offices involve the expectation of life-long tenure, in the absence of disturbing factors which may decrease the size of the organization. *Bureaucracy maximizes vocational security.* The function of security of tenure, pensions, incremental salaries and regularized procedures for promotion is to insure the devoted performance of official duties, without regard for extraneous pressures.[5]

[5]Robert K. Merton, *Social Theory and Social Structure,* rev. ed., The Macmillan Company, New York, 1957, p. 196. (Emphasis added. By permission.)

There is much evidence indicating that persons who become members of bureaucracies may value security above all else. This appears to be as true of those in the executive suite as it is of those on the assembly line.

A company that achieves a reputation of being an insecure place to work often has difficulty in recruiting. For example, a few years ago, a large nation-wide concern realized that a large percentage of its upper-middle and top management would be retiring within five to eight years. The company was anticipating a rapid growth during this same period. It began to step up its college recruiting. In fact, it began to stockpile personnel in its junior-executive training program. But two years after the stockpiling policy began, the company was presented with an extended strike. Overhead had to be reduced. Many management trainees were temporarily laid off and others were fired. After the strike was settled the company found it very difficult to recruit college graduates. The word was out: the company could not provide secure employment for its trainees.

INCOMPETENCY IN BUREAUCRACIES

Bureaucracy often develops into a sort of closed society where the loyal and faithful are promoted regardless of performance. In turn these managers promote other loyal and faithful subjects. Often the jobs in a bureaucracy are so structured, and policies, plans, rules and standard operating procedures so complete, particularly in middle- and lower-management jobs, that incompetence can be hidden. Decisions can be made by the book, and if the book doesn't cover the situation, then the problem is treated as an exception to be appealed to the next-higher decision-making level. Originality and creativity are not required—only an ability to read and apply regulations. Thus, it often does not become apparent that a manager is incompetent until after he has been appointed to a fairly high-level job that requires some imagination and initiative. By that time, this executive has built his own sphere of influence. Top-level management (perhaps itself seeking to avoid responsibility) may then transfer him to a noncritical job, kick him upstairs to a higher-pay, higher-status, but purely functionary job, or "shore him up" by providing him with a brilliant assistant.

SUMMARY

Bureaucracies have the advantage of bringing order and rationality into the organization. But persons in bureaucracies do not always behave in ways that will maximize the accomplishment of organizational objectives. Frequently individuals acting for their own personal benefit, as they see things in a bureaucracy, may perform dysfunctionally in terms of organizational goals. In a bureaucracy the very things that were originally designed to promote organizational effectiveness can be twisted to reduce organizational effectiveness. Strict lines of authority and responsibility, rigid procedures, and vocational security may have been originally designed to promote organizational effectiveness. Without alert management all of these features over time may tend to be viewed as ends in themselves rather than the means to organizational goals. On the other hand, a healthy organization will focus primarily on the objectives it wishes to attain and secondarily on the procedures necessary to that goal.

Bureaucracies do offer significant advantages; but bureaucracies also present significant opportunities for long-run inefficiency, and perhaps organizational stagnation and death.

FOR REVIEW AND DISCUSSION

1 Define a leader-oriented organization. Give an illustrative example from your own experience.

2 Define a patriarchal organization. Give an illustrative example from your own experience.

3 In your own words describe the following terms which characterize a bureaucratic organization: (a) specialized, (b) rational, (c) professional, (d) impersonal, (e) autonomous, and (f) stable.

4 Explain the meaning of the phrase "dysfunctional bureaucratic behavior." Illustrate your explanation with an example from your own experience.

5 Explain the meaning of the statement: "Some behavior is dysfunctional from the viewpoint of the organization, but that same behavior can be functional from the viewpoint of the individual." Could a manager's behavior be functional in terms of his department yet dysfunctional in terms of the larger organization within which his department is found? Explain your answer.

6 Describe each of the following types of bureaucrats, and explain how each avoids accepting appropriate responsibility. Illustrate each type with an example, preferably taken from your own experience: (a) the buck-passer, (b) the ostrich, and (c) the climber.

7 Describe each of the following types of bureaucratic behavior, showing how each can be dysfunctional. Illustrate each type with an example, preferably drawn from your own experience: (a) spreading responsibility, (b) hoarding authority, (c) filling the gap, (d) empire building, (e) delay of decisions, (f) formalism and ritualism, and (g) bureaucratic sabotage.

8 Explain the working-condition advantages that a bureaucracy can offer an employee.

9 Describe the special problems that a bureaucracy may have in eliminating incompetency and manpower that may no longer be needed.

10 Are bureaucracies found only in governmental organizations? Explain your anser.

CASES

A   Crescent Pipeline, Inc., transported finished petroleum products from the southwestern part of the country to the east through its pipelines. The company had been formed in 1945, and by 1948 it was in full operation. It required 600 employees in 1948 to operate the company effectively.

Through the years Crescent had taken advantage of technological improvements, and had automated most of its pumping facilities. By 1960 the company could have, according to the reliable estimates of one of its managers, operated efficiently with 300 employees. However, in 1960 the company had 550 persons on the payroll. Company profits had been satisfactory, and the policy of the company was not to lay anyone off. The management felt it owed a job to its loyal employees, and it planned to reduce its present work force by attrition through resignation, retirement, and death. It was estimated that it would require twenty-five years for this attrition process to balance company needs.

In 1960 Delta Pipeline Company constructed a parallel line that directly competed for Crescent's business. Delta offered lower rates to customers because its operations were more efficient than those of Crescent.

Almost overnight, Mr. Jacob, president of Crescent, was forced to recognize that he would have to discharge immediately 250 employees if Crescent were to survive and be competitive with Delta. Mr. Jacob deeply regretted this turn of events, because he knew that most of his employees could not get comparable jobs elsewhere. They were all over forty years of age now, and practically no firm would give a permanent job to an employee over forty. Furthermore, none of the employees qualified for retirement benefits with Crescent.

1 Why had Crescent not laid off unneeded employees? Do you think this policy was wise from the company's viewpoint? From the employee's viewpoint? Give the reasons for your answers.

2 If Delta had not begun to compete with Crescent is there any reason to think that Crescent would have changed its policy of no layoffs? Explain how such a practice may cause waste and inefficiency in any noncompetitive situation—say a governmental agency.

3 Suggest some different approaches that Crescent might have taken toward its problem of excess employees. Evaluate each of your proposals from the viewpoints of Crescent, its customers, its employees, and its competition (existing or potential).

B   Captain Blaylock, a supply officer, had the reputationn of being a cautious person. When a proposal came to him, his first step was to research his extensive library of regulations. Captain Blaylock rejected the vast majority of such proposals, citing the appropriate regulation that he had interpreted as prohibiting the desired action.

Captain Todd was also a supply officer in another unit on the same base. Captain Todd was usually receptive to a proposal, and if he thought the request would serve the objectives of the organization, he approved it even if it were contrary to regulations. Captain Todd spent very little time studying regulations, but he was aware that he often broke a regulation. When this was pointed out to him he said: "Sure I break regulations at times—everybody knows it. But nobody has ever criticized me for it. And I don't think they ever will as long as what I do is for the good of the organization. But sometimes I worry; I may get hung for it if somebody gets mad at me."

Major Mills, who supervised both Captains Blaylock and Todd, was considering which one to recommend for promotion.

    1 Which officer do you think Major Mills should recommend for promotion? Why?

    2 What are the advantages and disadvantages of the approach of each captain?

    C The consumer products division of the Naylor Corporation consisted of the marketing, production, research, accounting, and personnel departments. Each department had a full-time secretary.

Because of the seasonal demand for some of its products, the work of the secretaries in the consumer products division was often unbalanced. Usually when one department was temporarily overloaded, secretaries in other departments had free time available.

Each time the secretary of a department became overloaded, her departmental manager vigorously requested funds for additional secretarial work from Mr. Parks, the division manager. The reply Mr. Parks gave was to call the department heads into a meeting and request that those with extra secretarial time available should assist the overloaded departments. All department heads claimed that their secretaries were already overworked but that they would see what they could do.

After each of these meetings the department heads reluctantly shared a minimum amount of secretarial work. However, in every case the practice was discontinued within two weeks after the meeting called by Mr. Parks. Both the department heads and the secretaries resented the practice.

In each yearly budget every department continued to press for additional secretarial funds although it was apparent that the overall work load of the division did not justify additional funds.

    1 Why were the department heads and their secretaries reluctant to share the available time?

    2 What bureaucratic game is being played by the department heads and their secretaries? What is Mr. Parks's part in the game?

    3 What recommendations do you have for Mr. Parks? For the department heads?

FOR FURTHER STUDY

Additional sources can be found in the sources cited in the chapter.

Books

Michel Crozier: *The Bureaucratic Phenomenon,* The University of Chicago Press, 1964, chap. 7. This highly recommended chapter is a powerfully effective analysis of modern bureaucracy.

C. Virgil Gheorphui: *The Twenty-Fifth Hour,* trans. Rita Eddon, Alfred A. Knopf, Inc., New York, 1950, p. 307. A scathing criticism of impersonal, formal organization practices.

Eugene V. Schneider: "Causes of Industrial Bureaucracy," *Industrial Sociology,* McGraw-Hill Book Company, New York, 1957, pp. 77–81. An excellent explanation of six ways bureaucracy can increase efficiency in industrial organizations.

Victor A. Thompson: *Modern Organization,* Alfred A. Knopf, Inc., New York, 1961, chap. 2. This chapter describes a bureaucracy.

Articles

Warren G. Bennis: "Organization Development and the Fate of Bureaucracy," *Industrial Management Review,* Spring 1966. "Bureaucracy will not survive as the dominant form of human organization in the future."

S. N. Einstadt: "Bureaucracy, Bureaucratization, and Debureaucracy," *Administrative Science Quarterly,* December 1959. Literature approaches bureaucracy from two points of view. First, it is considered a mechanism created for the successful implementation of goals. Second, bureaucracy is looked upon as an instrument of power.

Robert K. Merton: "Bureaucratic Structure and Personality," *Social Forces,* 1940, pp. 560–568. The nature, advantages, and disadvantages of bureaucracy are analyzed.

Robert K. Merton: "The Unanticipated Consequences of Purposive Social Action," *American Sociological Review,* 1936, pp. 894–904. A still-relevant description of the limitations of bureaucratic organizations.

Philip Selznick: "Foundations of the Theory of Organization," *American Sociological Review,* 1948, pp. 25–28. The basic rationale of complex, structured organizations is described together with their intended and unintended consequences.

William H. Read: "The Decline of the Hierarchy in Industrial Organizations," *Business Horizons,* Fall 1965. Technological changes are forcing a new appraisal of the relations, authority, and responsibilities between people in a modern corporation. New arrangements of people and tasks, which break with bureaucratic tradition, will develop to obtain successful coordination of human efforts.

29
Quantitative Techniques for Managerial Use

It [quantitative analysis] promises to convert many problems which now seem too complex, too chaotic, too random, or too uncertain for treatment with anything other than intuition, experience, and judgment to ordered patterns which can be analyzed with a vast variety of tools already known and widely used in other disciplines.
ABE SHUCHMAN

The increasing complexity of organizational problems requires that improved methods of decision making be discovered and utilized. Thus, quantitative techniques for managerial use have been developed.

Quantitative techniques are particularly relevant to problems of complex business enterprises. This chapter will emphasize the use of quantitative techniques as they are applicable to business problems.

Basically, the application of managerial quantitative techniques involves the introduction of the element of quantities. Quantitative techniques involve the use of numbers, symbols, and mathematical techniques.

THE SCIENTIFIC METHOD IN MANAGEMENT

Quantitative techniques for organizational decision making are examples of the use of the scientific method by management.

Every thinking man, when confronted with seemingly baffling problems of life, has often felt that "there ought to be a law"—some explanation that will bring order out of chaos. Such thoughts may have occurred to the army recruit forced to stand in endless lines, to a motorist caught and rendered immobile by rush-hour traffic, and to the business manager trying to determine the best level of inventory for one of his products. Man has consistently searched for underlying principles that will explain such frustrating problems. In observing this tendency of man, John Pocock wrote:

> This feeling is an essential and basic motivation of all thinking people and has been in the mind of man from time immemorial. The ancient Persians felt it when they looked up at the stars and attempted to determine some rule for describing their erratic courses. The astronomer Brahe was similarly motivated when he brought together all the massive data concerning the movement of the stars and planets. So was Kepler as he carried on and worked these data into his studies. But Newton came along with his development of the laws of gravity and the laws of motion before the underlying "law of the heavens" was understood—and he had to invent differential and integral calculus to do it.[1]

So it is with management. Scientific management is the application of the scientific method of investigation, analysis, and solution to the problems of organizations. The use of the scientific method by management is an expression of a way of thinking, a frame of mind, and a method of approach to solving organizational problems. Thoughtful managers have not been satisfied with only subjective bases for solving their organizational problems. Scientific bases for decision making have therefore been developed.

The quantitative techniques presented in this chapter are examples of the implementation of the scientific method for managerial use. The basic premise of scientific management is a belief that organizational problems follow definable patterns. Management scientists think that systematic investigation will uncover those patterns. The discovered patterns generally are expressed in mathematical models or equations. We thereby are able to employ the many helpful techniques of mathematics and computers. Scientific management thus tends to replace decisions made on the basis of experience or intuition with decisions made by the scientific approach.

In summary, the scientific method offers the following potentialities for solving organizational problems:

1 Mathematical procedures can be used.

2 High-speed data processing with electronic computers is possible when data are quantified.

3 As an important by-product, the use of the scientific method will probably stimulate more logical thinking about organizational problems in general.

MATHEMATICS IN MANAGEMENT

Mathematics is the language of numbers, symbols, and their relationships. Through the use of mathematics, the factors in a problem can be quantified and related, thus pro-

---

[1]John W. Pocock, "Operations Research: A Challenge to Management," *Operations Research,* American Management Association, New York, 1956, p. 7. (By permission.)

viding a medium by which a quantitative solution may be obtained. Mathematical procedures useful for organizational problems range all the way from simple arithmetic to the complex higher mathematics—including differential and integral calculus, partial derivatives, and differential equations, etc.

ELECTRONIC DATA PROCESSING

The development of the electronic computer is one of the most significant events of the twentieth century. Electronic data processing has revolutionized the collection, processing, and storage of data for most larger organizations. Some observers feel that the eventual impact of the electronic computer on society will be comparable in scope to that of the industrial revolution. Business organizations have particularly taken advantage of the electronic computer. Clearly the electronic computer has significant implications for quantitative techniques for managerial use.

Capabilities of an Electronic Computer

The operations that an electronic computer performs are deceptively simple. Of course, when very large numbers of simple operations appear together in a problem (often the case), the task becomes complex indeed.

Although there are many types and sizes of computers, they all have a number of similar qualities. The valuable qualities of most electronic computers include the ability to:

1 *Perform operations of arithmetic* (adding, subtracting, multiplying, and dividing). Up to hundreds of thousands of these calculations can be performed per second, depending on the capabilities of the particular computer.

2 *Compare data.* For example, a computer can determine if one bit of data is equal to, greater than, or less than another bit of data, and it will carry out certain instructions based on its decisions. These logical transactions can be performed about as rapidly as arithmetic calculations.

3 *Store data.* Millions of bits of information can be stored in the "memory" of a computer.

4 *Retrieve data.* Any data stored in a computer can be retrieved and used by the computer in a fraction of a second.

5 *Process data accurately.* Despite its speed, an electronic computer almost never makes a mistake.

Without doubt, the fantastic computation, logic, speed, accuracy, and memory abilities of electronic computers make them potentially valuable for a number of organizational problems.

Businesses, for example, have found the electronic computer capable of performing operations in the areas of process control, product design, scheduling, accounting, and other areas. In another field, computers do the required lightning-fast calculations for the exploration of space.

Computer Use in Perspective

The preceding section has shown the tremendous capabilities of computers for certain applications. Nevertheless, the introduction of a computer in the typical organization has been accompanied by problems.

The introductory period   Inspired by the enthusiastic reports of pioneering companies about the great accomplishments of electronic data processing (EDP) and frustrated with the mounting load of paperwork, many companies began to install data-processing equipment. Thoughts such as "we want to stay ahead in the game" and "we can afford it" seem to have played a major role in the decision-making process. In a great number of companies this transition to EDP took place without first thoroughly investigating the implications of such a major change.

After a period of almost irrational computer enthusiasm, managers now take a more critical look at these costly, but hopefully cost reducing, devices. The period of the belief that the pure act of introducing data-processing equipment will result in cost savings and other advantages appears to be over. Computers, which often cost several hundred thousands of dollars per year merely to rent, must show impressive results indeed to justify their cost.

The nature of improvements   The resulting improvements in efficiency were often not due to the operation of the electronic data-processing equipment per se. Rather, many improvements seem to have been achieved by the streamlining of systems and procedures required for the computer. Studies have revealed that as much as 80 percent of the benefits realized could have been gained without installing the equipment at all, only by modernizing the previous manual systems. But apparently most organizations will not discipline their systems to such a degree, unless the discipline is rigidly enforced by a computer system. Even where the introduction of EDP has resulted in improvements, a significant part of that improvement may be attributed to the redesign of remaining manual operations.[2] For these reasons it may be safely stated that merely replacing manual operations by electronic data processing does not necessarily bring about savings in cost.

Some organizational problems   In some companies, EDP caused problems because it suddenly interrupted the traditional relationships among existing departments. Sometimes the impact on the organizational structure was so great that new organizational schemes had to be developed and adequate recognition for this new unit had to be found.

Only a few companies actually seem to have realized all the tangible and intangible

[2]John A. Postley, *Computers and People*, McGraw-Hill Book Company, New York, 1960, p. 76.

benefits which they expected. One study suggested that only a minority of companies received considerable benefits from their computer efforts and that for most of the companies, computers were still a relatively costly undertaking.[3] This study found that only nine out of twenty-seven companies, all leaders in their fields, have made EDP a profitable operation. The study concluded that inadequate recognition by top management of the implications and capabilities of EDP was probably the main reason for the often unsatisfactory results.

Often status considerations appear to have played a significant part in influencing the decisions of executives to acquire computers. An EDP rental service complained: "The smaller computer makes it possible for a company to justify a machine that it really does not need. . . . Too many executives still regard a computer, any computer, as a corporate status symbol."[4]

The Future of EDP

The development of the modern, high-speed electronic computer has probably done more to advance the use of complex quantitative techniques for organizational problems than any other single factor. Although the electronic computer performs only routine operations, it can perform these operations so quickly and at such low unit costs, as compared with other methods, that the computer has made feasible the solution of many problems heretofore impractical to solve.

There are many areas where computers do not offer significant advantages to organizations in the foreseeable future. For example, computers cannot set policies or create new ideas for new products or services. Computers basically can do only what they are told to do by their inventor—man. The output of a computer is no better than the data that man puts into it. "Garbage in yields garbage out" (GIGO), even if it is expressed in six digits.

Yet we can surely expect that computers will play an increasing role as they are improved and as their cost is reduced. Where particular organizational problems occur frequently and can be routinized and quantified the computer can provide truly astonishing results.

ADVANTAGES AND LIMITATIONS OF QUANTITATIVE TECHNIQUES

Effective use of quantitative techniques requires clear knowledge of their advantages and limitations. For some organizational problems, particularly problems that occur frequently, quantitative techniques often can be effective aids to decision making. But quantitative techniques have significant limitations, and subjective judgment is likely to remain a principal approach to decision making. This section presents a summary of the most important advantages and limitations of quantitative techniques.

---

[3]John T. Garrity, *Getting the Most out of Your Computer*, McKinsey & Company, Inc., Management Consultants, New York, 1963, 20 pp.

[4]Herbert E. Klein, "More Value for the Office Dollar," *Dun's Review and Modern Industry*, September, 1963, p. 176.

Advantages of Quantitative Techniques

Any decision, if necessary, can be made purely objectively, since quantitative methods are not required to make a decision. Decisions—good or bad—can be made without quantitative techniques. Why, then, are quantitative methods often helpful in making decisions? The answer is that quantitative techniques often provide better decisions than those obtained through purely subjective processes. This is true because quantitative techniques require clear assumptions and rational reasoning. Here is the principal strength and value of the quantitative approach. Other approaches to decision making such as judgment, whim, hunch, and caprice often produce inferior decisions. In addition to providing answers to problems, quantitative approaches may improve the overall quality of thinking in the organization. As one writer says:

> There is no escaping the iceberg analogy for quantitative analysis—the bare structure of equations through which values are to be found to get answers is the one-tenth that shows above the surface; the reasoning from which the equations derive, the qualifications attached to them, the preliminary steps to be completed before they are used and the interpretation of the answers when they are secured compose the hidden remainder.[5]

Quantitative techniques thus encourage and enforce disciplined thinking about organizational problems.

Limitations of Quantitative Techniques

Quantitative techniques have some substantial limitations. These limitations must be weighed against their advantages.

The inherent limitations of mathematical expressions   The first and most basic limitation of quantitative techniques has to do with the nature of mathematical models or equations, and quantitative techniques almost always involve the use of such mathematical expressions. Assumptions, either explicit or implicit, are incorporated in the derivation of an equation or model. We cannot emphasize too strongly that an equation may be correctly used for the solution of an organizational problem *only* when the underlying assumptions and variables in the model are present in the problem at hand. In short, prior to employing a particular equation or model, one must determine if the model is relevant. Ignoring this caution will result in a mistaken application to an inappropriate problem. Operations researchers, who use quantitative techniques in organizations, have often been accused of having many solutions without being able to find problems that fit.

Cost of quantitative techniques   Intuition and experience are often the primary bases for a decision. Grant wrote:

> Many [organizational] decisions . . . are made on the basis of guesswork, with very little

[5]Jack D. Rogers, "Perplexities in Economic Analysis for Equipment Decisions," *Advanced Management,* May 1958, p. 31.

attempt to consider the various possible alternatives and to judge the differences between them that are measurable in [quantitative] terms.[6]

Such a basis of decision making is very often justified. Indeed, there are multitudes of decisions which must be made from day to day in organizations and which could not be made economically on any other basis.

The cost of quantitative methods of problem solving is often quite high. Specialized persons skilled in the use of quantitative techniques are expensive. But a typical manager, exercising intuition and judgment, may be able to make a decision very inexpensively. Hence, we can expect that quantitative techniques will continue to be limited simply because they are not, in many cases, worth their cost.

Intangible factors   Thirdly, there are the intangible factors. Successful use depends upon proper managerial attitudes and policies. In the words of Churchman:

> The answer depends, not on a magic formula, but on the availability of data, the cooperation of members of your company, and the receptivity of your management, to mention just a few factors. There is not now, nor will there ever be, any formula that will immediately prove its worth in the solution of management problems.[7]

Quantitative approaches make no allowance for such intangible factors. But in many instances success or failure hinges upon the consideration of these nonmeasurable human factors. The successful use of quantitative methods depends upon the skill, attitude, and vigor with which they are employed.

SELECTED QUANTITATIVE TECHNIQUES

We now present a discussion of representative quantitative techniques used for managerial decision making. Our presentation is necessarily introductory and descriptive. The field of quantitative techniques for organizational decision making is complex and requires specialized training for detailed study.

Some business organizations have large staffs that specialize in the application of quantitative techniques to their problems. In a number of universities, students can take undergraduate and graduate degrees in this specialty. Obviously, intensive coverage of the field is beyond the scope of this book; students interested in additional work in quantitative analyses will find excellent sources in the footnotes. We also illustrate some of the more important quantitative techniques in the appendices at the end of this book. Our purpose here is to give a broad understanding of, rather than specialized proficiency in, quantitative analyses as techniques for assisting in organization decision making.

[6]Eugene L. Grant, *Principles of Engineering Economy,* 3d ed., The Ronald Press Company, New York, 1950, p. 4.

[7]C. West Churchman, "Operations Research: An Evaluation," *Advanced Management,* April 1954, p. 17. (By permission.)

Inventory Models

Much work has been directed toward the quantitative solution of inventory problems. The result is that a wide variety of models has been derived to fit many situations. These models help determine the most economic lot size to manufacture or to purchase.

Many formulas have been offered as aids in determining the economic lot size. They range from simple to complex, depending on assumptions made in their derivation.

There are two classes of cost factors in lot-size determination. Very large lots result in low unit costs because of the economies of mass production. Large lots also take advantage of quantity discounts and spreading order costs over larger quantities. Large lots, however, require large inventories with high storage costs. Small lots, on the other hand, cost relatively little to store, but they cost more per unit to manufacture or to purchase. The total yearly costs associated with a decision regarding the economic lot size includes the setup cost or order per lot, the unit cost of the product, and the cost of carrying inventory. We wish to find the lot size that will minimize the sum of these costs.

Figure 29-1 shows the inventory level through time for a typical situation. The average level of inventory is one-half the maximum inventory, or average inventory is one-half the lot size.

The economic lot size will be the lot size that minimizes total costs. Cost relationships are shown by the curves in Figure 29-2. The minimum point on the total cost curve determines the most economic lot size and may be found graphically or mathematically. Locating the low point on the total cost curve (ELS) is the solution determined by inventory models. Appendix A at the end of the book illustrates a mathematical solution to an inventory problem.

Linear Programming

Linear programming is a mathematical or graphical technique that can be used to determine the best use of scarce resources to accomplish a defined objective. An electronic

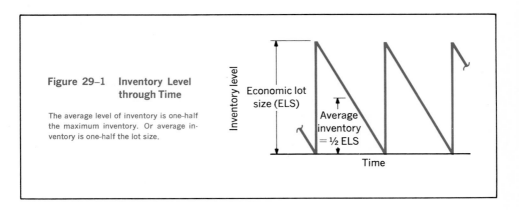

Figure 29–1   Inventory Level through Time

The average level of inventory is one-half the maximum inventory. Or average inventory is one-half the lot size.

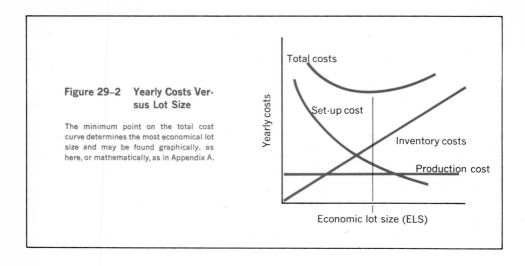

Figure 29–2   Yearly Costs Versus Lot Size

The minimum point on the total cost curve determines the most economical lot size and may be found graphically, as here, or mathematically, as in Appendix A.

computer is often used to assist in the mathematical solution of a linear-programming problem. But linear programming is not in any way a procedure for "programming" a computer. It is strictly an algebraic or graphical technique that, at least on relatively simple problems, can be used without an electronic computer. Complex problems generally require a computer simply because of the extremely large numbers of calculations required.

Linear programming can be applied to organizational problems such as:

1 Better use of the organization's resources.
2 Minimizing distribution costs.
3 Determining price-volume relationships.
4 Finding the optimum mix of products.

Simple examples will illustrate the areas in which linear programming can be used. For example, a company has three factories and four warehouses, all geographically separated. The problem is to find the best use of production and storage facilities to minimize freight costs in shipping the finished product from the three factories to the four warehouses. Linear programming may be used to find the solution.

In another area, an oil refinery can produce various proportions of fuel oil, gasoline, aviation fuel, and other products from its cracking plant, depending upon the type of crude oil used. The refinery can produce various proportions of these end products from a given crude, depending upon the refining process used. Because different crudes differ in price, and different refining processes vary in cost, additional variables are present. Assume the company has orders for definite quantities of end products. It must be decided which crudes to buy and which refining processes to use to produce the required amounts of end products at least cost, subject to the limitations of supply of crudes and the capacity of the plant.

Such a problem can be solved with linear programming. The solutions often are quite complex, and an electronic computer is generally required to perform the great number of calculations necessary.

When used to help solve this type of managerial problems, linear programming generally has the following well-defined characteristics:

1 The objective is to improve a current work situation so as to reduce costs, improve efficiency, increase profits, and so on.
2 Several alternative solutions to the problem are present, each of which would work. Linear programming, however, has as its objective finding the best solution or solutions.
3 Demand or requirements, as they are sometimes called, exist in every linear programming problem. Meeting a customer's required delivery date, for example, would be a demand typically found in linear programming problems.
4 The problem also presents certain restrictions, such as machine speed, machine capacity, warehouse space, and the like.
5 The results obtainable from the alternative solutions are significantly different.
6 And, obviously, to be solved by linear programming, the problem must be capable of being stated in quantitative terms.[8]

Appendix B at the end of the book illustrates the solution of a problem with linear programming.

The Break-even Chart

The break-even chart is a valuable but relatively simple technique for managerial decision making. A break-even chart clearly shows how different levels of sales affect the profits of a company. The chart yields a break-even point, which is the level of operations where income and costs are equal. Sales levels above the break-even point are profitable; sales levels below the break-even point are not profitable.

Simple break-even analysis commonly involves three assumptions: (1) that some costs are fixed regardless of sales volume, (2) that all remaining costs increase linearly with increasing sales volume, and (3) that the sales price is constant, regardless of sales volume. With these assumptions we can draw cost and revenue curves as straight lines on a graph.

We can illustrate the use of a break-even chart with an example. Assume the Jones Electronic Company has the following financial data:

$$\text{Sales price of product} = \$1.00 \text{ per unit}$$
$$\text{Variable costs for producing product} = \$0.60 \text{ per unit}$$
$$\text{Fixed costs} = \$20,000 \text{ per year}$$

Our problem is to find the break-even level of operations for the Jones Electronic Company. The solution using a break-even chart, in Figure 29-3, shows that the break-even

---

[8]Claude S. George, Jr., *Management in Industry*, 2d ed., Prentice-Hall, Inc., Englewood Cliffs, N.J., 1964, p. 44. Adapted by George from Nyles V. Reinfeld and William R. Vogel, *Mathematical Programming*, Prentice-Hall, Inc., Englewood Cliffs, N.J., © 1958, pp. 3–4. (Reprinted by permission of the publisher.)

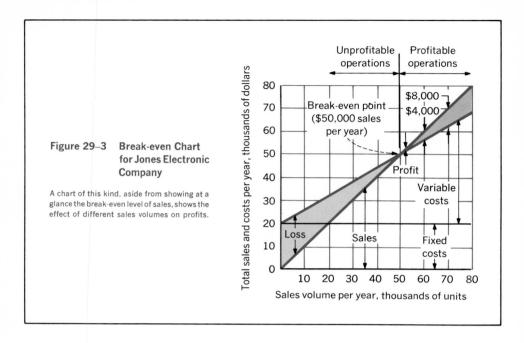

Figure 29-3   Break-even Chart for Jones Electronic Company

A chart of this kind, aside from showing at a glance the break-even level of sales, shows the effect of different sales volumes on profits.

level of sales for Jones Electronic Company is $50,000 per year. Sales below $50,000 per year will result in unprofitable operations; sales above $50,000 per year will return a profit.

In addition to showing the break-even level of sales, the break-even chart has the advantage of showing the effect of different sales volumes on profits. For example, again referring to Figure 29-3, we see that sales of $60,000 per year create profits of $4,000, and sales of $70,000 per year create profits of $8,000. Therefore, an increase in sales from $60,000 to $70,000, or approximately 17 percent, results in a 100 percent increase in profits, from $4,000 to $8,000. Thus, the break-even chart dramatically shows the influence of additional sales on profits. Increases in sales result in more than proportionate increases in profits, if fixed costs, variable unit costs, and price remain constant.

Queuing Theory

Queuing theory, often called the "theory of waiting lines," is a quantitative technique useful for determining the optimum number of service facilities. Queuing theory develops the relationships that are involved in waiting in lines.

The basic problem involved in waiting lines is to minimize the sum of two classes of cost: (1) the cost of waiting for service, and (2) the cost of providing service units. Customers waiting for service at a sales counter, planes waiting to land at an airport, machines waiting to be repaired, workers waiting on parts, and finished products waiting to be inspected are some examples.

The length of a line waiting to pass through a service facility depends on the rate and regularity of arrival at the facility and the rate of passage through the facility. If the arrival rate at the facility exceeds the service rate, the units seeking service will begin to form a line; a queue will develop.

The average service rate must always be made somewhat larger than the average arrival rate, otherwise a long waiting line will form. Thus, there must always be some idle or wasted time. The idle time, however, may often be reduced with queuing-theory analysis.

Game Theory

The analysis of competition between opposing factions is called "game theory." The competing elements may be the several firms in the industry. Competing elements also may be various internal departments of an organization that vie among themselves for the limited resources of the organization. Game theory provides a means of optimizing the allocation of available resources among competing demands.

The development of game theory may be credited chiefly to military strategists. It is a valuable aid in determining the proper allocation of limited war resources among the many competing demands of war. Game theory helps in making strategy decisions. It may be used to solve such problems as that of the fighter-plane pilot who has to decide when to fire his rockets. If his range is too long, his chance of hitting the target is small. On the other hand, the longer he waits, the greater becomes his own chance of being shot down. Through the use of game theory, the optimum range can be found.

There are basically two kinds of games, both of which may be illustrated by two types of coin matching. In the first type of game, each player makes a choice between matching with a penny or a nickel. If both coins are the same, that is, either both are pennies or both are nickels, the game is a stand-off. If both coins are not the same, the penny takes the nickel. In such a game it is always best strategy for either player always to play with a penny, for then he never loses. If a player used a nickel, he would run a risk of losing it without the offsetting chance of winning his opponent's nickel.

Such games, in which each opponent finds it always best to stick to one strategy, are called "single-strategy games." They are obviously not very interesting and certainly not often played. The situation could occur in warfare, however, if a general officer were pitted in a rifle duel with an enemy private. This is why the general usually stays behind the lines.

The other type of game may be illustrated by the usual coin matching in which each player chooses either heads or tails. If the coins match, the matcher wins; if they do not, the matchee wins. Should a player continue one strategy (for example, always playing heads), he would consistently lose because his opponent would soon discover and take advantage of this strategy or any other consistent pattern. The only safe way to play this game is to play heads and tails in a completely random manner, as by flipping the coins in the air. This type of game is called a "mixed-strategy game."

Competitive sports, such as football, are excellent examples of mixed-strategy games. A quarterback, for example, finds that his best strategy is randomly to mix his plays.

Mixed-strategy games are also seen in business situations. When one company's policies depend upon the reaction of another company, the situation can probably be seen as a mixed-strategy game. There are many examples in the area of marketing. For example, one company may design an advertising campaign. Game strategy thus considers a player's estimate of his opponent's probable actions.

Monte Carlo Method

Events in organizations often occur at random. This means simply that the *sequence* of occurrence is unpredictable. That is, no pattern of occurrence exists. The *frequency* of occurrence is another matter; it can be predicted.

Named after the famous gambling center, the *Monte Carlo method* is a technique that simulates random occurrences. Queuing theory and game theory are two examples of techniques that can use the Monte Carlo method. Both waiting lines and games involve random elements that can be simulated with the Monte Carlo method.

The Monte Carlo method can be used in queuing-theory analysis of scheduled and nonscheduled landings at an airport. The method can simulate many arrivals and landings that have the same properties as the actual arrivals and landings. An electronic computer can be used to perform the large number of computations required for such a problem.

Instead of using actual planes and airfields for a sample study, the whole job may be done by an analyst with the aid of the Monte Carlo method and other quantitative techniques. Theoretical analysis thus gives in a short time data equivalent to that of much counting and timing at an airport. Quantitative analysis could be used to determine the optimum scheduling of planes and airport facilities. Thus, the sum of costs of planes waiting to be serviced and the service costs can be minimized.

Search Theory

Search theory, like game theory, initially was developed by the military. Search theory originated from study of the problem of locating enemy submarines with limited detection resources.

A significant application of search theory in business has been to the problem of allocation of sales effort. Suppose a business has a limited number of salesmen who call on a wide variety of customers. Some of the customers are large and often place large orders. Some customers are small; orders from them will usually be relatively small. With a limited number of salesmen available, search theory indicates that the large customers should be visited more often than the small. With a very few salesmen, it would be economical to visit *only* the large customers.

Search theory helps to provide an answer to this problem and to some of its more subtle implications. For instance, optimum policy for the company might indicate that orders should be solicited from some small customers. Optimum policy for a salesman, from his own personal viewpoint, might be that he restrict his efforts solely to large customers. In other words, he might tend to maximize his sales per unit of sales effort at the expense of the additional volume the company would gain from making some sales to small customers. Search theory provides a means of reconciling these opposing tendencies. Optimum allocation, recognizing the divergent viewpoints, is obtained. The ultimate solution to such a problem might be to adjust the salesmen's commissions so that what is good for them is also good for the company. For such a problem, search theory may help to provide a means of optimizing the entire operation as well as the sub-functions of the operation.

Other Quantitative Techniques

The glossary of organizational quantitative analysis abounds in additional terms which have intriguing, sometimes awesome, sounds and connotations. Value theory, symbolic logic, information theory, subsystems, subproblems, statistical decision theory, automatic decision making, probability models, regression analysis, matrices, servomechanisms, state-probability method, and operational gaming are some examples. Though discussion of all these concepts is beyond the scope of this chapter, we can recognize that there are available extensive and varied quantitative techniques which can be applied to the solution of managerial decision problems.

SUMMARY

Quantitative methods of solving organizational problems sometimes produce better solutions than purely subjective means. Quantification requires that assumptions be explicit, that reasoning be logical, and that variables be expressed in their proper relationships. But since quantitative approaches are limited in their usefulness by assumptions, costs, and intangible factors, scientific management is necessary for their effective use. They are clearly not the only useful approach for solving organizational problems because subjective means remain valuable.

The extensive applicability of quantitative techniques to organizations is clear. But we need to remember that quantitative techniques are merely tools of analysis; they are not the complete decision-making process. As George wrote:

> Neither breakeven analysis, nor operations research, nor electronic data processing can make the final decision. They do, however, often suggest best alternatives based on quantita-

---

[9]Claude S. George, Jr., *op. cit.*, p. 61.

tive data. In the final analysis, of course, a manager still has to set objectives and decide whether or not to follow the solutions suggested by these devices.[9]

Quantitative analysis is a supplement to rather than a substitute for management; one must never lose sight of this fact. In the final analysis many organizational decisions will involve the human element.

FOR REVIEW AND DISCUSSION

1 Explain the advantages and limitations of using quantitative methods in the solution of organizational problems.

2 Describe the valuable qualities of an electronic computer.

3 Explain the statement: "The resulting improvements in efficiency were often not due to the operation of the electronic data processing equipment per se."

4 Have decisions by management to acquire a computer always been made on rational bases? Explain.

5 Define the term GIGO. What special importance does it have in the EDP field?

6 Explain the use of inventory models. What cost factors are involved?

7 What is linear programming? What are some types of problems that linear programming can help solve? What characteristics must a problem have if linear programming is to be used?

8 What are some types of problems for which queuing theory can be used? What happens if the demand for service is greater than the rate of service? Explain your answer.

9 For what types of business problems might game theory be helpful?

10 Explain some uses of the Monte Carlo method and search theory.

11 Do you think the day will come when all decisions in a business organization are made with the assistance of qualitative methods? Explain your answer.

CASES

A   Robert Bakery has the following accounting data:

$$\text{Fixed costs} = \$10,000 \text{ per year}$$
$$\text{Average sale} = \$0.60$$
$$\text{Variable costs for average sale} = \$0.30$$

Find the break-even level of sales. What would be the profit (or loss) at sales of $15,000 per year? At sales of $25,000 per year? Use a break-even chart in your solution.

B   (Refer to Appendix A) Mr. Stark, manager in charge of the inventory of Rex Industries, wishes to know the economic manufacturing lot size of a certain product. Each year sales of this item amount to 2,000 units. Setup costs are $100, and the other costs of manufacturing total $25 per unit. Mr. Stark has estimated that carrying an inventory costs 40 percent of the value of the inventory each year. Calculate the economic manufacturing lot size.

C   (Refer to Appendix B) Tom Jeffery, a salesman, spends all his working time calling on customers in the large Patton Building. There are a large number of retailers and wholesalers in the building—more than Tom would ever have time to call on. Tom is willing to work no more than an eight-hour day. He has a maximum budget for free samples to give to customers of $24 per day. Up to $24 of samples per working day are made available at no cost to Tom by his company, but there is no way he can get more samples.) Tom has found that the average wholesale call takes one hour, requires $2 worth of his samples, and returns him a commission of $4. For some reason, calls on wholesalers are so exhausting to Tom that he can make a maximum of seven wholesale calls each day. He has no such limitations on the less-tiring retail calls. The average call on a retailer takes thirty minutes, and requires $3 worth of samples. Like the wholesale calls, each retail call earns a commission for Tom of $4. Assume travel time between calls is insignificant. Solve by graphical linear-programming analysis.

  1 How many calls of each type should Tom make each day to maximize his income?
  2 How many hours would he work each day?
  3 What would be the total value of the samples he uses?
  4 What effect would Tom's limitation of no more than seven wholesale calls have on the answer?

FOR FURTHER STUDY

Additional sources can be found in the sources cited in the chapter.

Articles

James B. Boulden and Elwood S. Buffa: "Corporate Models: On-Line, Real-Time Systems," *Harvard Business Review,* July–August 1970. On-line, real-time, small-scale decision-making systems will be used eagerly by managers.

Robert Campbell: "The Eerie Interfact of Man and Machine," *Life,* Oct. 27, 1967, p. 72. Compares electronic computer capabilities with those of humans.

Gary W. Dickson and John K. Simons: "The Behavioral Side of MIS," *Business Horizons,* August 1970. Installation of management information systems may cause severe dysfunctional reactions from organizational members.

Roy N. Freed: "Get the Computer System You Want," *Harvard Business Review,* November–December 1969. Management failures have caused mismatches of corporate needs and computer systems.

Jay W. Forrester: "Industrial Dynamics—A Reply to Ansoff and Slevin," *Management Science,* May 1968. The directions, concepts, and potentials of the industrial dynamics approach are explained.

Robert A. Hammond: "Making O.R. Effective for Management," *Business Horizons,* Spring 1962. The total effectiveness of O.R. can be improved by careful planning

and close coordination between O.R. problem solvers and the solution imple-
menters.

Wesley R. Liebtag: "How an EDP Personnel Data System Works for Corporate Growth,"
Personnel, July–August 1970. The EDP personnel data for a large company is described.

Francis E. O'Meara: "The Challenge of Operations Research," *California Management
Review,* Summer 1965. In operational management research, the essential factor
has become a basic scientific principle—ask the right question.

John F. Rockhart: "Model-Based Systems Analysis: A Methodology and Case Study,"
Industrial Management Review II, Winter 1970. Model-based systems analysis provides a framework for further use of models to structure organizational problems.

Robert F. Vandell: "Management Evolution in the Quantitative World," *Harvard Business
Review,* January–February 1970. Uses of different quantitative tools for managerial
decision making are described.

30
Management and Systems Analysis

I must create a System, or be enslav'd by another Man's,
I will not Reason and Compare: my business is to Create.
  WILLIAM BLAKE

The word "system" has become commonplace in modern society. One can scarcely read the newspaper without finding "economic system," "escape system," and "social system." Management has become involved with systems theory and practice because organizations are systems in the truest sense of the word.

THE SYSTEMS CONCEPT

A system is a set of interrelated, interdependent, or interacting elements. It is an organized or complex whole; a combination of things forming a unitary whole. This definition is quite encompassing; it includes everything from an ant to a man to a bicycle to the cosmic universe.

The field of General Systems Theory has been developed in an effort to bring together many previously unrelated specialists to assist in the solution of common problems. Most investigations along this line have utilized one of two basic approaches:

1 Examination of the entire universe in pursuit of "underlying" similarities which are found in all areas of study.
2 Arrangement of theoretical constructs in a hierarchy of complexity corresponding to the complexity of the "individuals" of various disciplines and from static to more dynamic factors.[1]

In the first approach, phenomena such as growth, which is common to practically all living systems from the smallest cell to the largest business corporation, are examined in a search for analogies. In the second, an understanding of less complex systems is used as the stepping stone to the analysis of more complex ones. Regardless of the approach, the objective is the same—to analyze the functional interdependence between elements of a system, so that the whole may be better understood.

To illustrate, Scott uses Figure 30-1 to show the interdependence of the various parts

[1]Kenneth E. Boulding, "General Systems Theory—The Skeleton of Science," *Management Science*, April 1956, p. 200.

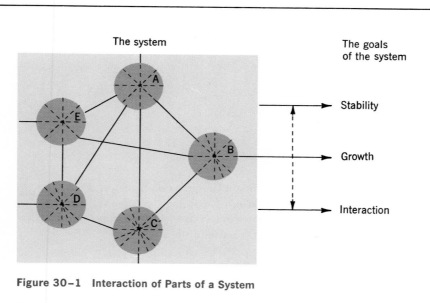

Figure 30–1   Interaction of Parts of a System

The parts of a system interact in accomplishing its goals.

Source: From William G. Scott, *Organization Theory*, Richard D. Irwin, Inc. Homewood, Ill., 1967, p. 124. Used with permission.

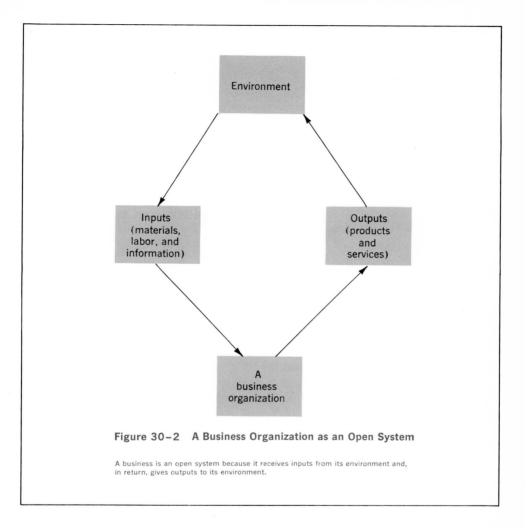

Figure 30–2   A Business Organization as an Open System

A business is an open system because it receives inputs from its environment and, in return, gives outputs to its environment.

of an organization.[2] In the diagram, the large box represents the system under consideration—the organization. The circles represent the parts of the system such as individuals (A), the formal organization (B), the informal organization (C), status and role-expectancy system (D), and the physical work environment (E). The lines illustrate the links between (solid) and within (dotted) the elements of the system. Finally, the arrows specify the goals of the system and the reasons for the interaction of the elements. A basic idea is that various elements, although possessing their own distinct objectives, contribute to the overall goals of the system through the process of mutual reinforce-

[2]See William G. Scott, *Organization Theory*, Richard D. Irwin, Inc., Homewood, Illinois, 1967, pp. 124–125.

ment. Consequently, the systems approach requires that the "whole" be investigated from the standpoint of the totality of the elements that compose it.[3] Thus, attention has been given in previous chapters to formal characteristics such as authority and accountability as well as the informal relationships that exist among men in organizations. Only after one has examined the various formal, informal, and environmental elements as well as the interconnecting processes can he hope to understand the organization as a whole system.

There are two basic types of systems, open and closed. A closed system is one that is self-contained and isolated from its environment. In the strict sense closed systems exist only in theory, for all real systems interact with their environment. Perhaps it is worth noting in passing that a problem of traditional management and organization theory was that it treated an organization largely as if it were a closed system. Now it is appreciated better that environmental elements are important, and there now is emphasis on treating organizations as open systems.

By far the most important type of system is the open system. An open system influences and is influenced by the environment through the process of "influence reciprocity," which results in a dynamic (changing) equilibrium. A business organization provides an excellent example of the process of influence reciprocity and, therefore, of an open system. As shown in Figure 30-2, a business takes inputs such as raw materials, labor, and information and converts them into products and services desired by consumers. Changing conditions in the environment can influence the operations of the firm.

For example, the producer of reciprocating engines for propeller-driven aircraft takes raw materials and technology from the environment. The manufacturer must also have knowledge of changing conditions. Through information it may be determined that the jet engine holds the promise of the future. The firm's continued existence can be assured only through research and development and other measures to provide products desired in the future.

MANAGEMENT OF SYSTEMS

If one could withdraw to some far away point and observe a complex organization, several things would become evident which are difficult to see from within. For instance, it would be easy to recognize that all complex organizations, businesses or otherwise, draw upon the environment for inputs, allocate these inputs, and combine them with internal factors to produce certain desirable outputs. The success of these outputs can then be determined by means of feedback.

Consider a university. It draws students and faculty from its environment, combines

[3]Paul Adler, Jr., "Toward a System of General Management Theory," *Southern Journal of Business,* July 1969, p. 112.

them in a proper mix, and supplies society with graduates. After the student graduates, the influence relationships continue. He and his fellow graduates practice their newly acquired skills, and the environment judges their success. If they are unsuccessful, the information flows back to the university, which then must correct accordingly. If they are successful as graduates, the institution is rewarded with a favorable reputation and resources.

As Figure 30-3 illustrates, four distinct stages can be described in the operation of an organization: the objective stage in which the goals of the system are formulated, the allocation stage wherein resources are combined and production initiated, the accomplishment stage where objectives are realized, and the feedback stage where the system evaluates its performance.

Objective Stage

Each stage is a subsystem of the larger system with its own inputs, operations, and outputs. The objective stage is the planning phase, or that period when the organization attempts to determine ways of coexisting with the environment while establishing performance standards and accomplishing its own specific goals. In other words, it attempts

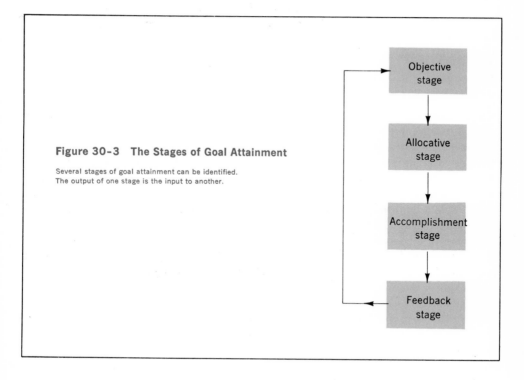

Figure 30-3   The Stages of Goal Attainment

Several stages of goal attainment can be identified. The output of one stage is the input to another.

to determine how it can achieve "symbiosis" (mutual beneficial living together of two dissimilar organisms) with its environment. A businessman seeks to establish a mutually beneficial relationship with federal and state regulatory agencies and the competitive environment. College presidents and football coaches are equally concerned with alumni associations, while ministers are sensitive to the thinking of their congregations.

During the objective stage special emphasis should be placed on strategic planning. Economic conditions, competitive circumstances, and numerous other such factors are important. The objective stage sets the overall goals of the organization.

Allocative Stage

The specific production process is set in the allocative stage. It is here that quantitative techniques have found their great application in providing systematic methods for combining resources and utilizing them in efficient ways.

Accomplishment and Feedback Stages

Once the information and physical raw materials are drawn together and systematically combined, the output of the system is obtained in the accomplishment phase.

Through feedback the objectives of the system are compared with actual output. The law of effect operates here, because if performance is satisfactory the process is reinforced. If not, alternations in the system's operations are required.

INFORMATION SYSTEMS

Effective management of an organization requires good information systems. Logical decision making requires an understanding of the circumstances surrounding an issue and knowledge of the alternatives available. The more pertinent and timely the information, the better the resulting decision. An organization has no natural memory other than the memory of the individuals within it. Since individuals come and go, administrators must develop extensive networks of reporting, or management information systems, to retain essential information over long periods of time. Few firms have been successful in developing totally adequate information systems for decision-making uses. A number of reasons have been advanced for this lack of success including inadequate efforts by top management, failure to make appropriate use of computer capabilities, and incorrect approaches to system design which have emphasized efficient processing more than the importance of the information.

Fortunately, recent trends indicate that better information systems are being developed in all types of organizations. For example, a law enforcement agency uses a complex computerized system for gathering and communicating relevant information from some ninety remote stations for use in decision making. Also, sophisticated information systems have been developed by utility companies that generate electrical power at a variety of locations. These systems provide "running" computations of costs at each producing plant, so that each unit of demand may be supplied, within certain limits, from the least expensive source. The computations include such factors as production and transportation costs.

FLOW CHARTING

Flow charting is a tool that is important in analyzing a system. Flow charting is particularly valuable in sequencing problems for electronic computer processing. It is a method of diagraming a problem in terms of the logical steps involved in its solution. This forces logical thinking and puts the problem into a form that can be programmed for a computer.

Consider the process of computing a student's grade in a given course. Figure 30-4 provides a flow chart of the steps involved. First, from the sum of all test scores, obtain a total. Next, compare the total with the established standard and assign the appropriate grade. When the logical steps are completed the student will be assigned the grade that corresponds to the quality of his work. Similar methods can be used to solve actual problems in the business environment.

For another example, consider the process involved in filling customer orders by a producer-distributor of specialized tools. Assume that the orders he receives can result in one of four possible courses of action. He can:

1 Fill the order from stock.

2 Assemble the item using standard parts and custom build the others in the regular production department.

3 Custom build all parts to unique specifications in the custom shop.

4 Refuse the order entirely because of an inability to construct for one reason or another.

Figure 30-5 illustrates, in flow chart form, the alternatives available. In this case, as in the previous one, the diagram makes explicit the range of action available to the supplier.

Flow charts can be used to design complex systems as well as to solve actual problems. In almost any problem where the solution depends upon logical sequencing of operations or the proper positioning of various types of equipment, the flow chart can be a valuable tool for analysis. Unfortunately, many problems—such as those involving non-quantifiable components—cannot be solved through logical analysis.

PROBLEMS OF SYSTEM DESIGN AND IMPLEMENTATION

Through the years men have felt mistrust for mechanical devices, even when machines have relieved them of the most exhaustive forms of physical labor. Although the fears of the rank-and-file worker were the dominant ones with respect to automation, managers and workers on all levels have at times shared the fear of the electronic computer.

The designer of any system should be particularly careful not to destroy company patterns or throw out all the "sacred cows" of the executives. Moreover, care must be

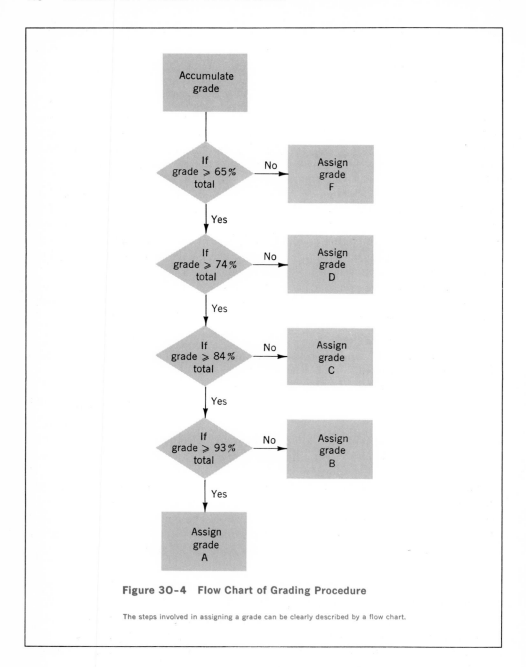

Figure 3O-4   Flow Chart of Grading Procedure

The steps involved in assigning a grade can be clearly described by a flow chart.

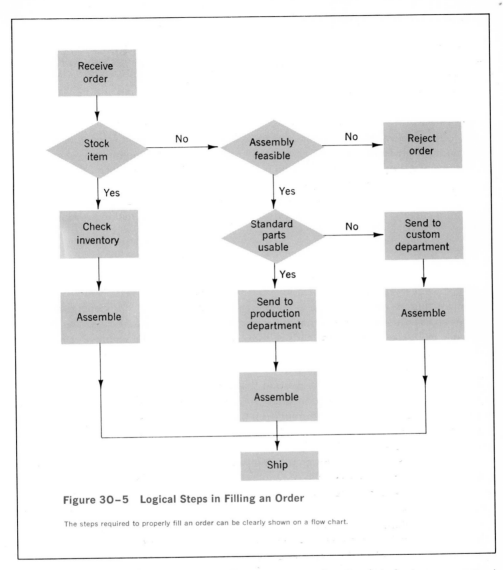

Figure 30–5   Logical Steps in Filling an Order

The steps required to properly fill an order can be clearly shown on a flow chart.

taken to align the system with established patterns. To illustrate, if employees are used to participating in decision formulation and implementation, they should be allowed to do so with respect to the system under consideration.

Middle- and lower-level managers likely will have another problem. They usually have a rather narrow perspective of the system as a whole. It may be difficult for them to identify with a "piecemeal" contribution and to project its relationship to the total system.

THE SYSTEMS CONCEPT AND THE FUTURE

Complex systems, both organizational and electronic, have been developed to perform almost unbelievable tasks. No doubt the future will witness equally fantastic accomplishments.

For instance, the systems concept allows one to think beyond the confines of a single organization. One example is the pooling of information processing capabilities among various firms. This now is practiced by banks and airlines.

Another interesting possibility is the application of management science techniques to the administration of public programs. Systematic procedures might better coordinate the actions of government agencies which at times engage in conflicting or overlapping projects because of information gaps.

Thus, the systems concept represents a promise for the future and a present challenge to managers, who have the responsibility of refining it and making it more meaningful.

SUMMARY

In recent years systems analysis has become important for managers. Systems analysis recognizes that an organization is a complex of interrelated and interdependent parts. Systems analysis also recognizes that the environment is important, because an organization receives inputs from it and sends outputs into it. Perhaps the greatest value of the systems approach is that with it one can get a clear concept of a large system composed of many smaller systems.

Systems analysis permits a recognition that the parts of a system, without effective coordination, do not necessarily contribute best to the larger system. In fact, if the goals of subsystems are substantially different from those of the larger system, suboptimization may occur. In such a case the subsystem works toward its goals but may not contribute adequately to higher goals.

Systems analysis focuses upon accomplishing goals, which is the reason for existence of the organization. From the systems point of view several steps in accomplishing goals can be identified. These include the objective, allocation, accomplishment, and feedback phases.

Systems analysis is closely related to flow charting, electronic data processing, and other sophisticated management technologies. These all can be extremely valuable, but they should always take into account the human resources of the organization. Systems analysis is relatively new, and the ultimate boundaries of its contributions remain to be discovered.

FOR REVIEW AND DISCUSSION

1 What does the term "symbiosis" mean as applied to organizational systems?

2 Define closed and open systems. Which type of system is a business organization? Why?

3 What is a flow chart? How can it be useful in designing systems and analyzing problems?

4 Make a list of the number of times you see the word "systems" during any given day. Analyze the contexts within which the word is commonly used.

5 Describe the objective, allocative, accomplishment, and feedback stages of goal accomplishment.

6 Make a flow chart, with at least ten boxes in it, of one of the following: obtaining a meal in a cafeteria, selecting and buying a car, preparing a hamburger, or grading fresh peaches.

CASES

A   ". . . the British created a civil service job in 1803 calling for a man to stand on the Cliffs of Dover with a spyglass. He was supposed to ring a bell if he saw Napoleon coming. The job was abolished in 1945."[4]

1 Why do you think the job was not abolished sooner?

2 How could a systems point of view result in earlier abolition of the job?

B   City University had been in existence for over 100 years. It became nationally prominent in the 1920s due to its outstanding faculty. During the early 1920s the University had been fortunate in receiving large sums of money, which were used to attract and pay its outstanding faculty.

Since its peak in the 1920s, the University's reputation has steadily deteriorated. The administration had continually complained that funds were inadequate to maintain its high reputation. However, a study by Mr. Sparks, a management consultant, revealed that total funds available to the University in 1970 and for the past three decades had been comparable to funds available to other universities with much higher reputations.

Mr. Sparks compiled the cost of instruction by departments of the University. The following table presents the relative costs of several selected departments.

DEPARTMENT	COST PER CREDIT HOUR
A	X
B	3X
C	20X
D	5X
E	2X

The five departments were comparable in their methods and levels of instruction. In other words, these were not departments which required special facilities, equipment, or faculty for instruction.

Further investigation revealed that with minor exceptions the new budget for each

[4]From Robert Townsend, *Up the Organization*, Alfred A. Knopf, New York, 1970, p. 93.

department each year since the 1920s had been last year's budget, plus the percent of new funds available to the University. In other words, every department in any given year received almost the same percentage increase.

During the past forty years substantial changes had occurred in the distribution of students in the various departments. For instance, Department A had from 1930 to 1970 increased its enrollment 500 percent. On the other hand, Department C's enrollment, for example, had decreased by 50 percent in the same period.

When Mr. Sparks presented his report to President Hopkins, he was taken aback by President Hopkins' response. After reviewing the report President Hopkins had said, "Well, this is all well and good, Mr. Sparks, but you can't run a university like a business."

   1 Do you agree with President Hopkins' comment? Why?

   2 Do you agree with the University's traditional budget policies? Why?

   3 Explain how a systems point of view can contribute to better administration of the university.

FOR FURTHER STUDY

Additional sources can be found in the sources cited in the chapter.

Articles

Kenneth E. Boulding: "General Systems Theory: The Skeleton of Science," *Management Science,* April 1956. This landmark paper shows how general systems theory can integrate and unify theories from different fields. Also, fields of study can be structured in a hierarchy. Several levels of organizations exist, ranging from simple to extremely complex. They all are interrelated.

Stanley E. Bryan: "Total Management Concept," *Business Topics,* Spring 1966. It is important to optimize the system with a total management concept.

James W. Cullington: "Age of Synthesis," *Harvard Business Review,* September–October 1962. There is a move toward an interdisciplinary "wholeness" view of business problems and away from looking at them only in a specialized, analytical fashion.

Richard A. Johnson, Fremont E. Kast, and James E. Rosenzweig: "Systems Theory and Management," *Management Science,* January 1964. The systems concept may be a conceptual scheme for integrated study of organizations and management.

Justin G. Longenecker: "Systems: Semantics and Significance," *S. A. M. Advanced Management Journal,* April 1970. A simple, lucid explanation of the systems concept.

William F. Pounds: "The Nature of Systems," *The Conference Board Record,* August 1970. Systems analysis is valuable because it defines the boundaries of a system and identifies the relevant variables.

Seymour Tilles: "The Manager's Job: A Systems Approach," *Harvard Business Review,* January–February 1963, pp. 73–81. A systems approach to management promises to provide the manager a way of taking advantage of the vast amount of knowledge now appearing and a framework in which to function.

31
Effective Management— An Overview

*The life-cycle thesis is myopic, for man's will determines
how long organizations live.*
  JOHN H. ABERNATHY

*Models of [organizations] are needed which provide for
the continuous generation and development of new
ideas, new programs, and new concepts.*
  JOSEPH W. TOWLE

You are probably a member of hundreds of organizations. It is also probable that you,
as shown by your study of this book, are preparing yourself for a managerial role. Or if
you are already a manager, you may be studying this book with a view toward improving
your managerial performance in your present position or to prepare yourself for larger
opportunities.

Whatever your reason for studying this book, it is highly important for you to understand the profound effect that you as a manager will have on your organizations. Perhaps
most important of all are the concepts and theories that you as the manager have about
the nature and functioning of your organizations. Your concepts and theories, as expressed in your managerial performance, will inevitably influence every facet of your
organizations. Every organization will eventually reflect the quality of its management.

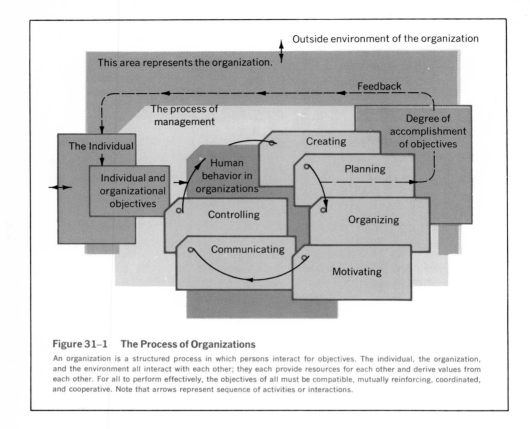

Outside environment of the organization

This area represents the organization.

Feedback

The process of management

Creating

Degree of accomplishment of objectives

The Individual

Planning

Individual and organizational objectives

Human behavior in organizations

Controlling

Organizing

Communicating

Motivating

Figure 31–1   The Process of Organizations

An organization is a structured process in which persons interact for objectives. The individual, the organization, and the environment all interact with each other; they each provide resources for each other and derive values from each other. For all to perform effectively, the objectives of all must be compatible, mutually reinforcing, coordinated, and cooperative. Note that arrows represent sequence of activities or interactions.

THE PROCESS OF ORGANIZATIONS

An organization is a structured process in which persons interact for objectives. Figure 31-1, which draws together many of the topics we have studied in this book, shows this dynamic process of organizations.

Referring to Figure 31-1, we trace step by step through the diagram the process of organization. Individuals are members of organizations because through their membership they expect to accomplish some of their personal objectives. These individual objectives when combined produce organizational objectives—compatible with but distinct from individual objectives. Organizational objectives are superordinate expressions of individual objectives; when organizational objectives are accomplished, individual objectives are also satisfied. Further, individual and organizational objectives are mutually reinforcing; successful achievement of one stimulates further effort toward the other, ad infinitum.

Managers, as shown in Figure 31-1, take individual and organization objectives (some of which may be developed in the managerial planning process) and, through the managerial functions of creating, planning, organizing, motivating, communicating, and controlling, cause the organization to accomplish its objectives. All of these functions comprise management of the core resource in organizations—human behavior. In turn, through their behavior all members of the organization can effectively employ other required resources.

When an organization is effective it reaches its objectives, which in turn provide feedback to produce values for each member. The member in turn does further work for the organization, thus continuing the organizational process.

While this process of organizations is in operation, there is continual interaction among the individual members, "the organization," and the environment in which the organization exists.

Thus, we summarize our study of organizations and management as a dynamic process. Each major subprocess has been studied in detail in previous chapters of this book.

INDIVIDUAL MAN—THE BASIC UNIT OF ORGANIZATIONS

A Problem of Complex Organizations

Individuals in our complex society run the risk of becoming immersed and submerged in the very organizations that were designed for their benefit. One authority expressed this problem as follows:

> We live today in a world of teeming population and vast urban conglomeration. The individual is part of immense organizations such as corporations, labor unions, farm organizations, and government bureaus. The individual sees himself as a kind of atom in a seemingly infinite society. The individual becomes a number, a cog in complex machinery, an object to be manipulated, a standardized unit that is expected to adjust to a norm.[1]

In a complex society a person may come to believe that some mythical "the government" or "the company" will take care of him, from cradle to grave. The "system" assumes real power, in his mind. Small wonder that he may come to reject his individual responsibility for himself and others under the illusion that some mythical organization will do his work for him.

The individual may also find it impossible to satisfactorily relate to that monster, the organization. Unable to comprehend their inner complexities, he may feel buffeted from all sides by organizations larger than himself, over which he has no control. Again his response may be a retreat from the main stream of life.

The individual cannot be expected to involve himself completely in something he does not understand, something of which he may be afraid, where he does not understand his own participation in all its marvelous complexity.

By going beneath the surface of the organization and focusing on the interaction and participation of individuals, we help extricate the individual from his organizational dilemma and predicament. If an individual understands organizations, he can relate to and be more deeply involved in them. His organizations then are no longer enormous, unknowable abstracts; rather they become simply the means whereby two or more

---

[1] An excerpt from the inaugural address of President Howard Bowen, The State University of Iowa, Iowa City, Iowa.

people work together to accomplish their compatible goals. An organization thus becomes an extension of the individual—a means for his self-expression rather than his submersion.

A central problem of organizations becomes clear: How to create effective organizations without loss of individuality. A significant part of the answer to this problem lies in a clear distinction between individual and organizational objectives.

The Importance of the Individual

The basic unit of any organization is the individual person. Everything done in organizations is done by individuals who are individually motivated. Everything that an individual does is designed to satisfy some need or objective of that individual. Individuals work for organizational goals because they see the accomplishment of organizational goals as means by which their individual goals can be accomplished.

Thus, we may have a key for solving in large part the problem of loss of individuality in organizations. Simply, we need to focus on the idea that individuals perform in organizations to accomplish their own goals. Individuals do not work, per se, to achieve organizational goals. It is the task of management to assure that individual and organizational goals are compatible. Thus, when an individual is working to accomplish something of value to himself he is at the same time helping to fulfill organizational objectives.

The clear understanding that individuals work to accomplish their own rather than organizational goals is of the utmost importance. Application of this concept offers maximum motivational advantage. In the past the distinction has not always been clear. The result has been confusion about the individual's role in organizations, poor approaches to motivation, and the subjugation of the individual to the organization.[2]

Clarification of the individual's role in organizations offers significant advantages to individuals, to organizations, and to the society at large.

The basic relationship between individual and organizational objectives is one of compatibility. Increased personal involvement in his organizations will increase when the individual sees himself accomplishing his goals along with compatible organizational goals.

WHY, WHAT, AND HOW?

In the most effective organizations the questions of why something is done or what is to be done will be asked and decided before the question of how something is done. Figure

---

[2] Failure to make the distinction clear has, in our view, been in large part responsible for the condition of contemporary society described eloquently in these popular books: David Riesman, *The Lonely Crowd,* Doubleday & Company, Inc., Garden City, N.Y., 1956; Sloan Wilson, *The Man in the Gray Flannel Suit,* Simon and Schuster, Inc., New York, 1955; William H. Whyte, *The Organization Man,* Simon and Schuster, Inc., New York, 1965.

Traditional management and organization theories may have contributed significantly to this problem. Specifically, the basic unit of study for organization and management theorists has often been the organization. The individual did not receive adequate emphasis because he was below the basic level of inquiry. To remedy this deficiency we, in this book, have insisted that the individual person is the basic unit of inquiry.

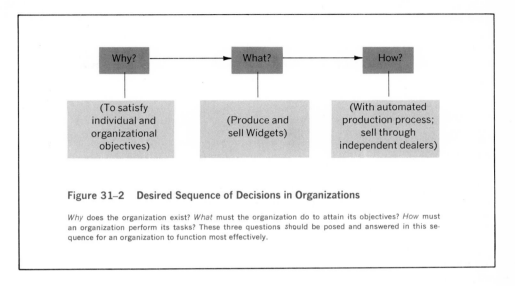

Figure 31–2 Desired Sequence of Decisions in Organizations

Why does the organization exist? *What* must the organization do to attain its objectives? *How* must an organization perform its tasks? These three questions should be posed and answered in this sequence for an organization to function most effectively.

31-2 illustrates this concept. As shown in Figure 31-2 managers of effective organizations will first and always keep in mind *why* the organization exists—to accomplish organizational objectives whose only purpose is to satisfy individual objectives. Next, managers decide *what* the organization is to do to accomplish these objectives—in our example, to produce and sell Widgets. Finally—and only *after* the two previous questions have been asked and satisfactorily answered—the question of *how* the organization is to perform its tasks is resolved. In this case "how" involves automated production with sales through independent dealers.

Although it is a subtle point, failure to keep continually in mind this simple means-ends chain is perhaps the greatest deficiency of modern management. Too often managers are concerned with how something is done without an adequate answer to the question of whether or not it ought to be done in the first place. Drucker pinpointed the futility of sole concern with method or procedure (how): "There is surely nothing quite so useless as doing with great efficiency what should not be done at all."[3]

LEADERSHIP OF DYNAMIC ORGANIZATIONS

In previous chapters of this book we have studied how managers perform the vital functions of creating, planning, organizing, motivating, communicating, and controlling the organization. These six functions describe the core of the manager's job. However, there are a number of additional managerial concepts that do not fit neatly into the six managerial functions as classified above. These leadership functions, although more intangible than the six managerial functions that we have already studied, may be critical to the success or failure of the organization. A leader's effect on an organization can be

[3] Peter Drucker, "Managing for Business Effectiveness," *Harvard Business Review*, May–June 1963, p. 54.

compared to the effect of an electron entering an atom, in the field of atomic physics. An electron with low energy (velocity) will merely be absorbed without substantially changing the atom. But a high energy electron will explode or significantly change the atom. Similarly a "low-energy" leader will have small effect on the organization; a "high-energy" leader, on the other hand, will profoundly affect the course of the organization.

Arbitrating

Often members disagree on the best decision for an organizational matter. An effective leader often will resolve the disagreement by *arbitrating,* or making the decision on the course of action to be taken. While we would hope that the leader will make the best or right decision, it often may be more important that he make *a* decision. For a decision is necessary to resolve the conflict to get the organization moving.

Suggesting

Suggestions are often employed by an adroit leader. The manager may say, "I believe it will be best to do it this way." Suggesting often permits the subordinate to retain his dignity and sense of participation more than if he were given a direct order. For the long term, the power of suggestion is likely to be a powerful tool in the manager's kit.

Supplying Objectives

A manager often personally supplies the objectives for the organization. In doing so the manager defines objectives which will allow members to work together. These organizational objectives do not usually appear automatically. Effective objectives are more often the result of conscious deliberate action. The manager must see that the organization is always supplied with suitable objectives.

Catalyzing

In organizations some force often is required to start or accelerate movement. A manager may provide this force. When he is doing this, he is acting as a catalyst. He stirs his subordinates to action.

Providing Security

In organizations personal security is often a significant factor. A manager can provide a large measure of security by maintaining a positive, optimistic attitude, even in the face of adversities. The founder of the IBM Corporation has been described thus: "When things were difficult and the sledding uphill, he could be very optimistic."[4] Such an ap-

---

[4] Thomas J. Watson, Jr., *A Business and Its Beliefs,* McGraw-Hill Book Company, New York, 1963.

proach when coupled with positive action can make highly successful leadership. After a while, the entire organization, for better or worse, tends to pick up the attitudes of its leaders.

Representing

A leader is usually the representative of his organization. He often speaks for the organization, stating the organization's position on matters with which it is concerned. In addition, the leader serves as a symbol of the organization; outsiders are likely to think of the whole organization in terms of their impression of the leader. If their impression of the leader is favorable they are likely to think well of the entire organization. On the other hand, if the leader makes a poor impression the reputation of the entire organization probably will suffer.

Inspiring

Many persons work more productively in organizations when their leader lets them know that the work they are doing is worthwhile and important. Thus a member is more likely to work toward organizational goals. When he is inspired, a member will enthusiastically accept organizational objectives and will work most effectively toward their accomplishment.

Praising

Everyone enjoys receiving praise for a job well done. Empty flattery will fail, but a sincere pat on the back for good work done will probably make a member pleased and help him to become involved with his work. Employees need to know that they are important, that their good work is appreciated, and that their manager has their interests sincerely at heart. Managers can help to satisfy these needs by sincere praise.

INCREASING PRODUCTIVITY IN ORGANIZATIONS

Productivity in organizations is determined to a great extent by the members' motivation and the degree to which their actions are directed toward organizational objectives. This relationship is shown by the equation:

$$P = f(M)\pm + f(D)_E^I \cdot \cdot \cdot + f(N)$$

That is, productivity is a function of motivation plus discipline plus a number of other factors that can be present in particular situations. The motivation may be plus (also called "positive," the "carrot," and "anxiety reducing") or minus (also called "negative," the "stick," and "anxiety producing"). Discipline is a measure of the extent of and the consistency with which the actions contribute toward objectives. Discipline may be internal (mature, self-actuating persons) or external (from a source outside the person).

Motivation may also be expressed with the following equation:

$M = f$ (aspirations — achievements)

This equation states that motivation for a person is a function of the degree to which his aspirations exceed his achievements.

When an organization member understands that successful achievement of his personal objectives is inextricably involved with successful accomplishment of organizational objectives, he is likely to work effectively. On the other hand if he does not see this connection, he is likely to work ineffectively. He will not see his work as a means of his own self-expression; he may simply "do time" on the job, serving his required forty hours per week but giving no more than minimum performance. He may see his job as simply a means of providing money which can be used to purchase his real satisfaction off the job. Such an attitude severely limits the productivity of organizations. This attitude can be overcome with benefits to all concerned if both managers and employees clearly understand the direct relationship of a member's productivity to the values he receives from the organization. This relationship is shown in Figure 31-3, which shows that an individual works toward organizational objectives which, when accomplished, bring economic, social, psychological, cultural, or other advantages to the individual. The cycle of productivity can continue indefinitely as long as both individual and organization objectives are achieved and when both sets of objectives continue to be compatible.

MANAGING FOR ORGANIZATIONAL RENEWAL

Organizations do not necessarily have an inherent life pattern or cycle. However, the lives of a number of things often associated with organizations do follow a pattern, as

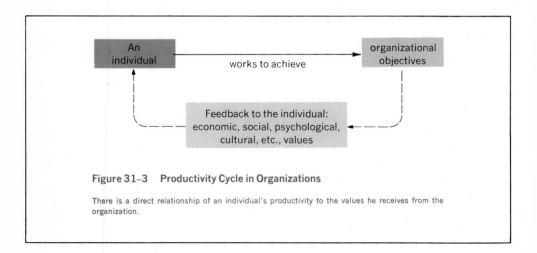

Figure 31–3 Productivity Cycle in Organizations

There is a direct relationship of an individual's productivity to the values he receives from the organization.

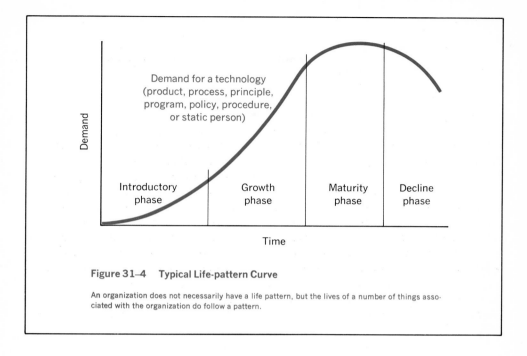

Figure 31–4   Typical Life-pattern Curve

An organization does not necessarily have a life pattern, but the lives of a number of things associated with the organization do follow a pattern.

shown in Figure 31-4.[5] In this figure we use the term "technology" to include particular products, processes, principles, programs, policies, procedures, or those persons who fail to mature or develop.

The life of a successful technology ordinarily includes four phases. In the introductory phase, the technology is started and perfected until there is a substantial demand for it. Next, the period of fastest growth occurs. After a time the market becomes saturated with this technology, or another technology may begin to replace it. Finally, rapid decline in the demand for the technology takes place.

Technology and Organizational Life

An organization that is associated with a particular technology will have the same life pattern as that technology. Such an organization will go in sequence through the introductory, growth, maturity, and decline phases; or the life of such an organization might be described in the following steps: (1) birth, (2) growth, (3) policy, (4) procedure, (5) theory, (6) religion, (7) ritual, and (8) last rites.

In this eight-step sequence, an organization is born and then has its growth. Policies

[5]Cf. Theodore Levitt, "Exploit the Product Life Cycle," *Harvard Business Review,* November–December 1965, pp. 81–94.

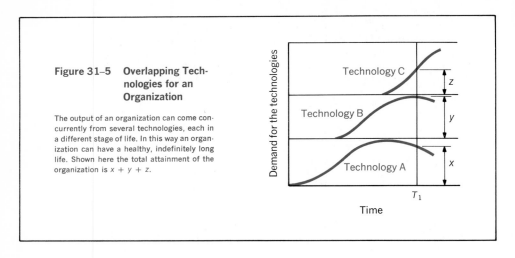

Figure 31–5 **Overlapping Technologies for an Organization**

The output of an organization can come concurrently from several technologies, each in a different stage of life. In this way an organization can have a healthy, indefinitely long life. Shown here the total attainment of the organization is $x + y + z$.

are developed to guide decisions, and these are carried out through procedures. These procedures are refined and made more efficient with theories about efficiency. In time, the organization may develop characteristics of a religion; it may worship the way it does things. Performance is by ritual; things are done by habit, without questioning. The death and last rites of the organization will ordinarily follow.

Unfortunately the steps listed above describe the life of too many organizations— perhaps the majority. But it does not have to be this way. Organizations can have a life pattern that does not necessarily lead to stagnation and death.

A Model for Organizational Renewal

An organization can have a healthy, indefinitely long life if it continually renews itself. Figure 31-5 shows how this renewal can occur, and that an organization is not inherently restricted to one technology that will eventually decline. Rather, the output of the organization may come concurrently from several technologies, each in a different stage of its life. Thus, the attainment of the organization shown in Figure 31-5 at time T_1 can be x from technology A, y from technology B, and z from technology C. Total attainment will be $x + y + z$.

If developing technologies are brought in to replace declining ones, the organization can have indefinite life. When the rate of introduction of the new technology is the same as the rate of withdrawal of the one being replaced, the organization can continue to be healthy without overall growth. An organization does not have to grow or die, but it does have to renew itself or die.

SUMMARY

An organization is a complex process of interaction which exists so that members can achieve personal objectives when they work toward organizational objectives. This organized process is likely to work best when individual members and managers understand this process and when managers effectively perform their managerial and leadership functions. One of the most important tasks of managers is to make sure that the things the organization does are the right things. It is easy to overemphasize how something is done without first determining whether or not it ought to be done at all.

Organizations can be renewed for indefinitely long life if managers will replace declining activities with activities for which there is an increasing demand. Thus we can provide for organizational renewal.

FOR REVIEW AND DISCUSSION

1 What effects do the concepts and theories that managers hold have on their organizations?

2 Summarize, in your own words, the concept of the process of organizations.

3 What is the basic unit in organizations? Explain the problems that individuals have had in satisfactorily relating to organizations.

4 Explain why it is important for an organization to have a clear concept of its objectives before a lot of attention is given to procedures and methods.

5 Describe each of the following functions that leaders perform in organizations. Illustrate each function with an example drawn from your own experience: (a) arbitrating, (b) suggesting, (c) supplying objectives, (d) being a catalyst, (e) providing security, (f) representing, (g) inspiring, and (h) praising.

6 Explain the relationship of motivation and discipline to productivity.

7 Explain the cycle of productivity in organizations. Do you agree with this statement: "The question of which comes first—individual or organizational objectives—is a sort of chicken-and-egg proposition. They must both be satisfied if the organization is to be effective." Explain your answer.

8 Explain the four phases in the typical life-pattern curve of a technology.

9 Explain the statement: "Organizations do not necessarily have an inherent life pattern or cycle." What happens, in terms of its length of life, to an organization that becomes attached to a single technology?

10 Explain the model for organizational renewal given in the chapter.

11 Does an organization have to grow or die? Explain your answer.

12 Explain the statement: "Individuals do not work, per se, to achieve organizational goals."

CASES

A   The Fairview Aluminum Door and Window Company was formed in the early 1950s. At that time the market for aluminum doors and windows was just beginning to be very large. In 1955 Fairview received $26.46 for its most popular window model. This price included a highly satisfactory profit margin.

In 1967 the market for aluminum doors and windows was larger than ever. However, the field had become saturated with manufacturers. Fairview received only $8.74 for the same popular model that it sold for $26.46 in 1955. Moreover, Fairview sales were higher than ever before. Many large improvements in production efficiency had been made since 1955, so that the cost of producing each item had gone down drastically. The product line of Fairview had not changed appreciably since 1955.

Despite its larger sales and lower costs, Fairview had lost money since 1960. After a meeting with Fairview creditors in 1967, Judge Radmore, referee in bankruptcy, appointed Mr. J. D. McCall, a local attorney, as trustee to administer the affairs of the company. Fairview could no longer meet its debts as they became due. Mr. McCall was sure that the management of the company had committed no fraud, and he also believed there was no evidence of mismanagement.

1 What caused Fairview's problems? Do you agree with Mr. McCall that there is no evidence of mismanagement of the company? Why? Do you think that the same mistakes Fairview made are often made by other firms? Give the reasons for your answer.

2 Mr. McCall was considering changing the name of the company to Fairview Industries, Inc. Evaluate his proposal. Might it have been better if this name had been given to the company when it was formed? Why?

B   Kyle College had been in existence for more than 150 years. Enrollment had gradually become larger until 1940 when the board of trustees froze total enrollment at 750 students. Kyle has always enjoyed a reputation of excellence.

Robert Milford has recently been appointed president of Kyle College. One of the first items that concerned him was whether he should request that the board of trustees remove the limitation on enrollment that had now been in effect for more than 25 years. President Milford was deeply concerned by a statement about organizations that he had heard many times. The statement was: "An organization must grow or die."

1 Should President Milford recommend to the board that the limitation be removed? Give the advantages and disadvantages of such a recommendation.

2 Do you agree with the statement: "An organization must grow or die." Explain your answer.

C   "Men," said Mr. Freeman, the sales manager, at the end of a long, inspiring talk, "we've got what it takes to do the job. I want every man here to go out and sell his new quota. You were all successful last year, and I'm looking forward to everyone joining the 100 percent club again. Just remember what your quota is, and you will get the job done."

1 Using this excerpt from his speech, evaluate Mr. Freeman as a leader, based on the criteria given in the text. What are the strong and weak points of his comments?

2 Is it possible that a more personal approach, directed at the needs of each salesman, might also be a motivation for him to sell his quota? Explain your answers. (HINT: See review and discussion questions 7 and 12, this chapter.)

FOR FURTHER STUDY

Additional sources can be found in the sources cited in the chapter.

Book

Chris Argyris: *Integrating the Individual and the Organization,* John Wiley & Sons, Inc., New York, 1964. "The incongruence between the individual and the organization can provide the basis for a continued challenge, which as it is fulfilled, will tend to help man to enhance his own growth and to develop organizations that will tend to be viable and effective."

Articles

Keith Davis: "Evolving Models of Organizational Behavior," *Academy of Management Journal,* March 1968. Managerial supervisory practices have evolved from an autocratic model, to a custodial model, to a supportive model, and there may be movement to a collegial model.

Peter F. Drucker: "Management's New Role," *Harvard Business Review,* November– December 1969. Today's managers have responsibilities that are vastly different from traditional ones.

Theodore Levitt: "Exploit the Product Life Cycle," *Harvard Business Review,* November– December 1965. "The concept of the product life cycle is known, but hasn't been used effectively or in a productive way. Knowledge and proper use of it can make the concept an effective managerial instrument of competitive power."

Leonard Sayles: "Whatever Happened to Management?" *Business Horizons,* April 1970. An evaluation of management education.

William G. Scott: "Organization Theory: An Overview and an Appraisal," *Journal of the Academy of Management,* April 1961. The development of classical, neoclassical, and modern management theory is described. This paper is an excellent summary of management and organization theory.

Herbert Sonthoff: "What Is the Manager?" *Harvard Business Review,* November–December 1964, pp. 24–36 and 188 ff. The manager is seen by others as an actor, catalyst, guardian, friend, owner, and technician.

32
Management in the Future

In every age there is a strain toward the organizational form that will encompass and exploit the technology of the time and express its spirit.
WARREN G. BENNIS

The preceding chapters have traced more than a century of management thought, with emphasis upon concepts of effective administration. Some of these concepts, such as the principle of specialization, were developed long ago and have remained relatively unchanged. Many others, such as those relating to motivating and controlling, have been developed almost entirely within the past twenty-five years or so. To a large extent they are reflections of changing socioeconomic conditions and of increased knowledge of the nature of man. New management and organization theories will be required in the future to deal with changes that will bring new and unique demands. In the past every generation has been able to rely upon a relatively high degree of stability. In the Stone Age society stayed pretty much the same for thousands of years; in the Middle Ages for a few hundred years; in the Industrial Revolution for ten to twenty years; but today an idea is scarcely recorded before it is revised by further experience.[1]

[1]Arthur W. Barber, "Not with a Bang, But a Bureaucratic Whimper," *Columbia Journal of World Business,* Winter 1966, p. 50.

Since change is inevitable, provisions must be made for the complications it presents. Change may assume a variety of forms, each with its unique problems.

TECHNOLOGICAL AND SOCIOLOGICAL CHANGES

Two convenient classifications of change are "sociological" and "technological." Technological changes, which are undoubtedly the most familiar, include any significant modification in products or services or in the ways they are produced. Sociological changes are those that alter established human relationships.

To illustrate the interplay of technological and sociological changes, consider the numerous technical advances taking place in the American iron and steel industry. Changes have been made over the past fifty to seventy-five years in the basic process by which most of our steel is produced. The open hearth process began to replace the Bessemer process around 1910. It remained the dominant means of steel making until about 1960, when a newer method, known as basic oxygen processing, became important. Today, this newer method accounts for about as much domestic steel production as does the open hearth. These and similar technical innovations overlap the sociological ones and affect the organizational relationships of workers.

One sociological reaction is in the level of employment itself. Since basic oxygen processing is much more efficient than open hearth, the same amount of steel can be produced by fewer men. Improved techniques used in steel production have reduced total employment, and many once booming areas are virtual ghost towns. Many miners and steel workers have been forced to find employment in industries requiring skill levels inferior to those they had developed.

The average steel worker, whether he be manager or laborer, can hardly escape the influence of the changes taking place. The miner who worked with a sense of pride and tradition throughout his youth finds himself in his middle age advising his sons to prepare for another profession. Meanwhile, the steel engineer gives his children similar advice. Resulting sociological consequences, both overt and covert, are enormous. Security is replaced by insecurity, and a sense of accomplishment is replaced by a feeling of doing something that is not so important. In the early 1970s a similar acute situation developed in the aerospace industry. Highly skilled and paid technical specialists suddenly found themselves without jobs because of reduced government spending in their industry. Most had never even considered the possibility of being without work.

Some of the most important future tests for managers may come in adjusting their organizations to meet accelerating rates of technological and sociological changes. On the other hand, the fascinating possibility exists that some societies will demand more security and tradition and less change. Witness the return in recent years to older styles of dress, for example. Psychologists have suggested that this may indicate a desire to "slow down" the society. If such a movement becomes dominant, it will affect management and organizations in countless ways.

INTERNATIONAL MANAGEMENT

Some highly significant trends of business to move increasingly to international operations are under way. For example, some 137 American corporations each have subsidiaries in from 10 to 14 countries. Dutch companies have 35 subsidiaries in the United States, while U.S. companies have 530 subsidiaries in Holland. Japan has 465 international companies located within her borders, of which 17 are based in West Germany, 33 in the United Kingdom, and 373 in the United States.[2]

This internationalization of business has created a number of new challenges for the management of multinational firms. Especially complicated is the evaluation of the organization's market potentials in the often unfamiliar economic, political, and social variables of other countries. Chances are that many readers of this text will work with such problems. Instead of moving to another part of the country—which was typical in the past fifty years—today's graduate has more and more of a chance to spend a large portion of his life working overseas.

One problem of international business is the structuring of multinational organizational relationships. Traditionally, firms have established headquarters organizations from which they retain full control over strategic planning and decision making. However, such factors as the isolation of top management from overseas operations, language barriers, and complex governmental regulations unique to specific locations have made this form of organization somewhat obsolete. As an alternative, international firms are often decentralized geographically, with area managers for the various localities. These managers often have great freedom from the parent company in running their operations. When a firm is thus decentralized each division is in a better position to respond to the culture in which it operates.

THE FUTURE AND THE ORGANIZATION MAN

The rising young businessman has been portrayed for years as the model of conformity. The "organization man," as he has come to be known, mechanically performed his tasks and fitted himself into the mold the firm provided. Today, however, many participants in organizations are quite different from their counterparts of a decade or two ago. This difference has come about primarily as the result of the "knowledge explosion" and the associated professionalization of employees. A recognition of this condition has prompted Bennis to suggest the need to alter many of our traditional ideas. He proposed the development of:

1 A new concept of man based on an increased knowledge of his complex and shifting needs.
2 A new concept of power based on collaboration and reason.
3 A new concept of organizational values based on humanistic-democratic ideals to replace the depersonalized mechanistic value system of bureaucracy.[3]

---

[2]Howard V. Perlmutter, "Some Management Problems in Spaceship Earth: The Megafirm and the Global Industrial Estate," *Academy of Management Proceedings*, August 1969, pp. 62.
[3]Warren G. Bennis, "Organizational Revitalization," *California Management Review*, Fall 1966, p. 55.

This new concept of man would recognize that the more highly educated and informed individual is not dependent upon a single firm, but is mobile and motivated by a more complex field of forces than the basic desires of food, clothing, and shelter. There is evidence that he needs intrinsic work, recognition, and social involvement. Often the large complex organization, unless tempered by such managerial techniques as participative decision making, can threaten the basic values of the more sophisticated employees.

The complex bureaucracy with its elaborate and impersonal hierarchy may come into conflict with the changing nature of man. The heavy influx of professional and scientific employees complicates hierarchical relationships. Scientists, for example, often have little organizational authority. The bureaucratic value system that rewards ability by promotion implies that individuals with lower ranks have lesser abilities. Several alterations have been suggested. One of the most common is the introduction of a dual hierarchy—one administrative and one technical. This creates a dual status and reward system designed to keep technical and professional employees in technical and professional positions, rather than encouraging or forcing them to move into administrative roles to satisfy the bureaucratic value system and their own status and income needs.

Thus, in organizations where tasks are nonroutine, where innovative and professional skills are required, and where organizational goals are abstract, some traditional approaches can be seriously questioned. Organizations such as hospitals, research institutions, and universities are particularly of concern here. Many of the traditional theories are simply not applicable in such organizations. The complex and changing characteristics of many organization members suggest the need to reexamine classic attitudes and to explore new philosophies of organization.

TOWARD A NEW PHILOSOPHY OF ORGANIZATION

It has been suggested that organizations are affluent with untapped human resources and creative potentials. Moreover, the argument continues, gifted employees are generally willing to contribute their talents but are unable to do so within the traditional framework.[4] For example, it has been suggested that many organizations have failed to open the channels of communication that allow for the free flow of potentially useful ideas from all members. Only through a free exchange of ideas can an organization continue its healthy and unending process of examining and modifying organizational objectives as they relate to individual goals, and achieve compatibility between them.[5]

Thus, the future demands adaptability, rather than excessive conformity. This does not mean a total absence of authority and a complete free-rein organization. Quite the contrary. To illustrate, a distinction was drawn between what one writer called "essential authority" and "substitutional authority."[6] Essential authority was defined as the mini-

[4]Raymond E. Miles, "The Affluent Organization," *Harvard Business Review,* May–June 1966, pp. 110–111.
[5]Rensis Likert, *New Patterns of Management,* McGraw-Hill Book Company, Inc., New York, 1961, p. 116.
[6]Robert Albanese, "Substitutional and Essential Authority," *Academy of Management Journal,* June 1966, pp. 140–141.

mum direction required to provide order and to arbitrate conflicts. Substitutional authority, on the other hand, is a temporary direction designed to assist the individual in self-development. Aimed at the common good of both the organization and the individual, it is self-destructive and encourages the member to mature to the point where it is no longer necessary.

No doubt everyone has noticed that in most universities freshmen are regulated more than juniors or seniors. Sometimes freshman women must be in their dormitories earlier than women in upper classes. Also, freshmen may be restricted as to where they may live, and they often are required to attend various orientation functions. However, as they progress to higher class standings, their restrictions are reduced. By the time they are seniors, hardly any absolute behavior patterns are required of them over and above those prescribed by society in general.

This type of administrative "fine-tuning" allows the student to come to the university as a formative adolescent and leave a mature and responsible adult. In the industrial context a similar development can be accomplished. Of course, the proper mixture of the two components will vary with every organization and depend to a great extent upon the characteristics of the workers, the characteristics of the leaders, and the general work situation itself.

The basic idea of the human resources movement is to assume that organization members can be developed to higher levels of fulfillment and productivity. The older idea was that members were static resources whom the manager should use as well as possible, but who did not generally possess developmental potential.

OUTLOOK FOR MANAGEMENT EDUCATION

The manager of the future will be constantly frustrated by the obsolescence of his experience. History and experience that once provided a sense of security and stability to preceding generations of managers will be of little comfort to future administrators. This is true because the managerial climate changes so quickly that outstanding solutions to problems in the past may be miserable failures in the present or future.

Managers will need to continually renew themselves. In some cases this will involve part-time participation in graduate programs or full-time participation in one of the numerous management development programs offered by colleges and universities throughout the nation. Perhaps we will even see the time when administrators will be granted periodic educational leaves of absence in order to keep abreast of their dynamic field.

Another equally important challenge in management education relates to the subject matter itself. Originally, the concentration in management literature was upon the "economic man" or the perfectly rational creature as just another productive natural resource. Later "psychological man" and "social man" with all his complex desires for acceptance and self-respect became the object of study. Today, and increasingly in the future, the successful manager will be required to become a behavioral scientist in the truest sense of the term and minister to the "total man"—a true integration of economic, psychological, and social man.

SUMMARY

A number of events have taken place in recent years that have significantly influenced established thinking concerning organizations. These include the knowledge explosion and the associated growth of technical and professional employees. The traditional bureaucratic philosophy, which has produced extremely high benefits in the area of technical efficiency, has often evolved as a threat to the values of better educated and better informed organizational participants. To overcome the numerous problems presented by this relatively new phenomenon, management must develop new ways of encouraging creativity and of bringing the goals of individuals into a compatible relationship with organizational objectives.

The ultimate goal is to have organizations that are highly productive and that contribute to personal development of every member.

FOR REVIEW AND DISCUSSION

1 What is meant by the term "obsolescence of experience"?

2 Define sociological and technological change. How are the two interrelated? Use examples in your explanation.

3 Why have international considerations become so important to managers in recent years? What are some of these considerations?

4 Explain the difference between essential and substitutional authority.

5 Do you agree with the statement: "Today's organizations are full of untapped human resources possessing great creative potential that we are failing to utilize"?

6 Explain the conflict between the work of scientists, engineers, and other professionals and the bureaucratic concept of organizational authority.

7 Explain the concept (human resources concept) that workers are resources to be developed by managers. How does this concept differ from tradition?

CASES

A The Cole Steel Company is being confronted by the public about its contribution to pollution. Every day a constant stream of black, yellow, and red smoke can be seen belching from the stacks of its open hearths.

Company management is presently considering converting its open hearths to basic oxygen processing furnaces. Such a move would require that 75 of the company's 500 employees be laid off. The change would, however, allow the installation of more modern facilities and substantially reduce the rate of pollution.

1 Should the company replace the open hearths?

2 Does the company have a responsibility for the displaced workers? If so, what responsibility?

B Rainier Electronics has experienced steadily increasing labor costs, especially in its wiring room where highly skilled craftsmen wire complete electrical circuits by hand. Last month the company purchased three precision machines to completely replace all manual wiring operations. Recognizing its social responsibility, Ranier Electronics has agreed to retrain all the displaced workers in lower skilled areas.

1 What effect do you think the company's action will have on morale?

2 Suggest a better way for the company to handle the problem.

C The Training Director of the James Service Company is planning his company's educational program for the coming year. He estimates that 50 percent of the company's managerial employees will participate in some form of education during this period. He is presently attempting to determine whether he should hold in-company training seminars or contact the local university and ask the faculty to formulate a series of courses specially designed for the company's needs. These would be held after work hours on the university campus.

1 What factors should he consider in arriving at his decision?

2 Which alternative should he select?

FOR FURTHER STUDY

Additional sources can be found in the sources cited in the chapter.

Book

Peter P. Schoderbek: "Prologue to the Future," *Management Systems,* John Wiley & Sons, Inc., New York, 1967, pp. 481–483. A prediction of the characteristics of future management practice.

Articles

H. Igor Ansoff: "The Firm in the Future," *Harvard Business Review,* September–October 1965. "Scientific and technological forces will bring drastic changes to the firm and the manager of the future. Management in the 1980s will definitely be different from what it is today."

H. Igor Ansoff and R. G. Brandenburg: "The General Manager of the Future," *California Management Review,* Spring 1969. The future general manager must be a communicator, systems architect, statesman, and sensitive citizen.

George J. Berkwitt: "The New Myths of Management," *Dun's Review,* September 1970. Certain contemporary myths wreck havoc on an organization.

Robert L. Dubin: "Management in Britain—Impressions of a Visiting Professor," *The Journal of Management Studies,* May 1970. The culture of industry in Britain is different from that in America.

Alan C. Filley and Robert J. House: "Profiles of the Future Management and the Future," *Business Horizons,* April 1970. Current management and organization thought is evaluated, and future trends are predicted.

Mason Haire: "A New Look at Human Resources," *Industrial Management Review II,* Winter 1970. A human resources view of manpower management is urged.

Raymond E. Miles: "Human Relations or Human Resources?" *Harvard Business Review,* July–August 1965. "Recent evidence indicates that managers have now adopted not one but two theories of participative leadership: a human relations approach for their subordinates, and a human resources approach for themselves."

Raymond E. Miles: "The Affluent Organization," *Harvard Business Review,* May–June 1966. Organizations can and should take the risks involved in developing and utilizing their human resources.

Barry M. Richman: "A Firsthand Study of Marketing in Communist China," *Journal of Retailing,* Summer 1970. Political structure, market structure, and sales organizations of Communist China are described.

Appendix A
Mathematical Solution for the Economic Lot Size

The fundamental problem in economic lot determination is that of finding the lot size which results in the lowest total cost. The economic lot size is determined mathematically by minimizing the total cost function.

ASSUMPTIONS

For this analysis the following assumptions are made:

Cost of setup is a fixed amount per lot and does not vary with lot size or the number of lots.

The unit price or cost is constant.

Storage costs vary directly and linearly with the size of inventory (the number of units in inventory).

Storage costs are assessed on units only while they are actually in inventory. Consequently, storage costs are computed on average—not maximum—inventory. This is equivalent to assuming that space not actually used by the product under consideration will always be used by some other product and, while being used by other products, will be assessed to those products.

Minimum inventory is zero units.

All items in a lot are manufactured instantaneously and move into inventory at the same time.

Consumption or usage is at a constant, linear rate.

CONSTRUCTION OF THE MODEL

The total yearly costs associated with a decision regarding the economic lot size for manufacturing varies with the setup cost per lot, the lot size, the cost of manufacturing, the cost of carrying inventory, and the number of units of the good required each year. Let these variables be represented by the following symbols:

T = total yearly costs

P = setup cost per lot

Q_a = lot size, units

D = unit price or cost of manufacturing (includes direct labor, materials, and overhead except setup cost)

I = inventory cost, a percentage cost factor per year of average inventory value allowing for the inventory costs of risk, obsolescence, storage, depreciation, and imputed interest on invested capital in the inventory, etc.

ELS = economic lot size, units

W = yearly demand, units per year

The total costs per period is the sum of three parts. First, there is the cost of setups. W is the yearly requirement in units, and Q_a equals the lot size in units; the number of setups per year equals W/Q_a. Furthermore, the setup cost per lot equals P; P times the number of setups gives the total cost of all setups during the year, which equals PW/Q_a. The magnitude of this term varies inversely with the size of the lot.

Next, there is the determination of the costs of production. Since D is the unit cost of manufacturing and W equals yearly requirement in units, then DW equals total costs of manufacturing for the year. The value of this term is independent of the lot size.

Finally, there is the determination of the cost of maintaining an inventory. Figure 29-1 shows the inventory level through time under the assumptions made for this model. The average level of inventory is one-half the maximum inventory. This is one-half of the lot size, or $Q_a/2$ units. Because D equals unit cost of manufacturing, then the average dollar value of the inventory is the average unit inventory times the cost per unit equals $DQ_a/2$. The term I gives the costs associated with the inventory, and is defined as a percentage cost factor of average inventory value. The cost of carrying the inventory per period equals the percentage cost factor times the average value of the inventory equals $IDQ_a/2$. Thus, the cost of carrying inventory varies directly with lot size.

The total year cost is expressed as the sum of the above three classes of costs. In mathematical form this may be written:

$$T = \frac{PW}{Q_a} + DW + \frac{IDQ_a}{2} \tag{1}$$

Figure 29-2 is a graphical representation of these costs.

The economic lot size will be the lot size for which T is minimum. In Figure 29-2 this is the lowest of all values of T [at this point the slope (steepness) of the total cost curve is zero]. This minimum point (or point of zero slope) of the curve may be found by elementary differential calculus.[1] Thus,

$$ELS = \sqrt{\frac{2PW}{ID}} \tag{2}$$

NUMERICAL EXAMPLE

The Alpha Company wishes to determine the most economic manufacturing lot size for one of its products. Each new lot requires a setup which costs $10. Manufacturing costs amount to $10 per unit, production is 1,000 units per year, and the yearly cost of carrying inventory totals 50 percent of the average value of the inventory. What is the most economic lot size to manufacture? What is the total yearly cost using the most economic lot size?

Solution

This problem may be solved with equation 2.

$$ELS = \sqrt{\frac{2PW}{ID}}$$

$$= \sqrt{\frac{2(\$10)\,(1,000)}{(0.50)\,(\$10)}} = 63 \text{ units, approximately}$$

[1]The derivative of T_u with respect to Q_a is:

$$\frac{dT_u}{dQ_a} = \frac{-PW}{Q_a{}^2} + 0 + \frac{ID}{2}$$

ELS may be found by setting

$$\frac{dT_u}{dQ_a} = 0$$

Then

$$\frac{-PW}{(ELS)^2} + \frac{ID}{2} = 0$$

From which

$$ELS = \sqrt{\frac{2PW}{ID}}$$

Thus, the Alpha Company will find it most economical to manufacture this product in lots of approximately 63 units. The total yearly costs if manufacturing is done in lots of 63 units may be found with equation 1.

$$T = \frac{PW}{Q_a} + DW + \frac{IDQ_a}{2}$$

$$= \frac{\$10\,(1,000)}{63} + \$10\,(1,000) + \frac{(0.50)\,(\$10)\,(63)}{2}$$

$$= \$10,316$$

Manufacturing in lots of 63 units will result in total yearly costs of $10,316.

OTHER CONDITIONS

The economic lot size under other conditions and assumptions may be found by similar approaches. We might note that we can keep a reserve stock (rather than assuming inventory goes to zero, we assume it normally goes to the level of the reserve stock) without changing the economic lot-size formula found above. We refer interested readers to the sources cited for inventory models in Chapter 29.

Appendix B
An Illustration of
Linear Programming

GRAPHIC SOLUTION

We illustrate linear programming by solving a problem of a firm producing gasoline-powered rotary lawn mowers. The firm purchases all parts in a finished condition; the only significant operations of the firm are painting, assembly, and testing. Two models are produced: a manual push-type mower and a self-propelled mower. Pertinent data for the two products are:

| | | HOURS REQUIRED FOR EACH UNIT | | |
KIND OF MOWER	UNIT SALE PRICE	ASSEMBLY	PAINTING	TESTING
Push-type	$50	1.0	0.2	0.0
Self-propelled	80	1.5	0.2	0.1

The departments have the following total number of hours available each week.

Assembly   600
Painting   100
Testing   30

Our problem is to find the best number of each product to produce, or the product mix that will provide maximum revenue. We can solve the problem graphically, as shown in Figure B-1.

The assembly department is capable of producing up to 600 ÷ 1.0 = 600 push-type units. We show this as point C on Figure B-1. If only self-propelled units were made 600 ÷ 1.5 = 400 units could be produced (point D). The limiting capabilities of the assembly department for different mixes of the two products is the line CD.

The painting department can produce up to 100 ÷ 0.2 = 500 units of either type. Limiting capabilities of the painting department are shown by the line AB.

Testing allows up to 30 ÷ 0.1 = 300 self-propelled units, but does not limit the possible production of push-type units. The limiting characteristics of the testing department are shown by the line rising vertically from point E.

Possible levels of operations are shown by the shaded polygon AGFEH. No operation outside this polygon is possible because of the constraints of the limited available resources. For example, we could not produce 100 push-type in addition to 400 self-propelled (point J). To produce at point J would require 100 (1.0) plus 400 (1.5) totals 700 assembly hours. Only 600 are available. Similarly, not enough testing hours are available for point J production. Since point J is not outside line AB, painting resources would allow point J production. But if one or more resources are not sufficient, production

**Figure B–1   Graphic Linear-pro-
graming Solution**

This is a graphic solution to the problem of finding the best number of each of two products to produce and the product mix that will provide maximum revenue. Although production anywhere within the shaded area is possible, the best solution will always be on the boundaries—in this case, at points A, G, F, or E. Which of these is the best of the four can be found by tabularly computing the revenue for each point.

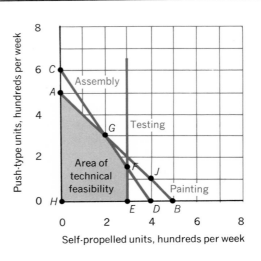

must be reduced to make enough of all resources available. Within the shaded area or along the boundaries of the shaded area (the x and y axes and lines *AG*, *GF*, and *FE*) production is feasible.

Although production anywhere within the shaded area is possible, the best solution always will be somewhere on the boundaries of that area. Specifically, revenue will be maximized at one of the levels of operations described by either points *A, G, F,* or *E.* We can find which point is best by computing the revenue for each point.

POINT	SELF-PROPELLED UNITS			PUSH-TYPE UNITS			TOTAL REVENUE
	NUMBER	PRICE	REVENUE	NUMBER	PRICE	REVENUE	
A	0	$80	0	500	$50	$25,000	$25,000
G	200	80	$16,000	300	50	15,000	31,000
F	300	80	24,000	150	50		31,500
E	300	80	24,000	0	50	0	24,000

Point *F* describes the optimum point of operations because it produces more revenue (total of $31,500) than either *A, G,* or *E.*

Relatively simple problems such as the one above can be solved by the graphic method. More complex problems can be solved by mathematical techniques. These mathematical techniques are beyond the scope of this book, but the reader may find information on them in the cited sources in the linear-programming section of Chapter 29.

Linear-programming techniques can be used to solve other types of problems. For example, linear programming could be used to determine which resource (assembly, painting, and testing hours in the above example) would be the best to increase if expanded operations were desired. Again, the reader is referred to the cited sources for information on other linear-programming procedures.

NameIndex

Subject Index